**COMMANDER
STEVEN HAINES
ROYAL NAVY**

International Humanitarian Law
and Human Rights Law

International Humanitarian Law and Human Rights Law

Towards a New Merger in International Law

Edited by
Roberta Arnold and Noëlle Quénivet

LEIDEN • BOSTON
2008

This book is printed on acid-free paper.

Library of Congress Cataloging-in-Publication Data

International humanitarian law and human rights law : towards a new merger in international law / edited by Roberta Arnold and Noelle Quenivet.
   p. cm.
  Includes index.
  ISBN 978-90-04-16317-1 (hardback : alk. paper) 1. Humanitarian law. 2. Human rights.
  I. Arnold, Roberta, 1974– II. Quénivet, Noëlle N. R.
  KZ6471.I5687 2008
  341.6'7—dc22
                                                                                  2008019606

ISBN   978 90 04 16317 1

Copyright 2008 by Koninklijke Brill NV, Leiden, The Netherlands. Koninklijke Brill NV incorporates the imprints Brill, Hotei Publishing, IDC Publishers, Martinus Nijhoff Publishers and VSP.

All rights reserved. No part of this publication may be reproduced, translated, stored in a retrieval system, or transmitted in any form or by any means, electronic, mechanical, photocopying, recording or otherwise, without prior written permission from the publisher.

Authorization to photocopy items for internal or personal use is granted by Brill provided that the appropriate fees are paid directly to The Copyright Clearance Center, 222 Rosewood Drive, Suite 910, Danvers, MA 01923, USA.
Fees are subject to change.

PRINTED IN THE NETHERLANDS

Contents

Introduction. The History of the Relationship Between International Humanitarian Law and Human Rights Law 1
Noëlle Quénivet

Part A

Concepts and Theories

Chapter I. Fundamental Standards of Humanity: A Common Language of International Humanitarian Law and Human Rights Law 15
Marco Odello

Chapter II. End Justifies the Means? – Post 9/11 Contempt for Humane Treatment 57
Agnieszka Jachec-Neale

Chapter III. Legal Conclusion or Interpretative Process? *Lex Specialis* and the Applicability of International Human Rights Standards 101
Conor McCarthy

Part B

Issues of Applicability

Chapter IV. Legal Reasoning and the Applicability of International Human Rights Standards During Military Occupation 121
Conor McCarthy

Chapter V. Triggering State Obligations Extraterritorially: The Spatial Test in Certain Human Rights Treaties 133
Ralph Wilde

Chapter VI. *DRC* v. *Uganda*: The Applicability of International Humanitarian Law and Human Rights Law in Occupied Territories 155
Tom Ruys and Sten Verhoeven

Part C

Issues of Implementation

Chapter VII. Individuals as Subjects of International Humanitarian Law and Human Rights Law 199
Cátia Lopes and Noëlle Quénivet

Chapter VIII. Concurrent Application of International Humanitarian Law and Human Rights Law: A Victim Perspective 237
Jean-Marie Henckaerts

Chapter IX. The Implementation of International Humanitarian Law by Human Rights Courts: The Example of the Inter-American Human Rights System 269
Emiliano J. Buis

Chapter X. "Collateral Damages" of Military Operations: Is Implementation of International Humanitarian Law Possible Using International Human Rights Law Tools? 295
Giovanni Carlo Bruno

Chapter XI. The Role of the UN Security Council in Implementing International Humanitarian Law and Human Rights Law 309
Gregor Schotten and Anke Biehler

Part D

The Protection of Specific Rights and Persons

Chapter XII. The Right to Life in International Humanitarian Law and Human Rights Law 331
Noëlle Quénivet

Chapter XIII. Protection of Women in International Humanitarian Law and Human Rights Law 355
Anke Biehler

Chapter XIV. Protection of Children in International Humanitarian Law and Human Rights Law 383
Vesselin Popovski

Chapter XV. Unaccompanied Minors and the Right to Family
  Reunification in International Humanitarian Law and Human Rights
  Law: The Iraqi Experience 403
  Kyriaki Topidi

Chapter XVI. Crossing Legal Borders: The Interface Between
  Refugee Law, Human Rights Law and Humanitarian Law in the
  "International Protection" of Refugees 421
  Alice Edwards

Part E
Specific Situations

Chapter XVII. Fair Trial Guarantees in Occupied Territory – The
  Interplay between International Humanitarian Law and Human
  Rights Law 449
  Yutaka Arai-Takahashi

Chapter XVIII. Terrorism in International Humanitarian Law and
  Human Rights Law 475
  Roberta Arnold

Chapter XIX. Judging Justice: Laws of War, Human Rights, and
  the Military Commissions Act of 2006 499
  Christian M. De Vos

Chapter XX. Targeted Killings and International Law: Law Enforcement,
  Self-defense, and Armed Conflict 525
  Michael N. Schmitt

Chapter XXI. Implementing the Concept of Protection of Civilians in
  the Light of International Humanitarian Law and Human Rights Law:
  The Case of MONUC 555
  Katarina Månsson

Conclusions 591
  Roberta Arnold

Index 593

Introduction

The History of the Relationship Between International Humanitarian Law and Human Rights Law

Noëlle Quénivet*

1. *Introduction*

The relationship between human rights law (HRL) and international humanitarian law (IHL), also called the law of war, did not draw much attention until the late 1960s. In contrast, nowadays, the way these two bodies of law interact is the focus of many scholarly writings and activities. Yet, the debate remains open as to how and when they apply and interrelate. In recent years academic literature has referred to the apparent "fusing,"[1] "meshing,"[2] "complementarity,"[3] "convergence"[4] or "confluence"[5] of these two areas of law.

This book aims to examine the current state of the law and the interpretations provided by various legal scholars. At the heart of the enquiry is whether the two bodies of law, IHL and HRL, have finally merged into a single set of laws.

---

* Dr. Noëlle Quénivet is a Senior Lecturer at the University of the West of England. She holds a LL.M. from the University of Nottingham (UK) and a Ph.D. from the University of Essex (UK). She is grateful to Bernard Dougherty for his comments.

[1] Felicity Rogers, *Australia's Human Rights Obligations and Australian Defence Force Operations*, 18 U. Tasmania L. Rev. 1, 2 (1999).

[2] Theodor Meron, *On the Inadequate Reach of Humanitarian and Human Rights Law and the Need for a New Instrument*, 77 Am. J. Int'l L. 589 (1983).

[3] René Provost, International Human Rights and Humanitarian Law (2002); Hans-Joachim Heintze, *On the Relationship between Human Rights Law Protection and International Humanitarian Law*, 856 Int'l Rev. Red Cross 789, 794 (2004) [hereinafter Heintze 2004].

[4] Raúl Emilio Vinuesa, *Interface, Correspondence and Convergence of Human Rights and International Humanitarian Law*, 1 YB Int'l Humanitarian L. 69–110 (1998); Asbjørn Eide, *The Laws of War and Human Rights – Differences and Convergences*, *in* Studies and Essays on International Humanitarian Law and Red Cross Principles in Honour of Jean Pictet 675–697 (Christophe Swinarski ed., 1984) [hereinafter Eide].

[5] Robert Q. Quentin-Baxter, *Human Rights and Humanitarian Law-Confluence of Conflict?*, 9 Austl. Y.B. Int'l L. 94 (1985).

2. IHL and HRL as Separate and Distinct Bodies of Law

At the inception of the discussion, both *corpora juris* were considered separate and distinct because, as many experts claimed, they historically emerged and developed independently from each other.[6] International humanitarian law developed early within public international law,[7] for it predominantly regulates inter-state relations. Moreover, some of the concepts used in IHL go as far back as the Middle Ages (e.g. idea of chivalry). While IHL mainly grew via customary law,[8] its first treaty codification dates back to 1864 when the Geneva Convention of August 22, 1864 for the Amelioration of the Condition of the Wounded in Armies in the Field was drafted.[9] This convention was followed by a range of treaties, each of them the product of the acknowledgment that individuals needed to be protected in times of armed conflict. Hence, as clearly stated by Cerna, IHL "evolved as a result of humanity's concern for the victims of war, whereas human rights law evolved as a result of humanity's concern for the victims of a new kind of internal war – the victims of the Nazi death camps."[10]

Consequently, human rights law only entered the field of public international law after the Second World War. Until then human rights had been granted to individuals via bills of rights[11] or, more generally, constitutional law[12] and in some

---

[6] *See* e.g. Michael Bothe, *The Historical Evolution of International Humanitarian Law, International Human Rights Law, Refugee Law and International Criminal Law, in* Crisis Management and Humanitarian Protection – Festschrift für Dieter Fleck 37 (Horst Fischer *et al.* eds., 2004); Leslie C. Green, *Human Rights in Peace and War: An Historical Overview, in* Crisis Management and Humanitarian Protection – Festschrift für Dieter Fleck 159 (Horst Fischer *et al.* eds., 2004); Leslie C. Green, *The Relations Between Human Rights Law and International Humanitarian Law: A Historical Overview, in* Testing the Boundaries of International Humanitarian Law 49 (Susan C. Breau & Agnieszka Jachec-Neale eds., 2006).

[7] G.I.A.D. Draper, *Humanitarianism in the Modern Law of Armed Conflicts, in* Armed Conflict and the New Law 3 (Michael A. Meyer ed., 1989) [hereinafter Draper 1989].

[8] For a clear presentation of how IHL rules developed, *see* Leslie C. Green, *Human Rights and the Law of Armed Conflict, in* Essays on the Modern Law of War 435 (Leslie C. Green ed., 1999) and Dietrich Schindler, *International Humanitarian Law: Its Remarkable Development and its Persistent Violation*, 5 Journal of the History of International Law 165–188 (2003) [hereinafter Schindler].

[9] Convention for the Amelioration of the Condition of the Wounded in Armies in the Field, (Aug. 22, 1864), 18 Martens Nouveau Recueil (ser. 1) 607, 129 Consol. T.S. 361.

[10] Christina M. Cerna, *Human Rights in Armed Conflict: Implementation of International Humanitarian Law Norms by Regional Intergovernmental Human Rights Bodies, in* Implementation of International Humanitarian Law 31, 34 (Frits Kalshoven & Yves Sandoz eds., 1989).

[11] Examples are the *Magna Carta* of 1215 the U.K. Bill of Rights of 1688, the French Declaration of the Rights of Man and of the Citizens of 1789, the U.S. Bill of Rights of 1791.

[12] "The demand for human rights, in the modern sense of the word, started as a liberal reaction, influenced by rationalist thinking in the 17th and 18th century, to the unfreedom caused by feudalism or monarchism." Eide, *supra* note 4, at 678.

exceptional cases international treaties providing protection to minorities. Shortly after the adoption of the United Nations Charter, which includes a set of articles dedicated to human rights, and the Universal Declaration of Human Rights on December 10, 1948,[13] a range of universal and regional instruments were designed to protect human rights.

However, at this early stage, because of the "underdevelopment" of HRL, the relationship between IHL and HRL was not discussed. Another reason for this unwillingness to scrutinize this relationship was the United Nations' reluctance to include the laws of war into its work because it "might undermine the force of *jus contra bellum*... and shake confidence in the ability of the world body to maintain peace."[14] Kolb notes that the 1948 Universal Declaration of Human Rights "completely bypasses the question of respect for human rights in armed conflict, while at the same time human rights were scarcely mentioned during the drafting of the 1949 Geneva Conventions."[15] A contrary viewpoint is presented by Schindler who argues that "the UN exerted a considerable, though little noticed, influence on [the outcome of the diplomatic conference that led to the adoption of the Geneva Conventions]. The efforts towards an international guarantee of human rights left an imprint on the Conventions."[16] In particular, he points out that Common Article 3 constitutes, in his opinion, a human rights provision since it aims to regulate the relationship between the state and its nationals in times of non-international armed conflicts.[17] Moreover the change of name of the body of law governing armed conflicts, i.e. from "law of war" or "law of armed conflict" to "international humanitarian law," reflects a different attitude towards it. Nevertheless, it is doubtful that at that time, such a view represented the majority.

---

[13] Universal Declaration of Human Rights, G.A. Res. 217A(III), U.N. Doc. A/810 (Dec. 10, 1948) [hereinafter UDHR].

[14] Robert Kolb, *The Relationship between International Humanitarian Law and Human Rights Law: A Brief History of the 1948 Universal Declaration of Human Rights and the 1949 Geneva Conventions*, 324 Int'l Rev. Red Cross 400, 409–419 (1998) [hereinafter Kolb]. *See also* Keith Suter, *Human Rights in Armed Conflicts*, XV Military Law and Law of War Review 400 (1976) [hereinafter Suter].

[15] *Id.*

[16] Schindler, *supra* note 8, at 170.

[17] *Id.* at 170–171. *See also* Louise Doswald-Beck & Sylvain Vité, *Origin and Nature of Human Rights Law and Humanitarian Law*, 293 Int'l Rev. Red Cross 95, 112 (1993) [hereinafter Doswald-Beck & Vité]; Joyce A.C. Gutteridge, *The Geneva Conventions of 1949*, 26 BYIL 300 (1949).

3. "Human Rights in Armed Conflicts"

Several events led to a growing interest in the issue: the adoption of the two international human rights covenants in 1966,[18] the conflicts in Vietnam and in Nigeria, and the Israeli occupation of Arab territories in 1967.[19] While the last two conflicts raised the difficult and practical issue of whether human rights law was applicable in times of armed conflict, the covenants, by creating a category of non-derogable rights,[20] explicitly acknowledged that certain human rights could be curtailed in armed conflict. It also ended the United Nations' trend to avoid dealing with armed conflicts.[21] Similar clauses are included in regional conventions such as the 1950 European Convention on Human Rights (ECHR),[22] and the 1969 American Convention on Human Rights.[23]

The 1968 Tehran Human Rights Conference, celebrating the 20th Anniversary of the UDHR, clearly raised the issue as to how both regimes interrelated. Doswald-Beck and Vité argue that it was "[t]he true turning point, when humanitarian law and human rights gradually began to draw closer."[24] Resolution No. XXIII called upon the U.N. General Assembly to "invite the Secretary General to study ... steps which could be taken to secure the better application of existing humanitarian international conventions and rules in all armed conflicts" and "[t]he need for additional humanitarian international conventions or for possible revision of existing Conventions to ensure the better protection of civilians, prisoners and combatants in all armed conflicts."[25] Remarkably, the resolution was entitled "Human Rights

---

[18] International Covenant on Civil and Political Rights, G.A. Res. 2200A (XXI), 21 U.N. GAOR (Supp. No. 16) at 52, U.N. Doc. A/6316 (Dec. 16, 1966), 999 U.N.T.S. 171, *entered into force* Mar. 23, 1976 [hereinafter ICCPR] and International Covenant on Economic, Social and Cultural Rights, G.A. res. 2200A (XXI), 21 U.N. GAOR Supp. (No. 16) at 49, U.N. Doc. A/6316 (1966), 993 U.N.T.S. 3, *entered into force* Jan. 3, 1976.

[19] Suter, *supra* note 14, at 395.

[20] Article 2(4) spells out "No derogation from articles 6 [right to life], 7 [prohibition on torture and inhuman treatment], 8 (paragraphs 1 and 2) [prohibition on slavery and servitude], 11 [prohibition on imprisonment for failure to fulfill a contractual obligation], 15 [prohibition on prosecution for offences which were not crimes when committed], 16 [right to recognition as a person before the law] and 18 [freedom of thought, conscience, and religion] may be made under this provision." ICCPR, *supra* note 18.

[21] Suter, *supra* note 14, at 400.

[22] European Convention for the Protection of Human Rights and Fundamental Freedoms, 213 U.N.T.S. 221, *entered into force* Nov. 4, 1950 [hereinafter ECHR].

[23] American Convention on Human Rights, O.A.S. Treaty Series No. 36, 1144 U.N.T.S. 123, *entered into force* July 18, 1978 [hereinafter ACHR].

[24] Doswald-Beck & Vité, *supra* note 17, at 95–119. See also Kolb, *supra* note 14, at 419.

[25] Resolution XXIII, adopted by the International Conference on Human Rights, Tehran, May 12, 1968, *available at* www1.umn.edu/humanrts/instree/1968a.htm (last visited October 8, 2007).

in Armed Conflicts" in order to satisfy those professing a separation between the two regimes. Indeed, fears were articulated that IHL may thereby be viewed as a branch of HRL. In those days, separatists claimed that the two underlying motivations of IHL, humanitarian considerations and self-interest, were not present in HRL norms.[26]

Yet, notwithstanding criticism, "human rights in armed conflicts" became "one of the most popular phrases in the United Nations political vocabulary"[27] in the beginning of the 1970s. It gained popularity although or maybe because it was unclear what it encompassed.[28] The drafter of the paper, Sean MacBride, equates the phrase with IHL,[29] which is highly disturbing since HRL in armed conflict and IHL are undeniably not the same. Later U.N. documents take a different stance inasmuch as they understand human rights as a peacetime concept. But, more generally, the expression "human rights law in conflict" seeks to provide protection to civilians caught in armed conflict. This explains why some scholars mainly focus on the Fourth Geneva Convention when dealing with this topic and assert that "the greatest departure made by the Geneva Law of 1949, which may be regarded as a manifesto of human rights for civilians during armed conflict, is the Fourth Convention relative to the Protection of Civilians."[30]

4. *Commonalities Between IHL and HRL*

In spite of the strong view expressed by separationists, the idea that IHL and HRL had several points of commonalities gained momentum in the early 1970s. At that time it was argued that the two *corpora juris* were not only related but also that "[t]he law of war [was] a derogation from the normal regime of human rights."[31] Furthermore, both sets of laws were "based in their fundamental nature upon the dignity and value of the individual being."[32]

See also "Respect for Human Rights in Armed Conflicts," GA Res. 2444 (XXIII), December 19, 1968, *available at* www.icrc.org/ihl.nsf/FULL/440?OpenDocument (last visited October 8, 2007).

[26] *See* discussion in Suter, *supra* note 14, at 405–413.
[27] Suter, *supra* note 14, at 394.
[28] *Id.* at 396–397.
[29] Sean MacBride, *Human Rights in Armed Conflicts*, Revue de Droit Pénal Militaire et de Droit de la Guerre 373–389 [1970].
[30] Leslie C. Green, *Human Rights and the Law of Armed Conflict*, *in* Essays on the Modern Law of War 435, 448 (Leslie C. Green ed., 1999).
[31] G.I.A.D. Draper, *The Relationship Between the Human Rights Regime and the Law of Armed Conflicts*, Isr. R.B. Hum. Rts. 191, 206 (1971).
[32] Draper 1989, *supra* note 7, at 4.

However this stance was only partially espoused by states. Indeed the two Additional Protocols to the Geneva Conventions,[33] while keeping the cleavage between the two regimes clear, "paid tribute to the world of human rights."[34] Several provisions acknowledge the existence of human rights norms while some read like a catalogue of human rights. For example, Article 72 AP I recognizes that besides the rules expressed therein as well as in the GC IV which deal with the protection of civilian and civilian objects there are "other applicable rules of international law relating to the protection of fundamental human rights during international armed conflict."[35] More specifically, the Commentary invokes human rights law as a source of such "applicable rules."[36] What is more, Article 75 AP I lists a series of fundamental guarantees for individuals who are in the power of a belligerent state. Undoubtedly, this catalogue of rights is reminiscent of human rights provisions and, more concretely, the guarantees spelled out in the ICCPR concerning the right to fair trial.[37]

In contrast, Draper argued in the late 70s that IHL and HRL were fundamentally distinct because of differing origins, theories, nature and purposes. Strongly opposed to the fusion or even overlap of the two regimes, he heralded that

> The attempt to confuse the two regimes of law is insupportable in theory and inadequate in practice. The two regimes are not only distinct but are diametrically opposed... at the end of the day, the law of human rights seeks to reflect the cohesion and harmony in human society and must, from the nature of things be a different and opposed law to that which seeks to regulate the conduct of hostile relationships between states or other organized armed groups, and in internal rebellions.[38]

---

[33] Protocol Additional to the Geneva Conventions of 12 August 1949, and Relating to the Protections of Victims of International Armed Conflicts (Protocol I), opened for signature Dec. 12, 1977, U.N. Doc. A/32/144, Annex I, II, (1977), *reprinted in* 16 I.L.M. 1391 (1977) [hereinafter AP I]; Protocol Additional to the Geneva Conventions of 12 August 1949, and Relating to the Protection of Victims of Non-International Armed Conflicts (Protocol I), June 8, 1977, 1125 U.N.T.S. 3 [hereinafter AP II].

[34] Doswald-Beck & Vité, *supra* note 17, at 95–119.

[35] Article 72 API, *supra* note 33.

[36] "[V]arious instruments relating to human rights spring to mind...In the first place, there is the Universal Declaration of 1948, but that Declaration represents, in its own words, a common standard of achievement for all peoples and all nations and does not constitute a legal obligation upon States. In the field under consideration here, there are three instruments binding the States which are Parties to them: a) the International Covenant on Civil and Political Rights; b) the European Convention for the Protection of Human Rights and fundamental freedoms; c) the American Convention on Human Rights." Yves Sandoz, Christophe Swinarski, Bruno Zimmerman, eds., Commentary on the Additional Protocols of 8 June 1977 to the Geneva Conventions of 12 August 1949, paras 2927–2928 (1996).

[37] Article 75 AP I, *supra* note 33. See comments by Doswald-Beck & Vité, *supra* note 17, at 113.

[38] G.I.A.D. Draper, *Humanitarian Law and Human Rights*, Acta Juridica 193, 205 [1979].

While recognizing that there are occasions when IHL and HRL do overlap, he contends that they cannot do so in any meaningful manner and, thus, IHL should be the governing body of law during armed conflict. Consequently, IHL is a "derogation from the normal regime of human rights."

Nevertheless, in 1990 experts adopted the so-called Turku Declaration of Minimum Humanitarian Standards that interlinked IHL and HRL. What is more, it mingled principles and norms that were present in both sets of laws and merged them into a single document. It proclaims principles "which are applicable in all situations, including internal violence, disturbances, tensions and public emergency, and which cannot be derogated from under any circumstances."[39] Although this declaration is the result of a private initiative, it was quickly integrated in the work of the United Nations and became what is now called "standards of humanity." Gradually the resolution and, thereby, its approach to the relationship between IHL and HRL gained recognition.

5. *IHL as the* Lex Specialis

The debate as to how IHL and HRL interrelate was again opened in 1996 when the International Court of Justice was asked whether the use of nuclear weapons breached any international law rules. It had been argued that nuclear weapons inherently violated the right to life as enshrined in Article 6 ICCPR.[40] The ICJ explained that since Article 6 sets forth a non-derogable right, it also applies in time of armed conflict. Yet, the ICJ added that this provision could not be interpreted so as to outlaw military operations, which *per se* are aimed at the killing of individuals:

> In principle, the right not arbitrarily to be deprived of one's life applies also in hostilities. The test of what is an arbitrary deprivation of life, however, then falls to be determined by the applicable *lex specialis*, namely, the law applicable in armed conflict which is designed to regulate the conduct of hostilities. Thus whether a particular loss of life, through the use of a certain weapon in warfare, is to be considered an arbitrary deprivation of life contrary to Article 6 of the Covenant, can only be decided

---

[39] Declaration of Minimum Humanitarian Standards, U.N. Doc. E/CN.4/Sub.2/1991/55 (Aug. 12, 1991).

[40] *See* the written statements of Malaysia, the Solomon Islands, and Egypt as cited in Christopher Greenwood, *Jus Ad Bellum and Jus In Bello in the Nuclear Weapons Advisory Opinion, in* International Law, the International Court of Justice and Nuclear Weapons 253 (Laurence Boisson de Chazournes & Philippe Sands, eds., 1999).

by reference to the law applicable in armed conflict and not deduced from the terms of the Covenant itself.[41]

Undoubtedly the ICJ declared that although IHL was the governing body of law applying in times of armed conflict, HRL continued to apply. It thereby recognized that while the interpretation of the right to life as encapsulated in the ICCPR might be affected by the application of the *lex specialis* rule, in other instances, the protection offered by HRL provisions might exceed that conceded by IHL.

This seminal statement led an entire generation of scholars to discuss the meaning of the expression *lex specialis* and, how the ICJ conceived the relationship between the two *corpora juris*. Generally, the *lex specialis* principle holds that when two norms collide, the more specific rule should be applied to provide content for the more general rule. For some authors the application of the *lex specialis* rule meant that in times of armed conflict IHL was the applicable law and HRL had to be discarded in the great majority of cases, for it was not appropriate. Speaking specifically about targeting, Watkin explains that "[r]ather than attempt to extend human rights norms to an armed conflict scenario, the appropriate approach is to apply the *lex specialis* of humanitarian law."[42] Some authors explain that, by adopting a *lex specialis* approach, the ICJ ignored "a large portion of human rights law, entirely disregarding the rights of those who are labeled as combatants."[43] As a result HRL is sidelined and replaced by IHL.

Another way to look at the *lex specialis* rule is to see it as a means to create a harmonious relationship between the two bodies of law since such a rule cannot be applied between two fundamentally incompatible set of laws. In particular, some authors contend that "the Court develop[ed] its reasoning by re-interpreting the law of armed conflict with a new-found emphasis on promoting humanitarian considerations."[44] Indeed, on several occasions, the ICJ explains that the rules and principles applicable in armed conflict are all related to considerations of humanity and that they are permeated with an "intrinsically humanitarian character."[45]

---

[41] Legality of the Threat or Use of Nuclear Weapons, Advisory Opinion, (July 8, 1996), I.C.J. Reports 1996, para. 25 [hereinafter Nuclear Weapons Opinion].

[42] Kenneth Watkin, *Controlling the Use of Force: A Role for Human Rights Norms in Contemporary Armed Conflict*, 98 Am. J. Int'l L. 1, 22 (2004) [hereinafter Watkin].

[43] David S. Koller, *The Moral Imperative: Toward a Human Rights – Based Law of War*, 46 Harv. Int'l L. J. 231, 261 (2005) [hereinafter Koller].

[44] Dale Stephens, *Human Rights and Armed Conflict – The Advisory Opinion of the International Court of Justice in the Nuclear Weapons Case*, 4 Yale Hum. Rts. & Dev. L.J. 1, 15 (2001) [hereinafter Stephens].

[45] Nuclear Weapons Opinion, para. 86.

6. IHL and HRL as Complementary or Distinctive Regimes

In order to explain the articulation of the relationship between IHL and HRL, scholars submitted a new theory, that of complementarity, which proclaimed that IHL and HRL are "not identical bodies of law but complement each other and ultimately remain distinct."[46] Detter advocates a horizontal view of IHL and HRL inasmuch as they are "*ratione materiae* interrelated fields, both raising the level of behaviour towards individuals and both concerned with the rights and protections of individuals."[47] In a nutshell, IHL and HRL are mutually supportive regimes. This is based on the idea that there is "considerable scope for reference to human rights law as a supplement to the provisions of the laws of war."[48]

Three types of arguments are made in this regard. First, HRL may fill in gaps in IHL. This is particularly the case when IHL rules are unclear or cover only certain situations. For example, the right to fair trial as protected in human rights treaties and developed by the jurisprudence of various international/regional courts/committees appears to be more comprehensive than the one enshrined in the Geneva Conventions and the Additional Protocols.

Second, HRL may provide specific mechanisms for implementing IHL provisions. Owing to the dearth or failure of IHL enforcement mechanisms (barring the exception of international criminal law) and the successful development of strict accountability mechanisms in HRL, individuals have turned towards human rights organs to adjudicate violations of IHL. Slowly these organs ventured into IHL, an area that used to be considered as separate and discrete. Despite the controversy surrounding the involvement as such organs in applying IHL, it is contended that human rights bodies "fill an institutional gap and give international humanitarian law an even more pro-human-rights orientation."[49] What is more, "incorporation of human rights principles of accountability can have a positive impact on the regulation of the use of force during armed conflict."[50]

Third, humanitarian considerations entered IHL at the end of the 19th century when the first conventions were drafted. It is contended that the humanitarian impulse set at that time gradually replaced concepts such as reciprocity,[51] an

---

[46] Heintze 2004, *supra* note 3, at 794.
[47] Ingrid Detter, The Law of War 161 (2000).
[48] Christopher Greenwood, *Rights at the Frontier: Protecting the Individual in Time of War*, in Law at the Centre, 277–293 (Barry Rider, ed., 1999) [hereinafter Greenwood].
[49] Theodor Meron, *The Humanization of Humanitarian Law*, 94 Am. J. Int'l L. 239, 247 (2000). *See also* Watkin, *supra* note 42, at 24.
[50] Watkin, *supra* note 42, at 34.
[51] *See* Stephens, *supra* note 44, at 11–12.

illustration of which being the Martens clause.[52] In light of this, experts argue that "[g]iven the relatively similar goals of these instruments, namely the protection and respect of humanity, it is difficult to accept... that the two streams of the law are 'diametrically opposed'."[53] As the International Criminal Tribunal for the Former Yugoslavia declared "[a] sovereignty-oriented approach has been gradually supplanted by a human being-oriented approach."[54]

This trend has been coined the "humanization of humanitarian law" by Theodor Meron who describes it in the following terms

> through a process of osmosis or application by analogy, the recognition as customary of norms rooted in international human rights instruments has affected the interpretation, and eventually the status, of the parallel norms in instruments of international humanitarian law.[55]

Despite this tendency, the doctrine of the separation of the two bodies of law continues to attract a number of scholars. Feinstein, for example, affirms that "the regime of international humanitarian law applicable in armed conflict situations and the regime of international human rights applicable in peacetime are mutually exclusive since there is a distinct contradiction between them."[56] Likewise, the European Union Guidelines on Promoting Compliance with International Humanitarian Law proffer that IHL and HRL "are distinct bodies of law and, while both are principally aimed at protecting individuals, there are important differences between them."[57]

Most arguments rely on the historical differences between these two areas. IHL was inspired and influenced by concepts of chivalry,[58] canonical notions of

---

[52] "Until a more complete code of the laws of war is issued, the High Contracting Parties think it right to declare that in cases not included in the Regulations adopted by them, populations and belligerents remain under the protection and empire of the principles of international law, as they result from the usages established between civilized nations, from the laws of humanity and the requirements of the public conscience." Convention with respect to the Laws and Customs of War on Land, July 29, 1989, preamble, 32 Stat. 1803, 1805, 187 Consol. T.S. 429, 431. For a discussion on the Martens clause, *see* Rupert Ticehurst, *The Martens Clause and the Laws of Armed Conflict*, 317 Int'l Rev. Red Cross 125 (1997).

[53] Stephens, *supra* note 44, at 13.

[54] Prosecutor v. Tadic, Case No. IT-94-1-AR72, Appeals Chamber, (October 2, 1995) para. 97.

[55] Theodor Meron, *The Humanization of Humanitarian Law*, 94 Am. J. Int'l L. 239, 244 (2000).

[56] Barry A. Feinstein, *The Applicability of the Regime of Human Rights in Times of Armed Conflict and Particularly to Occupied Territories: The Case of Israel's Security Barrier*, 4 Nw. J. Int'l Hum. Rts. 238, 301 (2005).

[57] European Union Guidelines on Promoting Compliance with International Humanitarian Law, 2005/C 327/04, para. 12, Official Journal of the European Union, December 21, 2005.

[58] As early as 1989, Draper argued that IHL witnessed a gradual elimination of the ideals of chivalry. Draper 1989, *supra* note 7, at 6.

immunity of noncombatants,[59] personal honor, and reciprocity and, accordingly, developed through the centuries. In contrast, HRL intends to protect individuals from the abuse of power by their own governments and human rights are mainly granted via treaties.

Another recurrent argument is that it is more practical to maintain the two as distinct bodies of law because IHL provides a more complete set of norms relating to basic standards of human dignity in the particular circumstances of armed conflict. In other words, because IHL has been specifically designed to apply in times of conflict, it is better suited to military operations. Furthermore, as most IHL treaties are being negotiated by military lawyers who are well acquainted with the exigencies of battle conditions, one assumes that the standards to which they agreed upon in the various conventions are of practical value, i.e. they will be abided by because they reflect the situation on the ground. As Greenwood explains war is "far too complex and brutal a phenomenon to be capable of being constrained by rules designed for peacetime."[60]

7. A Regained Interest in the Lex Specialis Rule

While scholars were debating how the two regimes interrelated, the ICJ grappled again with the issue in 2004. In its Advisory Opinion on the Legal Consequences of the Construction of a Wall in the Occupied Palestinian Territories, it confirmed that IHL was the *lex specialis*. Repeating its early pronouncement, the Court admitted that the right to life should be interpreted according to IHL but again stressed that HRL applied also during armed conflict "save through the effect of provisions for derogation of the kind to be found in article 4 of the [ICCPR]."[61] In an attempt to clarify the way the *lex specialis* rule works in practice, the ICJ asserted that there are three groups of rights: "some rights may be exclusively matters of...humanitarian law; others may be exclusively of human rights law; yet other may be matters of both these branches of international law."[62]

Unfortunately, the ICJ does not explain how to subdivide the rights into these categories,[63] how a particular right should be interpreted when it is a matter of both branches, and whether IHL is always the *lex specialis* even when HRL provisions

---

[59] Eide, *supra* note 4, at 677.
[60] Greenwood, *supra* note 48, at 277–293.
[61] Legal Consequences of the Construction of a Wall in the Occupied Palestinian Territories, Advisory Opinion, July 9, 2004, I.C.J. Reports 2004, para. 106.
[62] *Id.* para. 106.
[63] *See* the critique by Michael Dennis, *Application of Human Rights Treaties Extraterritorially in Times of Armed Conflict and Military Occupation*, 99 Am. J. Int'l L. 119, 133 (2005).

may be more specialized and accurate than those found in IHL.[64] As a result "a number of... experts characterized this analysis as utterly unhelpful."[65] This again has led to an upsurge of writing in the field and to a renewed battle between the proponents of the theories of complementarity and separation.[66]

H. *Issues Relating to the Relationship Between IHL and HRL*

As aforementioned this book aims to present the state of affairs between IHL and HRL and, thereby, show the current trend amongst scholars dealing with this issue.

The first chapter introduces the reader to the main concepts, tenets and theories relating to IHL and HRL. The second focuses on the applicability of the two regimes while the third examines the ways they are implemented. The fourth chapter provides an insight into the protection of specific rights and persons offered by IHL and HRL while the fifth chapter examines the relationship between these regimes in specific situations.

---

[64] For example, Martin argues that "some derogable ECHR rights can constitute the *lex specialis* in armed conflict and should be used to interpret provisions in the law of armed conflict." Francisco F. Martin, *The Unified Use of Force and Exclusionary Rules: Amplifications in Light of the Comments of Professors Green and Paust*, 65 Sask. L. Rev. 451, 453 (2002).
[65] Report of the Expert Meeting on the Right to Life in Armed Conflicts and Situations of Occupation, Geneva (Sept. 1–2, 2005), *available at* www.cudih.org/communication/droit_vie_rapport.pdf (last visited Sept. 4, 2007), at 19.
[66] *See* e.g. Koller, *supra* note 43, at 231.

Part A
Concepts and Theories

Chapter I

Fundamental Standards of Humanity: A Common Language of International Humanitarian Law and Human Rights Law

*Marco Odello**

1. *Introduction*

The second part of the 20th and the beginning of the 21st century have shown a change in the characteristics and nature of armed conflict and the different forms of violence.[1] Conventional war between States, but also other forms of conflict and violence, generally classified as non-international armed conflict, such as civil wars, national liberation conflicts, secessionist movements, etc. have been the cause of widespread suffering and destruction. More limited but very violent forms of violence which take place within a state, such as internal disturbances, riots, and widespread acts of terrorism may be the cause of human suffering. At the same time, the more active role of international actors, including both states and international organizations, provide examples of use of military force in international actions, including peace-keeping operations, humanitarian intervention, and international military missions.[2] In all the mentioned cases, the use of armed force, either by regular armies or by other kinds of more or less organized groups, such as guerrilla, paramilitary and terrorist groups, factions, etc, generally defined as non-state actors,[3] is a common element. Recent events related to the use of terrorist-like actions on the international scene have made the scenario even more complex, as non-state actors are not always considered to be bound by rules of international law.[4]

---

* Lecturer in Law, Department of Law & Criminology, University of Wales, Aberystwyth, United Kingdom.
[1] *See generally* Helen Durham & Timothy L.H. McCormack, The Changing Face of Conflict and the Efficacy of International Humanitarian Law (1999) [hereinafter Durham & McCormack].
[2] Garth J. Cartledge, *Legal Constraints on Military Personnel Deployed on Peacekeeping Operations*, in Durham & McCormack, *supra* note 1.
[3] The term non-state actors has different meanings. *See infra* for more details.
[4] Martin Sheinin, *Background Paper*, Presented at the International Expert Meeting held in Stockholm, 7–9 (Feb. 22–24, 2000); Asbjørn Eide et al., *Combating Lawlessness in Grey Zone Conflicts*

The changing pattern of modern armed conflict makes it difficult sometimes to apply the established rules of international law related to the use of force[5] and the protection of victims of armed conflict.[6] They were developed essentially for regular armies in the battlefield or in occupied territories. The main corpus of the laws of war and International Humanitarian Law (IHL)[7] is primarily framed on the concept of state obligations and enemy powers (usually another state or group of states). It is a state-centered system of legal rules,[8] whose obligations lie on states more than on individuals. However, this system has been significantly influenced by Human Rights Law (HRL), in particular after the Second World War, and more recently by legal developments under international criminal law.[9]

In contemporary conflicts the battlefield is not sufficiently or easily delimited, as the concept of combatant, as a regular army soldier, has lost most of its meaning. The civilian population is directly involved in the theatre of operations, and sometimes it becomes the main target of military operations, with devastating effects on the people who should not be involved in the conflict. The protection of victims of armed conflict is becoming increasingly difficult in case of undefined situations of violence, resulting in a widespread and indiscriminate violation of fundamental

---

Through Minimum Humanitarian Standards, 89 Am. J. Int'l L. 217 (1995).
[5] On the use of force *see generally*, Tarcisio Gazzini, The Changing Rule on the Use of Force in International Law (2005).
[6] *See generally* ICRC, International Humanitarian Law and the Challenges of Contemporary Armed Conflicts, 28th International Conference of the Red Cross and Red Crescent (Geneva, Dec. 2–6, 2003), Doc. 03/IC/09 (2003) [hereinafter International Humanitarian Law and the Challeges of Contemporary Armed Conflicts].
[7] On IHL there is a vast literature, among others see Yoram Dinstein, The Conduct of Hostilities under the Law of International Armed Conflict (2004); Leslie C. Green, The Contemporary Law of Armed Conflict (2d ed. 2000); Ingrid Detter, The Law of War (2d ed. 2000); Eric David, Principes de droit des Conflits Armés (2d ed. 1999); Judith Gardam, Humanitarian Law (1999); Christopher Greenwood, The Concept of War in Modern International Law, 36 Int'l & Comp. L. Q. 283 (1987); Darío Villaroel Villaroel y Joaquín González Ibáñez, El derecho internacional humanitario presente. Reflexiones y fórmulas desde la perspectiva europea, in Derechos Humanos, Relaciones Internacionales y Globalización (Joaquín González Ibáñez ed., 2006) [hereinafter Ibáñez].
[8] A different opinion is expressed by Detter who considers that war "is essentially a relationship by armed force between individuals, subject in varying degree to the Law of War," *see* Detter, *supra* note 7, at 5.
[9] *See generally* Claire de Than & Edwin Shorts, International Criminal Law and Human Rights (2003) [hereinafter de Than & Shorts]; Kriangsaak Kittichaisaree, International Criminal Law (2001); Elies van Sliedregt, The Criminal Responsibility of Individuals for Violations of International Humanitarian Law (2003); Hortensia D.T. Gutierrez Posse, *The Relationship between International Humanitarian Law and the International Criminal Tribunals*, 88 Int'l Rev. Red Cross 65–86 (2006).

human rights, such as the right to life, the prohibition of inhuman and degrading treatment, the prohibition of genocide, non-discrimination, etc.[10]

The international community, defined as the complex combination of states, international organizations, non governmental organizations, and other actors, such as corporations,[11] has been quite slow in addressing the issue with new ideas and strategies. Nevertheless, some interesting developments should be considered. One of the most important efforts to deal with this situation was proposed in 1990. A group of experts met at the Institute for Human Rights at Åbo/Turku in Finland. They adopted the so-called Turku Declaration on "Minimum Humanitarian Standards." The essential purpose of this document was based on the fact that "international law relating to human rights and humanitarian norms applicable in armed conflicts do not adequately protect human beings in situations of internal violence, disturbances, tensions and public emergency."[12] The previous year, the International Institute of Humanitarian Law in San Remo had organized the 14th Round Table on the issue of rules of humanitarian law governing the conduct of hostilities in non-international armed conflict. The results of that meeting were adopted by the Council of the Institute and widely diffused.[13]

Since then, jurists, experts, and institutions have discussed the idea of defining rules that should be applied – as a minimum requirement – in all situations of violence, with particular attention to undefined situations of internal conflict.[14] During the 1990s, international organizations, in particular the United Nations

---

[10] From the United Nations' point of view, see: Nicole Questiaux, Study of the Implications for Human Rights of Recent Developments concerning Situations Known as State of Siege or Emergency, U.N. Doc. E/CN.4/Sub.2/1982/15; Tenth Annual Report and List of States which, since 1 January 1985, Have Proclaimed, Extended or Terminated a State of Emergency, Presented by Mr. Leandro Despouy, Special Rapporteur Appointed pursuant to Economic and Social Council Resolution 1985/37, U.N. Doc. E/CN.4/Sub.2/1997/19 (June 23, 1997) [hereinafter Questiaux].

[11] On the concept of international community see: Dino Kritsiotis, *Imaging the International Community*, 13.4 Eur. J. Int'l L. 961 992 (2002).

[12] Institute for Human Rights at Åbo Akademy University, *Declaration on Minimum Humanitarian Standards* (1990), submitted to the U.N. Sub-Commission on Prevention of Discrimination and Protection of Minorities, U.N. Doc. E/CN/Sub.2/1991/55.

[13] International Institute of Humanitarian Law, Declaration on the Rules of International Humanitarian Law Governing the Conduct of Hostilities in Non-International Armed Conflicts, adopted by the Council Meeting in Taormina (Apr. 7, 1990), published in 278 Int'l Rev. Red Cross 404–408 (1990).

[14] On the subject there is a wide literature, for a general approach to the main issues, see: Theodor Meron, Human Rights in Internal Strife: Their International Protection (1987); Subrata Roy Chowdhury, Rule of Law in a State of Emergency (1989); Jaime Oraá, Human Rights in States of Emergency in International Law (1992); Joan Fitzpatrick, Human Rights in Crisis (1994); Laura Lopez, *Uncivil Wars: The Challenge of Applying International Humanitarian Law to Internal Armed Confllict*, 69 N. Y. U. L. Rev. 916–962 (1994).

and the International Committee of the Red Cross (ICRC), have been working on this important but very challenging and controversial issue. International lawyers have put forward ideas and proposals. Recent developments in international law try to provide solutions and better means of protection for victims of conflicts in unclear or borderline cases.

The identified rules, defined as Fundamental Standards of Humanity (FSH),[15] may be considered an effort to provide additional means for the protection of potential victims in situations of violence in cases where the applicability of either HRL or IHL, or both, is unclear.

The scope of this chapter is to analyze the idea of FSH, taking into particular account the work of the United Nations within the wider context and evolution of international law. This chapter will not focus on the complex relationship between IHL and HRL. The more modest aim consists in providing an account and discussion on the possible means for the protection of victims in unclear situations of violence, when IHL and HRL may leave some potential gaps. First, the reasons for the use of FSH will be addressed including a short historical introduction leading to the use of this expression. Second, the main legal development under discussion will be considered, taking into consideration the work of the United Nations and other international bodies on this topic. Third, the possible nature, content and applicability of the FSH will be analyzed on the basis of the evolution of contemporary international law. Finally, the possible definition and role of FSH will be considered.

2. *Justification for Fundamental Standards of Humanity*

Before starting the analysis of legal developments related to FSH it may be useful to provide the reasons why this idea was introduced at international level. The main justification resides in the theoretical and practical distinction made in international law between IHL and HRL.[16] The prevailing assumption related to

---

[15] Theodor Meron, *On the Inadequate Reach of Humanitarian and Human Rights Law and the Need for a New Instrument*, 77 Am. J. Int'l L. 589 (1983) [hereinafter Meron 1983]; Hernán Montealegre, *The Compatibility of a State Party's Derogations under Human Rights Instruments with its Obligations under Protocol II and Common Article 3*, 33 Am. U. L. Rev. 41, 43–44 (1983); Theodor Meron, *Towards a Humanitarian Declaration on Internal Strife*, 78 Am. J. Int'l L. 859 (1984) [hereinafter Meron 1984]; Theodor Meron, *Draft Model Declaration on Internal Strife*, 262 Int'l Rev. Red Cross 59 (1988) [hereinafter Meron 1988]; Peter Kooijmans, *In the Shadowland Between Civil War and Civil Strife: Some Reflections on the Standard-Setting Process*, in Humanitarian Law of Armed Conflict: Challenges Ahead – Essays in Honour of Frits Kalshoven (Astrid Delissen & Gerard Tanja eds., 1991).

[16] For a general account of the two legal branches of international law *see* René Provost, International Human Rights and Humanitarian Law (2002) [hereinafter Provost].

IHL and HRL is that they "constitute two wholly independent systems, allowing for the possibility of concurrent application to the same situation or, less happily, of the inapplicability of both systems."[17] But difficulties are encountered in the application[18] of these two sets of norms in some situations of violence, that today represent the great majority of concern for the violation of fundamental rights of individuals.[19]

2.1. *The Problem of Applicability*

One of the main issues related to the distinction between IHL and IHRL is their applicability in different circumstances.[20] It is generally accepted today that the strict traditional distinction between law of war, implying the application of IHL, and law of peace, when HRL should be applied, is not viable any more.[21] From the legal point of view the problem consists in defining which rules are applicable, in particular when the nature and classification of the conflict, internal violence or international military action is unclear. Common Article 2 to the four 1949 GC defines its applicability in case of an international armed conflict "to all cases of declared war or of any other armed conflict which may arise between two or more of the High Contracting Parties, even if the state of war is not recognised by one of them." The 1949 Geneva Conventions (GCs)[22] will apply also in case of "partial or total occupation of the territory of a High Contracting Party, even if the said occupation meets with no resistance."

---

[17] Provost, *id.* at 274.
[18] Adam Roberts, *The Laws of War: Problems of Implementation in Contemporary Conflicts, in* Law in Humanitarian Crises 13 (vol. I, 1995).
[19] *See* University of British Columbia, Human Security Center, *Human Security Report, War and Peace in the 21st Century*, 18 (2005) [hereinafter Human Security Report].
[20] There is an extensive literature on the relationship between IHL and IHRL, among others *see* G.I.A.D. Draper, *The Relationship between the Human Rights Regime and the Laws of Armed Conflict*, 1 Isr. Y.B. Hum. Rights 191 (19/1); Louise Doswald-Beck & Sylvain Vité, *International Humanitarian Law and Human Rights Law*, 293 Int'l Rev. Red Cross 94 (1993) [hereinafter Louise Doswald-Beck & Sylvain Vité]; Raúl Emilio Vinuesa, *Interface, Correspondence and Convergence of Human Rights and International Humanitarian Law*, 1 Y.B. Int'l Human. L. 69–110 (1998); Provost, *supra* note 16; Hans-Joachim Heintze, *On the Relationship between Human Rights Law Protection and International Humanitarian Law*, 86 Int'l Rev. Red Cross 798 (2004).
[21] *See* Carsten Stahn, 'Jus ad bellum', 'jus in bello'... 'jus post bellum'? – *Rethinking the Conception of the Law of Armed Force*, 17 Eur. J. Int'l L. 921, 922 (2007).
[22] The Geneva Convention for the Amelioration of the Condition of the Wounded and Sick in Armed Forces in the Field, Aug. 12, 1949, 75 U.N.T.S. 31, 32 [hereinafter GC I]; Geneva Convention for the Amelioration of the Condition of the Wounded, Sick and Shipwrecked Members of the Armed Forces at Sea, Aug. 12, 1949, 75 U.N.T.S. 85, 86 [hereinafter GC II]; Geneva Convention Relative to the Treatment to Prisoners of War, Aug. 12, 1949, 75 U.N.T.S. 135, 136 [hereinafter GC III]; Geneva Convention Relative to the Protection of Civilian Persons in Time of War, Aug. 12, 1949, 75 U.N.T.S. 287, 288 [hereinafter GC IV].

In case of non-international armed conflict, the applicable rules are mainly those provided by the common Article 3 to the four GCs and the 1977 Additional Protocol II.[23] The main problem of both rules is that they set a quite high threshold of the level of violence, so that the possible cases of application are quite limited.[24]

But situations of violent conflict are not limited to the inter-state and intra-state violence. The United Nations, mainly during the 1990s, has been increasingly involved in peace-keeping operations.[25] Other international organizations, such as the North Atlantic Treaty Organization (NATO), the European Union (EU), the Organization for Security and Cooperation in Europe (OSCE), the Organization of American States (OAS), and the African Union (AU) have deployed military missions, under different names and mandates, to foreign countries,[26] mainly under the umbrella of collective security,[27] and humanitarian protection in case of gross violations of human rights.[28] So-called "coalitions of the willing" have been established to fight international terrorism, sometimes using military means, and under the right to self-defense against a military attack.[29] This activity has been defined as "war" against terrorism,[30] an expression with unclear legal

---

[23] Protocol Additional to the Geneva Conventions of August 12, 1949, and Relating to the Protection of Victims of International Armed Conflicts, June 8, 1977, 1125 U.N.T.S. 3 (entered into force Dec. 7, 1978) [hereinafter AP I].

[24] On the difficult aplication of the 1977 AP II *see* Arturo Carrillo, *Hors de Logique: Contemporary Issues in International Humanitarian Law as Applied to Internal Armed Conflict*, 15 Am. U. Int'l L.Rev. 1, 66–97 (1999).

[25] *See generally* Nigel D. White, Keeping the Peace: the United Nations and the Maintenance of International Peace and Security (2d ed. 1997).

[26] These new forms of military action are based on the concept of collective responsibility to protect discussed in International Commission on Intervention and State Sovereignty, *Responsibility to Protect* (2001); U.N. High-level Panel on Threats, Challenges and Change, *A More Secure World: Our Shared Responsibility*, U.N. Doc. A/59/565 (Dec. 2, 2004); *see also* U.N.G.A. Res. 60/1 (Oct. 24, 2005), paras 138–139. On the issue *see* Gwyn Prins, *Lord Castlereagh's Return: the Significance of Kofi Annan's High Level Panel on Threats, Challenges and Change*, 81 International Affairs 373–391 (2005); Marco Odello, *Commentary on the United Nations' High Level Panel on Threats, Challenges and Change*, 10 JCSL 231–262 (2005).

[27] *See generally* Ademola Abass, Regional Organisations and the Development of Collective Security: Beyond Chapter VIII of the UN Charter (2004).

[28] Alexander Moseley & Richard J. Norman, Human Rights and Military Intervention (2002).

[29] On self-defence *see* Gazzini, *supra* note 5, Chapter IV.

[30] *See* Helen Duffy, The 'War on Terror' and the Framework of International Law (2005); Thomas M. Frank, *Terrorism and the Right to Self-Defence*, 95 Am. J. Int'l L 839 (2001). In favour of the use of force for self-defence, under Article 51 of the U.N. Charter, against an attack by terrorist groups *see* Davies Brown, *Use of Force Against Terrorism After September 11th: State Responsibility, Self-Defense and Other Reponses*, 11 Cardozo J. Int'l & Comp. L. 6 (2003); Sean D. Murphy, *Terrorism and the Concept of 'Armed Attack' in Article 51 of the U.N. Charter*, Harvard Int'l L.J. 43, 47–50 (2002). But see the critical analysis in the article by Gabor Rona, *Interesting Times for*

meaning[31] and possible dangerous consequences in terms of legal protection not only under IHL[32] but also under HRL.[33] These situations, sometimes defined as forcible methods short of war,[34] were not foreseen by traditional IHL and the application of international legal rules in the mentioned cases has not always been clear, due to their uneasy classification under international law.[35]

This is the reason why the issue of convergence and overlapping of IHL and HRL[36] is particularly relevant and it also led to the proposal of possible FSH applicable to all situations of violence falling short of the definitions provided by IHL treaties.

2.2. International Humanitarian Law

The traditional way how international law has addressed situations of military violence between or among states has been through the application of rules of the law of war. The development of rules on the conduct of hostilities, means and methods of warfare (Hague Law),[37] and the protection of individuals (Geneva

---

International Humanitarian Law: Challenges from the 'War on Terror', 17 Terrorism and Political Violence 157–173 (2005).

[31] Antonio Cassese, *Terrorism is Also Disrupting Some Crucial Legal Categories of International Law*, 12 Eur. J. Int'l L. 993 (2001); Steven R. Ratner, *Jus ad Bellum and Jus in Bello after September 11*, 96 Am. J. Int'l L. 905 (2002).

[32] *See* in particular International Humanitarian Law and the Challenges of Contemporary Armed Conflicts, *supra* note 6, at 17.

[33] *See* Paul Hoffman, *Human Rights and Terrorism*, 26 Hum. Rts. Q. 932 (2004); Alfred de Zayas, *Human Rights and Indefinite Detention*, 87 Int'l Rev. Red Cross 15 (2005); Colin Warbrick, *The European Response to Terrorism in an Age of Human Rights*, 15 Eur. J. Int. Law 989 (2004); Sabine von Schorlemer, *Human Rights: Substantive and Institutional Implications of the War Against Terrorism*, 14 Eur. J. Int. Law 265 (2003).

[34] Charles W. Kegley, Jr & Gregory A. Raymond, *Normative Constraints on the Use of Force Short of War*, 23 Journal of Peace Research 213 (1986).

[35] Tim Laurence, Humanitarian Assistance and Peacekeeping: An Uneasy Alliance? (1999); Michael Keren & Donald A. Sylvan, International Intervention: Sovereignty Versus Responsibility (2002); Simon Chesterman, Just War or Just Peace?: Humanitarian Intervention and International Law (2002).

[36] Jean Pictet, Humanitarian Law and the Protection of War Victims (1975); Dietrich Schindler, *Human Rights and Humanitarian Law: Interrelationship of the Laws*, 31 Am. U. L. Rev. 935 (1982); Jacques Meurant, *Humanitarian Law and Human Rights Law: Alike Yet Distinct*, 293 Int'l Rev. Red Cross 89 (1993). *See* introduction to the book.

[37] The treaties and rules concerning the means and methods of warfare include several treaties, among the most relevant: Convention (II) with Respect to the Laws and Customs of War on Land and its annex: Regulations concerning the Laws and Customs of War on Land. The Hague, 29 July 1899; Convention (IV) respecting the Laws and Customs of War on Land and its annex: Regulations concerning the Laws and Customs of War on Land. The Hague, 18 October 1907, Dietrich Schindler & Jiri Toman, The Laws of Armed Conflicts 263–264 (1988) [hereinafter Schindler & Toman]. The texts are available at www.icrc.org/ihl.nsf/TOPICS?OpenView.

Law) have merged in the contemporary *corpus* of IHL.[38] The scope of the law of war was related to the other main branch of international law, the law of peace. At the beginning of the 20th century, the generally accepted rule was that in case of armed conflict the law of war would apply, in other situations the law of peace would regulate inter-state relationships.[39] This rule was clearly stated in the following terms by the House of Lords in 1902: "the law recognises a state of peace and a state of war, but that it knows nothing of an intermediate state which is neither one thing nor the other."[40]

This clear-cut rule was easy to delineate, but difficult to apply in many circumstances, particulalry after the end of the Second World War. This difficulty was linked to the prohibition of the use of force[41] among states under Article 2 (4) of the U.N. Charter, with the consequent legal limitations on the right to use force (*jus ad bellum*),[42] and the unexpected development of human rights rules at international level, mainly through the United Nations[43] and other regional organizations, that started the debate on the relationship between IHL (*jus in bello*) and HRL,[44] and their applicability in different types of armed conflict. At the same time, the nature of the conflict has rapidly changed since the end of the Second World War. Situations of internal violence, and civil strife do not fit easily in the traditional criteria defined by the *jus in bello* and *jus ad bellum*.[45]

---

[38] The 1977 Additional Protocol I brings together the laws of Geneva and of the Hague, which until then had developed separately; *see* generally François Bugnion, *Law of Geneva and Law of The Hague*, 83 Int'l Rev. Red Cross 901 (2001); Legality of the Threat or Use of Nuclear Weapons, Advisory Opinion (July 8, 1996), 1996 ICJ Rep. 226, 256 [hereinafter Advisory Opinion on Nuclear Weapons].

[39] On the debate before the Second World War *see* Quincy Wright, When does War Exist? 26 Am. J. Int'l L. 362 (1932); William J. Ronan, *English and American Courts and the Definition of War*, 31 Am. J. Int'l L. 642 (1937).

[40] House of Lords, Lord MacNaghten, Janson v. Driefontein Consolidated Mines Ltd. [1902] AC 484.

[41] *See* generally Christine Gray, International Law and the Use of Force (2nd ed. 2004).

[42] *Report of the Secretary-General on Respect for Human Rights in Armed Conflicts*, U.N. Doc. A/7720 (1969) 11, para. 19.

[43] *See* in particular Resolution on Respect for Human Rights in Armed Conflicts, Res. 2444 (XXIII) (Dec. 19, 1968) reprinted in Schindler and Toman, *supra* note 37, at 263–264.

[44] Alessandro Migliazza, L'évolution de la réglementation de la guerre à la lumière de la sauvegarde des droits de l'homme, 37 Recueil des cours 142 (1972-III); U.N., Report of the Secretary-General on Respect for Human Rights in Armed Conflicts, U.N. Doc. A/8052 (1970).

[45] On the two categories of *jus ad bellum* and *jus in bello, see* Henri Meyrowitz, Le Principe de l'égalité des Belligérants devant le Droit de la Guerre (1970); Christopher Greenwood, *The Relationship Between* jus ad bellum *and* jus in bello, 9 Rev. Int'l Studies 221 (1983). On the use of force in general *see* Christine Gray, International Law and the Use of Force (2d ed. 2004).

It should be remembered here that one of the fundamental principles of IHL is that its rules would apply to any party to the conflict independently from the reasons which led to that particular conflict.[46] This automatic applicability of IHL would help the enforcement of the rules without relying on the categorization of a conflict, which in many cases can take a political dimension, particularly with the classification of some rebel groups under the label of terrorism.[47] On the other side, there are no international independent supervisory bodies which can declare the applicability of IHL and the classification of a situation of violence. This makes the enforcement of IHL quite difficult in many contemporary situations of violence.[48]

Despite the difficulties mentioned before, in case of armed conflict the rules of IHL is the relevant applicable law.[49] To define their applicability, the GCs and their two 1977 Additional Protocols (AP I[50] and AP II[51]) distinguish between different types of conflict.[52]

International armed conflicts are situations where two or more states are involved in the use of armed force. The full *corpus* of IHL is applicable. Wars of national liberation refer to armed conflicts when "peoples are fighting against colonial domination and alien occupation and against racist regimes in the exercise of their right to self-determination."[53]

Internal armed conflict or non-international armed conflict refers to situations that cannot be included in either of the previous categories.[54] Article 1(1) AP II states that the conflict

> must take place in the territory of a High Contracting Party between its armed forces and dissident armed forces or other organized armed groups which, under responsible

---

[46] François Bugnion, *Just Wars, Wars of Aggression and International Humanitarian Law*, 84 Int'l Rev. Red Cross 523 (2002).

[47] On the case of Chechnya *see* Aeyal M. Gross, *Human Proportions: Are Human Rights the Emperor's New Clothes of the International Law of Occupation?*, 35 Eur. J. Int. Law 1 (2007); William Abresch, *A Human Rights Law of Internal Armed Conflict: The European Court of Human Rights in Chechnya*, 16 Eur. J. Int. Law 741 (2005).

[48] This risk is particularly clear in the so-called war against terrorism, when states use war-like means and methods, but then they deny the application of IHL to alleged terrorists, and because they are considered illegal combatants, they are denied the protection of IHL.

[49] *See* International Humanitarian Law and the Challenges of Contemporary Armed Conflicts, *supra* note 6.

[50] AP I, *supra* note 23.

[51] Protocol Additional to the Geneva Conventions of 12 August 1949, and relating to the Protection of Victims of Non-International Armed Conflicts (June 8, 1977) [hereinafter AP II].

[52] For an analysis of the different types of armed conflicts *see* Detter, *supra* note 7, at 38–61.

[53] Article 1(4) AP I, *supra* note 50.

[54] Lindsay Moir, The Law of Internal Armed Conflict (2002) [hereinafter Moir].

command, exercise such control over a part of its territory as to enable them to carry out sustained and concerted military operations and to implement this Protocol.

These are more detailed conditions compared to the Common Article 3 to the four GC which refers to "armed conflict not of an international character occurring in the territory of one of the High Contracting Parties."

A fourth category of situations of violence is mentioned in Article 1(2) AP II defining "situations of internal disturbances and tensions, such as riots, isolated and sporadic acts of violence and other acts of a similar nature, as not being armed conflicts." The problem is that those situations of violence do not fit into the legal category of armed conflict and therefore IHL would not apply. They are dealt sometimes by states with internal security operations, which use police and military forces. At this stage, before discussing the problems related to the protection of victims of those types of conflict, the issues of HRL should be addressed.

2.3. *Human Rights Law*

Compared to IHL, international human rights law has developed and addressed a wide range of situations in the last sixty years.[55] It is impossible here to make reference to all the conventions, pacts, treaties, declarations, and resolutions dealing with human rights. It is important to point out that human rights law and rules have expanded to touch almost all kinds of situations, dealing with both individual and collective rights, and leading some scholars to describe this phenomenon as "proliferation of rights."[56]

It is accepted that HRL applies as a set of standard rules that pervades both international and national law. What is relevant to mention here is that international instruments of HRL also foresee the possibility of derogations in some cases and under specific conditions. Derogation from some human rights treaties[57] is allowed by the International Covenant on Civil and Political Rights (ICCPR)[58] and by regional instruments.[59] For the present analysis Article 4 ICCPR refers to a

---

[55] *See* Louis Henkin, The Age of Rights (1990); Louis Henkin, International Law: Policies and Values (1995); Jack Donnelly, Universal Human Rights in Theory and Practice (1989); Flavia Lattanzi, Garanzie dei diritti dell'uomo nel diritto internazionale generale (1983); from a more theoretical point of view *see* Costas Douzinas, The End of Human Rights (2000).

[56] Carl Wellman, The Proliferation of Rights: Moral Progress or Empty Rhetoric? (1999).

[57] There is wide literature on this subject. *See* the bibliography *supra* note 3.

[58] International Covenant on Civil and Political Rights, G.A. Res. 2200A (XXI), 21 U.N. GAOR Supp. (No. 16) at 52, U.N. Doc. A/6316 (1966), 999 U.N.T.S. 171 [hereinafter ICCPR].

[59] *See also*, Article 27, American Convention on Human Rights, O.A.S. Treaty Series No. 36, 1144 U.N.T.S. 123, entered into force July 18, 1978, reprinted in Basic Documents Pertaining to Human Rights in the Inter-American System, OEA/Ser.L.V/II.82 doc.6 rev.1 at 25 (1992) [hereinafter ACHR]; and Article 15, Convention for the Protection of Human Rights and Fundamental Freedoms, 213 U.N.T.S. 222, entered into force Sept. 3, 1953, as amended by Protocols Nos 3,

situation of "public emergency which threatens the life of the nation" when a state party to the covenant "may take measures derogating from their obligations under the present Covenant."⁶⁰ This means that some HRL provisions can be suspended or derogated apart from the so-called non-derogable rights, mentioned in Article 4(2). They include the right to life (Article 6); the prohibition of torture, cruel, inhuman and degrading treatment (Article 7); the prohibition of slavery (Article 8); the right not to be imprisoned on the ground of contractual obligation (Article 11); the right to criminal guarantees (Article 15); the right to recognition as a person (Article 16) and the fundamental freedoms of thought, conscience and religion (Article 18). Derogations suppose the fulfillment of criteria foreseen in Article 4 ICCPR. States can adopt measures "strictly required by the exigencies of the situation, provided that such measures are not inconsistent with their other obligations under international law" and do not involve discrimination. Furthermore, the state of emergency must be "officially proclaimed" and the state party must "immediately inform" the other states parties through the Secretary-General of the United Nations "of the provisions from which it has derogated and of the reasons by which it was actuated." Finally, the state party shall also inform, through the same procedure, all the other states parties "on the date on which it terminates such derogation."⁶¹ Considered under those terms, the system for derogation of HRL seems quite clear and efficient.⁶² In reality, states' abuses of emergency powers, including human rights derogation, are the most frequent cases of violation in internal conflict and violence.⁶³

 5, 8, and 11 which entered into force on Sept. 21, 1970, Dec. 20, 1971, Jan. 1, 1990, and Nov. 1, 1998 respectively [hereinafter ECHR].
⁶⁰ *See* U.N. Human Rights Committee, General Comment No. 29, States of Emergency, U.N. Doc. CCPR/C/21/Rev.1/Add.11, (Aug. 31, 2001). This document replaced General Comment No. 5 adopted in 1981 on the same subject.
⁶¹ Apart from legal limitations to the use of derogation powers by governments, some guidelines concerning the application of derogation clauses were developed by independent experts. *See* Joan F. Hartman, *Working Paper for the Committee of Experts on the Article 4 Derogation Provision*, 7 Hum. Rts. Q. 89 (1985); U.N. ECOSOC, Siracusa Principles on the Limitation and Derogation Provisions in the International Covenant on Civil and Political Rights, U.N. Doc. E/CN.4/1985/4, Annex (1985), 7 Hum. Rts. Q. 3 (1985).
⁶² One of the U.N. Reports on Fundamental Standards of Humanity seems to give little importance to the possibility of violations of human rights in case of derogation when it says that "constraints on the application of derogation clauses appear to provide a solid basis in international law for ensuring these clauses are not abused," U.N. Commission on Human Rights, Minimum Humanitarian Standards, Analytical Report of the Secretary-General Submitted Pursuant to Commission on Human Rights Resolution 1997/21, U.N. Doc. E/CN.4/1998/87 (Jan. 5, 1998), para. 57 [hereinafter U.N. Doc. E/CN.4/1998/87].
⁶³ *See* Institute for Human Rights at Åbo Akademy University, *Declaration on Minimum Humanitarian Standards* (1990), *supra* note 12.

2.4 Problems in Legal Protection

On the one hand, IHL is applicable for the protection of those taking part in the hostilities[64] and the civilian population in case of international and non-international armed conflict defined before. On the other hand, in situations of civil unrest, riots, etc., which fall below the threshold of Common Article 3 of the GC and AP II, states may proclaim a state of emergency and derogate a relevant part of HRL, but they do not have to apply IHL. In these circumstances, states also enjoy a certain margin of appreciation[65] concerning the characterization of the situation within their borders.[66] Here lies the problem and the high risk of gaps in legal protection of potential victims of violence.

It seems from experience that IHL legal instruments are not always adequate to address most present situations of conflict, mainly because standards fixed by IHL itself for their applicability are difficult to be matched in situations of internal violence. In many cases, states' concern regarding possible political consequences of the application of IHL, implying any possible sort of recognition of dissident armed groups, prevail on the issue of protection of victims in these types of conflict. The civilian population is targeted and no clear rules are applicable in that context. Despite the fact that states have a tendency to use military force in those situations, the rules of IHL, which should at least be known to military personnel,[67] do not always apply. In the meantime, HRL is not generally included in the training for military personnel, despite the fact that they should be the general rules applicable in situations where IHL does not apply.

Despite the adoption of the two 1977 Protocols to the four GCs to implement the international protection of victims in case of non-international armed conflict, the Diplomatic Conference,[68] which negotiated the texts of the APs, limited the scope of the provisions for those victims, on the one side by deleting some provisions which were proposed in the draft document of AP II prepared by the ICRC, and on the other side by defining a threshold of high intensity non-international armed conflict, therfore limiting the scope of application of AP II.[69] The 1977

---

[64] *See* International Humanitarian Law and the Challenges of Contemporary Armed Conflicts, *supra* note 32.
[65] *See* Branningan and McBride v. U.K., (1993) 17 EHRR 539, 590–591; Dominic McGoldrick, The Human Rights Committee 301(1991).
[66] Provost, *supra* note 16, at 277–279.
[67] There is a general obligation to disseminate IHL in the four GCs: GC I/II/III/IV, Arts. 47/48/127/144.
[68] Diplomatic Conference on the Reaffirmation and Development of International Humanitarian Law Applicable in Armed Conflicts was held in Geneva from 1974 to 1977; *see* Moir, *supra* note 54, at 91–96.
[69] *See* David Petrasek, *Moving Forward on the Development of Minimum Humanitarian Standards*, 92 Am. J. Int'l L. 557–558 (1998); Lindsay Moir, *The Historical Development of the Application of*

APs were not suitable to provide sufficient protection to victims of new forms of internal violence. In the meantime, the nature of violent conflicts has further changed, so that most situations of violence today occur within the border of a state under unclear legal rules.[70]

Despite the fact that the protection given by treaty law may be insufficient, it is important to make reference to customary law and general principles of international law that can be applied in conflict situations. In this case a powerful legal tool that can be used is the so-called Martens clause.[71] The Martens clause, a fundamental source for developments in IHL, included in most IHL treaties, has aquired customary character in international law.[72] In its original formulation in the Preamble of the 1899 Hague Convention II the clause states that

> Until a more complete code of the laws of war is issued, the High Contracting Parties think it right to declare that in cases not included in the Regulations adopted by them, populations and belligerents remain under the protection and empire of the principles of international law, as they result from the usages established between civilized nations, from the laws of humanity and the requirements of the public conscience.[73]

This clause provides an essential tool for the protection of persons affected by a conflict because

> the adoption of a treaty regulating particular aspects of the law of war does not deprive the affected persons of the protection of those norms of customary humanitarian law that were not included in the codification.[74]

Humanitarian Law in Non-International Armed Conflicts to 1949, 47 Int'l & Comp. L. Q. 337, 354–361 (1998).

[70] *See* Human Security Report, *supra* note 19.

[71] *See* Theodor Meron, The Humanization of International Law 16–29 (2006) [hereinafter Meron 2006]; Xavier Pons Rafols, *Revisitando a Martens: las normas básicas de humanidad en la Comisión de Derechos Humanos* in Soberanía del Estado y Derecho internacional: homenaje al profesor Juan Antonio Carrillo Salcedo (2005); Antonio Cassese, *The Martens Clause: Half a Loaf or Simply Pie in the Sky?*, 11 Eur. J. Int'l L. 187 (2000); Vladimir V. Pustogarov, *The Martens Clause in International Law*, 1 Journal of the History of International Law 125 (1999). On the historical origin and context of the Martens clause *see* Eric Myles, *"Humanity", "Civilization" and the "International Community" in the Late Imperial Russian Mirror: Three Ideas "Topical for Our Days"*, 4 J. Hist. Int'l L. 310 (2002).

[72] Corfu Channel Case (U.K. v. Albania), Merits, (Apr. 9, 1949), 1949 I.C.J. Rep. 4, at 22; Military and Paramilitary Activities in and against Nicaragua (Nicaragua v. U.S.A.), Merits, 1986 I.C.J. Rep. (June 27), 14, at 114 [hereinafter Nicaragua Case].

[73] Convention (II) with Respect to the Laws and Customs of War on Land and its annex: Regulation concerning the Laws and Customs of War on Land, 26 Martens Nouveau Recueil (ser. 2) 949, 187 Consol. T.S. 429, entered into force Sept. 4, 1900.

[74] Meron 2006, *supra* note 71, at 27.

Determining the evolution and rules of customary law is not an easy task. This can be done by addressing states' practice and their opinion regarding that practice as law.[75] Decisions by international tribunals and bodies, legal doctrine, and studies try to identify the content of that source of international law. It is not the purpose of this chapter to deal with this task. The more limited aim is to focus on the trends that show the international responses to fill the gap already identified.[76] The United Nations reports on FSH have identified two important tools that can help clarifying new customary rules in this area of international law: (1) the case-law developed by the International Criminal Tribunals for the Former Yugoslavia and Rwanda, and the adoption of the Rome Statute for a Permanent International Criminal Court; and (2) the study by the ICRC concerning the development of the rules of customary international law applying in both international and non-international armed conflicts.[77] The U.N. reports do not suggest and discuss new rules. They mainly make reference and reproduce the mentioned developments in international law.

2.5. *The Limits of HRL*

Compared to IHL, HRL shows some inadequacies to provide an appropriate protection in situations of conflict that have been underlined in the U.N. reports. Three elements must be taken into consideration: "the possibility of derogation, the position of non-State armed groups vis-à-vis human rights obligations, and the lack of specificity of existing standards."[78] Derogations have been considered before, and non-state actors will be mentioned later on in this chapter.

The lack of specificity of existing human rights rules is considered as a major weakness of human rights protection. This is due to the fact that the great majority of human rights norms are spelled out in fairly clear terms, but the means for their application and realization are usually quite unclear and vague.[79] Compared to IHL, human rights rules are difficult to be applied as they are formulated in general terms and no detailed obligations are set up for the possible violators. In this context, the development of well-defined rules and codes is considered to be useful "to make the protection of existing rights more effective by establishing

---

[75] On definition of customary law *see* Hugh Thirlway, *The Sources of International Law*, in International Law (Malcom Evans ed., 2d ed., 2006).

[76] For instance, Vigny & Thompson, *supra*, at 194 consider five sources.

[77] The ICRC had started developing the research work regarding the definition and development of customary law applicable in international and non-international armed conflict in 1995. This study was published as Jean-Marie Henckaerts & Louise Doswald-Beck, Customary International Humanitarian Law (3 volumes, 2005) [hereinafter CIHL].

[78] U.N. Doc. E/CN.4/1998/87, *supra* note 62, para 49.

[79] *See* in particular Louise Doswald-Beck & Sylvain Vité, *supra* note 20.

the obligations the right entails in specific circumstances."[80, 81] What is generally stressed is that there is no urgency for recognition or definition of further rights, but specific rules and clear guidelines are needed to apply existing rights that otherwise can remain as dead letter.

Finally, the position of non-state armed groups is considered to be important in the light of human rights obligations.[82] In situations of internal violence, where IHL is non applicable, non-state actors do not consider themselves bound by HRL. This reason is based on the fundamental assumption that HRL creates obligations for states and their agents. This point will be addressed in more detail later on.

3. *The Work of the International Community*

In this section the role and work of the international community will be addressed. This means taking into consideration bodies and actors which in different ways have contributed, and still contribute, to the identification and definition of standards applicable in all situations of violence. They include the United Nations, the ICRC, international tribunals and courts, governments, and legal scholars.

3.1. *The Idea of Fundamental Standards of Humanity*

The international community recognized the problems of the applicability of IHL and HRL, in particular the negative consequences on the protection of victims of violence. The United Nations approached the issue at an early stage affirming that some rules concerning human rights must be applied in internal armed conflicts.[83] Limitations on states of emergency declared by governments in case of "situations threatening the life of the nation" were foreseen in Article 4 of the 1966 International Covenant on Civil and Political Rights (ICCPR) which defined

---

[80] U.N. Doc. E/CN.4/1998/87, *supra* note 62, para 69.
[81] For instance, a good example of this kind of development is the U.N. Basic Principles on the Use of Force and Firearms by Law Enforcement Officials, Adopted by the Eighth United Nations Congress on the Prevention of Crime and the Treatment of Offenders, Havana, Cuba, Aug. 27–Sept. 7, 1990.
[82] On non-state actors *see* section D.1.b.*ii.*
[83] *See* U.N. G.A. Res. 2252 (1965); U.N. G.A. Res. 2444 (1968); U.N. G.A. Res. 2765 (1970); U.N. S.C. Res. 237 (1967) all stressing the fact that human rights must be respected by all the parties to a conflict. The 1968 International Conference on Human Rights declared that human rights principles must prevail during periods of armed conflict, Final Act of the International Conference on Human Rights (Teheran, 22 April–13 May 1968), U.N. Doc. A/Conf.32/41 (1968). *See* David Weissbrodt, *The Role of International Organizations in the Implementation of Human Rights and Humanitarian Law in Situations of Armed Conflict*, 21 Vanderbilt J. Trans. L. 313 (1988).

non-derogable human rights made applicable in all circumstances.[84] Nevertheless, at that time the two sets of rules, IHL and HRL, were still considered quite separate legal systems, applicable in different contexts.[85]

But legal scholars have identified a possible grey zone where the rules, based on the distinction between the two categories, left a legal vacuum, and therefore a risk for the protection of human beings.[86] In particular, during the 1980s, a series of important contributions related in particular to the clarification of limitations on states of emergency powers[87] and the respect of fundamental rights led to the proposal, made by Meron, of drafting a new instrument.[88]

The result of this international action was the adoption of the 1990 Turku Declaration of "Minimum Humanitarian Standards."[89] The justification of this declaration was based on

> the difficulties experienced in protecting human dignity in situations of internal violence that fall below the threshold of applicability of international humanitarian instruments but within the margin of public emergency;... These difficulties are compounded by the inadequacy of the nonderogable provisions of human rights instruments, the weakness of international monitoring and control procedures, and the need to define the character of the conflict situations...[90]

---

[84] *See also* Article 27 ACHR, *supra* note 59, and Article 15 ECHR, *supra* note 59; Rosalyn Higgins, *Derogations under Human Rights Treaties*, 48 BYBIL 281–283 (1976–1977).

[85] On the relationship between the IHL and HRL *see* introduction to the book.

[86] Georg Schwarzenberger, *Jus Pacis ac Belli? Prolegomena to a Sociology of International Law*, 37 Am. J. Int'l L. 460, 470 (1943); Jessup, *Should International Law Recognize an Intermediate Status Between War and Peace?* 48 Am. J. Int'l L. 98 (1954).

[87] Questiaux, *supra* note 10, on states of emergency, International Commission of Jurists, States of Emergency, Their Impact on Human Rights (1983), International Law Association, *1984 Paris Minimum Standards*, reprinted and accompanied by a comment of Lillich, in 79 Am. J. Int'l L. 1072 (1985), *The Siracusa Principles*, reproduced in 7 Hum. Rts. Q. 3 (1985); Jaime Oraá, Human Rights in States of Emergency in International Law (1992); Joan M. Fitzpatrick, Human Rights in Crisis: The International System For Protecting Rights During States Of Emergency (1994); Anna Lena Svensson-McCarthy, The International Law of Human Right and States of Exception (1998).

[88] Meron 1983, *supra* note 15; Meron 1984, supra note 15; Meron 1988, *supra* note 15.

[89] For the background of this document *see* Martin Scheinin, *Turku/Åbo Declaration of Minimum Humanitarian Standards (1990)*, paper presented at the Workshop organized by the International Council on Human Rights Policy & International Commission of Jurists (Geneva, Feb. 13–14, 2005).

[90] Theodor Meron & Allan Rosas, *A Declaration of Minimum Humanitarian Standards*, 85 Am. J. Int'l L. 375 (1991); Asbjørn Eide et al., *Combating Lawlessness in Grey Zone Conflicts through Minimum Humanitarian Standards*, 89 Am. J. Int'l L. 215 (1995).

The word "minimum"[91] implied the fact that some rules should be applied in all kinds of conflict, as a minimum guarantee for the protection of fundamental rights of individuals. The term "humanitarian" is very well known, widely used in the specialized legal language to refer to the set of rules applicable in armed conflicts. Nevertheless, the term "humanitarian" was used in a broader sense to imply the protection of human beings in situations of violence, and not only in the cases where the rules of IHL would apply. The use and definition of an accurate terminology are strictly associated to two major problems.

How can conflicts within a country be labeled? There are different terms and expressions that refer to situation of conflict, such as "armed conflict," "internal armed conflict," "internal conflict," "non-international armed conflict," "armed conflict not of an international character" and so on. In the U.N. study the general expression "internal violence" is adopted. The definition of this expression is given in the relevant U.N. documents, this is "to describe situations where fighting and conflict, of whatever intensity, is taking place inside countries, and without prejudice to any legal characterisation of the fighting for the purposes of applying international humanitarian law."[92]

Terminology issues are also strictly related to the individuation of groups who are involved in violent actions within a country. People who take arms in the context of a conflict might be defined as: terrorist groups, guerrillas, resistance movements, national liberation movements, insurgents, rebels, etc. In the U.N. study the terms "armed group" and "non-state armed group" are used "to describe those who take up arms in a challenge to government authority."[93] The issue of "motivations" of the group and the political aim of their fight are not taken into consideration in the report. So, there is no reference, for instance, to "terrorist" or "freedom fighter" groups. It is also stressed that the use of a neutral terminology does not justify the use of force by some groups that are frequently committing acts of terrorism during their activities.

3.2. *The Work of the United Nations*

In 1991 the Sub-Commission on Prevention of Discrimination and Protection of Minorities (U.N. Sub-Commission) received and analyzed the Turku Declaration.

---

[91] The word minimum has been criticised. The main risk of using the word minimum is that it can induce the parties involved in a conflict to apply a lower level of protection compared to the existing standards provided by international law. That means that, in some cases, the better standards achieved through international treaty and customary law could not apply. In the meantime, reference to humanitarian standards is limiting the field (area) of application to humanitarian law, with the risk of excluding other branches of international law, in particular, general human rights law.
[92] U.N. Doc. E/CN.4/1998/87, *supra* note 62, para. 6.
[93] *Id.* para. 7.

In 1994, it passed the same Declaration to the Commission on Human Rights (CHR) for its study, elaboration, and adoption.[94] In two subsequent resolutions, the Commission on Human Rights recognized the importance of further study of the issues related to internal violence.[95] Consequently, a special seminar was organized in Cape Town in 1996 and the result of that workshop submitted to the Commission on Human Rights.[96] In 1997, following the recommendations adopted at the international seminar held in Cape Town, the United Nations started dealing with the issue of humanitarian standards in a more systematic way. The very first idea was the elaboration of basic common rules applicable in all situations that should be grounded in both IHL and HRL existing rules.[97]

The documents under consideration take the form of reports of the Secretary-General of the United Nations. They are elaborated by officers of the United Nations High Commissioner for Human Rights who collect and organize new developments on the basis of legal writings, international documents, case-law, and comments by states and international organisations. Once prepared, they are submitted to the Commission on Human Rights for consideration and adoption.[98] As usually happens with those reports, there is a formal invitation by the Commission "to seek the views of and information from"[99] governments, U.N. bodies, human rights treaty bodies, mechanisms of the Commission, inter-governmental organizations, regional organizations, and non-governmental organizations "to comment on those issues."[100] This request has given raise to some comments from different bodies and institutions. They are relevant to show different positions related to the topic under discussion and may reveal interesting standpoints. Some states have also organized specific meetings on the topic.[101] Some of the comments are included

---

[94] U.N. Sub-Commission on Prevention of Discrimination and Protection of Minorities, Res. 1994/26.
[95] U.N. Commission on Human Rights, Res. 1995/29 and 1996/26.
[96] U.N. Doc. E/CN.4/1997/77/Add.1 (Jan. 28, 1997).
[97] Djamchid Momtaz, *The Minimum Humanitarian Rules Applicable in Periods of Internal Tension and Strife*, 324 Int'l Rev. Red Cross 455 (1998).
[98] Since the creation of the Human Rights Council by U.N.General Assembly res. 60/251 of 15 March 2006, and the abolition of the U.N. Commission on Human Rights, there seem to be no major changes in this procedure. The Human Rigths Council, by Decision 2/102 (Oct. 6, 2006) requested the Secretary General to "continue with the fulfilment of his activities, in accordance with previous decisions adopted by the Commission on Human Rights and to update the relevant reports and studies".
[99] This expression has been repeted in all relevant documents: *see* in particular U.N. Commission on Human Rights, Res. 1997/21 (Apr. 11, 1997).
[100] *See* all the relevant documents, *i.e.* E/CN.4/1997/21 (Apr. 11, 1997); comments and views received from states and U.N. bodies are included in U.N. Doc. E/CN.4/1998/87/Add.1 (Jan. 12, 1998).
[101] For instance, the seminar held in Stockholm (Sweden) in February 2000.

in annexes to the main reports[102] or are included in the same text of the report.[103]

In 1997, the Commission on Human Rights asked the Secretary-General to prepare a report "on the issue of fundamental standards of humanity."[104] Particular attention was devoted to the cooperation with the ICRC in the preparation of the report.[105] As a result, the U.N. Secretary-General submitted an analytical report on "Minimum humanitarian standards."[106] The report dealt with the following main topics:

- International human rights law and situations of internal violence;
- International humanitarian law and situations of internal violence;
- Advantages and disadvantages of identifying FSH;
- Individuation of the FSH; and
- The nature of an instrument concerning these standards.

The Commission on Human Rights in its Resolution 1998/29 adopted the report and asked the Secretary General to submit a further report on "Fundamental standards of humanity."[107] This second study analyzed issues which were identified in the previous report and needed further consideration.[108] This report was adopted by the Commission on Human Rights on April 28, 1999 by Resolution 1999/65. At the same time, the Secretary-General was requested "to continue to study and consult on this issue and to submit a report...taking into account comments received and relevant new developments." This work included consultations with member states, inter-governmental organizations, and non-governmental organizations. Since then, the United Nations has adopted a series of documents[109]

---

[102] U.N. Doc. E/CN.4/1998/87/Add.1, *supra* note 100.
[103] U.N. ECOSOC, *Report of the Secretary-General*, Annex to U.N. Doc.E/CN.4/1999/92, (Dec. 18, 1998) [hereinafter U.N. Doc. E/CN.4/1999/92], and the U.N. ECOSOC, *Report of the Secretary-General submitted persuant to Commission resoution 1999/65*, U.N. Doc. E/CN.4/2000/94 (Dec. 27, 1999).
[104] U.N. Commission on Human Rights, Res. 1997/21.
[105] CIHL, *supra* note 77.
[106] U.N. Doc. E/CN.4/1998/87, *supra* note 62, and Add.1, (Jan. 5, 1998). *See* Petrasek, *supra* note 69.
[107] U.N. Doc. E/CN.4/1999/92, *supra* note 103.
[108] The issues included:
  - The identification of crimes under international jurisdiction relevant to the protection of human dignity in situations of internal violence.
  - The international legal accountability of non-State actors.
  - The study by the ICRC on customary rules of international humanitarian law.
  - Developments concerning the possibility of State derogation from human rights obligation in case of emergency.
[109] U.N. Doc. E/CN.4/1999/92, *supra* note 107; and U.N. Doc. E/CN.4/2000/94 (Dec. 27, 1999), *supra* note 103; ECOSOC, *Report of the Secretary-General submitted persuant to Commission resolution 2000/69*, U.N. Doc. E/CN.4/2001/91 (Jan. 12, 2001); ECOSOC, *Report*

which have tried to highlight new developments in international law related to protection of victims in "situations of internal violence [that] pose a particular threat to human dignity and freedom."[110] The work of the United Nations aims at "strengthening the practical protection through the clarification of uncertainties in the application of existing standards in situations, which present a challenge to their effective implementation."[111] The reports do not pursue the development of new rules or the drafting of a new international document,[112] based also on the fact that "[p]rogress already achieved in this regard is largely based on the increasingly interplay between international human rights law, international humanitarian law, international criminal law, international refugee law and other bodies of law that may be relevant."[113]

Therefore, the attention should be focused on developments that have taken place in international law to identify how fundamental rules that should be applied in any situation are defined, and avoiding the risks linked to the classifications under IHL and HRL, for the protection of fundamental rights of any person which is a potential victim in situations of violence.

4. Developments in International Law

As mentioned before, the study conducted by the United Nations on the selection of standards that should be applied in situations of internal violence is still framed in quite general terms. It should be remembered that the standards under consideration are a very important, but also an extremely controversial issue. They deal with situations of violence that take place mainly within the borders of a state, therefore they may raise the concern of the same states that are also the victims of violence, as they can perceive the possibility of international interference into their national affairs.[114] In the following part the main issues that show trends in

---

of the Secretary-General submitted persuant to Commission on Human Rights Decision 2001/112, U.N. Doc. E/CN.4/2002/103 (Dec. 20, 2001); ECOSOC, *Report of the Secretary-General*, U.N. Doc. E/CN.4/2004/90 (Feb. 25, 2004); ECOSOC, *Report of the Secretary-General*, U.N. Doc. E/CN.4/2006/87 (Mar. 3, 2006); *see also* Jean-Daniel Vigny et Cecilia Thompson, *Fundamental Standards of Humanity: What Future?*, 20(2) Neth. Q. Hum. Rights 185 (2002).

[110] See U.N. Doc. E/CN.4/2002/103, para. 2; U.N. Doc. E/CN.4/2001/91, Id., para. 4; U.N. Doc. E/CN.4/2000/94, paras. 7–12; U.N. Doc. E/CN.4/1999/92, supra note 103, para. 3; U.N. Doc. E/CN.4/1998/8, para. 8.

[111] U.N. Doc. E/CN.4/2006/87, *supra* note 109, para. 3.

[112] *Id.* para. 3.

[113] *Id.*

[114] The case of the conflict in Chechnya may clarify this point quite well.

contemporary international law towards a common language between IHL and HRL will be provided.

4.1. *International Case Law*

International case law developed by international courts and tribunals has reached an unprecedented importance during the last decade. International courts created under human rights treaties have developed some important principles for the protection of human rights in situations of internal violence not covered by IHL. Furthermore, during the 1990s, the impressive development of international criminal jurisdictions and their case-law have clarified the interpretation of both IHL and HRL in situations of armed conflict. Case law is important for the interpretation and clarification of international rules, the identification of customary international law, all the more as judicial decisions are considered a subsidiary source of international law by Article 38(d) of the Statute of the ICJ.

4.1.1. *International Human Rights Courts*

International human rights courts were developed since the 1950s as supervisory bodies for the implementation and application of human rights treaties at regional level. The European Court of Human Rights, the Inter-American Commission and Court of Human Rights and the African Commission and Court on Human Rights are the most relevant examples. The original limitation of competence for the human rights courts to the application of human rights provision has been challenged in some cases. International case law, including the situation of human rights violations in Northern Cyprus after the Turkish invasion, cases involving South East Turkey security forces and the Kurdish separatists, and cases related to the troubles in Northern Ireland, show that the European Convention on Human Rights and Fundamental Freedoms[115] has been used to address the protection of human rights in the context of troubles and civil strife linked to military actions.[116] Since the *Cyprus* v. *Turkey* case[117] the European human rights bodies have recognized that the violation of human rights, some of which are also contained in Common Article 3 of the GC and in the 1977 AP II,[118] committed in "a situation of military action," or "civil strife"[119] fall within the jurisdiction of the European system for

---

[115] ECHR, *supra* note 84.
[116] *See* Aisling Reidy, *The Approach of the European Commission and Court of Human Rights to International Humanitarian Law*, 34 Int'l Rev. Red Cross 513–529 (1998).
[117] Cyprus v. Turkey, (1982) 4 E.H.R.R. 482. In this particular case Article 15 on derogation was not applicable as Turkey had not made a formal declaration of derogation.
[118] The Eur. Comm. H.R. found breaches of Article 2(1), right to life; Article 3, freedom from torture; Article 5(1), right to liberty; Article 1, Protocol 1, peaceful enjoyment of possessions; and Articles 13 and 14 ECHR, *supra* note 59.
[119] In the case Akdivar v. Turkey, (1997) 23 E.H.H.R. 143, at 186.

the protection of human rights.[120] In particular, the European Court of Human Rights affirmed that

> [t]he obligation to protect the right to life under [article 2], read in conjunction with the State's general duty under Article 1 of the Convention to 'secure to everyone within their jurisdiction the rights and freedoms defined in [the] Convention', requires by implication that there should be some form of effective official investigation when individuals have been killed as a result of the use of force by, *inter alios*, agents of the State.[121]

The Court has reaffirmed the applicability of HRL in recent cases concerning Chechnya. In considering a military operation, the Court affirmed that

> [i]n particular, it is necessary to examine whether the operation was planned and controlled by the authorities so as to minimize, to the greatest extent possible, recourse to lethal force. The authorities must take appropriate care to ensure that any risk to life is minimized.[122]

The Court applied HRL standards to the Chechen conflict due to the fact that Russia had not declared any state of emergency and no derogation from Article 15 of the European Convention on Human Rights was applicable. Therefore, the full European HRL could be applied to the case.[123]

A wider approach has been adopted by the Inter-American system. In examining situations of internal strife, both the Inter-American Commission on Human Rights and the Inter-American Court of Human Rights have applied not only HRL provisions but also IHL. The main example is *La Tablada* (*Abella*) case.[124] To justify its application of humanitarian law, the Commission affirmed that

> [i]ndeed, the provisions of common Article 3 are essentially human rights law. Thus, as a practical matter, application of common Article 3 by a State party to the American Convention involved in internal hostilities imposes no additional burdens on [a State], or disadvantages its armed forces *vis-à-vis* dissident groups. This is because Article 3 basically requires the State to do, in large measure, what it is already legally obliged to do under the American Convention.[125]

---

[120] *See* Aksoy v. Turkey, (1997) 23 EHRR 553; Kaya v. Turkey, E.C.H.R. Reports 1998-I, No. 65, 297; Güleç v. Turkey, E.C.H.R. Reports 1998-IV, No. 80, 1698; Ergi v. Turkey, E.C.H.R. Reports 1998-IV, No. 81, 1671.

[121] McCann and Others v. United Kingdom ECHR Series A, Vol. 324 (1996), para. 161, and Kaya v. Turkey, *supra* note 120, para. 86.

[122] Eur. Ct H.R., Isayeva, Yusupova and Bazayeava v Russia, Case No. 57947/00, 57948/00 and 57949/00 (Feb. 24, 2005), para. 171.

[123] *Id.* para 191.

[124] Inter-Am.CHR, Juan Carlos Abella v Argentina, Case No. 11.137, Report No. 55/97 (Nov. 18, 1997), para. 271.

[125] *Id.* p. 43, para. 158, note 19.

The justification for the application of human rights and humanitarian law in situations of emergency was grounded on Article 27(1) ACHR which states that derogation measures taken by states in time of emergency may "not be inconsistent with a State's other international legal obligations."[126] The Inter-American Court of Human Rights has addressed the issue of applicability of IHL in the *Las Palmeras*[127] case where the Court considered that neither the Commission nor the Court can make direct application of IHL and the Court has used IHL to interpret HRL norms.[128] This relationship has been further clarified by the Inter-American Commission on Human Rights by stating that

> in situations of armed conflict, the protections under international human rights and humanitarian law may complement and reinforce one another, sharing as they do a common nucleus of non-derogable rights and a common purpose of promoting human life and dignity. In certain circumstances, however, the test for evaluating the observance of a particular right, such as the right to liberty, in a situation of armed conflict may be distinct from that applicability in time of peace. In such situations, international law, including the jurisprudence of this Commission, dictates that it may be necessary to deduce the applicable standard by reference to international humanitarian law as the applicable *lex specialis*.[129]

It is generally assumed that the relationship between HRL and IHL is that between *lex generalis* and *lex specialis*.[130] The first is the general applicable law in all situations, whilst the latter provides more detailed rules applicable in situations defined as armed conflict (either international or non-international).

A further issue that shows the application of HRL by human rights courts in situations of conflicts is the so-called extra-territorial applicability of human rights obligations.[131] This is "primarily of relevance to international armed conflict, since

---

[126] For a discussion on the legal issues implied by the *La Tabalda* case, *see* Liezbeth Zegveld, *The Inter-American Commission on Human Rights and International Humanitarian Law: A Comment on the Tablada Case*, 324 Int'l Rev. Red Cross 505–511 (1998).

[127] Inter-Am.Ct H.R., Las Palmeras v. Colombia, Case No. 67, Judgment on preliminary Objections, (Feb. 4, 2000). On this case and the general use of IHL by the Inter-America Court of Human Rights *see* Fanny Martin, *Application du droit international humanitaire pour la Cour interaméricaine des droits de l'homme*, 83 Int'l Rev. Red Cross 1037–1065 (2001).

[128] A practice confirmed also in the *Bamaca Velazquez* case, IACHR, Bamaca Velazquez v. Guatemala, Judgment, Case No. 70 (Nov. 25, 2000).

[129] Inter-American Commission on Human Rights, Decision on Request for Precautionary Measures (Detainees at Guantanamo Bay, Cuba) (Mar. 12, 2002), (2002) 41 ILM 432.

[130] Advisory Opinion on Nuclear Weapons, *supra* note 38, para. 25; Legal Consequences of the Construction of a Wall in the Occupied Palestinian Territory, Advisory Opinion, (July 9, 2004), ICJ Rep. 2004, 43 ILM 1009 (2004), para. 106 [hereinafter Wall Advisory Opinion]; Heike Krieger, *A Conflict of Norms: The Relationship Between Humanitarian Law and Human Rights Law in the ICRC Customary Law Study*, 11 JCSL 265, 268–276 (2006).

[131] *See* generally Fons Coomans & Menno Kamminga (eds.), Extraterritorial Application of Human Rights Treaties (2004); Michael Dennis, *Application of Human Rights Treaties Extraterritorially in*

it is in such situations that a State is likely to be operating outside of its borders."[132] Despite the application of IHL in these cases the European Court of Human Rights,[133] the Human Rights Committee (HRC),[134] and the International Court of Justice (ICJ) have affirmed that the HRL obligations of a state extend to occupied territories not only in case of military occupation but also in other circumstances, as in the case where the state "is running a detention facility outside its borders."[135] This rule is based on the extraterritorial action of state agents, therefore representing the state, when they exercise control and authority over individuals. But this rule does not make clear if IHL and HRL apply concurrently, a problem that will be addressed at the end of this chapter.

4.1.2. *International Criminal Tribunals*

International criminal tribunals are a very new phenomenon in international law. The two most important examples, the Tokyo and Nuremberg Military Tribunals after the end of the Second World War, were not followed by any international criminal court until the beginning of the 1990s. The International Criminal Tribunal for the Former Yugoslavia (ICTY),[136] the International Criminal Tribunal for Rwanda (ICTR)[137] and the International Criminal Court (ICC)[138] are now a reality.[139] The first two tribunals have largely contributed to a new field of studies,

---

Times of Armed Conflict and Military Occupation, 99 Am. J. Int'l L. 119–141 (2005); Françoise Hampson & Ibrahim Salama, Working Paper on the Relationship between Human Rights Law and International Humanitarian Law, U.N. Sub-Commission on the Promotion and Protection of Human Rights, E/CN.4/Sub.2/2005/14 (June 21, 2005), paras. 78–92; Concluding Observations of the Human Rights Committee: Israel, CCPR/C/79/Add.93 (Aug. 18, 1998). For the relevant case law *see* ECHR, Loizidou v. Turkey (Preliminary Objections) 40/1993/435/414, paras 62–64; High Court of Justice, Queen's Bench Division, Divisional Court, R (Al-Skeini and others) v. Secretary of State for Defence (Dec. 14, 2004); Wall Advisory Opinion, *supra* note 130.

[132] Noam Lubell, *Challenges in Applying Human Rights Law to Armed Conflict*, 860 Int'l Rev. Red Cross 737, 739 (2005) [hereinafter Lubell].

[133] Öcalan v. Turkey, 46221/99 (2005) ECHR 282 (May 12, 2005).

[134] U.N. Humam Rights Committee. Communication No. 52/1979, U.N. Doc. A/36/40, 176 (July 29, 1981).

[135] Lubell, *supra* note 132, at 740.

[136] Statute of the International Tribunal, adopted by S.C. Res. 827, U.N. SCOR, 48th Sess., 3217th mtg. at 6, U.N. Doc. S/RES/827 (1993), 32 I.L.M. 1203 (1993).

[137] Statute of the International Tribunal for Rwanda, adopted by S.C. Res. 955, U.N. SCOR, 49th Sess., 3453d mtg. at 3, U.N. Doc. S/RES/955 (1994), 33 I.L.M. 1598, 1600 (1994).

[138] Rome Statute of the International Criminal Court, U.N. Doc. 2187 U.N.T.S. 90, entered into force July 1, 2002 [hereinafter ICC Statute].

[139] *See* Dominic McGoldrick, et al., The Permanent International Criminal Court: Legal and Policy Issues (2004); *see also* the thematic volume on: *International Criminal Tribunals*, 88 Int'l Rev. Red Cross (2006).

international criminal law,[140] that is relevant for the issues under discussion in this chapter. The importance of the jurisprudence of the ICTY and ICTR for the scope of determining the content and applicability of FSH resides particularly in the definition of international crimes and the clarification of either individual or groups criminal responsibility.[141]

4.1.2.1. International Crimes

Crimes under international law are relevant elements for the clarification of new trends in international law, in particular for determining the responsibility of non-state actors, and responsibility for gross human rights violations.[142] Crimes such as genocide, crimes against humanity, and war crimes in non-international armed conflict are important legal tools for the definition of FSH. With reference to the crime of genocide (Article 6) and the crimes against humanity (Article 7) there are no particular problems regarding their applicability in situations which do not fall within the legal definition of armed conflict. Both genocide and crimes against humanity defined in the ICC statute do not require a nexus with armed conflict.[143] Article 8, concerning war crimes in non-international armed conflict, gives opportunity for more debate. The ICC statute deals with war crimes in Article 8(2)(c) and Article 8(2)(e). But there is a very important limitation in the scope of application in case of non-international armed conflict. In fact, Article 8(2)(d) and (f) limit the scope of jurisdiction of the Court to "armed conflicts not of an international character and thus does not apply to situations of internal disturbances and tensions, such as riots, isolated and sporadic acts of violence or other acts of a similar nature."

Additionally, the jurisdiction over crimes envisaged by Article 8(2)(e) ICC statute[144] is limited by Article 8(2)(f) that refers only to "armed conflicts that take place in the territory of a State when there is protracted armed conflict." This means that there is little development in the jurisdiction of the ICC. The threshold imposed by both Common Article 3 of the GC and by AP II still limits the definition of "conflict not of an international character."

Despite these limitations, new developments in international law seem to attach important consequences for individuals who violate both IHL and HRL. The basic

---

[140] Kriangsaak Kittichaisaree, International Criminal Law (2001).
[141] *See* for instance William J. Fenrick, *The Development of the Law of Armed Conflict Through the Jurisprudence of the International Criminal Tribunal for the Former Yugoslavia*, 3 JCSL 197 (1998).
[142] *See* de Than & Shorts, *supra* note 9, Manisuli Ssenyonjo, *Accountability of Non-State Actors in Uganda for War Crimes and Human Rights Violations: Between Amnesty and the International Criminal Court*, 10 JCSL 405 (2005).
[143] *See* Christine Byron, *The Crime of Genocide*, and Timothy L.H. McCormack, *Crimes Against Humanity*, in The Permanent International Criminal Court: Legal and Policy Issues (2004).
[144] ICC Statute, *supra* note 138.

principle of individual criminal responsibility is actually recognized not only in the ICC Statute, but also by the Convention on the Prevention and Punishment of the Crime of Genocide,[145] that can be applied to "constitutionally responsible rulers, public officials or private individuals."[146] The same rules can be found in the Draft Code of Crimes Against the Peace and Security of Mankind[147] prepared by the International Law Commission. The relevant issue is that those acts are considered as international crimes not only when committed by a government,[148] but also by "any organisation or group,"[149] and by individuals[150] who are not necessarily acting on behalf of the state.

4.1.2.2. Accountability of Armed Non-State Actors

An important issue that must be considered for the protection of basic rights in internal conflicts is the involvement and responsibility of so-called non-state actors.[151] Armed non-state actors can be defined as armed groups that operate beyond state control,[152] and include dissident and more or less organized armed groups identified with different names.

It is noted that "armed groups, operating at different levels of sophistication and organization, are often responsible for the most grave human rights abuses."[153] The fundamental issue consists in understanding whether these groups are bound by IHL and/or HRL.

It is generally recognized that if non-state actors operate in a situation where IHL is applicable, those groups are legally bound by its rules.[154] If IHL is not

---

[145] Convention on the Prevention and Punishment of the Crime of Genocide, 78 U.N.T.S. 277, entered into force Jan. 12, 1951, adopted by the U.N.G.A. on Dec. 9, 1948.
[146] *Id.*, Article IV.
[147] Article 2, U.N. International Law Commission, Report 1996, Yearbook of the International Law Commission, 1996, vol. II (Part Two) [ILC Report 1996].
[148] Article 4, *id.*
[149] Article 25(d) ICC Statute, *supra* note 138.
[150] *Id.* Article 25 ICC Statute, *supra* note 138; Article 2, ILC Report 1996, *supra* note 147.
[151] The term non-state actors has a broad charaterization. It may include entities, groups and individuals acting outside state control, such as non-governmental organizations, multinational corporations, organized criminal groups, and armed groups, *see* Bass Arts, Math Noortmann, Bob Reinalda, Non-State Actors in International Relations (2001). *See generally* Andrew Clapham, Human Rights Obligations of Non-State Actors (2006); Philip Alston, Non-State Actors and Human Rights (2005).
[152] *See* David Petrasek, Ends and Means:Human Rights Approaches to Armed Groups 3 (2000); Caroline Holmqvist, *Engaging Non-State Actors in Post Conflicts Settings*, in Security Governance and Post-conflict Peacebuilding 45–46 (Alan Bryden & Heiner Hänggi eds., 2005).
[153] U.N. Doc. E/CN.4/1998/87, *supra* note 62, para 59.
[154] Common Article 3 to the 1949 GC states that: "in case of armed conflict not of an international character occurring in the territory of one of the High Contracting Parties, each Party to the conflict shall be bound to apply, as a minimum, the following provisions…" ICRC Study, Rule

applicable "the international legal accountability of such groups for human rights abuses is unclear (although clearly such acts should be penalized under domestic criminal law)."[155] Trends in international law to consider individuals subject to human rights rules are analyzed by the U.N. Secretary-General reports. Two basic doctrines and governmental positions are taken into consideration. The first and more conservative position affirms that, strictly legally speaking, those groups are not violating human rights. They can be considered ordinary criminals, accountable under national criminal law, but human rights violations as defined under international law are only binding on states, not on individuals or other groups not acting on behalf of a state. The second one considers that armed groups can violate human rights and should be held responsible for violations of human rights law. The U.N. study does not provide any clear solution to this problem justified by the fact that reaching a rushed conclusion on this difficult legal issue "might serve to legitimize actions taken against members of such groups in a manner that violates human rights."[156]

It should be noted that there is a trend to consider non-state actors to be bound by human rights law, both in legal writings[157] and in the U.N. Security Council practice[158] denouncing human rights abuses committed by armed non-state actors.

To tackle this important problem the U.N. study suggests that FSH could help in identifying basic obligations of non-state groups.[159] In particular, it addresses the issue of accountability with specific reference to crimes under international jurisdiction and the Statute of the International Criminal Court. Responsibility of

---

139; Article 25 ICC Statute, *supra* note 138; Prosecutor v. Dusko Tadic a/k/a "Dule", Decision on the Defence Motion for Interlocutory Appeal on Jurisdiction, Appeals Chamber, Case No. IT-94-1-AR72, (Oct. 2, 1995), paras 127 and 134 [hereinafter Tadic]; Dieter Fleck, *International Accountability for Violations of the* Ius in Bello: *The Impact of the ICRC Study on Customary International Humanitarian Law*, 11 JCSL 179 (2006) [hereinafter Fleck].

[155] U.N. Doc. E/CN.4/1998/87, *supra* note 62, para 60.

[156] *Id.*, para 64. *See also*: Report of the Meeting of Special Rapporteurs/Representatives, Experts and Chairpersons of Working Groups of the Special Procedures of the Commission on Human Rights and of the Advisory Services Programme, (Geneva, May 28–30, 1996), U.N. Doc. E/CN.4/1997/3, Annex, para. 44.

[157] Fleck, *supra* note 154, Dieter Fleck, *Humanitarian Protection Against Non-State Actors, in* Verhandeln für den Frieden/ Negotiating for Peace. Liber Amicorum Tono Eitel 79 (Jochen Abr. Frowein, Klaus Scharioth, Ingo Winkelmann & Rüdiger Wolfrum eds., 2003); Christian Tomuschat, *The Applicability of Human Rights Law to Insurgent Movements, in* Krisensicherung und Humanitärer Schutz – Crisis Management and Humanitarian Protection. Festschrift für Dieter Fleck (Horst Fischer, Ulrike Froissart, Wolff Heintschel von Heinegg & Christian Raap eds., 2004) [hereinafter Fischer].

[158] U.N. S.C. Res. 1019 (1995) and 1034 (1995); U.N. S.C. Res. 1400 (2002); U.N. S.C. Res. 1464 (2003); U.N. S.C. Res. 1468 (2003).

[159] *See generally* Liesbeth Zegveld, Accountability of Armed Opposition Groups in International Law (2002).

non-state actors is already recognized by conventions against piracy, by Article 4 of the Genocide Convention, and by Article 4 of the Convention Against Torture and Other Cruel, Inhuman or Degrading Treatment or Punishment.[160] These examples may prove either the "exception to the rule" or the starting point for a new approach to non-state actors responsibility under international law.[161]

4.1.2.3. Individual Criminal Responsibility

Individual criminal responsibility is an important tool that helps identifying the perpetrators of crimes under international law, and therefore the responsibility of both state and non-state actors. Individual direct responsibility under Article 7(1) and command responsibility under Article 7(3) ICTY Statute have been addressed. Any responsibility under Article 7(3) is subsumed under Article 7(1), and the same applies in case of commanders who incur criminal responsibility under the joint criminal enterprise doctrine through the acts of their subordinates.[162] The joint criminal enterprise presupposes that its participants, other than the principal perpetrator(s) of the crimes, share the perpetrators' joint criminal intent.[163] Therefore, the same type of joint criminal responsibility can be applied also to non-state actors that commit internationally defined crimes. Not only is the direct responsibility for acts committed by the accused foreseen, but also the case "[w]here the omission of an accused in a position of superior authority contribute (for instance by encouraging the perpetrator) to the commission of a crime by a subordinate, the conduct of the superior may constitute a basis for liability under article 7(1)."[164]

Therefore, individual criminal responsibility seems to provide justifications for the accountability of non-state actors for crimes such as genocide and crimes against humanity, that are committed in situations of violence not falling within the threshold of armed conflict.

4.1.3. *International Court of Justice*

The ICJ has dealt with several important cases related to IHL. Maybe, for the present purposes, the most well known is the *Nicaragua* case when the Court affirmed

---

[160] Convention against Torture and Other Cruel, Inhuman or Degrading Treatment or Punishment, G.A. Res. 39/46, [annex, 39 U.N. GAOR Supp. (No. 51) at 197, U.N. Doc. A/39/51 (1984)], entered into force June 26, 1987.

[161] For a discussion regarding the position of non-state actors in international law see Christopher Harding, *Statist Assumptions, Normative Individualism and New Forms of Personality: Evolving a Philosophy of International Law for the Twenty First Century*, 1 Non-State Actors and International Law 107 (2001).

[162] Prosecutor v. Kordic and Cerkez, Case No. IT-95-14/2-T, Trial Chamber, (Feb. 26, 2001), para. 371; Prosecutor v. Krstic, Case No. IT-98-33-T, (Aug. 2, 2001), para. 605.

[163] Prosecutor v. Milorad Krnojelac, Case No. IT-97-25-A, Appeals Chamber, (Sept. 17, 2003), para. 84.

[164] Prosecutor v. Kordic and Cerkez, *supra* note 162, para. 371.

that the norms enumerated in Common Article 3 to the GC are declaratory of substantive customary international law, and they constitute a minimum yardstick for all types of armed conflict.[165]

The 2006 Secretary-General report stresses the importance of the decisions taken by the ICJ. In particular, it refers to the Advisory Opinion on the construction of a wall in the occupied Palestinian territory by Israel,[166] and the case concerning the armed activities in the territory of the Congo.[167] In both cases the ICJ addressed the issue of the relationship between IHL and HRL. In the Advisory Opinion, the Court said that "the protection offered by human rights conventions does not cease in case of armed conflict."[168] The two branches of law are still different and may cover exclusive areas but there are rights that "may be matters of both these branches of international law."[169] The Court also confirmed the extraterritorial application of HRL "in respect of acts done by a State in the exercise of its jurisdiction outside its own territory" particularly in occupied territories.[170] In the case concerning armed activities in the territory of the Congo, the ICJ confirmed its position on the relationship between IHL and HRL referring to the Advisory Opinion.[171] The Court also considered that

> the acts committed by the [Uganda People's Defence Forces (UPDF)] and officers and soldiers of the UPDF are in clear violation of the obligations under the Hague Regulations of 1907, articles 25, 27 and 28, as well as articles 43, 46 and 47 with regard to obligations of an occupying Power. These obligations are binding on the Parties as customary international law.[172]

The Court also made reference to rules of both IHL and HRL stating that:

> Uganda also violated the following provisions of the international humanitarian law and international human rights law instruments, to which both Uganda and the Democratic Republic of the Congo are parties: Fourth Geneva Convention, articles 27 and 32 and well as article 53 with regard to obligations of an occupying Power; International Covenant on Civil and Political Rights, articles 6, paragraph 1, and 7; First Protocol Additional to the Geneva Conventions of 12 August 1949, articles 48, 51, 52, 57, 58 and 75, paragraphs 1 and 2; African Charter on Human and Peoples' Rights, articles 4 and 5; Convention on the Rights of the Child, article 38, paragraphs

---

[165] Nicaragua Case, *supra* note 72, para. 218. *See also* Theodor Meron, *The Geneva Conventions as Customary Law*, 81 Am. J. Int'l L. 348–370 (1987); U.S. Supreme Court, Hamdan v. Rumsfeld, Secretary of Defense, et al., 66–72, 548 U.S. ___ (2006).
[166] Wall Advisory Opinion, *supra* note 130, para. 163, (3) lit. A.
[167] Case Concerning Armed Activities on the Territory of the Congo (Democratic Republic of the Congo v. Uganda), Judgment (Dec. 19, 2005), I.C.J. Rep. 2005.
[168] Wall Advisory Opinion, *supra* note 130, para. 106.
[169] *Id*.
[170] *Id*. paras 107–113.
[171] Nicaragua Case, *supra* note 72, para. 216.
[172] *Id.*, para. 219.

2 and 3; Optional protocol to the Convention on the Rights of the Child, articles 1, 2, 3, paragraph 3, articles 4, 5 and 6.[173]

This led the Court to affirm that

> Uganda is internationally responsible for violations of international human rights law and international humanitarian law committed by the UPDF and by its members in the territory of the DRC and for failing to comply with its obligations as an occupying Power in Ituri.[174]

The Court did not consider the two sets of rules of IHL and HRL in separate way, but identified the rules applicable in the occupied territories using both IHL and HRL. In his separate opinion, Judge Simma considered that "at least the core of the obligations deriving from the rules of international humanitarian law and human rights law are valid *erga omnes*." That means they are the concern of all states and can be applied to any state.[175]

4.1.4. ICRC Study on Customary Law

One of the most important recent contributions to the clarification of rules applicable in situation of armed conflict is the study developed by the ICRC[176] concerning the development of the rules of customary international law applying in both international and non-international armed conflict.[177] The scope of the study was "to overcome some of the problems related to the application of international humanitarian treaty law."[178] Due to the fact that treaties apply only to states that have ratified them, and due to the limited regulation of non-international armed conflicts in IHL treaties, the study identified rules of general customary law that can be applied to all states, and to all parties to either international or non-international armed conflict. Also, a major outcome of the study is that the clarification of rules through state practice helps the interpretation of existing treaty law.[179]

It is not possible here to analyze the work of the ICRC. What is relevant for the purpose of identifying common rules of IHL and HRL is that

---

[173] *Id.*, para. 219.
[174] *Id.*, para. 220.
[175] I.C.J., Barcelona Traction Case, ICJ Reports (1970) 3, para. 3; Maurizio Ragazzi, The Concept of International Obligations Erga Omnes (2000); Christian J. Tams, Enforcing Obligations Erga Omnes in International Law (2005).
[176] During the 26th International Conference of the Red Cross and Red Crescent Movement, (December 1995), the ICRC was requested to prepare a report on customary rules of IHL, applicable in international and non-international armed conflicts.
[177] CIHL, *supra* note 77.
[178] Jean-Marie Henckaerts, *Study of Customary International Law: A Contribution to the Understanding and Respect for the Rule of Law in Armed Conflict*, 87 Int'l Rev. Red Cross 177, 175–212 (2005) [hereinafter Henckaerts].
[179] CIHL, *supra* note 77, at x, xxviii–xxx.

human rights law has been included in order to support, strengthen and clarify analogous principles of international humanitarian law. In addition, while they remain separate branches of international law, human rights law and international humanitarian law have directly influenced each other, and continue to do so, and this for mainly three reasons.[180]

The three reasons provided are on the one end "an assessment of conformity with human rights law at times involves a determination of respect for or breach of international humanitarian law"[181] as in the case of states of emergency; on the other end "international humanitarian law contains concepts the interpretation of which needs to include a reference to human rights law"[182] as in the definition of a regularly constituted court and the judicial guarantees. Secondly, HRL provisions are included in IHL treaties and IHL rules are found in modern HRL treaties. Thirdly, states and international organizations tend to scrutinize "the behaviour of States during armed conflict in the light of human rights law."[183]

The importance of the study for the purpose of clarification of FSH is that in Chapter 32 it identifies customary rules of both IHL and HRL that should apply in non-international armed conflict. Based on the fact that HRL applies at all times, the study takes into consideration HRL provisions as they contribute to define guarantees that apply also in states of emergency in a more detailed way than the basic provisions provided by the 1977 Additional Protocol II, and "has thus filled important gaps in the regulation of internal conflicts."[184] The study provides a list of 18 fundamental guarantees that

> apply to all civilians in the power of a party to the conflict and who do not take a direct part in hostilities, as well as to all persons who are *hors de combat*... these fundamental guarantees are overarching rules that apply to all persons.[185]

The guarantees include humane treatment, non-discrimination, prohibition of murder, of torture, inhuman and degrading treatment, prohibition of corporal punishment, mutilation, medical or scientific experiments, rape and other forms of sexual violence, slavery and slave trade, uncompensated or abusive forced labor, taking of hostages, use of human shields, enforced disappearance, arbitrary deprivation of liberty, right to a fair trial and prohibition of conviction without trial, non-retroactivity of criminal offences, principle of individual criminal responsibility,

---

[180] *Id.* at xxxi.
[181] *Id.*
[182] *Id.*
[183] *Id.*
[184] U.N. Doc. E/CN.4/2006/87, *supra* note 109, p. 6, para. 12. *See* Louise Doswald-Beck, *Filling the Protection Gap: Fundamental Standards of Humanity and the Relevance of Customary International Humanitarian Law*, Respect: The Human Rights Newsletter, 4 (June 6, 2005); Henckaerts, *supra* note 178.
[185] CIHL, *supra* note 77, Vol. I, at 299.

prohibition of collective punishment, respect for convictions and religious practices of civilians and persons *hors de combat*, respect for family life.[186]

Finally, a particularly positive outcome of identifying rules under IHL is their applicability to non-state actors involved in an armed conflict. In fact, it is generally accepted that HRL is binding on states only, while IHL binds both governments and armed opposition groups,[187] despite not being party to the relevant treaties, on the basis of general customary law, general principles of IHL, and treaty law.[188] From the point of view of the implementation and definition of obligations of rules in non-international conflicts this is a very important element that nevertheless needs further analysis and implementation to clarify the legal obligations of non-state actors.

4.1.5. *Other Developments in International Law*

Parallel to the mentioned developments in international law, it is also relevant to mention other important contributions by different bodies and practice that support the international effort in identifying FSH. In this section some of these contributions are provided.

The Human Rights Committee[189] is the body in charge of the supervision of the ICCPR. It also contributes to the clarification of HRL through its general comments to specific articles of the ICCPR. Two general comments, adopted in 2001 and 2004 respectively, are particularly relevant in this context: General Comment No. 29 on Article 4[190] and General Comment No. 31 on Article 2.[191] General Comment No. 29 is relevant as it deals with states of emergency, one of the possible situations where IHL and HRL find sometimes difficult application. The Comment refers to the ICC Statute, and the definition of crimes against humanity, as an important tool for the interpretation of Article 4 ICCPR. Furthermore, it makes reference to the obligations of states under IHL,[192] which cannot be violated under a state of emergency. General Comment No. 31 on obligations of states under the ICCPR confirms that

---

[186] *Id.* 299–379.
[187] See Christian Tomuschat, *The Applicability of Human Rights Law to Insurgent Movements, in Crisis Management and Humanitarian Protection, in* Fischer, *supra* note 157.
[188] *See* Sandesh Sivakumaran, *Binding Armed Opposition Groups*, 55 Int'l & Comp. L.Q. 369 (2006).
[189] On the Human Rights Committee *see generally* McGoldrick, *supra* note 65.
[190] *See supra* note 60.
[191] U.N. Human Rights Committee, General Comment No. 31, The Nature of the General Legal Obligation Imposed on States Parties to the Covenant, U.N. Doc. CCPR/C/21/Rev.1/Add.13 (May 26, 2004).
[192] See *supra* note 60, paras. 3, 9, 11, 16.

the Covenant applies also in situations of armed conflict to which the rules of international humanitarian law are applicable. While, in respect of certain Covenant rights, more specific rules of international humanitarian law may be specially relevant for the purposes of the interpretation of Covenant rights, both spheres of law are complementary, not mutually exclusive.[193]

The International Law Commission adopted in its fifty-third session, at second reading, the Draft Articles on Responsibility of States (ILC Articles).[194] These articles are considered an authoritative reference in international law in the area of state responsibility, and clarify the international responsibility of states for unlawful acts under international law.[195] It should be noted that due to the fact that the ILC Articles refer to the responsibility of states, "[t]he topic of the international responsibility of unsuccessful insurrectional or other movements...falls outside the scope of the present Articles, which are concerned only with the responsibility of States."[196]

For the purpose of identifying FSH, the ILC Articles provide several important elements.[197] In particular, the ILC Articles are relevant to clarify the obligations of states under both IHL and HRL. Circumstances that preclude wrongfulness listed in Part One, chapter V ILC Articles do not justify or excuse a breach of a state's obligation under a peremptory rule.[198] Peremptory rules, also defined as *jus cogens*, include the prohibition of aggression, IHL and HRL such as "genocide, slavery, racial discrimination, crimes against humanity and torture, and the right to self-determination."[199] Also, Part Two, chapter III, deals with serious breaches of obligations under peremptory norms of general international law, and the rule that all states are entitled to invoke responsibility for breaches of obligations to the

---

[193] See *supra* note 191, para. 11.
[194] Articles on the Responsibility of States for Internationally Wrongful Acts, adopted by the ILC on Aug. 10, 2001, Report of the International Law Commission on the work of its fifty-third session, Official Records of the General Assembly, Fifty-Sixth session, Supplement No. 10, U.N. Doc. A/56/10, chapter IV, section E. *See also* Draft Articles on Responsibility of States for Internationally Wrongful Acts with Commentaries (2001), Yearbook of the International Law Commission (2001) [hereinafter Draft Articles]. On state reponsibility *see* James Crawford, The International Law Commission's Articles on State Responsibility; Introduction, Text and Commentaries (2002); James Crawford and Simon Olleson, *The Continuing Debate on a UN Convention on State Responsibility*, 54 Int'l & Comp. L. Q. 959 (2005).
[195] ILC Articles, *Id.*, Draft Article 1 states: "Every internationally wrongful act of a State entails the international responsibility of that State."
[196] Draft Articles, *supra* note 194, Commentary to Article 10, para. 16.
[197] Due to the limitations of this work, this issue is mentioned in very general terms here. For a more detailed analysis, *see* U.N. Doc. E/CN.4.2002/103, *supra* note 109, paras 16–24.
[198] *See* Robert Kolb, *The Formal Source of* Ius Cogens *in Public International Law*, 53 Zeitschrift für Öffentliches Recht 69 (1998).
[199] Draft Articles, *supra* note 194, Commentary to Article 26, para. 5.

international community as a whole, the so-called obligations *erga omnes*.[200] They include, apart from the obligations already mentioned before, the prohibition of torture as defined in the Convention Against Torture and Other Cruel, Inhuman or Degrading Treatment or Punishment, and the basic rules of IHL defined by the ICJ "intrasgressible" in character.[201] As a consequence of international responsibility, injured states have the right to take countermeasures.[202] But this right is not unqualified, as Article 50 ILC Articles mentions obligations that "are sacrosanct" and include HRL and IHL prohibiting reprisals. In its commentary, the ILC used decisions by international tribunals, legal doctrine and practice of international bodies, in particular General Comment No. 8 of the Committee on Economic, Social and Cultural Rights for the consequences of economic sanctions on the civilian population, and in particular on children.[203]

Concerning international protection of children, it should be noticed that the 1989 Convention on the Rights of the Child,[204] and its 2002 Optional Protocol,[205] both HRL treaties, include provisions concerning the recruitment of children in armed conflict. In 2002 the U.N. Secretary-General called parties to conflicts to apply norms and standards protecting the recruitment and use of children in armed conflict, and provided a list of parties to conflicts, including governments and non-state actors that do not comply with international standards.[206] The U.N. Security Council adopted Resolution 1460 (2003) supporting the Secretary-General's report. This example shows the interrelationship between IHL and HRL and how the two areas of law are mutually influenced and can be applied for the protection of persons involved in situations of conflict.

Apart from the mentioned developments, other issues contribute to the improvement and corroboration of FSH. They include, for instance, the wider ratification of IHL and HRL international treaties. The adoption of rules and codes of conduct for specific categories of people or for specific circumstances, such as the

---

[200] *See supra* note 175.
[201] Advisory Opinion on Nuclear Weapons, *supra* note 38, para. 79; Draft Articles, *supra* note 194, Commentary to Article 40, para. 5.
[202] *See* Nigel White & Ademola Abass, *Countermeasures and Sanctions, in* International Law (Malcom D. Evans ed., 2d ed., 2006).
[203] Draft Articles, *supra* note 194, Commentary to Article 50, para. 7.
[204] Convention on the Rights of the Child, G.A. res. 44/25, annex, 44 U.N. GAOR Supp. (No. 49) at 167, U.N. Doc. A/44/49 (1989), entered into force Sept. 2, 1990.
[205] Optional Protocol to the Convention on the Rights of the Child on the involvement of children in armed conflicts, G.A. Res. 54/263, Annex I, 54 U.N. GAOR Supp. (No. 49) at 7, U.N. Doc. A/54/49, Vol. III (2000), entered into force Feb. 12, 2002.
[206] Secretary-General, Report of the Secretary-General on Children and Armed Conflict, U.N. Doc. S/2002/1299 (Nov. 26, 2002).

case of the 1979 Code of Conduct for Law Enforcement Officials,[207] the 1989 Principles on the Effective Prevention and Investigation of Extralegal, Arbitrary and Summary Executions,[208] and the 1990 Basic Principles on the Use of Force and Firearms.[209]

The dissemination of both IHL and HRL to the armed forces, as part of their training, and also to the general public, could improve their applicability. The conclusion of agreements at field level between humanitarian agencies, states, and non-state entities,[210] may implement the application of fundamental rules by all parties involved in the conflict. An interesting example is the case of agreements promoted by the humanitarian organization Geneva Call that provides a mechanism for the involvement of non-state actors in the application of the anti-personnel mine ban treaty.[211] As non state-actors cannot sign nor accede the treaty, they signed a "Deed of Commitment for Adherence to a Total Ban on Anti-Personnel Mines and for Cooperation in Mine Action" (DoC).[212] The "DoC holds non-state actors accountable to an anti-personnel mine ban and provides a platform for other humanitarian commitments."[213]

---

[207] Code of Conduct for Law Enforcement Officials, U.N. G.A. Res. 34/169, annex, 34 U.N. GAOR Supp. (No. 46) at 186, U.N. Doc. A/34/46 (1979).

[208] Principles on the Effective Prevention and Investigation of Extra-Legal, Arbitrary and Summary Executions, E.S.C. Res. 1989/65, annex, 1989 U.N. ESCOR Supp. (No. 1) at 52, U.N. Doc. E/1989/89 (1989).

[209] *See supra* note 81.

[210] For example, the Standards of Accountability to the Community and Beneficiaries for all Humanitarian and Development Workers in Sierra Leone, concluded in May 2002, and an Agreement on the Distribution of Humanitarian Aid and Assistance in Liberia, concluded on August 17, 2003 between the government of Liberia, Liberians United for Reconciliation and Democracy (LURD), the Movement for Democracy in Liberia (MODEL), ECOWAS, the United Nations and the African Union. On non-state armed groups humanitarian engagement *see generally* Max Glaser, Humanitarian Engagement with Non-State Armed Actors: The Parameters of Negotiated Access, HPN Network Paper No. 51 (2005), *available at* www.odihpn.org/documents/networkpaper051.pdf (last visited April 5, 2007); on Liberia see U.N. ECOSOC, Commission on Human Rights, *Preliminary Report of the Independent Expert, Charlotte Abaka*, U.N. Doc. E/CN.4/2004/113 (Feb. 16, 2004).

[211] Convention on the Prohibition of the Use, Stockpiling, Production and Transfer of Anti-personnel Mines and on Their Distruction, 36 I.L.M. (1997) 1507.

[212] Geneva Call, Deed of Commitment under Geneva Call for Adherence to a Total Ban on Anti-Personnel Mines and for Cooperation in Mine Action, *available at* www.genevacall.org/about/testi-mission/gc-deed-of-commitment.pdf (last visited June 21, 2007).

[213] U.N. Doc. E/CN.4/2004/90, *supra* note 109, para. 50.

5. Defining Fundamental Standards of Humanity

In the U.N. reports, the Secretary-General has identified the problems we have briefly indicated. There is usually a risk when a conflict starts to define its nature under international law. It is clearly stated that "to avoid lengthy debates on the definition of armed conflicts, the threshold of applicability of humanitarian law, and the legality under international law of derogations from human rights obligations"[214] new approaches are necessary. To this end, the report suggests that "the fundamental standards of humanity be applicable at all times, in all circumstances and to all parties."[215] However, this is still not an undisputed rule in international law.

5.1. The Nature of the Standards

States have presented comments on the legal nature of those rules affirmed in the Turku Declaration (Declaration) and those that are identified in the reports. There is a general assumption that there are enough rules but that there is also a gap between the law and the reality. Some states consider that the Declaration, as a non-binding instrument, is a weaker tool compared with legally binding instruments of international law.[216] Other states, such as Croatia, are prepared to support the "elaboration of an international instrument devoted to the protection of minimum core of inalienable rights."[217] The possibility is to adopt either a soft-law or a hard-law instrument that could "fill certain lacunae existing in the field of application of international human rights and humanitarian law standards in cases of internal disturbances and riots."[218] It is still difficult at this stage to clarify the legal nature of the FSH. In the concluding part some considerations will be provided on the nature of the rules, putting a particular emphasis on the legal problems that may arise when trying to fill the gap between IHL and HRL. Customary rules under IHL identified by the ICRC Study should be included.

5.2. List of Standards

The U.N. reports do not offer lists of standards and rules. In 1998, when the first U.N. report was released, it was said that it would be "premature" to provide a list.[219] The content of the Turku Declaration raised the interest of states, but some comments made a clear reference to the need of elaborating on the Martens

---

[214] U.N. Doc. E/CN.4/1999/92, *supra* note 103, para. 3.
[215] *Id.* para. 3.
[216] U.N. Doc. E/CN.4/1998/87/Add.1, *supra* note 100, para. 6 (Canada).
[217] *Id.* para. 52.
[218] *Id.* para. 52.
[219] U.N. Doc. E/CN.4/1998/87, *supra* note 62, para. 97.

Clause, as the clause was considered to be still vague. The goal of identifying the standards would include the definition "of more detailed and precise standards aiming at their proper implementation in the field."[220] Just to give an idea of the basic problems a list of issues to be addressed is given by the U.N. initial report on the basis of the rights and situations which should be addressed. The list is of course not exhaustive, as it is opened to incorporate new development in international law. The list includes abuses such as: deprivation of the right to life; torture and cruel, inhuman or degrading treatment; freedom of movement; the rights of the child; women's human rights; arbitrary deprivation of liberty and due process; and protection of civilian population. Specific rights that are already considered non-derogable under HRL are added, such as the prohibition of discrimination; the prohibition of servitude and slavery; the non-retroactivity of criminal law; the right of recognition as a person before the law; and the right to freedom of thought, conscience, and religion.[221]

The content of customary rules under IHL, already mentioned before, should be considered. Furthermore, the two customary law principles on the means and methods of warfare should be applicable. They provide that:

- the use of means and methods of warfare which are of a nature to cause superfluous injury or unnecessary suffering is prohibited,[222] and
- the use of weapons which are by nature indiscriminate is prohibited.[223]

These guarantees should aim at the protection of the civilian population and the protection of persons *hors de combat*.[224] It is also stressed by the U.N. report that the standards "would need to be stated in a way that was specific enough to be meaningful in actual situations, and yet at the same time be clear and understandable."[225]

5.3. *The Field of Application* Ratione Temporis

There is a general consensus of the states to consider the application of the standards "in all situations and at all times."[226] In general, states envisage the application of the standards to emergency situations and make reference to their national law

---

[220] U.N. Doc. E/CN.4/1998/87/Add.1, *supra* note 100, para. 57 (Croatia).
[221] U.N. Doc. E/CN.4/1999/92, *supra* note 103, para. 17.
[222] CIHL, *supra* note 77, Rule 70, 237.
[223] *Id.* Rule 71, 244.
[224] U.N. Doc. E/CN.4/1998/87/Add.1, *supra* note 100, para. 56 (Croatia). Common Article 3 of the 1949 GC mentions "members of armed forces who have laid down their arms and those placed hors de combat by sickness, wounds, detention, or any other cause."
[225] U.N. Doc. E/CN.4/1998/87, *supra* note 62, para. 98.
[226] U.N. Doc. E/CN.4/1998/87/Add.1, *supra* note 100, para. 89 (Norway).

regulating those situations.[227] Some positions agree with the fact that the standards should be applied "to everybody in every situation."[228] This should avoid the problem of qualification of the conflict determining the application of human rights or humanitarian law and "constitute a safety net independent of any assertion that a particular conflict is below the threshold of international humanitarian law treaties."[229] The distinction between international and non-international armed conflict was already avoided when defining the rules of IHL applicable by U.N. peacekeeping forces.[230] The ICC Statute maintains the distinction between international and non-international armed conflict, but it defines war crimes committed in all situations of armed conflict.[231] The ICRC study on customary law in the analysis of rules provides the distinction between international and non-international armed conflict, but in chapter 32, dealing with Fundamental Guarantees, including HRL, defines rules that apply in both types of conflict.

This trend has been confirmed by the ICTY which affirmed that "an armed conflict exists whenever there is a resort to armed force between states or protracted armed violence between governmental authorities and organized armed groups or between such groups within a state."[232] The problematic differentiation and threshold to identify non-international armed conflict and situations of internal violence and civil unrest which fall below the application of IHL has also been addressed by the ICTY in the *Celebici* case in which the Court held that the emphasis should be on the protracted extent of the armed violence and the organization of the parties involved.[233] In the *Tadic* case the ICTY considered both the minimum intensity of the conflict and the organization of the parties as fundamental criteria for the existence of the internal armed conflict.[234]

---

[227] *Id.* para. 4 (Botswana).
[228] *Id.* para. 74 (Finland).
[229] *Id.* para. 89 (Norway).
[230] Observance by United Nations Forces of International Humanitarian Law, U.N. Doc. ST/SGB/1999/13, Secretary-General's Bulletin (Aug. 6, 1999); Ray Murphy, *United Nations Military Operations and International Humanitarian Law: What Rules Apply to Peacekeepers?*, 14 Criminal Law Forum 153–194 (2003); Paolo Benvenuti, *The Implementation of Humanitarian Law in the Framework of Peacekeeping Operations*, *in* Law in Humanitarian Crises 83 (vol. I, 1995).
[231] Article 8(2)(c) and (e) ICC Statute, *supra* note 138.
[232] Tadic, *supra* note 154, para. 70.
[233] Prosecutor v. Delalic et al. (Celebici), Case No. IT-96-21, Trial Chamber Judgment, (Nov. 16, 1998), para. 184.
[234] Tadic, *supra* note 154, para. 70; Prosecutor v. Tadic, Case No. IT-94-1-T, Opinion and Judgement, (May 7, 1997), para. 564.

5.4. *The Field of Application* Ratione Materiae

The types of conduct regulated in case of conflict and internal violence conform the core of FSH. As already mentioned before, the idea is to protect people in situations of violence. This was clearly stated in the *Tadic* case by the Appeals Chamber:

> Why protect civilians from belligerent violence, or even ban rape, torture or other wanton destruction of hospitals, churches, museums or private property, as well as proscribe weapons causing unnecessary suffering when two sovereign States are engaged in war, and yet refrain from enacting the same bans or providing the same protection when armed violence has erupted 'only' within the territory of a sovereign State? If intenrnational law, while of course duly safeguarding the legitimate interest of States, must gradually turn to the protection of human beings, it is only natural that the aforementioned dichotomy should gradually lose its weight.[235]

Elaborating on the *Nicaragua* case,[236] that defined Common Article 3 to the GCs as a minimum set of rules for all types of armed conflict,[237] the ICTY has confirmed the existence and applicability of a common corpus of IHL regardless of the characterization of the conflict,[238] adding certain rules on means and methods of warfare, especially the ban on the use of chemical weapons and perfidious methods of warfare; and protection of certain objects such as cultural property.[239] It also considered that the general essence of rules and principles applicable to international armed conflicts extend to internal armed conflict.[240] This means that "(i) only a number of rules and principles governing international armed conflicts have gradually been extended to apply to internal conflicts; and (ii) this extension has not taken place in the form of a full and mechanical transplant of those rules to internal conflicts."[241]

5.5. *The Field of Application* Ratione Personae

As mentioned before, there is a problem concerning the individuation of the subjects who should be bound by the standards under consideration. There seem to be no doubt on the application of the standards by state agents. There are problems

---

[235] Tadic, *supra* note 154, para. 97.
[236] Nicaragua Case, *supra* note 72, para. 218
[237] Tadic, *supra* note 154, para. 102: "these rules reflect 'elementary considerations of humanity' applicable under customary international law to any armed conflict, whether it is of an internal or international character."
[238] Prosecutor v. Martic, Case No. IT-95-11-R61, Review of the Indictment Persuant to Rule 61, (Mar. 8, 1996) [hereinafter Martic].
[239] Tadic, *supra* note 154, paras 96–127; Martic, *supra* note 238, paras 10–18.
[240] Tadic, *supra* note 154, para. 126.
[241] *Id*. para. 126.

concerning the application of the same standards by non-state actors. To this end, it is interesting to note the fact that the Commission on Human Rights in its Resolution 1999/65 stated that the principles under consideration should govern "the behaviour of all persons, groups and public authorities." This means that the rules are applicable not only to states but also to other parties, and individuals as well. This seems to be the rule under international criminal law where the trends towards individual criminal responsibility are very clear. But still, under HRL states are the main subjects accountable for atrocities for violations of human rights, while under IHL all parties to the conflict have the responsibility for the application of IHL rules.

6. Conclusion

Several relevant issues arise from the legal point of view concerning the possible result of the work started by the United Nations on FSH. The definition of standards is under way. U.N. reports try to identify and keep a record of the main rules and principles that should be applicable in all situations of violence. They include the non-derogable rights under HRL, but also rules that have been identified by the ICRC Study on IHL customary law and relevant case-law by international tribunals and courts. Other rules on the conduct of state officials[242] and rules on the means and methods of warfare, and the limitations on the use of weapons would also be a relevant issue to be considered.[243]

There is not a clear definition of the final outcome of the study on FSH once they are identified by the United Nations. The Commission on Human Rights has not taken any decision on this issue. Statements by the Commission on Human Rights only addressed the "desirability of identifying principles." Since the creation of the Human Rights Council, which will discuss issues previously dealt before by the CHR, including the U.N. reports on FSH, there has not been any further development. The main question is whether, once and if the principles are identified, they would become a new legal instrument, a declaration, or a training tool, but also if it may be desirable to have a codified system of FSH.

If a new international instrument is negotiated, then new standards and clearer rules applicable in all situations should be identified. If a declaration will be adopted, possibly by the U.N. General Assembly, it could include new developments but

---

[242] For instance, other useful instruments in defining standards could be documents such as the Code of Conduct for Law Enforcement Officials, *supra* note 207, and the Basic Principles on the Use of Force and Firearms by Law Enforcement Officials, *supra* note 81.

[243] *See generally* David A. Koplow, Non-Lethal Weapons: The Law and Policy of Revolutionary Technologies for the Military and Law Enforcement (2006).

also restatements of the law and legal principles. If the United Nations and the international community have started working on this topic, it is due to the fact that, in many cases, international law does not provide adequate protection, not because there are not enough rules, but because the distinction between IHL and HRL still leaves the gaps in the legal regulation of situations of violence.

Suggestions provided by the U.N. reports are mainly toward the adoption of practical oriented outcomes that should strengthen the protection of victims of internal violence. FSH should fulfill the following purposes:

- Make clear the necessary clarifications and further elaboration of the law, and if they are required.
- Formulate a restatement that should reduce or prevent violations of the law.
- Give a practical educational tool both for training of members of the armed forces and for humanitarian workers acting in conflict areas.

At the same time, some potentially negative outcomes are envisaged:

- The risk of limiting the standards already achieved.
- The high political influence on many issues related to this topic.

The three options are all feasible. From the theoretical point of view, it may be relevant to clarify the fundamental rules applicable in times of violence. International rules are quite well defined, but still the problems of applicability of rules in cases that are considered short of war, such as humanitarian missions, peace-keeping operation and international policing actions should be better identified. Internal conflicts and situations of violence that fall below the threshold defined by the four GCs and related protocols should also be identified. And the legal position, rights and obligations of actors in the different types of situations need clarification. The risk of codification of the rules is that it might take a long time, and also the possibility of limiting the applicability of new rules that might be applicable in such an evolving and fluid situation.

It is important to keep in mind that the U.N. Secretary-General's reports make a constant reference to the two sets of norms of IHL and HRL. The research of common rules to both bodies of law is considered a fundamental methodology in identifying FSH. The specificity of IHL and HRL is not underestimated, but it is suggested that "in situations of internal violence – where there is considerable overlap and complementarity – this distinctness can be counter-productive."[244]

But still it is quite clear that despite the key trends identified in international law, the two sets of rule are not easily interchangeable. For instance, under IHL the use of lethal force, including collateral damages, is allowed with certain limitations,

---

[244] *Id.* para. 99.

but under HRL the right to life allows very limited exceptions.[245] Scholars do not agree on the level of integration, separation and priority, and applicability of the two branches of international law, and states are not always keen on applying basic rules for the protection of victims in conflict situations. Due to the actual problems of inefficient performance of the two separate sets of rights and inherent duties, a possibility of convergence or at least a form of "co-operation," as outlined in this chapter, is envisaged to achieve a better protection for the victims of violence. This integration is foreseen – and seems to be endorsed – by the 1999 U.N. report when it states that "[t]here is no reason why certain acts which may be unlawful in normal times and in situations of internal armed conflict should be lawful in situations of internal violence."[246]

It is a challenging task to clarify the forms of this interaction between two fundamental branches of international law. This development would be of course welcome, as it would give a clearer understanding of legal obligations for all actors involved in situations of violence and better protection of potential victims of violence.

It is significant that through the United Nations, the international community started addressing the legal implications related to situations of violence, in particular intra-state violence. This is one of the most important areas of concern for the protection of fundamental rights of millions of people around the world. At the beginning of the 21st century, after four centuries from the structuring of modern international law, legal rules and principles in the international system show the tension between a state-centered regime and the protection of fundamental rights of all human beings. This issue shows the difficult relationship between the recently broadly defined human security[247] and the interest of states.[248] As professor Meron suggests, it is possible to identify a trend towards "the humanization of international law," taking into account the influence of rules and principles developed by both IHL and HRL.[249] As the work started by the United Nations is still ongoing, it is not possible to provide a concluding statement on the matter. Nevertheless, international legal developments are relevant to show a trend in this area of law. Further legal analysis is needed to clarify the conundrum related to the legal definition of FSH. It will be also appropriate to see how states and other actors within the international community would further react to the definition of common rules applicable to all situations of violence, before addressing the practical issues concerning the application of the rules under consideration.

---

[245] On this issue *see* Louise Doswald-Beck, *The Right to Life in Armed Conflict: Does International Humanitarian Law Provide the Answer?*, 88 Int'l Rev. Red Cross 881 (2006).
[246] U.N. Doc. E/CN.4/1999/92, *supra* note 103, para. 25.
[247] Commission on Human Security, *Human Security Now* (2003).
[248] *See* Astri Suhrke, *Human Security and the Interests of States*, 30 Security Dialogue 265 (1999); Marco Odello, *¿Amenazas para la seguridad o amenazas para los individuos? El derecho internacional y los desafíos para la seguridad internacional*, *in* Ibáñez, *supra* note 7.
[249] *See* Meron 2006, *supra* note 71, Introduction.

Chapter II

End Justifies the Means? – Post 9/11 Contempt for Humane Treatment

*Agnieszka Jachec-Neale**

1. *Introduction*

In 1928 Supreme Court Justice Louise D. Brandeis warned:

> Decency, security, and liberty alike demand that government officials shall be subjected to the same rules of conduct that are commands to the citizen. In a government of laws, existence of the government will be imperilled if it fails to observe the law scrupulously. Our government is the potent, the omnipresent teacher. For good or for ill, it teaches the whole people by its example. Crime is contagious.[1]

Nearly eighty years after, one wonders how deeply relevant are those words in the context of the United States led "global war on terror." Many Americans and foreigners alike are perplexed, if not outraged by the practices introduced and implemented as a part of anti-terrorism measures aftermath the September 11, 2001 terrorist attacks. Sadly, the US is not the only state that conducts its counter-terrorist operations with sometimes subtle but persistent disregard of international legal standards and a respect for the human dignity, considered only an awkward impediment in the war against terrorists, where security is the overriding factor.

From the accounts of the widespread practice of arbitrary arrests all over the world, the approved and systematic use of torture either directly or by proxy, the use of inhumane detention conditions as a part of the "non-cooperation" punishments for detainees, accounts of humiliation and de-dignifying treatment of prisoners including desecrations of religious symbols to the five-year or longer incarcerations without any or appropriate judicial oversight, not to mention learning about charges, getting a lawyer or getting a trial for that matter – we faced the whole spectrum of

---

* Agnieszka Jachec-Neale is currently a doctoral student at the University of Essex (UK). She also teaches at the Centre for International Studies and Diplomacy at SOAS (London, UK). Her latest professional engagement was with the British Institute of International and Comparative Law (London, UK), where she served as Research Fellow for over two years.
[1] Olmstead v. U.S., Dissenting Opinion, 277 U.S. 438 (June 4, 1928), 485.

violations of international standards. Even rough estimations of "war on terror" detainees indicate that as many as 70,000 persons[2] could be imprisoned all over the world, including children and women and it is very likely they all experienced some of these practices at some point of time. These estimations can only be rough as the U.S. and other states' authorities have failed to inform the public on exactly how many detainees they keep in custody, whether in Afghanistan, in Iraq, or in the various states all over the world.

Traditionally, the counter-terrorism measures adopted by the states, internationally or nationally, were positioned in the law enforcement domain, where the dominating legal framework was that of human rights standards. Even if in numerous cases, the scale and intensity of violence emanating from the terrorist attacks might have reached a threshold of armed conflict (like in Chechnya or in the Northern Ireland conflicts), it was only the U.S. government declaring a campaign against the terrorist organizations and networks, like Al Qaeda in 2001, a first one to regard this fight as an armed conflict. Although a disputed determination, this view was subsequently recognized by the U.S. Supreme Court in the *Hamdan* case.[3] The Justices, arguably, agreed with the government that the laws of armed conflict were not only relevant in the war with Taliban authorities in Afghanistan (a part which is rather uncontested) but also in an ongoing fight against Al Qaeda and other terrorist organizations and networks.[4] The Court recognized this conflict as non-international in character by relying on a literate reading of Article 3 in conjunction with Article 2 common to all four 1949 Geneva Conventions.[5] The controversial reading of Article 3, thus far interpreted in a spirit and intention to be applicable in the civil wars, colonial or religious conflicts; being now also relevant

---

[2] Guantanamo and beyond: The Continuing Pursuit of Unchecked Executive Power, Amnesty International, AMR/51/063/2005 (May 13, 2005), at 4–5.
[3] Hamdan v. Rumsfeld548, U.S. 196, (June 29, 2006).
[4] *Id.* at 69ff.
[5] Article 3 common to all four 1949 Geneva Conventions, *see* infra note 7. The Article in parts reads as follows:
In the case of armed conflict not of an international character occurring in the territory of one of the High Contracting Parties, each Party to the conflict shall be bound to apply, as a minimum, the following provisions:
(1) Persons taking no active part in the hostilities, including members of armed forces who have laid down their arms and those placed 'hors de combat' by sickness, wounds, detention, or any other cause, shall in all circumstances be treated humanely, without any adverse distinction founded on race, colour, religion or faith, sex, birth or wealth, or any other similar criteria. To this end, the following acts are and shall remain prohibited at any time and in any place whatsoever with respect to the above-mentioned persons:
(a) violence to life and person, in particular murder of all kinds, mutilation, cruel treatment and torture;...
(c) outrages upon personal dignity, in particular humiliating and degrading treatment;'

to the global "war on terror" is further complicated by the sheer circumstances of the *Hamdan* case, linking it directly to the 2001 conflict in Afghanistan. This was however clearly an international armed conflict primarily against the Talibans, at that time the governing authority in Afghanistan state, which happened to accept the Al Qaeda presence and operations on and outside their soil.[6] The sole application of common Article 3, instead of the full set of Geneva Conventions to this conflict as a matter of treaty law and thus to all former Taliban supporters and subsequent U.S. detainees seems rather troubling. Consequently, however this interpretation indicated that at least the U.S. campaign is and will be considered in the context of an ongoing armed conflict, where not only international and domestic human rights rules but also more specifically international humanitarian law (IHL)[7] can and should be applied to. Without going into a comprehensive analysis of the Supreme Court's argument, the judgment reiterated the continuous and unconditional minimum obligation to treat humanely all those who are no longer taking an active part in the hostilities in all circumstances, whether ex-combatants or civilians, including those who might have resorted to the acts of terror. At first, this appears to be a well-intentioned and uncomplicated minimal requirement, yet the recent hugely problematic implementation verified this theoretical assumption. Taking the *Hamdan* ruling and the common Article 3 to all 1949 Geneva Conventions

---

[6] Following the literate method of interpretation, presumably, all acts and operations attributed to the United States on the territory of any country in the world (since all the States are now party to four 1949 Geneva Conventions) aimed at the suspected terrorists would be considered as a part of an ongoing non international armed conflict with Al Qaeda specifically and against any terrorist organization in general. Other interpretations assume the existence of a separate instance when armed force is used and the situation can be qualified as an armed conflict. A further question regards the position of third party/parties joining the US in this conflict, and whether they would similarly consider themselves as a part of a perpetual armed conflict in the first place and if so, of which type. Bearing in mind various treaty obligations, it is possible that the alternative approach towards the "war on terror" results in a substantively enhanced protection of the persons caught in the conflict.

[7] IHL is used synonymously with the laws of armed conflict, which comprise of the rules relative to the conduct of hostilities and the protection of victims, comprising of both treaty and the relevant customary norms. The main legal sources in this field consist of four 1949 Geneva Conventions, two of which will be referred to below as well as two Additional Protocols: Geneva Convention Relative to the Treatment to Prisoners of War, Aug. 12, 1949, 75 U.N.T.S. 135, 136 [hereinafter GC III] and Geneva Convention Relative to the Protection of Civilian Persons in Time of War, Aug. 12, 1949, 75 U.N.T.S. 287, 288 [hereinafter GC IV]; Protocol Additional to the Geneva Conventions of 12 August 1949, and Relating to the Protections of Victims of International Armed Conflicts, opened for signature Dec. 12, 1977, U.N. Doc. A/32/144, Annex I, II, (1977), *reprinted in* 16 I.L.M. 1391 (1977) [hereinafter AP I]; and Protocol Additional to the Geneva Conventions of 12 August 1949, and relating to the Protection of Victims of Non-International Armed Conflicts (June 8, 1977) [hereinafter AP II].

as the base, this paper will examine some of the problems associated with the effective implementation of the essential safeguards considered the integral elements of humane treatment, particularly the prohibition of torture and cruel, inhuman and other degrading treatment in the context of counter-terrorism measures. This paper is predominantly focused on the concept of humane treatment enshrined therein, the analysis of which is placed in the context of the recent developments in the field, including the reinterpretation of the prohibition of torture, the increased use of interrogation methods short of torture or other forms of ill-treatment[8] against suspected terrorist detainees, incommunicado and prolonged detention and detention conditions amounting to torture. As a result, the intrinsic relationship between IHL and human rights law is highlighted. Finally, consideration is given to the governmental policies and the existing law, the latter requiring a mere adherence and not re-adjustment in the ongoing campaign against the terrorists. The paper concludes by indicating the continued need to uphold the protections of individuals in all situations, including the fight against the terrorism through the reassertion of the centrality of the principle of human dignity.

2. Counter-terrorism in the Framework of International Law

Terrorism – generated violence should be considered in two dimensions, both interdependent and closely intertwined. First, it is necessary to distinguish between the deliberate acts of violence employing unpredictable and usually indiscriminate attacks against civilian population, including the authorities governing the state. These may be committed in the name of political or ideological ends. Such attacks, perceived as a direct threat to the security and stability of the state are usually met with some sort of self-defense response from the respective government. These responses may take various forms, depending on the intensity and the scale of the disruption caused. The state's reaction may too embody a predominantly violent conduct, whether in the framework of the domestic law enforcement or in the shape of more organized armed fighting, possibly including a complex military operations as well as the terror – based measures. The more complicated operationally and more intense and destructive in the impact the response is, the sooner we perceive the whole situation as an ongoing armed conflict and the particular circumstances then define the type of the conflict. If the original incidents were not met with a substantively violent response, even though they may be seen as acts of aggression, it would be difficult to frame them in an armed conflict context.

---

[8] The expression "ill-treatment" or "other forms of ill-treatment" is used here interchangeably to denominate cruel, inhuman or degrading treatment or punishment.

The July 7, 2005 London bombings and its aftermath, for example, represent specific and individual manifestations of terrorism which neither were responded to in a framework of armed conflict, nor generated any extensively violent state-imposed measures, with exception to the shooting of Jean Charles de Menezes on July 22, 2005.[9] Jean Charles was killed by unnamed police officers as a suspected terrorist during a faulty antiterrorist raid in connection to the July 21, 2005 attempted bombings in London, which followed the tragic events from July 7, 2005. One of the most disputed aspects of this incident were the counterterrorist procedures employed by the armed police when dealing with the suspect suicide bombers, in particular the rules permitting 'shoot to kill' suspects in the cases, where it is believed that the suspects are about to detonate explosives likely to result in mass casualties among the civilian population.[10] In fact, the new tactics in confronting potential suicide bombers were already discussed in late 2001, followed by a set of the guidelines under a code name "Operation Kratos,"[11] introduced in 2003.[12] Whilst still pending before the judicial authorities, it is worth recalling that this case was not the first time; similar tactics to prevent planned terrorist attacks were used by the British armed forces. In March 1988 in Gibraltar, members of the Special Air Service Regiment (SAS), the special forces unit of the British Army, shoot three Irish Republican Army operatives in an attempt to prevent them from operating a detonation device. Neither of the operatives had any explosives or detonators on them, although a timed car bomb linked to one of them was later recovered in Spain. This counterterrorism action, known as Operation *Flavius*, was subsequently scrutinized first during the jury inquest in Gibraltar and later by the European Court of Human Rights. The Court found, by a majority of ten to nine votes, that the killing of three IRA servicemen did not constitute a lawful use of force which was no more than "absolutely necessary" in defence of the individuals from unlawful violence as required by Article 22(a) of the European Convention

---

[9] A subsequent highly controversial inquiry (in one part still uncompleted) failed to implicate those criminally responsible for shooting an innocent man. Consequently, the Crown Prosecution Service (CPS) decided against pressing any charges due to insufficient evidence, which was uphold by the High Court in December 2006. Instead, the CPS put forward charges under section 3 of the Health and Safety at Work Act 1974 of failing to provide for the health, safety, and welfare of Jean Charles de Menezes by the Office of the Commissioner of Police of the Metropolis. These proceedings scheduled to begin in October 2007, can only result in a financial penalty.
[10] *Will Police now Shoot to Kill?*, BBC News, July 22, 2005.
[11] Suicide Terrorism, Metropolitan Police Authority Report (13), Oct. 27, 2005, *available at* www.mpa.gov.uk/committees/mpa/2005/051027/13.htm (last visited April 1, 2007).
[12] *Met Adopted Secret Shoot-to-Kill Policy in the Face of a New and Deadly Threat*, Financial Times, July 25, 2005.

of Human Rights [13] and by this infringing the victims' right to life.[14] Interestingly, this determination was based not on the assessment of the onduct of the soldiers who actually pulled the triggers (who were effectively exonerated based on obedience to the superior orders and their *mens rea* pointing to strong belief their actions were absolutely necessary to order to prevent the danger of mass killing)[15] but on the number of shortcomings in the authorities' organization and control over the whole operation. In particular, the Court stated that "the failure of the authorities to make sufficient allowances for the possibility that their intelligence assessments might, in some respects at least, be erroneous"[16] and that the soldiers automatic resort to lethal force:

> in this vital respect lacks the degree of caution in the use of firearms to be expected from law enforcement personnel in a democratic society, even when dealing with dangerous terrorist suspects, and stands in marked contrast to the standard of care reflected in the instructions in the use of firearms by the police which had been drawn to their attention and which emphasised the legal responsibilities of the individual officer in the light of conditions prevailing at the moment of engagement.[17]

The remaining nine judges contested the majority judgment precisely on these issues pointing out to the earlier findings of the then European Commission of Human Rights and the results of the inquest which both found that force was used lawfully. It was submitted that the Court asserted its position without a substantive justification.[18] Whether the Court's application of the established facts in the light of legal requirements was correct and sufficiently reasoned, the judgment revitalized a very much generic and perpetual in the situations of counter-terrorism caveat:

> On the one hand, they [the United Kingdom authorities] were required to have regard to their duty to protect the lives of the people in Gibraltar including their own military personnel and, on the other, to have minimum resort to the use of lethal force against those suspected of posing this threat in the light of the obligations flowing from both domestic and international law.[19]

Alongside with a growing pressure on the states to effectively implement their duty to suppress terrorism and to investigate and punish the terrorists, an increasing

---

[13] Convention for the Protection of Human Rights and Fundamental Freedoms [hereinafter ECHR], Nov. 4, 1950, Council of Europe, European Treaty Series No. 5.
[14] McCann and Others v. United Kingdom, Eur. Ct. Hum. H. R., Judgment (Sept. 27, 1995), A.324, para. 213.
[15] *Id.* para. 200.
[16] *Id.*
[17] *Id.* para. 212.
[18] Joint Dissenting Opinion of Judges Ryssdal, Bernhard, Thor Vilhjalmsson, Golcuklu, Palm, Pekkanen, Sir John Freeland, Baka and Jambrek in McCann and Others v. United Kingdom, *supra* note 14, para. 25.
[19] McCann and Others v. United Kingdom, *supra* note 14, para. 192.

concern involves a continued need to remain compliant with international and domestic obligations, particularly in the field of human rights and IHL.[20] Terrorism and counterterrorism measures can occur in the context of three factual situations (peacetime, an emergency threatening the security of the nation and an armed conflict), which affect the varied application of international law and in particular human rights norms. The normally full application of international human rights law during peacetime can be restricted during an emergency threatening the security and integrity of allowing the state to institute certain derogations. When the violence triggers or occurs in the context of the armed conflict, the human rights continue to apply parallel to the specific rules of IHL (whether restricted or not), however subject to the *lex specialis* rule. This position already indicated by the Inter-American Commission on Human Rights[21] was confirmed by the International Court of Justice (ICJ) in its Advisory Opinion on *the Legal Consequences of the Construction of a Wall in the Occupied Palestinian Territory*, which stated:

> that the protection offered by human rights conventions does not cease in case of armed conflict, save through the effect of provisions for derogation of the kind to be found in Article 4 of the International Covenant on Civil and Political Rights. As regards the relationship between international humanitarian law and human rights law, there are thus three possible situations: some rights may be exclusively matters of international humanitarian law; others may be exclusively matters of human rights law; yet others may be matters of both these branches of international law. In order to answer the question put to it, the Court will have to take into consideration both these branches of international law, namely human rights law and, as *lex specialis*, international humanitarian law.[22]

It should be noted that the sheer operation of terrorism in any situation does not affect the application of the particular normative framework, when the otherwise necessary conditions for such application are present.[23] Nonetheless, the involvement in the terrorist activity may bear on the legal status and the

---

[20] *See, e.g.*, U.N. Security Council [hereinafter S.C.] Res. 1456 (2003) and the reports of S.C. Counter-Terrorism Committee, the reports of the U.N. Independent Expert on the protection of human rights and fundamental freedoms while countering terrorism as well as the numerous multilateral treaties adopted on regional and international level, review of which is beyond this paper.

[21] *See*, Terrorism and Human Rights, Inter-American Commission on Human Rights, Report (Oct. 22, 2002), Organisation of American States, OEA/Sr.L/V/II.116, Doc. 5 rev. 1 corr., paras 29, 61 [hereinafter: IACHR Report] and also Inter-American Court of Human Rights Judgment in *Abella* (Argentina), Case No. 11.137, Report No. 5/97 and Annual Report of the IACHR, 1997, paras 158–159, 161.

[22] Legal Consequences of the Construction of a Wall in the Occupied Palestinian Territory, Advisory Opinion (July 9, 2004), 2004 I.C.J. Rep. 163, para. 106.

[23] IACHR Report, *supra* note 21, para. 19.

treatment of the persons suspected of such criminal activity, particularly in the course of hostilities.

1.1. *Peacetime and the Emergencies*

Resorting to terrorism is widely condemned as an unlawful criminal activity. The intention behind terrorist activity is to target the very essence of human being, human life. Even just the mere threat of mass killings can cause widespread psychological anxiety, not to mention the post-event trauma suffered by the victims, witnesses and all those who were in some way affected. Terrorist attacks resulting in any human casualties should be regarded as violations of human rights, possibly crimes against humanity when the legal requirements are satisfied.

Iniuria non excusat iniuriam, lawlessness does not justify lawlessness. The counter-terrorism measures must comply with all the domestic or international legal standards.

The absolute necessity to ensure compliance in accordance to human rights, IHL or refugee laws has been repeatedly stressed by various international bodies[24] and regional organizations[25] as well as reiterated in a number of international anti-terrorism treaties.[26] U.N. Secretary-General amply expressed the view shared by many:

> Human rights law makes ample provision for strong counter-terrorist action, even in the most exceptional circumstances. But compromising human rights cannot serve the struggle against terrorism. On the contrary, it facilitates achievement of the terrorist's objective – by ceding to him the moral high ground, and provoking tension, hatred and mistrust of government among precisely those parts of the population where he is most likely to find recruits.[27]

---

[24] *See, e.g.*, U.N. S.C. Res. 1456 of Jan. 20, 2003, U.N. Doc. S/RES/1456 (2003), U.N. World Summit Declaration 2005, adopted on 14–16 Sep. 2005, U.N. Doc. A/60/L.1, para. 85.

[25] *See, e.g.*, Council of Europe Guidelines on human rights and the fight against terrorism, adopted by the Committee of Ministers on July 11, 2002, H (2002) 004, see in particular Guidelines II–IV, U.N. Doc. S/RES/1624 (2005) para. 4; IACHR Report, *supra* note 21, paras 5, 22ff.; European Parliament, Recommendations on the Role of the European Union in Combating Terrorism (2001/2016 (INI)) (Sep. 5, 2001).

[26] *See, e.g.*, European Convention on the Suppression of Terrorism, European Treaty Series (ETS) 90 (Jan. 27, 1997); Convention to Prevent and Punish the Acts of Terrorism Taking the Form of Crimes Against Persons and Related Extortion that are of International Significance, OAS Treaty Series, No. 37 (Feb. 2, 1971); Inter-American Convention Against Terrorism, OAS General Assembly Resolution AG/RES. 1840 (XXXII-O/02) 2nd plenary session (June 3, 2002); Convention on the Prevention and Combating of Terrorism, Organization of African Unity, adopted at Algiers (July 13, 1999).

[27] U.N. Secretary-General K. Annan at the International Summit on Democracy, Terrorism and Security, Keynote speech (Mar. 10, 2005).

There is no doubt that human rights (albeit with the limitations and derogations) are applicable in all types of situations, as mentioned before, whether in peace, war or a time of other national emergencies, tensions and disturbances. There is no legal exception for terrorism in the application of these instruments, though they do recognize that the scope of the legal obligations may be modified due the exceptional circumstances. These modifications would be necessarily required by the exigencies of the situation for a limited period in order to protect the rule of law and democratic stability of the state. The European Court of Human Rights noted in the *Klass and Others* v. *Germany* case concerning the legitimacy of the secret surveillance:

> The Court, being aware of the danger such a law poses of undermining or even destroying democracy on the ground of defending it, affirms that the Contracting States may not, in the name of the struggle against espionage and terrorism, adopt whatever measures they deem appropriate.[28]

It is sometimes argued that the states should primarily recourse to making effective use of the limitation clauses, which should provide a sufficient legal framework operational in the situations of emergency.[29] This would normally be true only insofar derogable rights are considered, like Articles 8–11 ECHR.[30] Noteworthy, in *Brogan* v. *United Kingdom*[31] the European Court of Human Rights suggested that also in respect of some rights, which do not explicitly provide a possibility for limitations, like deprivation of liberty and a right to fair trial, law enforcement actions like an investigation of the terrorist offences may impose some restrictions on these rights.[32]

Any limitations must nevertheless satisfy the conditions of the legality (i.e. limitation should be clearly prescribed by the law, both domestic and international), the necessity (i.e. strictly in response to one of the listed objectives, most commonly national security, public order, health, morals or rights and freedoms of others) and the proportionality (measures allowed are in pursuance of legitimate aims). These conditions are very much required also in relation to derogations instituted

---

[28] Klass and Others v. Germany, European Court of Human Rights, Judgment (Sept. 6, 1978), Series A No. 28 (1978–1980), 2 EHRR 214, paras 48–50.

[29] Dominic McGoldrick, *The Interface between Public Emergency Powers and International Law*, 2 Int.'L J. Const. L. 380, 384–385 (2004).

[30] Similarly in General Comment No. 29: *States of Emergency (Article 4)*: Human Rights Committee, U.N. Doc. CCPR/C/21/Rev.1/Add.11 (Aug. 31, 2001), para. 5 [hereinafter General Comment No. 29].

[31] Brogan v. United Kingdom, Judgment (Nov. 29, 1988), Eur. Ct. H. R., 11 Eur. H. R. Rep. 117 (1989).

[32] *Compare* with Aksoy v. Turkey, Judgment (Dec. 18, 1996), Eur. Ct. H. R. Reports 1996–VI, No. 3, para. 68.

by the states,[33] but there are at least three additional constraints effectively raising a threshold of legality in the context of derogations.[34] First, the derogations are only allowed in a public emergency threatening the life of nation (Article 4 ICCPR, Article 15 ECHR) or threatening the independence or security of the State (Article 27 of American Convention on Human Rights.[35]) The emergency must be serious enough to threaten "the organised life of the community of which the state is composed"[36] even though it does not need to affect the whole population of such state.[37] Determination of such emergency is left to the national authorities under the margin of appreciation doctrine.[38]

Second, the derogations must be consistent with any other international obligations of the state, which implies consistency not only with other ratified human rights treaties but also other conventional and customary law as such.[39] This is of particular importance in relation to the international humanitarian law, which does not permit derogations from the similar protections enshrined in the relevant treaties or under the customary norms. The matter is further complicated by the fact that IHL treaties provide extended non-derogable protections compared to those proposed by human rights regulations.[40] In particular Article 3, common to all 1949 Geneva Conventions additionally prohibits any discrimination against those who are no longer taking part in hostilities as well as it provides for due process guarantees. Additional Protocol II to 1949 Geneva Conventions also contains some limitations on death penalty as well as the prohibition of forced displacement (Article 17).[41] Thus any derogation, imposed in the time of an armed conflict, contravening any of these provisions introduced by the state party to both relevant human rights and IHL treaties should be considered void.[42]

---

[33] General Comment No. 29, *supra* note 30, para. 8.
[34] Derogations cannot also be discriminatory solely on the ground of race, color, sex, language, religion or social origin. *See* Article 4, International Covenant on Civil and Political Rights, G.A. Res. 2200A (XXI), 21 U.N. GAOR (Supp. No. 16) at 52, U.N. Doc. A/6316 (Dec. 16, 1966), 999 U.N.T.S. 171, entered into force Mar. 23, 1976 [hereinafter ICCPR].
[35] American Convention on Human Rights, (Nov. 22, 1969), OAS Treaty Series No. 36, 1144 UNTS 123 [hereinafter AHCR].
[36] Lawless v. Ireland, Judgment (July 1, 1961), Eur. Ct. H. R Series A, No.25 para. 207.
[37] Ireland v. United Kingdom, Judgment (Jan. 18, 1978), Eur. Ct. H. R, Series A, No.3, para. 28.
[38] Aksoy v. Turkey, *supra* note 32, para. 68.
[39] Derogation under one human rights treaty is not valid in relation to any other treaties.
[40] Françoise Hampson, *Study on Human Rights Protection During Situations of Armed Conflict, Internal Disturbances and Tensions*, Council of Europe Committee of Experts for the Development of Human Rights, DH-DEV (2002) 001, para. 21.
[41] Similarly Article 4 ICCPR, *supra* note 34, covers also the non-discrimination and religious freedom.
[42] IACHR Report, *supra* note 21, para. 78.

Finally, some rights can never be subject to derogations. Each human rights treaty proscribes a slightly different set of rights,[43] but these ones seem to be most commonly invoked: right to life (with an exception to lawful acts of war under ECHR), prohibition of torture or cruel, inhuman or degrading treatment or punishment, prohibition of slavery and servitude or principle of legality in criminal law. Moreover, as mentioned above the rights fully protected by the laws of armed conflict are included in this category (like the prohibition of arbitrary deprivation of liberty, abductions or respect for the fundamental principle of fair trial).[44] The Human Rights Committee further stressed that even in state of emergency certain procedural rights, closely linked to the implementation of non-derogable rights (e.g. judicial guarantees including the presumption of innocence) must be fully observed.[45] Therefore, when assessing the need for a measure undertaken by the state during a period of derogation, the relevant human rights body will consider the function of the right and its particular relation to a non-derogable right.[46]

1.2. *Armed Conflicts*

This progressive interpretation of non-derogable rights may also appear to aim at the reconciliation of the differences in the scope of the protection provided in by IHL, as highlighted earlier. The Human Rights Committee implies that the existence of an armed conflict itself does not impact on the scope of human rights obligations, which scope can only be modified through a lawful derogation process; yet it views the gravity of the situations of armed violence, in which the derogations may be invoked, predominantly in the context of armed conflicts.[47] If the derogations were primarily allowed in emergencies like a war or internal armed conflict, they would be necessarily interpreted in the light of applicable norms of IHL.[48] A similar approach has been taken by the ICJ, which in one of its contentious cases found violations of international human rights law and IHL committed by Ugandan military forces on the territory of Democratic Republic of Congo, not

---

[43] ECHR indicates four non-derogable rights, ICCPR seven and ACHR eleven. It has to be noted however that while some of the enumerated rights are listed due to their unquestionable peremptory status, some other rights were included due to their nature, which nullifies the necessity for a derogation in any situations.
[44] The full list of the non-derogable rights in opinion of the Human Rights Committee is much longer and included the elements of the rights to remedies or of the minority rights. General Comment No. 29, *supra* note 30, paras 11–14.
[45] *Id.*
[46] General Comment 29, *supra* note 30, para. 16 and Françoise Hampson, *supra* note 40, para. 24.
[47] General Comment 29, *supra* note 30, para. 3.
[48] General Comment 31 [80]: *Nature of the General Legal Obligation Imposed on States Parties to the Covenant*, Human Rights Committee (May 26, 2004), U.N. Doc. CCPR/C/21/Rev.1/Add.13., para. 11.

only in the areas of military occupation, which is consistent with the previous *ditto* in the Advisory Opinion on *the Legal Consequences of the Construction of a Wall in the Occupied Palestinian Territory*,[49] but also in areas outside of Ugandan exercise of occupying power. Most importantly, it found violations of non-derogable rights (a right to life and the prohibition of torture) in conjunction to violations of the rules on the means and methods of combat, including relevant customary norms.[50] In making this assertion, the Court however failed to elaborate whether human rights violations were influenced by its interpretation of the violations of the laws of armed conflict and if so to what extent. As the matter remains unsettled, it seems that certain interpretational complications may possibly arise particularly in respect of the lawfulness of the detention and fair trial provisions.

Undoubtedly, this rather complicated marriage of human rights and IHL in armed conflict is exacerbated by the very nature of each of the set of laws. Human rights being applicable in all situations (albeit with the limitations and derogations if invoked), sets out rules binding on the states (officials, agents or any other persons acting on behalf of the states) in their relations with individuals as well as to some extend on the individuals themselves.

International humanitarian law governs only situations raising to the level of armed conflict, by regulating warfare among by all the parties to the conflict, including the non-state actor and providing for the protection of persons not engaged or no longer engaged in the hostilities.[51] In fact, the former further reinforces the latter through a set of key principles of military necessity and humanity, which in turn are supported by the principles of distinction and proportionality. The principle of humanity tames the military necessity principle by prohibiting using means and methods which would inflict suffering or destruction, which can be otherwise avoided in achieving the same military goal. This rule further reiterates humane protection to all persons, and in particular immunity from attack to non-combatants.[52] This is a necessary consequence of the operation of the principle of distinction, which puts on the warring parties an obligation to distinguish between civilian population and civilian objects and combatants and lawful military objectives at all times. The proportionality principle ties together

---

[49] *See* text accompanying note 22 above. ICJ has already previously referred to operations of the ICCPR in time of war, *see* Advisory Opinion on the *Legality of the Threat or Use of Nuclear Weapons* (July 8, 1996), ICJ Rep. 1996, para. 25.

[50] Case concerning Armed Activities on the Territory of the Congo (DRC v. Uganda) (Dec. 19, 2005), 2005 I.C.J. Rep. 116, para. 219.

[51] IHL does not regulate the internal tensions and disturbances or the isolated and sporadic acts of violence. Noteworthy Declaration of Turku /Abo of Dec. 2, 1990 proposed minimum humanitarian standards applicable in all situations, including the internal violence, disturbances, tensions, and the public emergency.

[52] In particular Article 3 common to the Geneva Conventions; Article 13 GC III, *supra* note 7; Article 14 GC IV, *supra* note 7; and Article 11 AP I and Article 4 AP II, *supra* note 7.

distinction and humanity rules, by prohibiting launching an attack which may be expected to cause incidental loss of civilian life, injury to civilians, damage to civilian objects, or a combination thereof, which would be excessive in relation to the concrete and direct military advantage anticipated.[53]

Crucial therefore to the analysis of the legal framework of armed conflict will be the intensity and the level of disruption in the first place (i.e. whether it attains a minimum threshold of the applicability) and the parties to the conflict.[54] Characterization of the realm of the organized armed violence in the context of international or non-international armed conflict will in many cases influence the scope of protections afforded to combatants and non-combatants.[55] The GC III provides a detailed account of the rules applicable in international armed conflicts in respect to combatants. The treaty specifies the scope of categories of persons entitled to POW status[56] as well as the particularities of the conditions of internment. The essential guarantee, however, is provided by Article 5 which requires a competent court to determine the status of all persons who have committed a belligerent act and have fallen into the hands of the enemy but there was doubt as to whether they would qualify as a POW under one of the categories stipulated in Article 4. Status determination standards were further reaffirmed, clarified and supplemented by Article 45 of AP I,[57] which introduced a presumption of POW status in instances when the person claimed or the Party upon s/he depended claimed such entitlement

---

[53] Articles 51, 52, 57 AP I, *supra* note 7.
[54] Article 23(g) of the Hague Regulations; Article 147 *in fine* GC IV, *supra* note 7; Article 51(1) *in fine* AP I, *supra* note 7.
[55] Applicable in international armed conflicts, the Geneva Conventions deal with the treatment of the wounded and sick in the armed forces in the field (Convention I), wounded, sick and shipwrecked members of the armed forces at sea (Convention II), Prisoners of War (GC III) and civilian persons (GC IV). Civilian persons include internally displaced persons, women, children, refugees, stateless persons, journalists and other categories of individuals (GC IV and AP I). Similarly, the rules applicable in non-international armed conflict (Article 3 common to the Geneva Conventions and AP II) deal with the treatment of persons not taking, or no longer taking part in the hostilities.
[56] Third Geneva Convention covers regular members of armed forces, including those who 'profess allegiance to a government or an authority not recognized by the Detaining Power' (Article 4A(1) and (3)). Further it grants POWs status to members of militias and other volunteer corps, belonging to the belligerent party, providing they satisfy four cumulative conditions (Article 4A(2)). The retained personnel (medical personnel and chaplains) although not considered Prisoners of War, were to be afforded protections associated with POW status enshrined in the Convention (Article 33). Civilians accompanying armed forces, members of the crews of the merchant marine and civil aircraft as well as civilians involved in *levée en masse* should too be afforded POW status similarly like interned former or current members of the armed forces belonging to occupied country. (Article 4B(1))
[57] Michael Bothe Et. Al., New Rules For Victims Of Armed Conflicts: Commentary on the Additional Protocols of 8 June 1977 to the Geneva Conventions of 12 August 1949 260 (1982) [hereinafter Bothe].

on his or her behalf to the Protecting Party. In cases of persons not detained as POWs (following the initial determination in accordance to Article 45(1)) and who are to be tried for offences arising out of hostilities, the Protocol designates a "judicial tribunal" as the relevant body to adjudicate when such persons wish nevertheless to assert their POW status. This Article also offers a guarantee of protections for all those who do not benefit from the combatant privilege but who joined the fighting. Those who fall into this group (like mercenaries, spies, civilians who do not benefit from protections of the GC IV or members of armed forces who forfeit their entitlement to POW status and treatment)[58] are entitled at all times to the protections of Article 75 AP I.[59] Article 75 reiterates a number of prohibitions (e.g. murder, torture of all kinds, or outrages upon personal dignity) and reinforces the obligation of humane treatment without discrimination. There is seems to be consensus that Article 75 could apply both as a treaty obligation and as customary norm.[60]

The basic principle based on nationality criterion introduced in Article 4 GC IV defines protected persons as those who find themselves in the hands of the belligerent party or Occupying Power of which they are not nationals.[61] Aliens in the territory of the belligerent party may be subject to assigned residence or internment only "if the Security of the Detaining Power makes it absolutely necessary."[62] Similarly, civilians in the occupied territories may be interned or assigned residence "if the Occupying Power considers it necessary, for imperative reasons of security."[63]

There are three situations in which any of the protected persons' liberty may be restricted. First, protected persons in the territory of a party to the conflict may be confined pending proceedings or serving a sentence involving loss of liberty.[64] They should be treated humanely in accordance to minimum of safeguards enshrined in Articles 27–34 of the Convention. Second, protected persons in the occupied

---

[58] For example those described in Article 44(3) AP I, following interpretation in, *id.* at 261ff.
[59] This problem is pertinent in a debate about the "enemy combatants," as termed by U.S. administration involving a large number of nationals of various States, either neutral or co-belligerent, who were captured in the course of 2001–2002 conflict in Afghanistan as well as 2003 conflict in Iraq (some as alleged supporters and members of the Al Qaeda organization) and who largely remain in the custody of U.S. As it seems a legal situation and the treatment so far afforded to these detainees does not satisfy the requirements of either GC III or GC IV or customary norms reflecting Article 75 AP I.
[60] Knut Dörmann, *The Legal Situation of 'Unlawful/Unprivileged Combatants'*, 85 Int. Rev. Red Cross 849 (2003).
[61] The Convention concerns itself with 'protected persons', who are de facto civilians. The AP I uses a notion of civilians, *see* Article 50(1) for a definition, *supra* note 7.
[62] Articles 41–42 GC IV, *supra* note 7. *See also* Prosecutor v. Delalic et al., ICTY Case No. IT-96-21, Appeals Chamber, Judgment (Feb. 20, 2001), paras 327–328.
[63] Article 78 GC IV, *supra* note 7.
[64] Article 37 GC IV, *supra* note 7.

territory may be subjected to detention as a result of proceedings for violation of the penal provisions promulgated by the Occupying Powers in accordance to Articles 64–65, including cases of espionage or sabotage. Articles 69–77 of the Convention safeguard the minimum of the afforded treatment during their detention. On the contrary, protected persons who do not commit a serious penal offence but one solely intended to harm an Occupying Power are subject to either imprisonment or internment proportionate to the offence committed (Article 68).

The GC IV further imposes restrictions on the protections if the protected persons are definitely suspected of or engaged in activities hostile to the security of that State or Occupying Power. The fundamental obligation of humane treatment as well as fair trial guarantees remain applicable nevertheless.[65]

In the context of non-international armed conflicts the most pertinent protection for persons under control of the adversary is enshrined in Common Article 3, which imposes more general requirements of humane treatment without adverse discrimination. It further prohibits violence to life, health and physical or mental well-being of the person. A more specific but still fairly limited set of measures applicable in all situations involving restriction of personal liberty, whether internment or detention, is laid out in Article 5 AP II.[66] Accordingly all persons deprived of liberty should be provided with sufficient food, drinking water, health and hygiene facilities as well as shelter from the weather and the dangers of conflict as well as they should be allowed to practice their religion and to receive relief. Paragraph 2 imposes additional obligations in respect to the conditions of the places of internment or detention as well as facilitation of the exchange of correspondence and medical assistance. Many sources indicate that Common Article 3 is declaratory of existing customary IHL.[67]

---

[65] Article 5. Note exceptional character of such derogation but also its temporal limitation.

[66] A set of fundamental and absolute guarantees reiterating these spelled out in common Article 3 is enshrined in Article 4 AP II. Yves Sandoz, Christophe Swinarski, Bruno Zimmerman, eds., Commentary on the Additional Protocols of 8 June 1977 to the Geneva Conventions of 12 August 1949 (1996), 1383–1395.

[67] Military and Paramilitary Activities in and against Nicaragua (Nicaragua v. U.S.A.), Merits, 1986 I.C.J. Reports (June 27), 14, at 218, 255; Prosecutor v. Tadic, Case No. IT-94-1, Appeals Chamber, Decision on the Defence Motion for Interlocutory Appeal on Jurisdiction (Oct. 2, 1995), paras 98, 117; Prosecutor v. Akayesu, Case No. ICTR-96-4-T, ICTR, Trial Chamber, Judgment (Sep. 2, 1998), paras 608–609, 618. Similarly Hans Peter Gasser, *A Measure of Humanity in Internal Disturbances and Tensions: Proposal for a Code of Conduct*, 262 Int. Rev. Red Cross 44 (1988) but compare with a critique of such approach in Theodor Meron, Human Rights And Humanitarian Norms As Customary Norms 25–27(1989).

3. Humane Treatment

In social sciences, humane treatment may appear as a relative concept, encompassing subjective cultural and emotive values. For the lawyer, the question will be not of what *is* humane treatment, rather what *is not* and whether, even if socially and ideologically condemned, it does constitute a violation of the relevant norms. Strikingly, even when all sciences agree in upholding protection of individuals through the reassertion of the principle of human dignity in all situations, the current policies proliferated under the "counterterrorism" slogan effectively force the re-evaluation of such a long established fundamental norm and moral principle. It took thousands of years of the civilized development for the humanity to reach the conclusion that torture and other forms of violence against human beings go against the very essence of human existence, inherent dignity and integrity. In the ICTY' view the humane treatment "principle is intended to shield human beings from outrages upon their personal dignity, whether such outrages are carried out by unlawfully attacking the body or by humiliating and debasing the honour, the self-respect or the mental well being of a person."[68] For the same reason, torture is an attractive means for the oppressors to achieve their ultimate goal of destroying a person without killing him/her.

Conceptually though, it is submitted that one must draw a distinction between what is the substance of a particular concept with its all encompassing elements and what may be considered as negation of that concept. In other words, what may constitute a violation of the prohibition of torture and other inhuman, cruel and degrading treatment or punishment (being the most fundamental elements of the right to humane treatment) might not necessarily always be illustrative of what torture or other forms of maltreatment is *sensu stricto*, but rather represent a positive obligation (procedural) attached to the prohibition. Such specific obligation may be an inherent part of the prohibition itself or may form a separate legal norm, materially linked to the original one.[69] Article 5 of the American Convention on Human Rights, under the "right to humane treatment", regards a right of an individual to have his/her physical, mental and moral integrity respected.[70] This formula is followed by the general prohibition of torture and other forms

---

[68] Prosecutor v. Furundzija, ICTY, Case No. IT-95-17/1-T, Trial Chamber, Judgment (Dec. 10, 1998), para. 183:
> The essence of the whole corpus of international humanitarian law as well as human rights law lies in the protection of the human dignity of every person, whatever his or her gender. The general principle of respect for human dignity is the basic underpinning and indeed the very *raison d'être* of international humanitarian law and human rights law; indeed in modern times it has become of such paramount importance as to permeate the whole body of international law.

[69] Soering v. United Kingdom, Eur.Ct. H. R., Judgment (July 7, 1989), 11 EHRR 439, para. 88.

[70] Article 5(1) AHCR, *supra* note 35.

of ill-treatment with the specific attention placed on an obligation of respect for the inherent dignity of a human person, especially when deprived of the liberty.[71] Concurrently, the African Charter of Human and Peoples' Rights first highlights the need to recognize and respect human dignity and ban exploitation and degradation of man as well as torture and alike practices.[72] In addition, the Inter-American Commission on Human Rights identifies another group, which consists of "other prerequisites for respect for physical, mental or moral integrity, including certain regulations governing the means and objectives of detention or punishment."[73] In this respect, the Commission refers to certain general conditions of detention as well as special protections afforded to particularly vulnerable individuals like children, women or aliens in the territory of the state.[74]

Recognizing therefore the centrality of the notion of torture and other inhuman treatment or punishment, the very essence of this concept will be the focus of this part of the text, whilst more specific obligations residual to the core of the prohibition shall form a part of the analysis in the subsequent part of this paper.

3.1. *Absolute Prohibition of Torture*

The law is clear – torturing people is absolutely and universally prohibited. This stems not only from the universal operation of the appropriate customary norm but also by virtue of the recognition of its *erga omnes* and *jus cogens* status, affirming it as one the highest non-derogable norms among other norms and principles of international law. The International Criminal Court for Former Yugoslavia (ICTY) observed:

> because of the importance of the values it protects, [the prohibition of torture] has evolved into a peremptory norm or jus cogens, that is a norm that enjoys a higher rank in the international hierarchy than treaty law and even 'ordinary' customary rules.... Clearly the jus cogens nature of the prohibition against torture articulates the notion that the prohibition has now become one of the most fundamental standards of the international community. Furthermore, this prohibition is designed to produce a deterrent effect, in that it signals to all members of the international community and the individuals over whom they wield authority that the prohibition of torture is an absolute value from which nobody must deviate.[75]

---

[71] *Id.* Article 5(2).
[72] Article 5 of African [Banjul] Charter of Human and People's Rights, Banjul (June 27, 1981); OAU Doc. CAB/LEG/67/3 rev. 5, ILM vol. 21 (1982), 58.
[73] IACHR Report, *supra* note 21, para. 150.
[74] *Id.* paras 167–179.
[75] *Id.* paras 153–154. *See also* General Comment No. 20: *Replaces General Comment 7 concerning Prohibition of Torture and Cruel Treatment or Punishment* (Article 7): U.N. Human Rights Committee (Mar. 10, 1992), U.N. Doc. HRI\GEN\1\Rev.1 at 30 (1994), paras 2–3; U.N. Committee Against Torture numerous conclusions and recommendations to the states parties, e.g. U.N.

The prohibition of torture and cruel, inhuman and degrading treatment is set out in all the major regional and international instruments governing both peacetime and conflict situations.[76] Article 4(2) ICCPR; Article 3 U.N. Torture Declaration;[77] Article 15 ECHR; Article 27(2) American Convention on Human Rights; and Article 4(c) of Arab Charter of Human Rights[78] all expressly exclude the possibility to derogate from this prohibition. *Ad hoc* international criminal courts and human rights bodies have both drawn from and supplemented the interpretational jurisprudence of the prohibition of torture and a general right to humane treatment, which will be subsequently considered alongside the human rights-focused sources.

The 1984 U.N. Convention against Torture and Other Cruel, Inhuman or Degrading Treatment and Punishment is fully dedicated to the protection of individuals against torture and other forms of ill-treatment, irrespective of the circumstances.[79] Article 2 (2) reiterates that "no exceptional circumstances whatsoever, whether a state of war or a threat or war, internal political instability or any other public emergency, may be invoked as a justification of torture." In the same spirit the European Court of Human Rights noted:

> Article 3 [ECHR], . . . enshrines one of the fundamental values of democratic society. Even in the most difficult of circumstances, such as the fight against organized terrorism and crime, the Convention prohibits in absolute terms torture or inhuman or degrading treatment or punishment.[80]

Doc. A/51/44 (1996), para. 211 (Egypt); A/52/44 (1997) para. 80 (Algeria); para. 258 (Israel); U.N. Doc. A/57/44 (2001), para. 90 (Russian Federation); U.N. Doc. A/58/44 (2002), para. 40 (Egypt); para. 51(Israel); para. 59 (Spain).

[76] Inter-American Convention to Prevent and Punish Torture, signed at Cartagena de Indias, Colombia, (Dec. 9, 1985), in Basic Documents Pertaining to Human Rights the Inter-American System, OEA/Ser.L/V/I.4 rev. 8 (May 22, 2001), at 83 [hereinafter Inter-American Torture Convention]. *See* e.g. Article 5 of the 1948 Universal Declaration of Human Rights; Article 7 ICCPR, *supra* note 34; Article 3 ECHR, *supra* note 13; Article 5 AHCR, *supra* note 35; Article 5 of the African Charter on Human and Peoples' Rights, *supra* note 72.

[77] The Declaration on the Protection of All Persons from Being Subjected to Torture and Other Cruel, Inhuman or Degrading Treatment or Punishment, G.A. Res. 3452 (XXX) (Dec. 9, 1975).

[78] Arab Charter on Human Rights, Council of the League of Arab States Resolution 5437 (102nd regular session) (Sep. 15, 1994), reprinted in 18 Hum. Rts. L.J. 151 (1997).

[79] U.N. Convention against Torture, G.A. Res. 39/46 (Dec. 10, 1984), entered into force on June 26, 1987,currently ratified by 144 States (as of April 19, 2007) [hereinafter CAT].

[80] Aksoy v. Turkey, *supra* note 32, para. 62, *see also* Tomasi v. France, Judgment (Aug. 27, 1992), European Court of Human Rights Series A, No. 241 para. 115, Al-Adsani v. United Kingdom, Judgment (Nov. 21, 2001), European Court of Human Rights, (No. 2) (35763/97) 34 EHRR 11, paras 59–61. *See also* Guideline IV of the Council of Europe Guidelines, *supra* note 25; Statement of the Committee against Torture in connection with the events of 11 September 2001 (Nov. 22, 2001), U.N. Doc. A/57/44 (2002), para. 17.

This Court and other human rights judicial and monitoring bodies upheld that even in times of armed conflict or public emergency threatening the life of the nation no exceptions or derogations are permissible.[81] This was fully endorsed by the ICTY reiteration of its peremptory status and absolute character[82] and in domestic jurisprudence. In *Pinochet (No. 3)*[83] the British House of Lords relied on the American *Siderman*[84] landmark opinion as persuasive authority to argue that the prohibition of torture had achieved the status of *jus cogens* already at the time of adoption of CAT. *Siderman* on the other hand referred to the 1980 ruling in *Filartiga* v. *Peña-Irala*[85] before the U.S. Second Circuit Court of Appeal, where Justice Kaufmann noted:

> Turning to the act of torture, we have little difficulty discerning its universal renunciation in the modern usage and practice of nations.... The international consensus surrounding torture has found expression in numerous international treaties and accords.... The substance of these international agreements is reflected in modern municipal i.e. national law as well. Although torture was once a routine concomitant of criminal interrogations in many nations, during the modern and hopefully more enlightened era it has been universally renounced.... Having examined the sources from which customary international law is derived – the usage of nations, judicial opinions and the works of jurists – we conclude that official torture is now prohibited by the law of nations. The prohibition is clear and unambiguous, and admits of no distinction between treatment of aliens and citizens.[86]

In recent years this over 20 years old recognition by U.S. judiciary of the unambiguous and clear prohibition of torture, universally applicable part of "laws of nations," gains even greater significance in the time when the executive attempts not only to undermine the content of the prohibition but even more disturbing, to question the ban in its entirety.

---

[81] *Id. see also* Chahal v. United Kingdom, Judgment (Nov. 15, 1996), Eur. Ct. H. R., Reports 1996-V, para. 79, General Comment No.20, *supra* note 75, para.3; *See also* Report of the Independent Expert on the Protection of Human Rights and Fundamental Freedoms while Countering Terrorism (R. K. Goldman), U.N. Doc. E/CN.4/2005/103 (Feb. 7, 2005), para. 49. Report of the U.N. Special Rapporteur on Torture (P. Kooijmans), U.N. Doc. E/CN.4/198 6/15 (1986), para. 3; for the Inter-American cases *see* e.g. Loayza-Tamayo *Case* (Peru), Inter-American Court Human Rights (Sep. 19, 1997), Series C No. 33, para. 57 or Castillo-Petruzzi et al. (Peru), Judgment (May 30, 1999) Series C No. 52, para. 197.

[82] Prosecutor v. Furundzija, *supra* note 68 para. 144.

[83] Regina v Bow Street Metropolitan Stipendiary Magistrate and others, ex parte Pinochet Ugarte (No. 3) [2000] 1 AC, 147, 247. *See also* Jones v. Ministry of Interior of Saudi Arabia, [2005] 2 WLR 808, Oct. 28, 2004, Court of Appeal, para. 108.

[84] Siderman de Blake v. Republic of Argentina, (9th Circuit Court of Appeal), 965 F. 2d 699 (May 22, 1992).

[85] Filartiga v. Peña-Irala, (2nd Circuit Court of Appeal), 630 F. 2d 876 (June 30, 1980).

[86] *Id.* at 884–885.

3.2. The Elements of the Concept

After examining of the relevant universal and regional human rights and IHL instruments, it is clear that the concept of inhuman treatment encompasses chiefly two categories of prohibited conduct. These comprise of torture and of other inhuman, cruel, and degrading treatment and punishment.

Starting our analysis with the notion of torture one must observe that although almost all major human rights and humanitarian law norms prohibit torture, hardly any provide any guidance as what torture means. The most comprehensive conventional definition, composed in the CAT, states that torture is characterized by:

> any act by which severe pain or suffering, whether physical or mental, is intentionally inflicted on a person for such purposes as obtaining from him or a third person information or a confession, punishing him for an act he or a third person has committed or is suspected of having committed, or intimidating or coercing him or a third person, or for any reason based on discrimination of any kind, when such pain or suffering is inflicted by or at the instigation of or with the consent or acquiescence of a public official or other person acting in an official capacity. It does not include pain or suffering arising only from, inherent in or incidental to lawful sanctions.[87]

The proviso, claimed to have attained customary status,[88] encapsulates the following elements: (a) the intentional (b) infliction, by act or omission, of severe pain or suffering, whether physical or mental, (c) which have occurred in order to obtain information or a confession, or to punish, intimidate or coerce the victim or a third person, or to discriminate, on any ground, against the victim or a third person.[89] Article 2 of the Inter-American Convention to Prevent and Punish Torture provides a similar, somehow wider definition. Torture under this treaty constitutes any act inflicted intentionally "on a person for purposes of criminal investigation, as a means of intimidation, as personal punishment, as a preventive measure, as a penalty, or for any other purpose" as well as "the use of methods upon a person intended to obliterate the personality of the victim or to diminish his physical or mental capacities, even if they do not cause physical pain or mental anguish."[90]

---

[87] Article 1 CAT, *supra* note 79. When considering torture as criminal conduct in the context of Common Article 3 to 1949 Geneva Conventions, ICTY observed that "[t]he crime of torture was defined by the Trial Chamber as the intentional infliction, by act or omission, of severe pain or suffering, whether physical or mental, for a prohibited purpose, such as obtaining information or a confession, punishing, intimidating, humiliating, or coercing the victim or a third person, or discriminating, on any ground, against the victim or a third person." The Prosecutor v. Kvocka et al., ICTY, Case No. IT-98-30/1-A, Appeals Chamber (Feb. 28, 2005) para. 289.

[88] Prosecutor v. Furundzija, *supra* note 68, para. 160.

[89] Prosecutor v. Brdjanin, ICTY, Case No. IT-99-36-T, Trial Chamber, (Sep. 1, 2004), para. 481.

[90] Article 2 Inter-American Torture Convention, *supra* note 76.

The ICTY, in assessing whether the threshold of severity of suffering or pain has been met, suggested that "the objective severity of the harm inflicted must be considered," as much as the "[s]ubjective criteria, such as the physical or mental condition of the victim, the effect of the treatment and, in some cases, factors such as the victim's age, sex, state of health and position of inferiority" as the seriousness of the pain or suffering sets torture apart from other forms of mistreatment.[91] The Court noted that the nature, purpose, and consistency of the acts committed were crucial factors in the objective severity assessment. It further stressed that:

> [w]ith respect to the assessment of the seriousness of the acts charged as torture, previous jurisprudence of the Tribunal has held that this should take into account all circumstances of the case and in particular the nature and context of the infliction of pain, the premeditation and institutionalisation of the ill-treatment, the physical condition of the victim, the manner and the method used and the position of inferiority of the victim. Also relevant to the Chamber's assessment is the physical or mental effect of the treatment on the victim, the victim's age, sex, or state of health. Further, if the mistreatment has occurred over a prolonged period of time, the Chamber would assess the severity of the treatment as a whole.[92]

When dealing with rape, the Court recommended that the social, cultural, and religious background of the victims should be also considered when assessing the severity of the alleged conduct, as they can exacerbate the ultimate suffering.[93]

The U.N. Human Rights Committee, in its General Comment on Article 7 of the ICCPR, indicated that the distinction between prohibited forms of mistreatment depends on the nature, purpose, and severity of the particular treatment.[94] The European Court of Human Rights further stressed the intensity and seriousness condition by holding that "the Convention, with its distinction between 'torture' and 'inhuman or degrading treatment', should by the first of these terms attach a special stigma to deliberate inhuman treatment causing very serious and cruel suffering."[95] It may thus be inferred that the level of severity affects the pain or suffering levels, while the treatment or punishment depends on the purpose and the context of the misconduct.

In relation to that, the European Commission on Human Rights indicated that torture is identifiable by the purpose of the treatment or punishment, such as the obtaining of information or confessions or the infliction of punishment and it is generally an aggravated form of inhuman treatment.[96] The Inter-American

---

[91] Prosecutor v. Brdjanin, *supra* note 89, paras 483–484.
[92] Prosecutor v. Limaj et al., ICTY, Case No. IT-03-66, Trial Chamber (Nov. 30, 2005), para. 237.
[93] *Id.*
[94] General Comment No. 20, *supra* note 75, para. 4.
[95] Ireland v. United Kingdom, *supra* note 37, para. 167.
[96] The Greek Case, 12 Y.B. Eur. Conv. on H.R., 1969, at 186.

Commission on Human Rights fully endorsed this approach[97] further distinguishing between the purpose (e.g. personal punishment or intimidation) and the intention (i.e. in order to produce a certain result).[98] Notably, the prohibited purpose must be a part of the motivation. Finally, the ICTY required a special, direct intent, as a pre-requisite i.e. the perpetrator must have intended to act in a way, which in the normal course of events would cause severe pain or suffering however irrespective of his/her motivation.[99]

Noteworthy, abandonment of CAT's requirement of "the consent or acquiescence of a public official or other person acting in an official capacity" (Article 1) represents another significant recent jurisprudential development. Over the time the ICTY has been developing this approach by indicating in 1998 that "[t]orture requires the act or omission to be 'committed by, or at the instigation of, or with the consent or acquiescence of, an official or other person acting in an official capacity'"[100] through the assertion that "[t]he fifth element of the crime of torture in a situation of armed conflict is 'at least one of the persons involved in the torture process must be a public official or must at any rate act in a non-private capacity, *e.g.*, as a de facto organ of a State or any other authority-wielding entity"[101] to the statement that "[u]nder international humanitarian law in general... the presence or involvement of a state official or of any other authority-wielding person in the process of torture is not necessary for the offence to be regarded as torture."[102] In other words, the Court arrived at the conclusion that the state actor requirement is inconsistent with the customary international law in relation to the criminal responsibility of an individual for torture outside of the framework of the Torture Convention.[103] The Court signalized that the nature of the committed act rather than the status of the perpetrator will be "the characteristic trait of the offence" for the purposes of the individual criminal responsibility. The Court noted that CAT was designed as human rights notion, which is built on the premise that human

---

[97] Luis Lizardo Cabrera (Dominican Republic), Case 10.832, Report No. 35/96, Annual Report of the IACHR 1997, paras 82–83.
[98] Raquel Martín de Mejía (Peru), Case 10.970, Report No. 5/96, Annual Report of the IACHR (1995), at 185.
[99] Prosecutor v. Kunarac, Kovac and Vokovic, ICTY, Case No. IT-96-23&23/1, Trial Chamber (Feb. 22, 2001), para. 486 and in Prosecutor v. Limaj et al, *supra* note 91, para. 238.
[100] Prosecutor v. Mucic et al., ICTY Case No. IT-96-21, Trial Chamber (Nov. 16, 1998), para 494–496.
[101] Prosecutor v. Furundzija, ICTY, Case No. IT-95-17/1, Appeals Chamber (July 21, 2000), para. 111.
[102] Prosecutor v. Krnojelac, ICTY, Case No. IT-97-25-T, Trial Chamber (Mar. 15, 2002), para. 188.
[103] *See also* Prosecutor v. Kvocka et al., ICTY, Case No. IT-98-30/1, Trial Chamber (Nov. 2, 2001), para. 139 and Prosecutor v. Kunarac, Kovac and Vokovic, ICTY, Case No. IT-96-23&23/1, Appeals Chamber (June 12, 2002), paras 146–148.

rights are predominantly violated by the states or governments.[104] The formulation of torture for the purposes of the ICC Statute seems to have adopted a similar approach, where a criminally responsible person would be considered as under whose control or in whose custody the victim has been subjected to the torture, devoid from a necessary connection to public authorities.[105]

3.2. Other Forms of Ill-Treatment

While torture is considered the most aggravated form of inhuman and degrading treatment, it differs from other forms by the existence of the specific "purpose", such as obtaining information or confessions or inflicting punishment.[106] Inhuman treatment, on the other hand, encompasses at least such treatment, which deliberately causes severe mental or physical suffering (or both) unjustifiable in the given circumstances.[107] "Justifiability" here does not mean that torture or inhuman treatment is ever justified, but merely indicates its potential relativity in application to the particular factual circumstances, for example criminal punishment is justified in cases of serious offences, however while instituted for a petty offence may be regarded as inhuman treatment.[108] In determining the existence and severity of inhuman treatment the following factors should be considered: the duration of the treatment, its physical and mental effects, the sex, age and state of health of the victim, before and after the suffering has been inflicted.[109] Noteworthy, even in the absence of the physical injuries, psychological and moral suffering accompanied by psychic disturbance may be declared inhuman treatment.

Inhuman treatment is deemed degrading if it is grossly humiliating before the others or it compels a victim to act against his/her will or conscience.[110] According to the Inter-American Court of Human Rights degrading element is characterized

---

[104] Prosecutor v. Brdjanin, *supra* note 89, paras 488–489, *see also* "[T]he Chamber notes that while the earlier jurisprudence of the Tribunal has reached different conclusions as to whether, for the crime of torture to be established, the alleged act or omission must be committed by, or at the instigation of or with the consent or acquiescence of an official or person acting in an official capacity, this issue is now settled by the Appeals Chamber. Under customary international law and the jurisprudence of the Tribunal it is not necessary that the perpetrator has acted in an official capacity." Prosecutor v. Limaj et al., *supra* note 81, para. 240.

[105] Article 7(2)(e), Rome Statute of the International Criminal Court, U.N. Doc. 2187 U.N.T.S. 90, entered into force July 1, 2002.

[106] Treatment and punishment tend to overlap materially and practically. Punishment can be a part of the treatment as much as the treatment may sometimes constitute punishment.

[107] The Greek case, *supra* note 96, 186, *see also* Luis Lizardo Cabrera, IACHR, *supra* note 97, paras 77–79.

[108] Claire Ovey, Robin C.A. White, Jacobs & White European Convention On Human Rights 60 (2002) [hereinafter Ovey & White].

[109] Ireland v. United Kingdom, *supra* note 37, para. 162.

[110] *Id.*

by the fear, anxiety, and inferiority induced for the purpose of humiliating the victim and breaking his physical and moral resistance, which can be further exacerbated by the vulnerability of an arbitrarily detained person.[111]

The human rights judicial bodies have signalized that the threshold of seriousness or severity of the induced pain or suffering is a relative concept and must be interpreted in the light of present-day conditions, to be able to adjust to the current realities.[112] Increasingly as a consequence, other distinction factors, like the context and purpose or premeditation of the employed force are gaining importance. In keeping with this approach Professor Nowak, U.N. Special Rapporteur on Torture, suggests that:

> In principle, every form of cruel and inhuman treatment, including torture, requires the infliction of severe pain or suffering.... Whether cruel or inhuman treatment can also be qualified as torture depends on the fulfillment of the other requirements in Article 1 CAT; mainly whether inhuman treatment was used for any purposes spelled out therein.[113]

This interpretation of the notion proposed in the context of human rights has indeed been adopted also by the *ad hoc* international criminal tribunals in the context of violations of IHL. The concept of inhuman treatment has been considered within the framework of grave breaches of the 1949 Geneva Conventions or AP I or serious violations of Article 3 common to the Geneva Conventions and, when committed as part of a widespread or systematic attack on any civilian population on national, political, ethnic, racial or religious grounds, as crimes against humanity and possibly genocide.

Particularly important for this debate will be the consideration of the inhumane treatment in the context of Common Article 3, indicated by the U.S. Supreme Court as applicable to U.S.-led anti-terrorism activities. This domestic determination is crucial for the assessment of any misconduct or abuse of the right to humane treatment generated during the U.S. campaign against terrorism as long as falls under the prohibited conduct under the mentioned Article 3.

---

[111] Loayza Tamayo Case, *supra* note 81, para. 57, citing Ribitsch v. Austria, Eur. Ct. H. R., Judgment (Dec. 4, 1995) Series A No. 336, para. 36.

[112] "[H]aving regard to the fact that the Convention is a 'living instrument which must be interpreted in the light of present day conditions... the Court considers that certain acts which were classified in the past as 'inhuman and degrading treatment' as opposed to 'torture' could be classified differently in the future. It takes the view that the increasingly high standard being required in the area of the protection of human rights and fundamental liberties correspondingly and inevitably requires greater firmness in assessing breaches of the fundamental values of democratic societies." Selmouni v. France, Eur. Ct. H. R., Judgment (July 28, 1999), 29 Eur. Ct. H. R. 403, para. 101. *See also* Luis Lizardo Cabrera Case, *supra* note 97, paras 82–83.

[113] Manfred Nowak, *What Practices Constitute Torture?*, 28 Hum. Rts. Q. 809, 822 ff. (2006) providing an ample analysis of the jurisprudence in support of that.

Before embarking on a study of the components of Article 3, it is worth briefly reiterating that IHL contains a vast range of protections aimed at the physical and mental integrity and well-being of the individuals. In the context of international armed conflict humane treatment, inclusive of protections from mutilations, medical and scientific experiments or acts of intimidation and insults of Prisoners of War, is secured by the GC III (Articles 13 and 14), and Article 4 of 1907 Hague Regulations whilst the same in respect to the protected persons who find themselves in the hands of the belligerent party or Occupying Power of which they are not nationals[114] is provided by the GC IV (Articles 27, 32 and 37 dealing with non-nationals detained in the territory of a party to a conflict). Furthermore, Article 75 AP I, which is considered to reflect a customary international norm, further strengthens these protections also in respect to all the persons in the power of the adverse party, especially if they cannot benefit from the conventional guarantees (e.g. when and for such time they took part in hostilities).[115] Finally, in the context of the specific non-international armed conflicts AP II lays out a more limited set of protections applicable in all situations involving restriction of personal liberty, whether internment or detention (Articles 4 and 5). The Conventions and the Protocols are much more specific in the regulation of many aspects of the general treatment of a person under the control of the adverse party such as the conditions for the quarters, food provision, medical treatments, clothing or interrogations. They also stipulate very specific safeguards relating to the vulnerable groups taking into consideration their age (children) or gender (women).[116]

Coming back to the humane treatment guarantees under common Article 3, it has been repeatedly acknowledged to be declaratory of existing customary IHL.[117] In substance it imposes more general requirements of humane treatment without adverse discrimination involving the prohibition of violence to life, health and physical or mental well-being of the person as well as some judicial guarantees to all persons taking no active part in the hostilities, whether combatants or non-combatants, unwilling or unable to fight due to sickness, injuries, capture and detention. In particular, the set out mandatory rules bar violence to life and person including

---

[114] The Convention concerns itself with "protected persons" based on the nationality criterion introduced in Article 4 GC IV, who are *de facto* civilians. AP I uses a notion of civilians, *see* its Article 50(1) for a definition.

[115] *Consult* also Article 11 AP I, *supra* note 7.

[116] More on discussion about the specific conditions of treatment of Prisoners of War and other person deprived of liberty under international humanitarian law *see* Agnieszka Jachec-Neale, *Status and Treatment of Prisoners of War and other Persons Deprived of their Liberty, in* Perspectives On The ICRC Study On Customary International Humanitarian Law (Susan C. Breau & E. Wilmshurst (eds.) forthcoming October 2007).

[117] *See supra* note 67.

mutilation, cruel treatment, and torture as well as outrages upon personal dignity, in particular, humiliating, and degrading treatment.

Similarly, like the human rights bodies, the ICTY took the position that the purpose and seriousness of the attack on the victim sets the torture apart from other forms of mistreatment. Even a very severe infliction of the pain but without the purpose or goal to attain a certain result would not qualify as torture.[118] Consequently, this suggests that other forms of ill treatment will be devoid of the specific purpose condition.

Starting with a vaguely described "violence to life and person" the Court initially noted that due its treaty formulation, this crime can be defined through a cumulation of the constitutive elements for murder, mutilation, torture, and cruel treatment.[119] Later on, however it refuted this approach altogether and declared that such a crime does not exist under customary law in the absence of any state practice in regards to the definition of this particular offence.[120] This does not imply that the separate elements, as mentioned above, cease to exist too.

In the ICTY's view cruel treatment constitutes an intentional act or omission, which, judged objectively, is deliberate and not accidental and which causes serious mental or physical suffering or injury. The act must constitute also a serious attack on human dignity.[121] The Court further held that cruel and inhuman treatment are materially the same offences in the framework of the grave breaches of the Geneva Conventions,[122] however the attack on dignity will distinguish cruel treatment from inhuman one. The Court confirmed that no prohibited purpose is necessitated for the act to amount to cruel treatment. Similarly, the outrages upon personal dignity do not require such purpose.[123] The definition of this offence rests very much on the notion of humiliation and destruction of human dignity. It encompasses an intentional act or an omission, which would generally be considered to cause serious humiliation, degradation or otherwise be the serious attack on human dignity.[124] The Court observed that violations of dignity will largely involve acts or omissions (or words), which not necessarily cause the long-term physical, harm, but are serious nevertheless.[125] Therefore, the humiliation or degradation must be

---

[118] Prosecutor v. Krnojelac, *supra* note 102, para. 180; Prosecutor v. Limaj et al., *supra* note 91, para. 239.
[119] Prosecutor v. Blaskic, ICTY, Case No. IT-95-14, Trial Chamber (Mar. 3, 2000), para. 182.
[120] Prosecutor v. Vasiljevic, ICTY, Case No. IT-98-32, Trial Chamber (Nov. 29, 2002), para. 203.
[121] Prosecutor v. Kordic and Cerkez, ICTY, Case No. IT-95-14/2, Trial Chamber (Feb. 26, 2001), para. 265.
[122] *Id.*
[123] Prosecutor v. Kvocka et al., *supra* note 103, para. 226.
[124] Prosecutor v. Kunarac et al., *supra* note 103, para. 161.
[125] Prosecutor v. Kvocka et al., *supra* note 103, para. 172.

real, so serious and intense that any reasonable person would be outraged.[126] In addition the ICTR noted that the elements of "humiliating or degrading treatment" under the Court Statute include "[s]ubjecting victims to treatment designed to subvert their self-regard. Like outrages upon personal dignity, these offences may be regarded as a lesser forms of torture; moreover ones in which the motives required for torture would not be required, nor would it be required that the acts be committed under state authority."[127] The European Court of Human Rights found that degrading treatment may arise from severe treatment based on racial or ethnic discrimination.[128]

Finally, as far as mutilation of the body parts is concerned, the ICTY has not developed much of jurisprudence except for stating that it can be an example of acts *per se* constituting torture.[129]

Indeed the examples from the illegal practice may be helpful and illustrative to highlight some differences between these converse forms of ill-treatment. Acts most commonly mentioned as those likely to constitute torture in the context of armed conflict include beating, sexual violence including rape, prolonged denial of sleep, food, hygiene, and medical assistance, as well as threats to torture or to kill the relatives.[130] Noteworthy, in certain circumstances rape and other forms of sexual violence may also amount to an outrage on the personal dignity, provided a serious attack on human dignity is present.[131] The use of detainees as human shields or trench-diggers may too be considered as inhuman or cruel treatment as it may constitute an outrage on personal dignity.[132]

Whilst the inappropriate conditions of the confinement in the Omarska camp in Bosnia, performing the subservient acts, being forced to relieve bodily functions in their clothing, and enduring the constant fear of being subjected to the physical, mental, or sexual violence in camps were all found to be outrages upon personal dignity,[133] deplorable material conditions at the Llapushnik/Lapusnik prison camp in Kosovo were considered to amount to cruel treatment.[134] Arbitrary

---

[126] Prosecutor v. Kunarac et al., *supra* note 103, para. 162.
[127] Prosecutor v. Musema, ICTR, Case No. ICTR-96-13-A, Trial Chamber (Jan. 27, 2000), para. 285.
[128] *See e.g.*, Cyprus v. Turkey, Judgment (May 10, 2001), Application No. 25781/94, Eur. Ct. H. R. 2001–IV.
[129] Prosecutor v. Kvocka et al., *supra* note 103, para. 144.
[130] *Id.*
[131] Prosecutor v. Furundzija, *supra* note 68, paras 172–173; Prosecutor v. Akayesu, *supra* note 117, para. 688.
[132] Prosecutor v. Blaskic, ICTY, Case No. IT-95-14-A, Appeals Chamber (July 29, 2004), para. 597.
[133] Prosecutor v. Kvocka et al., *supra* note 103, para. 173.
[134] Prosecutor v. Limaj et al., *supra* note 91, paras 288–289.

seizure, unlawful detention for prolonged periods and interrogations in certain situations however were not regarded as constituting cruel treatment.[135]

Human rights bodies were even more specific in indicating which acts may amount to torture and inhuman treatment, especially pertinent in analyzing anti-terrorist initiatives. These include in particular the conditions of detention and the conduct of interrogations, which will be comprehensively discussed in the subsequent part of this paper in the context of some recent examples of the abuses. Noteworthy, violations of human rights on the scale we have witnessed lately however are not incidental, they do appear to be institutionally supported by the policies predicated on the flawed premises and tenuous assumptions in acquiescence of disregard for human dignity. The most instructive of the examples of such occurrence comes from the United States and will be presented in more detail below.

4. *Sowing the Seeds and Reaping the Harvest*

In recent years, the use of torture (or alleged use of torture) and similar measures against terrorists has been alarmingly on sharp rise. One can identify three interrelated areas where the increase of such practices or a risk of using them can be clearly visible. The most common and obvious would be the situations of deprivation of liberty, when not only the conditions in detention, the instances of inhuman treatment *sensu stricto* but also the detention *per se* (if arbitrary, prolonged or *incommunicado*) are regarded as violations of the ban on torture and/or cruel, inhumane and degrading treatment or punishment. The prohibition of torture and other forms of mistreatment is usually enshrined in the relevant domestic legislation, but the domestic standard or its interpretation may differ from the international one. The most widely discussed example of such case is the U.S. interpretation of the torture definition, as it surfaced in the context of the ongoing counterterrorism campaign.

4.1. *Reinterpreting the Definition*

The 1994 Torture Statute,[136] the U.S. legislation implementing CAT into domestic legislation, was based on the understanding that the definition of torture and in particular other cruel, degrading and inhuman treatment or punishment would conform to an earlier U.S. law, including the Fifth, Eight and/or Fourteenth Amendments to the Constitution as well as previously adopted torture related

---

[135] *Id.* at para. 232.
[136] 18 U.S.C.§§ 2340–2340A (2000).

legislation, namely the Torture Victim Protection Act[137] (1990).[138] While the latter established civil procedures for the torture victims to recover damages for torture abuses overseas the former provided the mechanism for assessing criminal liability for both U.S. nationals and foreign nationals suspected of involvement in torturing individuals outside of the United States. Following the 9/11 attacks and the subsequent involvement in Afghanistan the Office of Legal Counsel of the U.S. Department of Justice was asked by the Counsel to President to prepare a memorandum regarding the standards of conduct for interrogation under the Torture Statute. The result of this request, known as Bybee's Memorandum, provided a controversially broad interpretation of the federal definition of torture.[139] The Memorandum suggested that for the act causing severe physical pain or suffering to amount to torture, it must "inflict pain...equivalent in intensity to the pain accompanying serious physical injury, such as organ failure, impairment of bodily function, or even death."[140] In accordance to the Torture Statute, an act specifically intended to inflict severe mental pain or suffering was considered an act of torture.[141] In so far mental pain or suffering was considered, the Memorandum contended that "it must result in significant psychological harm of significant duration, e.g., lasting for months or even years" to amount to torture under the statute, which was in line with the mentioned Reservations.[142] Finally, it advanced an argument that the interrogating officials under the authority of President could have invoked doctrines of self-defense and necessity in the fight against the terrorism to justify breaches of the U.S. international obligations.

The document was superseded in 2004 by the Memorandum prepared by the same Office of Legal Counsel as previously, but this time a message seemed rather

---

[137] 28 U.S.C.§ 1350 note.

[138] U.S. Reservations, Declarations, and Understandings to the Convention Against Torture and Other Cruel, Inhuman or Degrading Treatment or Punishment, Cong. Rec. S17486 01 (daily ed., Oct. 27, 1990) [hereinafter Torture Statute]. Reservation indicated that CAT's "cruel, inhuman or degrading treatment or punishment" would be applicable in so far it meant "cruel, unusual and inhumane treatment or punishment" in a light of Constitutional Amendments. Moreover, the reservation limited the geographical jurisdiction attached to a legal prohibition of inhuman treatment for the acts committed within U.S. territory or against U.S. nationals abroad.

[139] Memorandum from Jay S. Bybee, Assistant Attorney General, U.S. Dept. of Justice, to Alberto R. Gonzales, Counsel to the President (Aug. 1, 2002), at 1.

[140] *Id.*, at 1 and 6.

[141] Torture Statute, *supra* note 138, § 2340 (1).

[142] Bybee's Memorandum, *supra* note 139, at 8. Reservations defined mental pain or suffering as "prolonged mental harm caused by or resulting from – (A) the intentional infliction or threatened infliction of severe physical pain or suffering; (B) the administration or application, or threatened administration or application of mind altering substances or other procedures calculated to disrupt profoundly the senses or the personality; (C) the threat of imminent death; or (D) the threat that another individual will imminently be subjected to death, severe physical pain or suffering, or the administration or application of mind altering substances....", *supra* note 91.

different.[143] The author, Daniel Levin repudiated the earlier findings, which were based on irrelevant evidence and led to a wrong conclusion regarding the threshold of the "severity" of pain or suffering;[144] however even under this revised definition of torture, the previous Office of Legal Counsel opinions addressing issues related to treatment of detainees would have been the same.[145] Interestingly, in this context both of these legal opinions are nearly silent about the discussion on the prohibition of torture and other forms of ill-treatment in armed conflict. This was rather consistent with the earlier position of the Bush Administration regarding the non-applicability of the laws of armed conflict to the "war on terror" and in particular the non-applicability of the humane standards in questioning the detainees, which by the way "substantially reduce[d] the threat of domestic criminal prosecution."[146]

As one activist stated the Bybee's memo was not simply an academic exercise,[147] the Bybee's Memorandum served as legal basis for the quietly approved policy of intense and violent interrogations in the course of the 2001 Afghanistan and 2003 Iraq conflicts.[148] It was suspended only when the evidence of the horrific consequences of this policy, such as pictured in the gruesome photos from Abu Ghraib prison, already surfaced in the public domain. Bybee's opinion resonated in a series of concurrent and subsequent opinions, including the Haynes memorandum regarding the sixteen counter-resistance techniques, further approved by the Defence Secretary for the use in interrogations at the Guantanamo Bay detention camp.[149] The recommended techniques involved hooding, stress positions, isolation, stripping, deprivation of light, removal of religious items, forced grooming, and use of dogs.[150] They were all approved despite signals even from other governmental agencies indicating that some of the coercive techniques may constitute

---

[143] Memorandum from Daniel Levin, Acting Assistant Attorney General, U.S. Dept of Justice, to James B. Comey, Deputy Attorney General (Dec. 30, 2004), at 2.
[144] *Id.* at 8.
[145] *Id.* at 2.
[146] Alberto Gonzales, Memorandum to President Bush (Jan. 25, 2002).
[147] Elisa Massimino, Washington Director of Human Rights First, quoted in *New Torture Memo an Improvement but Raises More Questions* (Jan. 6, 2005), available at www.humanrightsfirst.org/media/2005_alerts/etn_0106_levin.htm (last visited Apr. 19, 2007).
[148] *See, e.g., An Investigation of Abu Ghraib*, Final Report of the Independent Panel to Review Department of Defense Detention Operations (James R. Schlesinger, Chairman) (August 2004), Cosimo Reports (2005) [hereinafter The Schlesinger Report].
[149] William J. Haynes II to the Secretary of Defense, Memorandum *Counter-resistance Techniques* (Nov. 27, 2002).
[150] The revised set of the aggressive interrogation techniques was issued in a response to a request from Guantanamo Bay camp Command to employ the harsher methods than those permitted thus far under the Army *Field Manual 34–52*. Donald Rumsfeld, *Memorandum* (Dec. 2, 2002).

a violation of the Torture Statute.[151] The application of some harsher techniques, those under Category III (except for the fourth one), although regarded a lawful, were made subject to expressed approval from the Defense Secretary. Subsequently established by the Department of Defense a working group conducted a study about the interrogation methods allowed in Guantanamo Bay, which resulted in another memorandum.[152] The subsequent document (dated April 2003) authorized isolation (technique X), removing the privileges from detainees (B), attacking or insulting their "egos" (I) or playing "Mutt and Jeff"- friendly and harsh interrogator as valid methods but subject of notification.[153] There was no mention of stress positions, use of dogs or stripping but infusing and manipulating the levels of fear (techniques: E, F, G) or of the environment (U) were still allowed. This Memo clearly recognized the techniques, which can be regarded as inhuman and/or prohibited by the Geneva Conventions.

Following a transfer to Iraq in 2003 of the ex-Guantanamo Bay Commander General Miller, who was claimed to have suggested the use of DOD policy guidelines on interrogation of detainees, General Sanchez signed a memorandum authorizing a number interrogations techniques adjusted for the applicability to a theatre of war, therefore presumably in line with the Geneva Conventions. Not only this document adopted techniques suggested in the April 2003 Memorandum in their entirety (so even those which were indicated as questionable in light of legal obligations) but also reinstated previously rejected techniques like the use of dogs, yelling, light and loud noise/music control, sleep management (effectively being a form of deprivation of the sleep), deception and finally the use of stress positions.[154] Other memos to the same effect followed shortly[155] until May 13, 2004, when a change of policy prompted another set of guidelines from General Sanchez prohibiting the use of the six interrogation methods previously accepted.[156]

---

[151] *FBI Legal Analysis of the Interrogation Techniques*, Memorandum (Nov. 27, 2002), at 3–4. Practices included hooding detainees, use of individual phobias including fear of dogs, exposure to cold weather or water, threats of killing or injuring the family members or using wet towel and dripping water methods of inducing a misperception of drowning, potentially also transferring detainees to the third state which allows such interrogation methods in order to obtain the required information.

[152] DOD Working Group Report on Detainee Interrogations (Apr. 4, 2003).

[153] Donald Rumsfeld, *Memorandum to the US Southern Command on Counter- Resistance Techniques in the War on Terror* (Apr. 16, 2003).

[154] Ricardo S. Sanchez, *Memorandum for Commander, US Central Command. CJTF-7 Interrogation and Counter-Resistance Policy* (Sep. 14, 2003).

[155] Ricardo S. Sanchez, *CJTF-7 Interrogation and Counter-Resistance Policy*, Memorandum for C2 and C3, Combined Joint Task Force Seven, Baghdad and Commander, 205th Military Intelligence Brigade, *Baghdad, Iraq* (Oct. 12, 2003).

[156] Inspection Report (although heavily redacted) of Brig. Gen. Charles Jacoby (June 26, 2004) into some 20 U.S. detention or holding centres in Afghanistan, released in June 2006, *available*

Whilst the Bush administration was facing strong international and growing domestic pressure, attempts to close all the potential gaps in the regulations of humane treatment whether on U.S. soil or custody were made both through judicial and legislative means to outbalance the executive suddenly unlimited powers. In order to reiterate rather than to introduce the prohibition of cruel, degrading or inhuman treatment, in December 2005 Congress amended the DOD 2006 Appropriations Act by adducing an explicit restatement of the prohibition.[157] In the same act, the authority of the Army Field Manual on Intelligence Interrogation was confirmed in regards of detainees in the custody or under effective control of the DOD. The amendment, known as the Detainee Treatment Act, as well as the subsequently adopted Military Commission Act[158] both distinguished between torture and other inhuman treatment in the spirit of the Bybee's recommendations, i.e. focusing on the severity threshold rather than the purpose and the context.[159] Accordingly, whilst the "severe" pain or suffering must be inflicted for the act to amount to torture, a "serious" one is required for cruel and inhuman treatment. Only "serious" pain here is defined in terms of bodily injury involving at least one of the following: substantial risk of death, extreme physical pain, burns or physical disfigurement of a serious nature, or significant loss or impairment of the function of a bodily member, organ or mental faculty.[160] The striking resemblance between what Bybee has defined as "severe" and what became "serious" pain and suffering in 2006 Military Commissions Act should not go unnoticed. One wonders how one can differentiate between the serious physical injury, such as organ failure or impairment of bodily function and the bodily injury involving extreme physical pain or significant impairment of the function of a bodily member or organ? The only distinguishable element between torture and inhuman treatment thus appears to be the prohibited purpose of the torture such as obtaining information or a confession, punishment, intimidation, coercion or any reason based on discrimination of any kind.[161] The ICTY, in relation to Bybee's Memo, after a brief review of the drafting history of CAT implied that the "severe" requirement of CAT offers lower level of the intensity of pain or suffering than suggested in this document.[162] The Court reasserted its earlier endorsement of the level of intensity as defined

---

at www.dod.mil/pubs/foi/detainees/JacobyReport.pdf (last visited Apr. 19, 2007) [hereinafter Jacoby's Report].

[157] Detainee Treatment Act of 2005, Pub.L.No. 109–148 enacted as title X of the Defence Appropriations Act, Sec. 1003, H.R. 2863, 109th Cong. 1st Sess., (Dec. 30, 2005).

[158] Military Commissions Act of 2006 (Oct. 17, 2006) Public Law 109–336, 120 Stat. 2600.

[159] *Id.* para. 950v (11)(A) and Sec. 6(b)(1)(B).

[160] *Id.* para. 950v (12)(B) and Sec. 6(b)(2)(D).

[161] *Id.* para. 950v (11)(A) and Sec. 6(b)(1)(B).

[162] Prosecutor v. Brdjanin, ICTY, Case No. IT-99-36-A, Appeals Chamber, Judgment (Apr. 3, 2007), paras 249–251.

by CAT remaining the same under customary international law and stressed that torture can include acts inflicting physical pain or suffering less severe than the pain accompanying serious physical injury such as organ failure or even death or any "extreme" pain or suffering. Clearly in light of such opinion, the Military Commission Act definition must be considered equally too restrictive as compared with the customary law standard.

Bearing in mind that when signing the Detainee Treatment Act, President Bush issued a "signing statement," in which he presented his interpretation of a law indicating that interrogation restrictions could be waived if the President, as Commander-in-Chief, relying on the military necessity thought this would assist maintain national security.[163] This was later clarified not to constitute a derogation from the absolute prohibition of torture;[164] however it arguably poses a certain potential caveat regarding the effective implementation of the prohibition of cruel and inhuman treatment, which although undoubtedly a customary international norm its *jus cogens* status remains unclear.[165]

Controversially, like the amendment attached to the Detainee Treatment Act enabled testimony obtained as a result of coercion to be used in Combatant Status Review Tribunals at Guantanamo Bay, the Military Commission Act allowed that evidence obtained through coercion prior to 2005 be admitted into trial if a military judge finds it "reliable" and serving the interests of justice. For evidence obtained after 2005, no coerced evidence could be admitted if a military judge determines that it was obtained through cruel or inhuman interrogation methods. Clearly, this provision contradicts the exclusionary rule enshrined in Article 15 of CAT, the 1975 U.N. Torture Declaration, The Guidelines on the Role of Prosecutors adopted by the Eighth United Nations Congress on the Prevention of Crime and the Treatment of Offenders,[166] whose principles were recognized in *Filartiga* v. *Peña Irala* as particularly assisting in the establishment of the customary prohibition

---

[163] Statement by the President of the United States, *Statement by President George Bush upon Signing*, (Dec. 30, 2005) *H.R. 2863*, 2005 U.S.C.C.A.N. S50.

[164] Consideration of Reports submitted by State Parties under Article 19 of the Convention, Conclusions and Recommendations of the Committee: United States of America, Committee Against Torture (July 25, 2006), U.N. Doc. CAT/C/USA/CO/2, at 2.

[165] Legal doctrine implies that if the State argues a persistent objector position to a particular norm of customary international law, it can be relieved from its effective application under its jurisdiction unless this particular norm represents *jus cogens* norm. [*see* Prosecutor v. Furundzija, *supra* note 68, paras 153–154] Accordingly, the limitation on cruel and inhuman treatment prohibition would have been effective in case of US "war on terror," if US have been consistently objecting to Common Article 3 prohibition in the context of this conflict, but this argument was effectively abrogated by *Hamdan* decision and subsequent legislative and policy changes.

[166] Principle 16 requires the prosecutors to refuse to use as evidence statements obtained by torture or other ill treatment, except in proceedings against those who are accused of using such means. U.N. Doc. A/CONF.144/28/Rev.1 at 189.

of torture.[167] In one of the recent cases focusing on the issue of admittance of confession obtained by "oppression" inclusive of torture, Britain's highest Court, the Law Lords found unanimously that evidence resulting from torture or other inhuman treatment was inadmissible in any proceedings, whether legal or administrative.[168] The Government's argumentation supporting the use of the evidence, which had been procured by the prohibited means in the hearings before UK's Special Immigration Appeals Commission (the body tasked with consideration of the deportation appeals of individuals believed to be a threat to national security) without complicity of the British authorities was categorically dismissed. The leading opinion Lord Bingham of Cornhill famously reaffirmed the significance of the prohibition:

> The issue is one of constitutional principle whether evidence obtained by torturing another human being may lawfully be admitted against a party to proceedings in a British court, irrespective of where, or by whom, or on whose authority the torture was inflicted. To that question I would give a very clear negative answer.... The principles of the common law, standing alone, in my opinion compel the exclusion of third party torture evidence as unreliable, unfair, offensive to ordinary standards of humanity and decency and incompatible with the principles which should animate a tribunal seeking to administer justice. But the principles of the common law do not stand alone. Effect must be given to the European Convention, which itself takes account of the all but universal consensus embodied in the Torture Convention.[169]

There have been however less positive judicial decisions in this context. In August 2005, Amnesty International reported that the Hamburg Supreme Court admitted as evidence the summaries of the interrogations of three terrorist suspects held in the undisclosed custody of U.S. authorities in the re-trial of Mounir al-Motassadeq, accused of assisting the organizers of September 11, 2001 attacks in the United

---

[167] *See also* General Comment No. 20, *supra* note 75, para. 12; Committee Against Torture: P.E. v. France, Communication No. 193/2001, U.N. Doc. CAT/C/29/D/193/2001 (Dec. 19, 2002), and Concluding Observations: United Kingdom (Nov. 25, 2004), U.N. Doc. CAT/C/CR/33/3, para. 5. For a comprehensive revision of the exclusionary rule *see* NGO submission before the House of Lords in the case A &Others (FC) v. Secretary of State for Home Department [2004] EWCA Civ 1123; [2005] 1 WLR 414, at 35–59, *available at* redress.org/casework/CaseofAHouseofLords.pdf (last visited Apr. 19, 2007).

[168] A & Others (FC) v. Secretary of State for Home Department, Appellate Committee of the House of Lords, Dec. 8, 2005, [2005] UKHL 71. In this case eight suspected terrorists, originally held in Belmarsh prison without charge even up to four years, alleged that some of the evidence relied upon the Home Office to issue the certificates under the 2001 Anti-Terrorism, Crime and Security Act and subsequently to support their case before the Special Immigration Appeals Commission came from statements obtained from the detainees in Guantanamo Bay or any other undisclosed custodial centers in Egypt, Jordan or Morocco by using the aggressive interrogation methods.

[169] *Id.* paras 51–52.

States.[170] The trial based on such disputable evidence resulted in a sentence of 15 years imprisonment, pronounced only in January 2007.

The prohibition of the use of information obtained under torture as evidence in any proceedings in accordance to CAT is only one of the several legal norms, which all are regarded to constitute broadly understood standards of humane treatment. Other positive obligations include a forefront obligation to abstain from involvement in practices amounting to torture or other ill-treatment and from deporting, extraditing or otherwise transferring any individual to the destination, where a person would be in danger of being subjected to torture and alike treatment. Other obligations also require the states to take effective preventive measures, investigate, and prosecute or extradite to countries seeking to bring to justice those suspected of the prohibited conduct or an obligation to afford effective remedies and reparation to the victims.[171] Whilst all of these obligations constitute fundamental and mutually reinforcing elements of the prohibition of torture and other forms ill-treatment, consideration of each of them would require a separate paper on its own. In this author's view, some of the most acute situations of abuse in recent years took place while during detention. There are three main specific types of the violations, which include use of torture or torture-like methods during interrogations, subjecting a person to the specific conditions in the custody, which are not imposed as a part of the interrogation process as well as prolonged and indefinite or *incommunicado* captivity as amounting to torture.

4.2. *Torture in Detention and Detention as Torture*

Some of the practices that have followed the set of the questionable memos have been documented in the Iraqi Abu Ghraib prison on the pictures of detainees being humiliated, subjected to torture and inhuman treatment. Even these photos could have been a part of torture, showed to the detainees to induce their fear. Alarming reports of similar accounts came from the prisons in Afghanistan while allegations of torture and similar ill-treatment of the prisoners in Guantanamo Bay camp surfaced.[172]

Accounts of beatings and using violence in different ways, using the environmental modification (switching off air conditioning for prolonged periods of

---

[170] *Germany: Hamburg Court Violates International Law by Admitting Evidence Potentially Obtained through Torture*, Amnesty International, AI Index: EUR 23/001/2005 (Aug. 18, 2006).

[171] Article 13 CAT, *supra* note 79; General Comment No. 31, *supra* note 48, para. 8, Cakici v. Turkey, Judgment (July 8, 1999), Eur. Ct. H. R., Rep. 1999–IV, para. 113.

[172] *See* for instance Human Rights Watch Reports (HRW): *Enduring Freedom: Abuses by U.S. Forces in Afghanistan* (March 2004), *The Road to Abu Ghraib* (June 2004), *Guantánamo: Detainee Accounts* (October 2004) or Physicians for Human Rights Report *Break Them Down: Systematic Use of Psychological Torture by U.S. Forces*, May 1, 2005; *Guantánamo and beyond*, Amnesty International, *supra* note 2.

time making the room temperature unbearably hot or on the contrary drastically turning it down, "short" shacking and chaining the detainees to floor in fetal position ever up to 24 hours causing them to urinate and defecate on themselves, stripping them naked for few days, gagging their whole heads with a duck tape just to stop them from chanting prayers, using dogs to intimidate the captives, sexual or religious humiliation acts experienced by the former detainees but also witnessed by the agents of the U.S. Federal Bureau of Investigation during their assignments in Guantanamo Bay are illustrative of the extent of the abuse.[173] Apparently, depravation of sleep, interviews with use of strobe lights and using loud music with alternate beats for sixteen hours for approximately four days would break anyone. An institutionalized system of rewards for the cooperation invertly promoted various levels of punishment for non-cooperation and non-compliance with the rules of detention, from removal of toothbrushes or towels to placement in solitary confinement, a dark freezing cold cell even up to four weeks.[174] The deliberate desecration of the Holy Koran and the purposely deprivation of running water necessary for religious practices could be considered as outrages on personal dignity in accordance to Article 3 common to the Geneva Conventions, if not for the fact that the outrages upon personal dignity prohibition has been conveniently omitted from the 2006 Military Commissions Act. The Act removed "outrages upon personal dignity" and "humiliating and degrading treatment" from the list of offences punishable under the U.S. War Crimes Act, making such regulation inconsistent with Common Article 3 to 1949 Conventions and thus also with the *Hamdan* ruling.[175]

The European Court of Human Rights already in 1979 recognized five particular interrogation techniques, known as "sensory deprivation" as amounting to inhuman treatment. These methods include wall-standing (forcing the detainees to remain for periods of some hours in a "stress position"); hooding (putting a hood over the detainees' heads and, at least initially, keeping it there all the time except during interrogation); subjection to noise; deprivation of sleep or deprivation of food and drink including subjecting the detainees to a reduced diet.[176] The Court

---

[173] *Detainee Positive Responses*, U.S. Federal Bureau of Investigation records of misconduct released only in early Jan. 2007, *available at* foia.fbi.gov/guantanamo/detainees.pdf (last visited Apr. 19, 2007); *Situation of Detainees at Guantánamo Bay*, Report of the Chairperson of the Working Group on Arbitrary Detention, Ms. Leila Zerrougui; the Special Rapporteur on the independence of judges and lawyers, Mr. Leandro Despouy; the Special Rapporteur on torture and other cruel, inhuman or degrading treatment or punishment, Mr. Manfred Nowak; the Special Rapporteur on freedom of religion or belief, Ms. Asma Jahangir and the Special Rapporteur on the right of everyone to the enjoyment of the highest attainable standard of physical and mental health, Mr. Paul Hunt, Feb. 15, 2006, U.N. Doc. E/CN.4/2006/120 [hereinafter: U.N. Rapporteurs' Report].
[174] *Detainee Accounts*, HRW, *supra* note 172, at 13–17.
[175] *Compare* Sec. 6(b)(1) (B) of the 2006 Military Commissions Act.
[176] Ireland v. United Kingdom, *supra* note 37, para. 96.

implied that these means only caused the actual body injury or intense physical or mental suffering, which led to acute psychiatric disturbances but also were intended to arouse the fear, anguish and the inferiority feelings with humiliating and degrading effects on the victims.[177] On the other hand severe beating to all parts of the body, using the so called "Palestinian hanging" technique (suspending the fully naked victim by the hands tied at the back of the neck), or rape for a period of over three days of the victim, who was also blind-folded, paraded naked and kept in a continued state of physical and mental pain for the purpose of obtaining information or confession amounted to torture.[178] In the *Tomasi* case a victim has been slapped, kicked, punched, made stand for long periods (in stress position) or naked in front of the open window and deprived of food over a period of two days in relation to his suspected involvement in terrorist activities in Corsica. The Court was adamant to point out that the requirements of the investigation and difficulties in the fight of terrorism cannot result in limits placed on the protection of the physical integrity of the individuals.[179]

If the beatings occurred over a short period of heightened tension and emotions without any other aggravating factors then it will be considered as inhuman treatment short of torture.[180] The European Court further stressed that rape, in particular, violates the physical and mental integrity and therefore constitutes an inherent part of the aggravated cruel and inhuman treatment, which, combined with other humiliating treatment, should be regarded as torture.

The Inter-American Commission and Court of Human Rights agreed with the European Court's opinion in that keeping the detainees hooded and naked and inflicting a drug called pentothal to facilitate the confessions or provision of information, imposing a restrictive diet even leading to malnutrition, applying electric shocks or keeping one's head under the water to the point of drowning, beatings and burning with cigarettes as well as threats of any of such practices or death were considered as inhumane treatment.[181] Interestingly, U.S. courts also found the acts such as severe beatings, threats of imminent death and mock executions, threats of removing extremities, burning (with the cigarettes), electric shocks to genitalia or threats to do so, rape or sexual assault or injury or threats of it, and forcing a prisoner to watch the torture of another person to constitute crime of torture.[182]

---

[177] *Id.* para. 167.
[178] *See* respectively: European Court of Human Rights: The Greek case, *supra* note 96, at 186; Aksoy v. Turkey, *supra* note 32, para. 64; Aydin v. Turkey (Sep. 5, 1997), Eur. Ct. H. R. 1997-VI, No. 50 paras 81–85.
[179] Tomasi v. France, *supra* note 80, para. 11.
[180] Egmez v. Cyprus, Judgment (Dec. 21, 2000), Eur. Ct. H. R., (2002) 34 EHRR 753, para. 78.
[181] IACHR Report, *supra* note 21, para. 161, also Loayza Tamayo Case, *supra* note 81, para. 57.
[182] Bybee's Memorandum, *supra* note 123, at 24.

Finally, as the Special Rapporteur on Torture reiterated in his 2004 report to the U.N. General Assembly:

> The Special Rapporteur has recently received information on certain methods that have been condoned and used to secure information from suspected terrorists. They notably include holding detainees in painful and/or stressful positions, depriving them of sleep and light for prolonged periods, exposing them to extremes of heat, cold, noise and light, hooding, depriving them of clothing, stripping detainees naked and threatening them with dogs. The jurisprudence of both international and regional human rights mechanisms is unanimous in stating that such methods violate the prohibition of torture and ill-treatment.[183]

Probably the most problematic conditions of detention,[184] apart from those instituted as a part of the inducing cooperation or investigation methods, included the prolonged confinement in the isolation cells (Maximum Security Units), unjustified excessive use of force by the Initial Reaction Forces[185] and the forced feeding of the hunger strikers. Prolonged solitary confinement, combined with excessively harsh conditions on numerous occasions for up to 18 months with only short breaks between the periods of isolation, have been considered excessive and amounting to inhuman treatment in violation of Article 7 ICCPR.[186] Although initially the European Commission of Human Rights observed that solitary confinement may fall within ambit of Article 3 ECHR depending on the particular conditions, the stringency of the measure, its duration, the effect pursued and its effect on the person concerned,[187] the subsequent findings of the European Court of Human Rights are more conservative. It appears that the solitary confinement on its own is not generally regarded as a violation of the prohibition of inhuman treatment. In the *Peers* case the Court asserted that incarceration in unventilated cells with no windows during the hottest time of the year combined with the fact that the victim had to share the toilet with his inmate diminished his human dignity and constituted degrading treatment. The Inter-American Court of Human Rights took a different approach in the context of a disappearance case in recognizing that "prolonged isolation and deprivation of communication are in themselves cruel and

---

[183] *Interim Report of the Special Rapporteur of the Commission on Human Rights on the Question of Torture and Other Cruel, Inhuman or Degrading Treatment or Punishment*, U.N. Doc. A/59/324 (2004), para. 17.
[184] For a brief comparison between Guantanamo Bay camp and Belmarsh prison *see Visit to Guantanamo Bay*, U.K. House of Commons Parliamentary Foreign Affairs Committee, Second Report of Session 2006–2007 (Jan. 21, 2007), HC44, at 13–14.
[185] For detailed account *see* U.N. Rapporteurs' Report, *supra* note 173, at 26.
[186] General Comment No. 20, *supra* note 75, para 6; similarly in Victor Rosario Congo (Ecuador), IACHR Case 11.427, Report No. 63/99, Annual Report of the IACHR (1999), paras 58–59, discussed also in the U.N. Rapporteurs' Report, *supra* note 173, at 25–26.
[187] "Complete sensory isolation coupled with complete social isolation can no doubt ultimately destroy the personality; this constitutes a form of inhuman treatment which cannot be justified by the requirements of security" as cited in Ovey & White, *supra* note 108, at 77.

inhuman treatment, harmful to the psychological and moral integrity of the person and a violation of the right of any detainee to respect for his inherent dignity as a human being" therefore finding a breach of the substantive prohibition of Article 5 of the Inter-American Convention on Human Rights.[188]

In December 2006 a new facility, known as Camp VI, opened in the Guantanamo Bay base. Reportedly the building contained more permanent isolation cells, completely sealed and with minimal contact with other human beings. Currently, approximately 385 individuals are being held on the base, ca. 285 of them being kept in isolation cells of different types, most however in the new maximum security confinement without access to natural light or fresh air.[189] Noteworthy, "separation" as an interrogation technique is also permitted, though subject to the special authority under the newest version of the U.S. Army Field Manual on Human Intelligence Collector Operations.[190] Separation is characterized by denial of communication with other inmates justified by "unique and critical operational requirements."[191] Separation in that sense very much resembles isolation. If a prolonged, solitary confinement is to be considered, in line with the U.N. Special Rapporteurs' report recommendations[192] as inhuman treatment, two-thirds of the current population of Guantanamo Bay is held in breach of the relevant international obligations as well as possibly the 2006 Military Commissions Act.

Setting aside the allegations of the brutal execution of the force-feeding of the detainees on the strike, which on its own may be considered at least in terms of inhuman treatment, the problem has more of an ethical dimension. Force-feeding, in view of the World Medical Association, which is contrary to an informed and voluntary refusal, is unjustifiable and when accompanied by threats, force, and the use of physical restraints may amount to inhuman or degrading treatment.[193]

---

[188] El-Megreisi v. Libyan Arab Jamahiriya, U.N. Human Rights Committee, Comm. No. 440/1990 CCPR/C/50/D/440/1990; Velasquez Rodríguez v. Honduras (Merits), Judgment (July 29, 1988), Inter-American Court of Human Rights, Series C, No. 4 (1988), para. 156. In the *Suárez Rosero* case, the same Court assessed that a 36-day detention and deprivation of any communication with the outside world constituted cruel, inhuman, and degrading treatment. Noteworthy, the victim was held in a damp poorly ventilated underground cell measuring approximately 15 square meters with 16 other prisoners, without the necessary hygiene facilities. Judgment (Nov. 12, 1997), Inter-American Court of Human Rights, Series C, No. 35, para. 91.

[189] *United States of America: Cruel and Inhuman: Conditions of Isolation for Detainees at Guantánamo Bay*, Amnesty International, AMR 51/051/2007 (Apr. 5, 2007).

[190] Army Field Manual, FM2–22.3 on Human Intelligence Operations (Sep. 6, 2006). Neither the Military Commission Act of 2006 nor this manual applies to the interrogations carried out by the Central Intelligence Agency.

[191] *See* sections M-2 and M-28 of the Manual for the more detailed description.

[192] U.N. Rapporteurs' Report, *supra* note 173, para. 87.

[193] World Medical Association Declaration on Hunger Strikers, adopted by the 43rd World Medical Assembly Malta, Nov. 1991 and revised in Oct. 2006, para. 3, *available at* www.wma.net/

According to the U.N. Special Rapporteur on Torture, force-feeding practices as well as certain actions of Initial Reaction Forces may also amount to torture if "it inflicts severe pain or suffering on the victims for the purpose of intimidation and/or punishment" and in that context the complicit role in torture of the medical professionals was highlighted.[194]

Many practices recorded in Guantanamo Bay were reported as "subtle" compared with the treatment of the detainees in Afghanistan.[195] Recollections of severe beatings, sometimes leading to possible deaths, hooding, striping naked, and parading in front of female guards, exposure to extreme cold, violent physical examinations, stress positions, isolation in poor conditions or aggressive sexual humiliation seem to run as a theme.[196] These augmented techniques were transplanted, officially approved, and extensively used later on in Iraq.[197] In both theatres, these techniques were used indiscriminately against all persons under the control of the U.S. forces, no matter that both situations represented international armed conflicts. During such conflicts some specific treatment may be accorded to specific groups of individuals depending on their status and/or their conduct over and above the fundamental standards of humane treatment, which as discussed in this paper always remain the legal minimum to be adhered to in all circumstances. Even if we accept the U.S. Supreme Court assertion that Common Article 3 to the Geneva Conventions is applicable in the fight against terrorism, it remains disputable whether the 2001–2002 conflict in Afghanistan should be subject to this interpretation and even more so to the uncontested conflict in Iraq. Taking into consideration the 2004 ICRC leaked report findings that most of the persons arrested and detained were civilians, one may conclude that most of the abuses were ultimately executed on civilians, most again declared that they had been arrested by mistake.[198] The report

---

e/policy/h31.htm (last visited Apr. 19, 2007), endorsed by the American Medical Association, Policy H-65.997 Human Rights (Feb. 10, 2006).

[194] U.N. Rapporteurs' Report, *supra* note 173, throughout.
[195] *Guantánamo and beyond*, Amnesty International, *supra* note 2, at 88.
[196] *Id.* at 84–89, *see also Enduring Freedom*, HRW, *supra* note 172; the Schlesinger Report, *supra* note 148, at 68 and Jacoby's Report, *supra* note 156.
[197] *See* Schlesinger Report, *supra* note 148, throughout and Investigation Report of Brig. Gen. Richard P. Formica into detention activities of Special Operation Forces in Iraq, Major Gen. A.M. Taguba, *Article 15–6 Investigation of the 800th Military Police Brigade*, at 16; Major G.R. Fay, *Article 15–6 Investigation of the Abu Ghraib Detention Facility and 205th Military Intelligence Brigade*, at 7; all *available at* www.dod.mil/pubs/foi/detainees/other_related.html (last visited Apr. 19, 2007), *Report of the International Committee of the Red Cross (ICRC) on the Treatment by the Coalition Forces of Prisoners of War and Other Protected Persons by the Geneva Conventions in Iraq during Arrest, Internment and Interrogation*, ICRC (Feb. 2004), throughout.
[198] *Id.* For example, in ongoing proceedings, seven British soldiers are charged with inhumane treatment of Iraqi civilian detained following a counter insurgency operation in Sep. 2003. One of the detainees died during custody allegedly due to severe physical. The case is currently pending

of Major Gen. Taguba, a military investigator, into Abu Ghraib practices findings indicates "numerous incidents of sadistic, blatant and wanton criminal abuses" and in some group of cases (detainees deemed to poses the "intelligence" value) also systemic. His list of examples of such abuses highlights the following treatment: arranging naked detainees in a pile and then jumping on them, positioning a naked detainee on a box, with a sandbag on his head, and attaching wires to his fingers, toes and penis to simulate electric torture; sodomizing with chemical lights and pouring the phosphoric liquid on detainees, threatening them with a loaded 9-mm pistol, rape on both male or female prisoners as well as using military working dogs (without muzzles) to intimidate detainees with threats of attack, which led in at least one case to biting and severely injuring a detainee.

Increasingly, the photographing and videotaping of many of these incidents were observed, some of the most humiliating conduct included videotaping and photographing naked male and female detainees; detainees forced into various sexually explicit positions or forced to masturbate themselves. The published pictures undoubtedly leave an uneasy impression of being not only a record of deliberate strategy of infusing fear and humiliation by using them during subsequent interrogations[199] but also evidence of some kind of amusement-smiles, "thumbs-up" and team hugs over the battered individuals. Whether civilians or prisoners of war, the law requires the captured individuals not only to be protected from acts of violence but also insults, intimidation, and public curiosity.[200] One has to call into question the purpose of such practices on the part of the perpetrators documenting their own misconduct, if they would not have genuinely thought it was all within an acceptable parameter of behavior; only that what is acceptable is not always lawful. The problem however of the disrespect for another human being appears to be far more comprehensive.

Only just released the U.S. Defense Department survey of the mental health of deployed U.S. Army and Marine Corps troops in Iraq shows that despite all the investigations, improved trainings and corrected legal positions in respect to torture in the war against terrorism, especially however during armed conflicts, suggests that less than half of soldiers (47 percent) and 38 percent of Marines believe that non-combatants should be treated with dignity and respect.[201] Well over one third of Marines (44 percent) and 41 percent of soldiers would allow torture if it would

---

on appeal before the House of Lords. Al Skeini & Others, R (on the application of) v. Secretary of State for Defence [2004] EWHC 2911 (Admin) The Court of Appeal, Judgment (Dec. 21, 2005) and Decision of High Court (Dec. 14, 2004).

[199] As mentioned in *Getting away with Torture*, HRW, Vol. 17 No. 1 (G) (Apr. 2005), at 23.
[200] Article 13 GC III and Article 27 GC IV, *supra* note 7.
[201] *Operation Iraqi Freedom 0507, Final Report*, Mental Health Advisory Team- IV (Nov. 17, 2006), at 34–42 (Battlefield Ethics) *available at* www.armymedicine.army.mil/news/mhat/mhat_iv/MHAT_IV_Report_17NOV06.pdf (last visited Apr.19, 2007).

help save the life of a Marine/ Soldier as well as to obtain important information about the insurgents. The other trend shows that the mistreatment involving insults and curses at non-combatants was exacerbated by having the member of the unit become a casualty (42 percent of soldiers and 50 percent of Marines) or when handling the dead bodies or human remains (54 percent of Marines and 48 percent of soldiers). These results depict the alarming degradation of the respect for the principles of dignity and humanity. The opponents, both civilians and combatants, appear to be annoying nobodies.[202] Striking is the easiness with which the soldiers would contemplate the infliction of torture, torture understood as extreme physical injury leading possibly to death, bearing in mind that torture is universally unlawful and unjustified in any circumstances.

5. Conclusions

The mistreatment of individuals deprived of their liberty has occurred probably in every war that has ever been fought, yet the recent practice is particularly shocking as it appears to be directed at diminishing or depriving an individual of dignity and humanity. These practices, which in many cases have been supported by state policy, strike at the very heart of international humanitarian law, the spirit of humanitarian values and respect for a human being during war, the most cruel of all times. The law as we know has not changed but the fighters and the goals of the fight may have done so. In this era when the rules of war with the limitations they impose are perceived as a hindrance to defeat of the enemy and ultimate victory, they are of utmost importance. Following the September 11, 2001 attack the U.N. Special Rapporteur on Torture, at that time, Sir Nigel Rodley, noted:

> However frustrating may be the search for those behind the abominable acts of terrorism and for evidence that would bring them to justice, I am convinced that any temptation to resort to torture or similar ill-treatment or to send suspects to countries where they would face such treatment must be firmly resisted. Not only would that be a violation of an absolute and peremptory rule of international law, it would be also responding to a crime against humanity with a further crime under international law. Moreover, it would be signalling to the terrorists that the values espoused by the international community are hollow and no more valid than the travesties of principle defended by the terrorists.[203]

This paper does not address a plentiful of other aspects debated in the context of humane treatment and in particular the prohibition of torture and other forms

---

[202] As cited in *The Road to Abu Graib*, HRW, *supra* note 172, at 24.
[203] Statement by the Special Rapporteur to the Third Committee of the General Assembly, delivered on Nov. 8, 2001, Annex III, U.N. Doc. E/CN.4/2002/76, at 14.

of ill-treatment. The catalogue of such problems encompasses proposals to legally sanction the use of torture in "ticking-bombs" scenarios, violations of the *non-refoulement* principle through extrajudicial transfers for aggressive interrogations to states commonly practicing the illegal methods and the apparently unlimited involvement of the U.S. Central Intelligence Agency in any of such activities, the problems with establishing the abuses and accountability issues. What this paper attempted to show is the essence of what humane treatment is considered to be or rather what universally it is accepted not to be. The analysis of the concept of the prohibited conduct aimed to illustrate that both branches of international law, the humanitarian and the human rights ones, in global and in regional dimensions, perceive the prohibition in broadly same terms. The dispute however remains as to the purposive reinterpretation of certain aspects of the concept, suited to political aims and not legal progress, translated into policy guidelines and embedded into the psychic of the individuals fighting with terrorism, which inevitably contributed if not led to a recent rise of violations, unprecedented in terms of scale and nature. Crime is contagious-

> If the government becomes a lawbreaker, it breeds contempt for law; it invites every man to become a law unto himself; it invites anarchy. To declare that in the administration of the criminal law the end justifies the means – to declare that the government may commit crimes in order to secure the conviction of a private criminal – would bring terrible retribution.[204]

---

[204] Olmstead v. U.S., *supra* note 1.

Chapter III

Legal Conclusion or Interpretative Process? *Lex Specialis* and the Applicability of International Human Rights Standards

Conor McCarthy*

1. *Introduction*

Few areas of international law exist in such close, but complex, proximity to other areas of legal regulation as international human rights law. The complexity of this interrelationship is particularly acute during times of armed conflict. While humanitarian law is conceived of specifically to address the kinds of situations which arise in warfare and the dynamics which underpins them, the relevance and applicability of human rights standards is more subtle and context dependent. As a result the relationship between these areas of law is, at times, fraught. International law seeks to fit these legal regimes together through a series of legal principles or maxims of interpretation. These interpretative maxims provide the primary mechanisms for the resolution of conflict, in particular the notions of *lex posterior derogat legi priori* – the idea that more recently assumed obligations prevail over those less recently assumed and *lex specialis derogare legi generali* – the notion that law specially tailored to a particular context takes precedence over generally applicable law.[1]

Considerable conceptual confusion shrouds these maxims of interpretation. Even their interrelationship is unclear. Some writers contend that *lex specialis* overrides *lex posterior*, others contend that it does not.[2] Further opacity surrounds how the

---

* Jesus College, Cambridge.
[1] The role of *lex posterior* and *lex specialis* is not necessarily limited to the resolution of normative conflict, occasionally they are used as a supplementary means of interpretation to direct the interpreter to a more elaborate or sophisticated set of applicable legal norms. For example, Sir Gerald Fitzmaurice, *The Law and Procedure of the International Court of Justice 1951–54: Treaty Interpretation and Other Treaty Points*, 33 BYIL 236 (1957). Other supplementary means of interpretation include interpretation *a contrario*, acquiescence, *contra proferentem*, *ejusdem generis* and *expressio unius est exclusio alterius*. *See* Anthony Aust, Modern Treaty Law and Practice 200–201 (2000).
[2] Daniel O'Connell & Ivan Shearer, The International Law of the Sea, Vol. I, 47 (1982). *Cf* Mark Villiger, Customary International Law and Treaties: A Manual on the Theory and Practice of the Interrelation of Sources 60 (2d ed., 1997) [hereinafter Villiger].

question of how *lex specialis* should properly be employed in legal reasoning, the controversy concerning whether and how human rights standards can be applied in occupied territory is indicative of this. This article will address in particular conceptual ambiguity on the latter point. It will examine the role *lex specialis* occupies in international legal reasoning. It will then seek to use these understandings to shed some further light on the issues of applicability where humanitarian law is concurrently applicable alongside human rights norms.

2. *The Nature of the Problem*

In its Advisory Opinion concerning the Legality of Nuclear Weapons, the ICJ stated that, except to the extent provided by lawful derogation, international human rights standards remained, "in principle" applicable in an armed conflict; however, "the test of what is an arbitrary deprivation of life...falls to be determined by the applicable lex specialis."[3] This was a relatively straightforward proposition for the Court to iterate in the context of the abstract question it had to address in that case. However, when faced with a more specific factual context in its Wall advisory opinion, it was necessary for the court to more fully address the complexity of the question of simultaneous applicability. It stated that:

> As regards the relationship between international humanitarian law and human rights law, there are thus three possible situations: some rights may be exclusively matters of international humanitarian law; others may be exclusively matters of human rights law; yet others may be matters of both these branches of international law. In order to answer the question put to it, the Court will have to take into consideration both these branches of international law, namely human rights law and, as lex specialis, international humanitarian law.[4]

The proposition that international human rights standards are, in some manner, applicable alongside humanitarian law during military occupation in spite of the general *lex specialis* character of the latter has been authoritatively and widely accepted, not just by the ICJ but also in a range of other authoritative determinations. Both U.N. Human Rights Committees have affirmed the applicability of human rights standards in contexts also falling within the purview of the laws of war, as has the European Court of Human Rights (ECHR).[5] The key issue of

---

[3] 1996 (I) ICJ Rep. 240.
[4] Legal Consequences of the Construction of a Wall in the Occupied Palestinian Territory, Advisory Opinion, (July 9, 2004) 2004 ICJ 131, at 35. [hereinafter The Wall Advisory Opinion]
[5] *See, inter alia*, Case concerning Armed Activities on the Territory of the Congo (DRC v. Uganda), (Dec. 19, 2005), 2005 I.C.J. Rep. 116, para. 179 [hereinafter DRC v. Uganda]; Committee on Civil and Political Rights, General Comment No. 6, Right to Life (1982), para. 2; General Comment No. 14, Nuclear Weapons and the Right to Life (1984); General Comment No. 29, States

applicability is therefore where and how these two legal regimes interrelate during armed conflict. There will inevitably be many circumstances where the applicable norms can only be derived from the specialized regime. However this paper will argue that the mere assignation of a body of principles as *lex specialis* is insufficient to achieve a full understanding of the applicable legal standards and the nature of the relationship between special rules, in this case the laws of war, and fundamental but more general norms. Several underlying issues are at play – the nature and purpose of the particular legal principles at stake, the context in which a particular principle is being applied, the nature of the relationship between the potentially conflicting regimes, and also the legal dynamics underpinning them.

3. *The Role of* Lex Specialis *in International Legal Reasoning*

Views as to the role and purpose of *lex specialis* in legal reasoning have a long lineage. Grotius wrote that in relation to those agreements which are to be regarded as equal, certain "should be given preference which is most specific and approaches most clearly to the subject at hand; for special provisions are normally more effective than those that are general."[6] The tentative phrasing adopted here is revealing; Grotius did not treat the principle as absolute – rather as a useful mechanism in the resolution of conflict in favour of the application of more effective specific rules in place of less effective general rules. Later Pufendorf[7] and then Vattel would adopt similar reasoning. Vattel, developing the work of Pufendorf, stated:

> Of two laws or two conventions, we ought (all other circumstances being equal) to prefer the one which is less general and which approaches nearer the point in question: because special matter admits of fewer exceptions than that which is general; it is enjoined with greater precision and appears to have been more pointedly intended.[8]

---

of Emergency, (2001) and Committee on Economic, Social and Cultural Rights, Consideration of Reports Submitted by State Parties (June 26, 2003), U.N. Doc. E/C.12/1/Add.90, para. 31. In a series of cases the ECHR has also applied human rights standards to circumstances of internal armed conflict. *See* Khashiyev and Akayeva v. Russia, Isayeva, Yusupova, Bazayeva v. Russia and Isayeva v. Russia, All ECtHR Chamber Merits, (Feb. 24, 2005), *available at* www.echr.coe.int. *See further* the Paris Minimum Standards of Human Rights Norms in a State of Emergency, 79 Am. J. Int'l L. 1072, 1073 (1985), U.N. Econ. & Soc. Council [ECOSOC], Comm. on Hum. Rts., Status of the International Covenants on Human Rights: Siracusa Principles on the Limitation and Derogation Provisions in the International Covenant on Civil and Political Rights, Annex, U.N. Doc. E/CN.4/1985/4 (Sept. 28, 1984), Special Rapporteur (L. Despouy), Tenth Annual Report on Human Rights and States of Emergency, U.N. Doc. E/CN.4/Sub.2/1997/19 (1997).

[6] Hugo Grotius, De Jure Belli Ac Pacis 428 (1625) [hereinafter Grotius].
[7] Samuel Von Pufendorf, De Jure Naturae Et Gentium 822 (1762).
[8] Emerich De Vattel, Law of Nations, § 316, 5th Rule (1758).

Thus Vattel attaches a clearer normative punch to earlier views about the nature of *lex specialis*. For Vattel voluntarism plays a key role in explaining, justifying, and understanding *lex specialis* – not only is it advisable for states to follow specially designed provisions as being more likely to lead to an effective disposition, but the special provisions also more closely reflect the deliberate will of those states agreeing to them, and therefore normatively merit being followed more closely.

In more recent times the place of *lex specialis* as a fundamental principle of international legal analysis has become entrenched. Although it finds no explicit place *eo nomine* in the Vienna Convention on the Law of Treaties (VCLT), it is nevertheless widely utilized as a means of treaty interpretation in accordance with Articles 31 and 32 of the VCLT.[9] However, its scope is not limited to treaties. It has a fundamental, though often not expressly acknowledged, role in distinguishing the scope of application of conventional and customary international law,[10] the former generally having priority over the latter by virtue of the *jus dispositivum* nature of most rules of custom.[11] *Lex specialis* and other concomitant interpretative principles such as *lex posterior* are generally not regarded as being customary rules *per se*. Schwarzenberger points out any tendency to so regard them would be challenged by the paradox of "the self-eliminating character" such customary maxims would develop.[12] Rather these maxims represent logical techniques.[13] However, these are not free-standing logical techniques. As suggested in the analysis of early jurists such as Grotius and Vattel, the "logic" which *lex specialis* furnishes legal reasoning with, is also, in itself, articulative of a bundle of underlying principles or values.

In its recent work on the subject the International Law Commission (ILC) has identified some of the concerns – both teleological and consequentialist – which *lex specialis* articulates. Echoing Vattel, it highlighted "the need to ensure the practical relevancy and effectiveness of the standard as well as to preserve what is often a useful guide to party intentions."[14] The Commission went on to say that these

---

[9] Martti Koskenniemi, Fragmentation of International Law: Difficulties Arising from the Diversification and Expansion of International Law, International Law Commission, 58th Session, U.N. Doc. A/CN.4/L.682 (April 13, 2006), at 38 [hereinafter ILC Fragmentation Report].

[10] *See* Villiger, *supra* note 2 and Sir Robert Jennings & Sir Arthur Watts (eds.), Oppenheim's International Law, Vol. I, 1270–1280 (9th ed., 1992) [hereinafter Jennings & Watts].

[11] Parties are entitled to derogate from such rules, establishing different rules governing their relations *inter se*. North Sea Continental Shelf Cases (Federal Republic of Germany/Denmark; Federal Republic of Germany/Netherlands) (Feb. 20, 1969) 1969 ICJ Rep. 42, para. 72 [hereinafter North Sea Continental Shelf Cases].

[12] *See* Georg Schwartzenberger, International Law as Applied by International Courts and Tribunals 472 (1957). However, general principles of interpretation, mentioned explicitly in the VCLT have been regarded as customary. *See* Territorial Dispute (Libyan Arab Jamahiriya v. Chad), (Feb. 3, 1994) 1994 ICJ Rep. 6, para. 41.

[13] Wilfred Jenks, *The Conflict of Law Making Treaties*, 30 BYIL 401, 436 (1953).

[14] ILC Fragmentation Report, *supra* note 9, at 40.

concerns "need, of course, to be balanced against countervailing ones: the hierarchical position of the relevant standard and other evidences of state intent."[15] Of course, at a deeper level the way in which interpretative techniques like *lex specialis* are employed in legal reasoning, and the relative emphasis which the process places on these various interests reveals much about the relative importance attached to concepts such as voluntarism, positivism, normativity and so forth in international law discourse. The discussion concerning the applicability of human rights standards during armed conflict must be seen in this context.

In broad terms therefore conceptions about the operation of *lex specialis* in legal reasoning can gravitate towards one of two tendencies – a kind of conclusory procedure or as more akin to an interpretative process. Before outlining some of the key characteristics of these a preliminary point is important. The following analysis is not meant to function as an analytic taxonomy of *lex specialis* in legal reasoning. Rather the point that will be developed here is that approaches to *lex specialis* in legal reasoning are not uniform, and that differences in the way in which the concept is used have a significant impact upon the legal conclusions reached. The analysis elaborated below is therefore meant as an analytical tool for delineating these differences and examining their significance.

Unfortunately, an examination of the legal reasoning involved in the application of *lex specialis* is complicated by the fact that the way in which the concept is used is often rather opaque. One reason for this conceptual opacity may stem from the fact that it often operates as a function of implicit rather than explicit legal reasoning – cited *en passant* as if involving the application of a relatively unsophisticated and uncontroversial legal principle. Jennings and Watts describe the concept as "expressive of common sense and normal grammatical usage."[16] On occasion, this will surely be the case.

However, the ease with which it can be applied is very much contingent on the legal and factual context which the interpreter faces. Frequently, judicial opinions will invoke the interpretative norm without a real explanation of how application of the reasoning connoted by the doctrine has led to the legal consequences cited.[17]

---

[15] *Id.*
[16] Jennings & Watts, *supra* note 10, at 1280.
[17] An early example of this kind of approach can be seen in the PCIJ case Mavrommatis Palestine Concessions, P.C.I.J. Series A, No. 2 (1924), at 31. Here the court was faced with two potentially conflicting treaties which had an impact upon its jurisdiction, the Mandate for Palestine and Protocol XII of the Treaty of Lausanne. After briefly addressing and dismissing two arguments in favour of the applicability of the Mandate, the Permanent Court went on the opine that "[o]n the contrary, in cases of doubt, the Protocol being a special and more recent agreement should prevail." More recently, in Armed Activities on the Territory of the DRC the ICJ assessed the lawfulness of Ugandan conduct in the Ituri province of the DRC against both the laws of military occupation and international human rights standards without discussion of the extent to which the laws of

The fact that a specifically tailored legal regime exists to address an issue is sometimes itself seen as sufficient to justify the application of those rules pertaining to that legal regime without reference to other norms. This can give an unfortunately conclusory or rhetorical quality to legal analysis relying on the doctrine. It means that its role in legal reasoning is paradoxically often concealed, though nonetheless very apparent because of its significant influence on legal outcomes.

Those relying on *lex specialis* argumentation in its more conclusory form appear to approach it as being akin to an heuristic mechanism. Through a form of typological reasoning, *lex specialis* is utilized as a straightforward instrumental device, revealing the applicability or non-applicability of a particular legal regime or body of legal principles.[18] The key aspect of this analysis is the characterization of a body of rules when considered systemically or *in toto*, usually by reference to the sophistication or particularity of the rules in addressing certain factual contexts or the perceived intention of state parties as to the specific context which a body of rules was purportedly designed to address.

Where it is determined that a body of principles can appositely be described as *specialis*, this is sufficient in itself to supplant a *generalis* legal framework.[19] It is in this sense that *lex specialis* functions, more as a legal conclusion than a mode of interpretation. Once *specialis* status has been determined there is little scope for mutual accommodation between the specialist and generalist regimes, the applicability of the former is treated as if almost an *a priori* function of its status.

This rather formalistic interpretative perspective has occasionally been deployed in academic writing. Dionisio Anzilotti described *lex specialis* norms as having the effect of displacement; he wrote "*in toto jure genus per speciem derogatur*; la norme de droit particulière l'emporte sur la norme générale."[20] Some of the criticisms of

---

military occupation should be applied *specialis* in such circumstances. DRC v. Uganda, *supra* note 5, paras 178–179.

[18] *Cf.* Jörg Kammerhofer, who frames *lex specialis* as the justification for breach of a general rule. Kammerhofer, *Unearthing Structural Uncertainty through neo-Kelsenian Consistency: Conflicts of Norms in International Law.* European Society of International Law, Research Forum paper, *available at* www.esil-sedi.eu/english/pdf/Kammerhofer.pdf (last visited June 6, 2007).

[19] The debate concerning the status and conditions of detention to which various kinds of participants in armed conflict are entitled is redolent with this kind of analysis. See, for example, Nathaniel Berman, *Privileging Combat? Contemporary Conflict and the Legal Construction of War*, 43 Colum. J. Transnat'l Law 1, 12 (2004). In this article Berman describes the nature of humanitarian law thus: "...lex specialis literally implicates matters of life and death, for its applicability may determine whether a particular killing is legally facilitated through its immunizations through international humanitarian law or is legally prohibited by international human rights law...." Berman continues, "[t]he construction of the scope of the combatants privilege is thus central to the construction of the line between the exceptional lex specialis of war and the normal lex generalis of human rights and crimes." *See also* Roy Schondorf, *Extra-State Armed Conflicts: Is there a Need for a New Legal Regime?*, 37 N.Y.U. J. Int'l Law and Pol. 1, 61 (2004).

[20] Dionisio Anzilotti, *Cours de droit international*, Tôme I (transl. by Gilbert Gidel), 103 (1929).

the ICJ's Wall Advisory Opinion have been structured on a similar premise. In addressing this subject Michael Dennis conducted a thorough schematic analysis of both the ICCPR and the ICESCR. He examined the structure and purpose of the conventions and also analysed their *travaux préparatoires* and state practice to assess the intention of states when the conventions were negotiated, concluding that:[21]

> In short, the best reading of the interrelationship between the ICCPR and international humanitarian law is the more traditional view that international humanitarian law should be applied lex specialis in determining what a state's obligations are during armed conflict or military occupation.[22]

Thus Dennis sees the *specialis* character of the relevant laws of war as supplanting conventional human rights obligations. The detailed and careful analysis he presents speaks to whether human rights standards and the law of military occupation can be considered *generalis* and *specialis* respectively. The fact that they are is determinative of the issue – the later must be applied to the exclusion of the former. States also occasionally rely on this form of reasoning as an explanation for often controversial legal policies, as the broad nature of the legal analysis involved reduces the scope for protracted argumentation on the applicability of certain pointedly sensitive norms. A good practical example of this approach is the recent controversy concerning the applicability of the Convention Against Torture (CAT) in times of war and in occupied territories.

In his testimony before the Committee Against Torture, John Bellinger, Legal Advisor to the U.S. Department of State, explained on behalf of the U.S. government that "our view is simply that U.S. detention operations in Guantanamo, Afghanistan, and Iraq are part of ongoing armed conflicts and, accordingly, are governed by the law of armed conflict, which is the *lex specialis* applicable to those particular operations."[23] Bellinger went on to argue that the CAT was only applicable to the *de jure* territorial jurisdiction of the U.S., and not to circumstances of military occupation where the U.S. only exercised de facto control.[24] The Committee in its final conclusions and recommendations found these arguments unmeritorious, stating:

---

[21] Michael Dennis, *Application of Human Rights Treaties Extraterritorially in Times of Armed Conflict and Military Occupation*, 99 Am. J. Int'l L. 119 (2005). This article is part of AJIL Agora: Wall in Occupied Palestinian Territory.

[22] *Id.*, at 139. Dennis expressed the same conclusions, *mutatis mutandis*, in respect of the ICESCR, at 141.

[23] Oral Statements by the United States Delegation to the Committee Against Torture (May 8, 2006), at 4, *available at* www.us-mission.ch/Press2006/CAT-May8.pdf (last visited June 6, 2007).

[24] Oral Statements by the United States Delegation to the Committee Against Torture, (May 5, 2006), at 16–17, *available at* www.us-mission.ch/Press2006/CAT-MAY5–SPOKEN.pdf (last visited June 6, 2007).

> The State party should recognize and ensure that the Convention applies at all times, whether in peace, war or armed conflict, in any territory under its jurisdiction and that the application of the Convention's provisions are without prejudice to the provisions of any other international instrument, pursuant to paragraph 2 of its articles 1 and 16.[25]

It went on to conclude that jurisdiction under the convention encompassed the notion of "de facto effective control" by "whichever military or civil authorities exercise such control."[26]

Particularly over the last decade, findings such as this by authoritative bodies means that typological approaches to *lex specialis* increasingly run counter to a growing and varied body of authoritative legal determinations which envisage some form of concurrent role for *generalis* and *specialis* norms, in particular in the fields of humanitarian and human rights law.[27] The categorical approach inherently leaves little room for such a mutual accommodation. At a more fundamental level the nature of the reasoning involved in this approach to *lex specialis* is also somewhat unsatisfactory.

As already noted, the fact that the characterizations, *lex specialis* and *generalis*, tend to be treated as if fully determinative of the applicable law, lends the categorical *lex specialis* reasoning a rather conclusory quality. The focus of argumentative discourse concerns the form of the legal norm in question. Once the appropriate assignation has been determined, the need for further argumentation or analysis is negated since the conclusion as to the applicability of a particular norm is thereby revealed. This can have the effect of concealing important aspects of the inherent legal reasoning – including articulation of those principles and purposes, mentioned earlier, which the concept of *lex specialis* comprises. The resultant lack of transparency is to the detriment of legal discourse. It tends to mask the underlying rationale for finding a body of law to be *specialis* and can obscure the extent to which importance was attached to factors such as the intent of state parties, the need for effectiveness, the normative weight attached to a body of rules and so forth. While it is quite appropriate and indeed necessary for these factors to be weighted carefully and differentially in a context sensitive manner, it is problematic for this analysis to be unarticulated and left to inference or speculation.

The categorical nature of the legal analysis also tends to oversimplify the factual and legal context in which the interpretative process takes place. The concepts of *specialis* or *generalis* are inevitably relative. They cannot be conceptualized or applied without reference to the legal context in which they are considered, nor

---

[25] Committee Against Torture, Conclusions and Recommendations of the Committee, United States of America, U.N. Doc. CAT/C/USA/CO/2 (July 25, 2006), paras 14–15.
[26] *Id.*
[27] A useful summary of case law relating to *lex specialis* is provided in the ILC Fragmentation Report, *supra* note 9, at 40–47.

can they be conceptualized in isolation from one another. Moreover, a conclusory approach also means that other nuanced factors relevant to the question of applicability are also afforded little space in this analysis, for example, the way in which even generalized frameworks, not tailored for a particular factual context, may, because of their more extensive usage, have areas of jurisprudence which speak to aspects of a particular factual scenario in a more sophisticated and relevant manner than the specially tailored law. This is especially so where the factor does not speak directly to the specificity or generality of a legal regime. In certain contexts, for example, it may be appropriate to attach less emphasis to the original intent of state parties. Partly as a consequence of this, conclusions can also be problematic. A categorical approach tends to abrogate the scope for more nuanced legal findings, most obviously through failing to allow space for an analysis which suggests the simultaneous, though not coterminous, applicability of both regimes in an appropriate context.

A further difficulty stemming from conclusory use of the *lex specialis* is that the reasoning imbibes a somewhat self-referential flavour. *Lex specialis* becomes both the legal justification and *de facto* consequence of the legal analysis. Justification is furnished through the strong, though unevaluated, connotations of "common sense," state intent and effectiveness which the concept is perceived to imply. Thus, the fact that a specialized framework exists is, in itself, seen as sufficient to provide legal justification for the consequences which flow from the classification. On the other hand, the synonymity between the status of *specialis* and the purported non-applicability of generalized rules, inhibits a thorough evaluation of underlying arguments whether based on voluntarism, effectiveness or normative superiority, and in so doing, completes the circularity of this kind of analysis.

A closely related difficulty is that of formalism. If the assignation of *lex specialis* status to a regime were to necessarily mean the non-applicability of a generalized regime then a sharp distinction must exist or be created between the two. However, one important aspect of reasoning which a conclusory approach often leaves hidden concerns the proper scope of the principle or rules which are purported to be *specialis*. Rarely do writings or opinions which appear to adopt this categorical approach articulate an explanation for the parameters of the framework which is purportedly *lex specialis*. For example, does a purportedly specialized legal regime encompass the treatment of POWs in international armed conflict, the treatment of all detainees in all armed conflict, or is it actually a more meta-legal question about the specialized character of humanitarian law more generally? What contextual factual and legal factors influence the setting of these parameters? Undoubtedly, sometimes these parameters will be clear, for example in narrow fields regulated by a single treaty.

However, this is not the case for areas such as international humanitarian law, regulated by a multiplicity of interwoven treaty standards and a range of fundamental customary norms. Indeed, an analysis which suggests that international humanitarian law as a whole should be regarded as *specialis* faces the challenge of how it can define parameters for humanitarian law without relying on arbitrary premises. For example, is it to be limited to the laws of war or are other areas of legal regulation, equally crucial to conflict, such as international refugee law (with its own strong human rights dimensions) to be included? If so, how can a sharp distinction between human rights and humanitarian law be sustained? On what basis is this multiplicity of interwoven rules to be untangled and distinguished?

In this context a conclusory approach to *lex specialis* is fundamentally problematic. In circumstances where two applicable but separate bodies of law seek to regulate a situation, one of which is specialized the other general, the two bodies of law need not be seen as radically distinct by mere function of the specialised nature of one. Instead these can be seen as existing along a spectrum of legal relevancy to the factual circumstances at issue. The various maxims of legal reasoning – and the underlying principles which give them impetus – help the interpreter to determine where along the spectrum a particular rule appears. *Lex specialis* cannot therefore properly be treated as a formalist technical rule which, upon heuristic application, reveals the applicable law. It is instead an interpretative construct, a maxim of legal reasoning which guides the interpreter towards those norms or bodies of law to be emphasised in the process of legal reasoning, those norms of most relevance. In a sense it encapsulates an argumentative framework for addressing questions of applicability and inapplicability.

4. Lex Specialis *as an Interpretative Process*

The crucial question is not then so much the assignation of the norm or regime as such, but instead a more engaged process of enquiry is necessary, utilizing those principles and precepts which underlie the concept. The legal analysis generated by less conclusory use of *lex specialis* allows for recognition of more nuanced factors in the process of interpretation and enables more carefully calibrated conclusions concerning applicability. This leaves space for less categorical outcomes while acknowledging that in some circumstances a degree of simultaneous applicability may exist. This is perhaps what the International Court of Justice had in mind in the Wall Advisory Opinion where it talked of the "three possible situations" as regards the relationship between humanitarian and human rights law – namely the applicability of one or other regime or in some circumstances the concurrent applicability of both.[28] Except for the most obvious cases a careful process of analysis is be necessary to determine which situation is pertinent, and what that means where there exists concurrent applicability.

---

[28] The Wall Advisory Opinion, *supra* note 4, para. 106.

From the discussion above the use of *lex specialis* in legal reasoning can be seen as being underpinned by two closely interrelated normative purposes. These are the idea of giving appropriate weight to the intention of those states which created the rule or rules in question, and the pursuit of relevancy and effectiveness in the application of legal norms in practical situations. The first of these is based on a normative voluntarist conception of procedural propriety, while the second is framed in consequentialist terms of substantive outcome.[29] These principles are not exhaustive of the kind of legal values which the concept of *lex specialis* articulates. Other principles could also be seen as encompassed by, or complementary to, these rather broad concepts, such as legal clarity, certainty, and predictability.

Nevertheless, the following analysis, without seeking to be definitive, will set out a range of factors that are meant as an elaboration of the principles which underlie *lex specialis* analysis with a specific view to casting further light on how the maxim acts as a bridge between human rights and the laws of war. The factors which will be emphasised, therefore, are those most pertinent to the application of human rights standards during an armed conflict. These are not meant as hard doctrinal rules or criteria but rather as compass points to assist in thinking about what it means to employ *lex specialis* in legal reasoning. The focus will be on the third of the situations identified by the court – "some rights... may be matters for both these branches of law." The key issue is how an interpretative process can determine whether a given right is a matter for both humanitarian and human rights law, and if so, how this miscegenetic relationship can be accommodated.

5. *Consentualism and Teleology in the Interpretative Process*

In many situations reference to state intent will occupy a crucial place in interpretation. Typically, where circumstances develop resulting in the emergence of new concerns, particularized rules, legal machinery and enforcement mechanisms are a standard response of states to address such challenges, in the process supplanting broad traditional customary principles. Where states create such a legal framework to derogate from customary *jus dispositivum*, the voluntary consent of states means that interpretation is likely to be relatively straightforward – the dispositive customary law can be set aside in favour of legal mechanisms and rules set out in *jus scriptum*.[30] The ICJ has taken the opportunity on several occasions

---

[29] See Martti Koskenniemi, From Apology to Utopia: The Structure of International Legal Argument 309 (2005).

[30] Hugh Thirlway expresses the matter thus: "It is universally accepted that – consideration of *jus cogens* apart – a treaty as *lex specialis* is law between the parties to it in derogation of the general customary law which would otherwise have governed their relations." Hugh Thirlway, *The Law and Procedure of the International Court of Justice*, 60 BYIL 147 (1989). *See further* Military and

to affirm the dispositive nature of most customary law (leaving aside the question of peremptory norms).[31] Thus state intent habitually occupies a primary role in interpretative reasoning leading to an uncontroversial outcome.

On the other hand, there are also circumstances where it is appropriate for less emphasis to be attached to state intent in the interpretative process, situations where state intent is not an overriding or strong consideration. This is an important consideration in relation to human rights treaties, the inherent nature of which justifies a more nuanced approach in addressing the intent of states parties.

In its Namibia advisory opinion the ICJ observed that "an international instrument must be interpreted and applied within the overall framework of the juridical system in force at the time of the interpretation."[32] On its face this statement, when taken with the obligation to interpret a treaty in light of its context, object, and purpose, seems like a rather unremarkable elaboration of principles enshrined in Article 31 VCLT. However, cumulatively recognition of these principles has a particular significance for the interpretation and application of international human rights norms. For interpretative purposes, the nature of international human rights treaties make them rather unlike other forms of legal instrument which regulate the conduct of states. Most treaties are based on the twin notions of national interest and reciprocity. They are negotiated and incarnated as a bundle of reciprocal rights and obligations which states enter into in pursuit of a vision of their own national and strategic interests.

For states entering into international agreements creating legal interests and burdens in this manner it is crucial for parties to have a clear sense of the situations in which they can expect to receive the benefits or endure the burdens which a treaty affords. Ambiguity in the development and application of these kinds of treaty standards would be a strong disincentive against utilizing such mechanisms in pursuit of national interest. Less altruistic means of pursuing national goals would, no doubt, acquire more prominence were this to be the case. In normative terms too, such dynamic processes of legal development – perhaps through teleological judicial pursuit of wider instrumental goals – would be difficult to justify given the nature of these conventions and the expectations of parties to them. If parties to an agreement meant it to function in a specialized manner attenuating the application of dispositive customary law, perhaps with new institutional enforcement

---

Paramilitary Activities in and against Nicaragua (Nicaragua v. United States of America), Merits (June 27, 1986) 1986 ICJ Rep. 14, para. 274.

[31] North Sea Continental Shelf Cases, *supra* note 11, para. 72; Case concerning the Continental Shelf (Tunisia v. Libyan Arab Jamahiriya), Judgment (Feb. 24, 1982), 1982 ICJ Rep. 3, para. 24

[32] Legal Consequences for States of the Continued Presence of South Africa in Namibia (South West Africa) notwithstanding Security Council Resolution, Advisory Opinion (June 21, 1971), 1971 ICJ Rep. 276, para. 31.

mechanisms, then the reciprocal and contractual nature of that agreement provides a strong imperative for the displacement of other legal regimes.

Some writers have sought to apply this framework to human rights treaties. However, this approach appears to overlook important, if subtle, differences in the nature of adjudication involved.[33] For human rights treaties, and perhaps other constitutive international instruments such as the Charter of the U.N., this sense of an agreement representing the *realpolitik* strategic pursuit of a national agenda is a less apposite framework of analysis. Other factors are at play. The tripartite relationship which states enter into when they ratify a human rights treaty fundamentally alters the nature of the legal relationship created, and thereby how such agreements must be interpreted. Human rights treaties do not primarily create substantive rights or legal benefits for states themselves, rather these rights flow to third parties, and are, primarily enforceable by such parties, almost entirely irrespective of the individual's prior personal conduct.

This was expressed by the ECHR at an early stage of its development in the seminal case of *Austria* v. *Italy*.

> [T]he obligations undertaken by the High Contracting Parties in the European Convention are essentially of an objective character being designed rather to protect the fundamental rights of individual human beings from infringement by any of the High Contracting Parties than to create subjective and reciprocal rights for the High Contracting Parties themselves.[34]

Thus the contractual sense in which performance by one party, or the lack thereof, alters the nature of the legal rights and obligations on another party is absent from human rights treaties, not least, of course, because those who receive benefits under these instruments are not party to them. In the consentualist sense too the nature of states' expectations in respect of human rights instruments are quite different from other forms of treaties. As the ECHR observed in *Austria* v. *Italy* human rights treaties are expressly entered into in pursuit of wider aspirations than connoted by the idea of strategic national interest, or reciprocal burdens and benefits. They are incarnations which are expressly created to affirm and pursue particular teleological goals. Purposive or teleological interpretation is a quotidian feature of human rights interpretation and adjudication. This is a view which has been quite expressly enunciated in the judicial pronouncements of human rights institutions. The ECHR, for example, has stated that:

---

[33] Laurence Helfer for example in writing about adjudication before the ECHR states that human rights tribunals "risk illegitimacy whenever they depart from an interpretation based on the intent of the original drafters." *See* Laurence Helfer, *Consensus, Coherence and the European Convention on Human Rights*, 26 Cornell Int'l L.J. 135 (1993).

[34] Austria v. Italy (Jan. 11, 1961), YBECHR Vol. 4, p. 116.

any interpretation of the rights and freedoms guaranteed has to be consistent with the general spirit of the Convention, an instrument designed to maintain and promote the ideals and values of a democratic society.[35]

In substantive terms this leads to human rights norms being treated not as static bodies of reciprocal legal obligations, but instead as "autonomous concepts"[36] subject to a "dynamic and evolutive"[37] interpretative approach, which seeks to render the rights "practical and effective, not theoretical and illusory."[38] A human rights convention is regarded as forming a "living instrument."[39] These aspects of the human rights discourse have been affirmed on numerous occasions in the judicial determinations of a variety of human rights institutions.

The function of human rights treaties is therefore a further reason why it would be inappropriate to attach overriding significance to a narrow conception of state intent in the interpretative process. Both in practical and theoretical terms such intent could not consistently function as if substantively determinative. In practical terms, many separate conflicting intents will be identifiable from the *travaux*. It is quite likely that even within the pronouncements of an individual state party, a certain cognitive dissonance will even have been manifested during the protracted and complex negotiations which led to the agreement under scrutiny. Thus, in practical terms the issue is not one of attenuating intent, but rather being realistic about where such intent can be said to exist at all. If "intent" is simply taken in the sense of negotiated outcome, then the text of the instrument itself is the only incarnation that can properly be characterized in this way. It is uncontroversial that there must be a strong sense of fidelity to the terms of an instrument in the articulation of rights based on its articles. Equally, this does not equate to mandating a purely textual approach to the interpretation of the scope of human rights

---

[35] Kjeldsen, Busk Madsen and Pedersen v. Denmark (Merits) (Dec. 7, 1976) Series A, No. 23, p. 27, para. 53.

[36] Engel and Others v. Netherlands (Merits) (June 8, 1976) Series A, No. 22 p. 34; Soering v. United Kingdom (July 7, 1989), Series A, No. 161, para. 87.

[37] In respect of Inter-American Court of Human Rights jurisprudence see, *inter alia*, Interpretation of the American Declaration of the Rights and Duties of Man within the Framework of the Article 64 of the American Convention on Human Rights, Advisory Opinion OC-10/89 (July 14, 1989) Series A, No. 10, para. 43; The Right to Information on Consular Assistance in the Framework of the Guarantees of the Due Process of Law, Advisory Opinion OC-16/99, (Oct. 1, 1999) Series A, No. 16, para. 144; *see also* the Concurring Opinion of Judge Cançado Trindade para. 3. For the ECHR see, *inter alia*, Stafford v. the United Kingdom (Merits) [GC] (May 28, 2002), ECHR 2002-IV, para. 68, and Christine Goodwin v. the United Kingdom (Merits) [GC], (July 11, 2002), ECHR 2002-VI, para. 74,.

[38] Artico v. Italy (Merits) (May 13, 1980), Series A, No. 37, at 16; *See also* Soering v. United Kingdom (Merits), *supra* note 36, para. 87.

[39] Tyrer v. United Kingdom (April 25, 1978) (Merits) Series A, No. 26, para. 31.

obligations. Any claim to do so would be entirely illusory in view of the open-textured language of human rights standards.

The idea of mapping approaches to intent from other treaties onto human rights instruments is also problematic at a more normative level. Like most legal norms human rights treaties provide standards against which actions or conduct can be assessed. However, human rights instruments also provide a prism through which other forms of law can be evaluated. This is particularly significant because the evaluative context in which human rights treaties operate is constantly evolving – societal change, social, technological, cultural, and political change are but a few aspects of this. The changing nature and conception of the state itself, its function, and role is another part of this.

This has, of course, many important consequences. To function properly as an evaluative instrument a necessary quality of human rights treaties is the ability to respond to continuously developing processes of evolution and change in a calibrated and flexible manner. Contextual circumstances and law which were not, and could not, have been envisaged at the time such instruments were agreed still fall for determination or evaluation under them. From a consentualist perspective this could not be anything other than in accord with the expectations of states parties.[40] Thus an interpretative process which places less emphasis on the perceptions or preconceptions of state parties at the time the treaty was negotiated does not only not emanate from a non-consentualist vision of international law, but such techniques are actually necessitated by the very nature of the treaties themselves, and the distinctive legal context created by the function, purpose, and expectation attaching thereto.

In terms of *lex specialis* therefore, the dynamic and autonomous organic development of human rights norms, the way in which such norms are interpreted in a manner which seeks to render the rights substantively meaningful, and the fundamental nature of the treaties themselves all indicate that state intent, at least in a narrow formalist sense, cannot be used as an overarching criterion through which the parameters of applicability of human rights treaties are set. In a wider sense though the underlying general intent of such treaties as manifested in their broader scheme and purpose does inform such interpretation, through recognition of the collective sense in which they affirm and seek to promote a shared vision of certain fundamental values. In this more teleological sense it is quite appropriate that cognisance of the underlying instrumental ambitions of the legal architects informs the interpretative construction of the edifice. This is precisely what state parties would expect when reaching an agreement of this sort.

---

[40] George Letsas, *The Truth in Autonomous Concepts: How to Interpret the ECHR*, 15 Eur. J. Int'l L. 279 (2004).

6. *Efficacy and Relevancy in the Interpretative Process*

As noted earlier the other concept which buttresses *lex specialis* is that of appositeness, encompassing notions of effectiveness and relevancy. Even early classical writers like Grotius were of the view that preference should be given to special provisions as they "most clearly approach the subject at hand" and are "normally more effective."[41] Where the legal context places less emphasis on intent as an aspect of interpretative enquiry these concepts tend to acquire a more pressing role in interpretative reasoning.

Thus, it is clear that often *lex specialis* tends to be characterized as being almost synonymous with clarity, efficacy, and relevancy. Generalis norms do not tend to be seen in this light. Judicial pronouncements often reflect this kind of proposition. In *Abella* v. *Argentina* the Inter-American Court of Human Rights stated that:

> the provisions of conventional and customary humanitarian law generally afford victims of armed conflicts greater or more specific protections than do the more generally phrased guarantees in the American Convention and other human rights instruments.[42]

In most circumstances this reasoning is not controversial. The processes of customary law formation are almost invariably slow, and recent trends towards rapid economic, social or environmental change mean that it is necessary to supplement basic standards with more tailored regimes.

Nevertheless, there is an inherent danger of oversimplification in this approach. Grotius implicitly acknowledges this in the passage cited above with his careful avoidance of adjectival superlatives in characterizing the significance of effectiveness. International law is not composed of layers of crude generalized norms interspersed with narrowly tailored specific regimes.[43] Often those bodies of rules which are of general application have a quite sophisticated and nuanced *corpus* of principles, capable of being calibrated to a range of different circumstances. Indeed, often this occurs precisely because of their general applicability, the wider range of varied circumstances which they encounter, and the incremental growth in refinement which this precipitates.

A further reason why specificity, in the sense of a large body of specially designed complex rules, cannot always be equated with effectiveness is because often effectiveness and relevance are a function of adaptability and evolution. In a real sense

---

[41] Grotius, *supra* note 6.
[42] Juan Carlos Abella v. Argentina (Merits) (1997) Inter-Am CHR Case 11.137, Report No. 55/97, OEA/Ser.L/V/II.95 Doc. 7 rev. para. 159.
[43] *See generally* David Koller, *The Moral Imperative: Towards a Human Rights Based Laws of War*, 46 Harv. J. Int'l Law 232 (2005).

therefore, *lex specialis* is not simply a question of law – how legally sophisticated are a set of rules? It is also a question of fact – how sophisticated and developed are the rules relative to the factual context in which they are being applied? Factual contexts change. The particularized fact patterns which required regulation by specialized norms will not themselves remain static. As a result those bodies of law which are specifically designed, or intended to address a specific question may need to be supplemented by other norms of a more flexible and broader kind to be capable of addressing a particular tension or problem adequately.

In semantic terms one could arguably consider both sets of principles to be *lex specialis* in these situations or simply as differentially but concurrently applicable. The terminology is less important than the fact of having given such considerations appropriate weight in the interpretative process. This leads to a final point concerning the relationship between *lex specialis*, effectiveness, and the dynamic factual and legal context. This is the question of how to determine the range of principles to be treated as *specialis* or *generalis* in the interpretative process.

In the critique of the categorical approach it will be recalled that proceeding by arbitrary typological distinctions was unsatisfactory. The first point which should be made in this respect is that where *lex specialis* is viewed less as a technical device than as an interpretative process this issue becomes less crucial. The non-binary approach to *specialis* and *generalis* means that this assignation is not the ultimate goal nor the determinative factor in legal reasoning. The question is therefore more simply what norms are relevant in the interpretative process in determining applicability? The answer to this is dependant not so much on the rules themselves, their structure, and content, but rather the particular factual context at issue. What rules are relevant to this factual context in terms of shedding light on arguments concerning intent, relevance, effectiveness and so forth?

7. Conclusion

In a very real sense then human rights and humanitarian law cohabit the same factual space during armed conflict. This article has sought to highlight some important aspects of the complex and nuanced interrelationship between these two bodies of law, focusing on *lex specialis* as the central bridge between them. Although the application of *lex specialis* can, at times, provide a relatively straightforward means of resolving legal conflict, often the superficial simplicity of the concept conceals its normative and practical complexity. It is true, to the point of tautology, to state that the laws of war are appropriately applied *lex specialis* in the situations where they are applicable. However, conclusory forms of *lex specialis* would see this fact, in itself, as being dispositive of questions of applicability and as dispensing with the need for further interpretation and argumentation. This may be a convenient approach to legal analysis but it is not a thorough one.

Inevitably, processes and methods of interpretation speak to those interests and values which we regard as important in the legal order. The very act of interpretation is also an implicit articulation of the significance of certain concepts and their proper place in the legal order. The two interests which *lex specialis* most obviously articulates are voluntarism and efficacy. When *lex specialis* as a legal concept is dissected it becomes readily apparent that the binary idea of an applicable category of *specialis* against an inapplicable category of *generalis* cannot be justified in terms of those normative principles which underpin the very concept itself. Seeing *lex specialis* as a form of reasoning in an interpretative process does not detach or condense all the layers of complexity which cleave to the concept, nor does it remove interpretation from those values and principles which are articulated. It simply unpacks the concept and identifies relevant considerations in a transparent manner. Ultimately, this sees the interpretative maxim as being a form of legal argumentation, as "art not science," with all of the strengths or fallibilities which that may entail.[44]

In short, the strength of a legal conclusion rests simply on the strength of argumentation inherent in the legal reasoning. Whether the *lex specialis* status of a norm actually has the effect of displacement, primacy of some other consequence cannot simply be determined simply by a conclusion as to the status of that norm – it depends on the legal reasoning which arrives at that outcome. In this sense therefore applicability is a function of process not conclusion.

---

[44] Myres McDougal, Harold Lasswell & James Miller, The Interpretation of Agreements and World Public Order: Principles of Content and Procedure 39–45 (1967); Richard Falk, The Status of Law in International Society (1970).

Part B
Issues of Applicability

Chapter IV

Legal Reasoning and the Applicability of International Human Rights Standards During Military Occupation

*Conor McCarthy**

1. Introduction

The transformation in the law of military occupation from the relatively obscure position it has until recently occupied in international legal scholarship, to one of its most topical and widely discussed areas has been as rapid as it is unsurprising. The invasion and subsequent occupation of Iraq in 2003, the surge in violence in the Middle East associated with the Second Intifada in 2000, and to a lesser extent the controversy surrounding the International Court of Justice's advisory opinion in the *Wall* case[1] have, combined with a range of other factors, served to propel this area of legal discourse to an elevated level of importance.

In addition to international humanitarian law a range of other international legal regimes speak to issues which arise during military occupation. Human rights issues play an important, if at times overshadowed, role in this.[2] International refugee law and international criminal law also provide relevant standards. In many ways, military occupation scenarios form a factual crucible for various intersecting legal regimes because of the nature and number of interests in tension or conflict. Inevitably these various socio-political tensions are regulated at the international level by a variety of legal regimes, with different innate systemic and doctrinal approaches to such issues. The relationship which is the focus of this paper is that of international human rights standards which vertically regulate the relationship between a state and private individuals or groups, and international humanitarian

---

* Jesus College, Cambridge.
[1] Legal Consequences of the Construction of a Wall in the Occupied Palestinian Territory, Advisory Opinion, (July 9, 2004), 2004 I.C.J. Rep. 131 [hereinafter The Wall Advisory Opinion].
[2] *See generally* John Dugard, *Enforcement of Human Rights in the West Bank and the Gaza Strip*, in International Law and the Administration of International Territories 461 (Emma Playfair ed. 1992).

law which, at least in orthodox terms, horizontally regulates the relationship between groups or individuals acting on behalf of states.[3]

The orientation of these regimes is not without analytical significance. In many ways it maps the nature of the practical tensions which arise during a foreign military intervention. In broad terms there are two kinds of conflicted relationship which it has proved necessary for law to address. The first is the horizontal interstate relationship between two sovereign entities – the rights of one and the obligations of the other. Both conventional and customary international humanitarian law, in particular the Hague Regulations 1907, are tailored quite directly to regulating the legal stresses inherent in this relationship.

On the other hand, a concurrent legal dynamic concerns the relationship between the population of the occupied territory and the state apparatus of the foreign occupying power. While the population of the occupied territory are likely not to feel any sense of loyalty or fidelity to the occupying power, and in fact, a strong sentiment of resentment may rapidly develop, a certain degree of cooperation is inevitably necessary for even a basic level of civil administration and public order.[4] International human rights norms have extensive experience of addressing these kinds of issues, containing a rich supply of jurisprudence regulating important questions such as the tension between the interests of the individual and measures taken in pursuit of public order. Nevertheless, the presence of two legal regimes speaking to the same issues, but with a rather different orientation means that tension is inevitable. A fundamental question is therefore how these relationships can be reconciled.

Lex specialis is one of the central concepts which international legal reasoning uses to bridge these differences. The presence of a wide range of intersecting and potentially applicable legal regimes during military occupation results in a particularly crucial role for *lex specialis* in the analysis of the legal rules and principles applicable to military occupation. The various distinctive legal aspects of the law of military

---

[3] For a variety of reasons, including the influence of international criminal law this paradigm has shifted somewhat. In general terms, international criminal law transects these conventional relationships through imposing individual criminal responsibility for internationally unlawful criminal conduct irrespective of whether the act was ostensibly committed on behalf of a state. Further indication of this trend can be seen in Meron's contention that a process of "humanizing" humanitarian law has occurred in recent years. Theodor Meron, *The Humanization of Humanitarian Law*, 94 Am. J. Int'l L. 239 (2000) and also *War Crimes Law Come of Age*, 92 Am. J. Int'l L. 262 (1998). For example, in discussing the significance of the inclusion of crimes against humanity and crimes derived from Common Article 3 in the ICC Statute Meron points out that this "connotes a certain blurring of international humanitarian law with international human rights law and thus an incremental criminalization of serious violations of human rights," Meron, *The Humanization of Humanitarian Law, id.* at 468.

[4] On the legal problems associated with this tension see, Major Richard Baxter, *The Duty of Obedience to a Belligerent Occupant*, 27 Brit. Y.B. Int'l L. 235 (1950).

occupation also play into this interpretative process. The following discussion will therefore seek to provide an overview of this process, addressing the applicability of human rights standards in the context of military occupation.

2. Interpretative Reasoning and the Law of Military Occupation

Unlike many other aspects of the laws of war, the applicability of a military occupation regime is not premised on the notion of an armed conflict as such. The standard for applicability of the law of military occupation is that territory "is considered occupied when it is actually placed under the authority of the hostile army."[5] It is not therefore required that an armed conflict *per se* is occurring between two states for the law of military occupation to be applicable. Indeed, it is quite possible that there may be no hostilities occurring in the occupied territory. Certainly, in practice, a military occupation will invariably result from an armed intervention.[6] This is not, however, to say that an "armed conflict" will necessarily last for the duration of the military occupation for the purposes of the laws of war. Article 6 GC IV extends the application of certain provisions well beyond the general close of military operations.[7] Particularly in a prolonged occupation, it is quite possible for armed resistance to subside, or subside during certain periods.[8] Thus the relative applicability of the law of military occupation and the general laws of war are not inevitably legally coterminous.

In these circumstances a central tenet in interpretative reasoning underpinning a *generalis/specialis* distinction between human rights and humanitarian law – the idea that only the specialized regime is adequately tailored to the particularized

---

[5] The article also goes on to state that "[t]he occupation extends only to the territory where such authority has been established and can be exercised." Article 42, Hague Convention IV (1907): Respecting the Laws and Customs of War on Land, with annexed Regulations [hereinafter HR].

[6] The meaning attributed to "armed conflict" is of course a matter of scholarly debate. (See Leslie Green, The Contemporary Law of Armed Conflict 70 (2nd ed. 2000) However, the ICRC commentary to the Common Article 2 of the Geneva Conventions 1949 states that: "Any difference arising between two states and leading to the intervention of armed forces is an armed conflict within the meaning of article 2 even if one of the parties denies the existence of a state of war." Jean Pictet (ed.), Commentary I Geneva Convention 32 (1952).

[7] Geneva Convention Relative to the Protection of Civilian Persons in Time of War, Aug. 12, 1949, 75 U.N.T.S. 287 [hereinafter GC IV].

[8] For a detailed examination of the various problems in a military occupation which extends over long periods of time *see* generally, Adam Roberts, *Prolonged Military Occupation: The Israeli Occupied Territories Since 1967*, 84 Am. J. Int'l L. 44 (1990).

circumstances at hand – is much less well founded.[9] Where military occupation exists in the absence of a significant armed conflict the nature of the operations involved – maintaining security, public order and law enforcement – is rather akin to the kind of challenges which pertain during international territorial administrations. The phenomenon of territorial administration is a subject which has received considerable academic attention in recent years.[10] Traditionally it has been treated as analytically separate from military occupation even if showing a "strong family resemblance."[11] During international territorial administrations, the strong tendency has been for human rights to be regarded as paramount, while the primacy of international humanitarian law has largely been limited to military occupations by states in circumstances where their actions have been unauthorized or unacknowledged by the Security Council.

International human rights standards have a long history of being applied in territorial administrations regulating the inevitable tensions between the indigenous population and the outside authority.[12] This approach can be seen clearly in the Report of the Panel on U.N. Peace Operations.[13] Human rights standards have provided a principled framework through which areas as diverse as law and order,

---

[9] Emmerich de Vattel expressed the point thus:
> Of two laws or two conventions, we ought (all other circumstances being equal) to prefer the one which is less general and which approaches nearer the point in question: because special matter admits of fewer exceptions than that which is general; it is enjoined with greater precision and appears to have been more pointedly intended.

Emerich De Vattel, Law of Nations, § 316, 5th Rule (1758). For a more detailed analysis of the nature of *lex specialis* reasoning and the legal principles which it articulates, see Chapter III, Conor McCarthy, Legal Conclusion or Interpretative Process? Lex Specialis and the Applicability of International Human Rights Standards.

[10] At a broader level, the degree of developing law and practice in the post-conflict arena has led some to argue that a putative tripartite structure for the regulation of armed conflict in international law is developing – the two traditional strands (*jus ad bellum* and *jus in bello*) being supplemented by a third – *jus post-bellum*. See Christine Bell, *Peace Agreements: Their Nature and Legal Status*, 100 Am. J. Int'l L. 373 (2006); Carsten Stahn, *Jus ad bellum', jus in bello'… 'jus post bellum'?: Rethinking the Conception of the Law of Armed Force*, 17 Eur. J. Int'l L. 943 (2006); Brian Orend, *Jus Post Bellum*, 31 Journal of Social Philosophy 117 (2000).

[11] Richard Caplan, International Governance of War Torn Territories: Rule and Reconstruction 3 (2005) [hereinafter Caplan].

[12] The Brahimi Report (U.N. General Assembly and Security Council, Report of the Panel on U.N. Peace Operations, U.N. Doc. A/55/305–S/2000/809 (Aug. 21, 2000) (prepared by Lakhdar Brahimi) [hereinafter Brahimi Report]) contains extensive discussion about the implications of international human rights standards on such operations. The academic literature on territorial administrations also contains a similarly voluminous discussion. See, inter alia, Simon Chesterman, You, The People: The United Nations, Transitional Administration and State-Building (2004) and Caplan *supra* note 11.

[13] Although the Brahimi Report contained extensive detailed discussion of the role of human rights standards in such operations, international humanitarian law was only dealt with in passing.

the control of law enforcement powers, problems concerning discriminatory practices or the re-establishment of mechanisms for the administration of justice can be addressed.[14] In Kosovo and East Timor, UNMIK and UNTAET[15] both faced the problem of resuscitating the municipal legal systems and respecting local law while ensuring that the application of these laws did not perpetuate existing problems or antagonize local sensibilities. In seeking to reconcile these difficulties both missions decided that the applicable law during the respective international administrations of these territories would remain domestic legal norms but only insofar as they were compatible with internationally recognized human rights standards.[16]

Of course, this is not to suggest that there have not been controversies in the scope and nature of the application of human rights principles in such contexts. Nevertheless, these difficulties have not been seen as justification for the *a priori* exclusion of their applicability, rather the application and cognisance of human rights standards has often made an important contribution to addressing practical problems.

The similarity between these two kinds of legal institutions demonstrates that much of the scepticism about the instrumental viability of applying human rights standards to a military occupation is unfounded.[17] This also has implications for applicability reasoning based on a *specialis* premise of relevancy and appositeness in relation to the law of military occupation. The fact that human rights standards are considered instrumentally effective and appropriate during territorial administrations undermines an argumentative approach to military occupations which frames the law of military occupation as narrowly tailored and effective *specialis* against international human rights standards as unrefined and inapposite *generalis*.

Moreover, the report did not at any stage address the law of military occupation nor the extent to which it may be relevant in U.N. peace operations.

[14] Caplan, *supra* note 11, at 64–65.

[15] The full titles for these administrations are respectively the United Nations Interim Administration Mission in Kosovo and United Nations Transitional Administration Mission in East Timor.

[16] UNMIK Reg. No. 1999/1, On the Authority of the Interim Administration in Kosovo (July 25, 1999), and UNTAET Reg. No. 1999/1, On the Authority of the Transitional Administration in East Timor (Nov. 27, 1999). The applicable law was a particularly controversial question in Kosovo with ethnic Albanians strongly objecting to Yugoslav laws remaining applicable notwithstanding the necessary compliance with international human rights standards. Later in 1999 UNMIK decided that the applicable law would in fact be the law in force before the revocation of Kosovo's autonomy on March 22, 1989 (*see* UNMIK Reg. No. 1999/24).

[17] Indeed it is arguable that there is little justification in principled legal terms for distinguishing international territorial administrations from military occupations, except in so far as mandated by Security Council resolutions. Distinguishing such operations on the basis of the consent of the host state is often rather fictive. *See further* Steven Ratner, *Foreign Occupation and International Territorial Administration: The Challenges of Convergence*, 16 Eur. J. Int'l L. 695 (2005).

In circumstances of military occupation the conflict is often not straightforwardly between *generalis* norms, which are crude and unmeasured and *specialis* humanitarian law which is tailored and effective. In many contexts during a military occupation human rights standards with their extensive jurisprudence and experience in addressing specific kinds of legal controversy provide much more detailed, elaborate and sophisticated guidance for interactions between state agencies and the civilian population, and the conflicting interests therein, than those set out in the relevant rules of humanitarian law.

Before addressing certain specific situations where international human rights standards could supplement the law of military occupation an important preliminary question concerns the status of such international norms for the occupying power.

The seminal provision in this respect is Article 43 of the Hague Regulations which obliges the Occupying Power to respect "unless absolutely prevented the laws in force in the country."[18] At first glance this appears something of a double-edged sword. The Occupying Power is itself bound to respect human rights obligations "in force" in the country, on the other hand it also appears bound to respect and enforce domestic laws in the country which may run fundamentally counter to particular international human rights standards – for example, discriminatory rules about the ethnicity of individuals who can hold public office.

Dealing with the latter point first, there is a strong argument that in circumstances where certain laws in force in an occupied territory run fundamentally counter to obligations in international human rights law – whether in the form of customarily binding rules on both states or rules conventionally binding on either – the occupying power would for the purposes of the Hague Regulations be "absolutely prevented" from respecting such norms by operation of law.[19] The ordinary meaning of the term offers no indication that the concept "absolutely prevented" must be limited to circumstances of practical factual and not legal imperatives. The same argument could be made in relation to the duty to respect penal provisions under Article 64 GC IV.

There is a strong argument that international human rights obligations – whether customary or conventional – binding upon the state whose territory is occupied

---

[18] Only the French text is actually authoritative. It reads as follows:
L'autorité du pouvoir ayant passé de fait entre les mains de l'occupant, celui-ci prendra toutes les mesures qui dépendent de lui en vue de rétablir et d'assurer, autant qu'il est possible, l'ordre et la vie public, sauf empêchement absolu, les lois en vigueur dans le pays.
Article 43 HR, *supra* note 7. *See also* Article 64 of Geneva Convention IV which deals with respecting penal laws in force.

[19] *See* Marco Sassoli, *Legislation and Maintenance of Public Order and Civil Life by Occupying Powers*, 16 Eur. J. Int'l L. 661, 676 (2005).

should be considered laws "in force" for the purposes of Article 44 HR. It would be a rather anomalous position were international law to permit human rights standards, applicable against the sovereign government of a state, to be rendered inapplicable in the territory once occupied, removing the population from its protection, simply by virtue of the international, rather than municipal, origin of those obligations. If the population of the occupied territory's own government is legally obliged to respect certain standards of conduct in relation to them, then there seems no reason to suppose that the occupying power would not, by the same token, be similarly obliged to respect such standards under Article 43 in its treatment of the population of the occupied territory. The creation of a sharp dichotomy between international and domestic legal obligations based on their legal origin, irrespective their similarly obligatory quality, would be unsustainable.

3. Specialized Human Rights Standards

There are several fields where human rights standards may offer particularly tailored and specialized guidance in the context of military occupations. A good example of this is in the field of education. Under Article 50 GC IV the occupying power is under an obligation to "cooperate with the national and local authorities, to facilitate the proper working of all institutions devoted to the care and education of children." However, little more detailed guidance than this is stipulated. A range of issues concerning the nature and substance of educational provision may arise during an occupation which are not addressed by the laws of military occupation. One example of this is the use of ideology in the course of education. This is a problem common to areas emerging from conflict. Richard Caplan notes that in Eastern Slavonia, Croatia the teaching of recent history (1989–1997) was a hugely contentious issue. This aspect of children's education was immersed in such a high degree of controversy that the United Nations had to negotiate a five-year moratorium with the government preventing schools from covering this subject matter in the Danube region.[20]

While the law of military occupation does not address these tensions in great detail international human rights jurisprudence has some relevant and relatively sophisticated principles. These principles serve as much as waymarks to good practice as much as constraints on state behaviour. The Committee on Economic, Social and Cultural Rights (CESCR) has authoritatively interpreted the relevant provisions of the International Covenant on Economic Social and Cultural Rights

---

[20] Caplan, supra *note* 11, at 109.

and its provisions relevant to these concerns. Article 13(3) of the Covenant provides for liberty of educational choice.[21]

In General Comment 13 the CESCR interpreted Article 13(3) as permitting "public school instruction in subjects such as the general history of religions and ethics if it is given in an unbiased and objective way, respectful of the freedoms of opinion, conscience and expression."[22] The ECHR has also addressed these questions directly in the case of *Kjeldsen* v. *Denmark* setting out some very clear principles on permissible forms of public education. In the course of a fairly extensive judgment the court stated:

> the State, in fulfilling the functions assumed by it in regard to education and teaching, must take care that information or knowledge included in the curriculum is conveyed in an objective, critical and pluralistic manner. The State is forbidden to pursue an aim of indoctrination that might be considered as not respecting parents' religious and philosophical convictions. That is the limit that must not be exceeded.[23]

General Comment 11 concerns states obligations in respect of primary education. This includes the creation of a plan of action where the state has been unable to secure compulsory primary education free of charge for all. Given the general principle that sovereignty does not pass to the occupier and the specific obligation in the Hague Regulations to respect the laws in force in the occupied territory, where such a plan of action exists this should form the basis for educational provision during the occupation.[24]

Certain compulsory elements of this plan of action are worthy of note. The first is that the provision of primary education for every child is a compulsory not discretionary obligation – albeit within the confines of progressive realization. The Committee elaborates upon this criterion in the following manner. Neither parents guardians nor the state is entitled to treat access to primary education as optional.[25] In addition to the obligatory nature of primary educational provision the Committee intimates "that the education offered must be adequate in quality,

---

[21] The precise wording of Article 13(3) Covenant is as follows:
States Parties to the present Covenant undertake to have respect for the liberty of parents and, when applicable, legal guardians to choose for their children schools, other than those established by the public authorities, which conform to such minimum educational standards as may be laid down or approved by the State and to ensure the religious and moral education of their children in conformity with their own convictions.
[hereinafter ICESCR].

[22] CESCR General Comment 13, U.N. Doc. E/C.12/1999/10 (Dec. 8, 1999), para. 28.

[23] Kjeldsen v. Denmark, (Merits) (1976) Series A, No. 23, p. 27, para. 53.

[24] *Supra* note 19. It seems unsustainable to create a distinction between pre-existing policies pertaining in the occupied territory and the laws existing in the territory since the later is created by and implemented through a range of legal and legislative measures.

[25] *Id.* para. 6.

relevant to the child and must promote the realization of the child's other rights."[26] Although the reference to quality is somewhat elliptical it can probably be surmised that at the very least the education must conform to the aims and objectives of education as interpreted in General Comment 13.

First, these are said to reflect the fundamental purposes and principles of the United Nations as reflected Articles 1 and 2 of the Charter. Further, they are said to entail that education "be directed to the human personality's sense of dignity, it shall enable all persons to participate effectively in a free society, and it shall promote understanding among all ethnic groups, as well as nations and racial and religious groups."[27] The most fundamental objective of education under the covenant is said to be that it is "directed to the full development of the human personality."[28]

Although these standards are open textured and broadly framed they do provide further strong indication that failure to provide educational opportunities, or discrimination in access to those opportunities or in the substantive provision of education services would be impermissible under the Covenant. Particularly in a prolonged occupation – and irrespective of issues of extraterritorial applicability – taken together these obligations suggest that failure to meet these various requirements would be in violation of Article 43 HR in respect of territories where the Covenant was in force. In this way the Covenant can be seen as providing further elaboration on educational obligations incumbent upon the occupying power by virtue of Article 50 GC IV.

A further area in which international human rights law helps provide more specialized and elaborate principles to guide the conduct of an occupying power is in respect of obligations concerning adequate access to and provision of food.[29] Armed conflict interferes with the right to food at each stage of the nutrition cycle. Article 55 GC IV provides that "to the fullest extent of the means available to it, the occupying power has the duty of ensuring the food and medical supplies of the population...."[30] There is little further elaboration of the nature and quality of this broad imperative, or how the "extent of the means available to it" is to be assessed. Once again, there is a fairly developed body of international human rights principles and instruments relevant to these questions.

Article 11(1) ICESCR recognizes the right to an adequate standard of living including adequate food.[31] In General Comment 12 the CESCR provides further

---

[26] *Id.*
[27] *Supra* note 23, General Comment 13, para. 4. Internal quotation marks omitted.
[28] *Id.*
[29] *See generally* Jelena Pejic, *The Right to Food in Situations of Armed Conflict: The Legal Framework*, 83 Int'l Rev. Red Cross 1097 (2001).
[30] Where the resources of the occupied territory are inadequate the occupying power is obliged to bring in the necessary supplies. Article 55 GC IV.
[31] The status of the right to food in respect of customary international law is uncertain. It is arguable that the core element of the right to food is a customary obligation. However, it is doubtful that

interpretation of this provision.[32] In its opening remarks the General Comment notes the important role played by armed conflict in inhibiting the realization and implementation of the right to food.[33] In particular the Committee notes "the prevention of access to humanitarian food aid in internal conflicts or other emergency situations" as an important and common way in which the right can be violated by "states or entities insufficiently regulated by states."[34]

These statements are particularly significant in the current discussion for two reasons. First, they provide clear indication of the Committee's authoritative view that the right to food and its cognate principles are relevant in situations of armed conflict. In addition to the question of applicability the statements also speak in more substantive terms to the way in which a state incurs positive obligations pursuant to the right to food not merely to refrain from preventing access to food or even to facilitate its realization but also in some circumstances to control non-state entities which inhibit the realization of the right.

Given the tension between the positive nature of the state obligations in respect to food and the potential practical limits on its capacity to guarantee adequate food to all those under its control the caveat "to the fullest extent of the means available to it" under Article 55 GC IV acquires a particular importance. Jurisprudence under the Covenant may have a pointed relevance to the interpretation of this provision as Article 2(1) ICESCR couches the Covenant's obligations, including the right to food, in a similar caveat.

As noted in General Comment 12, Article 2(1) obliges states to undertake steps "to the maximum of its available resources" with a view to the progressive realization of the rights contained in the convention.[35] The Committee highlights three levels of human rights obligation in relation to the right to food – the obligations to respect, protect, and fulfill, the later incorporating an obligation to facilitate and to provide. The obligation to protect requires states to take measures to ensure that private enterprises or individuals do not act in a manner which prevents access to adequate food or otherwise inhibits the realization of the right. The obligation to fulfill goes further requiring that the state "must pro-actively engage in activities intended to strengthen people's access to and utilization of resources and means

---

the more burdensome components of Article 11 are part of customary law. *See* Smith Narula, *The Right to Food: Holding Global Actors Accountable Under International Law*, 44 Colum. J. Transnat'l L. 691 (2006). *See further* Margret Vidar, *The Right to Food in International Law*, United Nations Food and Agriculture Organization, *available at* www.fao.org/Legal/rtf/statemts/vidar03.pdf (last visited May 1, 2007).

[32] CESCR General Comment 12, U.N. Doc. E/C.12/1999/5 (May 12, 1999).
[33] *Id.* para. 5.
[34] *Id.* para. 19.
[35] *Id.* para. 17. *See also* General Comment 3, U.N. Doc. E/1991/23 (Dec. 14, 1990).

to ensure their livelihood, including food security."³⁶ Whenever an individual or group is unable, for reasons beyond their control, to enjoy the right to adequate food by the means at their disposal, states have the obligation to see that the core of that right is satisfied directly.³⁷

The Committee goes on to point out that although the obligations in relation to the right to food are of progressive realization, "violations... occur when a state fails to ensure the satisfaction of, at the very least, the minimum essential level required to be free from hunger." This essential minimum level amounts to a "core content" of the right to food which the Committee defines as "the availability of food in a quantity and quality sufficient to satisfy the dietary needs of individuals, free from adverse substances, and acceptable within a given culture."³⁸

However, inability and unwillingness to comply with the right are to be distinguished. Where a state seeks to rely on arguments of inability, the onus is on the state to demonstrate that "every effort has been made to use all resources at its disposal in an effort to satisfy, as a matter of priority, those minimum obligations."³⁹ The requirement under Article 2(1) of the Covenant – to seek, if necessary, international assistance and cooperation, is also significant in this context, as a state will not be able to demonstrate that it has in fact taken all reasonable steps to satisfy its obligations where it has failed to seek international support to ensure the availability and accessibility of food.⁴⁰

In the context of military occupation these standards have particular resonance. It is not enough for the occupying power to simply ensure that the civilian population does not starve, nor to refrain from inhibiting the work of humanitarian relief organizations as they seek to assist the population. The occupier may also be required to take a variety of other more proactive steps to ensure the economic and physical accessibility of food. This may include a need for the occupying power to make certain market interventions to prevent inflationary pressures placing basic foodstuffs beyond the ordinary household, or may involve ensuring that military or security measures do not interfere unduly with procurement or allocation processes in the food production cycle.⁴¹

Particular concern must also be paid to certain vulnerable groups. Undoubtedly, the population displacement which occurs during armed conflict dislocates large numbers of people from their habitual sources of nutrients or their own means of food production. Those living in infrastructurally damaged urban areas also experience similar problems in procuring food. Proactive steps by the occupying

---

³⁶ *Id.* para. 15.
³⁷ *Id.* para. 15.
³⁸ *Id.* para. 8.
³⁹ *Id.* para. 17.
⁴⁰ *Id.* para. 17.
⁴¹ *See further* para. 13 *id.*

power will therefore be necessary to safeguard the minimum food security of these sections of the civilian population.

8. *Conclusion*

Education and adequate food are two examples of areas where, during military occupation, human rights jurisprudence complements the obligations laid out in the laws of war. The depth of experience of applying and adjudicating upon contentious human rights questions in many different contexts has resulted in the development of some quite sophisticated and nuanced standards. Of course, much depends on the precise nature of the military occupation in question. Nevertheless, as has been seen, in a variety of ways human rights standards are sometimes very well tailored to addressing precisely the kinds of factual tensions which arise during military occupation. They have a sophistication and flexibility which enables them to carefully address practical problems arising during a military occupation and in providing further detailed guidance about how the nature and extent of the obligations which fall upon the occupying power are to be assessed. This sophistication and particularity must be taken carefully into consideration in legal reasoning, especially in the application of the *lex specialis* maxim. Human rights standards therefore have an important role to play both in guiding the behavior of an occupying power and in assessing the legality of that conduct.

Chapter V

Triggering State Obligations Extraterritorially: The Spatial Test in Certain Human Rights Treaties

*Ralph Wilde**

1. *Introduction*

Determining whether state obligations apply to a particular area of activity usually involves asking whether the activity in question falls within the scope *ratione materiae* of the obligations in question, and whether the connection between the state and the activity meets the requirements of the relevant responsibility norms. When the activity under consideration takes place outside the state's territory, however, a further question must be resolved: do the obligations in question apply to the state at all, given the extraterritorial nature of the location? This question is at issue for two legal regimes which, in terms of subject-matter, are potentially relevant to extraterritorial state activity: the law of occupation and international human rights law. Without an answer in the affirmative, the norms in these two areas of law are not in play, regardless of whether as a matter of fact the state is acting in a manner that speaks to the kinds of issues, notably concerning the treatment of individuals, they seek to regulate.

The trigger for the law of occupation, and one of the two triggers for the human rights law concept of "jurisdiction" extraterritorially, are based on a *spatial* concept of territorial control. The interplay between the approaches taken in each case on the question of what type of control is required mediates the extent to which the field of activity covered by the two areas of law overlaps. Since debate on what these approaches are is highly contested, there is considerable uncertainty and disagreement as to the scope of their parallel application.

A complete and comparative analysis of the various aspects of the spatial tests in these two areas of law is beyond the scope of a piece of this length. Instead, the focus is narrowed considerably to a particular aspect that has been the subject of

---

* UCL Faculty of Laws, www.ucl.ac.uk/laws/wilde. Thanks to Dr. Silvia Borelli for research assistance. This research was supported by the Leverhulme Trust. This piece is an updated reproduction, with permission, of an article published in the Israel Law Review, vol. 40, issue 2 (2007).

significant judicial comment in recent years: the spatial test in human rights treaties on civil and political rights. What light do these determinations shed on the meaning of the scope of the spatial test, thereby mediating the degree to which the human rights obligations at issue will apply, potentially overlapping with the law of occupation?

In the judicial treatment of the spatial test in this area of human rights law, one can identify various suggestions that coverage is limited to a sub-set of extraterritorial state activities involving territorial control occurring as a matter of fact. The effect of these suggestions, which is sometimes explicitly acknowledged when they are made, is that a situation of territorial control by a foreign state might trigger that state's obligations in the law of occupation, but not its obligations in human rights law. This article conceptualizes these suggestions in four categories, and offers a critical appraisal of each, by way of contributing to understandings of their significance for the scope of the law in this area.

This piece begins in part 2 by explaining the concept of "jurisdiction" used in the human rights treaties under evaluation to determine their field of application, how this concept is understood in the extraterritorial context and, within this general issue, the contours of the spatial test that will be the focus of the present piece. In Part 3 the equivalent trigger in the law of occupation is explained in overview.

Part 4, the heart of the piece, explains and critically analyses four different suggestions that have been made as to understandings of "jurisdiction" as territorial control which have the potential to attenuate the scope of this concept to a sub-set of the situations of extraterritorial control as a matter of fact. The first suggestion is that "jurisdiction" maps onto the meaning of this term in general international law, thereby supposedly limiting applicability to extraterritorial situations that enjoy some sort of international legal sanction. The second suggestion is that "jurisdiction" as a matter of human rights law only exists exceptionally, that this exceptionalism is somehow autonomous from the exceptional nature of extraterritorial activities as a matter of fact, and the former is more exceptional than the latter. The third suggestion is that the test includes a requirement that the state is in a position to exercise civil administration; without this capacity, the obligations are not triggered. Finally, the fourth suggestion is that control must be exercised "overall" and that the concept of jurisdiction cannot accommodate situations involving varying degrees of control.

2. The 'Jurisdiction' Test in the Main Human Rights Treaties on Civil and Political Rights

2.1. Treaty Provisions

The main international human rights treaties on civil and political rights, the International Covenant on Civil and Political Rights (ICCPR), the American Convention on Human Rights (ACHR) and the European Convention on Human Rights (ECHR) and their Protocols, and the Convention on the Rights of the Child (CRC), conceive state responsibility for securing the rights they contain only in terms of the state's "jurisdiction."[1] Under the Convention Against Torture (CAT), the state is obliged to take measures to prevent acts of torture "in any territory under its jurisdiction."[2] Thus it is necessary to establish whether a situation falls within the state's "jurisdiction" before the obligations in these instruments are in play.[3]

The International Covenant on Economic, Social and Cultural Rights (ICESCR), by contrast, does not contain any general reference to the arena of application.[4] However, in Article 4 the steps that the state is obliged to take to achieve the full

---

[1] Article 1, European Convention for the Protection of Human Rights and Fundamental Freedoms 213 U.N.T.S. 221 (Nov. 4, 1950) [hereinafter ECHR]; Article 2, International Covenant on Civil and Political Rights, G.A. Res. 2200A/XXI, Dec. 16, 1966, U.N. Doc. A/6316 (Dec. 19, 1966), 999 U.N.T.S. 171 (entry into force on Mar. 23, 1976) [hereinafter ICCPR]; Article 1, American Convention on Human Rights, O.A.S.T.S. No. 36, O.A.S. Off. Rec. OEA/Ser. L/V/II.23, Doc. 21, Rev. 6 (Nov. 22, 1969), (entry into force on July 18, 1978) [hereinafter ACHR]; Article 2, Convention on the Rights of the Child, G.A. Res. 44/25, Annex, 44 U.N. GAOR Supp. No. 49, U.N. Doc. A/44/49 (Nov. 20, 1989) (entered into force Sept. 2, 1990) [hereinafter CRC]. The ICCPR formulation is slightly different from the others in that applicability operates in relation to those "within [the state's] territory and subject to its jurisdiction." This issue is addressed below, note 8. The American Declaration of the Rights and Duties of Man, adopted by the Ninth International Conference of American States, Bogotá, Colombia, 1948, OAS Res. XXX (1948), although not containing a reference to "jurisdiction," has been understood to operate as if it did; *see, e.g.*, Coard v. United States of America, Case 10.951, Inter-American Commission of Human Rights, OEA/ser. L/V/II.106.doc.3rev, para. 37 [hereinafter Coard v. United States]. Note that the ECHR and its Protocols have separate provisions on applicability to overseas territories; *see, e.g.*, Article 56 of the ECHR. The African Charter on Human and Peoples' Rights (OAU Doc. CAB/LEG/67/3 rev. 5, June 27, 1981) does not contain the "jurisdiction" conception of responsibility.

[2] Article 2, Convention Against Torture and Other Cruel, Inhuman or Degrading Treatment or Punishment, G.A. Res. 46, U.N. GAOR, 39th Sess., Supp. No. 51, U.N. Doc. A/39/51 (Sept. 28, 1984) [hereinafter CAT].

[3] But cf. the special regime for applicability in overseas territories under the ECHR and its Protocols, and the reference to "territory" in the ICCPR (*see supra* note 1 and *infra* note 8).

[4] Although the state's obligations in relation to the provision of primary education are conceived in terms of "metropolitan territory or other territories under its jurisdiction" *See* Article 14, International Covenant on Economic, Social and Cultural Rights, 993 U.N.T.S. 3 (Dec. 19, 1966) [hereinafter ICESCR].

realization of economic, social, and cultural rights are not explicitly conceived in a manner limited to such realization within the state's territory, and in the *Wall Advisory Opinion* the International Court of Justice (ICJ) seemed to assume that in the extraterritorial context the "jurisdiction" test from the ICCPR could also be applied to the ICESCR.[5]

It is clear that a state's "jurisdiction" covers its own territory under its control; less clear are the precise circumstances in which this can subsist extraterritorially.[6] No definition of the term is given in the treaties that use it, and the extraterritorial meaning of it has been discussed in relatively few cases and other authoritative statements.[7]

---

[5] *See* Article 2, *id.* and Legal Consequences of the Construction of a Wall in the Occupied Palestinian Territories, Advisory Opinion (July 9, 2004), 2004 I.C.J. Rep. 163, para. 112 [hereinafter Wall Advisory Opinion].

[6] Given the approach taken by the European Court of Human Rights in relation to the Russian presence in Transdniestria, there is a question as to whether it covers the state's territory that is not under its control. *See, e.g.*, Ilascu and Others v. Moldova and Russia, Application No. 48787/99, European Court of Human Rights [Grand Chamber], Reports 2004-VII (Jul. 8, 2004), in particular paras 310–335.

[7] *See* Wall Advisory Opinion, *supra* note 5, paras 107–113; Case concerning Armed Activities on the Territory of the Congo (DRC v. Uganda), (Dec. 19, 2005), 2005 I.C.J. Rep. 116, paras 216–217 [hereinafter Armed Activities on the Territory of the Congo]; Human Rights Committee, General Comment No. 31 on Article 2 of the Covenant: The Nature of the General Legal Obligation Imposed on States Parties to the Covenant, U.N. Doc. CCPR/C/74/CRP.4/Rev.6 (2004), para. 10 [hereinafter General Comment No. 31]; Lopez Burgos v. Uruguay, Communication No. R.12/52, Human Rights Committee, Supp. No. 40, at 176, U.N. Doc. A/36/40 (1981); Lilian Celiberti de Casariego v. Uruguay, Communication No. R.13/56, Human Rights Committee, Supp No. 40, at 185, U.N. Doc. A/36/40 (1981); M. v. Denmark, Application No. 17392/90, European Commission on Human Rights, (Oct. 14, 1992), 73 DR 193; Drozd and Janousek v. France and Spain, Application No. 12747/87, European Court of Human Rights, 14 EHRR 745 (1992); Loizidou v. Turkey (Preliminary Objections), Application No. 15318/89, European Court of Human Rights [Grand Chamber], Preliminary Objections, Series A, No. 310 (1995) (Mar. 23, 1995), para. 62 [hereinafter Loizidou (Preliminary Objections)]; Loizidou v. Turkey, Application No. 15318/89, European Court of Human Rights [Grand Chamber], Merits, Reports 1996-VI (Dec. 12, 1996), paras 52–56 [hereinafter Loizidou (Merits)]; Illich Sanchez Ramirez v. France, Application No. 28780/95, European Commission on Human Rights (June 24, 1996), 86 D.R. 155; Cyprus v. Turkey, Application No. 25781/94, European Court of Human Rights [Grand Chamber], Reports 2001-IV (May 10, 2001), para. 77; Banković v. Belgium and 16 Other Contracting States, Application No. 52207/99, European Court of Human Rights [Grand Chamber], Admissibility Decision, Reports 2001-XII (Dec. 12, 2001) [hereinafter Banković v. Belgium]; Issa and Others v. Turkey, Application No. 31821/96, European Court of Human Rights (Nov. 16, 2004); Ilascu and Others v. Moldova and Russia, *supra* note 6; Isaak and Others v. Turkey, Application No. 44587/98, European Court of Human Rights, Admissibility Decision (Sept. 28, 2006); Coard v. United States, *supra* note 1, paras 37, 39, 41; Committee Against Torture, Consideration of Reports Submitted by States Parties under Article 19 of the Convention, Conclusions and Recommendations: United States of America, U.N. Doc. CAT/C/USA/CO/2 (July 25, 2006), para. 15 [hereinafter CAT:

2.2. General Approach to Extraterritorial Applicability

In the case law and other authoritative statements on the ICCPR, the ECHR, the ACHR, and the CAT, the term "jurisdiction" has been understood in the extraterritorial context in terms of the existence of a factual connection between the state and either the territory in which the relevant acts took place – a *spatial* connection[8] –

USA Report]. As mentioned *supra* in note 2, obligations in the ICCPR are owed to "all individuals within a state's territory and subject to its jurisdiction." Given the clear affirmation by the Human Rights Committee and the International Court of Justice that the ICCPR can apply extraterritorially, it would seem that jurisdiction can operate as a basis for applicability independently of territory. For academic commentary *see, e.g.*, Christopher Lush, *The Territorial Application of the European Convention on Human Rights: Recent Case Law*, 42 ICLQ 897 (1993); Theodor Meron, *Extraterritoriality of Human Rights Treaties*, 89 Am. J. Int'l L. 78 (1995); Joachim Frowein, *The Relationship Between Human Rights Regimes and Regimes of Belligerent Occupation*, Israel Yearbook of Human Rights 1 [1998]; Pasquale De Sena, *La nozione di giurisdizione statale nei trattati sui diritti dell'uomo* (2002); Matthew Happold, *Bankovic v. Belgium and the Territorial Scope of the European Convention of Human Rights*, 3 EHRLR 77 (2003); Alexander Orakhelashvili, *Restrictive Interpretation of Human Rights Treaties in the Recent Jurisprudence of the European Court of Human Rights*, 14 Eur. J. Int'l L. 529 (2003); Kerem Altiparmak, *Bankovic: An Obstacle to the Application of the European Convention on Human Rights in Iraq?*, 9 JCSL 213 (2004); Orna Ben-Naftali & Yuval Shany, *Living in Denial: The Application of Human Rights in the Occupied Territories*, 37 Israel Law Review 17 (2003–2004); Silvia Borelli, *Casting Light on the Legal Black Hole: International Law and Detentions Abroad in the 'War on Terror'*, 87 Int'l Rev. Red Cross 39 (2005); Gregory H. Fox, *The Occupation of Iraq*, 30 Geo. J. Int'l L. 195, 270–278 (2005); Kenneth Watkin, *Controlling the Use of Force: A Role for Human Rights Norms in Contemporary Armed Conflict*, 98 Am. J. Int'l L. 1 (2004); Michael J. Dennis, *Application of Human Rights Treaties Extraterritorially in Times of Armed Conflict and Military Occupation*, 99 Am. J. Int'l L. 119 (2005); Olivier De Schutter, Globalization and Jurisdiction: Lessons from the European Convention on Human Rights, NYU School of Law, Center for Human Rights and Global Justice Working Paper No. 9 (2005), *available at* www.nyuhr.org/docs/wp/DeSchutter%20Globalization%20and%20Jurisdiction.pdf (last visited June 13, 2007); Michal Gondek, *Extraterritorial Application of the European Convention on Human Rights: Territorial Focus in the Age of Globalization?*, 52 NILR 349 (2005); Ralph Wilde, *Legal 'Black Hole'?: Extraterritorial State Action and International Treaty Law on Civil and Political Rights*, 26 Mich. J. Int'l L. 739 (2005); Ralph Wilde, *The 'Legal Space' or 'Espace Juridique' of the European Convention on Human Rights: Is It Relevant to Extraterritorial State Action?*, 10 EHRLR 115 (2005); Adam Roberts, *Transformative Military Occupation: Applying the Laws of War and Human Rights*, 100 Am. J. Int'l L. 580 (2006) [hereinafter Roberts, *Transformative Military Occupation*]; and the contributions in Fons Coomans & Menno Kamminga (eds), Extraterritorial Application of Human Rights Treaties (2004) [hereinafter Coomans & Kamminga].

[8] *See, e.g.*, Wall Advisory Opinion, *supra* note 5, paras 107–113; General Comment No. 31, *supra* note 7, para. 10; Loizidou (Preliminary Objections), *supra* note 7, para. 62; Loizidou (Merits), *supra* note 7, para. 52; Cyprus v. Turkey, *supra* note 7, paras 75–77; Banković v. Belgium, *supra* note 7, generally, and in particular paras 70 and 75; Issa and Others v. Turkey, *supra* note 7, paras 69–70; Ilascu v. Moldova and Russia, *supra* note 6, paras 314–316; Isaak and Others v. Turkey, Application No. 44587/98, European Court of Human Rights, Admissibility Decision (Sept. 28, 2006) at 19; CAT: USA Report, *supra* note 7, para. 15.

or the individual affected by them – a *personal* connection.[9] Although there is less authoritative commentary on the extraterritorial applicability of the CRC, the meaning of "jurisdiction" under this instrument is arguably similar. The ICJ appeared to assume this in affirming the applicability of this treaty to Israel's presence in the occupied Palestinian territories in the *Wall Advisory Opinion*.[10]

2.3. Jurisdiction as Control over Territory

Extraterritorial jurisdiction understood spatially conceives obligations as flowing from the mere fact of territorial control – if the state controls territory, the state is responsible for what happens in it. Whether or not the state has title over the territory, and/or its presence there is or is not lawful, is irrelevant.[11]

This perhaps reflects a principle of state responsibility in international law generally, as articulated in the *Namibia Advisory Opinion* of the ICJ in 1971, where the Court stated that South Africa, who at the time was unlawfully occupying Namibia, was

> accountable for any violations... of the rights of the people of Namibia. The fact that South Africa no longer has any title to administer the Territory does not release it from its obligations and responsibilities under international law towards other States in respect of the exercise of its powers in relation to this Territory. Physical control of a territory, and not sovereignty or legitimacy of title, is the basis of State liability for acts affecting other States.[12]

---

[9] *See, e.g.*, General Comment No. 31, *supra* note 7, para. 10; Lopez Burgos v. Uruguay, *supra* note 7, para. 12.3; Celiberti de Casariego v. Uruguay, *supra* note 7, para. 10.3; M v. Denmark, *supra* note 7, at 93; Illich Sanchez Ramirez v. France, *supra* note 7, at 155; Banković v. Belgium, *supra* note 7, generally, and in particular para. 75; Issa v. Turkey, *supra* note 7, para. 71; Isaak v. Turkey, *supra* note 7, at 19–21; Coard v. United States, *supra* note 7, paras 37, 39, 41; CAT: USA Report, *supra* note 7, para. 15.

[10] Wall Advisory Opinion *supra* note 5, para. 113. In paras 108–111 the ICJ discusses the potential for the term "jurisdiction" under the ICCPR to subsist extraterritorially, concluding in the affirmative. After considering the position under the ICESCR, it turns to the CRC, and concludes extraterritorial applicability simply on the basis that obligations in that instrument are conceived in relation to the state's "jurisdiction." One can perhaps conclude that this assumption is made in the light of the Court's earlier discussion about the meaning of the same term in the ICCPR, and on the basis that the term has the same meaning in both instruments, since otherwise the Court would have to conduct a similar enquiry into the meaning of "jurisdiction" in the CRC to that it conducted in relation to the ICCPR.

[11] This is discussed in more detail below in Section D. 5.

[12] Legal Consequences for States of the Continued Presence of South Africa in Namibia (South West Africa) Notwithstanding Security Council Resolution 276 (1970), Advisory Opinion, 1971 I.C.J. Rep. 16, para. 118.

What, then, does the requirement of territorial control involve?[13] The general contours of the test are set out in a *dictum* from the *Loizidou* case before the European Court of Human Rights, which, together with the later *Cyprus v. Turkey* case, concerned the question of Turkey's responsibility for certain aspects of the situation in Northern Cyprus because of its military presence there following its invasion in 1974 and the declaration of the Turkish Republic of Northern Cyprus in 1983. In a *dictum* contained in both the 1995 judgment on preliminary objections and the 1996 judgment on the merits, the European Court of Human Rights stated that:

> the responsibility of a Contracting Party may . . . arise when as a consequence of military action – whether lawful or unlawful – it exercises effective control of an area outside its national territory. The obligation to secure, in such an area, the rights and freedoms set out in the Convention derives from the fact of such control[14]

The spatial test for triggering applicability, then, is "effective control of an area," and the consequences of this are a generalized "obligation to secure the rights" in the area in question.[15]

3. *The Trigger in the Law of Occupation*

Understanding the trigger for the application of legal obligations extraterritorially in terms of control exercised over foreign territorial space echoes the approach taken by the law of occupation. Under the Hague Regulations, the test for occupation is when territory "is . . . placed under the authority of the hostile army"[16] and "extends . . . to the territory where such authority has been established and can be exercised."[17] Common Article 2 to the Geneva Conventions provides for

---

[13] On this test for jurisdiction, *see* Loizidou (Merits), *supra* note 7; Loizidou (Preliminary Objections) *supra* note 7; Cyprus v. Turkey, *supra* note 7; Banković v. Belgium, *supra* note 7; Issa v. Turkey, *supra* note 7; Ilascu and v. Moldova and Russia, *supra* note 6; R (on the application of Al-Skeini and others) v. Secretary of State for Defence [2004] EWHC 2911 (Admin) [hereinafter Al-Skeini (HC)]; R (on the application of Al-Skeini and others) v. Secretary of State for Defence [2005] EWCA Civ 1609 [hereinafter Al-Skeini (CA)]; Al-Skeini and others v. Secretary of State for Defence [2007] UKHL 26 [hereinafter Al-Skeini (HL)]; CAT: USA Report, *supra* note 7, para. 15.

[14] Loizidou (Preliminary Objections), *supra* note 7, para. 62, cited in Loizidou (Merits), *supra* note 7, para. 52.

[15] *See also* Cyprus v. Turkey, *supra* note 7, para. 77. Further aspects of the test are discussed below in Section D.4 and 5.

[16] Article 42 (1), Hague Regulations Respecting the Laws and Customs of War on Land (annex to the Convention (IV) Respecting the Laws and Customs of War on Land, The Hague (Oct. 18, 1907), Martens Nouveau (Series 3), vol. 3, 461. *See* more generally *id.*, Articles 42–46.

[17] *Id.*

applicability "to all cases of partial or total occupation of the territory,"[18] and this regime is understood to apply in circumstances where the foreign occupier does not enjoy title.[19] What exactly these tests require is a matter of controversy.[20]

A useful overview of some of the arguments made here is provided by the following statement by Daniel Thürer of the International Committee of the Red Cross (ICRC):

> exercise of authority... permits at least two different interpretations. It could, *first*, be read to mean that a situation of occupation exists whenever a party to a conflict is exercising some level of authority or control over territory belonging to the enemy. So, for example, advancing troops could be considered an occupation, and thus bound by the law of occupation during the invasion phase of hostilities. This is the approach suggested by Jean Pictet in the 1958 'Commentary to the Fourth Geneva Convention.'
>
> An *alternative, and more restrictive approach*, would be to say that a situation of occupation only exists once a party to a conflict is in a position to exercise the level of authority over enemy territory necessary to enable it to discharge *all* the obligations imposed by the law of occupation, i.e. that the invading power must be in a position to substitute its own authority for that of the government of the territory. This approach is suggested by a number of military manuals. For example the new British Military Manual proposes a two-part test for establishing the existence of occupation:

---

[18] *See, e.g.*, Article 2, Geneva Convention Relative to the Protection of Civilian Persons in Time of War, (Aug. 12, 1949), 75 U.N.T.S. 287. *See* more generally *id.*, Articles 27–34 and 47–78.

[19] *See, e.g.*, Eyal Benvenisti, The International Law of Occupation 4 (1993) [hereinafter Benvenisti].

[20] For academic commentary on occupation law generally, *see, e.g.* Benvenisti (*supra* note 19), in particular at 3–6; Adam Roberts, *What is a Military Occupation?*, 55 BYIL 249 (1984), in particular at 300; Jean S. Pictet (ed.), *The Geneva Conventions of 12 August 1949, Commentary to the IV Geneva Convention Relative to the Protection of Civilian Persons in Time of War* 21–22 (1958), Commentary to Article 2 (2); Gerhard von Glahn, Law Among Nations: An Introduction to Public International Law (1995), ch. 25; Allan Gerson, Israel, the West Bank and International Law (1978); David Kretzmer, The Occupation of Justice: The Supreme Court of Israel and the Occupied Territories (2002); UK Ministry of Defence, The Manual of the Law of Armed Conflict (2004); Arnold Wilson, *The Laws of War in Occupied Territory*, 18 Transactions of the Grotius Society 17 (1932); Allan Gerson, *Trustee Occupant: The Legal Status of Israel's Presence in the West Bank*, 14 Harv. Int'l L.J. 1 (1973); Daniel Thürer, Current Challenges to the Law of Occupation, Speech delivered at the 6th Bruges Colloquium, Oct. 20–21, 2005, *available at* www.icrc.org/web/eng/siteeng0.nsf/html/occupation-statement-211105?opendocument (last visited June 13, 2007) [hereinafter Thürer]; Hans-Peter Gasser, *Protection of the Civilian Population*, ch. 5 *in* The Handbook of Humanitarian Law in Armed Conflicts 240–279 (Dieter Fleck ed., 1995) and sources cited therein; David Scheffer, *Beyond Occupation Law*, 97 Am. J. Int'l L. 842 (2003); Sylvain Vité, *L'applicabilité du droit international de l'occupation militaire aux activités des organisations internationale*, 86 Int'l Rev. Red Cross 9 (2004); Nehal Bhuta, *The Antinomies of Transformative Occupation*, 16 Eur. J. Int'l L. 721 (2005); Steven R. Ratner, *Foreign Occupation and International Territorial Administration: The Challenges of Convergence*, 16 Eur. J. Int'l L. 695 (2005); Roberts, *Transformative Military Occupation, supra* note 7.

[f]irst, that the former government has been rendered incapable of publicly exercising its authority in that area; and, secondly, that the occupying power is in a position to substitute its own authority for that of the former government.

On the basis of this approach the rules on occupation would not apply during the invasion phase and in battle areas. What is clear, however, is that it is not necessary for a state to control the entirety of another State's territory, for occupation to exist. It is sufficient for authority to be established over any portion of another state's territory.[21]

As already explained, it is beyond the scope of a piece of this length to delve further into the debate as to the test for the trigger in the law of occupation; the point of the foregoing overview is to flag up the broader context to the analysis that will follow on the debate on the spatial trigger in human rights law.

4. Attenuating Human Rights Law Applicability

4.1. Introduction

The differences of views on what level of control is required to trigger the law of occupation echo the debates in relation to the human rights treaties under evaluation. This section offers a critical evaluation of four issues discussed in the case-law, each of which allowing a position to be taken which serves to attenuate extraterritorial applicability.[22]

The first two issues concern the meaning of extraterritorial jurisdiction in the context of human rights law generally: it has been suggested that this meaning might reflect the concept of "jurisdiction" in general international law, and there is a question as to whether it only covers an "exceptional" sub-set of extraterritorial activities. The third and fourth issues relate to the "effective control" heading of "jurisdiction" in particular. Here, it has been suggested that the state must be in a position to exercise civil authority in order to meet the test. Moreover, there is a debate as to whether the test covers only control exercised "overall," or also control of a lesser kind.

---

[21] Thürer, *supra* note 20 (footnotes omitted).

[22] One such idea which will not be addressed is the notion that human rights treaties only apply extraterritorially when states are acting in the territory of other states who are also parties to the same treaty. Thus for extraterritorial action occurring in the territory of a non-party state or non-state entity, the obligations are inapplicable. This has become a topic of debate following the observations of the European Court of Human Rights in relation to the "espace juridique" of the Convention in the *Banković* case: see *Banković, supra* note 7, para. 80; for commentary, see, *e.g.*, the works by Orakhelashvili, Altiparmak and Wilde cited in *supra* note 7 above; *see also* Rick Lawson, *Life After Bankovic: On the Extraterritorial Application of the European Convention on Human Rights, in* Coomans & Kamminga, *supra* note 7, 131.

In different ways, these four issues mediate the general question of how broad or how narrow a range of extraterritorial state activities falls within "jurisdiction" defined as spatial control. This in part determines the degree of overlap in the circumstances where human rights law and the law of occupation apply.[23]

4.2. "Jurisdiction" in Public International Law

A concept called "jurisdiction" exists in general international law. What relevance, if any, has this general concept for understandings of the term in the human rights treaties under evaluation? The general international law concept of "jurisdiction" is concerned with rules prescribing the particular circumstances where a state is legally permitted to exercise its legal authority over a particular situation (*e.g.*, prosecuting its own nationals for crimes committed abroad).[24]

In the *Banković* case concerning the NATO bombing of a radio and television station in Belgrade as part of the broader bombing campaign of what was then the Federal Republic of Yugoslavia in 1999 explained in terms of preventing atrocities in Kosovo, the European Court of Human Rights seemed to suggest that the meaning of "jurisdiction" in the ECHR reflects the meaning of that term in public international law generally.[25] However, insofar as the Court intended to make this suggestion, it does not fit with how the Court and other authoritative bodies have approached the issue in other cases, which is to define extraterritorial jurisdiction as simply a factual test, regardless of whether such a situation is lawful. For example, the Court held that Turkey's presence in Northern Cyprus constituted exercise of jurisdiction for ECHR purposes because of the degree of control exercised, stressing that such jurisdiction could subsist on this basis regardless of the legality of the exercise of control.[26]

---

[23] Another issue mediating the degree of overlap is the extent to which the applicability of each area of law is determined by the subject matter at issue. On the applicability of human rights obligations in war time, see the derogation provisions of the various international instruments for the protection of human rights: Article 4 ICCPR, *supra* note 1; Article 15 ECHR, *supra* note 1; Article 27, ACHR, *supra* note 1; *see* also *Coard* (*supra* note 1), paras 39–42; Legality of the Threat or Use of Nuclear Weapons, Advisory Opinion (July 8, 1996), 1996 I.C.J. Rep., paras 24–25; Wall Advisory Opinion, *supra* note 5, paras 105–106.

[24] *See, e.g.*, Rosalyn Higgins, Problems and Process: International Law and How We Use It (1994), chapter 4; Ian Brownlie, Principles of Public International Law (2003), chapter 15; Malcolm N. Shaw, International Law (2003), chapter 12; Francis A. Mann, *The Doctrine of Jurisdiction in International Law*, 111 Recueil des Cours 1 (1964–I); Francis A. Mann, *The Doctrine of International Jurisdiction Revisited after Twenty Years*, 186 Recueil des Cours 8 (1984-III); Michael Akehurst, *Jurisdiction in International Law*, 46 BYIL 145 (1972–1973).

[25] Banković v. Belgium, *supra* note 7, paras 59–61.

[26] Loizidou v. Turkey (Preliminary Objections), *supra* note 7, para. 62; Loizidou v. Turkey (Merits), *supra* note 7, paras 52–56. *See* also Cyprus v. Turkey, *supra* note 7, para. 77.

As for the ICCPR, the U.N. Human Rights Committee stated in General Comment No. 31 that the principle of making available the enjoyment of Covenant rights to all individuals regardless of nationality,

> applies to those within the power or effective control of the forces of a State Party acting outside its territory, *regardless of the circumstances in which such power or effective control was obtained.*[27]

So the state could be exercising extraterritorial jurisdiction without a valid international legal basis for doing so, and its human rights obligations would not be inapplicable simply by virtue of the illegality.

Clearly the notion that human rights obligations do not apply if the action in question is not itself lawful is perverse; moreover, the foregoing evidence suggests that it is contradicted by the approach taken in the jurisprudence, other than the general statement which the European Court of Human Rights made in *Banković* but failed to apply to the facts of the case. Of course, to say that to constitute "jurisdiction" for the purpose of applicability of human rights obligations, action need not constitute a valid exercise of "jurisdiction" in general international law terms or be, in a broader sense, legally authorized, is not to say that action with this lawful basis cannot also constitute "jurisdiction" for human rights purposes. All it suggests is that one cannot find the meaning of "jurisdiction" in human rights law from a different concept with the same name in another area of international law.

4.3. De facto *and* de jure *Exceptionalism*

However controversial and important extraterritorial state action is in the world, and however fundamental to the interests of the state and those in the territory affected it may be in certain cases, taken as whole it is exceptional when compared with the presence and activities of state authorities within their territories. Thus in the *Wall Advisory Opinion* mentioned earlier the ICJ stated in relation to the ICCPR that,

> …while the exercise of jurisdiction is primarily territorial, it may sometimes be exercised outside the state territory.[28]

The Court went on to say that:

> Considering the object and purpose of the…Covenant…it would seem natural that, even when such is the case, States parties to the Covenant should be bound by its provisions.[29]

---

[27] General Comment No. 31, *supra* note 7, para. 10, emphasis added.
[28] Wall Advisory Opinion, *supra* note 5, para. 109.
[29] *Id.*

Here, then, the Court is being descriptive about the exercise of jurisdiction in the sense of a state presence (the particular activity performed by Israel at issue before it) reflecting the fact that states do not normally engage in this activity *as a matter of fact* outside their territory.

In the *Banković* case, the European Court of Human Rights made a similar observation, that jurisdiction is "essentially" territorial, with extraterritorial jurisdiction subsisting only in "exceptional" circumstances.[30] However, in this observation the European Court, perhaps influenced by the idea, mentioned earlier, of limiting the meaning of extraterritorial jurisdiction to that which is legally permissible, seemed to suggest that somehow the "exceptional" character of extraterritorial jurisdiction should be understood not only in a purely factual sense; it should also have purchase in defining the boundaries of the meaning of "jurisdiction" in international human rights law in a limited fashion, and should do so in an autonomous manner from the factual exceptionalism.

The autonomous nature of this exceptionalism creates the possibility that even if a state *is* acting "exceptionally" as a *matter of fact* outside its territory, such a situation might not fall within its "jurisdiction" for the purposes of human rights law.

The *Banković* case was the first case to adopt such an approach, which is not found in earlier ECHR cases, or the jurisprudence of other international human rights treaty bodies, including the U.N. Human Rights Committee, or in the decision of the International Court of Justice in the *Wall Advisory Opinion*. The approach was, however, picked up at certain stages of the *Al-Skeini* case in the English courts concerning the applicability of the United Kingdom's human rights obligations to its presence in Iraq, although by way of simple recitation only.[31] It remains to be seen whether this idea has traction more generally, but insofar as it is adopted it serves to attenuate the range of circumstances in which jurisdiction is understood to subsist extraterritorially as a matter of law from the full scope of extraterritorial state activities as a matter of fact.

4.4. *Being Able to Exercise Civil Administration*

The third potentially limiting consideration for understandings of the spatial meaning of "jurisdiction" is whether or not the capacity to exercise civil administration a requirement for the "effective control" test. In the *Banković* case, the European Court made the following general statement on the issue of effective control:

> the case-law of the Court demonstrates that its recognition of the exercise of extra-territorial jurisdiction by a Contracting State is exceptional: it has done so when

---

[30] Banković, *supra* note 7, para. 67.
[31] *See* Al-Skeini (HC), *supra* note 13, paras 245 and 269; Al-Skeini (CA), *supra* note 13, paras 75–76.

the respondent State, through the effective control of the relevant territory and its inhabitants abroad, as a consequence of military occupation or through the consent, invitation or acquiescence of the Government of that territory exercises all or some of the public powers normally to be exercised by that Government.[32]

Here the Court underlines a feature of the factual backdrop to the Northern Cyprus cases not actually emphasized in its earlier consideration of the exercise of jurisdiction in them. For the Court in *Banković* the issue is control over territory that is not only "effective" but also involves the exercise of "some or all of the public powers normally to be exercised" by the local government. Whereas indeed such powers were exercised by Turkey in Northern Cyprus, their exercise was not seen as a prerequisite to the exercise of jurisdiction by the Court in the Northern Cyprus cases: the only issue was the exercise of "effective control."

Whereas this statement from *Banković* touches on some of the factual circumstances in relation to which the court had previously found the exercise of jurisdiction (cf. the phrase "it has done so"), it would be wrong to conclude that the capacity to exercise public authority was actually one of the *salient* facts, and thus part of the test for jurisdiction as territorial control, in those previous cases. Indeed, it is notable in this regard that in its application of the law to the facts of the case in *Banković*, the Court made no statement, either explicit or implicit, touching on the question of whether or not the relevant acts – the bombing – involved the exercise of powers normally to be exercised by the local government.[33] In fact, the Court dismissed the contention that the bombing constituted jurisdiction on other grounds, namely that aerial bombardment did not constitute "effective control" of territory.[34]

Despite this, the question of whether the capacity to exercise public governmental powers is part of the test for applicability is still a live one. In the *Al-Skeini* case, the U.K. government argued in the affirmative, suggesting that it does not exercise public authority in Iraq, and so the ECHR is not applicable to it there on the basis of jurisdiction as territorial control. It was suggested that the obligations in the ECHR by their nature presuppose the exercise of civil administration, and so the trigger for applicability must include this capacity. If it did not, the law would apply in circumstances where the state was incapable of fulfilling the applicable obligations. It was also suggested that the exercise of control amounting to the exercise of civil administration involving the widespread implementation of rights in the ECHR would be prohibited by the other main area of applicable law, the law of occupation.

---

[32] Banković v. Belgium, *supra* note 7, para. 71.
[33] *Id.* paras 75–76.
[34] *See* the discussion in the paragraphs cited *supra* note 33.

These arguments found favour with Lord Justice Brooke in the Court of Appeal, as illustrated in the following passage from his opinion:

> Unlike the Turkish army in northern Cyprus, the British military forces had no control over the civil administration of Iraq...
>
> In my judgment it is quite impossible to hold that the UK... was in effective control of Basrah City for the purposes of ECHR jurisprudence at the material time. If it had been, it would have been obliged, pursuant to the *Bankovic* judgment, to secure to everyone in Basrah City the rights and freedoms guaranteed by the ECHR. One only has to state that proposition to see how utterly unreal it is. The UK possessed no executive, legislative or judicial authority in Basrah City, other than the limited authority given to its military forces, and as an occupying power it was bound to respect the laws in force in Iraq unless absolutely prevented... It could not be equated with a civil power: it was simply there to maintain security, and to support the civil administration in Iraq in a number of different ways.[35]

In a similar vein, Lord Brown stated at the House of Lords stage of the same case that

> ...except when a state really does have effective control of territory, it cannot hope to secure Convention rights within that territory... Indeed it goes further than that. During the period in question here it is common ground that the UK was an occupying power in Southern Iraq and bound as such by Geneva IV and by the Hague Regulations [occupation law]. Article 43 of the Hague Regulations provides that the occupant "shall take all the measures in his power to restore and ensure, as far as possible, public order and safety, while respecting, unless absolutely prevented, the laws in force in the country."... The occupants' obligation is to respect "the laws in force", not to introduce laws and the means to enforce them (for example, courts and a justice system) such as to satisfy the requirements of the Convention. Often (for example when Sharia law is in force) Convention rights would clearly be incompatible with the laws of the territory occupied.[36]

For Brooke LJ, the test for territorial control must include a capacity to exercise public authority, because it is only in such circumstances that the state would actually be in a position to fulfill its obligations in the ECHR. In other words, the Convention cannot be applicable in a generalized sense when the state does not enjoy such authority, since the obligations it contains in part presuppose such enjoyment.

Under these approaches, then, a particular instance of foreign state territorial control can meet the test for applying the law of occupation while not meeting the test for human rights law, in part because of the obligations that flow from the first area of law (being bound to respect local laws unless absolutely prevented).

---

[35] *See* Al-Skeini (CA), *supra* note 13, paras 123–124 (Lord Justice Brooke).
[36] Al-Skeini (HL), *supra* note 13.

However, these assertions rest on a series of assumptions which are left unexplained and which are, when considered, difficult to sustain.[37] In the first place, it is assumed that human rights law properly applied, with all the advantages of limitation clauses, derogations and, for the ECHR, the margin of appreciation, would actually oblige the state to exercise public authority both generally and in particular in a manner that would put it at odds with obligations under the law of occupation. This is questionable even if one focuses only on human rights law, let alone the Security Council authority given to the coalition states in Iraq which, indeed, in another case about Iraq, *Al Jedda*, the United Kingdom is seeking to argue trumps its obligations under the ECHR.[38]

In the second place, this argument presupposes the validity of a particular approach to the relationship between different areas of international law, without having explained the basis for this validity. A clash between two areas of law is feared, and a solution to this clash offered by defining the applicability of one area of law so as to remove it from being in play, without explaining the basis for choosing this particular method of norm clash resolution. Perhaps one has to accept that there are two mutually contradictory regimes of law in play; that there is normative confusion. Perhaps, in the alternative, the standard techniques available to mediate the relationship between overlapping regimes of law, including the concept of *lex specialis*, might actually lead to a harmony of standards.[39] Perhaps the drastic approach of rendering human rights law entirely inapplicable is preferable to these other approaches to the issue, but its status as such cannot be assumed, as is suggested by his use of it.

An equally plausible scenario, of course, in the light of both the ECHR itself and its relationship to other areas of law, is that a relatively modest set of substantive obligations would actually subsist, qualitatively and quantitatively different from those in play in the state's own territory, even if derived from the same legal source. The possibility of this lies behind the following *dictum* from Lord Justice Sedley in the Court of Appeal stage of *Al-Skeini*:

> No doubt it is absurd to expect occupying forces in the near-chaos of Iraq to enforce the right to marry vouchsafed by Art. 12 or the equality guarantees vouchsafed by Art. 14. But I do not think effective control involves this. If effective control in the jurisprudence of the [European Court of Human Rights] marches with international

---

[37] *See* also the disagreement by Lord Justice Sedley, Al-Skeini (CA), *supra* note 13, para. 195.
[38] *See* R. (on the application of Al-Jedda) v. Secretary of State for Defence [2005] EWHC 1809 (Admin.); R. (on the application of Al-Jedda) v. Secretary of State for Defence [2006] EWCA Civ. 327. And of course the law of occupation itself contains obligations concerning the promotion of law and order and the protection of human rights. *See* generally the sources cited *supra* note 20.
[39] *See* Fragmentation of International Law: Difficulties Arising from the Diversification and Expansion of International Law, Report of the Study Group of the International Law Commission (finalized by Martti Koskenniemi), U.N. Doc. A/CN.4/L.682, (April 13, 2006).

humanitarian law and the law of armed conflict, as it clearly seeks to do, it involves two key things: the de facto assumption of civil power by an occupying state and a concomitant obligation to do all that is possible to keep order and protect essential civil rights. It does not make the occupying power the guarantor of rights; nor therefore does it demand sufficient control for all such purposes. What it does is place an obligation on the occupier to do all it can.

If this is right, it is not an answer to say that the UK, because it is unable to guarantee everything, is required to guarantee nothing.[40]

In addition to these arguments about what the test actually requires, two further arguments have been made in the *Al-Skeini* litigation defending this requirement as a matter of principle. In the first place, it is suggested that to have human rights law apply in circumstances where the state was not entitled to exercise public authority would undermine the right of the local population to govern their own affairs. At the Court of Appeal stage, Brooke LJ stated that:

> It would...have been contrary to the Coalition's policy to maintain a much more substantial military force in Basrah City when its over-arching policy was to encourage the Iraqis to govern themselves. To build up an alternative power base capable of delivering all the rights and performing all the obligations required of a contracting state under the ECHR at the very time when the IGC had been formed, with CPA encouragement, as a step towards the formation by the people of Iraq of an internationally recognized representative Government...would have run right against the grain of the Coalition's policies.[41]

Here, then, a fear is expressed that being bound by human rights law in the absence of a public authority prerogative would require the coalition in Iraq to become more involved in Iraqi governmental matters rather than, as is intended, to reduce its presence, transferring power to local bodies as soon as possible. Another way of putting this is to suggest that applying human rights law might somehow cut against the right of internal self-determination.[42]

Again, such an approach fails to appreciate how human rights properly applied in the occupation context, both on its own terms and in consequence of its interplay with occupation law, might actually not have this effect. It also ignores the fact that human rights law contains a right – the right of self-determination – whose application might lead to a special meaning given to other obligations in human rights law in the particular occupation context. Although that right is not contained in the ECHR, it is of course brought into the frame through the general approach of interpreting Convention rights wherever possible so as to be in harmony with other international law.[43]

---

[40] Al-Skeini (CA), *supra* note 13, paras 196–197 (Lord Justice Sedley).
[41] *Id*. para. 125 (Lord Justice Brooke). *See also id*. para. 126.
[42] *Id*. para. 125 (Lord Justice Brooke).
[43] A right of self-determination is contained in Article 1 ICCPR, *supra* note 1; Article 1 ICESCR, *supra* note 1. On the interpretative approach to the ECHR referencing other legal obligations, *see*

The second, related argument of principle is that the obligations of the ECHR are culturally specific and thereby inappropriate for application in situations taking place outside their cultural context. In *Al-Skeini* Brooke LJ raises a concern that applying the ECHR to the United Kingdom in Iraq might involve inculcating "the common spiritual heritage of the member states of the country [sic] of Europe"[44] (misquoting a phrase from the ECHR *Golder* case)[45] in "a predominantly Muslim country."[46] At the House of Lords stage of the same case Lord Brown states that unless an ECHR contracting state

> ... is within the area of the Council of Europe, it is unlikely... to find certain of the Convention rights it is bound to secure reconcilable with the customs of the resident population.[47]

Discussing areas where the obligation to secure Convention rights would be supposedly incompatible with local law (and so the obligation to respect local law in law of occupation), Lord Brown gives a single example: "where Sharia law is in force."[48]

Brooke LJ's orientalist positioning of Islam and Europe as normative opposites implicitly renders invisible the Muslim people who live in Council of Europe countries, including Turkey, which one imagines the judge would regard as "a predominantly Muslim country." Although Lord Brown is not so extreme, his suggestion that Sharia law and the "customs of the local population" are necessarily going to be incompatible with the obligations in the ECHR fails to consider the significance of other human rights treaties which contain the same rights as the

---

Article 53 ECHR, *supra* note 1; Article 31(3)(c) Vienna Convention on the Law of Treaties, 1155 U.N.T.S. 331 (May 23, 1969); Golder v. United Kingdom, European Court of Human Rights, Judgment (Feb. 21, 1975), Series A, No. 18 (1975), para. 35; Loizidou v. Turkey (Merits), *supra* note 7, para. 43; Al Adsani v. United Kingdom, Application No. 35763/97, European Court of Human Rights [Grand Chamber], Reports 2001-XI (Nov. 21, 2001), para. 55; Fogarty v. United Kingdom, Application No. 37112/97, European Court of Human Rights [Grand Chamber], Reports 2001-XI (Nov. 21, 2001), para. 35; McElhinney v. Ireland, European Court of Human Rights [Grand Chamber], Reports 2001-XI (Nov. 21, 2001), para. 35; Banković v. Belgium, *supra* note 7, para. 57; Kalogeropoulou and Others v. Greece and Germany, European Court of Human Rights, Reports 2002-X, (Dec. 12, 2002), para. D (1) (a); Mamatkulov and Askarov v. Turkey, Applications Nos. 46827/99 and 46951/99, European Court of Human Rights [Grand Chamber], Reports 2005-I (Feb. 4, 2005), para. 111; Bosphorus Hava Yollari Turizm Ve Ticaret Anonim Sirketi v. Ireland, Application No. 45036/98, European Court of Human Rights, Judgment (June 30, 2005), para. 150.

[44] Al-Skeini (CA), *supra* note 13, para. 126 (Lord Justice Brooke).
[45] Golder v. United Kingdom, *supra* note 43, para. 34. Here the word "States" is capitalized, and reference is made to the "Council", not "Country", of Europe, which denotes the regional grouping under whose aegis the ECHR was adopted.
[46] Al-Skeini (CA), *supra* note 13, para. 126 (Lord Justice Brooke).
[47] Al-Skeini (HL), *supra* note 13, para. 129.
[48] *Id.* para. 129.

ECHR and may be binding on the state of Iraq anyway – one thinks in particular here of the International Covenant on Civil and Political Rights.[49]

Crude chauvinism aside, is there not a valid point that applying a regime of law that has in part been formulated with a particular sub-global political community in mind to people living in territories outside that community is inappropriate? Here, one recalls the much-misunderstood "legal space" *dictum* from the *Banković* case.[50] At the House of Lords stage of *Al Skeini*, Lord Rodger discussed this *dictum* and observed that

> The essentially regional nature of the Convention is relevant to the way that the court operates. It has judges elected from all the contracting states, not from anywhere else. The judges purport to interpret and apply the various rights in the Convention in accordance with what they conceive to be developments in prevailing attitudes in the contracting states. This is obvious from the court's jurisprudence on such matters as the death penalty, sex discrimination, homosexuality and transsexuals. The result is a body of law which may reflect the values of the contracting states, but which most certainly does not reflect those in many other parts of the world. So the idea that the United Kingdom was obliged to secure observance of all the rights and freedoms as interpreted by the European Court in the utterly different society of southern Iraq is manifestly absurd.[51]

For Lord Rodger, if the European Court of Human Rights interpreted the meaning of "jurisdiction" on the basis of territorial control so as to include situations in territories not in states that are parties to the European Convention, it would "run the risk ... of being accused of human rights imperialism."[52]

It might be thought that, if anything, subjecting the U.K. presence in Iraq to the regulation of human rights law would have the effect of mitigating, not exacerbating, the colonial nature of the occupation. However, for Lord Rodger, it would make it worse – or, if a colonial comparison is not accepted when considering the very existence of the U.K. presence, would render a non-colonial situation colonial. Such an argument suggests that even if the courts may not be able to review the legality of the conduct of war and the existence of U.K. troops in foreign countries, they can ensure, at least, that such practices are somehow less "colonial" by ensuring that an obligation to override local cultural norms does not operate.

Such an idea, however, assumes that the law properly applied would not permit distinctions to operate as between a state's own territory and foreign territory under its control and, indeed, might even oblige the state to respect, not override,

---

[49] Iraq ratified the ICCPR on 25 January 1971; see *Status of Multilateral Treaties Deposited with the Secretary-General available at* http://untreaty.un.org/ENGLISH/bible/englishinternetbible/partI/chapterIV/treaty6.asp (last visited 10 July 2007).
[50] *See supra* note 22.
[51] Al-Skeini (HL), *supra* note 13, para 78.
[52] *Id.* para. 78.

certain local customs. In the light of the Strasbourg organs' general willingness to utilize the relevant devices contained in the ECHR, and their invented "margin of appreciation" doctrine, to accommodate both the needs of contracting states and the differences between particular situations, this is difficult to sustain.

To suggest that the application of human rights law in the occupation context would involve obligations that presuppose the occupier enjoying full public powers, and oblige the occupier to hold back from transferring powers to local people, and be unable to take into account differing cultural norms as between the people of the occupying state's own territory and the population of the occupied territory constitutes a remarkably unimaginative and simplistic approach to the issue. At the very least, as formulated in the *dicta* extracted above, it rests on a series of assumptions which are left unproved.

4.5. *The Degree of Territorial Control*

The fourth and final issue concerning the spatial test for applicability is of a quantitative nature: the question of the degree of control required for the test of "effective control" to be met. A key point of contention is whether only one approach – overall control – is correct, or whether a second approach – sliding scale or cause and effect control – is also possible.

4.5.1. *Overall Control*

The first approach to the meaning of "effective control," "overall control," originates from the Northern Cyprus cases.[53] In its judgment on the merits in *Loizidou*, the European Court of Human Rights stated that

> [Turkey's] army exercises effective overall control over that part of the island. Such control, according to the relevant test and in the circumstances of the case, entails her responsibility for the policies and actions of the "TRNC" [the local Turkish Cypriot regime]... Those affected by such policies or actions therefore come within the "jurisdiction" of Turkey for the purposes of Article 1 of the Convention...[54]

On the facts in Northern Cyprus, the Court emphasized that Turkey exercised effective control operating "overall," in such circumstances, it was unnecessary to identify whether the exercise of control was detailed.[55] So if the state is in overall control of a territorial unit, everything within that unit falls within its "jurisdiction," even if at lesser levels powers are exercised by other actors (e.g. if particular activities are devolved to other states or local actors).[56]

---

[53] *See also* Issa v. Turkey, *supra* note 7, paras 74–75.
[54] Loizidou (Merits), *supra* note 7, para. 56 and Loizidou (Preliminary Objections), *supra* note 7, paras 63–64.
[55] *Id.*
[56] *See also* Cyprus v. Turkey, *supra* note 7, para. 77.

4.5.2. *"Sliding Scale"/"Cause and Effect"*

What of control operating in a lesser sense? In the *Banković* case, which was decided in 2001, the applicants proposed the idea of "sliding scale" or "cause and effect" jurisdiction: obligations apply insofar as control is exercised; their nature and scope is set in direct proportional relation to the level of control.[57] The European Court rejected this argument; for it the concept of jurisdiction could not be "divided and tailored in accordance with the particular circumstances of the extra-territorial act in question."[58] However, in the later *Issa* case of 2004, the Court, having concluded that Turkey did not exercise "overall control" in the area of Northern Iraq in question, did not end its consideration of whether the Turkish presence constituted the exercise of "jurisdiction." Rather, it went on to consider "whether at the relevant time Turkish troops conducted operations in the area where the killings took place."[59] If the troops had been doing this, which the Court found on the facts they had not, jurisdiction would have subsisted. Unfortunately, the Court failed to indicate whether at this stage it was considering jurisdiction as territorial control, but if it was, one might discern a more receptive attitude towards the broader cause-and-effect concept than in the earlier case of *Banković*.

This concept was picked up in the Court of Appeal stage of the *Al-Skeini* case by Lord Justice Sedley, who considered the idea that applicability might depend not on "enforceability as a whole" but "whether it lay within the power of the occupying force to avoid or remedy the particular breach in issue."[60] Although he acknowledged that this was blocked by the *Banković dictum*, he rejected the underlying logic of the *dictum* and suggested that the European Court of Human Rights might sooner or later revisit it.[61]

5. *Conclusion*

In the extraterritorial context, the norms triggering the applicability of the law of occupation and the main treaties on civil and political rights are governed by contested notions of territorial control. This paper has explored some of the different

---

[57] Banković v. Belgium, *supra* note 7, para. 75.
[58] *Id.* paras 75–76.
[59] Issa v. Turkey, *supra* note 7, para. 76.
[60] Al-Skeini (CA), *supra* note 13, para. 198 (Lord Justice Sedley).
[61] *Id.* paras 201–202. The idea of dividing and tailoring was criticized at the House of Lords stage. *See* in particular paras 79–80 (Lord Rodger) and 128–30 (Lord Brown). The alternative understanding of jurisdiction not covered in detail in this article, that of control over individuals rather than control over territory, is, however, clearly significant in rendering human rights obligations applicable even when the territorial control test is not met; *see supra* note 9 and accompanying text.

arguments relating to human rights law which have the effect of attenuating the circumstances in which it applies extraterritorially, thereby potentially creating a situation where the law of occupation is in play and human rights law is not. Two of these arguments, concerning a supposed link with the general international law concept of "jurisdiction" and the notion of "exceptional" applicability are, respectively, of doubtful and uncertain relevance. The third argument, rooted in a requirement that the state must be in a position to exercise civil authority, found favor in certain *dicta* in the *Al-Skeini* case, but, it has been suggested, on the basis of reasoning that is, at best, insufficient. The fourth argument, limiting applicability to situations of "overall" control, excluding lesser forms of control on a "cause-and-effect" or "sliding scale" basis, although seemingly rejected by the European Court of Human Rights in the *Banković* case, may find favour in the future, including with that Court itself given its pronouncement in the later case of *Issa*.

Although these arguments are made in different ways and their credibility and authority varies, taken together they demonstrate that the law in this area is as highly contested as it is underdeveloped. The issues they raise promise to be the key sites of future argumentation and norm development on the extraterritorial application of human rights law, determining the scope of this application and so the extent to which the operation of human rights norms overlaps with that of occupation norms.

Chapter VI

DRC v. *Uganda*: The Applicability of International Humanitarian Law and Human Rights Law in Occupied Territories

Tom Ruys* and Sten Verhoeven**

1. *Introduction*

In its judgment of December 19, 2005 in the *Case concerning Armed Activities on the Territory of the Congo* (*DRC* v. *Uganda*)[1] the International Court of Justice (ICJ) has for the second time affirmed the simultaneous application of international humanitarian law and human rights law to occupied territories, be it in circumstances significantly different from those under consideration in the *Palestinian Wall* Advisory Opinion.[2] Unlike in the latter case, the Court did not dwell on the criteria for the extraterritorial application of international human rights instruments, but confined itself to the conclusion that these instruments are applicable "in respect of acts done by a State in the exercise of its jurisdiction outside its own territory," before listing the provisions violated by Uganda. Nevertheless, the Court's affirmation of its earlier ruling in the specific circumstances of Uganda's invasion of Congolese territory, together with its finding that Article 43 of the Hague Regulations (HR) comprises the obligation to take measures "to secure respect for the applicable rules of international human rights law and international humanitarian law," generates important consequences that may reverberate well beyond the Great Lakes region.

The present chapter delves deeper into these issues by examining the possible thresholds for application of international humanitarian law (IHL) on belligerent

---

* Research Fellow of the Fund for Scientific Research Flanders, Institute of International Law, University of Leuven (Belgium).
** Assistant at the Institute of International Law, University of Leuven (Belgium).
[1] Case concerning Armed Activities on the Territory of the Congo (DRC v. Uganda), (Dec. 19, 2005), 2005 ICJ Rep. 116 [hereinafter DRC v. Uganda].
[2] Legal Consequences of the Construction of a Wall in the Occupied Palestinian Territory, Advisory Opinion (July 9, 2004), 2004 ICJ Rep. 163 [hereinafter Palestinian Wall].

occupation on the one hand and international human rights law on the other hand as well as the possible interplay between the two groups of norms in relation to occupied territories. The chapter begins with a summary of the Court's ruling in *DRC* v. *Uganda*. Subsequently, we will examine the Court's interpretation of the concept of "occupation" in IHL. Part three turns to the extraterritorial applicability of human rights instruments in occupied territories. Part four focuses on the interplay of IHL and human rights norms in terms of normative content. The chapter concludes with some final observations.

2. *Synopsis of the Judgement*

On December 19, 2005, the ICJ delivered its judgment in the *Armed Activities on the Territory of the Congo* case between the Democratic Republic of Congo and Uganda (*DRC* v. *Uganda*).[3] The Court condemned Uganda for the unlawful use of force and for violations of IHL and human rights law. In turn, it found that the DRC had violated its obligations under the 1961 Vienna Convention on Diplomatic Relations by seizing property from the Ugandan embassy and maltreating Ugandan diplomats.

Although the judgment only concerns the dispute between the DRC and Uganda, the armed conflict in the territory of the DRC (1998–2003) was a Gordian knot of different sub-conflicts, both internal and international. In all, eight African nations were involved in the "Great War of Africa" as well as about 20 armed groups.[4] An estimated three to four million people died. Millions more fled their homes. The complexity of the conflict is illustrated by the fact that the DRC also filed applications against Burundi and Rwanda before the ICJ. Neither of these cases reached the merits stage: the former was removed from the docket at the request of the DRC; the latter case was found inadmissible due to a lack of jurisdiction.[5]

The origins of the conflict can be traced back to the ousting of the Congolese (then Zairian) President Mobute Ssese Seko by Laurent-Desiré Kabila, with the backing of Rwanda and Uganda. In the initial period following the coup, the DRC

---

[3] Remark: the present section only provides a brief overview of the main legal issues of the judgment. For a more extensive analysis of the case, *see*: Phoebe N. Okowa, *Case concerning Armed Activities on the Territory of the Congo (Democratic Republic of the Congo v. Uganda)*, 55 I.C.L.Q. 742–753 (2005); Sten Verhoeven, *Case concerning Armed Activities on the Territory of the Congo*, 45 Revue de Droit Militaire et de Droit de la Guerre 355–368 (2006).

[4] The eight countries are: the DRC, Uganda, Rwanda, Burundi, Sudan, Angola, Zambia, and Zimbabwe.

[5] *See*: Armed Activities on the Territory of the Congo (DRC v. Rwanda), (Feb. 3, 2006), 2006 ICJ Rep. 126; Armed Activities on the Territory of the Congo (DRC v. Burundi), Order (Jan. 30, 2001), 2001 ICJ Rep. 3.

and Uganda worked closely together, *inter alia* in the field of counter-insurgency. However, as time went on, the DRC sought to substantially limit the influence of Uganda and Rwanda on its territory, a policy shift that led to a gradual deterioration of the relations between the countries. Following a failed coup by the Chief of Staff, a Rwandan national, President Kabila on July 28, 1998 announced in the press that all foreign troops had to leave the country. From early August onwards, Rwanda and Uganda augmented their troop presence and began to seize successive parts of Congolese territory. The situation aggravated badly as various African states sided either with the DRC or with Uganda and Rwanda. Added to this was the presence of numerous armed groups engaged in hostilities against the government and each other.

In casu, the DRC claimed that the statement of July 28, 1998 provided the direct impetus for the Ugandan invasion and alleged that Uganda had organized military and paramilitary activities against the DRC amounting to aggression. Uganda objected that its initial armed presence was based on a treaty concluded between the two countries with the aim of eliminating anti-Ugandan elements in the eastern border region. Subsequently it had been forced to act in self-defense, since the DRC was creating ties with Sudan, Chad and rebel movements fighting against Uganda. According to Uganda, troop presence had only been strengthened when it became clear that the number of Sudanese troops in the DRC was rising (para. 39). The Court deduced from these arguments that Uganda claimed that: in the period from May 1997 until September 11, 1998, the DRC had consented to the presence of its troops; in the period between September 11, 1998 and July 10, 1999 it was exercising its right to self-defense; and, that from July 10, 1999 onwards the DRC had again consented to the presence of Ugandan troops as a result of the Lusaka Agreement and subsequent agreements providing in a ceasefire and a phased withdrawal of foreign troops (para. 92).

Addressing the legality of the Ugandan intervention, the Court first looked into the issue of consent. Concerning the first period (from May 1997 until September 11, 1998) it found that President Kabila closely cooperated with Uganda and allowed it to station troops in eastern Congo in order to combat anti-Ugandan groups (para. 36). This cooperation was subsequently formalized by the Protocol on Security along the Common Border of April 27, 1998. However, as the Court rightly spelled out, the actual consent antedated the Protocol – the Protocol merely resulted in a third Ugandan battalion being installed in the DRC. Consequently, the source of this consent was not linked to the Protocol and could be withdrawn at any time irrespective of procedures for the termination of treaties. The situation changed on July 28, 1998, when President Kabila requested the removal of foreign troops. Although the Court conceded that the initial statement was ambiguous *vis-à-vis* the presence of Ugandan troops, subsequent statements at the Victoria Falls Summit made clear that the DRC no longer consented hereto (para. 53). Since withdrawal of consent was not subject to any formalities (para. 47), the Court concluded that the presence of Ugandan troops was no longer desired from August 8, 1998, i.e. the closing date of the Victoria Falls Summit. Concerning the period after July 10, 1999, the Court examined the roles of the Lusaka Ceasefire Agreement, the Harare and Kampala Disengagement Plans and the Luanda Agreement. These documents installed a ceasefire between the various parties to the conflict and provided for a phased withdrawal of foreign troops, including by Uganda.[6] According to the Court, none of these instruments provided for a (renewed) consent to the presence of Ugandan troops. Instead, they merely reflected the situation on the ground without addressing the legal questions involved, and only laid down a *modus operandi* for withdrawal (para. 99). Consequently, the Court concluded that the DRC had only consented to the presence of Ugandan troops until August 8, 1998.

The ICJ subsequently examined the submission of Uganda that it was acting in self-defense. Uganda contended that the territory of the DRC was used by its enemies, most notably Sudan and the Allied Democratic Forces (ADF), who were allegedly supplied by Sudan and the DRC. It claimed that Sudan had bombed Ugandan forces and the DRC had encouraged and facilitated attacks against Uganda. Hence, Operation Safe Haven, launched after the promulgation of the Ugandan "High Command Document" on September 11, 1998, constituted a necessary measure in response to "secure Uganda's legitimate security interests." The Court rejected the Ugandan arguments one by one. Thus, it found that Operation Safe Haven had already commenced in August 1998, before the issuing of the "High Command Document" (paras 109 and 115). Secondly and more importantly, it noted that the *objectives* of Uganda were not consonant with the law of self-defense. Indeed, the "High Command Document" made no reference whatsoever to armed attacks that had already occurred against Uganda. The Court denounced the justification given as being "essentially preventative," thereby implicitly rejecting the possibility of preventive self-defense (para. 143).[7] Furthermore, the Court found no proof of attacks by armed bands imputable to the DRC within the sense of Article 3(g) of the Definition of Aggression,[8] which could justify the exercise of the right

---

[6] The Lusaka Ceasefire Agreement provided *inter alia* for the scheduled withdrawal of all foreign troops from the DRC. When it became apparent that the initial timetable agreed upon was not realistic, this issue was further elaborated by the Harare and Kampala Disengagement Plans. However, the DRC and Uganda concluded a subsequent agreement, the Luanda Agreement concerning the withdrawal of Ugandan troops and the normalization of relations, changing the Lusaka Ceasefire Agreement without resulting in protest of the other parties.

[7] While the Court implicitly rejected the possibility of preventive self-defense (against non-imminent armed threat), it refrained from taking any position *vis-à-vis* the legality of pre-emptive self-defense (against an imminent attack). Instead, the Court merely repeated its position in the *Nicaragua* case, namely that it "expressed no view on the issue."

[8] Definition of Aggression, Annex to G.A. Res. 3314 (XXIX) (Dec. 14, 1974).

to self-defense (paras 146–147).⁹ In conclusion, the Court found that the intervention of Uganda was of such magnitude and duration that it should be considered to be a grave violation of the prohibition on the use of force (Article 2(4) of UN Charter). However, despite an explicit request by the DRC, the Court stopped short from qualifying the intervention as an act of "aggression," an approach that was criticized by a number of ICJ Judges.¹⁰

The second claim of the DRC concerned alleged Ugandan violations of IHL and international human rights law on Congolese territory. In this respect, the Court first examined whether Uganda could be considered an occupying power in the sense of Article 42 HR. To this end, it assessed whether it could be proven that the Ugandan military forces had substituted their own authority for that of the DRC (para. 173).¹¹ After answering this question in the positive, the Court concluded that Uganda was responsible for violations of IHL and human rights committed by its own forces in the occupied territory. It moreover stated that Uganda bore responsibility for violations by other armed groups if it had failed to abide by its duty of vigilance as an occupying power. In a second stage the Court scrutinized whether Uganda was bound by various humanitarian law and human rights instruments, whether violations had taken place, and whether they were attributable to Uganda (paras 205–221), thereby concluding that Uganda had indeed violated several provisions of IHL and human rights law.

In a third submission, the DRC claimed that Uganda had illegally exploited its natural resources in violation of IHL and the principle of permanent sovereignty over natural resources. Uganda objected that the alleged facts were not proven and were in any case not imputable to Uganda. Whereas the Court held that the principle of permanent sovereignty was not applicable to occupied territory (para. 244), it nonetheless determined that Uganda had breached the prohibition of pillage, laid down in Article 47 HR and Article 33 of the Fourth Geneva Convention (GC IV) (para. 250).

The last submission of the DRC concerned alleged violations of the ICJ Order of Provisional Measures of July 1, 2000.¹² Although the Court noted that the DRC had not provided any proof to support its claim, it nevertheless found Uganda in

---

⁹ The Court's insistence on the need for imputability of attacks by non-state armed groups to a state was criticized by a number of judges. See in particular: DRC v. Uganda, *supra* note 1, Separate Opinion of Judge Kooijmans, paras 19–31 and Separate Opinion of Judge Simma, paras 7–15.

¹⁰ *Id.* Separate Opinion of Judge Elaraby, paras 9–19; Separate Opinion of Judge Simma, paras 2–3. The Court's silence inspired Judge Simma to the following reveries: "So, why not call a spade a spade? If there ever was a military activity before the Court that deserves to be qualified as an act of aggression, it is the Ugandan invasion of the DRC. Compared to its scale and impact, the military adventures the Court had to deal with in earlier cases...border on the insignificant."

¹¹ See Section C.2.

¹² DRC v. Uganda, Order (July 1, 2000), 2000 ICJ Rep. 111.

breach of the Order since the conduct for which is was held responsible in the earlier part of the judgment went against the provisions of the Order (paras 262–265).

Uganda itself also submitted two counterclaims. Firstly, it argued that the DRC itself had committed acts of aggression on the grounds that Uganda had, since 1994, been the victim of military operations carried out by hostile armed groups based in the DRC and supported or tolerated by successive Congolese governments (para. 276). The Court however ruled that there was insufficient evidence that the DRC (then Zaire) was involved in anti-Ugandan armed activities; that neither Uganda nor Zaire were in the position to effectively combat those rebel groups, and, that at the end of the period under revision the DRC was entitled to support such groups since it was exercising its right to self-defense (paras 298, 301 and 304). Secondly, Uganda claimed that Congolese armed forces had carried out attacks on the Ugandan embassy in Kinshasa, confiscated Ugandan property and maltreated diplomats and other Ugandan nationals present on the premises of the mission and at the airport. The DRC challenged the admissibility of the second counter-claim, but was only partially successful. On the one hand, the Court found the claim of alleged mistreatment at the airport of Ugandan nationals, not enjoying diplomatic status, to be inadmissible because of a lack of exhaustion of local remedies, a necessary condition for the exercise of diplomatic protection. On the other hand, it ruled that there was sufficient evidence to prove that the DRC had violated the embassy and had maltreated Ugandan diplomats as well as other Ugandan nationals present on the embassy premises in contravention of the 1961 Vienna Convention on Diplomatic Relations (para. 333).

This brief synopsis of the judgment illustrates that what was initially a matter of consensual presence of foreign troops on Congolese territory gradually turned into the large-scale use of armed force between the DRC and Uganda, triggering the rules of IHL relating to international armed conflicts, in particular the rules concerning belligerent occupation. Let us now have closer look at the Court's findings on this issue.

3. *Occupation*

3.1. *Applicability of Thresholds and the Laws of Occupation*

Whereas inhabitants of occupied territories long enjoyed little if any rights at all, their position has greatly improved through the insertion in the 1907 Hague Regulations and the 1949 Fourth Geneva Convention of a series of provisions dealing specifically with occupation.[13] The provisions are founded on the idea that

---

[13] Hans-Peter Gasser, *Protection of the Civilian Population*, in The Handbook of Humanitarian Law in Armed Conflicts 209, 240 (Dieter Fleck ed., 1995) [hereinafter Gasser].

an occupying power does not acquire sovereignty over occupied territory and that occupation is only a temporary situation. Hence, the rights of the occupier are limited to the extent of that period and existing laws and structures should generally be left unaltered. Together they create a wide-ranging regime for the protection of inhabitants of occupied territory that goes much further than the general provisions applicable to civilians in armed conflicts. This regime contains a number of broad obligations, such as the duty to take measures to restore and ensure, as far as possible, public order and safety (Article 43 HR, *cf.* infra). It also contains numerous specific rules *inter alia* addressing the protection of civilian property and the possibility to impose taxes or to organize compulsory labor.

Given the far-reaching nature of these rights and duties, the question emerges as to what situations qualify as "occupations" in the sense of the Hague Regulations and the Fourth Geneva Convention. According to Article 42 HR, territory is considered occupied when it is actually placed under the authority of the hostile army. The occupation extends only to the territory where such authority has been established and can be exercised. Common Article 2(2) of the Geneva Conventions makes clear that this qualification extends beyond the realm of traditional "belligerent occupations" and also covers situations where the occupation of state territory meets with no armed resistance (hence the present use of the more generic term "occupation").[14]

The picture that emerges is that the actual control exercised directly by an occupier through the physical presence of its armed forces forms the key to the application of the aforementioned rules.[15] The label used by the occupying power to describe its activities, whether "administration," "invasion," "trusteeship" or plain "occupation," is of no significance; Nor is the motivation of the occupier. Occupations may indeed cover a wide range of goals. They may aim at implementing territorial claims, at acquiring control over natural resources, at preventing the use of territory as a base of attack by armed groups, at re-establishing order and stability in a

---

[14] *See* Eyal Benvenisti, The International Law of Occupation 4 (2004) [hereinafter Benvenisti]. The ambit of the laws of occupation is further enlarged as a result of Article 1(3) of the First Additional Protocol of the Geneva Conventions, which equates conflicts in pursuit of self-determination or against colonial or racist regimes with international armed conflicts.

[15] Adam Roberts, *What is a Military Occupation?*, 55 B.Y.B.I.L. 249, 252 (1984) [hereinafter Roberts, Military Occupation]; Conor McCarthy, *The Paradox of the International Law of Military Occupation: Sovereignty and the Reformation of Iraq*, 10 J.C.S.L. 43, 45 (2005) [hereinafter McCarthy].

collapsed state (sometimes termed "transformative military occupation,")[16] etc.[17] Furthermore, it makes no difference whether an occupation was approved by the U.N. Security Council or not. The qualification ultimately boils down to a factual test, determined by the situation on the ground. This becomes all the more clear if one considers the authentic French text of Article 42 HR, which considers a territory as occupied "*lorsqu'il se trouve placé de fait sous l'autorité de l'armée ennemie*" (the wording "*de fait*" was somewhat inaccurately translated as "actually" instead of "in fact.")

Still, the actual application of the laws of occupation causes some disagreement, both in relation to the so-called invasion phase and in relation to the elements to be used for the factual test. Two views exist as to the law applicable to troops advancing in enemy territory.[18] On the one hand, it is argued that a situation of occupation exists whenever a party to a conflict is exercising some level of authority or control over territory belonging to the enemy, including during the invasion phase of hostilities. This approach is based on the idea that Common Article 2 (1) and (2) of the Geneva Conventions purports to give a broader meaning to the concept of "occupation" than does Article 42 HR. It finds some support in a number of other provisions, such as Article 6 GC IV, which refers to occupations which continue after the end of military operations.[19] Pictet in the 1958 Commentary to the GC IV affirms the view that the notion of "occupation" was given a broader meaning than in relation to the Hague Regulations: "So far as individuals are concerned, the application of the Fourth Geneva Convention does not depend upon the existence of a state of occupation within the meaning of the Article 42 referred to above. The relations between the civilian population of a territory and troops advancing into that territory, whether fighting or not, are governed by the present Convention. There is no intermediate period between what might be termed the invasion phase and the inauguration of a stable regime of occupation.... [A]ll persons who find themselves in the hands of a Party to the conflict or an Occupying Power of

---

[16] This type of occupation has recently attracted scholarly attention in the wake of the U.S. intervention in Iraq and has stirred up debates regarding the tension between the need for political and economic reform and the respect for existing laws and structures in occupied territory. *See* for example Adam Roberts, *Transformative Military Occupation: Applying the Laws of War and Human Rights*, 100 Am. J. Int'l L. 580–622 (2006) [hereinafter Roberts, Transformative Military Occupation]; McCarthy, *supra* note 15.

[17] *See* for example Roberts, Transformative Military Occupation, *supra* note 15, at 300. Roberts lists no less than seventeen types of occupation divided in three categories: wartime and post-war occupation, peacetime occupation, and other possible categories.

[18] *See* Daniel Thürer, *Current Challenges to the Law of Occupation*, Oct. 20–21, 2005, *available at* www.icrc.org/web/eng/siteeng0.nsf/html/occupation-statement-211105?opendocument (last visited May 11, 2007) [hereinafter Thürer].

[19] *See* Roberts, Transformative Military Occupation, *supra* note 15, at 253–254.

which they are not nationals are protected persons."[20] Pictet hereby refers to the example of invading troops taking civilians with them while withdrawing, arguing that such conduct would constitute a breach of Article 49 GC IV which prohibits the deportation or forcible transfer of persons from occupied territory.

The alternative approach claims that a situation of occupation only comes into existence once a party to a conflict is in a position to exercise the level of authority over enemy territory necessary to enable it to discharge *all* the obligations imposed by the laws of occupation.[21] Thus, Gasser suggests that the law of occupation is intended to apply in stable situations.[22] Its rules do not apply until the forces invading a foreign country have established actual control over a certain territory. Such control presupposes that through their physical presence the invading troops can actually assume the responsibilities attached to an occupying power, including the ability to issue directives to the inhabitants of the conquered territory and to enforce them. This, he argues, does not create a legally unprotected period, since all other provisions of IHL such as the "general protection" of Part II GC IV or the rules on targeting and distinction continue to apply throughout the invasion period.

The U.K. Manual of the Law of Armed Conflict follows a similar line of view and argues that patrols or commando units which move on or withdraw after carrying out their mission do not normally occupy territory since they are not there long enough to set up an administration.[23] When hostilities continue in enemy territory, occupation only arises in areas coming under control of the adverse party, provided that measures are taken to administer the areas in question. To determine whether a state of occupation exists, two conditions must be satisfied according to the U.K. Manual: firstly, the former government must have been rendered incapable of publicly exercising its authority in that area; and, secondly, the occupying power must be in a position to substitute its own authority for that of the former government. In similar vein, the position adopted in the U.S. Field Army Manual 27–10 is that the laws of occupation only apply to actual occupation, which presupposes "invasion plus taking firm possession of enemy territory for the purpose of holding it."[24] It should however be noted that, while the U.S. Manual denies the *de jure* applicability of the laws of occupation to situations of mere invasion, it nevertheless argues that these rules should, as a matter of policy,

---

[20] Oscar M. Uhler & Henri Coursier, Geneva Convention relative to the Protection of Civilian Persons in Time of War: Commentary 60 (1958) [hereinafter Uhler & Coursier].

[21] *See* Thürer, *supra* note 18.

[22] Gasser, *supra* note 13, paras 526–527.

[23] U.K. Ministry of Defence, The Manual of the Law of Armed Conflict 275–276 (2004) [hereinafter U.K. Ministry of Defence].

[24] U.S. Department of the Army, *Field Manual 27–10: the Law of Land Warfare*, (July 18, 1956), *available at* www.globalsecurity.org/military/library/policy/army/fm/27–10/index.html (last visited May 11, 2007) Rules 352–356 [hereinafter U.S. Department of the Army].

be observed as far as possible in areas through which troops are passing and even on the battlefield.

Recently the controversy was before the International Criminal Tribunal for the Former Yugoslavia (ICTY) in the *Naletilic and Martinovic* case.[25] Here, the ICTY Trial Chamber defines occupation as a transitional period following invasion and preceding the agreement on the cessation of hostilities. It furthermore states that the law of occupation only applies to those areas actually controlled by the occupying power. This should be determined on a case by case basis, taking account of the relevant times and places. So far this reasoning seems to follow the more restrictive approach. This is also illustrated by the fact that the ICTY includes a list of guidelines to establish occupation, which largely builds on the aforementioned military manuals.[26] However, the Court subsequently adopts the view expounded by Pictet that the word "occupation" has a wider meaning for the purpose of GC IV than it has in Article 42 HR (paras 221–222). The Court hereby makes a distinction between the protection of individuals on the one hand, and property or other matters on the other hand. Whereas in the latter case, the laws of occupation only come into play when "actual authority" arises, for the purpose of individuals' rights, a state of occupation exists as soon as individuals fall into "the hands of the occupying power." Thus, according to the ICTY, violations of the provisions on forcible transfer or unlawful labor could arise whenever civilians fall into the hands of the opposing power, regardless of the stage of hostilities. This approach corresponds to the "maximalist position" of the International Committee of the Red Cross that whenever – even in the so-called invasion phase – persons come within the power or control of a hostile army they should be ensured the protection of the GC IV as a minimum.[27]

3.2. *The Court's Approach in* DRC *v.* Uganda

In the *DRC* v. *Uganda* case, the debate concerning the commencement of a state of occupation would seem particularly interesting in respect of the fact that the advance of the UPDF (the Ugandan army) into Congolese territory developed over a relatively long span of time. Indeed, as the report of the Porter Commission – an

---

[25] Prosecutor v. Naletilic and Martinovic, Case No. IT-98-34-T, Trial Chamber I, (Mar. 31, 2003), paras 210–223 [hereinafter Naletilic and Martinovic].
[26] *Id.* para. 217, footnotes 584–588. The Court refers to the military manuals of the United States, the United Kingdom, New Zealand, and Germany *inter alia* to support the view that an occupying power must be in a position to substitute its own authority for that of the occupied authorities, which must have been rendered incapable of functioning publicly, and; that battle areas may not be considered as occupied territory.
[27] Thürer, *supra* note 18. Speaking on behalf of the ICRC, Thürer notes that this may be considered a premature qualification of a situation as occupation but argues that the aim of this approach is to maximize protection of affected persons.

independent tribunal of inquiry established by Uganda in 2001 – and the claims of the contending parties demonstrate, from August 1998 onwards, a growing number of Congolese locations were captured by Ugandan troops (paras 72–91). While the exact dates of capture are often contested, it is fair to say that the Ugandan advance only came to an end in July 1999 when a ceasefire was concluded.[28]

Yet, the Court chose not to go into the details of the practicalities of the Ugandan advance, instead opting for a general examination of whether Congolese territory was actually placed under the authority of the hostile army. In this regard, the Court argued that it needed to satisfy itself "that the Ugandan armed forces in the DRC were not only stationed in particular locations but also that they had substituted their own authority for that of the Congolese government" (para. 173). The Court first observed that the territorial limits of a zone of occupation could not simply be determined by drawing a line connecting the locations where Ugandan troops were present. It subsequently stressed the (undisputed) fact that General Kazini, commander of the UPDF in the DRC, created the new "province of Kibali-Ituri" in June 1999 and appointed Ms. Adèle Lotsove as its Governor. Regardless of whether or not General Kazini acted in violation of his orders in doing so and was punished as a result – as Uganda contends –, the Court determined that this conduct was "clear evidence of the fact that Uganda established and exercised authority in Ituri as an occupying power" (para. 176).

The fact that the Court refrained from pronouncing on the application of the laws of occupation to troops advancing in enemy territory may be a missed opportunity to clarify the existing law on this issue, yet it is an understandable one as the Court's findings concerning violations hereof refer to the post-invasion-period (paras 206–212). This silence should therefore not be interpreted as rendering support to the restrictive approach to applicability. On the other hand, even though it correctly observed that the creation of a structured military administration is not a prerequisite for military occupation and even though it rightly attributed General Kazini's conduct to Uganda, the Court seems to have relied all too heavily on formal administrative elements in establishing the applicability of the laws of occupation. This creates a double-edged misperception that such formal administrative steps are 1) sufficient and 2) necessary for a state of occupation to come into existence.

Firstly, while the creation of a separate province and the appointment of a "provisional Governor" may be important indications that a state has established authority over (part of) another state's territory, Judge Parra-Arranguren correctly points out that this does not necessarily imply that the former state is also in a position

---

[28] The DRC even claimed that a number of towns were taken after the conclusion of the ceasefire agreement, yet the Court found that there existed insufficient evidence to make a finding in this regard (paras 88–90).

to exercise this authority in the sense of Article 42 HR.[29] The role and strength of the occupying troops are crucial. Indeed, as indicated above, a true (post-invasion) occupation presupposes that through their physical presence the occupying troops are able to issue directives to the inhabitants of the conquered territory and enforce them.[30] This does not mean that the occupying power must keep troops permanently stationed throughout the area.[31] In the words of the U.S. Army Field Manual: "It is sufficient that the occupying force can, within a reasonable time, send detachments of troops to make its authority felt within the occupied district. It is immaterial whether the authority of the occupant is maintained by fixed garrisons or flying columns, whether by small or large forces, so long as the occupation is effective."[32] In this regard, while the Court admits that occupation presupposes the stationing of troops in particular locations, it does not respond to Uganda's claims that it had deployed only a small number of troops in Congolese territory – "fewer than 10.000 soldiers at the height of the deployment" – and that it was the rebels of the MLC and the RDC "which controlled and administered these territories, exercising *de facto* authority" (para. 170). In fact, the Court says virtually nothing about troop deployment, but merely "notes" that according to MONUC observers, the UPDF was in effective control in Bunia, the capital of Ituri (para. 175). However, it seems hard to imagine how effective control over Bunia could automatically be equated with actual control over a province of some 65.000 km² and home to a dozen different rebel groups.[33] Thus, one might sympathize with Judge Parra-Aranguren's criticism that the Court should have shed more light on the role of the UPDF in comparison to Rwandan troops and various rebel groups present in Ituri in order to gain a better understanding of which areas were occupied by Uganda at which times. The outcome of such an examination might have been the same, yet the legal analysis would have been more convincing.

Secondly, although the Court explicitly states that it would be irrelevant whether or not Uganda had established a structured military administration (para. 173), its emphasis on formal administrative steps and its reference to the "substitution of authority" create the impression that formal measures are necessary for the law of occupation to apply. The reference to "substitution of authority" acquires particular meaning in light of the difference between the double standards used in the U.K. and U.S. Manuals respectively.[34] On the one hand, both Manuals overlap to the extent that they require that the occupation has rendered the former government incapable

---

[29] DRC v. Uganda, *supra* note 1, Separate Opinion of Judge Parra-Aranguren, para. 33.
[30] Gasser, *supra* note 13, paras 526–527.
[31] U.K. Ministry of Defence, *supra* note 23, at 276.
[32] U.S. Department of the Army, *supra* note 24, para. 356.
[33] *See* also DRC v. Uganda, *supra* note 1, Separate Opinion of Judge Parra-Aranguren, para. 33.
[34] U.K. Ministry of Defence, *supra* note 23, at 275; U.S. Department of the Army, *supra* note 24, para. 355.

of publicly exercising its authority in the area. On the other hand, the U.K. Manual merely demands that the occupying power is in a "position to substitute" its own authority for that of the former government, whereas the U.S. Manual presumes that the occupying power should have "successfully substituted" authority. The Court's wording seems to correspond to the latter, more restrictive version. However, the former version seems to be more suitable, as it better reflects the *raison d'être* of the law of occupation, i.e. the protection of the civilian population.[35] Indeed, the danger of the restrictive approach and – *in extenso* – of the Court's reliance on formal measures is that the applicability of the law of occupation is made conditional upon the occupying power taking active steps to administer the occupied territory. This may be understandable from a historical perspective: at the time the Hague Regulations were adopted, the establishment of a system of administration by the occupant was widely accepted as mandatory in literature as well as in practice.[36] Today, however, the term "occupation" has acquired a pejorative connotation and occupants for a variety of reasons prefer not to establish such a direct administration.[37] Instead, as Benvenisti argues, "[t]hey [purport] to annex or establish puppet States or governments, make use of existing structures of government, or simply refrain from establishing any form of administration. In these cases, the occupants [tend] not to acknowledge the applicability of the law of occupation to their own or their surrogates' activities, and when using surrogate institutions [deny] any international responsibility for the latter's actions."[38] Given this evolution, making the applicability of the law of occupation conditional upon deliberate measures to administer territory would turn things upside down. Occupying powers cannot escape their obligations under IHL by not engaging in such measures. To the contrary, these obligations are activated as soon as the occupying power acquires the *capacity* to administer territory and in turn create the responsibility to implement this capacity. Occupying powers cannot turn their back on the power vacuum and institutional vacuum they have often created themselves. The application of the law of occupation cannot be left to the discretion of the occupying power.[39]

---

[35] Several authors refer the "possibility" or "capacity" to assert authority. *E.g.* Lassa Oppenheim and Hersch Lauterpacht, International Law: a Treatise. Vol. 2 Disputes, War and Neutrality 435 (1952); Gasser, *supra* note 13, para. 527. *See also* DRC v. Uganda, *supra* note 1, Separate Opinion of Judge Kooijmans, paras 43–45.

[36] Benvenisti, *supra* note 14, at 4–5, 212.

[37] The occupation of Iraq following the US-UK intervention is rather exceptional in this regard. Section 1, para. 1 of Coalition Provisional Authority Regulation Number 1 of May 16, 2003 states that the CPA "shall exercise powers of government temporarily in order to provide for the effective administration of Iraq during the period of transitional administration ...," text *available at* www.cpa-iraq.org/regulations/20030516_CPAREG_1_The_Coalition_Provisional_Authority_.pdf (last visited May 11, 2007).

[38] Benvenisti, *supra* note 14, at 5.

[39] Thürer, *supra* note 18.

This reading is supported by the Oxford Manual adopted by the Institut de Droit International in 1880.[40] According to Article 41 of the Manual, territory is regarded as occupied "when, as the consequence of invasion by hostile forces, the State to which it belongs has ceased, in fact, to exercise its ordinary authority therein, and the invading State is alone in a position to maintain order there."

In this regard, one may wonder whether the Court has not passed too lightly on the possibility that the territory occupied by Uganda extended beyond the province of Ituri. The Court rejected this option on the double grounds that the DRC did not provide any specific evidence to show that authority *was exercised* by Ugandan armed forces in any areas other than in the Ituri district and that the evidence presented to the Court did not support the view that rebel groups were "under the control" of Uganda in the sense of the ILC's Draft Articles on State Responsibility (para. 177 *juncto* para. 160). On the other hand, as argued by Judge Kooijmans, the invasion by the UPDF directly enabled Congolese rebel movements to bring the north-eastern provinces under their control.[41] Uganda moreover provided training and military support to at least one of the most important rebel groups, the MLC (para. 160). Finally, while the rebel groups may have exercised *de facto* authority over these provinces, the UPDF nevertheless continued to occupy certain airports (e.g. Kisangani airport) and other strategic locations (one may think for example of barracks or extraction sites). For these reasons, Judge Kooijmans claims that Uganda should have been considered as the occupying power in these locations at least until the Lusaka Ceasefire Agreement of July 10, 1999 "upgraded" the two main rebel movements (the MLC and the RCD) to formal participants in the national Congolese dialogue and – together with the central Congolese government – vested them with the primary responsibility for the re-establishment of an integrated state administration in the relevant provinces.[42]

Whether or not Uganda should have been considered as an occupying power in territories outside the Ituri district would seem to depend on the question whether its armed presence in certain strategic locations sufficed to put it in a position to maintain order in (part of) the said locations (e.g. by enforcing orders). If this were the case, the lack of attributability of the actions of rebel groups to Uganda should not exclude the application of the law of occupation to Uganda's conduct in these territories. "Capacity", it seems, is the key element.

---

[40] Institut de Droit International, The Laws of War on Land, (Sept. 9, 1880), reproduced in Dietrich Schindler & Jiri Toman, The Laws of Armed Conflicts 36–48 (1988).
[41] DRC v. Uganda, *supra* note 1, Separate Opinion of Judge Kooijmans, paras 48–49.
[42] *Id.* paras 50–54.

4. Extra-Territorial Applicability of Human Rights Instruments

4.1. General

After determining that Uganda acted as the occupying power in Ituri, the ICJ found that it was under the obligation, pursuant to Article 43 HR, to take all the measures in its power to restore, and ensure public order and safety in the occupied area. According to the Court, this obligation comprised the duty to secure respect for the applicable rules of international human rights law and IHL (para. 178). The Court subsequently repeated its earlier findings from *Palestinian Wall* that "the protection offered by human rights conventions does not cease in case of armed conflict, save through the effect of provisions for derogation."[43]

While the Court in *Palestinian Wall* went at great lengths to justify the extra-territorial application of human rights obligations to the Occupied Palestinian Territories (OPT) on behalf of Israel,[44] in *DRC* v. *Uganda* it deemed such rambles superfluous. Instead, the Court merely reaffirmed that "international human rights instruments are applicable 'in respect of acts done by a State in the exercise of its jurisdiction outside its own territory'" (para. 216).[45] After listing the relevant human rights instruments, the Court found that Uganda had violated:

- Article 6(1) of the International Covenant on Civil and Political Rights (ICCPR) and Article 4 of the African Charter on Human and Peoples' Rights (ACHPR) (the right to life);
- Article 7 of ICCPR and Article 5 of ACHPR (the prohibition against torture and cruel, inhuman or degrading treatment or punishment), and;
- Article 38(2) and (3) of the Convention on the Rights of the Child (CRC) and Articles 1, 2, 3(3), 4, 5 and 6 of the Optional Protocol to the Convention on the Rights of the Child (concerning child soldiers).

At first sight *DRC* v. *Uganda* seems to add little new to the advisory opinion on the *Palestinian Wall*. Nevertheless, the judgment is of great symbolic importance. Indeed, the laws of war were long seen as the only branch of international law applicable to occupations. Many authors stressed that human rights were meant to operate in peacetime and would be superseded by IHL in wartime.[46] Others added that human rights could not apply extraterritorially, arguing for example that the *travaux préparatoires* of the ICCPR make clear that a state's obligations under

---

[43] Palestinian Wall, *supra* note 2, para. 106.
[44] *Id.* paras 107–113.
[45] *See id.* paras 111–113.
[46] *See* Roberts, Transformative Military Occupation, *supra* note 16, at 589–592; Yoram Dinstein, *Human Rights in Armed Conflict: International Humanitarian Law, in* Human Rights in International Law: Legal and Policy Issues 350 (Thedor Meron ed., 1985) [hereinafter Dinstein].

the Convention only apply within its territory *and* subject to its jurisdiction,[47] a phrase which should not be read disjunctively.[48] Yet, this position has increasingly come under strain as a result of a growing body of international jurisprudence confirming that international human rights law may apply extraterritorially to occupied territories. Thus, the European Commission of Human Rights and the European Court of Human Rights have done so in relation to Turkey's occupation of northern Cyprus.[49] The Inter-American Commission of Human Rights did the same with regard to the U.S. invasion of Grenada and Panama.[50] Likewise, in the *Al Skeini* case, the U.K. Court of Appeal recognized the possible application of the European Convention on Human Rights (ECHR) to the occupying powers in Iraq.[51] Furthermore, the Human Rights Committee (HRC) has stressed that Israel is bound by the ICCPR with regard to its conduct in the Occupied Palestinian Territories,[52] as has the Committee on Economic, Social and Cultural Rights in relation to the obligations under the International Covenant on Economic, Social and Cultural Rights (ICESCR).[53] Given these developments, it seems that there now exists general agreement between these bodies that if a state exercises effective control over foreign territory, for example as a result of military occupation, the human rights treaties to which it is a party are applicable to its conduct in that

---

[47] Article 2(1) International Covenant on Civil and Political Rights, G.A. Res. 2200A (XXI), 21 U.N. GAOR Supp. (No. 16) at 52, U.N. Doc. A/6316 (1966), 999 U.N.T.S. 171 [hereinafter ICCPR].

[48] *E.g.* Michael J. Dennis, *Application of Human Rights Treaties Extraterritorially in Times of Armed Conflict and Military Occupation*, 99 Am. J. Int'l L. 119, 122–127 (2005) [hereinafter Dennis]; Manfred Nowak, *The Effectiveness of the International Covenant on Civil and Political Rights: Stocktaking after the First Eleven Sessions of the UN Human Rights Committee*, 1 Human Rights L. J. 136, 156 (1980).

[49] Cyprus v. Turkey, Application Nos. 6780/74, 6950/75, 2 Eur.Comm.H.R. Dec. & Rep. 125 (1975) [hereinafter Cyprus v. Turkey 1975]; Cyprus v. Turkey, Application No. 8007/77, 13 Eur.Comm.H.R. Dec. & Rep. 85 (1978) [hereinafter Cyprus v. Turkey 1978]; Cyprus v. Turkey, Application No. 25781/94, 86–A Eur.Comm.H.R. Dec. & Rep. 104 (1986); Loizidou v. Turkey (Preliminary Objections), (Mar. 23, 1995), Series A Vol. 310 [hereinafter Loizidou (Preliminary Objections)].

[50] Salas and Others v. the United States (U.S. Military Intervention in Panama), Report No. 31/93, Case No. 10.573, (Oct. 14, 1993), Ann. Rep. I.A.C.H.R. 312 (1999) [hereinafter Salas and Others]; Coard and Others v. the United States (U.S. Military Intervention in Grenada), Report No. 109/99, Case No. 10.951, (Sept. 29, 1999), Ann. Rep. I.A.C.H.R. (1999) [hereinafter Coard and Others].

[51] U.K. Court of Appeal, The Queen (on the application of Mazin Mumaa Galteh Al Skeini and Others) v. The Secretary of State for Defence, Case No. C1/2005/0461, C1/2005/0461B, (Dec. 21, 2005), E.W.C.A. Civ. 1609 (2005) [hereinafter Al Skeini Case].

[52] HRC, Concluding Observations: Israel (Aug. 21, 2003), U.N. Doc. CCPR/CO/78/ISR, para. 11.

[53] Committee on Economic, Social and Cultural Rights (CESCR), Concluding Observations: Israel (May 23, 2003), U.N. Doc. E/C.12/1/Add.90, paras 15 and 31.

foreign territory.⁵⁴ This reasoning has moreover been supported by political bodies such as the Security Council⁵⁵ or the Parliamentary Assembly of the Council of Europe.⁵⁶

In light of this evolution it will not come as a surprise that the opponents of extraterritorial application of human rights have become a dying breed. This, however, is not to say that they no longer exist. As Roberts makes clear: "The general principle that human rights law can apply to military occupations is now widely, but by no means universally, accepted."⁵⁷ Even after the ICJ's assertion in *Palestinian Wall* that the ICCPR, the ICESCR and the CRC are applicable in respect of acts done by a state in the exercise of its jurisdiction outside its own territory, some attempted to erode this finding. Thus, Dennis argued that "the ICJ's conclusion... appears to have been based upon the unusual circumstances of Israel's prolonged occupation. It therefore remains unclear whether the opinion should be read as generally endorsing the view that the obligations assumed by States under international human rights instruments apply extraterritorially during situations of armed conflict and military occupation."⁵⁸ The significance of *DRC v. Uganda* is exactly that it demonstrates that the ICJ's finding was not merely inspired by the exceptional circumstances in the OPT, but should indeed be read as a general confirmation of the extraterritorial application of international human rights instruments in relation to the exercise of jurisdiction abroad. Contrary to the *Palestinian Wall* advisory opinion, *DRC v. Uganda* does not confine the discussion on extraterritorial application to specific human rights instruments. Rather, it emphasizes in broad and unmistakable terms that (all) "international human rights instruments are applicable 'in respect of acts done by a State in the exercise of its jurisdiction outside its own territory', particularly in occupied territories" (para. 216). Moreover, the facts underlying *DRC v. Uganda* exclude the excuse that the Court's appeal to international human rights law was inspired by any exceptional circumstances. Contrary to the situation in the OPT (which have been under Israeli occupation since 1967) the Ugandan occupation of Congolese territories did not last for an unusually long period of time. As mentioned before, Uganda began to occupy successive locations in Eastern Congo from August 1998 onwards; the advance of its troops seems to have continued until July 1999. It gradually withdrew some of its battalions from June 2000 onwards. Full withdrawal was completed in June

---

⁵⁴ Fons Coomans & Menno T. Kamminga, *Comparative Introductory Comments on the Extraterritorial Application of Human Rights Treaties, in* Extraterritorial Application of Human Rights Treaties 1, 3 (Fons Coomans & Menno T. Kamminga eds., 2004) [hereinafter Coomans & Kamminga] [hereinafter Coomans & Kamminga eds].
⁵⁵ *E.g.*, S.C. Res. 1456, U.N. Doc S/RES/1456 (2004) (June 8, 2004).
⁵⁶ Parliamentary Assembly Council of Europe, Resolution 1386 (June 24, 2004), para. 17.
⁵⁷ Roberts, Transformative Military Occupation, *supra* note 16, at 595.
⁵⁸ Dennis, *supra* note 48, at 122.

2003.⁵⁹ In sum, by affirming in general terms its ruling in *Palestinian Wall*, the ICJ seems to have delivered the *coup de grâce* to the remaining dissenting voices in the debate on the extraterritorial application of international human rights law.

4.2. What Thresholds? The "State Agent Authority" and "Effective Control of an Area" Tests

While *DRC* v. *Uganda* may well have silenced for good the opponents of extraterritorial application *per se*, it is evident that plenty of outstanding issues remain unresolved. A crucial issue is of course to determine how the applicable norms of IHL and human rights law interact in practice. This matter will further be examined in the following section. First, however, we will look deeper into the precise threshold for the extraterritorial application of human rights. The idea is not to provide a complete overview of relevant case law but rather to examine how the respective thresholds of the laws of occupation and international human rights law relate to one another.

Although various international human rights instruments use divergent wordings to establish their applicability and although some do not incorporate an explicit provision to this end, there clearly exists a great deal of commonality.⁶⁰ The key element for all these instruments is the "exercise of jurisdiction." In the *Bankovic* case the European Court of Human Rights states that this concerns an "essentially territorial" concept, "other bases of jurisdiction being exceptional and requiring special justification."⁶¹ Nonetheless, two categories of extraterritorial jurisdiction have acquired wide recognition. One is related to a state's control over *persons* outside its own territory and is characterized by "state agent authority" (SAA). The other is related to a state's control over foreign *territory* and is more accurately characterized as "effective control of an area" (ECA).⁶²

Extraterritorial applicability as a result of "state agent authority" has been confirmed by a large body of human rights jurisprudence. Already in the 1970s the European Commission of Human Rights used this line of reasoning to hold Turkey

---

⁵⁹ Hence, the Ugandan occupation of Ituri does not seem to qualify as a "prolonged occupation." While recognizing the deficiencies of any attempt to define this concept, Adam Roberts characterized "prolonged occupations" as occupations that last more than five years and extend into a period when hostilities are sharply reduced, i.e., a period at least approximating peacetime. *See* Adam Roberts, *Prolonged Military Occupation: the Israeli-Occupied Territories since 1967*, 84 Am. J. Int'l L. 44, 47 (1990).

⁶⁰ An overview of these jurisdiction provisions can be found in Coomans and Kamminga eds., *supra* note 54, at 271–274.

⁶¹ Bankovič v. Belgium and 16 other Contracting States, Application No. 52207/99, (Grand Chamber, Dec. 12, 2001), 41 I.L.M. 517 (2002), para. 61 [hereinafter Bankovič].

⁶² *See e.g.*, Al Skeini Case, *supra* note 51, para. 49.

accountable for human rights violations in northern Cyprus.[63] Turkey argued that northern Cyprus was under the exclusive jurisdiction of an entity known as the Turkish Federated State and that it had neither annexed a part of the island nor established a military or civil government there. The Commission rejected this plea, arguing that "authorized agents of a State, including...armed forces...bring any other persons or property 'within the jurisdiction' of that state, to the extent that they exercise authority over such persons or property. Insofar as, by their acts or omissions, they affect such persons or property, the responsibility of the State is engaged."[64] The Commission subsequently used this test to determine that persons who had been confined in detention centers or in private residences had been under the "actual control" of the Turkish army but also applied it in relation to access to property. The European Court has copied the line of reasoning developed by the European Commission of Human Rights to judge the compatibility with human rights standards of the detention or abduction of individuals by security forces acting abroad.[65] The SAA threshold has also been used by other human rights bodies. In *Lopez* v. *Uruguay* and *Celiberti* v. *Uruguay*, for example, the HRC found Uruguay guilty of violating the ICCPR as a result of kidnappings carried out by Uruguayan security forces acting abroad.[66] Moreover, in its communications with ICCPR member states, the Committee has occasionally stressed the application of the Convention to states' military forces acting abroad. It did so *inter alia* with regard to Belgian soldiers taking part in UNOSOM II in Somalia[67] as well as with regard to detention facilities in Bosnia-Herzegovina controlled by Croatian military factions.[68] Finally, in May 2004, the Committee endorsed General Comment 31 which abandons in general terms the disjunctive reading of Article 2(1) ICCPR.[69] According to this document "the enjoyment of Covenant rights...must...be

---

[63] *See* Cyprus v. Turkey 1975, *supra* note 49; Cyprus v. Turkey 1978, *supra* note 49; Chrysostomos v. Turkey, 68 Eur.Comm.H.R. Dec. & Rep. 216 (1991).
[64] Cyprus v. Turkey 1975, *supra* note 49, at 135.
[65] *E.g.* Öcalan v. Turkey, Application No. 46221/99 (May 12, 2005): "It is common ground that, directly after being handed over to the Turkish officials by the Kenyan officials [in Kenya], the applicant [Öcalan] was under effective Turkish authority and therefore within the 'jurisdiction' of that State for the purposes of Article 1 of the Convention" (para. 91).
[66] HRC, Delia Saldias de Lopez v. Uruguay, Communication No. 52/1979, U.N. Doc. CCPR/C/OP/1 at 88 (1984); HRC, Lilian Celiberti de Casariego v. Uruguay, Communication No. 56/1979, U.N. Doc. CCPR/C/OP/1 at 92 (1984). *See also* HRC, Mabel Pereira Montero v. Uruguay, Communication No. 106/1981, U.N. Doc. Supp. No. 40 (A/38/40) at 186 (1983).
[67] HRC, Concluding Observations: Belgium (Nov. 19, 1998), U.N. Doc. CCPR/C/79/Add.99, para. 14 (1998).
[68] HRC, Concluding Observations: Croatia (Dec. 28, 1992), U.N. Doc. CCPR/C/79/Add.15, paras 7 and 10 (1992).
[69] HRC, General Comment No. 31: Nature of the General Legal Obligation Imposed on States Parties to the Covenant (May 26, 2004), U.N. Doc. CCPR/C/21/Rev.1/Add/13.

available to all individuals...who may find themselves in the territory *or* subject to the jurisdiction of the State Party."[70] Like the aforementioned bodies, the Inter-American Commission for Human Rights has applied the SAA test, for example, with regard to the indefinite detention of aliens by the U.S. at Guantanamo Bay or with regard to the detention of civilians during the U.S. military intervention in Grenada in 1983.[71]

As suggested above, extraterritorial applicability may also flow from the fact that a state exercises effective control over foreign territory as a consequence of a military occupation or through the consent, invitation or acquiescence of the government of that territory. In *Loizidou* v. *Turkey*,[72] for example, the European Court held that a state is in principle accountable for violations of rights that occur in territories over which it has physical control, even if the territory is administered by a local administration. *In casu*, the Court found it obvious that Turkey had effective control over northern Cyprus given the fact that more than 30,000 Turkish military personnel were engaged in northern Cyprus. For this reason, it was unnecessary to determine whether Turkey actually exercised detailed control over the policies and actions of the authorities of the so-called Turkish Republic of Northern Cyprus (TRNC). Responsibility for the policies and actions of the TRNC resulted automatically from Turkey's effective control over the territory. In *Cyprus* v. *Turkey*,[73] the Court affirmed that "[h]aving effective overall control over northern Cyprus, [Turkey's] responsibility cannot be confined to the acts of its own soldiers or officials...but must also be engaged by virtue of the acts of the local administration which survives by virtue of Turkish military and other support. It follows that...Turkey's 'jurisdiction' must be considered to extend to securing the entire range of substantive rights set out in the Convention..., and that violations of those rights are imputable to Turkey."[74] The validity of the ECA-test has been recognized by a number of other human rights bodies, such as the U.N. Com-

---

[70] *Id.* para. 10.
[71] *E.g.* Coard and Others, *supra* note 50; Rafael Ferrer-Mazorra and others v. the United States (U.S. Detentions in Guantanamo), Report No. 51/01, Case No. 9903, (Apr. 4, 2001), Ann. Rep. I.A.C.H.R. 1188 (2000). *See* Christina M. Cerna, *Extraterritorial Application of the Human Rights Instruments of the inter-American System*, *in* Coomans & Kamminga eds., *supra* note 54, 141–174 [hereinafter Cerna].
[72] Loizidou (Preliminary Objections), *supra* note 49; Loizidou v. Turkey, Application No. 15318/89, (Dec. 18, 1996), 23 EHRR 513 (1997) [hereinafter Loizidou (Merits)].
[73] Cyprus v. Turkey, (May 10, 2001), D.C. 183–186 (2001), paras 77–78 [hereinafter Cyprus v. Turkey 2001].
[74] *Id.* para. 77.

mittee against Torture,⁷⁵ the HRC (*inter alia* in General Comment 31),⁷⁶ and the Committee on Economic, Social and Cultural Rights.⁷⁷

The jurisprudence of the European Court sheds further light on the scope of "effective control." Thus, in *Bankovic* the Court made clear that the bombing by NATO forces of Serbian territory did not amount to effective control of the area,⁷⁸ suggesting instead that effective control presupposed the exercise of "all or some of the public powers normally to be exercised by" the government of the relevant territory.⁷⁹ In *Issa* v. *Turkey*,⁸⁰ the Court rejected the claim that Turkey exercised effective control over northern Iraq during the six-week-period in 1995 when its armed forces conducted military operations in the region. It argued that – notwithstanding the large number of Turkish troops involved – a number of elements distinguished this situation from the one in northern Cyprus. In the latter case, the troops had been present over a much longer period and had been stationed throughout the whole territory. Moreover, northern Cyprus was constantly patrolled and had checkpoints on all main lines of communication.⁸¹ In *Ilascu* v. *Moldova and Russia*,⁸² the Court noted that the control exercised by the Moldovan government over the separatist region of Transdniestria remained limited to such matters as the issue of identity cards and custom stamps⁸³ and was therefore insufficient to amount to effective control.⁸⁴ The Court nevertheless found "effective control" on

---

[75] Committee against Torture (CAT), Conclusions and Recommendations: United Kingdom of Great Britain and Northern Ireland – Dependent Territories (Dec. 10, 2004), U.N. Doc. CAT/C/CR/33/3, para. 4.

[76] HRC, Concluding Observations: Israel (Aug. 18, 1998), U.N. Doc. CCPR/C/79/Add.93, para. 10: "The Committee is therefore of the view that, under the circumstances, the Covenant must be held applicable to the occupied territories and those areas of southern Lebanon and West Bekaa where Israel exercises effective control." *See a contrario* HRC, Concluding Observations: Lebanon (Apr. 1, 1997), U.N. Doc. CCPR/C/79/Add.78, paras 4–5.

[77] CESCR, Concluding Observations: Israel (Dec. 4, 1998), U.N. Doc. E/C.12/1/Add.27, para. 8: "The Committee is of the view that the State's obligations under the Covenant apply to all territories and populations under its effective control." Dennis nevertheless argues that the value of the CESCR's observations should not be overestimated, given the fact that the Committee was not constituted to render authoritative interpretations of Covenant rights. *See* Dennis, *supra* note 48, at 128.

[78] Bankovič, *supra* note 61, paras 61–71.

[79] *Id.* para. 71.

[80] Issa v. Turkey, Application No. 31821/96, (Nov. 6, 2004), paras 65–82 [hereinafter Issa].

[81] *Id.* para. 75.

[82] Ilascu and others v. Moldova and Russia, Application No. 48787/99, (July 8, 2004), D.C. 196/200 [hereinafter Ilascu].

[83] *Id.* para. 329.

[84] The Court nonetheless argued that, even in the absence of effective control over the Transdniestrian region, Moldova still has a positive obligation under Article 1 ECHR to take the diplomatic, economic, judicial or other measures that it is in its power to take to secure to the applicants the rights guaranteed by the Convention. *Id.* para. 331.

behalf of Russia on the grounds that Russia had contributed militarily and politically to the creation of the so-called "Moldovan Republic of Transdniestria;" that Russian troops were present in the region; *et cetera*.[85] All these facts proved that the Moldovan Republic of Transdniestria remained under the effective authority, or at least under the decisive influence, of the Russian Federation.[86]

The distinction between "state agent authority" and "effective control of territory" has important implications. For instance, the SAA test requires that the acts or omissions which are at the roots of an alleged human rights violation can be imputed to the state. If a state has effective control over foreign territory, state attributability is not required in order to hold the controlling state accountable for human rights violations by local officials or by armed groups which survive by virtue of its support or acquiescence. Furthermore, the scope of relevant human rights obligations is significantly narrower with regard to state agent authority than with regard to effective control over territory. In the former case, states are only required to respect those human rights obligations that they affect,[87] whereas a state exercising effective control is required to secure the entire range of substantive rights of the conventions to which it is a party.[88]

4.3. *Comparison of IHL and Human Rights Law Thresholds*

If we transplant these principles to situations of occupation, it seems that the SAA-test is especially relevant in the so-called invasion phase, whereas effective control of territory seems to correspond to situations of actual occupation. As mentioned before, considerable disagreement exists as to whether the law of occupation applies throughout the invasion phase. The ICTY has adopted an intermediate position between the "gradual" and the "all-or-nothing" approach by suggesting that the laws of occupation dealing with the protection of individuals are triggered as soon as an individual falls into "the hands of the occupying power."[89] Yet, with regard to human rights law, it is now widely accepted that the relevant norms apply whenever an individual is abducted, detained or otherwise held by a state acting outside its own territory. Such a situation not only entails negative obligations, such as the duty to refrain from torture and inhuman or degrading treatment, but also positive obligations, such as the duty to take measures to prevent physical abuse from

---

[85] *Id*. paras 377–394.
[86] *Id*. para. 391.
[87] Cyprus v. Turkey 1975, *supra* note 49, at 135. *See* Noam Lubell, *Challenges in Applying Human Rights Law to Armed Conflict*, 37 Int'l Rev. Red Cross 737, 739–740 (2005).
[88] *See e.g.* Cyprus v. Turkey 2001, *supra* note 73, para. 77; *see* however Lord Justice Sedley, Al Skeini Case, *supra* note 51, paras 195–197.
[89] Naletilic and Martinovic, *supra* note 25, paras 210–223.

happening or to undertake investigations into the deaths of individuals during detention.[90] Beyond these situations where the victim of a human rights violation is – at the material time – under the control of the state agents and where a direct relationship between the two can straightforwardly be identified, it is not clear to what cases the SAA paradigm may be applied. The European Commission of Human Rights has applied the test to the protection of property, notably in relation to the taking of houses and land, looting and robbery, and destruction of certain property by Turkish forces in northern Cyprus or by persons acting under the direct orders or authority of the Turkish forces,[91] but this position has so far found little following before the other human rights bodies. An issue that remains particularly controversial is whether SAA jurisdiction also arises when extraterritorial killings are not preceded by detention or abduction. The Inter-American Commission of Human Rights seemed to answer this question affirmatively in the *Brothers to the Rescue* case, which dealt with the alleged downing by a Cuban military aircraft of two civilian airplanes belonging to an anti-Castro organization in international airspace, resulting in the death of the four persons on board.[92] The Commission declared the case admissible on the grounds that the acts of the agents of the Cuban state, although outside their territory, placed the civilian pilots of the "Brothers to the Rescue" organization under their authority.[93] However, in *Bankovic*, the European Court took the opposite position by rejecting that the bombing by NATO forces of the Serbian broadcasting corporation RTS constituted an exercise of jurisdiction by these states.[94] In the absence of effective control over northern Iraq on behalf of Turkey, the European Court in *Issa* v. *Turkey*[95] went on to examine whether the Iraqi shepherds killed during Turkey's military operation were otherwise under the authority or control of Turkey. Due to a lack of evidence

---

[90] *See e.g.* Cyprus v. Turkey, Applications Nos. 6780/74 and 6950/75, (July 10, 1976), 4 E.H.R.R. 482, 537 (1976) [hereinafter Cyprus v. Turkey 1976]; Al Skeini Case, *supra* note 51, para. 108 *et seq.*

[91] Cyprus v. Turkey 1976, *supra* note 90, at 548.

[92] Armando Alejandre Jr. and Others v. Cuba (Brothers to the Rescue), Report No. 86/99, Case No. 11.589, (Sept. 29, 1999), Ann. Rep. I.A.C.H.R. 586 (1999) [hereinafter Brothers to the Rescue Case]. *See* also Cerna, *supra* note 71, at 156–159.

[93] Brothers to the Rescue Case, *supra* note 92, paras 23–25.

[94] Bankovič, *supra* note 61. The authors follow the approach that the Court's distinction between extraterritorial conduct inside and outside the *espace légal* of the ECHR should not be interpreted as an additional threshold for the applicability of the Convention. In any event, the HRC does not subscribe to such a doctrine. *See* Coomans & Kamminga, *supra* note 54, at 4–5; Rick Lawson, *Life after Bankovic: On the Extraterritorial Application of the European Convention on Human Rights*, in Coomans & Kamminga eds., *supra* note 54, 83, 113–115; Michael O'Boyle, *The European Convention on Human Rights and Extraterritorial Jurisdiction: A Comment on 'Life after Bankovic'*, in Coomans & Kamminga eds., *supra* note 54, 125, 137.

[95] *Issa*, *supra* note 80, paras 65–82.

that Turkish troops were present in the particular village the Court was unable to establish jurisdiction. Extraterritorial killing not preceded by arrest was furthermore discussed by the U.K. Court of Appeal in the *Al-Skeini* case.[96] In his leading judgment, Lord Justice Brooks rejected that such situations involved an exercise of jurisdiction, arguing instead that "control" presupposes that troops "deliberately and effectively restrict someone's liberty."[97] This was not the case for individuals who were at liberty in a city street, at home, or driving a vehicle when they were shot by British soldiers. It is interesting to note that in the same case, Lord Justice Sedley took the absolutely opposite approach, stating that "the one thing British troops did have control over, even in the labile situation described in the evidence, was their own use of lethal force."[98] Such a position comes close to the "cause and effect" approach, which was also hinted at by the Inter-American Commission of Human Rights,[99] and according to which human rights are implicated whenever the use of military force has resulted in non-combatant deaths, personal injury, and/or property loss. The latter approach may, however, be a bridge too far. It is hard too see how civilians, killed in the midst of hostilities, would be under the authority and control of the state involved. It could be argued that this requires some degree of stability; some control over the circumstances in which the killings took place. If the killing would be the result of a pre-planned operation, and/or would not be connected to a context of ongoing hostilities, there may indeed be room for accepting the exercise of jurisdiction. An even stronger case could be made when the extra territorial killing results from a pre-planned operation carried out with the consent or support of the host state, as was the case with the 2002 U.S. Predator strike against Al Qaeda suspects in Yemen.[100]

In any event, no such problems are present when there is "effective control" over foreign territory. As mentioned before, such a context activates the entire range of substantive rights set out in the relevant human rights instruments – be it that some of these rights may be superseded by the *lex specialis* norms of IHL or may be derogated from (cf. *infra*) in times of public emergency. The question that arises next is whether the existence of a state of occupation in the sense of the Hague Regulations and the GC IV automatically entails "effective control" for the purpose of extraterritorial application of human rights. In *DRC* v. *Uganda* the ICJ seems to answer this question in the affirmative as it declares that the obligation

---

[96] Al Skeini Case, *supra* note 51.
[97] *Id*. paras 109–110.
[98] *Id*. para. 197.
[99] Salas and Others, *supra* note 50.
[100] For further information on the facts, *see* Norman G. Printer, *Use of Force against Non-state Actors under International Law: An Analysis of the U.S. Predator Strike in Yemen*, 8 U. C. L. A. J. I. L. & Foreign Affairs 331, 335–336 (2003); *Missile Strike Carried out with Yemeni Cooperation – Official Says Operation Authorized under Bush Finding*, The Washington Post, Nov. 6, 2002.

of occupying powers under Article 43 HR comprises "the duty to secure respect for the applicable international human rights law" (para. 178). However, when the U.K. Court of Appeal delivered its judgment in the *Al-Skeini* case (two days after the *DRC* v. *Uganda* judgment), Lord Justice Brooke explicitly rejected the arguments made by the claimants to the effect that occupation for the purposes of the Hague Regulations must necessarily be equated with effective control of the occupied territory for ECHR purposes.[101] According to Lord Justice Brooke: "[I]t is quite impossible to hold that the U.K., although an occupying power for the purposes of the Hague Regulations and [the Fourth Geneva Convention], was in effective control of Basrah City for the purposes of ECHR jurisprudence at the material time. If it had been, it would have been obliged ... to secure to everyone in Basrah City the rights and freedoms guaranteed by the ECHR. One only has to state that proposition to see how utterly unreal it is. The UK possessed no executive, legislative or judicial authority in Basrah City, other than the limited authority given to its military forces.... It could not be equated with a civil power: it was simply there to maintain security, and to support the civil administration in Iraq in a number of different ways ... It would indeed have been contrary to the Coalition's policy to maintain a much more substantial military force in Basrah City when its over-arching policy was to encourage the Iraqis to govern themselves."[102] This reasoning seems somewhat at odds with the European Court's finding in *Loizidou* v. *Turkey*[103] and *Ilascu* v. *Moldova and Russia*[104] that the *de facto* administration of a territory by a local administration does not impede "effective control" by a third state if the said administration is itself controlled by or under the decisive influence of the latter state. As is the case for determining a state of occupation, the key issue in finding "effective control" is the physical control over a territory though the presence of military personnel. This boils down to a factual test, decisive elements for which are – obviously – the number of troops, but also the length of their stay, their dispersal, and their capacity to patrol an area.[105] Whereas supremacy in the air alone does not fulfil the requirements of actual occupation,[106] the European Court in *Bankovic* similarly denounced the idea that aerial bombing as such produces effective control over territory.[107] In sum, the criteria for applicability of the laws of occupation and international human rights law to occupied territory seem to be largely analogous. In combination with the ICJ's statement in *DRC* v. *Uganda* (at para. 178) this creates a strong presumption that a state of occupation also

---

[101] Al Skeini Case, *supra* note 51, para. 127.
[102] *Id.* paras 124–125.
[103] Loizidou (Preliminary Objections), *supra* note 49; Loizidou (Merits), *supra* note 72.
[104] Ilascu, *supra* note 82.
[105] *Id.* para. 75.
[106] Gasser, *supra* note 13, at 243.
[107] Bankovič, *supra* note 61.

entails effective control for the purpose of international human rights law. Thus, once a state of occupation exists there would be no need to enter into a detailed examination of the circumstances of every incident to establish the applicability of relevant international human rights law. Only if part of the occupied territory would (again) turn into a battle area would effective control be lost,[108] both for the purposes of the law of occupation and for the purposes of international human rights law. One may therefore wonder if it would not have made more sense for the U.K. Court of Appeal in discussing the exceptional circumstances in and around Basrah City to state that the ECHR applied extraterritorially, while taking account of the context in determining whether its provisions had actually been violated and taking account of the *lex specialis* of IHL. The latter consideration brings us to the normative interplay between IHL and human rights.

5. Interplay Between IHL and Human Rights Law in Occupied Territory

The Court's ruling in *DRC* v. *Uganda* that human rights law and IHL apply simultaneously to occupied territories generates important consequences, both on the procedural and the substantive level. Firstly, depending on the ratification of relevant instruments, human rights law may sometimes provide victims in occupied territories with access to human rights implementation mechanisms such as the European Court of Human Rights or the Human Rights Committee (HRC). Apart from this important aspect – which will not be explored in the present context – simultaneous application of human rights law and IHL also creates additional rights for civilians and parallel obligations for occupying powers. This raises the question as to how the relevant provisions of IHL and human rights law interact in practice.

The latter issue was first addressed by the ICJ in its *Nuclear Weapons* advisory opinion.[109] Here, the Court famously stated that the right to be free from arbitrary deprivation of life continues to apply in times of armed conflict, yet it quickly added that infringements of this right should be determined by the *lex specialis* of IHL. Unfortunately, given the widely divergent protection of life under human rights law and under IHL, little is clarified by this statement. Slightly more illuminating is the Court's more recent ruling on the *Palestinian Wall*, where it envisaged three possible scenarios: some rights may be exclusively matters of IHL; others may be exclusively matters of human rights law; yet others may be matters of both these branches of

---

[108] Gasser, *supra* note 13, at 528.
[109] Legality of the Threat or Use of Nuclear Weapons, Advisory Opinion (July 8, 1996), 1996 ICJ Rep. 226, para. 25.

international law.¹¹⁰ Again, however, the Court gave no concrete examples of these respective categories. In *DRC* v. *Uganda*, the Court subsequently confined itself to repeating its earlier *dicta* in the aforementioned advisory opinions.¹¹¹

It should moreover be noted that human rights jurisprudence is not conclusive in this regard: the European Court has had the opportunity to dwell upon the interplay between the two bodies of law, but has been very hesitant to explicitly apply IHL,¹¹² although its American counterpart has applied humanitarian law to determine whether or not there was a violation of human rights.¹¹³

Despite the brevity of the Court's *dicta*, the issue of interplay is rather complex. Dinstein for instance lists six variations of interplay between both regimes.¹¹⁴ For the present purposes, however, we will limit our examination to interaction in situations of occupation. In this regard, building on the three scenarios spelled out by the ICJ, different situations can be discerned. Some acts may be governed by a specific rule of IHL which has no equivalent counterpart under human rights law. An example hereof would be Article 25 GC IV, according to which all persons in the territory of a party to the conflict, or in a territory occupied by it, shall be enabled to give news of a strictly personal nature to members of their families, wherever they may be, and to receive news from them. In other situations, human rights law may complement IHL by regulating behavior which is not dealt with under IHL. An illustration is provided in the *DRC* v. *Uganda* case, where the Court made use of the CRC and the Optional Protocol to the CRC to hold Uganda accountable for the recruitment of child soldiers. Thirdly, situations occur where both regimes regulate the same behavior. If there is no discrepancy between the respective norms, no problems arise. This is for example the case with regard to the prohibition on torture, where human rights jurisprudence may be employed to interpret human rights law and IHL. On the other hand, where there exists (partial) contradiction between the two sets of norms, as is the case in relation to the protection of human life, for example, the difficulty is to identify which aspect of human rights law is superseded by the *lex specialis* of IHL and which aspect remains applicable to fill the *lacunae* or incertitudes left open by humanitarian law.

A complete study of the interaction between human rights law and IHL is beyond the scope of this contribution. Instead, we will limit our examination to certain aspects of interaction in occupied territories. First, we will examine the conditions

---

¹¹⁰ Palestinian Wall, *supra* note 2, para. 106.
¹¹¹ DRC v. Uganda, *supra* note 1, paras 216–217.
¹¹² Loizidou (Merits), *supra* note 72; Ergi v. Turkey, Application No. 23818/93, (July 28, 1998), 81 ECHR (1998-IV); Isayeva v. Russia, Application No. 57950/2000, (Feb. 24, 2005).
¹¹³ Abdella case, Case No. 11.137, (Nov. 18, 1997), paras 155–156; Bamaca-Velasquez Case, 70 Series C (2000).
¹¹⁴ Dinstein, *supra* note 46.

under which a state may derogate from human rights provisions and whether such derogation may be limited to the occupied territory. Secondly, we will address the relation between human rights obligations and the duty of the occupying power to guarantee public order and life.[115] Finally, the problematic interplay between the two sets of rules will be illustrated by reference to the ruling in *DRC* v. *Uganda* on the issue of natural resources.

5.1. *Derogation of Human Rights in Times of Emergency*

While human rights are not automatically shelved during armed conflicts or in occupied territories, they may nonetheless be suspended in exceptional circumstances. Indeed, most human rights instruments contain provisions, such as Article 4 ICCPR – which was applicable in *DRC* v. *Uganda* – or Article 15 of ECHR, which allow states parties to take measures derogating from the greater part of their obligations (at least from those rights that are not "*notstandfest.*") As the provisions themselves indicate, derogation is nonetheless bound to stringent conditions.

A first criterion establishes that derogation is only possible "in times of public emergency which threatens the life of the nation." War as such is not mentioned in Article 4 ICCPR, but is nonetheless referred to in Article 15 ECHR and Article 27 of the American Convention on Human Rights (ACHR). In general, the presence of an armed conflict provides a *prima facie* example of a "public emergency." However, it would be false to assume that the existence of an armed conflict automatically fulfils this requirement.[116] A case by case approach is needed, taking account of the factual circumstances. The NATO bombing campaign against the former Republic of Yugoslavia, for example, clearly did not threaten the life of the participating NATO member states and could therefore not have been invoked by these states to justify any curtailing of human rights.

The requirement of "public emergency" presupposes the existence of "an exceptional situation of crisis or emergency which affects the whole population and constitutes a threat to the organized life of the community of which the State is composed."[117] This definition was further elaborated by the European Commission of Human Rights in the *Greek* Case.[118] In particular, the Commission emphasized

---

[115] The English translation of Article 43 HR obliges the occupying power to guarantee public order and safety. However, this is an unfortunate translation of the authentic French text laying down the obligation to guarantee "l'ordre et la vie publics." Unfortunately, the French text of the judgement literally translates the official English text of the judgement.
[116] Hernán Montealegre, *The Compatibility of a State Party's Derogation under Human Rights Conventions with its Obligations under Protocol II and Common Article 3*, 33 Am. Univ. L. Rev. 43 (1983–84).
[117] Lawless v. Ireland (No. 1), Application No. 332/57, (Nov. 14, 1960), Y.B. ECHR 438 (1961).
[118] Greek Case, Application Nos. 3321/67, 3322/67, 3323/67, 3324/67, Report of Nov. 5, 1969, Y.B. ECHR 72 (1969).

that a public emergency must be actual or imminent; that the effect must involve the whole nation; that the continuance of the organized life of the community must be threatened, and; that the dangers must be such that normal measures do not suffice to remedy the situation. The need for a public emergency to affect the whole nation seems to have been discarded by the European Court in *Ireland v. UK*,[119] in which the Court examined a derogation limited to Northern Ireland. On the other hand, the fact that Ireland did not dispute the state of emergency, could explain why the Court did not devote much attention to the issue.[120] In any event, preparatory documents of the HRC again suggest that derogation requires a threat to the nation as a whole.[121]

A second condition states that derogation is only possible to the extent that it is required by the exigencies of the situation. In other words, the measures taken should be proportionate to the danger facing the state, both in terms of scope and duration. This also entails that states cannot use the "opportunity" to suspend human rights whose derogation is not necessary and that they cannot take measures that are overly restrictive: If the same result could be obtained by employing less restrictive measures, Article 4 ICCPR will be violated. Nevertheless, states do appear to have a certain margin of discretion, as they are normally in the better position to choose appropriate remedies to overcome the emergency.[122] The European Court moreover made clear that derogation measures may and should be adjusted when the situation improves.[123] On the other hand, if a state restricts its derogation measures absent any alteration in the situation, this may indicate that the initial measures overstepped the "exigencies standard." In any event, Article 4 ICCPR stresses that derogation measures may not be discriminatory. Nor may they be inconsistent with states' other obligations under international law. As a result, in cases of armed conflict, a significant derogation of human rights will not be allowed if this would run counter to humanitarian law provisions, which will serve as minimum standards in the emergency situation.[124]

Lastly, states wishing to derogate have to issue a notification. Article 4 ICCPR, for example, requires states to immediately inform the other state parties of the

---

[119] Ireland v. United Kingdom, Application No. 5310/77, (Jan. 18, 1978), 2 EHRR 25 (1979) [hereinafter Ireland v. UK].

[120] John Quigley, *The Relation between Human Rights Law and the Law of Belligerent Occupation: Does an Occupied Population Have a Right to Freedom of Assembly and Expression?*, 12 Boston College Int'l and Comp. L. Rev. 26 (1989).

[121] *Id.* at 26; Marc Bossuyt, Guide to the "Travaux Préparatoires" of the International Covenant on Civil and Political Rights 86 (1987); *similarly* Joan F. Hartman, *Derogation from Human Rights Treaties in Public Emergencies*, 22 Harvard Int'l L.J. 16 (1981).

[122] Ireland v. UK, *supra* note 119, para. 220.

[123] *Id.* para. 220.

[124] For example States may derogate from Article 14 ICCPR, but they should respect the judicial safeguards laid down in the Geneva Conventions and Additional Protocol I.

provisions from which they plan to derogate as well as to provide adequate reasons. Termination of the measures should likewise be communicated. In practice, however, states tend to only give very general justifications.[125] More importantly, the HRC has stated that a state's failure to comply with the notification requirement does not deprive it of its substantive rights of derogation while considering an individual complaint and has considered the possibility of derogation in the absence of a state's reliance on it.[126] In this respect, one could wonder whether the ICJ should not have followed the same line of reasoning by indicating that although Uganda had not made a derogation notification, it should look into the conditions of Article 4 ICCPR. On the other hand, the fact that the ICJ only considered alleged violations of human rights that were clearly non-derogable (the right to life and the prohibition against torture) or specifically envisaged situations of armed conflict (the provisions relating to the recruitment of child soldiers) probably explains why the Court did not raise the possibility of a "public emergency."

Taking the requirements of Article 4 ICCPR into consideration, could an occupying power issue derogation measures limited to the occupied territory? Despite some practice limiting derogation to a part a state's territory (cf. *supra*),[127] it is submitted that such measures are not always permissible since – as mentioned before – the public emergency should in principle threaten the entire nation. Depending on the circumstances, it may be that an occupation of enemy territory meets this requirement. For instance, if the occupied territory is contiguous to the territory of the occupying power and resistance movements carry out cross-border attacks, this might constitute a threat to the entire nation (one might think of the situation in Israel and the OPT). Conversely, if only sporadic resistance actions take place within the occupied territory, this will not normally constitute a public emergency.[128] Again a case-by-case approach is necessary, examining whether there exists an actual or imminent threat. It is perfectly possible that an invasion meets no resistance whatsoever. In conclusion, occupation does not automatically constitute a public emergency in the sense of Article 4 ICCPR or other derogation clauses. Hence, in principle human rights law will apply side by side with IHL.

---

[125] *See* derogation made by Israel, mentioned by the Palestinian Wall, *supra* note 2, para. 127; *see also* derogation made by the United Kingdom, HRC, U.N. Doc. CCPR/C/2, 12.

[126] Dennis, *supra* note 48, at 135.

[127] Especially, the United Kingdom has derogated from the European Convention on Human Rights, but limited this derogation to the six counties of Northern Ireland. Ireland v. UK, *supra* note 119, para. 212.

[128] In this respect, it has been argued that a grave emergency or disturbance taking place in a part of the territory of a State, could allow for derogation since although it might not affect the nation as a whole, it could still affect the whole nations' public order. However, if the situation can be dealt with by normal measures and the normal State apparatus, a derogation will not be possible; *see* Mohamed M. El Zeidy, *The ECHR and States of Emergency: Article 15 – A Domestic Power of Derogation from Human Rights Obligations*, 4 San Diego Int'l L. J. 284–285 (2003).

5.2. The Duty to Restore and Maintain Public Order and Life

5.2.1. Restoring and Maintaining Public Order and Life

In its judgment the ICJ held Uganda responsible not only for breaches of IHL and human rights law committed by its armed forces, but also for breaches committed by individuals.[129] This seems to be a correct application of Article 43 HR, which requires that immediately after the ending of hostilities occupying powers should restore as far as possible the public order in the occupied territory and should take steps to bring daily life back to normal. As administrators over the territory, they must restore the normal functioning of society and guard public order. Consequently, an occupying power must not only make sure that its own forces do not commit unlawful acts against the local population, but must in turn prevent private individuals or armed bands from attacking the local inhabitants. In similar vein the obligation of states to ensure within their jurisdiction the enjoyment of international human rights[130] is not solely limited to the (negative) duty not to unlawfully intervene in this enjoyment, but is also framed as a positive obligation to take steps against individuals infringing the human rights of others.[131]

Still, the interplay between Article 43 HR and human rights law requires careful scrutiny. The duty to restore public order and life has been interpreted by occupying powers as a possibility to intervene in many aspects of public life or social activities.[132] As a *lex specialis* norm it also seems to allow for the curbing of human rights if public order so requires, even if no human rights derogation was made at all. Yet, the latter possibility is not unlimited, as the second part of the same article requires occupying powers to respect the laws in force in occupied territory *unless absolutely prevented*. The two dimensions of Article 43 HR imply a careful balance of interests. On the one hand, they reflect the basic idea underlying the regime of occupation, according to which the occupier does not become the sovereign of the

---

[129] DRC v. Uganda, *supra* note 1, para. 178 *juncto* paras 248–250.
[130] Article 2 ICCPR, *supra* note 47; Article 1 Convention for the Protection of Human Rights and Fundamental Freedoms, (Nov. 4, 1950), 213 U.N.T.S. 221 (entered into force Sept. 3, 1953) [hereinafter ECHR]; Article 1 American Convention on Human Rights, O.A.S. Treaty Series No. 36, 1144 U.N.T.S. 123, entered into force July 18, 1978, reprinted in Basic Documents Pertaining to Human Rights in the Inter-American System, OEA/Ser.L.V/II.82 doc.6 rev.1 at 25 (1992); Article 1 African Charter on Human and Peoples' Rights (Banjul Charter) (June 27, 1981) 21 I.L.M. 59.
[131] HRC, General Comment No. 31, *supra* note 69, para. 8; A. v. The United Kingdom, Application No. 25599/94, (Sept. 23, 1998), 27 EHHR (1999), para. 22; Osman v. United Kingdom, Application No. 23452/94, (Oct. 28, 1998), 29 EHHR (1998), para. 115; Velasquez Rodriguez Case, (July 29, 1988), 4 Series C (1988), para. 172.
[132] Roberts, Transformative Military Occupation, *supra* note 16, at 588; McCarthy, *supra* note 15, at 62.

occupied territory, but merely acts as a temporary administrator.[133] Hence, the laws in existence cannot normally be altered since they have been enacted by the lawful sovereign and changing them would constitute an usurpation of sovereignty. In this regard, it should be noted that the laws in existence not only comprise those rules laying down rights and obligations, but also those dealing with procedure, administration, and judicial organization.[134] On the other hand, an overly narrow focus on the legislative *status quo* could undermine the obligation of the occupier to restore and maintain public order and safety, equally contained in Article 43.

Given the fact that the curtailment of human rights normally requires legislative action, the same appraisal is needed when such measures are envisaged. This is equally true if an occupying power contemplates legislative action in order to fulfill its human rights obligations in occupied territories. Before elaborating on these two aspects, we should first recall that the restoration and maintenance of public order and life should in the first place be done by the existing local authorities and courts, unless the courts were instructed to enforce discriminatory laws or when judges have resigned for reasons of public conscience pursuant to Article 56 GC IV.[135]

5.2.2. *The Power to Restrict or Ensure Human Rights*

If the laws in existence would absolutely prevent the restoration and maintenance of public order and civil life, the occupying power can put them aside (Article 43 HR). The phrase "unless absolutely prevented" makes clear that this constitutes an exceptional possibility. Article 64 GC IV further concretizes the scope for legislative action.[136] According to this provision, the occupying power may suspend criminal laws if they constitute a threat to its security or an obstacle to the application of the Fourth Geneva Convention (and of the Hague Regulations). Moreover, the occupier can enact provisions altering existing laws which are essential to enable it to fulfill its obligations as an occupying power, to maintain the orderly government of the territory, and to ensure its security, as well as that of the members and property of the occupying forces or administration, and of the establishments and lines of communication used by them. Classical examples hereof are the abolishing of laws criminalizing the lack of resistance to resist enemy forces and the putting aside of laws allowing citizens to bear arms. In any event, there are a number of

---

[133] Benvenisti, *supra* note 14, at 6; this follows also implicitly from the wording of Article 43 HR, establishing that the authority of the legitimate power has *in fact* passed into the hands of the occupant. Furthermore, it can equally be deduced from Article 55 HR, laying down that the occupying power is considered to be an administrator and usufructary of public real estate property.
[134] Article 64 GC IV; Benvenisti, *supra* note 14, at 17.
[135] Uhler & Coursier, *supra* note 20, at 336.
[136] Article 154 GC IV; Uhler & Coursier, *supra* note 20, at 335.

procedural safeguards if an occupying power wishes to adopt new criminal laws. Firstly, it should publish them before coming into force (Article 65 GC IV); secondly, if the new criminal laws concern security matters enumerated in Article 64 GC IV, the occupying power may hand over the accused to its properly constituted, non-political military courts, sitting in the occupied territory (Articles 66 GC IV). The penal provisions should furthermore be in accordance with general principles of law, in particular with the principle of proportionality. The death penalty is not allowed, save in certain circumstances (Articles 67–68 GCIV). These safeguards are moreover reinforced by Article 75 (4) of the First Additional Protocol,[137] which offers a similar protection in relation to criminal prosecution as do human rights conventions. From this we may conclude that, on the one hand, Article 43 HR does indeed allow for the possibility to lawfully restrict human rights to ensure public order, but on the other hand IHL also provides for some safeguards similar to human rights law. In particular, IHL may be invoked to set aside certain rights such as the right to freedom of assembly, the right to freedom of expression, and the right to liberty.[138] On the other hand, one should not omit that if there is no remarkable resistance of the local population and no threat to the security of the occupying power, human rights, as regulated by the (national and international) laws in existence should be fully applied. Last but not least, it should be pointed out that human rights provisions themselves often provide that the rights enshrined therein may be subject to restrictions in order to ensure public order, irrespective of the existence of an armed conflict or a situation of occupation.[139]

The reverse question is whether the occupying power may adopt legislation in order to fulfill (rather than curb) its human rights obligations. Three situations come to the fore: firstly, the laws in existence in the occupied territory may run counter to the human rights obligations of the occupying power; secondly, the laws in existence may implement human rights in a different way than does the occupying power; lastly, the laws in existence may provide for certain human rights which are not adopted by the occupying power.

---

[137] Protocol Additional to the Geneva Conventions of August 12, 1949, and Relating to the Protection of Victims of International Armed Conflicts, June 8, 1977, 1125 U.N.T.S. 3 (entered into force Dec. 7, 1978) [hereinafter AP I].

[138] In relation to the right to liberty, Article 78 GC IV establishes that if the Occupying Power considers it necessary, for imperative reasons of security, to take safety measures concerning persons living in the occupied territory, it may, at the most, subject them to assigned residence or to internment – which is more restrictive than Article 9 ICCPR.

[139] *See e.g.* Article 12 ICCPR (right to liberty of movement), Article 14(1) ICCPR (possibility to restrict the press from all or part of a criminal trial), Article 18 ICCPR (right of freedom of thought, conscience and religion), Article 19 ICCPR (right to hold opinions without interference), Article 21 ICCPR (right of peaceful assembly), *supra* note 47.

As regards the first situation, Article 64 GC IV provides that states may change the existing laws in question if they would infringe upon IHL. Consequently, humanitarian law provides minimum standards that should be respected at all times and that overlap to some extent with human rights law. With regard to civil and political rights for example, Article 27 GC IV obliges occupying powers to respect protected persons, in particular to show respect for their persons, their honor, their family rights, their religious convictions and practices, and their manners and customs. Protected persons must moreover at all times be treated humanely and be protected against all acts of violence or threats thereof. On this basis, discrimination of a group based on religion, race, or ethnicity will not be permitted.[140] As a result, if the laws of the occupied territory would infringe upon the rights of a minority, the occupying power must set them aside. Furthermore, Article 51 GC IV prohibits compulsory labor, unless in certain circumstances. Apart from the aforementioned provisions, it should also be stressed that if rules of IHL remain too vague, guidance can be sought in human rights law,[141] which has better enforcement machinery from which states may deduce more concrete rules to apply to the given situation. Moreover, making abstraction of the measures taken to restore and maintain public order, it seems that the occupying power must provide for the same protection of civil and political rights as in its own territory.

In relation to economic, social, and cultural rights, IHL also provides for some minimum guarantees. Article 50 GC IV for example establishes that the occupying power is obliged together with the national and local authorities, to facilitate the proper working of all institutions devoted to the care and education of children. Article 51 GC IV states that workers have the right to a fair wage and have to perform work consistent with the national regulations and safeguards. Article 52 GC IV provides that all measures aiming at creating unemployment or at restricting the opportunities offered to workers in an occupied territory, in order to induce them to work for the occupying power, are prohibited. Furthermore, the occupying power has to make sure that the civilian population has sufficient access to basic utilities, drinking water and food (Articles 55–56 GC IV). The question then arises whether the occupying power should provide for the same level of economic, social, and cultural rights as in its own territory. The problem is that the development of these rights occurs gradually. Indeed, as Article 2 ICESCR indicates, states commit themselves to take steps to "progressively realize" these rights to the maximum of their available resources. In this regard, taking account of the possible short duration of the occupation and the damage caused by the hostilities, it might be too burdensome for an occupying state to organize the same level of protection

---

[140] Uhler & Coursier, *supra* note 20, at 335.
[141] Benvenisti, *supra* note 14, at 189; Hans-Joachim Heintze, *On the Relationship between Human Rights Law Protection and International Humanitarian Law*, 856 Int'l Rev. Red Cross 795 (2004).

in an occupied territory. However, it seems that the longer the occupation lasts, the more efforts should be made to improve the economical, social, and cultural rights of the population in order to escape infringements thereof. This "temporal" factor, may explain why the ICJ held Israel accountable for breaches of economic, social, and cultural rights in *Palestinian Wall*, whereas in *DRC* v. *Uganda* it confined itself to an assessment of civil and political rights and the issue of child soldiers, despite the fact that both the DRC and Uganda were parties to the ICESCR and despite the DRC's invocation of the latter convention as being pertinent in the case before the Court.[142]

In sum, if the laws in existence manifestly and flagrantly infringe the human rights by which the occupying power is bound, it is obliged to change them and to provide in any event for a minimum protection consistent with IHL. To interpret the minimum standards, it can moreover have recourse to human rights jurisprudence. The occupying power will also be under an obligation pursuant to international human rights law to grant civil and political rights. With respect to economic, social, and cultural rights, it should not only provide the minimum protection under IHL, but is also required to do all reasonable efforts to attain a certain level of protection of these rights in the short term, be it that this may fall below the protection of these rights in its own state. On the long term however, the occupier must strive for an equal level of protection.

The second of the three situations spelled out above concerns the possibility that the occupying power and the state whose territory is occupied have both ratified human rights conventions but have implemented them differently. For instance, certain human rights may be limited by law on the basis of good morals, but the conception of good morals may diverge in the respective states. Here, the occupying power should respect the local laws pursuant to Article 43 HR and Article 64 GC IV. It cannot repel the local laws and replace them on the grounds of its own conception of good morals. The same goes for economic, social, and cultural rights: the laws of the occupied territory can be based on different policy choices, which the occupying power should respect. Of course, as has been mentioned, Article 43 HR and Article 64 GC IV do allow for restrictions and changes in order to protect the security of the occupying power.

In the last hypothesis the occupying power is not a party to human rights conventions which are however ratified by the state whose territory is occupied. In this situation, the occupying power has to respect the laws of the occupied territory, again provided lawful changes in the existing laws pursuant to Article 43 HR and Article 64 GC IV.

---

[142] Mémoire de la République Démocratique du Congo, 147, No. 3.58, *available at* www.icj-cij.org/docket/files/116/8321.pdf (last visited May 11, 2007).

5.3. *The Issue of Natural Resources*

The last submission of the DRC, concerning the illegal exploitation of natural resources, demonstrates the problematic nature of the interplay between the two bodies of law. The DRC argued that the Ugandan exploitation of Congolese natural resources breached IHL as well as the principle of permanent sovereignty over natural resources. Uganda objected that the alleged facts were either not proven or not imputable. Ultimately, the Court did find Uganda in breach of international law, but only on the basis of IHL.

To justify the exclusion of the principle of permanent sovereignty over natural resources as a legal basis for its ruling, the Court succinctly held that this principle – albeit part of customary international law – is not applicable to situations of occupation (para. 244). This conclusion might be correct, but nevertheless seems too boldly stated. Undoubtedly, the principle was in the first instance conceived as the economic corollary of the political and legal appeal for decolonization and self-determination.[143] Yet, this does not necessary entail that it is limited to those instances. For instance, the principle also plays a role in relation to foreign investment: in essence the principle of permanent sovereignty over natural resources vests control over natural resources in the state which decides how they should be exploited in favor of its peoples.[144] Consequently, if a foreign state invades and sets up a system of exploitation of the natural resources of the other state, it usurps this right. This is not necessarily the same as state-organized plunder or pillage since an occupying power can issue concessions to private actors which would then exploit the natural resources. Moreover, the principle has played a role in relation to occupation since it was invoked by the General Assembly in the context of the OPT.[145] Therefore, it seems to be premature to exclude the right of permanent resources over natural resources in the context of foreign occupation.

On the other hand, it has to be admitted that the laws of occupation will be more suitable to address the issue of exploitation of natural resources in occupied territories. Firstly, its rules are more concrete than the general principle of permanent sovereignty. Secondly, they are also more flexible since natural resources may be used and exploited in case of requisitioning of public goods and to use certain goods as a usufructuary.[146] Despite these arguments, it cannot be denied that the permanent sovereignty over natural resources is intrinsically linked with

---

[143] Rudolf Dolzer, *Permanent Sovereignty over Natural Resources and Economic Decolonization*, 7 Human Rights L. J. 221 (1986).

[144] Emeka Duruigbo, *Permanent Sovereignty and Peoples' Ownership of Natural Resources in International Law*, 38 George Washington Int'l L.Rev. 30 (2006).

[145] *See* G.A. Res. 58/229, U.N. Doc. A/RES/58/229 (2003); G.A. Res. 59/251, U.N. Doc. A/RES/59/251 (2004); G.A. Res. 60/183, U.N. Doc. A/RES/60/183 (2005).

[146] Articles 53 and 55 HR.

the human right to self-determination.¹⁴⁷ Since human rights remain applicable in armed conflicts and situations of belligerent occupation,¹⁴⁸ it could be argued that a state invading another state, putting (parts of) its territory under its control and exploiting the natural resources, is infringing the right to self-determination and its corollary principle of permanent sovereignty over natural resources, even though it is respecting the laws of occupation. This is evidenced by Article 1(4) AP I, which provides that the armed struggle of peoples fighting for self-determination falls within the scope of the Protocol and is thus considered an international armed conflict to which the rules of occupation apply. This is not limited to peoples fighting colonial domination, but also includes struggles against racist regimes and alien occupation. Furthermore, the ICJ in *Palestinian Wall* has taken the position that by constructing the wall in the OPT, Israel breached the right to self-determination of the Palestinian people.¹⁴⁹ In the *Case concerning East-Timor* Portugal similarly argued that the concluding of a delimitation treaty of the continental shelf of East Timor, invaded and annexed by Indonesia, violated the principle of self-determination and permanent sovereignty over natural resources.¹⁵⁰ Consequently, it seems the right to self-determination and permanent sovereignty over natural resources could still be applicable in situations of belligerent occupation. In this regard, it should be noted that Article 21 ACHPR, which was held applicable by the Court in the dispute before it, establishes similarly that all peoples must freely dispose of their wealth and natural resources, that this right has to be exercised in the exclusive interest of the people, and that in no case shall a people be deprived of it. Yet, the Court found no violation of this right, although it mentioned Article 21(2) of the same convention (para. 245).

After dismissing the principle of permanent sovereignty, the Court nonetheless retains IHL as the legal foundation of the DRC's claim. Unfortunately, the Court refrains from setting out the legal regime applicable to the exploitation of natural resources in occupied territory. In fact, it merely states that it is proven that Uganda has violated its obligations under IHL, in particular the prohibition on pillage enshrined in Article 47 HR and Article 33 GC IV. The Court subsequently observes that, pursuant to Article 21(2) ACPHR, in case of spoliation, the dispossessed people shall have the right to recovery of property and compensation damages (para. 245). Finally, the Court also asserts that in the territory it occupied

---

¹⁴⁷ Article 1 ICCPR, *supra* note 47; Article 1 International Covenant on Economic, Social and Cultural Rights, G.A. res. 2200A (XXI), 21 U.N.GAOR Supp. (No. 16) at 49, U.N. Doc. A/6316 (1966), 993 U.N.T.S. 3, entered into force Jan. 3, 1976.

¹⁴⁸ Subject to derogations contained in human rights treaties and to the *lex specialis* of IHL. Palestinian Wall, *supra* note 2, para. 106.

¹⁴⁹ Palestinian Wall, *supra* note 2, para. 122.

¹⁵⁰ Case concerning East-Timor (Portugal v. Australia), (June 30, 1995), 1995 ICJ. Rep., para. 19.

Uganda violated its duty of vigilance by not taking adequate measures to prevent pillage from occurring.

Yet, with all respect to the wisdom of the Court, the matter is much more complex than its ruling seems to indicate. Of course, the Court should not deal with each violation or with the specifics of the system set up to exploit the natural resources, but it could nonetheless have presented the appropriate legal framework to consider whether the exploitation in the case at hand was lawful or not. A first point is that under IHL, the exploitation is not prohibited *per se*: since states are interested to exploit the natural resources of the occupied territory in order to sustain their military efforts, there is no general proscription.[151] However, despite the possibility of exploitation, the Hague Regulations equally provide in the protection of state and private property. From these provisions we can deduce the applicable rules.

During occupation, the general rule is that private property belonging to the citizens of the enemy combatant has to be respected and cannot be confiscated (Article 46 HR). This rule is absolute and no exceptions are accepted.[152] The protection of public property is more complex. With regard to immovable goods, the Hague Regulations determine that the occupying state has to be considered as an administrator and usufructary. Movable state property was traditionally subject to the right of booty, yet the Hague Regulations broke with this longstanding practice: Article 53 HR determines that the occupying power can only seize those objects which can be useful for military operations. Furthermore, the occupier may demand requisitions in kind and services provided they are destined for the needs of the occupation army; proportionate to the resources of the country; not leading to the participation of inhabitants in military operations against their own country; and take into account the needs of the population of the occupied territory (Article 55 GC IV). In principle, contributions in kind have to be paid in cash, but if this is impossible a receipt must be handed over, and payment is to follow as soon as possible (Article 52 HR). From this brief overview one can conclude that state property enjoys lesser protection than private property: movable state assets which may be used for military purposes will become spoils of war and upon seizure will become the property of the occupying state without compensation. Examples include means of transportation, weapons, munitions, but also cash, funds, and realizable securities, arguably also gold bars and other valuable metals or minerals. Immovable state property is subject to administration and usufruct by the occupying power.

---

[151] Gerhard von Glahn, The Occupation of Enemy Territory, A Commentary on the Law and Practice of Belligerent Occupation 20–21 (1957).

[152] Stanislaw E. Nahlik, *La protection internationale des biens culturels en cas de conflit armé*, 120 Recueil des Cours 92 (1967–I).

Applying the aforementioned rules to the *DRC* v. *Uganda* case, a more nuanced image comes to the forefront. Indeed, even though the ICJ's conclusion is undoubtedly correct,[153] it seems that some activities might have been lawful under the laws of occupation. One of the most important activities concerned the mining of minerals, in particular gold, diamonds, and coltan. Under the national laws of Zaire/DRC all subterranean minerals are the property of the state.[154] Consequently, it has to be determined whether these goods are immovable or movable. Immovable goods are goods which cannot be moved by themselves or by any outside force.[155] As a result, the soil and its appurtenants – including its subterranean resources and its superstructures (buildings e.a.) – are to be considered as immovable, as are forests, crops, waters, et cetera.[156] Therefore, the rights of the occupant are limited to administration and usufruct over mines. Whether "usufruct" has a separate Roman law meaning in the Hague Regulations or should be interpreted by reference to the national law of the occupied territory pursuant to Article 42 HR, the concept essentially boils down to the use and gaining of the benefits and yields of the property without however impairing the substance of the usufruct.[157] This entails that new mines may not be established, while mines that are already open and operating may be subject to usufruct.[158] The usufructuary must moreover be confined to the normal exploitation of existing mines, meaning that mines can only be exploited in the same way as before the establishing of usufruct or according to local customs.[159] Consequently, Uganda had the right to exploit existing state-owned mines in a normal way, or as a *bonus pater familias*. Yet, it could not

---

[153] *See* U.N. Report of the Panel of Experts of the Illegal Exploitation of Natural Resources and Other Forms of Wealth of the Democratic Republic of the Congo, para. 32 and following, *available at* www.un.org/News/dh/latest/drcongo.htm (last visited May 11, 2007), speaking of mass scale looting.

[154] Article 3 Constitution of Zaire (1994); Article 9 Constitution of DRC (2006); Article 1 Ordonnance-Loi No. 81-013 (1981), J.O. 15 April 1981; Article 3 Loi No. 007/2002 (2002), J.O. 15 July 2002 (special edition).

[155] Article 528 Code Civil; Article 528 Code Civil Belge; Article 335 Codigo Civil Español (definition of movable goods as goods which move by themselves or by extraneous force).

[156] Article 3–3 and Article 5–20 Nederlands Burgerlijk Wetboek; Article 518 Code Civil; Article 518 Code Civil Belge; Article 812 Codice Civile; § 1031 *juncto* § 926 Bürgerliches Gesetzbuch; Article 334 Codigo Civil Español.

[157] Article 578 Code Civil; Article 578 Code Civil Belge; Article 981 Codice Civile; § 1036 (2) Bürgerliches Gesetzbuch; Article 467 Codigo Civil Español. *See* also Guano Case (1901), 15 UNRIAA 367.

[158] Article 598 Code Civil; Article 598 Code Civil Belge; Article 987 Codice Civile; Article 476 Codigo Civil Español; this is confirmed by the Military Manuals of the United States and the United Kingdom, which establish that an Occupying Power may work the mines, entailing that only existing mines could be exploited: U.S. Department of the Army, *supra* note 24, at para. 402; U.K. Ministry of Defence, *supra* note 23, para. 610.

[159] Article 598 Code Civil; Article 598 Code Civil Belge; Article 987 Codice Civile.

overexploit those mines, or establish new ones. The same applies to timber and plantations (e.g. rubber and coffee): an usufructary may log forests for timber and harvest the yields, but they may not do so in an excessive way and should ensure the substance of the usufruct.[160] Moreover, the occupying power may sell the fruits of the immovable state property[161] and may give concessions to operate the mines, albeit under the same strict conditions and respecting the national legislation of the occupied territory concerning concessions. As a result, it will not be allowed to give concessions automatically to nationals of the occupying power.

Yet, this is not the end of the matter. Frequently, states will grant concessions to private corporations to exploit the natural resources. Under international law, these concessions are regarded as private property.[162] Consequently, as Article 46 HR provides that private property must be respected and cannot be confiscated; mines, plantations and forest given in concession enjoy a far-reaching protection. The occupying power is entitled to ask inhabitants for requisitions in kind, but only for the need of the occupying army and if compensation is paid. As a result, the occupying army may not requisition private property for conducting commercial activities or to sell it to other private persons which use the requisitioned object for commercial purposes.[163] Another possibility is that the occupying power seizes private property belonging to one of the categories listed in Article 53 HR. For instance, it could be argued that some private property – minerals, rubber, semi-manufactured goods – could be qualified as "munitions of war." "Munitions of war" are indeed not limited to munitions as such, but may also include objects susceptible of direct military use.[164] Of course, it depends on factual circumstances whether objects are susceptible of direct military use, but in general minerals, timber or rubber need extra industrial processing before being used directly for military appliances. In any event, if private property is seized, this does not transfer title, since there is at all times a duty to restore the property or a subsidiary duty to pay compensation.[165] Consequently, the seized private property may not be used for commercial purposes or to boost the economy of the homeland.[166]

---

[160] Articles 590–594 Code Civil; Articles 590–594 Code Civil Belge; Articles 989–992 Codice Civile; Articles 483–485 Codigo Civil Español.
[161] Alan Gerson, *Notes and Comments: Off-Shore Oil Exploration by a Belligerent Occupant: The Gulf of Suez Dispute*, 71 Am. J. Int'l L. 730 (1977).
[162] Lighthouses Arbitration between France and Greece (1956), 12 UNRIAA 806–807; N.V. Bataafsche Petroleum Maatschappij v. War Damage Commission (1956), 23 ILR 819.
[163] Gasser, *supra* note 13, 259; Edward R. Cummings, *Oil Resources in Occupied Arab Territories*, 9 J. Int'l L. & Econ. 584 (1974) [hereinafter Cummings].
[164] Cummings, *id.* at 579; U.S. Department of the Army, *supra* note 24, at para. 410.
[165] Cummings, *id.* at 574–575.
[166] *Id.* at 575.

In conclusion, while the exploitation of natural resources by Uganda was undoubtedly inconsistent with the laws of occupation, it seems the Court should at least have outlined the main rules governing the matter. Indeed, its function is not solely restricted to establish state responsibility for breaches of international law, but also to set out, interpret, and apply the law in a concrete case.

6. Conclusion

The *Case concerning Armed Activities on the Territory of the Congo* unequivocally confirms the Court's finding in *Palestinian Wall* that international human rights law applies whenever states exercise jurisdiction extraterritorially, even in times of armed conflict. It refutes the idea that the Court's earlier ruling was inspired by the exceptionally long duration of Israel's occupation of the OPT, thereby dealing a heavy blow to opponents of extra-territorial application of human rights. Instead, the Court suggests that whenever a state occupies foreign territory in the sense of Article 42 HR, it is automatically obliged to ensure respect not only for the laws of occupation, but also for the applicable rules of human rights law, be it that the threshold used by the ICJ to establish the existence of a state of occupation seems open to questioning. This implies that an occupier may be held responsible for acts of its armed forces infringing these rights, but also for violations by private individuals which it failed to prevent. The Court's finding generates potentially far-reaching negative and positive obligations for occupying powers, which in turns necessitates clarification of the complex interplay between human rights law and the *lex specialis* of IHL. However, while the authors welcome the *dictum vis-à-vis* the applicability of human rights and while it would be difficult to disagree with the end verdict, the Court's reasoning is somewhat sketchy in many respects. Indeed, it has failed to give more flesh to the interplay between the two bodies of law. It steered clear from applying ESC rights or from examining the legislative powers of occupying powers in relation to human rights, instead confining itself to briefly enumerating the human rights provisions breached by Uganda. Hence, states still miss guidelines to apply both bodies of law simultaneously. In this regard, the Court may have missed an important opportunity to clarify the relationship between the two regimes.

Part C
Issues of Implementation

Chapter VII

Individuals as Subjects of International Humanitarian Law and Human Rights Law

Cátia Lopes* and *Noëlle Quénivet***

1. *Introduction*

As states have always been considered as the only subjects of international law, they were granted extensive rights and duties under international law. Legal personality is understood as the capacity of subjects of international law to enter into treaties and to act in an autonomous way. Hence, their powers are not derived from other legal entities. Only states have international legal personality to the fullest extent. However, they are not the only subjects of international law. Individuals, for example, are also conferred rights and duties, possess the ability to seize international courts and are also obliged to respect international rules.

Initially, individuals were only marginally involved on the international legal plane. Their conduct was regulated through the prohibition of piracy and certain war crimes which were, in fact, duties imposed upon a state to cooperate with other states in the suppression of the crime.[1] Further, rights were conceded under conventional law, e.g., providing human or commercial rights for which the individual was only a third party beneficiary as these treaties were aimed at states too.

Therefore, individuals were objects of international law, i.e. individuals could only be beneficiaries of the international law system inasmuch as states took action on behalf of individuals and, thereby, protected their rights on the international plane. For, it is common knowledge that the primary intention of international law is to regulate relations between states[2] and not relations between states and individuals.[3]

---

* Cátia Lopes is a LL.M. Candidate at King's College London.
** Dr. Noëlle Quénivet is a Senior Lecturer at the University of the West of England. She holds a LL.M. from the University of Nottingham U.K. and a Ph.D. from the University of Essex U.K.
[1] *The Status of the Individual in International Law*, 100 Am. Soc'y Int'l L. Proc. 249 (2006).
[2] Case of the S.S. Lotus (France v. Turkey), PCIJ, Series A, No. 10, at 18 (1927).
[3] As Doswald-Beck explains "[i]t is an obvious truism that international law is primarily aimed at regulating relations between States, human rights law notwithstanding." Louise Doswald-Beck,

However, as Lauterpacht affirms "the fact that individuals are normally the object of international law does not mean that they are not, in certain cases, the direct subjects thereof."[4] Indeed, the 20th century has seen the emergence of other subjects of international law, such as individuals, insurgents, belligerents, etc. The Nuremberg and the Tokyo trials as well as the Universal Declaration of Human Rights are a testimony to this fundamental change. This was indeed the very start of the assertion of the individual as an entity endowed with rights and duties under international law.

Straight after WWII states agreed that individuals should enjoy basic rights and freedoms and enshrined these in the United Nations Charter which called for the protection and "respect for human rights and fundamental freedoms for all without distinction as to race, sex, language or religion."[5] The Charter ushered in a worldwide movement of "internationalisation of human rights and… humanisation of international law."[6] Four years later the Universal Declaration of Human Rights[7] (UDHR) was enacted. Although it is a declaratory instrument with non-binding rules, it provides for a general human rights outline to be followed by governments since many of its articles are today considered as reflecting customary international legal norms. The UDHR constitutes the birth of international human rights law (HRL) in the sense that, rather than individuals receiving rights from their own states via the constitution or a bill of rights, they are conceded rights by international law.

In international humanitarian law (IHL), the negotiations of the draft texts authored by the International Committee for the Red Cross (ICRC) in consultation with states which culminated in the four Geneva Conventions of 1949 (GCs)[8] showed that states were prepared to inscribe in treaty law the fact that individuals had certain rights and duties. This ambitious approach taken by the ICRC is

---

Implementation of International Humanitarian Law in Future Wars, in The Law of Armed Conflict into the Next Millennium 52 (Michael N. Schmitt & Leslie C. Green eds, 1998).

[4] Hersch Lauterpacht, International Law 639 (1955).

[5] Article 1(3) U.N. Charter.

[6] Thomas Buergenthal, *Human Rights: A Challenge for the Universities*, 31 UNESCO Courier 25, 28 (1978).

[7] Universal Declaration of Human Rights, G.A. Res.217A (III), U.N. GAOR, 3d. Sess., at 71, U.N. Doc. A/810 (1948) [hereinafter UDHR].

[8] The Geneva Convention for the Amelioration of the Condition of the Wounded and Sick in Armed Forces in the Field, Aug. 12, 1949, 75 U.N.T.S. 31, 32; Geneva Convention for the Amelioration of the Condition of the Wounded, Sick and Shipwrecked Members of the Armed Forces at Sea, Aug. 12, 1949, 75 U.N.T.S. 85, 86; Geneva Convention Relative to the Treatment to Prisoners of War, Aug. 12, 1949, 75 U.N.T.S. 135, 136 [hereinafter GC III]; Geneva Convention Relative to the Protection of Civilian Persons in Time of War, Aug. 12, 1949, 75 U.N.T.S. 287, 288 [hereinafter GC IV].

notably exhibited in the provisions relating to the prosecution of grave breaches of the GCs. Indeed, although the prosecution of individuals for international crimes was already thought of after WWI, its acceptance in treaty law only dates back to the Geneva Conventions of 1949. However, on the international level the prosecution of individuals for crimes under international law only started thanks to the establishment of the *ad hoc* international criminal tribunals (International Criminal Tribunal for the Former Yugoslavia[9] and International Criminal Tribunal for Rwanda)[10] and the creation of the International Criminal Court.[11] These have enabled the prosecution of individuals without the interposition of domestic rules, for violations of the law of war and of certain fundamental human rights, including crimes against humanity.

As a result of these two concurrent processes individuals are not only protected by states which must guarantee a certain set of rights but they are also the subject of duties. It is clear now that individuals have acquired international legal personality and become right- and duty-holders under international law. Yet, it is unclear how the two regimes, i.e. international humanitarian law and human rights law, relate in this regard.

For example, while the individual can claim the right to life under HRL this right seems to be denied *prima facie* by IHL since the latter allows or at least tolerates killing, and wounding of innocent human beings not directly involved in the armed conflict e.g. civilians who are victims of collateral damage. Meron assimilates this with a boxing match where "pummelling the opponent's upper body is fine; hitting below the belt is proscribed"[12] and therefore, while the rules of the game are followed, the cause of suffering, deprivation of freedom, and death is to a certain extent permitted.

Individuals cannot claim that their right to be absolutely free from military attacks has been violated; for, first, there is no such right under IHL and, second, there is no legal forum examining such issues. On the other hand, HRL condemns such acts inasmuch as it provides for the full protection of the physical integrity and human dignity of individuals. Indeed, it bestows individuals with absolute rights, such as the right of freedom from torture, ill or degrading treatment. Under this second *corpus juris* individuals whose lives have been endangered can apply to a competent court against their own government. In a nutshell, while individuals enjoy certain

---

[9] Statute of the International Criminal Tribunal for the Former Yugoslavia, S.C. Res. 827, U.N. Doc. S/RES/827 (May 25, 1993) [hereinafter ICTY Statute].

[10] Statute of the International Criminal Tribunal for Rwanda, S.C. Res. 955, U.N. Doc. S/RES/955 (Nov. 8, 1994) [hereinafter ICTR Statute].

[11] Rome Statute of the International Criminal Court, U.N. Doc. 2187 U.N.T.S. 90, entered into force July 1, 2002 [hereinafter Rome Statute].

[12] Theodor Meron, *The Humanization of Humanitarian Law*, 94 Am. J. Int'l L. 240 (2000) [hereinafter Meron].

rights according to one set of laws, these same rights are denied by another set of laws. Furthermore the implementation mechanisms appear to be different.

Consequently, these two doctrines are often analysed with regards to their differences without noting their complementarity. Yet, it must be stressed that IHL is considered as the *lex specialis* of HRL[13] and that the two *juris corpora* must be understood as interactive.[14] In particular, Meron notes that the law of war is implanted in HRL and is shifting its parameters to embrace the protection of individuals more generally.[15]

Under these two legal regimes individuals are endowed with substantive and procedural rights and duties. Substantive rights and duties are those given effect by bilateral or multilateral agreements, or by international customary law and are often recognised as part of *jus cogens*. In contrast procedural rights are dependent on the recognition by the state of the legal personality of the individual. This chapter first discusses the position of individuals as right- and then as duty-holders under the two legal regimes.

2. Individuals as Right-holders

The discussion concerning individuals as right-holders of the provisions embedded in IHL and HRL treaties is quite a complex one. While it is clear from the terminology that HRL aims to endow individuals with rights, on the other hand it appears that under IHL the primary right-holders are states. The seminal point is, however, whether individuals have rights according to IHL.

2.1. International Human Rights Law

Although it seems that the individual is generally considered as a subject of international law, i.e. holder of rights, he/she has few means to enforce them. Indeed, a crucial issue is whether such rights are directly applicable to individuals. The lack of enforcement means does not however signify that the individual does not possess such rights.

2.1.1. The Rationale for Granting Individuals Rights under HRL

It can be affirmed that to a certain extent it is the state that, via the ratification of an international instrument, bestows human rights on individuals and confers the duty to protect them upon itself and, in case it fails to do so, upon an interna-

---

[13] Legality of the Threat or Use of Nuclear Weapons, Advisory Opinion, (July 8, 1996), I.C.J. Reports 1996, para. 25.
[14] Meron, *supra* note 12, at 239–278.
[15] *Id.*

tional body. In the *Jurisdiction of the Courts of Danzig* Case the Permanent Court of International Justice accepted that it was open to states to create and confer enforceable (by national courts) rights on individuals.[16]

Although this jurisprudence is well established, it must yet be underlined that it is remarkable that individuals receive their rights via an international legal instrument that binds *states* in their relation to each other. This particular set of relationships is governed by the Vienna Convention on the Law of Treaties of 1969[17] which includes a mechanism for which treaties become juridical acts at the time states express their consent to be bound by it. The time of the ratification of an international treaty is crucial, as it stands at the foremost of the concession of rights to the individual. Moreover, this Convention includes the principle of *pacta sunt servanda* under Article 26[18] which imposes an obligation upon the parties ratifying the treaty to be bound by and respect it. The commitment of compliance with the provisions under a human rights treaty allows for individuals to benefit from the rights assigned to them.

It is irrefutable that HRL is directed at individuals and not states[19] and, therefore, one may wonder why a state would agree to enter into such agreements especially because it is common practice that states confer such rights via municipal law.[20] Enacting a Bill of Rights, as illustrated by the case of the United States, is a way to bestow rights under constitutional law. Nonetheless, constitutional law has a limited scope since it only affects the citizens of a certain state and the rights are interpreted according to the particular interests of the state.[21] In other words, human rights under constitutional law are not allocated in the view to best protect the individual but under a balance of interests between the individual and the state. In contrast, HRL confers universal rights, aiming at protecting individuals regardless of their

---

[16] Jurisdiction of the Courts of Danzig Case, PCIJ, Advisory Opinion No. 15, Series B. No. 15, at 17.
[17] The Vienna Convention on the Law of Treaties, 1969, 1155 UNTS 331 [hereinafter VCLT].
[18] The article provides as: "Every treaty is binding upon the parties to it and must be performed by them in good faith." *Id.*
[19] *See* in particular Human Rights Committee, General Comment No. 24: Issues Relating to Reservations Made upon Ratification or Accession to the Covenant or the Optional Protocols thereto, or in Relation to Declarations under Article 41 of the Covenant, U.N. Doc. CCPR/C/21/Rev.1/Add.6 (Nov. 2, 1994), para. 17.
[20] The initial notion of human rights law "is linked to the constitutional concept of the rule of law – the inherent limitations on the exercise of absolute power by a sovereign or Parliament." Rhona K.M. Smith, Textbook on International Human Rights 5 (2007) [hereinafter Smith].
[21] This explains why "human rights law was initially developed inside the respective nations, dealing with national matters" that were not connected to international issues and interests. Asbjørn Eide, *The Laws of War and Human Rights-Differences and Convergences, in* Studies and Essays on International Humanitarian Law and Red Cross Principles in Honour of Jean Pictet 675, 676–677 (Christophe Swinarski ed., 1984).

"race, sex, language or religion"[22] and, thus, provides a protection that does not hinge upon state interests or policies.

Hence, the international community encourages states to enter into such international agreements with the aim of protecting human dignity and the physical integrity of individuals. Unfortunately, often, the ratification of human rights treaties is merely symbolic, for it asserts publicly the interest of the state in the protection of human rights. As a matter of fact, accession to a particular human rights treaty increases the state's standing as a human rights law promoter, which, in turn, enhances its reputation and improves its relations with other subjects of international law. Several other reasons for formally joining such agreements may be highlighted: it deflects foreign criticism[23] and more powerful states may have exercised significant political/economic pressure upon certain states.[24] Other classical motives are linked to internal factors, such as international and civil war, population and economic constraints, which have shown to affect negatively human rights protection.[25] As a result those states are keener on accepting rules relating to HRL. Another principal motive for states to join such treaties is the legal obligation imposed as a member of the United Nations[26] since one of the United Nations' vital purposes, as listed under Article 1(3) U.N. Charter, is the achievement of international cooperation "in promoting and encouraging respect for human rights and for fundamental freedoms for all without distinction as to race, sex, language, or religion." Moreover, the "universal" status of the imposition in favour of human rights issues is enshrined in Article 56 whereby all members of the United Nations "pledge themselves to take joint and separate action in cooperation with the Organization for the achievement of the purposes set forth in Article 55."[27]

---

[22] Article 55(c) U.N. Charter.
[23] David P. Forsythe, *The United Nations and Human Rights, 1945–1985*, 100 Polit. Sci. Quart. 249–269 (1985); Thomas Buergenthal, *The Normative and Institutional Evolution of International Human Rights*, 19 Hum. Rts Q. 703 (1997) [hereinafter Buergenthal].
[24] Jack Donnelly, Universal Human Rights in Theory and Practice (1989). In particular the foreign policy of Jimmy Carter placed human rights on the international political agenda and led to changes in many countries. See Buergenthal, *supra* note 23, at 712.
[25] David R. Davis & Michael D. Ward, *Deaths and the Disappeared in Contemporary Chile*, 34 J. Conflict Resolution 449–475 (1990); Conway W. Henderson, *Conditions Affecting the Use of Political Repression*, 35 J. Conflict Resolution 120–142 (1991); Conway W. Henderson, *Population Pressures and Political Repression*, 74 Soc. Sci. Quart. 322–333 (1993); Neil J. Mitchell & James M. McCormick, *Economic and Political Explanations of Human Rights Violations*, 40 World Polit 476–498 (1988); Steven C. Poe & C. Neal Tate, *Repression of Human Rights to Personal Integrity in the 1980s: A Global Analysis*, 88 Amer. Polit. Sci. Rev. 853–872 (1994); Linda Camp Keith, *The United Nations International Covenant on Civil and Political Rights: Does It Make a Difference in Human Rights Behavior?*, 36.1 Journal of Peace Research 100 (1999) [hereinafter Keith].
[26] Buergenthal, *supra* note 23, at 706–708.
[27] Article 56 U.N. Charter.

In addition, states are encouraged to establish impartial mechanisms that adjudicate claims brought by individuals whose rights have been violated.

Many stages must be passed before the legal standing of the individual is recognised. First, the international treaty, which confers rights upon individuals, must be negotiated, signed, and ratified. Often, this conventional instrument only contains substantive rights. Treaties such as the International Covenant on Civil and Political Rights,[28] the European Convention of Human Rights,[29] and the Inter-American Convention on Human Rights[30] describe the rights of individuals but are restricted since they are not self-executing but reliant upon domestic law.

Second, states must recognise that individuals have a procedural right to bring a claim before an international body, be it judicial or quasi-judicial.[31] Sometimes the clause bestowing individuals with procedural rights is enshrined in the original treaty (see e.g. Article 34 ECHR)[32] while in others a protocol needs to be added (see e.g. ACHPR).[33] Therefore, individuals are from the very beginning confined in the scope of their international claim since it is only possible to lodge a complaint against a state which recognises the individual's standing.

2.1.2. *Substantive Rights*

The concept of substantive rights describes general rights granting the individual the power to act or behave in a particular way despite the government's desire to the contrary. Such rights are "arranged in a series of assertions, each assertion setting forth a right that all individuals have by virtue of the fact that they are human"[34] and they differ from treaty to treaty.[35] Thus, human rights law focuses on the rights of the recipients of a certain treatment.

---

[28] International Covenant on Civil and Political Rights, G.A. Res. 2200A (XXI), 21 U.N. GAOR Supp. (No. 16) at 52, U.N. Doc. A/6316 (1966), 999 U.N.T.S. 171.

[29] Convention for the Protection of Human Rights and Fundamental Freedoms, 213 U.N.T.S. 222, entered into force Sept. 3, 1953, as amended by Protocols Nos 3, 5, 8, and 11 which entered into force on Sept. 21, 1970, Dec. 20, 1971, Jan. 1, 1990, and Nov. 1, 1998 respectively [hereinafter ECHR].

[30] American Convention on Human Rights, O.A.S. Treaty Series No. 36, 1144 U.N.T.S. 123, entered into force July 18, 1978, reprinted in Basic Documents Pertaining to Human Rights in the Inter-American System, OEA/Ser.L.V/II.82 doc.6 rev.1 at 25 (1992) [hereinafter IACHR].

[31] Eleventh Protocol to the European Convention for the Protection of Human Rights and Fundamental Freedoms, May 11, 1994, Europ. T.S. No. 155, Article 34.

[32] ECHR, *supra* note 29.

[33] African Charter on Human and Peoples' Rights (Banjul Charter) (June 27, 1981), 21 I.L.M. 59 [hereinafter ACHPR].

[34] Louise Doswald-Beck & Sylvain Vité, *Origin and Nature of Human Rights Law and Humanitarian Law*, 293 Int'l Rev. Red Cross 95, 101 (1993).

[35] For instance, under the ICCPR some of the substantive rights include: right to life; freedom from torture; liberty and security of person; right to a fair trial; privacy; freedom of thought, conscience, religion and belief; freedom of opinion, expression and information; freedom of assembly; freedom of association; right to take part in public affairs, etc. International Covenant on Civil and Political

Human rights have been described as "universal, indivisible and interdependent and interrelated" under the Vienna Declaration and Programme of Action of the World Conference on Human Rights.[36] Nonetheless, many writers[37] accept the classification of human rights in three different generations, which represent the constant development within the doctrine of human rights. It should be noted, however, that the term "generation" does not comprise the replacement of rights but the addition of rights, with different nature and characteristics, accomplished with time. In other words, the three generations do not replace but complete each other.

The first generation embraces the primary rights of security, property, and political participation (as seen in the French and U.S. bills of rights). The rights under this generation are often denominated as "negative" since states have to abstain from taking actions in violation of those rights. In addition and integrated within the UDHR are the so-called "positive rights" under the second generation. These require the state to progressively take actions to guarantee, for instance, socio-economic rights, such as the right to welfare, education, and leisure. Finally, the third and most recent (only since the last two decades of the 20th century) generation of human rights includes such rights as the right to development,[38] the right to peace,[39] and the right to a clean/healthy environment.[40] The third generation is composed of "collective rights" which, unlike the previous generations, are rather vague and complex to apply to individuals. Many of the reasons why such applicability is difficult lay on the holders of the rights and duties. For instance, under the third generation rights are bestowed upon collective entities[41] which makes it confusing when determining who is entitled to which rights. Another setback is that it is often argued that for a right to exist, it is imperative that a duty be

---

Rights, G.A. Res. 2200A (XXI), 21 U.N. GAOR (Supp. No. 16) at 52, U.N. Doc. A/6316 (Dec. 16, 1966), 999 U.N.T.S. 171, entered into force Mar. 23, 1976 [hereinafter ICCPR].

[36] World Conference on Human Rights, Vienna Declaration and Programme of Action, Vienna, June 14–25, 1993, U.N. Doc. A/Conf.157/24 (Oct. 13, 1993), para. 5.

[37] *See* e.g. Ran Hirschl, *"Negative" Rights vs. "Positive" Entitlements: A Comparative Study of Judicial Interpretations of Rights in an Emerging Neo-Liberal Economic Order*, 22 Hum. Rts Q. 1060–1098 (2000).

[38] *See* "Alternative approaches and ways and means within the United Nations System for improving the effective enjoyment of human rights and fundamental freedoms." G.A. Res. 36/133 (Dec. 14, 1981) where it is declared "that the right to development is an inalienable human right." This is followed by the Declaration on the Right to Development, G.A. Res. 41/128, (Dec. 4, 1986) [hereinafter DRD].

[39] *See* the Declaration on the Rights of People to Peace (G.A. Res. 39/11 (Nov. 12, 1984)) which proclaims that "the people of our planet have a sacred right to peace."

[40] Proclaimed for the very first time in the U.N. Conference on the Human Environment in Stockholm 1972.

[41] *See* e.g. the Declaration on the Right to Development which refers to human beings and peoples. DRD, *supra* note 38.

imposed on someone in relation to that right (either, not to interfere or to provide such right). Particularly relating to the right to development, it is unclear whether peoples have rights against their own states or whether poorer states have entitlements vis-à-vis other states. Hence, not all substantive rights are directly granted and applicable to individuals, in particular third generation rights. The latter do not set out specific measures to be taken, instead, they express agreed objectives and goals the international community has undertaken to pursue.

Moreover, since substantive rights are enshrined in treaty law, only states that have ratified such treaties are bound. Another limitation relates to the fact that some human rights treaties, unlike the ICCPR, are not of universal scope. The ECHR,[42] the IACHR,[43] and the ACHPR[44] guarantee rights on the regional level. Even more restrictive is the fact that only members of the Council of Europe can become party to the ECHR and only members of the Organisation of American States can ratify the IACHR.

These conventions can also be criticised with regards to their scope. An oddity is that according to treaty law states concede these rights not only to their nationals but also to any person under their jurisdiction. For example, asylum-seekers,[45] foreigners[46] and refugees[47] have successfully claimed violations of their human rights under the ECHR.[48]

---

[42] ECHR, *supra* note 29.
[43] IACHR, *supra* note 30.
[44] ACHPR, *supra* note 33.
[45] For instance, in the case of Limbuela, where asylum seekers were left destitute, the Secretary of State for the Home Department sought reliance on conventional rights enshrined in the ECHR and, more specifically, on Article 3. R (Limbuela) v. SSHD [2005] UKHL 66, [2005] 3 WLR 1014.
[46] Another guarantee offered by the ECHR is to avoid deportation to a state where a risk of persecution exists as illustrated in the case of Soering. In this case the Court found that the United Kingdom would violate the ECHR should it return the alien, a USA citizen, to the United States if he were to be served the death row. Jens Soering v. The United Kingdom, Application No. 14038/88 ECHR, (July 7, 1989).
[47] A refugee, while in the territory of a contracting state, enjoys all the guarantees that the ECHR provides for persons within the jurisdiction of a state party. Article 8, concerning private and family life, is also regularly invoked in circumstances where the deportation of a person may lead to a serious and irreparable disruption of his or her private or, even more so, family life. In the specific case of Mubilanzila Mayeka the ECHR assisted individuals with refugee status in Canada. This case concerned a five year old who was detained alone in Belgium when travelling with her uncle to join her mother, a refugee living in Canada. Mubilanzila Mayeka and Kaniki Mitunga v. Belgium, Application No. 13178/03 ECHR, (Oct. 12, 2006).
[48] Ireneu Cabral Barreto, *The Status of Refugees in the Countries Where They Seek Asylum*, Proceedings of the 2nd Colloquy on the European Convention on Human Rights and the Protection of Refugees, Asylum-Seekers and Displaced Persons, Strasbourg, May 19–20, 2000, at 65.

Although at first sight it appears that a broad range of individuals enjoy rights under the ECHR, it must be stressed that not every individual can benefit from such substantive rights. Indeed treaty law often provides for jurisdictional restrictions. The ECHR asserts that "The High Contracting Parties shall secure to everyone within their jurisdiction the rights and freedoms defined in Section I of this Convention." In other words, only individuals under the jurisdiction of a contracting party can claim rights entrenched therein. The statement is based on a decision of the European Court in the *Bankovic* case where several citizens of the Former Republic of Yugoslavia claimed that their right to life had been violated by the aerial attacks carried out by the NATO states.[49] Although the judges acknowledge that the Convention is a "living instrument," they adopt a restrictive interpretation inasmuch as they declare that the states participating in the military intervention did not "exercise...all or some of the public powers normally to be exercised by [a] Government."[50] Such a narrow reading has been criticised by certain authors. As Schäfer notes it is difficult to imagine how the bombing of a building cannot be considered as an exercise of sovereign power.[51] Indeed, it is possible to contend that the state whose planes attacked the bridge exercised its executive jurisdiction extraterritorially, for the planes were used as a tool of state policy. In contrast, it must be noted that the Inter-American Commission on Human Rights[52] as well as the Human Rights Committee[53] have adopted a wider interpretation.

Another way for individuals to benefit from human rights provisions is via international customary law inasmuch as this allows granting human rights to individuals without the barrier of nationality or jurisdiction. A classic paradigm is the UDHR, based on customary rules, which is not binding but consistently applied by states. Consequently, "it flows into the municipal legal system of countries becoming enforceable legal protections."[54] Moreover, the United Nations via the Human Rights Council (former Human Rights Commission) investigates possible breaches of human rights, as defined by the United Nations Charter, the UDHR and other treaties ratified under the auspices of the said international organization,

---

[49] Banković v. Belgium and 16 Other Contracting States, ECHR, Application No. 52207/99, Admissibility Decision, (Dec. 12, 2001).

[50] *Id.* para. 71. *See also* Ilascu and Others v. Moldova and Russia, ECHR, Application No. 48787/99 (Jul. 8, 2004).

[51] Bernhard Schäfer, *Der Fall Bankovic oder wie eine Lücke geschaffen wird*, 3 MenschenRechtsMagazin 149, 156 (2002).

[52] Coard v. United States of America, Case 10.951, Inter-American Commission of Human Rights, OEA/ser.L/V/II.106.doc.3rev (Sept. 29, 1999).

[53] Lopez Burgos v. Uruguay, Communication No. R.12/52, Human Rights Committee, Supp. No. 40, at 176, U.N. Doc. A/36/40 (1981) and Lilian Celiberti de Casariego v. Uruguay, Communication No. R.13/56, Human Rights Committee, Supp No. 40, at 185, U.N. Doc. A/36/40 (1981).

[54] Julie Cassidy, *Emergence of the Individual as an International Juristic Entity: Enforcement of International Human Rights*, 9 Deakin L. Rev. 534, 554 (2004) [hereinafter Cassidy].

and thereby ensure that states comply with HRL standards.[55] Indeed, under Resolution 1503[56] and as amended by Resolution 2000/3 (entitled Procedure for Dealing with Communications concerning Human Rights),[57] the Human Rights Council via the Sub-Commission on the Promotion and Protection of Human Rights is allowed to examine individual complaints for evidence of a pattern of abuses.

However, not all human rights are considered of customary nature and therefore limitations regarding nationality and jurisdiction are still strong impediments to the enjoyment of such rights. For instance, not all civil and political rights, which protect individuals from government abuse of power, and economic, social, and cultural rights, which are the basis for adequate standards of living that will ensure human dignity, are embedded within the provisions of the UDHR. Some rights will only be applicable to individuals within the jurisdiction of the convention/covenant; consequently, reducing the scope of applicability of that particular right. As pinpointed by Meron, two categories of human rights can be distinguished: the fundamental and the peremptory (*jus cogens*)[58] human rights.[59] Those classed as *jus cogens* norms are accepted and recognized by the international community and prevail over treaty law. Accordingly, *jus cogens* rights are not restricted by reference to nationality or jurisdiction, thereby allowing for the enforcement of the most vital human rights to individuals.

As a conclusion, as Buergenthal explains "a definition of international law that did not today recognize the individual as the direct beneficiary of international human rights law and, to that extent, a subject of international law, would be blind to contemporary legal and political realities."[60]

2.1.3. *Procedural Rights*
In addition to being accorded substantive rights under HRL, individuals also enjoy procedural rights. As Teitel underlines "[the individual's] new subjectivity is evident in the heightened enforcement of the expanded norms, which are directed beyond States to persons and peoples."[61] Procedural rights usually refer to statutory or common law rights that administer official settlements.[62] To a certain extent procedural rights are a continuation of substantive rights since they provide for

---

[55] Ian Brownlie, Principles of International Law 554 (1973).
[56] ECOSOC, Resolution 1503 (XLVIII), U.N. Doc. E/4832/Add.1 (May 27, 1970).
[57] ECOSOC, Resolution 2000/3, U.N. Doc. E/RES/2000/3 (June 16, 2000).
[58] *See* Article 53 VCLT, *supra* note 17.
[59] Meron, *supra* note 12, at 239–278.
[60] Buergenthal, *supra* note 23, at 708.
[61] Ruti G. Teitel, *Humanity's Law: Rule of Law for the New Global Politics*, 35 Cornell Int'l L.J. 355, 363 (2002).
[62] Larry Alexander, *Are Procedural Rights Derivative Substantive Rights?* 17 Law and Philosophy 23 (1998).

their application. Yet, it must be stressed that there is no automaticity between substantive and procedural rights, for "the capacity to possess... rights does not necessarily imply the capacity to exercise those rights oneself."[63]

Generally claims can be made at two levels: national and international. National claims are those which are lodged by the individual to assert his/her rights under national law (e.g. rights under the Bill of Rights in the United States) whereas international procedural rights are employed when individuals claim their internationally granted rights (e.g. rights under the ECHR).

International conventions endow individuals with procedural rights that allow them to demand the proper application of HRL within the domestic legal system. As a consequence, national courts play an essential role in the protection of an individual's rights. When an individual's right has been encroached upon, the individual can make a claim under domestic law. Such a system has two main advantages. Firstly, it is often the case that the claim is made in the territory where the violation occurred and, therefore, the means of investigation and evidence are within easier reach. Secondly, it should be remembered that if all claims were made at the international level, international bodies would be managing an enormous set of files which would result in massive delays and great injustice notably due to the dearth of information. It is predominantly for these reasons that all domestic remedies must be exhausted before a claim is transferred to an international body.

Such a system is in place under the ECHR before any claim reaches the European Court of Human Rights in Strasbourg. In other words, an individual can only request the implementation of his/her rights if the municipal provisions or case-law are inconsistent with the ones provided by the ECHR. Therefore, under Article 26 ECHR, an individual may only bring a case under the Commission within 6 months from the date in which the final decision was taken where all remedies were exhausted under domestic provisions.[64] It can thus be argued that, at the European level, individuals' procedural rights depend upon the state's failure to deal appropriately with a claim. Other treaties have espoused similar approaches. For instance, Article 5(2)(b) of the Optional Protocol to the ICCPR imposes upon individuals the obligation to exhaust municipal remedies.[65] In contrast, the ACHPR adopts a slightly different approach since it imparts that the exhaustion of all domestic remedies is not necessary in cases where the Commission opines that such remedies were non-existent or that the procedure for achieving them was excessive.[66] Consequently, the individual's initial ability to protect his/her rights is

---

[63] Peter Pazmany University Case, PCIJ, Series A/B, No. 61 (1933), at 231.
[64] ECHR, *supra* note 29.
[65] Optional Protocol to the International Covenant on Civil and Political Rights (Dec. 16, 1966), 999 U.N.T.S. 302.
[66] *See* Article 50 ACHPR, *supra* note 33.

to a certain extent dependent on the fact that these are recognised by the state and that the latter provides available remedies to enforce them.

As a result, this mechanism imposes upon states the responsibility to ensure that their legislation complies with international human rights treaties and that their courts deliver judgments in line with HRL jurisprudence. Thus, one can claim that the fewer claims are brought against a state on the international level, the more the state complies *prima facie* with international human rights standards. As a result, the system put in place by states in HRL treaties can be said to be self-enforcing. Indeed, a state, that might have ratified the treaty to appear well on the international level, ends up having to change its behaviour with regards to human rights because it otherwise faces numerous claims brought by its citizens which in turn bring shame upon the state. The formal and highly visible commitment to human rights should make the state more willing to improve its performance.[67] Hence, the state feels compelled to implement the treaty provisions and adapt its behaviour to the new standards as this is the only possibility to obtain a natural decrease in the number of cases brought before international bodies.

Although individual complaint mechanisms vary from treaty to treaty, they all share similar objectives and procedures. Each mechanism provides for a body or forum before which individuals, from those states that have specifically endorsed this procedure, may allege that the government has violated treaty-based HRL.[68] Such states expressly authorise an impartial international body to examine the allegation and decide upon whether the government has in fact encroached upon the human rights guaranteed in the said treaty. The ECHR was the first human rights treaty to give individuals standing to file cases directly with the appropriate judicial body.[69]

One must however wonder what is the authoritativeness and enforceability of these international decisions. Taking the impressive example of the European system where (at present) all states parties to the ECHR must consent to the European Court of Human Rights jurisdiction, this system has undoubtedly surpassed all the expectations since its decisions have been respected and implemented by the states without exception.[70] The substantial majority of states parties to the ECHR apply it faithfully and routinely; although a number of the newer states find it challenging to live up to their obligations. It is indeed the process of internalizing the values of the ECHR in domestic legislation and national governments that places the European Court as a constitutional court in matters of civil and political

---

[67] Keith, *supra* note 25, at 95–118.
[68] Douglas Donoho, *Human Rights Enforcement in the Twenty-First Century*, 35 Ga. J. Int'l & Comp. L. 1 (2006) [hereinafter Donoho].
[69] Thomas Buergenthal, *The Evolving International Human Rights System*, 100 Am. J. Int'l L. 83 (2006).
[70] *Id.*

rights where individuals are gradually conferred legal standing. This system should therefore be taken as a model of enforcement.

Regrettably, not all human rights treaties have such enforcement mechanisms or records as the example of the Inter-American system shows. The Human Rights Committee, which receives communications from individuals who claim to be the victims of violations of rights enshrined in the ICCPR,[71] knows of similar problems.[72] In the opinion of Douglas Donoho[73] this is due to the ambiguous legal status of the decisions made and the absence of enforcement mechanisms, although this poor record should also be blamed on the lack of voluntary compliance from the states parties. This matter is governed by a common sense of contradiction since on the one hand, the parties do not voluntarily follow the decisions of international bodies, however, on the other, they provide individuals with a right to lodge complaints at an international level.

In this context, it is recognised that modern human rights treaties offer individuals a mechanism that allows them to break away from the classical intermediation. Individuals have acquired the right to lodge complaints on the international level independently from the intervention of their states of nationality. Once a specific state has agreed to the existence of an individual complaint mechanism, the state cannot intervene on behalf of the individual anymore since this would defeat the very aim of the individual complaint mechanism which is to give an independent voice to the individual on the international level. In such a hypothetical case, the procedure would be devoid of value since the state would be representing not only the individual but also itself in the same proceedings.[74]

At present the individual may not only impose the compliance by states of their obligations under the covenants and conventions but may also stand before a competent international court to defend his/her case.

---

[71] Alexander Orakhelashvili, *The Position of the Individual in International Law*, 31 Cal. W. Int'l. L.J. 241 (2001).

[72] Indeed, according to the 2002 Report of the Human Rights Committee, there was a 30% compliance rate with the decisions (Report of the Human Rights Committee, Vol. 1, 225, U.N. Doc. A/57/40 (2002)) and in 2004 deep concern was expressed by the HRC with regards to the "increasing number of cases where States parties fail to implement the Committee's" final views on individual petitions (Report of the Human Rights Committee, Vol. 1, 256, U.N. Doc. A/58/40 (2004)).

[73] Donoho, *supra* note 70, at 1.

[74] An intermediary solution was designed under the old system of the ECHR whereby the commission represented the individual before the Court. At that time, individuals did not have standing to bring a case before the Court, therefore only states and the Commission would directly participate in the proceedings. This system suffered some change with the adoption of Protocol No. 11 to the Convention which abolished the Commission and conceded individuals, for the first time, the right to access the Court directly. Protocol No. 11 to the Convention for the Protection of Human Rights and Fundamental Freedoms, Restructuring the Control Machinery Established Thereby, May 11, 1994, 33 ILM 943 (1994).

2.2. International Humanitarian Law

The relative dearth of rights accorded to individuals in IHL stands in stark contrast to the numerous rights that individuals are endowed with by way of international human rights treaties. Indeed, IHL seems on its face to grant individuals very few substantive and procedural rights.

2.2.1. Substantial Rights

In IHL, the primary right-holders are states. The seminal point is, however, whether individuals have rights according to the conventions, for they only offer "protection" to the individuals. It is indeed true that, "th[e] conventions are centred on the notion of protection of persons"[75] as they focus on "protected persons" such as civilians in the hands of the enemy and prisoners of war.

It should nevertheless be noted that the definition of "protected persons," such as under the Fourth Geneva Convention, only applies to persons which are nationals of a state with which the occupying power is at war. Therefore, nationals of a neutral or cobelligerent state who find themselves in the territory of a belligerent state are not protected persons while their state of nationality maintains normal diplomatic representation in the state where they are found.[76] However, the ICTY introduced in the *Tadic* case[77] another definition of protected persons, independent of nationality. The Trial Chamber came to the conclusion that the victims could not be considered "protected persons" because they were not "in the hands of a party to the conflict of which they were not nationals." In contrast, the Appeals Chamber adopted a different position by replacing the nationality requirement of protected persons by the dual factors of allegiance to, and effective protection by, the state.[78] Therefore, the new standard which was adopted for determining a protected person's status extends to all victims in need of such status in international armed conflicts.[79]

---

[75] Marie-Pierre Besson de Vezac, *Les sanctions des violations des conventions de Genève du 12 aout 1949*, 3 Droit et Defense 4 (1997) [hereinafter de Vezac].

[76] Meron, *supra* note 12, at 257.

[77] Prosecutor v. Tadic, Case No. IT-94-1-AR72, Appeal on Jurisdiction (Oct. 2, 1995) [hereinafter Tadic 1995].

[78] For this revolutionary change to succeed, the Appeals Chamber explained that the nationality requirement was not vital either under the explicit provisions of the Geneva Conventions or according to their *travaux préparatoires*. To buttress its viewpoint the Court referred to the position of refugees or nationals of a neutral state who have lost their effective (or diplomatic) protection. The inadequacy of the criterion of nationality was noted with regards to the manner in which IHL provides protection to civilians.

[79] However, one must note that the law of international armed conflict does not always offer better protection for victims than the law of non-international armed conflict. The former offers protection to persons who are located in the hands of a belligerent depending on a number of factors: the status of the particular person (civilian or combatant) and the status of the territory on which the

The aim of the regime of "protected persons" under IHL is to offer protection and assistance to those individuals who do not play a role in the hostilities. According to the Geneva Conventions, there are four categories of "protected persons:" the sick and wounded, medical personnel, civilians, and prisoners of war, all of which are granted specific rights.

In addition to the protective regime offered by IHL which endows individuals with certain rights, it is contended that treaty law also holds special rights for individuals by virtue of the GCs and their APs.[80] Indeed, it is contended that Common Article 6/6/6/7 reflects the tendency to refine individual rights over time and introduces into IHL the idea of *jus cogens* in the protection of rights granted to "protected persons" inasmuch as it declares that "no special agreement shall...restrict the rights which [the Convention] confers upon [the individuals protected by GCI]."[81] The use of the specific word "rights" demonstrates that individuals are indeed granted rights according to conventional humanitarian law instruments. Illustrative and often cited examples are the right of POWs to refuse repatriation and the language used in the broad catalogue of human rights protections of Article 75 API.[82]

2.2.2. Procedural Rights

Yet, that individuals may have rights under international law does not automatically mean that they can enforce these rights on the international level. As a matter of fact, states are particularly cautious to keep the monopoly of justice in the international order.[83]

It should be pointed out that the enforcement mechanisms of IHL differ from those of HRL. Whereas IHL is mainly implemented by inter-state, i.e. traditional, means and has only recently integrated the individual in its enforcement mecha-

---

individual is found. In this regard, one must pinpoint that it is often difficult to precisely determine who is a combatant and who is a civilian and, furthermore, it is often nearly impossible to establish that a particular party to the conflict acts as an occupying powers. In contrast, the law of non-international armed conflict protects persons according to the actual situation the particular individual is in. These rules appear to be more appropriate to the often chaotic situations of many contemporary conflicts. *See* Common Article 3 GCs, *supra* note 8; Protocol Additional to the Geneva Conventions of 12 August 1949, and Relating to the Protection of Victims of Non-International Armed Conflicts, opened for signature: Dec. 12, 1977, 1125 UNTS 609 [hereinafter Additional Protocol II].

[80] Jann K. Kleffner, *Improving Compliance with International Humanitarian Law Through the Establishment of an Individual Complaints Procedure*, 15 LJIL 237, 244–245 (2002).
[81] Common Article 6/6/6/7GC, *supra* note 8.
[82] George Aldrich, *Individuals as Subjects of International Humanitarian Law*, in Theory of International Law at the Threshold of the 21st Century: Essays in Honour of Krzysztof Skubiszewski 851, 855 (Jerzy Makarczyk ed., 1996).
[83] Patrick Daillier & Alain Pellet, Droit International Public 701 (1999).

nism, HRL has, from the inception, offered individuals a significant place in the implementation system.

As IHL emerged by the end of the 19th century, it also opted for classical means of law enforcement. International law being solely state-centric at that period of time and wars involving only state actors, state responsibility was conceived as the primary implementation mechanism. The law of war was driven by "collective responsibility, with the attendant collective sanctions of classical international law: belligerent reprisals *in bello* and war reparations *post bellum*."[84] This position has not changed much since the rules set forth in the GCs and the APs are not self-executing and, thus, "individuals are not allowed to file a claim in order to obtain compensation."[85]

By the end of the conflict, the parties to the conflict, i.e. the states, sign a peace treaty and in some cases request reparations. However, reparations are more predicated on *jus ad bellum* norms than on violations of the laws of war perpetrated by the states.[86] This means that reparations are usually imposed on the defeated side. Post-conflict arrangements between states also include the negotiation of compensation.[87] Whereas in the past such money was awarded to the state as national courts regularly rejected individual claims,[88] a more recent mechanism set up after the 1990–1991 Gulf conflict provides that individuals may also be awarded compensation based on state responsibility.

Another way for states to obtain reparation for violations of international law[89] and more particularly of the laws of war is to lodge a complaint before an international court such as the International Court of Justice (ICJ) or before an *ad hoc* arbitration tribunal. The ICJ was requested on numerous occasions to adjudicate, amongst others, issues relating to IHL.[90] Another glaring example is the arbitral

---

[84] Georges Abi Saab, *International Criminal Tribunals and the Development of International Humanitarian and Human Rights Law, in* Liber Amicorum Judge Mohammed Bedjaoui 649, 650 (Emile Yakpo & Tahar Boumedra eds., 1999).

[85] Federico Sperotto, Violations of Human Rights during Military Operations in Chechnya, Working Paper No. 41 (Feb. 1, 2007), *available at* www.du.edu/gsis/hrhw/working/2007/41-sperotto-2007.pdf (last visited Sept. 5, 2007).

[86] Adam Roberts, *Implementation of the Laws of War in Late-Twentieth-Century Conflicts, in* The Law of Armed Conflict into the Next Millennium 359, 367 (Michael N. Schmitt & Leslie C. Green eds., 1998) [hereinafter Roberts].

[87] *See* Article 3 of the Hague Convention Respecting the Laws and Customs of War on Land, with Annex of Regulations, Oct. 18, 1907, 36 Stat. 2277; T.S. 539.

[88] Rudolf Dolzer, *The Settlement of War-Related Claims: Does International Law Recognize a Victim's Private Right of Action? Lessons After 1945*, 20 Berkeley J. Int'l L. 296, 299 (2002).

[89] Case Concerning the Factory at Chorzów, PCIJ, Series A, No. 17 (1928).

[90] Military and Paramilitary Activities in and against Nicaragua (Nicaragua v. U.S.A.), Merits, 1986 I.C.J. Reports (June 27), 14; Legality of the Threat or Use of Nuclear Weapons, Advisory Opinion, (July 8, 1996), I.C.J. Reports 1996.

court established upon the agreement of the Federal Democratic Republic of Ethiopia and the Government of the state of Eritrea in December 2000. The first partial award extensively dealt with IHL issues and notably with the treatment of POWs.[91]

The conventions pertaining to IHL also provide for specific implementation mechanisms that have, unfortunately, often been ignored or side-stepped.[92] For example, the Geneva Conventions provided for the institution of Protecting Powers to supervise and implement the rules of warfare.[93] Another international instrument that appeared in Article 90 AP I was the International Fact-Finding Commission that has, since its inception in the beginning of the 90s, never been engaged in settling accounts.[94] These mechanisms are however designed to facilitate communication between states.

Another classical example of enforcing IHL is the limited recourse to reprisals against a state perceived to be violating the law mentioned in AP I.[95] Yet, as Meron explains "[t]he very idea of reprisals, which impose collective responsibility on the many for violations by a few, is antithetical to the notion of individual responsibility so fundamental to human rights."[96]

From the foregoing it is evident, that, at no stage does the individual have any legal standing in IHL. The only possibility according to general international law, is with the intermediation of his state of nationality by a device called "diplomatic protection."[97] Indeed, in the past, "in the absence of an independent legal personality for the individual, if his rights were violated by a foreign State, it was the State of which the victim was a citizen which was authorised to bring a claim for violation of his rights."[98] An excellent illustration of this method of "individual complaint",

---

[91] See Kate Greenwood, *Arbitrating Responsibility for Violations of IHL: The Eritrea-Ethiopia Claims Commission*, Bofaxe 263E, Institute for International Law of Peace and Armed Conflict (Dec. 12, 2003).

[92] Martin Fanny, *Le droit international humanitaire devant les organes de contrôle des droits de l'homme*, 1 Droits Fondamentaux 121 (2001).

[93] Article 8 GC I, Article 8 GC II, Article 8 GC III, Article 9 GC IV, *supra* note 8. *See* also Article 5 Protocol Additional to the Geneva Conventions of 12 August 1949, and Relating to the Protections of Victims of International Armed Conflicts (Protocol I), opened for signature Dec. 12, 1977, U.N. Doc. A/32/144, Annex I, II, (1977), *reprinted in* 16 I.L.M. 1391 (1977) [hereinafter AP I].

[94] Kenneth Keith, *International Humanitarian Fact-Finding Commission: Its Potential*, 5 AJHR 101–108 (1999); Frits Kalshoven, *The International Humanitarian Fact-Finding Commission: A Sleeping Beauty*, 4 HuV-I 213–216 (2002).

[95] Roberts, *supra* note 88, at 370.

[96] Meron, *supra* note 12, at 250.

[97] *See* Annemarieke Vermeer-Künzli, *As If: The Legal fiction in Diplomatic Protection*, 18 Eur. J. Int'l L. 37–68 (2007).

[98] Javaid Rehman, International Human Rights Law. A Practical Approach 2 (2003). *See also* Cassidy, *supra* note 54, at 539.

albeit not related to IHL, is the *Mavromattis* case before the Permanent Court of International Justice in which the individual had requested his state, Greece, to intervene on his behalf against the United Kingdom.[99] Yet, "by taking up the case of one of its subjects and by resorting to diplomatic action or international judicial proceedings on his behalf, a State is in reality asserting its own rights – its rights to ensure, in the person of its subjects, respects for the rules of international law."[100]

In another context, outside the scope of state responsibility, victims of the crimes committed by a person found guilty by the ICTY or the ICTR of violations of the laws of war may be returned their property acquired by criminal conduct or apply to a competent body to obtain compensation on the national level, provided there is such an institution. While in the first case, i.e. restitution, victims cannot *proprio motu* start the proceedings,[101] in the case of compensation they do have the right to initiate the proceedings. Unfortunately, as of now, none of these mechanisms has ever been used. Yet, they all show that the individual needs to refer the matter to the state if he/she wants reparations for violations of IHL.

In the current state of law, this necessity for the individual to relate to his/her state of nationality seems outdated because more and more it is the individual himself whose house has been destroyed or demolished and his/her family who has been killed or injured. A simple glance at the last few international armed conflicts triggering the applicability of the full range of IHL norms, e.g. the American intervention in Iraq in March/April 2003 and the NATO intervention in Kosovo in 1999, demonstrates that the armed forces are increasingly involved in zero-casualty warfare.[102] In turn, the civilian population suffers from the effects of armed conflict.[103] Furthermore "the scale and frequency of serious infractions of existing rules have been greater than in earlier decades."[104] This human suffering is all the more incomprehensible as, so it seems, individuals are left without remedy except via their own state.

As a conclusion, individuals may have rights under international law but that does not automatically mean that they can enforce these rights on the international level. It should be pointed out that the enforcement mechanisms of IHL differ from those of HRL. Whereas IHL is mainly implemented by inter-state, i.e. traditional,

---

[99] Mavromattis Palestine Concession (Jurisdiction) Case, PCIJ Reports, Series A, No. 2 (1924), at 12.
[100] *Ibid.*
[101] Susanne Malmstöm, *Restitution of Property and Compensation to Victims, in* Essays on ICTY Procedure and Evidence in Honour of Gabrielle Kirk McDonald 373, 376 (Richard May et al. eds., 2001).
[102] A.P.V. Rogers, Zero-Casualty Warfare, 837 Int'l Rev. Red Cross 165–181 (2000).
[103] Human Rights Watch, Civilian Deaths in the NATO Air Campaign, Feb. 2000, Vol. 2 No. 1 (D) and Amnesty International, 'Collateral Damage' or Unlawful Killings?, EUR 70/18/00, June 8, 2000.
[104] Roberts, *supra* note 88, at 360.

means and has only recently integrated the individual in its enforcement mechanism, HRL has, from the inception, offered individuals a significant place in the implementation system. From the foregoing it is clear that HRL grants individuals more rights than IHL does. This is linked to the different origins of the two legal regimes: IHL is meant to regulate the behaviour of states in armed conflict while HRL aims at protecting individuals from the state.

3. *Individuals as Duty-holders*

There is no doubt that in both HRL and IHL, the duty-bearers are the states. In HRL, individuals are not bound by the provisions of human rights treaties; *prima facie* only states are. Yet, a closer analysis reveals that individuals also have duties under HRL. In contrast, it is evident from IHL provisions that individuals have duties.[105] The best illustration is the prosecution of war criminals before *ad hoc* international courts such as the International Military Tribunals for Nuremberg[106] and for Tokyo[107] and the more recent International Criminal Tribunal for Yugoslavia[108] and for Rwanda.[109] Moreover, individuals have been or will be hauled before hybrid courts, mixing national and international elements, such as the Special Tribunal for Sierra Leone[110] or the courts in East Timor,[111] Bosnia Herzegovina,[112] Kosovo,[113] and Cambodia.[114]

---

[105] Edoardo Greppi, *The Evolution of Individual Criminal Responsibility under International Law*, 835 Int'l Rev. Red Cross 531–553 (1999).

[106] Charter of the International Military Tribunal, in Agreement for the Prosecution and Punishment of the Major War Criminals of the European Axis (London Agreement), 58 Stat. 1544, E.A.S. No. 472, 82 U.N.T.S. 280, Aug. 8, 1945.

[107] International Military Tribunal for the Far East arts. 1, 6, 1589 T.I.A.S. 20, Jan. 19, 1956.

[108] ICTY Statute, *supra* note 9.

[109] ICTR Statute, *supra* note 10.

[110] Agreement between the United Nations and the Government of Sierra Leone on the Establishment of a Special Court for Sierra Leone, 2178 U.N.T.S. 38342, Jan. 16, 2002 [hereinafter Statute of the Special Court for Sierra Leone].

[111] UNTAET, Regulation No. 2000/15, On the Establishment of Panels with Exclusive Jurisdiction over Serious Criminal Offences, UN Doc. UNTAET/REG/2000/15 (June 6, 2000).

[112] Section 1 for War Crimes, The Court of Bosnia Herzegovina. For general information on the Chambers, *available at* www.sudbih.gov.ba/?jezik=e (last visited May 4, 2007).

[113] U.N. Interim Administration Mission in Kosovo, Appointment and Removal from Office of International Judges and International Prosecutors, U.N. Doc. UNMIK/REG/2000/6 (Jan. 12, 2001).

[114] Agreement between The United Nations and The Royal Government of Cambodia Concerning The Prosecution Under Cambodian Law Of Crimes Committed During The Period Of Democratic Kampuchea, (June 6, 2003), *available at* www.eccc.gov.kh/ (last visited May 4, 2007) [hereinafter Statute of the ECCC].

3.1. International Human Rights Law

It is a fact that obligations are generally not imposed upon individuals under HRL instruments; the obligation to comply with treaty provisions is upon the states that ratify such treaties. However, states can agree that individuals have duties under HRL. Yet, even in this case, only states can be brought before international courts, for, obligations enshrined in HRL treaties are by and large understood in terms of state responsibility. Duties imposed on individuals can be divided into two categories: duties imposed either directly via a clear provision or indirectly as the result of the application of certain provisions. Furthermore, certain human rights violations have been criminalised via a new legal field, international criminal law. As Buergenthal explains "[i]f individuals are deemed to have ever greater rights under the international law of human rights, it makes sense to impose corresponding duties on them not to violate those rights and, if appropriate, to hold them internationally responsible for their violation."[115]

3.1.1. Direct Duties

The UDHR states that "[e]veryone has the duties to the community in which alone the free and full development of his personality is possible."[116] Although it does not clearly enforce specific duties upon the individual, this provision reminds the individual that he/she has certain obligations which are encapsulated in an international legal document.

The ACHPR is oftentimes cited as the only international human rights treaty that imposes direct duties upon individuals (see Part I Chapter II).[117] As Robertson explains

> [T]he States concerned wished to put forward a distinctive conception of human rights in which civil and political rights were seen to be counter-balanced by duties of social solidarity, just as they are complemented by economic and social rights and supplemented by peoples' rights.[118]

These duties are specifically outlined due to the discrepancy concerning the conception of an individual under the ACHPR and the conception of human rights under other international instruments. Indeed, in Africa the conception of the individual is one of a person integrated in society and not of an abstract

---

[115] Buergenthal, *supra* note 23, at 719.
[116] Article 29 UDHR, *supra* note 7.
[117] One must however underline that Article 32 IACHR also refers to the relationship between duties and rights. IACHR, *supra* note 30.
[118] Arthur H. Robertson & John G. Merrills, Human Rights in the World: An Introduction to the Study of the International Protection of Human Rights 216 (1989); Claude E. Welch Jr., *The African Commission on Human and Peoples' Rights: A Five-Year Report and Assessment*, 14 Hum. Rts Q. 43–61 (1992).

and isolated entity.[119] "Duties are at once the consequence of one's membership of society and the pre-requisite to one's possessing membership of the society."[120] In contrast, under the Western view, human rights may be invoked when an individual is in conflict with a group. Therefore, it is possible to state that under the African perception, the individual must comply with his/her duties under the Charter to ensure the development of its society and integration in harmony.[121] All these duties vary according to the age, sex, and position/role of the individual in the society which means that there is no set of defined rules.[122] This, of course, is a cause of concern when these duties are transformed from moral into legal duties which require clarity in definition and scope. Moreover, according to the African approach, such duties are owed to individuals depending on the recipients' needs rather than on a set of pre-defined rules.

These duties towards a group comprise, for instance, the duty of children towards their parents to maintain them in case of need; the duty to preserve the harmonious development and cohesion of the family (Article 29(1)); the duty to promote, safeguard, and reinforce mutual respect and tolerance (Article 28); the duty to serve the national community by placing one's physical and intellectual abilities at its service (Article 29(2)) or by paying taxes imposed by law in the interest of society (Article 29(6)); the duty to preserve and strengthen positive African cultural values (Article 29(7)); and the duty to contribute to the promotion and achievement of African unity (Article 29(8)).

It is often strenuous to identify the recipient of a particular duty. Some duties are owed to specific individuals, others to larger units such as the family, the society or the state and can accordingly be grouped. For instance, individuals are said to have duties to their "family;" however, it is difficult to ascertain what the specific term "family" entails in this context[123] or what the specific implications are of

---

[119] According to Benedek, "[t]he human rights approach to be found in traditional African societies is characterized by a permanent dialectical relationship between the individual and the group, which fits neither into the individualistic nor the collectivistic concept of human rights." Wolfgang Benedek, People's Rights and Individuals' Duties as Special Features of the African Charter on Human and Peoples' Rights, *in* Regional Protection of Human Rights by International Law: Emerging African System 59, 63 (Philip Kunig et al. eds., 1985). *See also* Mkau Wa Mutua, *The Banjul Charter and the African Cultural Fingerprint: An Evaluation of the Language of Duties*, 35 Va. J. Int'l L. 339 (1995).

[120] Annemarie Devereux, *Should 'Duties' Play a Larger Role in Human Rights? A Critique of Western Liberal and African Human Rights Jurisprudence*, 18 U.N.S.W.L.J. 464, 474 (1995).

[121] B. Obinna Okere, *The Protection of Human Rights in Africa and the African Charter on Human and Peoples' Rights: A Comparative Analysis with the European and American Systems*, 6 Hum. Rts Q. 141–159 (1984).

[122] Devereux, *supra* note 120, at 475.

[123] Ouguergouz argues that it should be understood to refer to extended families. Fatsah Ouguergouz, The African Charter on Human and Peoples' Rights: A Comprehensive Agenda for Human Dignity and Sustainable Democracy in Africa (2003).

having such a duty.[124] Addis notes that these difficulties arise with regard to the great majority of the duties under the Charter, e.g. the duty to "contribute...to the promotion and achievement of African Unity" (Article 29(8)) or the duty to "serve his national community by placing his physical and intellectual abilities at its service" (Article 29(2)). The view can be taken that these duties may be simply aspirational and not enforceable. However, if that is the case, the existence of legal duties or rights which are deemed to be unenforceable under the law will undermine the legal status of the entire document by leading people to view them as declaratory and hortatory rather than as binding and enforceable.

Another issue noted by Addis[125] is the possible contradiction between the enforcement of certain duties and specific rights under the Charter. For instance, the duty under Article 29(5): "to preserve and strengthen the national independence and the territorial integrity of his country...," may be invoked by regimes in order to silence dissent on especially divisive national issues or on matters involving the treatment of ethnic minorities. However, Mutua refutes the idea that there is a clash between these duties and rights; rather, he understands this combination as the possibility for individuals to adhere to live in harmony with the community.[126]

In this framework it is argued that "rights do not simply grow out of duties and that some duties do not have corresponding rights."[127] This, in a Western oriented human rights document, inevitably leads to both theoretical and practical problems since it is assumed that for an individual to be able to claim a right, another entity must have a corresponding duty so that this right can be enforced. Furthermore, if the duty-holders as well as the right-holders can be better identified, then the state is also in a better position to enforce the obligations or, at least, mediate such obligations.[128] In other words, it assists the state in understanding how it can fulfil its obligations according to HRL.

On the face of it, it seems that duties are expressed in terms which are incapable of enforcement because "'duties' are either considered too wide or too lacking in foundation or empowerment for effective enforcement."[129] In particular, it is argued that because they are perceived as a matter of morality and personal sacrifices,

---

[124] Adeno Addis, *Review of The African Charter on Human and Peoples' Rights: A Comprehensive Agenda for Human Dignity and Sustainable Democracy in Africa by Fatsah Ouguergouz*, 98 Am. J. Int'l L. 879–883 (2004).

[125] *Id.*

[126] *See* M. Mutua, *The African Human Rights System: A Critical Evaluation*, 2000, *available at* hdr.undp.org/docs/publications/background_papers/MUTUA.PDF (last visited Oct. 25, 2007) [hereinafter Mutua].

[127] Devereux, *supra* note 120, at 469.

[128] *Id.* at 479.

[129] *Id.* at 466.

rather than law, they are less enforceable.[130] First, one must pinpoint the person to whom the duty is owed, second one must ensure that there is a correlated right since "where there is a direct correlation between right and duty, prospects for the enforcement of both may be enhanced."[131] As seen earlier, there is no direct correlation between duties and rights and, hence, conflicts cannot be solved in the classical legal manner known to HRL. Consequently Mutua recommends that the language of duties should be more focussed on the precise meaning, content, conditions of compliance and application of such duties. He also expresses a need for some clarification of the status of duties in the Charter, the definition of their moral and legal dimensions and their implications of enforcement.[132]

As Devereux stresses " '[d]uties' are regarded as part of the 'law' of the community and are enforced in a similar manner as other laws-primarily through custom and religion."[133] The state-enforced system of human rights is ill-conceived to sanction individual breaches of duty to another. This is notably due to the fact that it is difficult for the state to establish that a particular individual is not fulfilling his/her duties to the best of his/her abilities and competence.[134] To enforce these general duties, it seems that the state can only educate and train individuals so as to ensure that they are aware of their duties. Indeed, if these duties are not a mere aspiration, the state is under a duty to inculcate the principles and ideals of the Charter and to elucidate the community in relation to their own obligations and duties.[135]

Overall, it is clear that individuals have duties according to HRL; yet, it appears that there are several impediments, notably owing to the theoretical foundation of the concept of "duties," that prevent their enforcement both on the national and international level.

3.1.2. *Indirect Duties*

Other duties may be classified as indirect inasmuch as they concern certain limitations to the general rights granted to individuals under human rights instruments.[136]

---

[130] *See* the discussion in *id*. at 471.
[131] Guy Powles, *Duties of Individuals: Some Implications for the Pacific of Including 'Duties' in 'Human Rights' Documents*, 22 Victoria U. Wellington L. Rev. 49, 53 (1992).
[132] Mutua, *supra* note 126.
[133] Devereux, *supra* note 120, at 476.
[134] Ziyad Motala, *Human Rights in Africa: A Cultural, Ideological and Legal Examination*, 12 Hastings Int'l & Comp. L. Rev 373, 403 (1989).
[135] *See* Article 25 ACHPR: "States parties to the present Charter shall have the duty to promote and ensure through teaching, education and publication, the respect of the rights and freedoms contained in the present Charter and to see to it that these freedoms and rights as well as corresponding obligations and duties are understood." ACHPR, *supra* note 33. *See* Umozurike Oji Umozurike, *The African Charter on Human and Peoples' Rights*, 77 Am. J. Int'l L. 902, 907 (1983).
[136] Wa Mutua, *supra* note 119, at 368–369.

These limitations are enforced in order to prevent the abuse of rights in the general interest of society.[137] In other words, limitations in the exercise of rights and freedoms become duties every person owes to any other person because "someone's right to do something correlates with the duty of another not to interfere."[138]

For example, the UDHR generally imposes a restriction on the exercise of rights for the non-interference with the rights of others, the rules of morality, and general welfare in a democratic society under Article 29(2). Following the trail, the IACHR explains that "[t]he rights and freedoms of each individual shall be exercised with due regard to the rights of others, collective security, morality and common interest."[139] As a result, "[i]ndividuals are asked to reflect on how the exercise of their rights in certain circumstances might adversely affect other individuals or the community. The duty is based on the presumption that the full development of the individual is only possible where individuals care about how their actions would impact on others."[140]

A classical illustration of limitations of the enjoyment of certain rights is contained in the right of freedom of expression.[141] This freedom is embedded in all human rights charters[142] and is well recognised on the national level for countless reasons: it promotes the self fulfilment of the individual regarding its spiritual and mental development spiritually and mentally;[143] it constitutes an instrument for the quest for truth, the advancement of theories and problems solutions;[144] and it develops political debate and therefore can be linked to the very essence of democracy.[145]

---

[137] William Abresch, *A Human Rights Law of Internal Armed Conflict: The European Court of Human Rights in Chechnya*, 16 Eur. J. Int'l L. 741, 766 (2005).

[138] Devereux, *supra* note 120, at 470. In particular, someone's right is only exercisable to the extent that it does not impinge upon the right of another person and any court will have to determine which right should be given priority in the given context. Smith, *supra* note 20, at 165–166.

[139] Article 27(2) IACHR, *supra* note 30.

[140] Wa Mutua, *supra* note 119, at 369.

[141] "Limitations attached to rights represent the qualifications which must often attend the exercise by A of a right in the face of B's competing rights. Thus, A's rights to freedom of expression may be limited by the need to protect B from the invasion of his privacy and defamation." Françoise Hampson, *Human Rights and Humanitarian Law in Internal Conflicts*, in Armed Conflict And The New Law: Aspects of the 1977 Geneva Protocols and the 1981 Weapons Convention 55, 56 (Michael Meyer ed., 1989).

[142] *See* e.g. Article 19 UDHR, *supra* note 7; Article 19 ICCPR, *supra* note 35; Article 10 ECHR, *supra* note 29; Article 9(2) ACHPR, *supra* note 33.

[143] R v. Home Secretary ex parte Simms [2000] 2 AC 115 [hereinafter Simms].

[144] Abrams v. United States, [1969] 395 U.S. 444.

[145] Simms, *supra* note 143; *See* also statement by Lord Bridge in Hector v. Attorney General of Antigua and Barbuda [1990] 2 AC 312: "Any attempt to stifle or fetter…criticism [of those who hold an office in the government] amounts to political censorship of the most insidious and objectionable kind."

Indeed, although freedom of speech, in its various expressions, i.e. political, commercial, obscene and violent, is a very important right in a democratic society, it is however restricted.[146] The European Court of Human Rights proffers that different types of speech enjoy different kinds of protection under Article 10 ECHR. In the landmark ruling of *Handyside* v. *UK*, the Court determined that freedom of expression

> is applicable not only to 'information' or 'ideas' that are favourably received or regarded as inoffensive or as a matter of indifference, but also to those that offend, shock or disturb the State or any sector of the population. Such are the demands of that pluralism, tolerance and broadmindedness without which there is no 'democratic society.'[147]

The Court noticeably applies a categorical approach to free speech. In the case of *Sunday Times* v. *UK*, the Court added that "exceptions [to freedom of speech] must be narrowly interpreted and the necessity for any restrictions must be convincingly established."[148] Hence, racism was consistently held to be beyond the final limit of protected expression[149] because it squarely falls within the ambit of the prohibition of manifestly unfounded activities as outlined in Article 17 ECHR.[150] Consequently, it is possible to view Article 17 ECHR as an in-built safety mechanism, designed to prevent provisions of the Convention from being invoked in favour of activities contrary to its text or spirit,[151] i.e. allowing for certain acts to impinge on the rights granted to individuals by the Convention.

---

[146] Canada takes a rather generous approach in the interpretation of free-speech as it accepts any type of speech apart from incitement to violence. The American approach categorizes speech according to the weight it has in society.

[147] Handyside v. United Kingdom, ECHR, Application No. 5493/72 (Dec. 7, 1976), para. 49.

[148] Sunday Times v. The United Kingdom (No. 2), Application No. 6538/74, (April 26, 1979), para. 50.

[149] *See* Glimmerveen and Hagenbeek v. The Netherlands, ECHR, Applications Nos. 8348/78 and 8406/78, (Oct. 11, 1979).

[150] Article 17 reads "Nothing in this Convention may be interpreted as implying for any State, group or person any right to engage in any activity or perform any act aimed at the destruction on any of the rights and freedoms set forth herein or at their limitation to a greater extent than is provided for in the Convention." ECHR, *supra* note 29.

[151] For instance, cases concerning e.g. the Holocaust denial (Garaudy v. France, ECHR, Application No. 65831/01, (June 24, 2003)), the exhibition of obscene material (Müller and others v. Switzerland, ECHR, Application No. 10737/84 (May 24, 1988)), defamation in relation to war crimes convictions (Lingens v. Austria, ECHR, Application No. 9815/82 (July 8, 1986)), the incitement of hatred (Özgür Gündem v. Turkey, ECHR, Application No. 23144/93 (March 16, 2000) or of violence (Gerger v. Turkey, ECHR, Application No. 24919/94, (July 8, 1999)) have been declared inadmissible under Article 17 ECHR. *See also* Tarlach Mc Gonagle, *Freedom of Expression and Limits on Racist Speech: A Difficult Symbiosis*, 13 Interights Bulletin 135 (2001) [hereinafter Mc Gonagle].

The Human Rights Committee also applies a strict test of justification, yet, only when "provided by the law and necessary (a) For respect of the rights or reputations of others; (b) For the protection of national security or of public order (ordre public), or of public health or morals."[152]

The narrow nature of these tests generally proves that HRL instruments have become tremendously important vehicles for promoting freedom of expression.[153] From the above discussion it can be concluded that HRL treaties grant rights to individuals under certain restrictions, imposing on the individual a duty to obey these restrictions in a way not to interfere with the rights conceded to other individuals.

3.1.3. *International Criminal Law*

The concept of individual liability, which emerged after WW II but only grew in importance with the establishment of the International Criminal Tribunals, permits the imposition of duties upon individuals. It is particularly interesting to apply it to cases where mass violations of human rights have been committed because it allows for the "punishment" of the state via its representatives. As Smith notes "[t]he trial and judgments of the International Military Tribunal at Nuremberg of major war criminals added further fuel to the embryonic international human rights movement."[154]

Under the principle of individual liability individuals are held responsible for human rights violations. Indeed the "international community [has been forced] to explore ways not only to hold the state responsible, but also to act directly against individuals whom the state is too weak or unwilling to punish."[155] For many years, mass violations of human rights were left unpunished. The state could plan and instigate mass murders within its borders without suffering any legal repercussions. As a result the state and its ruling elite would be free to violate HRL. National laws would often provide for general amnesties for all those involved in these crimes and international law did not have the tools to deal with violations of such a nature.[156]

---

[152] *See* Article 19 ICCPR, *supra* note 35.
[153] Clearly not all complaints regarding freedom of expression have been upheld, especially when Article 19 is considered in conjunction with Article 20, which prohibits "any propaganda for war," and "any advocacy of national, racial or religious hatred that constitutes incitement to discrimination, hostility or violence." *See* Faurisson v. France Decision, Communication No. 550/1993 (Nov. 8, 1996). In contrast, in the case of W.G. Party v. Canada the HRC explained that the dissemination of anti-semitic messages by telephonic means "clearly constitute[s] the advocacy of racial or religious hatred" under Article 20(2). W.G. Party v. Canada Communication No. 104/1981 (April 6, 1983). For an analysis, *see* Mc Gonagle, *supra* note 151.
[154] Smith, *supra* note 20, at 25.
[155] Buergenthal, *supra* note 23, at 718.
[156] *See* for example the incapacity of human rights courts to deal with gross violations of human rights. Aisling Reidy, Françoise Hampson & Kevin Boyle, *Gross Violations of Human Rights: Invoking the*

This needed to be changed. As the Nuremberg Tribunal explained "Crimes against international law are committed by men, not by abstract entities."[157] "[G]uilty individuals could no longer hide behind the abstract structure of the state."[158] As a result, leaders, who formulate governmental policies and direct their actions into channels which are criminal under international law, are personally and individually responsible for such crimes.[159]

Hence, certain violations of HRL have been criminalised on the international plane.[160] For example, whereas under classical HRL, mass killings are called "gross violations of human rights," under international criminal law, they are called crimes against humanity. Yet, they describe the same types of crimes.

It is worth considering that crimes against humanity originated in the preamble of the 1907 Hague Convention, which codified the customary law of armed conflict based on existing state practices deriving from such values and ideals perceived as to constitute the "laws of humanity." The Nuremberg Charter firmly established crimes against humanity in positive international law, adding that they could be committed "during or before the war." This requirement established a connection of crimes against humanity and war crimes or a crime against peace.

Decades later discussions as to whether crimes against humanity can only happen in the context of an armed conflict are still taking place. The ICTY Statute links crimes against humanity to an armed conflict.[161] As a result, although constrained by the language of the ICTY Statute, the ICTY Appeals Chamber correctly observed that the requirement of a nexus to armed conflict was peculiar to the Nuremberg Charter and had not been followed in subsequent instruments.[162] Hence, it was largely argued that the ICTY Statute did not reflect contemporary international law regarding that particular provision.[163] In contrast, other statutes, e.g. the Statute for the Special Court for Sierra Leone, the ICTR Statute and the Rome Statute, contain no references to a nexus to armed conflict. They affirm that crimes against

---

European Convention on Human Rights in the Case of Turkey, 15 NQHR 173 (1997). *See* more generally Robert Cryer, Håkan Friman, Darryl Robinson, Elizabeth Wilmshurst, An Introduction to International Criminal Law and Procedure 9 (2007) [hereinafter Cryer et al.].

[157] Trial of the Major War Criminals before the International Military Tribunal Proceedings, vol. I Nuremberg, 1947, at 234.

[158] Cassidy, *supra* note 54, at 552.

[159] Principles of International Law Recognized in the Charter of the Nuremberg Tribunal and in the Judgment of the Tribunal, U.N. Doc. A/CN.4/SER.A/1950/Add.1 (1950).

[160] In fact "crimes against humanity evolved to protect persons from gross human rights abuses including those committed by their own government." Cryer et al., *supra* note 156, at 1.

[161] Article 5 ICTY Statute, *supra* note 9.

[162] Tadic 1995, *supra* note 77, paras 140–141. *See* Darryl Robinson, *Defining "Crimes Against Humanity" at the Rome Conference*, 93 Am. J. Int'l L. 43–57 (1999) [hereinafter Robinson].

[163] *See* Phyllis Hwang, *Defining Crimes Against Humanity in the Rome Statute of the International Criminal Court*, 22 Fordham Int'l L.J. 485 (1998).

humanity can occur not only during armed conflict but also during peacetime or civil strife. This result was essential to the practical effectiveness of the ICC in responding to large scale atrocities committed by governments against their own communities.[164] The great majority of delegations present at the Rome negotiations argued in favour of the disconnection between crimes against humanity and war crimes. In their opinion the inclusion of the armed conflict nexus would be contrary to the post-Nuremberg developments, as observed in statements of the International Law Commission (ILC)[165] and in instruments addressing specific crimes against humanity, such as the Genocide Convention and the Apartheid Convention.[166]

Consequently, it can be seen that, as time goes by, individuals are now subject to prosecution for the most egregious violations of human rights and that international tribunals and courts are closing the gap between IHL and HRL.

3.2. *International Humanitarian Law*

In contrast to HRL, IHL instruments contain scores of duties, some of which are incorporated in treaty law whereas others are established in customary international law.

3.2.1. *Duties according to Treaty Law*

IHL imposes many duties upon individuals under treaty law. It is often said that the GCs have been the first conventional instrument to introduce the notion of individual criminal responsibility. This must however be refuted, for the Charters of the Nuremberg and Tokyo Tribunals, both international treaties, "defined a series of criminal offences for which individuals could be held accountable."[167]

The Geneva Conventions require states to incorporate penal provisions with regards to the "grave breaches" (articles 49 GC I, 50 GC II, 129 GC III, and 146 GC IV) in their domestic legislation. A similar provision is encapsulated in Article 85 AP I. Because grave breaches are considered as the most flagrant violations of

---

[164] See Robinson, *supra* note 162.
[165] ILC commented with respect to its 1996 draft Code of Crimes that "[t]he definition of crimes against humanity in the present article does not include the requirement that an act was committed in times of war.... The autonomy of crimes against humanity was recognized in [the instruments subsequent to the Nuremberg Charter] which did not include this requirement." Report of the International Law Commission on the work of its forty-eighth session, *Official Records of the General Assembly, Fifty-first Session, Supplement No. 10* (A/51/10 and corrigendum), Chap. II., Article 18, Commentary, para. 6. See Robinson, *supra* note 162.
[166] Robinson, *ibid.*
[167] Hortensia D.T. Gutierrez Posse, *The Relationship between International and Humanitarian Law and the International Criminal Tribunals*, 88 Int'l Rev. Red Cross 65, 66 (2006) [hereinafter Gutierrez Posse].

IHL, states are required to criminalise such acts.[168] In addition, the state is obliged to stop other violations of the Conventions[169] or take necessary measures to ensure their suppression[170] but is not required to criminalise such acts.

The so-called grave-breaches system, often confused with war crimes,[171] is implemented together with the principle of *aut dedere aut judicare* (duty to extradite or prosecute in international law) which applies no matter where the grave breach was committed.[172] Indeed state parties are required to search for persons alleged to have committed such breaches or who have ordered them to be committed, and to bring them before their courts. If a state does not wish to prosecute the alleged offender, then the Conventions give the state the option and obligation to extradite the individual to a state that is willing to prosecute the alleged criminal. This suggests that the international community regards such crimes as deserving special attention. This consensus indirectly imposes on states signatories to the Conventions a duty to enact the legislation necessary to provide effective domestic jurisdiction.[173]

However, this principle has been often criticised. In fact, for the correct application of the present doctrine, three problems must be addressed:

> first, the status and scope of application of this principle under international law; second, the hierarchy among the options embodied in this rule, provided that the requested State has a choice; third, practical difficulties in exercising *judicare*.[174]

It is also necessary to consider whether there are competing interests or obligations to extradite or if this is just a matter of discretion of the states concerned.

---

[168] For a more detailed explanation as to how national criminal legislation adopted to sanction violations of IHL should be drafted, *see* Maria T. Dutli, *National Implementation Measures of International Humanitarian Law: Some Practical Aspects*, 1 YB Int'l Humanitarian L. 245, 249 (1998) [hereinafter Dutli].

[169] De Vezac, *supra* note 75, at 6.

[170] Knut Dörmann, *Individual and State Responsibility in the Field of International Humanitarian Law*, 18 RSQ 78, 79 (1999) [hereinafter Dörmann].

[171] "The notion of war crimes is broader than that of grave breaches because it covers, in addition to the acts [listed in the Geneva Conventions and Additional Protocol I], other serious violations of the rules of international humanitarian law, either customary or treaty-based, regardless of whether such violations are committed in situations of international or of non-international armed conflict." Dutli, *supra* note 168, at 249.

[172] Article 49 GC I, *supra* note 8; Article 50 GC II, *supra* note 8 ; Article 129 GC III, *supra* note 8; Article 146 GC IV, *supra* note 8.

[173] *See* Colleen Enache-Brown & Ari Fried, *Universal Crime, Jurisdiction and Duty: The Obligation of Aut Dedere Aut Judicare in International Law*, 43 McGill Law Journal / Revue De Droit De McGill 613 (1998) [hereinafter Enache-Brown & Fried].

[174] Michael Plachta, *Aut Dedere Aut Judicare: An Overview of Modes of Implementation and Approaches*, 6 Maastricht J. 332 (1999).

States are requested to prosecute *all* individuals, not only their own nationals, suspected of having perpetrated grave breaches. Not only are states reluctant to take firm action against their own nationals;[175] they often do not have the necessary legislation to prosecute war criminals. As a result, it is contended that the GCs provide a basis for universal jurisdiction regarding grave breaches notably in the grave breaches provision itself but also in Common Article 1 that requests states to "respect and ensure respect." With time, this provision has been widely regarded as implying a universal obligation of states to seek implementation of the Conventions.[176] Yet, in practice, most states are not properly equipped to tackle such issues. Further, the few attempts made by states, such as Belgium, led to serious diplomatic incidents with the state whose nationals had been suspected of having committed a grave breach and, finally to the withdrawal of the law.[177] Nevertheless, generally, it is argued that the proper implementation of the Geneva Conventions decreases the possibility of impunity to a minimum level especially if the principle of universal jurisdiction is adequately used. For, if all signatories to the Conventions are *bona fide* implicated in the prosecution or extradition of a perpetrator of a specific international crime, there is little room for war criminals to escape prosecution.[178]

Although it appears that a series of duties is being imposed upon individuals, one must remember that these duties stem from treaties that bind states. In other words, it is ultimately the state that bears responsibility on the international level, should it fail to implement the provisions of the Geneva Conventions and Additional Protocol pertaining to grave breaches. Consequently, owing to the very nature of international treaties, duties are imposed upon individuals via the state and these duties can only be enforced by the state (according to municipal law) and via the state (in pursuance of the principle of state responsibility). The two classical methods of enforcement, municipal law and state responsibility, are again the predominant means to bind individuals to international law.

---

[175] Dörmann, *supra* note 170, at 79.
[176] *Id.* at 81. For a different view *see* Birgit Kessler, *Die Durchsetzung der Genfer Abkommen von 1949 in nicht- internationalen bewaffneten Konflikten auf Grundlage ihres gemeinsamen Art. 1* 65–66 (2001).
[177] Markus Rau, *Das Ende der Weltrechtspflege? Zur Abschaffung des belgischen Gesetzes über die universelle Verfolgung völkerrechtlicher Verbrechen*, 4 HuV-I 212–216 (2003).
[178] "[E]ach [party] shall be under the obligation to search for persons alleged to have committed or to have ordered to be committed...grave breaches and shall bring such persons, regardless of their nationality, before its own courts." Article 49 GC I, *supra* note 8; Article 50 GC II, *supra* note 8; Article 129 GC III, *supra* note 8; Article 146 GC IV, *supra* note 8. *See also* Enache-Brown & Fried, *supra* note 173.

Even the various documents relating to international criminal law, that have influenced and been influenced by norms in the field of IHL, are based on state consent. The Statutes of the IMT,[179] the IMTFE,[180] and the ICC[181] contain lists of acts that can be prosecuted, i.e. duties imposed upon the individuals directly by an international treaty. The only exceptions to the rule are the tribunals that were established via a Chapter VII U.N. Security Council Resolution.

3.2.2. *Duties according to Customary International Law*

Similarly to the grave breaches system under treaty law, it is argued that customary international law provides for some duties to individuals.

Already in 1872 Gustave Moynier, one of the co-founders of the ICRC, published the first known draft statute for an international criminal court.[182] Almost 40 years later the first concrete proposal to set up an international tribunal to adjudicate violations of the laws and customs of war committed by Germans during WW I was adopted. Unfortunately, the anticipated High Tribunal never came into being as Germany promised to undertake national trials. However, proceedings were only initiated against twelve defendants although Germany had been handed a list of 896 defendants.[183] Due to the failure of the Leipzig trials, the Allied Powers agreed in the Moscow Declaration, which was issued even before the end of WW II, that the prosecution of alleged war criminals should not be left in the hands of the state, but handed over to international tribunals,[184] the International Military Tribunals at Nuremberg and for the Far East in Tokyo. Although heavily criticised, these tribunals clearly established the principle of individual liability that sustains the entire edifice of international criminal law. Duties were imposed upon individuals and international tribunals directly enforced these duties. Despite this progress, reliance on national laws to prosecute war criminals never ceased. Unfortunately, the post WW II period showed how inadequate the exclusive reliance on national enforcement of international criminal law was[185] and that, once again in the history of public international law, international tribunals to judge acts committed

---

[179] IMT Statute, London Agreement (Aug. 8, 1945).
[180] IMTFE Statute, Special Proclamation, Establishment of an International Military Tribunal for the Far East (Jan. 19, 1946), TIAS No. 1589, at 3.
[181] *See* Article 8 Rome Statute, *supra* note 11.
[182] Christopher K. Hall, *The First Proposal for an International Criminal Court*, 322 Int'l Rev. Red Cross 57 (1998).
[183] Timothy McCormack, *The Importance of Effective Multilateral Enforcement of International Humanitarian Law, in* Making the Voice of Humanity Heard: Essays on Humanitarian Assistance and International Humanitarian law in Honour of HRH Princess Margriet of the Netherlands 319, 324 (Liesbeth Lijnzaad, Johanna van Sambeek & Bahia Tahzid-Lie eds., 2004).
[184] *Id.* at 327.
[185] *Id.* at 329.

by individuals were necessary. Thanks to the establishment of the ICTY and the ICTR and later of the International Criminal Court individual liability was then anchored in international law. Hence, it is now clear that according to customary international law individuals have duties under international law relating to armed conflicts.

Bearing in mind the wide range of international statutes defining international crimes, it can be observed that each statute contains a list of war crimes, i.e. crimes that can only be committed in the situation of an armed conflict. The only exception to the rule is the ICTY Statute, according to which there are two categories of crimes that must be linked to armed conflict in order to fall within the jurisdiction of the Court: war crimes and crimes against humanity. Under other Statutes, because of the disconnection between an armed conflict and crimes against humanity, the only crimes that can be perpetrated in times of armed conflict are war crimes.

Generally, war crimes are those violations of the laws of war committed during an international armed conflict and that incur individual criminal responsibility. The Rome Statute[186] takes this traditional approach towards war crimes, albeit it also includes the latest developments in the field.[187] Indeed, the crimes listed under the ICC can be divided into four categories:

- The grave breaches of the Geneva Conventions;
- The "other serious violations of the laws and customs applicable in international armed conflict, within the established framework of international law;"
- The serious violations of Common Article 3 of the Geneva Conventions;
- The "serious violations of the laws and customs applicable in armed conflicts not of an international character."

In pursuance of the latest international law developments, the armed conflict nexus has been broadened to enclose non-international armed conflict, thereby widening the scope of application of the prohibition of such crimes. Indeed, while it was initially only possible to attach individual liability to crimes perpetrated in international armed conflicts, it is now possible to prosecute individuals for crimes committed in times of non-international armed conflict. For example, violations of the laws and customs of war, listed notably under Common Article 3 to the GCs which regulates conduct in non-international armed conflict, may now be prosecuted directly before international tribunals without the interposition of national law.[188] At the time of the drafting of the Conventions, its introduction achieved a compromise acceptable to states which favored the restrictive application of IHL to

---

[186] *See* Article 8 Rome Statute, *supra* note 11.
[187] *See* Hans-Heinricht Jescheck, *War Crimes*, in Encyclopaedia of Public International Law 294 (Rudolf Bernhardt ed., 1981).
[188] Meron, *supra* note 12, at 253.

non-international armed conflict. While all states agreed that Common Article 3 only repeated well established rules of warfare and minimum standards to be complied with in any type of conflict, the article does not provide for any enforcement mechanism. Consequently, states are now compelled to adopt national laws penalising violations of Common Article 3.

There have been, however, recent efforts made to expand the scope of Common Article 3 offering more protection to the victims of non-international armed conflicts by setting standards in military manuals, offering training to armed forces in humanitarian laws, enacting national legislation and fixing accountability on individuals who are responsible for violating such provision. As noted by Gandhi, these developments blurred not only the traditional distinction between international and non-international armed conflicts, but also resulted in the blurring of the conceptual boundaries between non-international armed conflicts, war crimes, "crimes against humanity" and "obligation *erga omnes*."[189]

During the discussions approving the ICTY Statute, several states firmly maintained that the obligations contained in Common Article 3 as well as AP II could be imposed on individuals.[190] As a result, the Security Council endowed the Tribunal with jurisdiction over both international and non-international armed conflicts,[191] specifically mentioning that it could prosecute individuals violating the laws or customs of war. Yet, it "did not explicitly provide for, not did it exclude, the criminalization of serious violations of the laws or customs of war if they were committed within the context of an internal armed conflict."[192] The *Tadic* case[193] constitutes the first judicial affirmation that certain violations of Common Article 3 entail individual criminal responsibility by virtue of customary international law. The Court thereby settled a number of questions regarding the possible prosecution of certain violations of Common Article 3. It explained that for a breach of the said provision to constitute a war crime it must be demonstrated that the prohibition in question constituted a crime under customary international law at the time of its commission and that the violation must be of a serious nature.[194] Only such a breach entails individual criminal responsibility under the Statute of the ICTY. In contrast, the Statute of the ICTR recognised that war crimes could be committed

---

[189] M. Gandhi, C*ommon Article 3 of Geneva Conventions, 1949 in the Era of International Criminal Tribunals*, 11 ISIL YB IHL RL (2001), *available at* www.worldlii.org/int/journals/ISILYBI-HRL/2001/11.html (last visited Oct. 25, 2007).
[190] Gutierrez Posse, *supra* note 167, at 73.
[191] Tadic 1995, *supra* note 77, para. 72.
[192] Guenael Mettraux, International Crimes and the ad hoc Tribunals 130 (2005).
[193] Tadic 1995, *supra* note 77.
[194] Tadic 1995, *supra* note 77, paras 90–91.

in the context of a non-international armed conflict[195] and did not need to fulfil any particular requirements.

The ICTY Appeals Chamber explained the rationale for its decision in the following terms: "to maintain a distinction between the two legal regimes and their criminal consequences in respect of similarly egregious acts because of the difference in nature of the conflicts would ignore the very purpose of the Geneva Conventions, which is to protect the dignity of the human person."[196] Hence, "[f]rom the Statutes of the ICTY and the ICTR and from their jurisprudence interpreting international humanitarian law, it emerges that violations of the prohibitions contained in common Article 3 constitute war crimes in any situation of armed conflict."[197] Consequently one can safely affirm that Common Article 3 imposes duties upon individuals, irrespective of the nature of the armed conflict and in pursuance of the customary nature of that provision.

Originally, violations of the laws of war by soldiers could only be tried by the courts of their country of nationality or those of the captor state. At present, the principle of universal jurisdiction enables third countries to try violations of the laws and customs of war irrespective of the nationality of the perpetrator, the nationality of the victim or the place where the crime was committed. This principle "assumes that every state has an interest in exercising jurisdiction to combat egregious offences that states universally have condemned."[198] This interest may rely on its economic or social nature. In terms of reputation for example, it is not deniable that the principle of universal jurisdiction reflects the wide consideration and acceptance of international values whose protection is understood to favour the common interests of all members of the world community. Accordingly, states prosecute certain offences due to the fact that the object of legal protection is particularly commendable according to customary or treaty law, and the injury is generally recognized as punishable.[199] This shows that the principle of universality stands for the reduction of the impunity gap, ensuring that all individuals who have breached their duties according to IHL are being reprehended.

Obviously, IHL imposes more duties on individuals than HRL. Again this can be linked to the origins of the two legal regimes. However, the latest developments

---

[195] ICTR Statute, *supra* note 10.
[196] Prosecutor v. Delalic et al., Case No. IT-96-21-A, Appeal Judgment, (Feb. 20, 2001) para. 172.
[197] Gutierrez Posse, *supra* note 167, at 77.
[198] Kenneth C. Randall, *Universal Jurisdiction under International Law*, 66 Texas L.R. 785, 788 (1998). *See also* Enache-Brown & Fried, *supra* note 173.
[199] *See* Rudolf Wolfram, *The Decentralized Prosecution of International Offenses Through National Courts*, 24 Israel Y.B.H.R. 183, 185 (1995). *See also* Enache-Brown & Fried, *supra* note 173.

in both HRL and IHL, in particular via the criminalisation of many IHL principles and HRL norms, show that more and more duties are imposed on individuals.

4. Conclusion

This chapter discussed the position of the individual as a right- and duty-holder under the regimes of HRL and IHL.

The present chapter started by analysing the rights held by individuals under the two doctrines. Under the first regime the substantial rights provided to individuals under the various human rights treaties were considered with relation to the idea that human rights are provided by the state directly to the individual, yet bearing in mind that membership in a treaty is also beneficial to the state itself. It must also be noted that the nationality nexus has been removed since all human beings enjoy these rights, notably via customary international law and the status of some human rights as peremptory norms. Procedural rights under HRL were also considered both in national and international courts. The right to lodge a complaint at the international level is, again, a courtesy of the state to implement the substantive rights granted via conventional instruments. On the other hand, the discussion regarding the second regime (IHL), which is often much related to the rights of states and not of individuals, showed that the Geneva Conventions and Additional Protocol I grant substantial rights to individuals. With regards to procedural rights under IHL, a great discrepancy between the rights of states and those of individuals was pinpointed. However, the latter may make use of the "diplomatic protection" system or of the human rights mechanisms. The procedural rights mechanisms under the two regimes differ in the way that HRL confers rights directly on individuals whereas IHL provides for an inter-state mechanism.

In the second section, the duties imposed on individuals were examined with regards to the two doctrines. The initial proposition that HRL grants more rights to individuals than it imposes duties (direct or indirect) was partially refuted. Indeed, the ACHPR enumerates direct duties of individuals. Moreover, the restrictions contained in all international human rights instruments provide for the indirect duty of compliance within the limits imposed in the name of the prevention of the abuse of power or rights. What is more, the development of international criminal law and the evolution of the concept of individual criminal liability have also led to an upsurge of duties imposed upon individuals, duties that can be found both in HRL and in IHL. The principles of *aut dedere aut judicare* and that of universal jurisdiction also assisted not in the creation but in the implementation of duties to the extent that the immunity gap has been severely reduced.

The states, as principal subjects of IHL and HRL, have proved to be willing to grant individuals a place in public international law by endowing them with rights and duties for an active interaction with the international community. A close observation of the issues discussed above clearly shows that in the last century the position of the individual is developing and expanding beyond expectations and that both in IHL and HRL, the individual is being bestowed with rights and obligations. Moreover, an increasing number of mechanisms are being designed to ensure that such rights and obligations are upheld.

Chapter VIII

Concurrent Application of International Humanitarian Law and Human Rights Law: A Victim Perspective

*Jean-Marie Henckaerts**

1. *Introduction*

While the concurrent application of international humanitarian law and human rights law is by no means new,[1] it is increasingly being tested in practice. The current, renewed interest in the subject of the relationship between international

---

* Legal Adviser, Legal Division, International Committee of the Red Cross (ICRC). The views expressed in this article reflect those of the author and not necessarily those of the ICRC. The author would like to thank his colleagues Iris Müller for her excellent research assistance, as well as Cordula Droege for general advice on the content of this contribution and for specific information on national and international case-law. This contribution is adapted from an article which first appeared in International Law & Human Rights Discourse, Vol. I, 2007, pp. 95–124.

[1] For early treatment of the subject *see*, e.g., Richard R. Baxter, *Human Rights in War*, 31 Bulletin of the American Academy of Arts and Sciences 4 (1977); Igor P. Blischchenko, *Conflit armé et protection des droits de l'homme*, 18 Revue de droit contemporain 23 (1971); Aristidis Calegoropoulos-Stratis, *Droit Humanitaire et Droits de l'Homme. La protection de la personne en période de conflit armé* (1980); Viktor M. Chkhikvadze, *Armed Conflict and Human Rights*, 11 International Affairs 43 (1979); Vida Čok, *Le développement du droit international humanitaire au point de vue des droits de l'homme*, 27 Jugoslovenska Revija za Medunarodno Pravo – Revue Yougoslave de Droit International 121 (1980); G.I.A.D. Draper, *The Relationship between the Human Rights Regime and the Laws of Armed Conflict*, 1 Israel Yearbook of Human Rights 191 (1971); G.I.A.D. Draper, *Human Rights and the Law of War*, 12 Va. J. Intl L. 326 (1972); Sean McBride, *Human Rights in Armed Conflict: The Inter-relationship between the Humanitarian Laws and the Law of Human Rights*, 9 Military Law and Law of War Review 373 (1970); Henri Meyrowitz, *Le droit de la guerre et les droits de l'homme*, 88 RD Publ. 1095 (1972); Alessandro Migliazza, *L'évolution de la réglementation de la guerre à la lumière de la sauvegarde des droits de l'homme*, 137 Rec. des cours de l'Ac. de droit int'l 143 (1972); M. Mushkat, *The Development of International Humanitarian Law and the Law of Human Rights*, 21 GYBIL 150 (1978); Waldemar A. Solf, *Human rights in Armed Conflict: Some Observations on the Relationship of Human Rights Law to the Law of Armed Conflict*, in World in Transition: Challenges to Human Rights, Development and World Order 41 (Henry H. Han ed., 1979); Dietrich Schindler, *Human Rights and Humanitarian Law: Interrelationship of the Laws*, 31

humanitarian law and human rights law appears to be inspired by the judicial review of military action in a number of cases, both domestic and international, on the basis of human rights law. This chapter argues that this trend is largely due to victims' search for a forum in order to obtain remedies for violations of their rights during armed conflict.

The structure of this chapter is informed by the main differences between both branches of international law, namely their historic origin, their judicial enforcement and their scope of application. It then looks at the concurrent application of international humanitarian law and human rights law in practice.

The term "concurrent" or "simultaneous" application is used in this chapter, rather than "parallel" application, as it seems to most accurately reflect the phenomenon under discussion. Concurrent application implies that it is possible that both bodies of law apply at the same time to the same issue and, as a result, overlap or interplay. A "parallel" application would, strictly speaking, not allow for any overlapping spheres of application or any interplay. This chapter also argues that the concurrent application of both branches of international law requires that, in relevant cases, they be interpreted in the light of each other.

2. *Historic Origin*

Historically, human rights law and humanitarian law have developed separately.[2] Whereas human rights law has grown out of domestic, constitutional law, humanitarian law has its roots in international law.

The origin of human rights law can be traced back to the movement to protect the individual against government abuse and led to the recognition and protection of what are now called civil and political rights. In Western civilization, this development can be traced back, *inter alia*, to the *Magna Carta* of 1215. A second wave of rights, now called economic, social, and cultural, gained recognition during

---

Am. U.L. Rev. 935 (1982) and Keith D. Suter, *An Inquiry into the Meaning of the Phrase "Human Rights in Armed Conflict"*, 15 Rev. dr. pén. mil. 393 (1976).

[2] *See generally* Michael Bothe, *The Historical Evolution of International Humanitarian Law, International Human Rights Law, Refugee Law and International Criminal Law*, *in* Crisis Management and Humanitarian Protection – Festschrift für Dieter Fleck 37 (Horst Fischer *et al.* eds., 2004) [hereinafter Fischer]; Leslie C. Green, *Human Rights in Peace and War: An Historical Overview, in* Crisis Management and Humanitarian Protection – Festschrift für Dieter Fleck 159 (Horst Fischer *et al.* eds., 2004); Leslie C. Green, *The Relations Between Human Rights Law and International Humanitarian Law: A Historical Overview, in* Testing the Boundaries of International Humanitarian Law 49 (Susan C. Breau & Agnieszka Jachec-Neale eds., 2006) [hereinafter Breau & Jachec-Neale eds.]; and Robert Kolb, *The Relationship between International Humanitarian Law and Human Rights Law: A Brief History of the 1948 Universal Declaration of Human Rights and the 1949 Geneva Conventions*, 324 Int'l Rev. Red Cross 409 (1998).

the era of industrialization when the individual sought protection through collective action in situations of sickness, unemployment, and old age, among others.[3] Most if not all constitutions of the world today include a bill of rights recognizing an important array of rights, often enforceable through individual petitions. These constitutional rights are complemented and implemented by a vast system of legislation and administrative regulations.

It is only since the Second World War, however, that these rights have been recognized under international law. Although there were precedents of human rights protection under international law during the interwar period, in particular the protection of minority rights, it is only since the adoption of the Charter of the United Nations that "human rights" have fully become a subject of international law.[4] The development of "international" human rights law since the U.N. Charter is well known and includes, first and foremost, the adoption of the Universal Declaration of Human Rights on December 10, 1948 (now Human Rights Day), followed by a series of international conventions, both universal and regional.

International humanitarian law, on the other hand, has its roots in international law. From the outset humanitarian law has dealt with hostile relations between states. As such, it has fallen squarely within the traditional concept of international law as a body of law regulating inter-state relations. The first treaty codification of universal ambit was the Geneva Convention of August 22, 1864 for the Amelioration of the Condition of the Wounded in Armies in the Field which sought to tackle the main humanitarian problem of the day, as vividly described in Dunant's "A Memory of Solferino,"[5] i.e. the collection and care for wounded soldiers. This was followed by a range of treaties, updating previous treaties in the light of new practice, expanding the scope of protected persons and limiting the means and methods of warfare as technology developed. For example, whereas the first Geneva Convention of 1864 only dealt with wounded soldiers in the field, by 1929 it had been updated for the second time,[6] and an

---

[3] The protection of economic, social, and cultural rights in both human rights law and humanitarian law is beyond the scope of this article. *See generally*, Noam Lubell, *Challenges in Applying Human Rights Law to Armed Conflict*, 860 Int'l Rev. Red Cross 737, 751–753 (2005). On the right to humanitarian assistance, *see*, e.g., Ruth Abril Stoffels, *Legal Regulation of Humanitarian Assistance in Armed Conflict: Achievements and Gaps*, 855 Int'l Rev. Red Cross 515 (2004). On the right to food, *see*, e.g., Jelena Pejic, *The Right to Food in Situations of Armed Conflict: The Legal Framework*, 844 Int'l Rev. Red Cross 1097 (2001). On the right to education, *see*, e.g., Sohbi Tawil, *International Humanitarian Law and Basic Education*, 839 Int'l Rev. Red Cross 581 (2000).

[4] *See* Articles 1(3) and 55(c) Charter of the United Nations.

[5] Jean Henry Dunant, Un souvenir de Solférino (1862).

[6] Convention for the Amelioration of the Condition of the Wounded and Sick in Armies in the Field (July 27, 1929), 47 Stat. 2074, 118 L.N.T.S. 303. The 1929 Convention replaces a previous update of the 1864 Convention adopted in 1906 (Convention for the Amelioration of the Condition of the Wounded in Armies in the Field, (Aug. 22, 1864), 18 Martens Nouveau Recueil (ser. 1)

entirely new convention dealing with the treatment of prisoners of war had been adopted.[7]

As is well-known, these treaties were further updated in 1949 and in 1977. The four Geneva Conventions of 1949[8] and their Additional Protocols of 1977[9] provide an extensive regime for the protection of persons who do not or no longer participate in armed conflict, including civilians. Indeed, as warfare moved into cities and villages, it increasingly affected civilians and new rules were needed for the protection of this important category of persons.

The regulation of the means and methods of warfare in treaty law goes back to the 1868 St. Petersburg Declaration,[10] the 1899[11] and 1907 Hague Conventions[12] and the 1925 Geneva Gas Protocol[13] and has most recently been addressed in the

---

607, 129 Consol. T.S. 361). *See* Additional Articles relating to the Condition of the Wounded in the Field, Oct. 20, 1868; Convention for the Amelioration of the Condition of the Wounded and Sick in Armies in the Field (July 6, 1906).

[7] Geneva Convention Relative to the Treatment of Prisoners of War (July 27, 1929), 47 Stat. 2021, 118 L.N.T.S. 343.

[8] The Geneva Convention for the Amelioration of the Condition of the Wounded and Sick in Armed Forces in the Field, Aug. 12, 1949, 75 U.N.T.S. 31, 32; Geneva Convention for the Amelioration of the Condition of the Wounded, Sick and Shipwrecked Members of the Armed Forces at Sea, Aug. 12, 1949, 75 U.N.T.S. 85, 86; Geneva Convention Relative to the Treatment to Prisoners of War, Aug. 12, 1949, 75 U.N.T.S. 135, 136; Geneva Convention Relative to the Protection of Civilian Persons in Time of War, Aug. 12, 1949, 75 U.N.T.S. 287, 288 [hereinafter GC IV].

[9] Protocol Additional to the Geneva Conventions of 12 August 1949, and Relating to the Protections of Victims of International Armed Conflicts (Protocol I), opened for signature Dec. 12, 1977, U.N. Doc. A/32/144, Annex I, II, (1977), *reprinted in* 16 I.L.M. 1391 (1977) [hereinafter AP I]; Protocol Additional to the Geneva Conventions of 12 August 1949, and Relating to the Protection of Victims of Non-International Armed Conflicts (Protocol I), June 8, 1977, 1125 U.N.T.S. 3 [hereinafter AP II].

[10] Declaration Renouncing the Use, in Time of War, of Certain Explosive Projectiles (Nov. 29/ Dec. 11, 1868), 18 Martens Nouveau Recueil (ser. 1) 474, 138 Consol. T.S. 297.

[11] *See* e.g. Declaration (IV, 1) to Prohibit for the Term of Five Years, the Launching of Projectiles and Explosives from Balloons, and Other Methods of Similar Nature, (July 29, 1899), 26 Martens Nouveau Recueil (ser. 2) 994, 187 Consol. T.S. 456; Hague Declaration (IV, 2) Concerning the Prohibition of the Use of Projectiles Diffusing Asphyxiating Gases (July 29, 1899), 26 Martens Nouveau Recueil (ser. 2) 998, 187 Consol. T.S. 453; Hague Declaration (IV, 3) Concerning the Prohibition of the Use of Expanding Bullets (July 29, 1899), 26 Martens Nouveau Recueil (ser. 2) 1002, 187 Consol. T.S. 459.

[12] *See* e.g. Hague Declaration (XIV) Prohibiting the Discharge of Projectiles and Explosives from Balloons (Oct. 18, 1907), 3 Martens Nouveau Recueil (ser. 3) 745, 205 Consol. T.S. 403; Hague Convention (VIII) Relative to the Laying of Automatic Submarine Contact Mines (Oct. 18, 1907), 3 Martens Nouveau Recueil (ser. 3) 580, 205 Consol. T.S. 331.

[13] Protocol for the Prohibition of the Use in War of Asphyxiating, Poisonous or Other Gases, and of Bacteriological Methods of Warfare (June 17, 1925), 94 L.N.T.S. 65.

1972 Biological Weapons Convention,[14] the 1977 Additional Protocols, the 1980 Convention on Certain Conventional Weapons and its five Protocols,[15] the 1993 Chemical Weapons Convention[16] and the 1997 Ottawa Convention banning anti-personnel landmines.[17] The protection of cultural property in the event of armed conflict is regulated in detail in the 1954 Hague Convention and its two Protocols.[18] The 1998 Statute of the International Criminal Court contains a list of war crimes subject to its jurisdiction.[19] The protection of children and the recruitment of child soldiers are regulated in the 1989 Convention on the Rights of the Child[20] and the 2002 Protocol on the involvement of children in armed conflict.[21]

Notwithstanding this high degree of codification, customary humanitarian law continues to play an essential role today in the legal regulation of armed conflict.[22] But whether as treaty law or as customary law, humanitarian law has essentially always been part of international law. Over time, the denomination of "law of

---

[14] Convention on the Prohibition of the Development, Production, and Stockpiling of Bacteriological (Biological) and Toxin Weapons and on Their Destruction (Apr. 10, 1972), 1015 U.N.T.S. 163.

[15] Convention on Prohibitions or Restrictions on the Use of Certain Conventional Weapons Which May Be Deemed to Be Excessively Injurious or to Have Indiscriminate Effects (Oct. 10, 1980), 1342 U.N.T.S. 137, 19 I.L.M. 1524; CCW Protocol on Non-Detectable Fragments (Protocol I), (Oct. 10, 1980), 1342 U.N.T.S. 168, 19 I.L.M. 1529; CCW Protocol on Prohibitions or Restrictions on the Use of Mines, Booby-Traps and Other Devices (Protocol II), (Oct. 10, 1980), 1342 U.N.T.S. 168, 19 I.L.M. 1529. This protocol was amended in 1996. Protocol on Prohibitions or Restrictions on the Use of Mines, Booby-Traps and Other Devices as Amended on 3 May 1996 (Protocol II to the 1980 Convention as amended on 3 May 1996), 1125 U.N.T.S. 609, 19 I.L.M. 1206; CCW Protocol on Prohibitions or Restrictions on the Use of Incendiary Weapons (Protocol III), (Oct. 10, 1980), 1342 U.N.T.S. 171, 19 I.L.M. 1534; CCW Protocol IV on Blinding Laser Weapons,(Oct. 13, 1995), 35 I.L.M. 1218; CCW Protocol V on Explosive Remnants of War, (Nov. 27, 2003), U.N. Doc. CCW/MSP/2003/ 2 (entered into force Nov. 12, 2006).

[16] Convention on the Prohibition of the Development, Production, Stockpiling and Use of Chemical Weapons and on Their Destruction (Jan. 13, 1993), 1015 U.N.T.S. 163.

[17] Convention on the Prohibition of the Use, Stockpiling, Production and Transfer of Anti-Personnel Mines and on Their Destruction (Sept. 18, 1997), 36 I.L.M. 1507.

[18] The Convention for the Protection of Cultural Property in the Event of an Armed Conflict (May 14, 1954), 249 U.N.T.S. 240.

[19] Rome Statute of the International Criminal Court, adopted on July 17, 1998 by the U.N. Diplomatic Conference of Plenipotentiaries on the Establishment of an International Criminal Court, entered into force, July 1, 2002, U.N. Doc. A/CONF.183/9 (1998) [hereinafter ICC Statute].

[20] Convention on the Rights of the Child, G.A. Res. 44/25, Annex, 44 U.N. GAOR Supp. No. 49, U.N. Doc. A/44/49 (Nov. 20, 1989) (entered into force Sept. 2 1990) [hereinafter CRC].

[21] Optional Protocol to the Convention on the Rights of the Child on the Involvement of Children in Armed Conflict, G.A. Res. 54/263, Annex I, U.N. Doc A/RES/54/263 (May 25, 2000) (entered into force Feb. 12, 2002).

[22] *See* Jean-Marie Henckaerts, *Study on Customary International Humanitarian Law: A Contribution to the Understanding and Respect for the Rule of Law in Armed Conflict*, 857 Int'l Rev. Red Cross 175 (2005).

war" has changed to "law of armed conflict" and "international humanitarian law" but all three terms are now used interchangeably. It is also sometimes referred to with the Latin phrase *ius in bello*,[23] the law that applies in war, as opposed to *ius ad bellum*, the law that applies to resort to war. As resort to the use of force in international relations is, in principle, prohibited, it may be better to speak of *ius contra bellum*.[24]

In addition to their different origins, human rights law and humanitarian law have developed differently in several other ways. For example, in human rights law, regional organizations, in particular the Council of Europe, the Organization of American States and the Organization of African Unity, now the African Union, have successfully developed regional human rights conventions which are widely ratified by their member states. Humanitarian law, both treaty law and customary law, remains essentially a body of law of universal ambit.

This is particularly relevant in the area of enforcement where the regional human rights mechanisms have proved to be the most effective in terms of offering individual remedies to victims of human rights abuse (see below). The availability of these remedies, and the lack thereof under humanitarian law, combined with the substantive rights covered have increased the attraction of victims to seek justice for violations committed during armed conflict under human rights law and procedures.

3. *Judicial Enforcement*[25]

In the area of judicial enforcement, human rights law and humanitarian law have gone distinctly different routes. In particular, numerous international judicial and quasi-judicial mechanisms have been established under human rights law, which provide an opportunity for victims to bring a petition against the offending state,

---

[23] *See* Robert Kolb, Ius in Bello. Le droit international humanitaire des conflits armés, (2002). *See also* Robert Kolb, *Origin of the Twin Terms jus ad bellum/jus in bello*, 320 Int'l Rev. Red Cross 553 (1997).

[24] Article 2(4) Charter of the United Nations. *See* Robert Kolb, Ius contra bellum. Le droit international relatif au maintien de la paix (2003).

[25] A comparison of enforcement through other means, such as via diplomatic measures by third States (*see*, e.g., duty to ensure respect for humanitarian law according to common Article 1 of the Geneva Conventions and customary international law), civil society, NGOs, and the media, UN and regional organisations, enquiry and fact-finding procedures, and the work of the ICRC, is beyond the scope of this article. *See generally* Marco Sassòli, *Mise en oeuvre du droit international humanitaire et du droit international des droits de l'homme: une comparaison*, 43 ASDI 24 (1987) and César Sepúlveda, *Interrelationships in the Implementation and Enforcement of International Humanitarian Law and Human Rights Law*, 33 Am. U. L. Rev. 117 (1984).

after exhausting all available and effective domestic remedies. The mechanisms that establish a system of individual petition include:

3.1. *Universal Human Rights Instruments (in chronological order)*

International Convention on the Elimination of All Forms of Racial Discrimination (1965):[26]

> According to Article 14(1) of the Convention
> [a] State Party may at any time declare that it recognizes the competence of the Committee [on the Elimination of Racial Discrimination] to receive and consider communications from individuals or groups of individuals within its jurisdiction claiming to be victims of a violation by that State Party of any of the rights set forth in this Convention.[27]

Optional Protocol to the International Covenant on Civil and Political Rights (1966):[28]

> According to Article 1 of the Optional Protocol,
> [a] State Party to the Covenant that becomes a party to the present Protocol recognizes the competence of the [Human Rights] Committee to receive and consider communications from individuals subject to its jurisdiction who claim to be victims of a violation by that State Party of any of the rights set forth in the Covenant.[29]

Convention against Torture and Other Cruel, Inhuman or Degrading Treatment or Punishment (1984):[30]

> According to Article 22(1) of the Convention
> [a] State Party to this Convention may at any time declare under this article that it recognizes the competence of the Committee [against Torture] to receive and consider

---

[26] International Convention on the Elimination of All Forms of Racial Discrimination, opened for signature Dec. 21, 1965 (entered into force on Jan. 4, 1969) [hereinafter CERD].

[27] As of January 17, 2007, there were 173 States party to the Convention on the Elimination of All Forms of Racial Discrimination and 49 of them had made the declaration under Article 14. The individual complaints mechanism of the Convention became operative on December 3, 1982, when ten States had become bound by declarations under Article 14. Information on the status of ratification of universal human rights treaties can be found at www.ohchc.org/english/countries/ratification/index.htm (last visited Aug. 19, 2007).

[28] International Covenant on Civil and Political Rights, G.A. Res. 2200A (XXI), 21 U.N. GAOR Supp. (No. 16) at 52, U.N. Doc. A/6316 (1966), 999 U.N.T.S. 171 [hereinafter ICCPR].

[29] As of January 17, 2007, there were 160 States party to the International Covenant on Civil and Political Rights and 109 had ratified the Optional Protocol. The Optional Protocol became operative on March 23, 1976, three months after the date of the deposit of the tenth instrument of ratification. *See id.*

[30] Convention against Torture and Other Cruel, Inhuman or Degrading Treatment or Punishment, G.A. Res. 39/46, [annex, 39 U.N. GAOR Supp. (No. 51) at 197, U.N. Doc. A/39/51 (1984)], entered into force June 26, 1987 [hereinafter CAT].

communications from or on behalf of individuals subject to its jurisdiction who claim to be victims of a violation by a State Party of the provisions of the Convention.[31]

Optional Protocol to the Convention on the Elimination of All Forms of Discrimination against Women (1999):[32]

According to Articles 1 and 2 of the Optional Protocol, a state party to the Protocol recognizes the competence of the Committee on the Elimination of Discrimination against Women to receive and consider communications "submitted by or on behalf of individuals or groups of individuals, under the jurisdiction of a State Party, claiming to be victims of a violation of any of the rights set forth in the Convention by that State Party."[33]

The acceptance of an individual complaints mechanism pursuant to a declaration by states parties is also provided in Article 77 of the International Convention on the Protection of the Rights of All Migrant Workers and Members of Their Families (1990).[34] However, a declaration by at least ten states party to the Convention is required for the complaint mechanism under Article 77 to come into force. No such declaration has been made to date.

Similarly, no individual complaints mechanism exists at present under the International Covenant on Economic, Social and Cultural Rights.[35] However, in 2003, the UN Commission on Human Rights established an open-ended Working Group to consider options regarding the elaboration of an optional protocol to the Covenant.[36] After this mandate had been renewed for two further years by the Commission,[37] the newly established Human Rights Council renewed the mandate of the working group in 2006 for two further years and requested the Chairperson

---

[31] As of January 17, 2007, there were 144 States party to the Convention against Torture and 59 of them had made the declaration under Article 22. The individual complaints mechanism became operative on June 26, 1987, at the same time as the Convention itself, more than 5 States having made declarations under Article 22 prior to that date. *See id.*

[32] Convention on the Elimination of All Forms of Discrimination Against Women, opened for signature Mar. 1, 1980, 1249 U.N.T.S. 14 (entered into force on Sept. 3, 1981) [hereinafter CEDAW].

[33] The Optional Protocol entered into force on December 22, 2000. As of January 17, 2007, there were 185 States party to the Convention and 78 had ratified the Optional Protocol. *See id.*

[34] International Convention on the Protection of the Rights of All Migrant Workers and Members of their Families, G.A. Res. 158, 45th Sess., U.N. Doc. A/RES/45/158 (Dec. 18, 1990) [hereinafter Migrant Workers Convention].

[35] International Covenant on Economic, Social and Cultural Rights, 993 U.N.T.S. 3 (Dec. 19, 1966) [hereinafter ICESCR].

[36] *See* U.N. Commission on Human Rights, Res. 2002/24 (April 22, 2002), para. 9(f) and Res. 2003/18 (April 22, 2003), para. 12. *See also* ECOSOC, Decision 2002/254, (July 25, 2002), para. (b) endorsing the Commission's plan to establish the open-ended Working Group.

[37] U.N. Commission on Human Rights, Res. 2004/29 (April 19, 2004), para. 14(a).

to prepare "a first draft optional protocol," including draft provisions on individual communications, to be used as a basis for further negotiations.[38]

3.2. Regional Human Rights Instruments (in chronological order)

European Convention for the Protection of Human Rights and Fundamentals Freedoms (1950):[39]

According to Article 34 of the European Convention, as amended by Protocol No. 11 of November 11, 1994, the European Court of Human Rights "may receive applications from any person, non-governmental organisation or group of individuals claiming to be the victim of a violation by one of the High Contracting Parties of the rights set forth in the Convention or the protocols thereto."[40] Already under the original 1950 version of the Convention, individuals could bring a complaint against a State party; however, recognition of the right of individual petition was optional and could only be exercised against a State party which had accepted it.[41] Today, all 46 member States of the Council of Europe are party to the Convention and have accepted *ipso facto* the jurisdiction of the Court to receive individual applications.[42]

American Declaration of the Rights and Duties of Man (1948/1965):[43]

The Inter-American Commission on Human Rights was established by the Organization of American States (OAS) in 1959, in order to further respect for human rights as already proclaimed in the 1948 American Declaration of the Rights and Duties of Man. In 1965, the Commission was authorized by the Second Special Inter-American Conference to examine individual petitions or complaints regarding specific cases of human rights violations by OAS member States.[44]

---

[38] Human Rights Council, Res. 20006/3 (June 29, 2006), para. 3.
[39] Council of Europe, Convention for the Protection of Human Rights and Fundamental Freedoms, 213 U.N.T.S. 222, entered into force Sept. 3, 1953, as amended by Protocols Nos 3, 5, 8, and 11 which entered into force on 21 Sept. 1970, 20 Dec. 1971, 1 Jan. 1990, and 1 Nov. 1998 respectively [hereinafter ECHR].
[40] Information on the Convention can be found on the Council of Europe Treaty Office site: conventions.coe.int/Treaty/EN/v3MenuTraites.asp (last visited Aug. 19, 2007).
[41] *See* Article 25(1) of the original version of the Convention, *supra* note 39.
[42] *See id.*
[43] American Declaration of the Rights and Duties of Man, O.A.S. Res. XXX, adopted by the Ninth International Conference of American States (1948), reprinted in Basic Documents to Human Rights in the Inter-American System, OEA/Ser.L.V/II.82 doc.6 rev.1 (1992).
[44] Final Act of the Second Special Inter-American Conference, OAS Official Records, OEA/Ser. C/I.13, 1965, pp. 32–34.

American Convention on Human Rights (1969):[45]

> According to Article 44 of the American Convention
> [a]ny person or group of persons, or any nongovernmental entity legally recognized in one or more member states of the Organization [of American States], may lodge petitions with the [Inter-American] Commission [on Human Rights] containing denunciations or complaints of violation of this Convention by a State Party.

Today, the Inter-American Commission on Human Rights, in its examination of individual petitions, applies the American Convention on Human Rights in cases brought against states which are a party to that instrument, while with regard to those states which have not ratified the Convention; it applies the 1948 American Declaration. To date, the OAS has 35 member states, 24 of which have ratified the Convention.[46]

According to Article 61 of the American Convention, "[o]nly the States Parties and the Commission shall have the right to submit a case to the [Inter-American] Court [of Human Rights]" and according to Article 62, the Court only has jurisdiction vis-à-vis those States that have made a declaration to accept the jurisdiction of the Court. Out of the 24 states party to the American Convention, 21 have made such a declaration accepting the contentious jurisdiction of the Court.[47]

African Charter on Human and Peoples' Rights (1981):[48]

> According to Article 55 of the African Charter,
> [b]efore each Session, the Secretary of the [African] Commission [on Human and Peoples' Rights] shall make a list of the communications other than those of States parties to the present Charter and transmit them to the members of the Commission, who shall indicate which communications should be considered by the Commission. A communication shall be considered by the Commission if a simple majority of its members so decide.

To date, all 53 member states of the African Union (AU) are party to the Charter.[49]

Protocol to the African Charter on Human and Peoples' Rights on the Establishment of an African Court on Human and Peoples' Rights (1998):[50]

---

[45] American Convention on Human Rights, O.A.S. Treaty Series No. 36, 1144 U.N.T.S. 123, entered into force July 18, 1978, reprinted in Basic Documents Pertaining to Human Rights in the Inter-American System, OEA/Ser.L.V/II.82 doc.6 rev.1 at 25 (1992) [hereinafter ACHR].

[46] Information on the status of ratification of the American Convention can be found at www.oas.org/juridico/english/Sigs/b-32.htm (last visited Aug. 19, 2007).

[47] See www.corteidh.or.cr/index.cfm (last visited Aug. 19, 2007).

[48] African Charter on Human and Peoples' Rights, adopted June 27, 1981, O.A.U. Doc. CAB/LEG/67/3 Rev. 5, 21 I.L.M. 58 (1982), arts. 27–29.

[49] Information on the status of ratification of the African Charter can be found at www.africa-union.org/root/au/Documents/Treaties/treaties.htm (last visited Aug. 19, 2007)

[50] Protocol to the African Charter on Human and Peoples' Rights on the Establishment of an

According to Article 5 of the Protocol, the African Court on Human and Peoples' Rights set up under the Protocol, "may entitle relevant Non Governmental organizations (NGOs) with observer status before the Commission and individuals to institute cases directly before it, in accordance with article 34(6) of this Protocol." The latter article provides that the Court may only receive petitions from NGOs and individuals against states which have made a declaration accepting the competence of the Court to receive such cases. The Protocol came into force on January 25, 2004. To date, there are 23 states party to the Protocol.[51]

As can be seen from the above overview, the right of individual petition before human rights committees and courts is now well established and is available for a wide array of rights and vis-à-vis a large number of states. The remedies offered by these judicial and quasi-judicial bodies are additional to those offered by domestic law, which are also extensive in many states. This is particularly so due to the fact that human rights law has its origin in domestic legal systems and these systems are generally well developed in comparison with the international legal system. The purpose of the adoption of the international instruments is to ensure a minimum (not uniform) level of protection, while states may offer higher standards of protection in domestic law.

As a result of this elaborate system of individual petition, an extensive body of international human rights case law has developed interpreting the scope of the rights enshrined in the various treaties. The content of this body of case law is further enhanced by the concluding observations regarding state reports and general comments on specific treaty provisions elaborated by the various committees set up within the United Nations in order to administer the main human rights treaties of universal ambit.[52]

Under international humanitarian law, such a system of individual petition does not exist, nor does a system of state reporting.[53] Instead, the judicial enforcement of international humanitarian law has been pursued in the main through criminal law.

African Court on Human and Peoples' Rights, adopted June 9, 1998, OAU Doc. OAU/LEG/EXP/AFCHPR/PROT (III).

[51] *See id.* (when accessed on January 17, 2007, the website did not indicate which states party to the Protocol made a declaration accepting the competence of the Court to receive petitions from NGOs and individuals).

[52] A system of State reporting exists under the seven main universal human rights treaties. *See* Article 9 CERD, *supra* note 26; Article 40 ICCPR, *supra* note 28; Article 16 ICESCR, *supra* note 35; Article 18 CEDAW, *supra* note 32; Article 19 CAT, *supra* note 30; Article 44 CRC, *supra* note 20; Article 73 Migrant Workers Convention, *supra* note 34. In addition to issuing concluding observations on specific country reports, the committees established under these treaties also have the power to issue "general comments" or "general recommendations" and have done so in practice with a varying degree of intensity.

[53] *See* Liesbeth Zegveld, *Remedies for Victims of Violations of International Humanitarian Law*, 851 Int'l Rev. Red Cross 497 (2003). For a specific proposal to establish an individual petition system, *see* Jann Kleffner & Liesbeth Zegveld, *Establishing an Individual Complaints Procedure for Violations*

An enforcement system based on criminal law has several disadvantages, however, from the point of view of the victims of the violations, as well as from the point of view of the development and interpretation of the law.

Firstly, victims do not have access to international (or "mixed") criminal courts or tribunals. A limited, but important exception is provided for in Article 75 of the Statute of the International Criminal Court which provides in part:

1. The Court shall establish principles relating to reparations to, or in respect of, victims, including restitution, compensation and rehabilitation. On this basis, in its decision the Court may, either upon request or on its own motion in exceptional circumstances, determine the scope and extent of any damage, loss and injury to, or in respect of, victims and will state the principles on which it is acting.
2. The Court may make an order directly against a convicted person specifying appropriate reparations to, or in respect of, victims, including restitution, compensation and rehabilitation.

    Where appropriate, the Court may order that the award for reparations be made through the Trust Fund provided for in article 79.
3. Before making an order under this article, the Court may invite and shall take account of representations from or on behalf of the convicted person, victims, other interested persons or interested States.[54]

Although this represents a positive development, it remains to be seen how this system will operate in practice. Criminal procedures before domestic courts, where victims can act as *partie civile*, or civil procedures for damages before domestic courts, may also offer a solution to this problem.

Secondly, international (or "mixed") criminal procedures for the prosecution of perpetrators of serious violations of humanitarian law have mainly been set up on an *ad hoc* basis, i.e. selective in geographical and temporal scope of application. They have generally been established after the commission of serious violations on a large scale, in places such as former Yugoslavia, Rwanda, and Sierra Leone. Again, the establishment of the International Criminal Court may eventually overcome this deficit. The existence of domestic criminal legislation on serious violations of humanitarian law may also help to overcome this deficit. However, such legislation does not exist in every state today.

Thirdly, the prosecutorial policies of the international (or "mixed") criminal tribunals seem to restrict investigation and prosecution to a limited number of "high value" cases. It is unlikely that "minor" offenders will be prosecuted before these international or "mixed" courts or tribunals, even though their acts may have had significant consequences for the victims. In theory, and also increasingly in practice, this limitation is overcome through the complementary work of national courts and tribunals. However, there are still relatively few national war crimes prosecutions.

---

of International Humanitarian Law, 3 Yearbook of International Humanitarian Law 384 (2000).

[54] Article 75 ICC Statute, *supra* note 19.

Fourthly, the judicial enforcement of humanitarian law mainly operates under the principles of individual criminal responsibility, whereby named individuals are indicted, prosecuted, and possibly convicted, whereas the enforcement of human rights law operates under the principles of state responsibility whereby the state, and no named individual, assumes responsibility. It seems obvious that states and their military and political leaders are more willing to submit to the latter type of responsibility. No doubt, the mere existence of international or "mixed" criminal courts and tribunals, as well as their national counterparts, has had a deterrent effect on the commission of serious violations of humanitarian law, although it is difficult to measure this effect with any precision.

These characteristics of international, "mixed" or national criminal procedures and the lack of an individual complaints mechanism proper to humanitarian law may explain the current tendency to pursue remedies for violations of humanitarian law under human rights law and procedures. As long as humanitarian law does not offer proper remedies to victims, this trend is likely to continue and may even increase.

Finally, one result of this state of affairs is that case law on humanitarian law mainly deals with war crimes and is limited to a few categories of war crimes, mostly related to the treatment of persons. Until an individual petition system for humanitarian law exists, it is unlikely that the law will be clarified to the extent witnessed within the area of human rights law. Some rules of humanitarian law which have existed for decades, such as the prohibition to commit acts or threats of violence, the primary purpose of which is to spread terror among the civilian population,[55] are only now being tested in court for the first time,[56] and other rules, such as the prohibition of causing excessive civilian losses, have never been tested in court at all.

4. Scope of Application

There is extensive state practice to the effect that human rights law continues to apply during armed conflict.[57] The resolutions adopted at the International Conference on Human Rights in Teheran in 1968 and by the U.N. General Assembly the same year referred to "human rights in armed conflict," whereas the content of the resolutions related primarily to international humanitarian law.[58]

---

[55] See Article 51(2) AP I, *supra* note 9 and Article 13(2) AP II, *supra* note 9. These rules have existed since at least 1977.
[56] See Prosecutor v. Stanislav Galić, Case No. IT-98-29-T, Judgment, (Dec. 5, 2003) and Case No. IT-98-29-A, Judgment (Nov. 30, 2006).
[57] This section is based on Jean-Marie Henckaerts & Louise Doswald-Beck, Customary International Humanitarian Law 303–305 (Vol. I, 2005).
[58] International Conference on Human Rights, Teheran, Res. XXIII (May 12, 1968); U.N. G. A., Res. 2444 (XXIII) (Dec. 19, 1968).

However, the approach changed shortly afterwards. U.N. General Assembly Resolution 2675 (XXV) on basic principles for the protection of civilian populations in armed conflict, adopted in 1970, referred to the four Geneva Conventions in its preamble, and specifically to the Fourth Geneva Convention too, as well as to "the progressive development of the international law of armed conflict." In its first operative paragraph, the resolution stated that "fundamental human rights, as accepted in international law and laid down in international instruments, continue to apply fully in situations of armed conflict."[59] Since then, the understanding that both human rights law and humanitarian law apply in armed conflict has been confirmed by numerous resolutions condemning violations of both these areas of law in specific armed conflicts and by U.N. investigations into violations of both areas of law within armed conflict situations.

Human rights violations have been condemned, for example, in the context of armed conflict or military occupations in Afghanistan,[60] Iraq,[61] Sudan,[62] Russia,[63] former Yugoslavia,[64] and Uganda.[65] The United Nations has also conducted investigations into violations of human rights, for example in connection with the conflict in Liberia,[66] Sierra Leone,[67] Israel's military occupation of the Palestinian

---

[59] U.N. G. A. Res. 2675 (XXV) (Dec. 9, 1970) (adopted by 109 votes in favour, none against and 8 abstentions), preamble and para. 1.

[60] U.N. G. A. Res. 52/145, U.N. Doc. A/RES/52/145 (Dec. 12, 1997) (adopted by consensus), para. 2 ("notes with deep concern the intensification of armed hostilities in Afghanistan") and para. 3 ("condemns the violations and abuses of human rights and humanitarian law, including the rights to life, liberty and security of person, freedom from torture and from other forms of cruel, inhuman or degrading treatment or punishment, freedom of opinion, expression, religion, association and movement.")

[61] U.N. Commission on Human Rights, Res. 1992/60 (March 3, 1992), preamble (paras 3, 6 and 8) indicating respectively that the resolution is guided by, *inter alia*, the international covenants on human rights and the Geneva Conventions of 1949, that it expresses "deep concern at the grave violations of human rights and fundamental freedoms during the occupation of Kuwait" and notes "with grave concern the information to the effect that the treatment of prisoners of war and detained civilians does not conform to the internationally recognised principles of humanitarian law." There are similar statements in U.N. G. A. Res. 46/135, U.N. Doc. A/RES/46/135 (Dec. 17, 1991).

[62] U.N. Commission on Human Rights, Res. 1996/73 (April 23, 1996).

[63] U.N. Commission on Human Rights, Res. 2000/58 (April 25, 2000), preamble (para. 10) ("the need to...observe international human rights and humanitarian law in situations of conflict") and para. 4 (calling on Russia to "investigate promptly alleged violations of human rights and breaches of international humanitarian law committed in the Republic of Chechnya.")

[64] U.N. S. C., Res. 1019, U.N. Doc. S/RES/1019 (1995) (Nov. 9, 1995); U.N. S. C., Res. 1034, U.N. Doc. S/RES/1034 (1995) (Dec. 21, 1995); U.N. G. A. Res. 50/193, U.N. Doc. A/RES/50/192 (Dec. 22, 1995); U.N. Commission on Human Rights, Res. 1996/71 (April 23, 1996).

[65] U.N. Commission on Human Rights, Res. 1998/75 (April 22, 1998).

[66] U.N. Secretary-General, Progress Report on UNOMIL, U.N. Doc. S/1996/47 (Jan. 23, 1996).

[67] U.N. Secretary-General, Progress Report on UNOMSIL, U.N. Doc. S/1998/750 (Aug. 12, 1998).

territories,[68] Iraq's military occupation of Kuwait,[69] and the situation in Afghanistan during and after the Soviet occupation.[70] The U.N. High Commissioner for Human Rights also has national offices that monitor and promote respect for both human rights and humanitarian law in non-international armed conflict.[71]

The reports of the investigations into the situation in Afghanistan from 1985 onwards and into the situation in Kuwait during the Iraqi occupation, as well as states' reaction to them, are examples of the acceptance of the simultaneous applicability of both areas of international law.

The various reports of the U.N. Special Rapporteurs for Afghanistan referred to aspects of both human rights and humanitarian law, for example, in the report submitted to the U.N. Commission on Human Rights in 1987.[72] This report was commended in a resolution adopted by consensus by the U.N. Commission on Human Rights, in which it expressed concern that "the Afghan authorities, with heavy support from foreign troops, are acting...without any respect for the international human rights obligations which they have assumed," voiced "its deep concern about the number of persons detained for seeking to exercise their fundamental human rights and freedoms, and their detention contrary to internationally recognized standards", noted "with concern that such widespread violations of human rights...are still giving rise to large flows of refugees," and called on

---

[68] U.N. Commission on Human Rights, Res. S-5/1 (Oct. 19, 2000), para. 6 (decided "to establish...a human rights inquiry commission...to gather and compile information on violations of human rights and acts which constitute grave breaches of international humanitarian law by the Israeli occupying Power in the occupied Palestinian territories.") Its first and last preambular paragraphs refer specifically to human rights treaties and to humanitarian law treaties respectively.

[69] U.N. Commission on Human Rights, Res. 1991/67 (March 6, 1991), para. 9 (mandated a Special Rapporteur "to examine the human rights violations committed in occupied Kuwait by the invading and occupying forces of Iraq.")

[70] U.N. Economic and Social Council, Decision 1985/147 (May 30, 1985), approving U.N. Commission on Human Rights, Res. 1985/38 (May 13, 1985) "to extend for one year the mandate of the Special Rapporteur on the question of human rights and fundamental freedoms in Afghanistan and to request him to report to the General Assembly...and to the Commission [on Human Rights]...on the situation of human rights in that country," reprinted in U.N. Doc. E/1985/85, p. 44. The mandate was renewed on many occasions. *See* U.N. Doc. A/52/493 (Oct. 16, 1997), the introduction to which lists the reports submitted by Special Rapporteurs for Afghanistan between 1985 and 1997. For more practice, *see* Daniel O'Donnell, *Trends in the Application of International Humanitarian Law by United Nations Human Rights Mechanisms*, 324 Int'l Rev. Red Cross 481 (1998).

[71] For example, the field office in Santafé de Bogotá, Colombia, established by agreement in November 1996, which has the mandate to monitor the situation and to "promote respect for and observance of human rights and international humanitarian law in Colombia." (*see* www.unhchr.ch/html/menu2/5/colombia.htm (last visited Aug. 17, 2007)).

[72] U.N. Commission on Human Rights, Special Rapporteur on the Situation of Human Rights in Afghanistan, Report, U.N. Doc. E/CN.4/1987/22 (Feb. 19, 1987).

"the parties to the conflict to apply fully the principles and rules of international humanitarian law."[73]

The report on the Iraqi occupation of Kuwait examined issues such as arbitrary arrest, disappearances, right to life, right to food, right to health in the light of the provisions of the ICCPR and the ICESCR, but also of international humanitarian law. In particular, the report states that "there is consensus within the international community that the fundamental human rights of all persons are to be respected and protected both in times of peace and during periods of armed conflict."[74] Resolutions adopted by the U.N. General Assembly and by the U.N. Commission on Human Rights on the situation of human rights in Kuwait under Iraqi occupation in 1991 expressed these bodies' appreciation of the Special Rapporteur's report.[75]

Even though it is clear that, in principle, human rights law continues to apply during armed conflict, there are a number of legal and technical issues that may complicate its actual application. These issues relate to (1) the material and temporal scope of application of human rights law, (2) the personal scope of application of human rights law, and (3) the geographic scope of application of human rights law.

4.1. *Material and Temporal Scope of Application*

Whereas humanitarian law only applies in relation to situations of armed conflict and to acts related to the armed conflict,[76] human rights law applies at all times.

---

[73] U.N. Commission on Human Rights, Res. 1987/58 (March 11, 1987), paras 2, 7, 9 and 10.
[74] U.N. Commission on Human Rights, U.N. Doc. E/CN.4/1992/26 (Jan. 16, 1992), para. 33; *see* also the introduction to this report by Walter Kälin and Larisa Gabriel, which catalogues and analyses the bases for the applicability of both human rights law and humanitarian law during armed conflict and occupation, reprinted in Walter Kälin (ed.), Human Rights in Times of Occupation: The Case of Kuwait (1994).
[75] U.N. G. A. Res. 46/135, U.N. Doc. A/RES/46/135 (Dec. 17, 1991) (adopted by consensus), para. 2; U.N. Commission on Human Rights, Res. 1991/67, (March 6, 1991) (adopted by 41 votes in favour, 1 against and no abstentions), para. 1.
[76] In addition to regulating the actual conduct during armed conflict, humanitarian law also contains many rules which continue to apply after the end of hostilities but which relate to acts committed during the conflict and which continue to have adverse effects, such as rules relating to the return of cultural property, compensation to victims, repatriation of prisoners, investigation of alleged war crimes and prosecution of the perpetrators, the granting of amnesty for mere participation in hostilities, accounting for the missing, maintaining grave sites, etc. In addition, humanitarian law requires certain measures to be taken by states not party to a conflict, either in peacetime such as the teaching of humanitarian law to armed forces, the dissemination of humanitarian among the civilian population, the setting up of Information Bureaux, and the marking of cultural property; or with respect to an armed conflict in a third State or between third States, in particular the obligation to ensure respect for humanitarian law *erga omnes* by exerting their influence, to the degree possible, to stop violations.

However, by the terms of the International Covenant on Civil and Political Rights, as well as the European and American Conventions on Human Rights, derogations from certain rights are possible in times of public emergency, such as situations of armed conflict. In general, derogations are not permissible under humanitarian law.[77]

4.1.1. Permissible Derogation from Human Rights Law

Historically, the European Convention on Human Rights (1950) was the first international treaty to specifically include a provision allowing for derogations from certain rights "in time of war or other public emergency threatening the life of the nation."[78] Subsequently, the International Covenant on Civil and Political Rights (1966) provides that derogation is possible "in time of public emergency which threatens the life of the nation."[79] The American Convention on Human Rights (1969) provides that derogation is possible "in time of war, public danger, or other emergency that threatens the independence or security of a State Party."[80] It is interesting to note that both the European and American Conventions on Human Rights specifically refer to war as a type of public emergency threatening the life of the nation. The International Covenant does not refer to war as it was adopted in the framework of the United Nations which had as its main aim to work for the avoidance of war.

However, derogation is the exception and is always limited. State authorities have to show that a public emergency exists which threatens the life of the nation and must officially proclaim its existence. If an armed conflict occurs, a state will need to consider whether the situation is one that amounts to an emergency "threatening the life of the nation." According to international case law, this phrase does not require that the whole nation be involved in the emergency but that the essence of the emergency consists of the fact that the normal application of human rights law – taking into account limitations that are allowed in relation to a number of rights for public safety and order – cannot be ensured in view of the nature of the emergency. If that is the case, a state party to a human rights treaty is entitled to declare a state of emergency and inform the appropriate organs, as required by the treaty concerned – or else the state continues to be bound by the whole treaty.[81]

---

[77] The only exception being that limited derogations from some rights provided for in the Fourth Geneva Convention are permitted under the conditions set out in Article 5 thereof. GC IV, *supra* note 8.
[78] Article 15(1) ECHR, *supra* note 39.
[79] Article 4(1) ICCPR, *supra* note 28.
[80] Article 27(1) ACHR, *supra* note 45.
[81] For a more complete description of the interpretation of these treaties by the treaty bodies in relation to detention, judicial guarantees and states of emergency, *see* Louise Doswald-Beck & Robert

If these conditions are met, i.e. an emergency exists and it is officially proclaimed, certain measures may be taken to derogate from some rights "to the extent strictly required by the exigencies of the situation" while other, enumerated rights may never be derogated from (*see* below). Hence, derogation by no means involves the automatic and complete suspension of all rights.

It should be noted in this respect that it is the consistent practice of human rights treaty bodies to insist on a strict interpretation of the requirement that derogation measures during a state of emergency be limited "to the extent strictly required by the exigencies of the situation." The Human Rights Committee stressed that:

> This requirement relates to the duration, geographical coverage and material scope of the state of emergency and any measures of derogation resorted to because of the emergency... The mere fact that a permissible derogation from a specific provision may, of itself, be justified by the exigencies of the situation does not obviate the requirement that specific measures taken pursuant to the derogation must also be shown to be required by the exigencies of the situation. In practice this will ensure that no provision of the Covenant, however validly derogated from, will be entirely inapplicable to the behaviour of a State party.[82]

The European and Inter-American Courts of Human Rights have taken the same approach when examining derogation measures from specific rights, stressing the need for safeguards so that the essence of the right is not totally eliminated, as well as the requirement of proportionality so that the measures are only those strictly required.[83]

Interestingly, the African Charter of Human and Peoples' Rights contains no derogation clause.[84] However, limitations to rights are allowed on the basis of Article 27(2) which states that "the rights and freedoms of each individual shall

---

Kolb, Judicial Process and Human Rights: United Nations, European, American and African Systems, Texts and Summaries of International Case-Law (2004).

[82] U.N. Human Rights Committee, General Comment No. 29, States of Emergency, U.N. Doc. CCPR/C/21/Rev.1/Add.11, (Aug. 31, 2001), para. 4 [hereinafter General Comment No. 29].

[83] *See*, e.g., European Court of Human Rights, Fox, Campbell and Hartley v. UK, Judgment (Aug. 30, 1990), Series A No. 182, para. 32; G.R. Lawless v. Ireland (Merits), Judgment (July 1, 1961), Series A No. 3, para. 37; Brannigan and McBride v. UK, Judgment (May 26, 1993), Series A No. 258-B, paras 43 and 61–65; Aksoy v. Turkey, Judgment (Dec. 18, 1996), Reports of Judgments and Decisions 1996-VI, paras 83–84; Inter-American Court of Human Rights, Castillo Petruzzi and Others case v. Peru, Judgment (May 30, 1999), Series C No. 52 (1999), para. 109.

[84] It is noteworthy that other human rights treaties similarly do not contain a derogation clause, including the International Covenant on Economic, Social and Cultural Rights and the Convention on the Rights of the Child. In its advisory opinion on Legal Consequences of the Construction of a Wall in the Occupied Palestinian Territory, the International Court of Justice thus held that the rights enshrined in these instruments are entirely applicable in occupied territory. Legal Consequences of the Construction of a Wall in the Occupied Palestinian Territory, Advisory Opinion, (July 9, 2004), ICJ Rep. 2004, 43 ILM 1009 (2004), para. 106 [hereinafter Advisory Opinion on the Wall].

be exercised with due regard to the rights of others, collective security, morality and common interest." In practice, this has been strictly interpreted by the African Commission on Human and Peoples' Rights. In a case concerning killings and disappearances during a civil war, the Commission confirmed that no derogation was possible under the African Charter on Human and Peoples' Rights, and that the government remained responsible for securing the safety and liberty of its citizens and for conducting investigations into murders.[85] In another case, the Commission confirmed that no derogations from the Charter were possible and added that limitations imposed upon rights under Article 27(2) of the African Charter "must be strictly proportionate with and absolutely necessary for the advantages which follow. Most important, a limitation may not erode a right such that the right itself becomes illusory."[86]

Finally, by the terms of the ICCPR, a state may only derogate from its obligations "provided that such measures are not inconsistent with their other obligations under international law."[87] The European and American Conventions on Human Rights contain the same requirement.[88]

In its General Comment 29 on states of emergency, the Human Rights Committee underlined and illustrated the relevance of humanitarian law in the application of this requirement:

> Furthermore, article 4, paragraph 1, requires that no measure derogating from the provisions of the Covenant may be inconsistent with the State party's other obligations under international law, particularly the rules of international humanitarian law.
> ... States parties may in no circumstances invoke article 4 of the Covenant as justification for acting in violation of humanitarian law or peremptory norms of international law, for instance by taking hostages, by imposing collective punishments, through arbitrary deprivations of liberty or by deviating from fundamental principles of fair trial, including the presumption of innocence.[89]

This built-in limitation is further evidence of the fact that the concurrent application of human rights law and humanitarian law was explicitly foreseen and taken into account when human rights treaties were adopted.

---

[85] African Commission on Human and Peoples' Rights, Civil Liberties Organisation v. Chad, Communication No. 74/92, 18th Ordinary Session, Praia, (Oct. 11, 1995), 9th Annual Activity Report, paras 21–22.
[86] African Commission on Human and Peoples' Rights, Constitutional Rights Project v. Nigeria, Communication Nos. 140/94, 141/94 and 145/95, 26th Ordinary Session, Kigali (Nov. 1–15, 1999), 13th Annual Activity Report 1999–2000, Doc. AHG/222 (XXXVI), Annex V, paras 41–42.
[87] Article 4(1) ICCPR, *supra* note 28. *See also* General Comment No. 29, *supra* note 82, para. 9.
[88] Article 15(1) ECHR, *supra* note 39; Article 27(1) ACHR, *supra* note 45.
[89] General Comment No. 29, *supra* note 82, paras 9 and 11.

4.1.2. Non-Derogable Rights

Even though some rights may be derogated from under strict conditions, as outlined above, other rights may never be derogated from at all.

In 1950, the European Convention only included a short list of non-derogable rights:[90]

- Right to life (Article 2), "except in respect of deaths resulting from lawful acts of war";
- Prohibition of torture or inhuman or degrading treatment or punishment (Article 3);
- Freedom from slavery or servitude (Article 4(1)); and
- Freedom from *ex post facto* laws (principle of legality) (Article 7).

By 1966, the International Covenant on Civil and Political Rights had extended this list to include:[91]

- Right to life (Article 6);
- Prohibition of torture or cruel, inhuman or degrading treatment or punishment (Article 7);
- Freedom from slavery and the slave-trade (Article 8(1));
- Freedom from servitude (Article 8(2));
- Prohibition of imprisonment merely for inability to fulfil a contractual obligation (Article 11);
- Freedom of *ex post facto* laws (principle of legality) (Article 15);
- The right to recognition as a person before the law (Article 16); and
- The right to freedom of thought, conscience and religion (Article 18).

It should be noted that the Human Rights Committee has stated that the provisions of the Covenant that are not listed as non-derogable contain elements that cannot, in its opinion, be made subject to lawful derogation. It has cited the following examples:

(a) All persons deprived of their liberty shall be treated with humanity and with respect for the inherent dignity of the human person. Although this right, prescribed in Article 10 of the Covenant, is not separately mentioned in the list of non-derogable rights in Article 4(2) the Committee believes that here the Covenant expresses a norm of general international law not subject to derogation. This is supported by the reference to the inherent dignity of the human person in the preamble to the Covenant and by the close connection between Articles 7 and 10.

(b) The prohibitions against taking of hostages, abductions or unacknowledged detention are not subject to derogation. The absolute nature of these prohibitions,

---

[90] Article 15(2) ECHR, *supra* note 39.
[91] Article 4(2) ICCPR, *supra* note 28.

even in times of emergency, is justified by their status as norms of general international law.

(c) The Committee is of the opinion that the international protection of the rights of persons belonging to minorities includes elements that must be respected in all circumstances. This is reflected in the prohibition against genocide in international law, in the inclusion of a non-discrimination clause in Article 4 itself (paragraph 1), as well as in the non-derogable nature of Article 18.

(d) As confirmed by the Rome Statute of the International Criminal Court, deportation or forcible transfer of population without grounds permitted under international law, in the form of forced displacement by expulsion or other coercive means from the area in which the persons concerned are lawfully present, constitutes a crime against humanity. The legitimate right to derogate from Article 12 of the Covenant during a state of emergency can never be accepted as justifying such measures.

(e) No declaration of a state of emergency made pursuant to Article 4(1), may be invoked as justification for a state party to engage itself, contrary to Article 20, in propaganda for war, or in advocacy of national, racial or religious hatred that would constitute incitement to discrimination, hostility or violence.[92]

The 1969 American Convention contains the most extensive list of non-derogable rights and includes, in general, "the judicial guarantees essential for the protection of such rights" as being non-derogable:[93]

– Right to juridical personality (Article 3);
– Right to life (Article 4);
– Right to humane treatment (Article 5);
– Freedom from slavery (Article 6);
– Freedom from *ex post facto* laws (principle of legality) (Article 9);
– Freedom of conscience and religion (Article 12);
– Rights of the family (Article 17);
– Right to a name (Article 18);
– Rights of the child (Article 19);
– Right to a nationality (Article 20);
– Right to participate in government (Article 23); and as mentioned above
– "the judicial guarantees essential for the protection of such rights."[94]

The fact that a right is non-derogable means that even in situations of armed conflict states remain responsible, *per se*, to guarantee these rights to all persons under their jurisdiction. Furthermore, the fact that several non-derogable rights significantly

---

[92] General Comment No. 29, *supra* note 82, para. 13.
[93] Article 27(2) ACHR, *supra* note 45.
[94] *Id.*

overlap with provisions of humanitarian law further underlines their particular relevance in times of armed conflict. Contrarily, the argument can easily be made that the rights that have not been listed as non-derogable but which are recognized under humanitarian law should also be non-derogable in practice. Indeed, if states have agreed, under humanitarian law, to respect certain rights in times of armed conflict, including civil war, there would be, *prima facie*, no justification for ever derogating from these rights in other, less serious situations of public emergency. The Human Rights Committee has used this argument in its General Comment No. 29 on states of emergency to state that certain elements of the right to a fair trial are, in fact, non-derogable:

> As certain elements of the right to a fair trial are explicitly guaranteed under international humanitarian law during armed conflict, the Committee finds no justification for derogation from these guarantees during other emergency situations. The Committee is of the opinion that the principles of legality and the rule of law require that fundamental requirements of fair trial must be respected during a state of emergency. Only a court of law may try and convict a person for a criminal offence. The presumption of innocence must be respected. In order to protect non-derogable rights, the right to take proceedings before a court to enable the court to decide without delay on the lawfulness of detention, must not be diminished by a State party's decision to derogate from the Covenant.[95]

4.2. *Personal Scope of Application*

Whereas humanitarian law applies to all parties to the conflict, including armed opposition groups, human rights treaty law is only binding upon states themselves.[96] This means that acts committed by state armed forces, and other groups for which the state bears responsibility, are fully covered by human rights treaties, whereas acts committed by armed opposition groups are not. Under specific circumstances, responsibility for violations of human rights treaties could still be attached to the state for violations committed by armed opposition groups. This would be the case, for example, where it is established that the state had failed to adequately protect the right to life of its citizens.[97]

---

[95] General Comment No. 29, *supra* note 82, para. 16.
[96] By their terms, human rights treaties only bind states parties. On the other hand, it can be argued, e.g. on the basis of the practice of the U.N. Security Council and General Assembly, that under customary human rights law armed opposition groups have certain obligations, particularly if they control part of the territory. For an analysis of practice in this respect, *see*, e.g., Christian Tomuschat, *The Applicability of Human Rights Law to Insurgent Movements, in* Fischer, *supra* note 2, at 573.
[97] This may be the result, for example, of a failure on the part of the state to carry out an effective investigation into allegations of unlawful deprivation of the right to life. *See*, e.g., Human Rights Committee, General Comment No. 6 (Article 6), (July 30, 1982), para. 4; Civil Liberties Organisation v. Chad, *supra* note –, para. 22; Selçuk and Asker v. Turkey, Judgment (April 24, 1998); Kaya v.

4.3. Geographic Scope of Application

International humanitarian law has been specifically designed to apply in any territory, whether national or foreign, where armed conflict takes place. Human rights treaties, on the other hand, specify that they are to be applied by states party thereto wherever they have jurisdiction. The question thus arises whether human rights treaties apply outside national territory, for example during a military occupation.[98] The requirement of jurisdiction has been interpreted as meaning that human rights law applies wherever state organs have *effective control* over an area outside national territory or whenever they exercise *authority and control* over a person abroad.

Article 2 ICCPR specifies that "[e]ach State Party to the present Covenant undertakes to respect and to ensure to all individuals within its territory and subject to its jurisdiction the rights recognized in the present Covenant." State practice has interpreted this somewhat widely. For example, the U.N. Special Rapporteur for Iraqi-occupied Kuwait was instructed by states to report on respect for or the violation of human rights by Iraq in Kuwait, even though Kuwait could not be considered to be its "territory" and recognition of any formal jurisdiction had not occurred. As mentioned above, the Special Rapporteur analysed the implementation of the provisions of the Covenant by Iraq in Kuwait and his report was welcomed by states.

The Human Rights Committee has also held that Article 2 ICCPR does not stand in the way of the extraterritorial application of the Covenant. In a case concerning the arrest and detention of a dissident Uruguayan national by Uruguayan forces in Argentina, the Human Rights Committee held that it would be "unconscionable" to interpret Article 2 of the Covenant "so as to permit a State party to perpetrate violations of the Covenant on the territory of another State, which violations it

---

Turkey, Judgment, (March 28, 2000), para. 108 and Avsar v. Turkey, Judgment (July 10, 2001), paras 394 and 408; Inter-American Commission on Human Rights, Case 10.559 (Peru), Report (March 1, 1996), Section V(2); Inter-American Court of Human Rights, Velásquez Rodríguez Case, Judgment (July 29, 1988), para. 181.

[98] *See generally*, John Cerone, *Out of Bounds? Considering the Reach of International Human Rights Law*, Center for Human Rights and Global Justice, New York University School of Law, Working Paper No. 5, 2006 [hereinafter Cerone]; Cordula Droege, *The Interplay between International Humanitarian Law and International Human Rights Law in Situations of Armed Conflict*, 40 Israel L. Rev. (forthcoming 2007); Matteo Tondini, *UN Peace Operations: The Last Frontier of the Extraterritorial Application of Human Rights*, 44 The Military Law and the Law of War Review 175 (2005) and Jochen Abr. Frowein, *The Relationship Between Human Rights Regimes and Regimes of Belligerent Occupation*, 28 IYHR 1 (1998).

could not perpetrate on its own territory."[99] In its General Comment 31, the Committee therefore stated that:

> States Parties are required by article 2, paragraph 1, to respect and to ensure the Covenant rights to all persons who may be within their territory and to all persons subject to their jurisdiction. This means that a State party must respect and ensure the rights laid down in the Covenant to anyone *within the power or effective control* of that State Party, even if not situated within the territory of the State Party.... This principle also applies to those within the power or effective control of the forces of a State Party acting outside its territory, regardless of the circumstances in which such power or effective control was obtained, such as forces constituting a national contingent of a State Party assigned to an international peace-keeping or peace-enforcement operations.[100]

The jurisprudence of the Human Rights Committee has confirmed this approach, in particular in situations of military occupation,[101] as well as with regard to national troops taking part in peacekeeping operations.[102]

Article 1 of the European and American Conventions on Human Rights specify that the Conventions are to be applied by States Parties to persons "within their jurisdiction" and "subject to their jurisdiction," respectively. This has been interpreted by their treaty bodies as meaning that the Conventions apply in areas abroad over which they have "effective control" and that they apply to persons over whom they have authority and control. In *Loizidou* v. *Turkey* in 1995, concerning the situation in northern Cyprus, the European Court of Human Rights held that a

---

[99] Human Rights Committee, López Burgos v. Uruguay, U.N. Doc. CCPR/C/13/D/52/1979 (July 29, 1981), para. 12(3); *see also* Celiberti v. Uruguay, U.N. Doc. CCPR/C/13/D/56/1979 (July 29, 1981), para. 10(3). *See generally* Dominic McGoldrick, *Extraterritorial Application of the International Convenant on Civil and Political Rights, in* Extraterritorial Application of Human Rights Treaties 41 (Fons Coomans & Menno T. Kamminga eds., 2004) and Martin Scheinin, *Extraterritorial Effect of the International Covenant on Civilian and Political Rights, in* Extraterritorial Application of Human Rights Treaties 73 (Fons Coomans & Menno T. Kamminga eds., 2004) [hereinafter Coomans & Kamminga eds.].

[100] Human Rights Committee, General Comment No. 31, Nature of the General Legal Obligation Imposed on States Parties to the Covenant, U.N. Doc. CCPR/C/21/Rev.1/Add.13 (May 26, 2004), para. 10 (emphasis added). *Contra* Michael Dennis, *Application of Human Rights Treaties Extraterritorially in Times of Armed Conflict and Military Occupation*, 99 Am. J. Int'l L. 119 (2005).

[101] *See, e.g.*, Human Rights Committee, Concluding Observations on Cyprus, U.N. Doc. CCPR/C/79/Add.39 (Sept. 21, 1994), para. 3; Concluding Observations on Israel, U.N. Doc. CCPR/C/79/Add.93 (Aug. 18, 1998), para. 10; Concluding Observations on Israel, U.N. Doc. CCPR/CO/78/ISR (Aug. 21, 2003), para. 11.

[102] *See, e.g.*, Human Rights Committee, Concluding Observations on Belgium, U.N. Doc. CCPR/C/79/Add.99 (Nov. 19, 1998), para. 14; Concluding Observations on the Netherlands, U.N. Doc. CCPR/CO/72/NET (Aug. 27, 2001), para. 8; Concluding Observations on Belgium, U.N. Doc. CCPR/CO/81/BEL (Aug. 12, 2004), para. 6.

State party is bound to respect the Convention "when as a consequence of military action – whether lawful or unlawful – it exercises effective control of an area outside its national territory."[103] In the case of *Banković* against seventeen NATO member States, the European Court confirmed that it applied the European Convention extra-territorially when a

> State, through the effective control of the relevant territory and its inhabitants abroad as a consequence of military occupation or through the consent, invitation or acquiescence of the Government of that territory, exercises all or some of the public powers normally to be exercised by that Government.[104]

In later cases, the Court further specified that acts committed against an individual, while under the control of state agents, also engage state responsibility, for example during arrest and detention abroad and during a military operation abroad.[105] The United Kingdom Court of Appeals has understood the case law of the European Court of Human Rights in a similar way and followed it.[106] The same yardstick of authority and control has been used by the Inter-American Commission on Human Rights to evaluate the extraterritorial applicability of the American Convention on Human Rights.[107]

---

[103] Loizidou v. Turkey, Preliminary Objections, Judgment (March 23, 1995), Series A Vol. 310, para. 62. *See also* Loizidou v. Turkey, Judgment (Dec. 18, 1996), Reports 1996-VI, § 56 and Cyprus v. Turkey, Judgment (May 10, 2001), Reports 2001-IV, para. 77 ("effective *overall* control.")

[104] Banković v. Belgium, the Czech Republic, Denmark, France, Germany, Greece, Hungary, Iceland, Italy, Luxembourg, the Netherlands, Norway, Poland, Portugal, Spain, Turkey and the United Kingdom, Decision as to Admissibility (Dec. 12, 2001), para. 71.

[105] Öcalan v. Turkey, Judgment, (March 12, 2003), para. 93 (Turkey was held responsible for the treatment of the applicant during his arrest and detention by Turkish agents in Kenya) and Issa and others v. Turkey, Judgment (Nov. 16, 2004), para. 71 (Turkey was held responsible for the treatment of Kurdish shepherds in Northern Iraq after a Turkish military incursion). For an analysis of the case-law of the European system, *see*, e.g., Luigi Condorelli, *La protection des droits de l'homme lors d'actions militaires menées à l'étranger*, Collegium, No. 32, Summer 2005, College of Europe, Bruges, p. 89 and Rick Lawson, *Life after* Banković*: On the Extraterritorial Application of the European Convention on Human Rights*, *in* Coomans & Kamminga eds., *supra* note 99, at 83.

[106] Court of Appeals, R v. the Secretary of State for Defence, ex parte Al-Skeini and others, Judgment (Dec. 21, 2005), paras 62–112. *See* Philip Leach, *The British Military in Iraq – The Applicability of the espace juridique Doctrine under the European Convention on Human Rights*, 3 Public Law 448 (2005).

[107] Inter-American Commission on Human Rights, Case 11.589, Armando Alejandre Jr. and Others v. Cuba, Report No. 86/99 (Sep. 29, 1999), paras 24–25; Case 10.951, Coard v. the United States, 109/99 (Sept. 29, 1999), para. 37. For an analysis of the case-law of the Inter-American system, *see*, e.g., Douglass Cassel, *Extraterritorial Application of Inter-American Human Rights Instruments*, *in* Coomans & Kamminga eds., *supra* note 99, at 175; Christina Cerna, *Extraterritorial Application of the Human Rights Instruments of the Inter-American System*, *in* Coomans & Kamminga eds., *supra* note 99, at 141; Cerone, *supra* note 98; John Cerone, The Application of Regional Human

In situations of non-international armed conflict the issue of extraterritorial application of human rights law should not pose itself, except in situations where hostilities spill over into the territory of a third state. In such situations, the same practical questions as those faced in situations of international armed conflict and occupation would occur.

5. Concurrent Application

In international as in national law, it is not infrequent that rules from two or more branches of the law are relevant and apply to one particular event or situation. However, when these rules apply concurrently and are in a conflict that cannot be reconciled, resort is to be had to rules to resolve such a conflict. One such rule, for example, is that a later rule trumps an earlier one (*lex posterior derogat priori*).[108] Another rule is that a more specific rule trumps a more general rule (*lex specialis derogat generali*).[109] There are not many examples, however, whereby so-called "general" rules of human rights law would be in conflict with "more specific" rules of humanitarian law. The most obvious example would be the legal regime applicable to prisoners of war. This regime is contrary to human rights law in at least one important aspect, as it does not allow such prisoners to challenge their detention in court (through a so-called writ of *habeas corpus*). So the specific regime for prisoners of war deviates from and trumps the human rights requirement of *habeas corpus*. The prisoner-of-war regime is not entirely contrary to human rights law, however, as it does not actually amount to an arbitrary deprivation of liberty. Indeed, the prisoner-of-war regime is firmly established in the Third Geneva Convention, which is universally ratified. The grounds for the deprivation of liberty of prisoners of war are well-established in practice, namely denying the enemy of its combatants, members of armed forces, until the end of active hostilities. In addition, certain procedures for the supervision of prisoner of war camps exist.

Rights Law Beyond Regional Frontiers: The Inter-American Commission on Human Rights and US Activities in Iraq, ASIL Insight, *available at* www.asil.org, posted Oct. 25, 2005.

[108] *See*, e.g., Jean Salmon (ed.), *Dictionnaire de Droit International Public*, Bruylant, Brussels, 2001, pp. 651–652 [hereinafter Salmon].

[109] *See id*. 652. *See generally* Martti Koskenniemi, Study on the Function and Scope of the Lex Specialis Rule and the Question of "Self-Contained Regimes", International Law Commission, U.N. Doc. ILC (LVI)/SG/FIL/CRD.1 and Add 1 (2004); Anja Lindroos, *Addressing Norm Conflict in a Fragmented Legal System: The Doctrine of* Lex Specialis, 74 Nordic Journal of International Law 24 (2005) and Joost Pauwelyn, *Conflict of Norms in Public International Law: How WTO Law Relates to Other Rules of International Law* 385–439 (2003).

The continued internment of prisoners of war after the end of active hostilities, on the other hand, would amount to an arbitrary detention as the reasons for internment no longer exist.

Most other issues that have come up in practice do not in fact concern a conflict between human rights law and humanitarian law but rather imprecision in human rights law, or contrarily, in humanitarian law. Therefore the main question in practice is rather when and to what extent human rights law should be interpreted in the light of humanitarian law and *vice versa*.

The most obvious example of this issue is the protection of the right to life under human rights law. There is no inherent conflict between the right to life, as formulated in human rights treaties, and the rules on the conduct of hostilities under humanitarian law. Human rights treaties only prohibit the "arbitrary" deprivation of the right to life. While in peacetime situations, the criterion of arbitrariness has an important role to play, e.g. in the evaluation of the use of lethal force by law enforcement officials, it also serves to accommodate the continued application of the right to life during armed conflict; a deprivation of life in armed conflict which is consistent with humanitarian law would not be arbitrary.[110] The European Convention on Human Rights uses a slightly different formulation to arrive at the same result, prohibiting the intentional deprivation of life but listing the permissible exceptions to this prohibition. While this list does not include lawful acts of war, the right to life in the derogation clause of the Convention is listed as non-derogable "except in respect of death resulting from lawful acts of war." The lawfulness of such "acts of war" has to be assessed on the basis of the specific rules of humanitarian law.

In its advisory opinion on the Legality of the Threat or Use of Nuclear Weapons in 1996, the International Court of Justice confirmed the continued applicability of human rights law within armed conflict, including the non-derogable right to life. The Court also held that in a situation of armed conflict the human right to life has to be interpreted in the light of humanitarian law:

> The Court observes that the protection of the International Covenant of Civil and Political Rights does not cease in times of war, except by operation of Article 4 of the Covenant whereby certain provisions may be derogated from in a time of national emergency. Respect for the right to life is not, however, such a provision. In principle, the right not arbitrarily to be deprived of one's life applies also in hostilities. The test of what is an arbitrary deprivation of life, however, then falls to be determined by the applicable *lex specialis*, namely, the law applicable in armed conflict which is designed to regulate the conduct of hostilities. Thus whether a particular loss of life, through

---

[110] It can be argued, however, that in addition to humanitarian law, human rights law still has some import on the interpretation of the right to life in armed conflict; *see* Louise Doswald-Beck, *The Right to Life in Armed Conflict: Does International Humanitarian Law Provide All the Answers?*, 88 Int'l Rev. Red Cross 881 (2006).

the use of a certain weapon in warfare, is to be considered an arbitrary deprivation of life contrary to Article 6 of the Covenant, can only be decided by reference to the law applicable in armed conflict and not deduced from the terms of the Covenant itself.[111]

It seems that the Court used the term *lex specialis* in its ordinary meaning as the "special law" that deals with an issue in more detail, and not in the technical meaning, as a device to solve a contradiction between two rules, as there is no inherent contradiction between the prohibition to "arbitrarily" deprive someone of his or her right to life and the rules on the conduct of hostilities under humanitarian law. It is interesting to note that the Court only referred to "*lex specialis*" as such and not to the conflict rule "*lex specialis derogat generali.*" The Court thus endorsed the use of humanitarian law in interpreting the concept of "arbitrary" deprivation of the right to life within the specific context of armed conflict. The judgment cannot be read to suggest that humanitarian law replaces human rights in its entirety during situations of armed conflict. Such a reading would contradict the very wording of the judgment as well as the express terms of the relevant treaties.

The Court made this clear in its subsequent advisory opinion on the Legal Consequences of the Construction of a Wall in Occupied Palestinian Territory:

> More generally, the Court considers that the protection offered by human rights conventions does not cease in case of armed conflict, save through the effect of provisions for derogation of the kind to be found in Article 4 of the International Covenant on Civil and Political Rights. As regards the relationship between international humanitarian law and human rights law, there are thus three possible situations: some rights may be exclusively matters of international humanitarian law; others may be exclusively matters of human rights law; yet others may be matters of both these branches of international law. In order to answer the question put to it, the Court will have to take into consideration both these branches of international law, namely human rights law and, as *lex specialis*, international humanitarian law.[112]

While the Court distinguished between three categories of rights, it did not specify the content of each of these categories, however.

---

[111] Legality of the Threat or Use of Nuclear Weapons, Advisory Opinion (July 8, 1996), 1996 ICJ Rep. 226, para. 25. For commentary *see*, e.g., Louise Doswald-Beck, "*International Humanitarian Law and the Advisory Opinion of the International Court of Justice on the Legality of the Threat or Use of Nuclear Weapons*, 316 Int'l Rev. Red Cross 35 (1997) and Dale Stephens, *Human Rights and Armed Conflict: The Advisory Opinion of the International Court of Justice in the Nuclear Weapons Case*, 4 Yale Hum. Rts. & Dev. L.J. 1 (2001).

[112] Advisory Opinion on the Wall, *supra* note 84, para. 106. For commentary *see*, e.g., Susan C. Breau, *The Humanitarian Law Implications of the Advisory Opinion on the Legal Consequences of the Construction of a Wall in the Occupied Palestinian Territory, in* Breau & Jachec-Neale eds., *supra* note 2, at 191 and Michael Kelly, *Critical Analysis of the International Court of Justice Ruling on Israel's Security Barrier*, 29 Fordham Int'l L.J. 181 (2005).

On the basis of its Statute, the ICJ can apply any branch of international law that is relevant. The human rights treaty bodies, on the other hand, are more restricted, in principle, as they are set up by a treaty that exhaustively defines the rights they have to monitor. Hence, they can only import humanitarian law concepts through interpretation, for example through the interpretation of the derogation clauses or the interpretation of the concept of "arbitrary" deprivation of the right to life. An attempt by the Inter-American Commission to have the Court declare certain state acts in violation of Article 4 ACHR (right to life) as well as common Article 3 of the 1949 Geneva Conventions was rejected by the Court which stated that it only had the competence to determine whether acts of states were compatible with the Convention itself, but not with the 1949 Geneva Conventions.[113] This put to rest the attempt by the Commission to apply humanitarian law directly which had started a few years earlier in the *Tablada* Case.[114] The Court's position, however, appears to be logical and, more importantly, does not stand in the way of the Court (or the Commission) relying on humanitarian law to interpret the arbitrariness of a deprivation of the right to life under Article 4 of the Convention in a situation of armed conflict. The European Court has also been hesitant to explicitly refer to humanitarian law, even though its terms would clearly allow for it, for example, to assess whether a deprivation of life "resulting from lawful acts of war" would violate the Convention. So far the Court has, rightly or wrongly, preferred to assess the lawfulness of acts committed in situations of conflict under the terms of the Convention, even though a strong flavour of humanitarian law language is sometimes given.[115]

---

[113] Inter-American Court of Human Rights, Las Palmeras Case, Judgment on Preliminary Objections (Feb. 4, 2000), Ser. C No. 67 (2000), para. 33 ("The result of this operation will always be an opinion in which the Court will say whether or not that norm or that fact is compatible with the American Convention. The latter has only given the Court competence to determine whether the acts or the norms of the States are compatible with the Convention itself and not with the 1949 Geneva Convention"). *See* Fanny Martin, *Application du droit international humanitaire par la Cour interaméricaine des droits de l'homme*, 844 Int'l Rev. Red Cross 1037 (2001).

[114] Inter-American Commission on Human Rights, Juan Carlos Abella v. Argentina, Case No. 11.137 (Oct. 30, 1997), Report No. 55/97, OEA/Ser/L/V/II.95, Doc. 7 rev., p. 271. See Liezbeth Zegveld, *The Inter-American Commission on Human Rights and International Humanitarian Law: A Comment on the Tablada Case*, 324 Int'l Rev. Red Cross 505 (1998).

[115] *See*, in particular, Ergi v. Turkey, Judgment (July 28, 1998), Reports of Judgments and Decisions 1998-IV, para. 79 ("The responsibility of the State is not confined to circumstances where there is significant evidence that misdirected fire from agents of the State has killed a civilian. It may also be engaged where they fail to take all feasible precautions in the choice of means and methods of a security operation mounted against an opposing group with a view to avoiding and, in any event, to minimising, incidental loss of civilian life."). *See also* Özkan v. Turkey, Judgment (April 6, 2004), para. 406 and the so-called Chechen cases Isayeva, Yusupova and Bazayeva v. Russia, Judgment (Feb. 24, 2005), para. 177 and Isayeva v. Russia, Judgment (Feb. 24, 2005), para. 176.

The reverse question – when and to what extent humanitarian law can be interpreted in the light of human rights law – is less tested, as there is no humanitarian law court as such, other than criminal courts and tribunals. However, if *lex specialis* as a principle other than conflict solving applies to the concurrent application of international humanitarian law and human rights law, it ought to work in both directions.[116] There clearly are areas where human rights law is the more specific body of law that has addressed issues in more detail. In some of these areas, humanitarian law treaties expressly provide that human rights law continues to apply. Article 72 AP I thus provides that the provisions on fundamental guarantees in Article 75 AP I are additional to "other rules of international law relating to the protection of fundamental human rights during international armed conflict." Similarly, the preamble of Additional Protocol II recalls that, in addition to its provisions, "international instruments relating to human rights offer a basic protection to the human person." This is particularly relevant in interpreting and applying the provisions of Protocol II which mirror human rights principles, such as those concerning fundamental guarantees (Article 4), deprivation of liberty (Article 5) or penal prosecutions (Article 6).[117] In these areas, human rights law is the more specific law and ought to be relied upon to interpret protection under humanitarian law during armed conflict.

The explicit references to human rights law in the Additional Protocols indicate that the latter cannot be read as an exhaustive listing of rights in armed conflict and that humanitarian law can be interpreted in the light of human rights law to the extent that it continues to apply in armed conflict. While the latter point may of course pose a problem for certain rights, it should be underlined that a number

---

See William Abresch, *A Human Rights Law of Internal Armed Conflict: The European Court of Human Rights in Chechnya*, 16 Eur. J. Int. Law 741 (2005); Michael Bothe, *Die Anwendung der Europäischen Menschenrechtskonvention in bewaffneten Konflikten – eine Überforderung*, 65 ZaöRV 615 (2005); Hans-Joachim Heintze, The European Court of Human Rights and the Implementation of Human Rights Standards During Armed Conflict, 45 GYIL 60 (2002); Aisling Reidy, *The Approach of the European Commission and Court of Human Rights to International Humanitarian Law*, 34 Int'l Rev. Red Cross 513 (1998); Peter Rowe, *The Application of the European Convention on Human Rights during an International Armed Conflict*, in International Conflict and Security Law – Essays in Memory of Hilaire McCoubrey 185 (Richard Burchill, Nigel D. White & Justin Morris eds, 2005).

[116] *See also* Orna Ben-Naftali & Yuval Shany, Living in Denial: The Application of Human Rights in Occupied Territories, 37 Israel L.Rev. 17 (2003–2004) and Nancie Prud'homme, Lex Specialis: *Oversimplifying a More Complex and Multifaceted Relationship?*, 40 Israel L.Rev. (forthcoming 2007).

[117] An area in which human rights law is more developed than international humanitarian law is the prohibition of arbitrary deprivation of liberty, particularly in non-international armed conflict. *See*, e.g., Jelena Pejic, *Procedural Principles and Safeguards for Internment/Administrative Detention in Armed Conflict and Other Situations of Violence*, 858 Int'l Rev. Red Cross 375 (2005).

of important rights are explicitly listed as non-derogable and that others have been similarly recognised in state practice and jurisprudence (see above).

7. Conclusion

The fact that human rights law continues to apply during armed conflict is borne out by the terms of human rights treaties, state practice and international case law, including that of the ICJ. This article has sought to provide an overview of the different origins and enforcement mechanisms of human rights law and humanitarian law. On this basis it has argued that the interest of victims to pursue remedies under human rights law and procedures is at the origin of the renewed interest in the concurrent application of both branches of international law. However, the enforcement by courts or committees of specific rights in the context of armed conflict is subject to a number of technical hurdles, including the following:

- the right has to be materially applicable, i.e. non-derogable or not (validly) derogated from;
- the state has to be responsible for the behaviour in question because it is attributable to it, most commonly because it had been committed by state agents;
- the state has to have jurisdiction over the acts when committed extraterritorially, i.e. the acts have taken place in an area under effective overall control of the state or the acts involve persons over whom the state exercises authority and control.

Most importantly, in relevant cases, human rights law has to be interpreted in the light of humanitarian law. This is particularly the case for the protection of the right to life, which will almost invariably be at issue during an armed conflict. Though the import of this right, it is possible that human rights courts and committees will exercise even greater judicial review of action in armed conflict in the future than is already the case. Such a development would be the logical consequence of the lack of sufficient enforcement mechanisms for victims under humanitarian law. In the face of violations of their person, dignity or property, victims will inevitably search for a forum.

Chapter IX

The Implementation of International Humanitarian Law by Human Rights Courts: The Example of the Inter-American Human Rights System

Emiliano J. Buis[*]

1. *Introduction*

It remains an obvious fact that, from a theoretical point of view, the relationship between human rights law (HRL) and international humanitarian law (IHL) can no longer be neglected. Even if IHL is only applicable during situations of armed conflicts, it has been widely accepted that both branches of law share a basic hardcore of well-defined rules, which aim at the protection of the human person[1] and constitute a homogenous legal *corpus*. Due to this close articulation and the absence of courts specifically created to decide on IHL violations, human rights tribunals have been traditionally understood as an effective way of attributing responsibility to states for the violation of humanitarian law.[2] It is therefore

---

[*] Associate Professor in Public International Law and International Humanitarian Law, Faculty of Law, University of Buenos Aires, Argentina. Associate Professor in Public International Law and Human Rights Law, University of the Centre of the Province of Buenos Aires (UNICEN), Azul, Argentina. Professor in International Humanitarian Law, School of National Defence (EDENA), Ministry of Defence, Argentina. I would like to thank hereby the editors of the book for helpful suggestions and comments. For all the errors overlooked and advice spurred, I am, obviously, solely responsible.

[1] *See* Section 1 Chapter 1.

[2] "As the implementation mechanisms of that law are insufficient and the elaboration of State reports and individual complaints procedures is not to be expected for it in the very near future, the existing human rights procedures gain in practical importance" (Hans-Joachim Heintze, *On the Relationship between Human Rights Law Protection and International Humanitarian Law*, 86 Int'l Rev. Red Cross 812 (2004)). On the overstep of enforcement mechanisms, see Francisco Forrest Martin, Stephen J. Schnably, Richard Wilson, Jonathan Simon & Mark Tushnet, International Human Rights and Humanitarian Law. Treaties, Cases, and Analysis (2006).

possible to discuss how the mechanisms for enforcing HRL are used to implement the specific rules of IHL.[3]

However, this traditional way to explore the connection between human rights courts and IHL does not seem so precise and neat once the decisions and reports issued by the supervising mechanisms are examined. Even if nothing within the set of humanitarian law rules seems to impede their practical application by human rights courts, the situation becomes different as soon as the particular jurisdiction and competence of each tribunal is addressed. In this sense, the Inter-American Human Rights system, as a regional mechanism dealing with the protection of human rights in the continent, has found it difficult to take in hand the matter of its competence to refer to IHL when a specific situation of internal conflict is submitted. In fact, once precedents are studied, it turns out to be quite obvious that the Inter-American system itself has been always faced to concrete problems arising from the application *per se* of the main humanitarian conventional instruments which seem to be related to the more general provisions of the American Convention of San José (ACHR).[4]

In the framework of this grey situation, this paper reviews the relationship between IHL and HRL on the one hand, and the applicable laws and competent fora on the other. By briefly examining the vocabulary used by the regional Commission and the Court – in order to shed some light on the expressions denoting the ways in which IHL and HRL intermingle – I seek to demonstrate how and to which extent regional mechanisms to protect human rights are (or not) legally able in their praxis to make direct recourse to a set of rules – exclusively applicable in times of armed conflicts – that is not explicitly available in their own framework of competence.

---

[3] The importance of the decisions of tribunals dealing with HRL in the promotion of IHL is undeniable, as it has been demonstrated in the recent ICRC Study on Customary Rules of International Humanitarian Law (Jean-Marie Henckaerts & Louise Doswald-Beck eds., 2005). Nevertheless, to what precise extent the regional human rights case law is suitable to examine the protection of individuals in the context of armed conflicts has been analysed by Heike Krieger, *A Conflict of Norms: The Relationship between Humanitarian Law and Human Rights Law in the ICRC Customary Law Study*, 11(2) J. Confl. & Sec. L. 265 (2006).

[4] American Convention on Human Rights, signed Nov. 22, 1969, O.A.S.T.S. No. 36, O.A.S. Off. Rec. OEA/Ser. L/V/II.23, Doc. 21, Rev. 6 (1969) [9 I.L.M. 673 (1970)], entry into force on July 18, 1978) [hereinafter ACHR]. On this aspect, *see* Lindsay Moir, *Decommissioned? International Humanitarian Law and the Inter-American Human Rights System*, 25 Hum. Rights Quart. 182 (2003) [hereinafter Moir].

2. IHL and HRL: Convergence and/or Opposition

As all the contributions to this collective volume suggest, the true nature of the ways in which HRL and IHL relate to each other has never been considered a simple task to deal with. In historical terms, the legal inconvenience of describing this relationship soon made two contradictory opinions make their way in contemporary doctrine. On the one hand, some legal scholars support an "integrationist" view, overstating the importance of their similarities and tending to promote the merger of what they considered two intimately related branches of law.[5] On the other, some scholars subscribe to a "separatist" approach, considering that IHL and HRL are two distinct and almost incompatible systems, whose unification might become not only useless but also dangerous for an appropriate and consistent protection of individuals.[6]

The danger acknowledged by this last perspective is clearly perceived in those interstitial areas in which neither HRL nor IHL seem fully applicable, like internal disturbances or tensions.[7] We know *a priori* that human rights shall be protected

---

[5] In fact, this positive position favors considering the existence of a unique international legal system that globally aims at protecting human beings, the laws of armed conflict only representing one of its kinds. Mario Madrid-Malo Garizábal, *Convergencia y complementariedad del derecho internacional humanitario y el derecho internacional de los derechos humanos*, in Conflicto armado y derecho humanitario (1994), Ramiro Píriz Ballón, *El derecho internacional humanitario y la proteccion de la persona humana en los conflictos armados no internacionales: hacia nuevas formas de aplicación de sus principios y normas*, in Héctor Gros Espiell *Amicorum Liber*: Persona Humana y Derecho Internacional 1185 (Vol. II, Héctor Gros Espiell ed., 1997), Raúl E. Vinuesa, *Interface, Correspondence and Convergence of Human Rights and International Humanitarian Law*, 1 YB of Int'l Humanitarian Law 69 (1998), Sylvain Vité, Les procedures internationales d'établissement des faits dans la mise en œuvre du droit international humanitaire 50 (1999), Gabriella Venturini, *Diritto umanitario e diritti dell'uomo: rispettivi ambiti di intervento e punti di confluenza*, 14 Rivista internazionale dei diritti dell'uomo 49 (2001), Antônio A. Cançado Trindade, El Derecho Internacional de los Derechos Humanos 249 (2001), René Provost, International Human Rights and Humanitarian Law (2002).

[6] On these two contradictory theses, *see* Robert Quentin-Baxter, *Human Rights and Humanitarian Law – Confluence or Conflict*, 9 Austl. Y.B. Int'l L. 94 (1985), Hans-Peter Gasser, *International Humanitarian Law and Human Rights Law: Joint Venture or Mutual Exclusion?*, 45 German YB of Int'l L. 149 (2002) and Alexander Orakhelashvili, *The Interaction between Human Rights and Humanitarian Law: A Case of Fragmentation?*, Paper presented at the Institute for International Law and Justice Colloquium, New York University, Feb. 26, 2007. Concerning the difference between both branches, especially in the confusion that mat arise from the language employed, *see* Noam Lubell, *Challenges in Applying Human Rights Law to Armed Conflict*, 87 Int'l Rev. Red Cross 737 (2005).

[7] *See* Yoram Dinstein, *The International Law of Civil Wars and Human Rights*, 6 Isr. YB of Hum. Rights 62 (1976), Asbjørn Eide, *Troubles et tensions intérieurs*, in Les dimensions internationales du droit humanitaire 279 (UNESCO & Institut Henri Dunant, 1986), Rosemary Abi-Saab, Droit

in all times, with the sole exception of the limits imposed by national security or public order.⁸ If the scope and intensity of disturbances increase, so as to put a nation at stake, a state of emergency can be declared, as provided by treaty, some rights can be suspended.⁹ However, at this moment IHL rules might still not be applicable because the threshold of applicability, i.e. an armed conflict, has not yet been reached.¹⁰ As a result, during internal tensions individuals become unprotected in the midst of a legal lacuna. The paradox is evident: just when human beings need the highest degree of assistance, IHL and HRL happen to overstep in a disorganized manner and, therefore, efficacy cannot be properly achieved.¹¹ With this

---

humanitaire et conflits internes. Origines et évolution de la réglementation internationale (1986), Hernán Salinas Burgos, *The Application of International Humanitarian Law as Compared to Human Rights Law in Situations Qualified as Internal Armed Conflict, Internal Disturbances and Tensions, or Public Emergency, with Special Reference to War Crimes and Political Crimes*, in Implementation of International Humanitarian Law 1 (Frits Kalshoven & Yves Sandoz eds., 1989), Françoise Hampson, *Human Rights and Humanitarian Law in Internal Conflicts*, in Armed Conflict and the New Law 53 (Michael A. Meyer ed., Vol. II, 1993), Rosemary Abi-Saab, *Human Rights and Humanitarian Law in Internal Conflicts*, in Human Rights and Humanitarian Law. The Quest for Universality 107 (Daniel Warner ed., 1997), Tom Hadden & Colin Harvey, *The Law of Internal Crisis and Conflict*, 833 Int'l Rev. Red Cross 119 (1999).

⁸ Cf. Article 4 of the International Covenant on Civil and Political Rights (G.A., Res. 2200A/XXI, Dec. 16, 1966, 52, U.N. Doc. A/6316 (1966), 999 U.N.T.S. 171, entry into force on March 23, 1976); Article 15 of the European Convention for the Protection of Human Rights and Fundamental Freedoms (Nov. 4, 1950, 213 U.N.T.S. 221) and Article 27 ACHR, *supra* note 4. On these situations of emergency, *see* Anna-Lena Svensson-McCarthy, The International Law of Human Rights and States of Exception: With Special Reference to the Travaux Préparatoires and Case-Law of the International Monitoring Organs (1998), Leandro Despouy, Los derechos humanos y los estados de excepción (1999).

⁹ In fact, IHL conventional instruments explicitly exclude situations of internal disturbances and tensions, such as riots, isolated and sporadic acts of violence such as riots from its field of application (cf. Article 1(2) Protocol Additional to the Geneva Conventions of 12 August 1949, and Relating to the Protection of Victims of Non-International Armed Conflicts (Protocol II), June 8, 1977, 1125 U.N.T.S. 609). Only when these activities become generalized and develop into a non-international armed conflict Common Article 3 to the four Geneva Conventions becomes statutorily applicable, cf. Hortensia D.T. Gutiérrez Posse, *La aplicación del artículo tres común a los cuatro Convenios de Ginebra de 1949 en las situaciones de tensión interna*, Rev. Jur. de Buenos Aires 17 (1999–2000). On the legal characteristics of this state of exception, *see* Daniel O'Donnell, *States of Exception*, 21 Rev. of the Int'l Comm'n of Jurists 52 (1978).

¹⁰ Theodor Meron, *On the Inadequate Reach of Humanitarian and Human Rights Law and the Need for a New Instrument*, 77 Am. J. Int'l L. 589 (1983). On the complex concept of armed conflict, *see* Mónica Pinto, *La noción de conflicto armado en la jurisprudencia del Tribunal Penal Internacional para la ex Yugoslavia*, 78 Lecciones y Ensayos 297 (2003).

¹¹ Louise Doswald-Beck & Sylvain Vité, *Le droit international humanitaire et les drois des droits de l'homme*, 800 Int'l Rev. Red Cross 99 (1993). It is, precisely, in these disturbances that convergence between IHL and HRL should become more evident (Antônio Cançado Trindade, *Desarrollo de las relaciones entre el derecho internacional humanitario y la protección internacional de los derechos humanos en su amplia dimensión*, 16 Rev. I.I.D.H. 44 (1992)).

problem in mind, it must be said that some steps forward have been taken by the negotiation of certain legal texts trying to join several aspects from IHL and HRL, in order to create a merged *corpus* of minimal principles that should be applicable both in times of peace and war.[12]

A hardcore of fundamental guarantees, nevertheless, cannot be suspended or derogated even if a situation of emergency has been declared. These basic rights, which are inherent to the dignity of all human beings, constitute a common ground which is shared by HRL and IHL.[13] The right to life, the prohibition of torture and inhumane treatment, the prohibition of slavery and serfdom, as well as the respect for basic judicial principles, for instance, must be respected in all times and constitute a *noyau dur* provided and consecrated by both HRL and IHL.[14] In this sense, these similar patterns of elementary rights that must be protected in every circumstance tend to attach very closely the systems of protection created to control HRL and IHL. In fact, both branches of international law address a common objective: the protection of individuals when they are not able to defend themselves.[15]

---

[12] Asbjørn Eide, Allan Rosas & Theodor Meron, *Combating Lawlessness in Gray Zone Conflicts through Minimum Humanitarian Standards*, 89 Am. J. Int'l L. 215 (1995); Allan Rosas, *Human Rights at Risk in Situations of Internal Violence and Public Emergency: Towards Common Minimum Standards* 165, *in* The Future of Human Rights Protection in a Changing World: Fifty Years since the Four Freedoms Address. Essays in Honour of Torkel Opsahl (Asbjørn Eide & Jan Helgesen eds., 1991). Similar reflections have motivated the *Declaration of Minimum Humanitarian Standards* (Adopted by Meeting of Experts at Human Rights Institute of Abo Akademi in Turku, Finland, U.N.Doc. E/CN.4/Sub.2/1991/55 (1990)). This instrument proclaims the applicability of a number of basic rules to all situations, including those in which violence, internal disturbances, tensions or exceptional public danger are present. The provisions, drafted by legal experts and related both to HRL (like the prohibition of torture or the availability of *habeas corpus*) and IHL (as the necessary humane treatment that must be granted to injured and sick people, for instance), are not derogable under any circumstance (cf. Theodor Meron & Allan Rosas, *A Declaration of Minimum Humanitarian Standards*, 85 Am. J Int'l L. 375 (1991) and Hans-Peter Gasser, *New Draft Declaration of Minimum Humanitarian Standards*, 282 Int'l Rev. Red Cross 328 (1991)). After the approval of these principles, an international seminar was conducted in South Africa on September 1996 to discuss these minimal standards of humanity that ought to be respected onwards in every situation of violence (Rapport de l'Atelier international sur les règles humanitaires minimales, Cape Town, Sept. 27–29, 1996, Doc. ONU E/CN 4/1997/77/Add.1, Jan. 28, 1997). Cf. Anna-Lena Svensson-McCarthy, *Minimum Humanitarian Standards: From Cape Town Toward the Future*, 53 Rev. of the Int'l Comm. of Jurists 1 (1994).

[13] Djamchid Momtaz, *Les règles humanitaires minimales applicables en période de troubles et tensions internes*, 831 Int'l Rev. Red Cross 487 (1998).

[14] "Today there can no longer be any doubt: international humanitarian law and international human rights law are near relations." (Robert Kolb, *The Relationship Between International Humanitarian Law and Human Rights Law – A Brief History of the 1948 Universal Declaration of Human Rights and the 1949 Geneva Conventions*, 324 Int'l Rev. Red Cross 409 (1998)).

[15] Arthur H. Robertson, *Humanitarian Law and Human Rights, in* Études et essais sur le droit international humanitaire et sur les principes de la Croix-Rouge /Studies and essays on international humanitarian law and Red Cross principles, en l'honneur de/in honour of Jean Pictet

consequence – the protection of victims of the armed conflicts or use forbidden means and methods of warfare. But this does not imply that all judicial mechanisms of control (whether international, regional or national) can attribute responsibility to the state for the violation of IHL rules. This general observation, which might seem quite elementary, has not been always clear if we follow doctrine and case law, and the Inter-American Human Rights system might provide an interesting example of this hesitating behavior.

3. IHL in the Experience of the Inter-American Human Rights System

Several control mechanisms, composed by a series of procedures created by international organizations to scrutinize human rights in the absence of a specific centralized power, have been established by the will of states throughout the second half of the 20th century. Expert committees, political commissions (like the U.N. Commission on Human Rights), and judicial organs integrated by independent judges constitute different bodies instituted with the purpose of investigating, conciliating, and taking decisions on the protection of HRL around the globe.[19] Nevertheless, the possibility of invoking and applying IHL in the framework of these systems, when an armed conflict is identified, has been largely discussed by scholars as a result of the lack of explicit provisions on the matter.[20] The inexistence of specific

---

[19] On the characteristics and particular differences of these universal and regional mechanisms, which include contentious and non-contentious procedures, *see* Mónica Pinto, *Mecanismos de protección internacional de los derechos humanos*, in Jornadas sobre sistema penitenciario y derechos humanos 69 (1997), *Sistemas de protección internacional de los derechos humanos*, 2 Justicia y derechos del niño 27 (2000), *inter alia*. On the protection systems available in times of armed conflict, *see* Allan Rosas, *International Monitoring Mechanisms in Situations of Armed Conflicts*, in Monitoring Human Rights in Europe. Comparing International Procedures and Mechanisms 221 (Arie Bloed, Liselotte Leicht, Manfred Nowak & Allan Rosas eds., 1993).

[20] Bertrand G. Ramcharan, *The Role of International Bodies in the Implementation and Enforcement of Humanitarian Law and Human Rights Law in Non-International Armed Conflicts*, 33 Am. Univ. Law Rev. 99 (1993), Marco Sassòli, *Mise en oeuvre du droit international humanitaire et du droit international des droits de l'homme: une comparaison*, 43 Annuaire Suisse de Droit Int'l 24 (1987), Jean-François Flauss, *Le droit international humanitaire devant les instances de contrôle des conventions européennes et interaméricaine de droits de l'homme*, in Les nouvelles frontières du droit international humanitaire 117 (Jean-François Flauss ed., 2003). On the problems of implementation of IHL in the universal control system, see Daniel O'Donnell, *Trends in the Application of International Humanitarian Law by United Nations Human Rights Mechanisms*, 324 Int'l Rev. Red Cross 481 (1998) [hereinafter O'Donnell]. On the questions arising from the application of IHL in the framework of the European System, see more specifically Aisling Reidy, *The Approach of the European Commission and Court of Human Rights to International Humanitarian Law*, 324 Int'l Rev. Red Cross 513 (1998) and Christina Cerna, *Human Rights in Armed Conflict: Implementation of International Humanitarian Law Norms by Regional Intergovernmental Human Rights Bodies*,

courts dealing with IHL violations has transformed human rights monitoring mechanisms into useful fora to discuss states' compliance with its principles, even if in practice this procedure is far from being simple or uniform.

Forming part of these mechanisms, regional systems play an essential role. The Inter-American Commission on Human Rights (the Commission), created in 1959, is an autonomous and permanent organ of the Organization of American States (OAS), whose mandate is formulated both in the OAS Charter and the American Convention on Human Rights.[21] Since 1965, its independent members, elected by the General Assembly of the OAS, have been given the explicit authorization to examine specific cases of human rights violations in the continent. As a mechanism of control, the Commission has the task of receiving, analyzing, and investigating individual petitions alleging violations of specific human rights protected by the ACHR. The Inter-American Court of Human Rights (IACtHR), established in 1979 and located in San José, Costa Rica, constitutes the second body in the regional system for the promotion and protection of human rights and freedom, representing its judicial institution.[22]

It is widely known that every mechanism designed with the purpose of enforcing legal provisions depends on the mandate engraved by the instrument that created or constituted the system. In this sense, the conventional document which stands as the basis for the activities of the different mechanisms serving to uphold and promote basic rights – especially at a regional level – needs to identify the precise field of applicability of each legal body. As we will see, the identification of clauses describing the competence *ratione materiae* of a commission or a court is fundamental

---

in Implementation of International Humanitarian Law 31 (*supra* note 7). Articles and papers dealing with the Inter-American System will be specifically quoted and discussed in the following section.

[21] The ACHR incorporated the rights that had been previously included in the American Declaration of the Rights and Duties of Man, O.A.S. Res. XXX, Chap. 2, Articles XXIX–XXXVIII, adopted by the Ninth International Conference of American States (1948), reprinted in Basic Documents to Human Rights in the Inter-American System, OEA/Ser.L.V/II.82 doc.6 rev.1 (1992). It was the very first instrument dealing with human rights in a broad sense and general perspective.

[22] On the Inter-American system, *see*-among others-the general works by Juliane Kokott, Das interamerikanische System zum Schutz der Menschenrechte (1986); Rafael Nieto Navia, Introducción al sistema interamericano de protección a los derechos humanos (1993); David J. Harris & Stephen Livingstone (eds.), The Inter-American System of Human Rights (1998); Cecilia Medina, *Toward Effectiveness in the Protection of Human Rights in the Americas*, 8 Transnational Law & Comparative Problems 337 (1998); Héctor Faúndez Ledesma, El sistema interamericano de protección de los derechos humanos: aspectos institucionales y procesales (1999), Christina M. Cerna, *Inter-American System for the Protection of Human Rights*, 95 Am. Soc. of Int'l L. Proceedings 75 (2001). On the Commission, see Anna Schreiber, The Inter-American Commission on Human Rights (1970) and Mónica Pinto, La denuncia ante la Comisión Interamericana de Derechos Humanos (1993). On the IACtHR, *see* Scott Davidson, The Inter-American Court of Human Rights (1992) and Jo M. Pasqualucci, The Practice and Procedure of the Inter-American Court of Human Rights (2003).

in order to understand the characteristics of the violations that can be stated and legally presented to the control system and to know beforehand which violations cannot be analyzed and discussed in the staging of that procedure.

3.1. *The Inter-American Commission: From Applying IHL to Using it as a Tool of Interpretation*

The ACHR establishes the basic criteria for the competence of the Inter-American Commission in its Article 44, which provides that only denunciations or complaints of violations to the treaty itself by state parties can be dealt with and can provide a basis for proceedings. This text clearly implies, for instance, that those rules related to HRL which are specifically included in the text of the Convention might be applied and, therefore, that only breaches to the constitutive instrument can be prosecuted. According to the article, there does not seem to be any possibility for the Commission to examine possible violations of other international treaties, since it would fall outside the narrow scope of material application spelled out in the Convention. If not, it would imply that an obligation can be imposed against a state without its consent, thereby breaching the content of Article 34 of the Vienna Convention on the Law of Treaties[23] which declares that obligations can only be created for a state if that state has expressly accepted them.

Nevertheless, in several reports the Commission has aimed at justifying the necessary application of IHL to specific situations presented by individuals against state parties. With the positive intention of granting a more specific protection to victims of internal armed conflicts, the Commission initially developed a number of arguments tending to generate a ground for the application of IHL as an independent source of obligations for state parties to the treaty.[24]

The *Abella* report is probably the most illustrative example of these efforts.[25] When analyzing the situation – some forty-two civilians had taken up weapons and, allegedly fearing a new *coup d'état*, attacked for almost thirty hours the military

---

[23] Vienna Convention on the Law of Treaties, signed May 23, 1969, 1115 UNTS 331, entry into force on Jan. 27, 1980.

[24] For a structural and very clear description of all these arguments, *see* Moir, *supra* note 4, at 191–199. It must be said here that a first attempt to deal with this problem took place in Disabled People's International et al. v. United States (Application No. 9213, Inter-Am. C.H.R. 184, OEA/Ser. L/V/II.71, doc. 9 rev. 1 IV.C(3) (April 17, 1987)). We shall not discuss here this precedent since it was an isolated situation and the Commission only limited itself to accepting the presentation without offering or presenting any concrete explanation to justify its position; see David Weissbrodt & Beth Andrus, *The Right to Life during Armed Conflict: Disabled People's International v. United States*, 29 Harvard Int'l L.J. 59 (1988).

[25] Juan Carlos Abella v. Argentina, Report No. 55/97, Case 11.137, Inter-Am. C.H.R. 271, OEA Ser. L/V/II.98, Doc. 6 Rev. (1998). The report was adopted on Nov. 18, 1997 [hereinafter Tablada Case].

barracks of La Tablada in January 1989 –, the Commission had to answer to the argument of the surviving attackers that both HRL and IHL had been violated by Argentina when responding to the assault. In paragraph 156, the Commission concluded that, as a result of careful planning and coordination, the military operation was not to be considered just an internal disturbance but a real internal armed conflict, and thus Common Article 3 was applicable.[26] The problem, in fact, was to justify a direct application of this provision to the situation, given the limits of competence imposed by Article 44 of the Convention.

In the first place, an explanation based on the articles of the ACHR was put forward. According to the Commission, Articles 25, 27(a), 29(b) and 64(1) were relevant to decide that IHL can be effectively applied. Let us focus here, for a few seconds, on those arguments.

In paragraph 163, the Court argued that since IHL treaties had been incorporated into Argentinean national legislation, Article 25 might allow their violations to be addressed by the Commission. The text of the article explains that every individual is entitled to a domestic judicial remedy if a violation of any human right recognized by the legislation (constitution or laws) of the state concerned happens to occur. Therefore, the Commission considered that the text implies an authorization to deal with questions of IHL when violations of Article 25 are exposed.

As far as Article 27(a) is concerned, the Commission invoked the existence of a general possibility of derogating from several provisions listed in the ACHR when a state of public emergency is declared. In this sense, as we have explained, the Commission identified a number of rights that cannot be derogated because they constitute the hardcore of protection, where both HRL and IHL overlap and should be applied. The article provides that the allowed derogations must always comply with other obligations that a state can be engaged to by means of other positive rules of international law. Therefore, even if we are dealing with the suspension of human rights, this implies that the rest of the international obligations assumed by the state remains in force. It was clearly thought to be the case of IHL,[27] which seems to constitute a useful tool for protecting individuals in these situations of exception since its provisions can never be derogated.

Article 29(b) is quoted by the Commission in order to justify the validity of the *pro homine* principle throughout the ACHR. According to the norm, no provision of the Convention shall be interpreted as "restricting the enjoyment of exercise of

---

[26] It should be said here that the frequent reference to Common Article 3 to the four Geneva Conventions in the scope of the Inter-American system can also be understood in its close attachment to HRL rules. Since it deals with internal armed conflicts, its text – considered to codify a miniature treaty – points to the relationship between a state and an *internal* group of individuals, establishing a similar pattern as the one consolidated in HRL where states are faced to the necessary protection of their *own* population.

[27] Jaime Oraá, Human Rights in States of Emergency in International Law 195 (1992).

any right or freedom recognized by virtue of the laws of any State Party by virtue of another convention to which one of the said states is a party." As a conclusion, the Commission stated in paragraph 165 that in those situations where there are differences between legal standards governing the same or similar rights in the American Convention and IHL treaties, "the Convention is duty bound to give legal effect to the provision(s) of that treaty with the higher standard(s) applicable to the right(s) or freedom(s) in question." Therefore, the consequence is made explicit immediately after: "If that higher standard is a rule of humanitarian law, the Commission should *apply* it."[28]

What the Commission postulated here is that, in the case of an armed conflict, IHL definitely contains the clauses which are more favorable to the individual. The verb "*apply*" shows that, according to the Commission, violations of IHL could be definitely analyzed by the Inter-American system, despite the explicit negative principle sustained by Article 44 ACHR. In order to deal with this contradiction, the report clarifies that the reference to IHL rules in order to establish the state's responsibility does not mean adding new international obligations but reinforcing the ones already contained in the Convention: "Article 3 basically requires the state to do, in large measure, what is already legally obliged to do under the American Convention."[29]

Finally, in the same report the Commission also made an important reference to Article 64(1) ACHR, which establishes that the states which are members of the OAS "may consult the Court regarding the interpretation of this Convention or *of other treaties* concerning the protection of human rights in the American states" (emphasis added). In fact, the Inter-American Court had considered in an Advisory Opinion that the expression "other treaties" could refer to legal instruments not directly approved or negotiated in a regional level,[30] so the Commission interpreted that IHL conventions were easily included in the text and thus could be invoked when discussing the alleged violations by a state.

---

[28] Tablada Case, *supra* note 25, para. 165 *in fine*. On IHL as a *lex specialis*, *see* Legality of the Threat or Use of Nuclear Weapons, Advisory Opinion, 1996 ICJ 240 (June 8, 1996), para. 25 (emphasis added).

[29] Tablada Case, *supra* note 25, para. 158. On this overlap, the ICJ recently considered that, even if some matters only correspond to IHL and some other exclusively to HRL, several situations can be simultaneously addressed under both branches of law (Legal Consequences of the Construction of a Wall in the Occupied Palestinian Territory, Advisory Opinion, I.C.J. 131 (June 9, 2004), para. 106).

[30] "Other Treaties" Subject to the Consultative Jurisdiction of the Court (American Convention on Human Rights, Article 64), Advisory Opinion OC-1/82, Inter-Am. Ct. H.R. (Ser. A) No. 1 (Sept. 24, 1982). In paragraph 43, the Court considered that "the Commission has properly invoked in some of its reports and resolutions 'other treaties concerning the protection of human rights in the American states', regardless of their bilateral or multilateral character, or whether they have been adopted within the framework or under the auspices of the Inter-American system." On this opinion, *see* Thomas Buergenthal, *The Advisory Practice of the Inter-American Human Rights Court*, 79 Am. J. Int'l L. 1, 5–8 (1985).

It seems certain that all these arguments based upon the articles of the ACHR, as a whole, are quite weak from a legal standpoint.[31] Article 25, for instance, only authorizes a competence to address the allegations of violations of the right to obtain a judicial remedy and not to apply the whole *corpus* of IHL instruments as the Commission might have tended to interpret. Article 27, on the other hand, is only valid if the IHL rules which can be applied correspond and concur with the substantive norms of the Convention and not in any circumstance.[32] Besides, it seems difficult to justify the applicability of IHL rules if a state does not derogate the rules, since in those situations it is evident that Article 27 cannot be applied.[33] Concerning Article 29, the treaty makes clear that the Commission is required to take due notice of and, when appropriate, give legal effect to applicable IHL rules in those situations where the ACHR and IHL instruments apply concurrently. This means that IHL as the more favorable clause cannot be invoked independently and should be considered together with the relevant HRL statutes.[34] Finally, in relationship to Article 64(1), one could argue that the Advisory Opinion referring to its content did not mention IHL or concerned its rules in an explicit way. In conclusion, as Zegveld notices, "none of the arguments presented by the Commission seems to provide compelling authority for an unqualified application of international humanitarian law."[35]

Despite the notorious flaw represented by the exaggerated interpretation of the Commission's ability to examine IHL violations, *Abella* has not been isolated in its main ideas or logical reasoning. In fact, two other reports from the same year seem to arrive to similar conclusions by making use of a parallel (and equally critizable) argumentation.

In a report adopted almost simultaneously, *Ribón Avilán*,[36] the Commission quoted Article 25 ACHR and explained that a close examination of Colombia's respect of IHL was made possible by the incorporation of the treaties on armed conflicts to the national legislation.[37] Since both IHL and HRL contain a number of common provisions dealing with the protection of individuals in times of

---

[31] This has been very well remarked by Liesbeth Zegveld, *The Inter-American Commission on Human Rights and International Humanitarian Law: A Comment on the Tablada Case*, 38 Int'l Rev. Red Cross 505 (1998) [hereinafter Zegveld].

[32] *See id.*, at 510.

[33] *See* Moir, *supra* note 4, at 197.

[34] *See id.* at 195.

[35] *See* Zegveld, *supra* note 31, at 510–511.

[36] Arturo Ribón Avilán v. Colombia, Report No. 26/97, Case 11.142, Inter-Am. C.H.R. 444, OEA Ser. L/V/II.98, Doc. 6 Rev. (1998). The report was adopted on Sept. 30, 1997 [hereinafter Ribón Avilán Case], and dealt with the death of eleven Colombian citizens who were allegedly killed when surrendering after a clash between an armed dissident group called M-19 and the national army.

[37] *Id.* paras 177–178.

internal armed conflict, the Commission could conclude that both branches of law had to be respected, for "Common Article 3 of the Geneva Conventions and the American Convention guarantee these rights...and the Commission should *apply both bodies of law*."[38]

Just as we described in *Abella*, the use of the verb "apply" here is also clearly problematic in the scope of the competence granted to the Commission by the ACHR, as Colombia noticed when presenting its own arguments. Following the same logical guidelines, however, the Commission also considered here that this necessary application of common Article 3 did not imply further obligations for Colombia, since its content was already broadly contained in the Convention of San José: "the *application* of Common Article 3 to a State party to the American Convention does not impose additional burdens on the State."[39] Again the direct application of IHL is made relative and softened by the argument that no unexpected burdens were generated, as if the justification for recourse to IHL rules rested on the overlapping of their content with the HRL norms referred to in the treaty. On this basis, the Commission could consider that not only the ACHR has been breached in its content, but *also* the Geneva provision dealing with the basic regulations in internal conflicts, as the following sentence allows to understand: "the victims were executed extrajudicially by state agents in a clear *violation of* Common article 3 of the Geneva Conventions *as well as* the American Convention."[40]

Also in 1997, the Commission drafted the report on *Bustíos Saavedra* on similar grounds.[41] When examining the responsibility of the Peruvian state for the violation of several articles of the ACHR as a result of the murder of Hugo Bustíos and the injuries caused to another journalist, Alejandro Arce, the Commission made reference to a similar pattern of reasoning and finally asserted that Peru "*has also violated* common article 3 of the Geneva Conventions."[42] Once again, the words mentioned become interesting under the light of the main provision of competence provided by Article 44 ACHR; in this sense, through the verb "violate", the passage suggests that IHL ought to be independently and additionally applied to the situation and that therefore, apart from the strict examination of the articles of the Convention which had been violated, the state was *also* considered responsible for the *autonomous* breach of the content of Common Article 3.

Interestingly enough, the Commission continued to use the verb "*violate*" and related terms to indicate the failure of states to respect IHL rules applicable to internal armed conflicts in subsequent reports, reinforcing the idea that international

---

[38] *Id.* para. 174 (emphasis added).
[39] *Id.* para. 172 (emphasis added).
[40] *Id.* para. 134 (emphasis added).
[41] Hugo Bustíos Saavedra v. Peru, Report No. 38/97, Case 10.548, Inter-Am. C.H.R. 753, OEA Ser. L/V/II.98, Doc. 6 Rev. (1998). The report was adopted on Oct. 16, 1997.
[42] *Id.* para. 88 (emphasis added).

responsibility arising from breaches to IHL treaties could be unquestionably stated by the Inter-American system beyond the traditional violation of the articles of the ACHR. However, a slight modification in these general considerations can be perceived.

In three different reports, the Commission concluded, for example, that El Salvador "*violated*... common Article 3 of the Four Geneva Conventions of 1949 and Article 4 of Protocol II,"[43] "*has violated* the right to life enshrined in Article 4 of the American Convention, *together with* the principles recognized in common Article 3 of the Geneva Conventions of 1949"[44] and "*has violated*...Article 4 of the American Convention, *in conjunction with* the principles codified in common Article 3,"[45] respectively. The Commission also stated that Colombia "*is responsible for the violation* of the right to life pursuant to Article 4 of the American Convention *and* common Article 3 of the Geneva Conventions."[46]

The syntax of these expressions is more than significant. In *Parada Cea* the object of the violation is directly related to two specific provisions of the Geneva instruments, following the precedent of the *Bustíos Saavedra* report. In *Ellacuría*, however, the Commission made reference not to the infringement of concrete instruments on IHL but to the violation of a specific right contained in the ACHR and to some *principles* which are merely *acknowledged* in Common Article 3. IHL norms are, in the latter example, not directly included in the determination of El Salvador's responsibility; they are mediated through the inclusion of the word "principles." A similar conclusion might be reached when considering the terms "*principles codified*" employed by the Commission in *Romero y Galdámez*. In these two remarks, Common Article 3 is not said to have been violated, but some basic principles which that article only happens to translate.

In this subtle use of language, the Commission seems to postulate a more moderate approach than in previous reports. What is more, the particular use of the expressions "*together with*" and "*in conjunction with*" allows to place IHL next to HRL and not to consider its rules as autonomously attributable to the state.

---

[43] Lucio Parada Cea et al. v. El Salvador, Report No. 1/99 (adopted on Jan. 27, 1999), Case 10.480, Inter-Am. C.H.R. 531, OEA Ser. L/V/II.102, Doc. 6 Rev. (1999), para. 160 (emphasis added).
[44] Ignacio Ellacuria, S.J. et al. v. El Salvador, Report No. 136/99 (adopted on Jan. 22, 1999), Case 10.488, Inter-Am. C.H.R. 608, OEA Ser. L/V/II.106, Doc. 3 Rev. (1999), para. 237 (emphasis added).
[45] Monsignor Oscar Amulfo Romero y Galdámez v. El Salvador, Report No. 37/00 (adopted on Apr. 13, 2000), Case 10.481, Inter-Am. C.H.R. 671, OEA Ser. L/V/II.106, Doc. 3 Rev. (1999), para. 72 (emphasis added).
[46] José Alexis Fuentes Guerrero v. Colombia, Report No. 61/99 (adopted on Apr. 13, 1999), Case 11.519, Inter-Am. C.H.R. 466, OEA Ser. L/V/II.106, Doc. 7 Rev. (1999), para. 67 (emphasis added).

In *Fuentes Guerrero*, finally, it is also the right to life prescribed by Article 4 ACHR that has been violated. In an ambiguous sentence, the structure of the phrase seems to indicate through the conjunction "*and*" that the same right is considered to be simultaneously protected by HRL and IHL, so both branches are supposed to apply concurrently. Nevertheless, if read under the light of previous references, it is not clear whether the objects of the violation are "the right of life pursuant to Article 4 of the American Convention", on the one side, *and* the whole "common Article 3", on the other, or if it is only the right of life (enshrined in both articles, connected by the "*and*") that happens to be considered as violated. The consequence of understanding the sentence in one way or another carries a different weight to the Commission's observation, since the first interpretation takes the conclusion closer to the extreme pronouncement elaborated in *Abella, Ribón Avilán* or *Bustíos Saavedra*, whereas the second reading would rather place Fuentes Guerrero in a moderate line similar to the precepts of *Ellacuría* or *Romero y Galdámez*.

A later report issued on Colombia leaves ambiguity aside and shows a more radical reversal in the Commission's perspective. In *Riofrío Massacre*, despite the declarations of the petitioners asking to assert the state's responsibility for violations of both HRL and IHL, the Commission contradicted its own previous approach and, in the context of an internal armed conflict, only decided to affirm that the murder of thirteen civilians was a clear violation of Article 4 ACHR, without including any final reference to the applicability of Common Article 3.[47]

Moir has suggested that the general evolution in the view of the Commission, from an original position tending to apply directly IHL to a less radical opinion, can be explained by the strength of the Inter-American Court jurisprudence that denied the direct reference to IHL rules in the regional system.[48] Nevertheless, if the cases decided by the judicial institution are revisited, it is possible to discover a slight uncertainty of thought as well, which finally endorses a less problematic position in legal terms.

3.2. IHL in the Inter-American Court: A Similar Hesitation or a More "Legalistic" Approach?

As we have seen, the Commission has been dealing with the possible implementation of IHL in several reports since 1997, where it has considered that both branches of law are indubitably connected. In the first precedents, it reaffirmed that IHL should be applied as a *lex specialis* whenever it seems to be more adequately suited

---

[47] Riofrío Massacre (Colombia), Report No. 62/01 (adopted on Apr. 6, 2001), Case 11.654, Inter-Am. C.H.R. 758, OEA Ser. L/V/II.111, Doc. 20 Rev. (2000), para. 58.
[48] Moir, *supra* note 4, at 212: "Since the Court's pronouncements, the Commission seems to have realized the error of its ways, and is now prepared to use humanitarian law in order to determine violations of human rights law."

to the situations under examination, even if its rules do not belong to the American Convention. According to the Commission, this solution helped providing more specific standards for analysis when alleged violations happened in the context of hostilities.

Notwithstanding this evolution, a traditional opposition between the Commission and the Court has been assessed, since with opposite arguments the IACtHR overturned these initial positions by stating that only the ACHR and general PIL could be applied by the tribunal, excluding thus IHL from its legal competence.[49] As we will try to show, this dualist approach is, at least, oversimplified.

We consider as a preliminary statement that one of the most ordinary errors in examining the Court's position concerning the possibility of applying IHL in cases submitted to its competence consists in starting by the decision on preliminary measures taken in *Las Palmeras* in February 2000.[50] If to a certain extent it is possible to agree that this was the first case in which the IACtHR explored and gave an answer to the problems of making direct reference to the specific law of armed conflicts, the truth is that *Las Palmeras* was not an isolated decision and cannot be conceived as such. As the Inter-American case-law shows, the judges had previously had the opportunity of addressing the difficulty of including other treaties to the traditional scope provided by the ACHR, and the examination of these texts becomes extremely useful to address the conclusions reached in *Las Palmeras*.

In *Paniagua Morales*,[51] for example, the Court had clearly decided that a violation of an instrument different from the ACHR could be judged within the framework of the Inter-American system. Hence, it affirmed that Guatemala violated Article 5 ACHR *and* Articles 1, 6 and 8 of the Inter-American Convention on Torture.[52] A few months later, the IACtHR considered in *Villagrán Morales*,[53] on the basis of similar arguments,[54] that Guatemala "*violated* Articles 1, 6 and 8 of the Inter-American Convention to Prevent and Punish Torture."[55] Since this case concerned the massacre of five street children, the IACtHR went on to analyze the possibility of referring to more specific rules protecting minors and concluded that, as a whole,

---

[49] On the complex relationship between the Commission and the IACtHR, *see* Cecilia Medina, *The Inter-American Commission on Human Rights and the InterAmerican Court of Human Rights: Reflections on a Joint Venture*, 12 Hum. Rights Quart. 439 (1990).

[50] Las Palmeras Case, Preliminary Objection, Judgment (Feb. 4, 2000), Inter-Am Ct. H.R. (Ser. C) No. 67 (2000) [hereinafter Las Palmeras Case 2000].

[51] Paniagua Morales et al. Case, Judgment (Mar. 8, 1998), Inter-Am Ct. H.R. (Ser. C) No. 37 (1998).

[52] *Id.* para. 136 (emphasis added). Inter-American Convention to Prevent and Punish Torture, Dec. 9, 1985, OAS Treaty Series No. 67, reprinted in 25 I.L.M. 519 (1986).

[53] Villagrán Morales v. Guatemala ("Street Children" Case), Judgment (Nov. 19, 1999), Inter-Am Ct. H.R. (Ser. C) No. 63 (1999) [hereinafter Street Children Case].

[54] *Id.* paras 247–248.

[55] *Id.* para. 252 (emphasis added).

"the American Convention and the Convention on the Rights of the Child form part of a very comprehensive international *corpus juris* for the protection of the child that should help this Court establish the content and scope of the general provision established in Article 19 of the American Convention."[56] In this opportunity, then, another additional treaty – the Convention on the Rights of the Child –[57] was not specifically applied with the ACHR but was examined in order to help interpret the contents of a concrete clause of the regional human rights instrument (in this case, Article 19).

The landmark case of *Las Palmeras* should be explained in this background context. Following some investigations arisen from the extra-judicial execution of at least six individuals by the Colombian Police Force, the Commission submitted the case to the Court in July 1998 by means of the use of a linguistic expression recalling its contemporary reports. By reproducing some previous precepts, the Commission required the IACtHR to decide on Colombia's responsibility for the violation of "the right to life, embodied in Article 4 of the Convention *and* Article 3, common to all the 1949 Geneva Conventions."[58] It is obvious that the sentence translates – with the coordination "*and*" – a double reading which is identical to the ambiguity we identified in *Fuentes Guerrero*. In any case, the difference between the two positions is notorious as far as the result is concerned.

When offering an answer to the second preliminary objection presented by Colombia – which was related to the question of whether the Commission had competence to apply IHL – the IACtHR considered, by the majority of votes, that despite the broad faculties granted by the ACHR for the promotion and protection of human rights, the Commission was restricted by the text of the treaty and could only "refer *specifically* to rights protected by that Convention" when submitting a case to the Court.[59]

An analogous reckoning was put forward *vis-à-vis* the issue of applicability of IHL by the tribunal itself, postulated in the third preliminary objection. In this sense, the IACtHR also decided to reject explicitly the Commission's opinion in this regard by explaining that IHL cannot be applied in the Inter-American system: "In order to carry out this examination, the Court interprets the norm in question and analyzes it in the light of the provisions of the Convention. The result of this operation will always be an opinion in which the Court will say whether or not that norm or that fact is compatible with the American Convention. The latter has *only* given the Court competence to determine whether the acts or the norms of

---

[56] *Id.* para. 194.
[57] Convention on the Rights of the Child, G.A. Res. 44/25, Annex, 44 U.N. GAOR Supp. No. 49, U.N. Doc. A/44/49 (1989) (entered into force Sept. 2, 1990).
[58] Las Palmeras Case 2000, *supra* note 50, para. 12 (emphasis added).
[59] *Id.* para. 34 (emphasis added).

the States are compatible with *the Convention itself*, and *not* with the 1949 Geneva Conventions."[60] In this sense, the Court considered that Article 62 ACHR is more than explicit when rejecting the possibility of basing its competence in other conventions: "The jurisdiction of the Court shall comprise all cases concerning the interpretation and application of the provisions of *this* Convention that are submitted to it."[61] A contrary position would also run against the content of Article 33, when it limits the competence to "matters relating to the fulfillment of the commitments made by the States Parties to *this* Convention."

Therefore, if we follow the tribunal's way of thinking, it is possible to assume that Common Article 3 of the Geneva Conventions can become useful only as an effective tool of interpretation when dealing with the possible violation of HRL norms in period of civil war or internal hostilities. This observation, however, is not new. The value of IHL as an appropriate instrument to understand and illuminate a specific rule of the ACHR in the particular context of a non-international armed conflict, which the IACtHR developed in *Las Palmeras*, had already been noticed in the Commission's reports but had remained obscured by the more radical position of postulating the direct application of IHL. In fact, in *Ribón Avilán* the Commission had stated that in order to identify whether casualties were legitimate military targets it was necessary to "refer to and apply definitional provisions and relevant rules from humanitarian law as authoritative sources which provide orientation in the resolution of these cases."[62] Additionally, and with a very similar measured vocabulary, in *Abella* the task of the Commission was mildly described as attempting to "necessarily look to and apply definitional standards and relevant rules of humanitarian law as sources of authoritative guidance in its resolution of this and other kinds of claims alleging violations of the American Convention in combat situations."[63]

Nevertheless, whereas the Commission confirmed in both paragraphs this principle as a general basis and then proposed the joint application of IHL and HRL rules, the Court stated that the interpretative function of allusions to the law of armed conflicts is taken as the *only* possible effect of quoting IHL when assessing international responsibility in the regional system. To the IACtHR, every other use of IHL exceeding this guidance is not allowed according to the ACHR.

In a contribution published soon after the release of the decision in *Las Palmeras*, Martin heavily criticized the position of the Court.[64] By resuming the importance of the precedent reports issued by the Commission, the author considered that the

---

[60] *Id.* para. 33 (emphasis added).
[61] *Id.* para. 32 (emphasis added).
[62] Ribón Avilán Case, *supra* note 36, para. 173.
[63] Tablada Case, *supra* note 25, para. 161.
[64] Fanny Martin, *Application du droit international humanitaire par la Cour interaméricaine des droits de l'homme*, 844 Int'l Rev. Red Cross 1037 (2001).

judgment represented a step backwards in the need to ensure the necessary complementarity between IHL and HRL, since it managed to erase the previous efforts made by the Commission. However, this argument does not seem strong enough. Even if we agree that there is a close relationship between IHL and HRL and that their rules must be considered together in order to provide a more efficient protection of individuals in particularly harsh times of armed conflicts, the consideration that IHL must be directly applied by a human rights tribunal presents, at least, an essential legal obstacle which seems hard to overcome. In fact, appealing to IHL instruments in order to discern a state's responsibility when the treaty that gives origin to the protective mechanism does not authorize their inclusion constitutes a complicated conflation between applicable law and jurisdiction. A situation might be perfectly well covered by both branches of law if the state ratified the appropriate conventions, but that overstep does not mean that a specific tribunal has to take into account both legal *corpora* when addressing the alleged violations.

Martin also considers – among other arguments – that the content of Common Article 3 to the Geneva Conventions is obligatory to all states because of its international customary character[65] and that therefore it must be referred to and applied by HRL tribunals. We can agree on the first point of her comment. Nonetheless, instead of bringing a solution to the problem of applying IHL, the whole statement rather displaces the discussion creating some additional difficulty: if the question does not concern the application of conventional norms anymore but the incorporation of international custom as a source of obligations, we should immediately ask ourselves if the ACHR permits the autonomous implementation of custom – together with the relevant HRL articles – when proclaiming the core of responsibility.

Perhaps Martin is rather thinking of the possibility of conceiving the provisions contained in Common Article 3 as *jus cogens* obligations, as it has been suggested and explained elsewhere.[66] I think, in particular, that the references to the "*principles*

---

[65] *Id.*, at 1049: "La Cour interaméricaine manque donc une occasion d'intégrer le droit humanitaire dans la sphère des mécanismes de protection des droits de l'homme au prix d'un moindre effort: il suffisait pour elle de consacrer le caractère coutumier de l'article 3 commun." On the customary nature of humanitarian law, *see* Mohamed El Kouhene, Les garanties fondamentales de la personne en droit humanitaire et droits de l'homme 233 (1986).

[66] See the Opinion of Judge Antônio Cançado Trindade (paras. 40–41) in the Serrano-Cruz Sisters v. El Salvador, Judgment (Nov. 23, 2004), Inter-Am. Ct. H.R. (ser. C) No. 118 [hereinafter Serrano-Cruz Sisters Case]. To understand the nature and the current implications of these rules, that are so fundamental to the international community that no State can derogate from them, as well as their close relationship with humanitarian principles codified in the Geneva Conventions, *see* now Christian J. Tams, Enforcing Obligations *Erga Omnes* in International Law (2005) and the collective work Christian Tomuschat & Jean-Marc Thouvenin eds., The Fundamental Rules of the International Legal Order: Jus Cogens and Obligations Erga Omnes (2006), *inter alia multa*. In fact, the ICJ has asserted that Common Article 3 to the Geneva Conventions is one of "the

recognized" or "*principles codified*" in Article 3, as described in the quotations we extracted from *Ellacuría* and *Romero y Galdámez* respectively, are pointing to this last direction. In this hypothesis, it must be said that it is not Article 3 as such – i.e. as an integral part of the Geneva Conventions – that should be applied by the Inter-American bodies, but the imperative content which the norm happens to describe: this does not mean *applying* IHL or deciding on a state's responsibility for violating an IHL treaty, but establishing a general web of basic obligations attributable to every subject of general PIL, which can help to define the specific substance of human rights rules in a very particular context of armed fighting or warfare.

Despite this negative interpretation, the measured and "legalistic" holding of the decision in the *Las Palmeras* case was soon reproduced in later decisions.

In the Court's judgment of *Bámaca Velásquez*,[67] the Commission had also requested the Court to decide on the responsibility of Guatemala for the violation not only of several articles of the ACHR but also of "Articles 1, 2 and 6 of the Inter-American Convention to Prevent and Punish Torture *and* Article 3 common to the Geneva Conventions."[68] However, the Court came back to its precedent and expressed that it was not possible to decide on the basis of other instruments different from the ACHR, although a comparative view can authorize an observation related to additional violations not comprised in the regional treaty: "Although the Court lacks competence to declare that a State is internationally responsible for the violation of international treaties that do not grant it such competence, it can *observe* that certain acts or omissions that violate human rights, pursuant to the treaties that they do have competence to apply, also violate other international

---

fundamental general principles of humanitarian law" (Case Military and Paramilitary Activities in and against Nicaragua (paragraph 194)). It was conceived as part of the elementary considerations of humanity that states must abide by and, therefore, as a minimum yardstick which states ought to respect in every situation of armed conflict (Merits, 1986 I.C.J. 14, para. 218). *See* Pierre-Marie Dupuy, *Les considérations élementaires d'humanité dans la jurisprudence de la Cour internationale de Justice*, *in* Droit et Justice. Mélanges en l'honneur de Nicolas Valticos 117 (René-Jean Dupuy ed., 1999). On this specific consideration, *see* Vincent Chetail, *The Contribution of the International Court of Justice to International Humanitarian Law*, 85 Int'l Rev. Red Cross 235 (2003) and Dinah Shelton, *Are there Differentiations among Human Rights? Jus Cogens, Core Human Rights, Obligations Erga Omnes and Non-Derogability*, *in* The Status of International Treaties on Human Rights 159 (2006). The same ICJ had conceived that *erga omnes* obligations derive, *inter alia*, from "the principles and rules concerning the basic rights of the human person" (Case Concerning the Barcelona Traction, Light and Power Co., Ltd., I.C.J. Reports 1970, 3, para. 34). As such, the protection of the hardcore rights promoted by HRL and IHL can be conceived as an imperative obligation for all states (Roberto Ago, *Droit des traités à la lumière de la Convention de Vienne*, RCADI I, No. 134, 324 (1971)). *See* also Antonio Gómez Robledo, El ius cogens internacional. Estudio histórico-crítico 166–167 (2003).

[67] Bámaca Velásquez v. Guatemala, Judgment (Nov. 25, 2000), Inter-Am. Ct. H.R. (ser. C) No. 70.
[68] *Id.* para. 2 (emphasis added).

instruments for the protection of the individual, such as the 1949 Geneva Conventions and, in particular, common Article 3."[69]

The sentence clarifies the limits imposed by the *Las Palmeras* case, since its language elucidates a difference between those treaties that can be directly *applied* in accordance with the granted competence and those "other" treaties which can only be *observed* as they rest outside that scope *ratione materiae*.

In addition to this, the following paragraph reinforces the idea that IHL instruments – and especially Common Article 3 of the four Geneva Conventions – can only be mentioned with the purpose of offering an interpretative background for HRL rules: "Indeed, there is a similarity between the content of Article 3, common to the 1949 Geneva Conventions, and the provisions of the American Convention and other international instruments regarding non-derogable human rights (such as the right to life and the right not to be submitted to torture or cruel, inhuman or degrading treatment). This Court has already indicated in the *Las Palmeras* Case, that the relevant provisions of the Geneva Conventions may be taken into consideration *as elements for the interpretation* of the American Convention."[70] In order to explain the nature of the interpretative device acknowledged by the judgment, the overlapping content of the humanitarian clause contained in Article 3 and the respective provisions in the ACHR is once again revealed.

The vocabulary employed in this passage by the IACtHR can be discovered elsewhere. In the *Serrano-Cruz Sisters* case, the same path was confirmed. It was also established there that the relevant provisions contained in the Geneva Conventions could be taken as *elements of interpretation* of the ACHR.[71] More recently, this interpretative aim of referring to IHL has been confirmed in the *Mapiripán Massacre* case too, where the IACtHR also reiterated that responsibility for IHL could not be declared by the Court but that humanitarian rules could be useful to achieve a better interpretation of the ACHR when dealing with states' responsibility or with some specific aspects of the alleged violations.[72]

As a whole, then, the Court gives a special importance to the contextualization of human rights in the broader scope of PIL and in the more specific scope of IHL. This argumentative strategy agrees and complies with the intention, frequently expressed by its judges, of providing a dynamic interpretation of the relevant rules contained in the ACHR. Thus, in *Villagrán Morales*, it was concluded that an "evolutive interpretation of international protection instruments" should be achieved.[73] By reproducing a previous statement, the Court was able to confirm

---

[69] *Id.* para. 208 (emphasis added).
[70] Las Palmeras Case 2000, *supra* note 50, para. 209 (emphasis added).
[71] Serrano-Cruz Sisters Case, *supra* note 66, para. 119.
[72] "Mapiripán Massacre" v. Colombia, Judgment (Sept. 15, 2005), Inter-Am. Ct. H.R. (ser. C) No. 134., para. 115.
[73] *Id.* para. 193.

here that "this evolutive interpretation is consequent with the general rules of the interpretation of treaties embodied in the 1969 Vienna Convention. Both this Court...and the European Court...have indicated that human rights treaties are living instruments, the interpretation of which must evolve over time in view of existing circumstances."[74] In the logical scheme of the IACtHR expressed in these sections, if the HRL set of rules needs to be studied and defined in the framework of a dynamic context, then the reference to specific tools of interpretation – as it happens with IHL – becomes a consistent, functional, and helpful strategy to update the content of the ACHR in concrete circumstances.

According to this complex case-law, how should we consider the experience of the Inter-American system, then? To sum up, in these ups-and-downs of the regional organs, we have seen that the higher pretensions consecrated in *Abella* or *Ribón Avilán* ended up being restrained by more recent reports and decisions that consolidate a strict reading of the competence of the Commission and the Court. The initial will of the Commission to go beyond this legal edge was replaced by a much moderate position in which IHL seems to be implemented exclusively:

a) when the content of its provisions coincide with the non-derogable rights explicitly protected in the ACHR, as it happens for instance with the right to life, and
b) as far as it remains useful to elucidate or understand better the HRL provisions in a period when peace is absent, so human rights norms become interpreted through the prism offered by IHL.

These two conditions, generally presented as separate,[75] constitute in fact a single argument. As the two sides of a coin, interpretation is only possible as long as the content of the IHL rule is able to reproduce the protected right in the context of an armed conflict.

The legal issue, however, is still far from being solved. In 2003 the Commission revised its precedents and seemed to reinforce its new reasoning with a temperate and clear reference to both justifications for implementing IHL. In the report on the detained individuals in Guantanamo by U.S. forces,[76] the relationship between

---

[74] The Right to Information on Consular Assistance in the Framework of the Guarantees of Due Process of Law, Advisory Opinion, Advisory Opinion OC-16/99 (October 1, 1999). Series A No. 16, para. 113.
[75] Moir, *supra* note 4, at 191–194, for instance, considers that the "necessary interpretative device" and the "substantive overlapping" represent two different justifications which were advanced in order to explain the Commission's competence to apply IHL.
[76] Precautionary Measures in Guantanamo Bay (Cuba), Inter-Am. C.H.R. (Mar. 13, 2002) in 41 I.L.M. 532 (2002). *See* Dinah Shelton, *The Legal Status of the Detainees at Guantanamo Bay: Innovative Elements in the Decision of the Inter-American Commission on Human Rights of 12 March*

IHL and HRL was once again discussed under the light of the specific competence of the Inter-American control bodies. As opposed to previous circumstances, it was no longer here a question of facing an internal armed conflict, regulated by Common Article 3 or Additional Protocol II, but dealing with an international armed conflict. After recalling that the mandate given by OAS members referred to the supervision of the member states' observance of those human rights prescribed under the American Declaration of the Rights and Duties of Man, the Commission made clear that it was possible with this purpose to look to and apply definitional *standards* and relevant rules of international humanitarian law in interpreting the appropriate instruments in times of war.

The argument of the *lex specialis* was placed now in the context of these standards, and the verb *apply* reappeared in the report only to refer to IHL as a tool of interpretation: "in situations of armed conflict, the protections under international human rights and humanitarian law may complement and reinforce one another, sharing as they do a common nucleus of non-derogable rights and a common purpose of promoting human life and dignity. In certain circumstances, however, the test for evaluating the observance of a particular right, such as the right to liberty, in a situation of armed conflict may be distinct from that applicable in time of peace. In such situations, international law, including the jurisprudence of this Commission, dictates that it may be necessary to deduce the applicable standard by reference to international humanitarian law as the applicable *lex specialis*."

Nonetheless, on the same topic, in July 2006 the Commission, during its 125th Period of Sessions celebrated in Guatemala, issued Resolution No. 1/06 urging the United States to close the Guantanamo Bay facility without delay and to remove the detainees in full accordance *both* with international HRL and IHL.

Despite this general principle of joint application of the two branches of international law, it must be said in general that only HRL – as contained in the ACHR – remains applicable to the cases submitted to the Commission and to the Court. *Contrario sensu*, IHL stays outside the limits of the conventional competence. We should bear in mind, however, that the exclusion is not absolute: the value of humanitarian stipulations for interpretative purposes is indisputable.[77]

2002, 23 Hum. Rights Law J. 13 (2002); Manuel Pérez González & José Luis Rodríguez Villasante y Prieto, *El caso de los detenidos de Guantánamo ante el derecho internacional humanitario y de los derechos humanos*, 54 Rev. española de dcho. Int'l 11 (2002), María del Pilar Pozo Serrano, *La Comisión Interamericana de Derechos Humanos solicita a Estados Unidos que adopte medidas cautelares en relación con los detenidos en Guantánamo*, 54 Rev. española dcho. Int'l 1018 (2003), Brian D. Tittemore, *Guantanamo Bay and the Precautionary Measures of the Inter-American Commission on Human Rights: A Case for International Oversight in the Struggle Against Terrorism*, 6 Hum. Rights Law Rev. 378 (2006).

[77] O'Donnell, *supra* note 20.

In this context, it must be underlined that references to IHL as means of interpretation do not imply a direct reference to the content of its conventional clauses. A different approach would be as incorrect as assuming that a state can be considered responsible for the breach of certain provisions contained in the Preamble of a treaty in addition to the violation of its articles.

4. Conclusion: *The Need to Implement IHL by Means of Interpretative References or Contextualizing Guidelines*

As expressed in the introduction, my purpose in this chapter was related to the legal assessment of some hesitations on the implementation of IHL in the framework of the Inter-American human rights system, in order to suggest through the use of a specific vocabulary a diachronic reading of the application of IHL and its main consequences.

It remains clear, to wrap up, that IHL and HRL are closely related, within the great area of PIL, in the objective of protecting individuals by the imposition of fundamental obligations. However, this common aim – enshrined in a shared hardcore of rights and duties – does not wipe away the fact that they are finally different legal *corpora* and that, as a consequence, in their articulation it is impossible to confuse or blend their rules.

The experience of the Inter-American system has proven to be fruitful in order to understand some general problems related to the true nature of IHL rules when used by a human rights control mechanism.[78] In this sense, it must be concluded that regional commissions or tribunals dealing with HRL violations, built over very specific treaties defining their competence, do not contemplate the legal duty of addressing breaches to IHL in an independent manner, since in general they

---

[78] As opposed to this developments reached in the Inter-American Commission and Court, where the inclusion or exclusion of IHL has been always motivated, neither the European system for the protection of HRL nor the African one have dealt with the applicability of IHL and have traditionally rejected *de facto* humanitarian rules from their sphere of competence (Fanny Martin, *Le droit international humanitaire devant les organes de contrôle des droits de l'homme*, 1 Droits fondamentaux 119 (2001)). On the European cases, *see* Cyprus v. Turkey, Applications 6780/74 & 6950/75, Report of the Commission of July 10, 1976; Ergi v. Turkey, Application 23818/94, Judgment (July 28, 1998) and Isayeva, Yusupova and Bazayeva v. Russia, Applications 57947/00, 57948/00 & 57949/00, Judgment of Feb. 24, 2005. On this last case, *see* William Abresch, *A Human Rights Law of Internal Armed Conflict: The European Court of Human Rights in Chechnya*, 16 Eur. J. Int'l L. 741 (2005). On the African experience, *see* African Commission on Human and People's Rights, Civil Liberties Organization v. Chad, No. 74/92. Decision of Oct. 11, 1995 (cf. Louise Doswald-Beck, *Human Rights Law and Humanitarian Law. Are there some Individuals Bereft of all Legal Protection?*, 98 Am. Soc'y Int'l L. Proc. 353, 356 (2004)). This general lack of precedents in other regional control mechanisms turns the Inter-American discussions even more significant.

include the possibility of asserting responsibility only for the violation of the articles contained in the convention itself. This fact, of course, is aligned with the political will of states, that engage to respect specific obligations which are included in the negotiated text of conventions and may not be forced to comply with obligations which do not arise from the positive rules that were accepted and that the state explicitly decided to respect (whether they find their binding force in treaties or custom). It seems evident, as a consequence, that compliance with IHL rules cannot be directly supervised by a human rights tribunal unless formally stated in its constitutive instrument.

The contrary position, elaborated mainly by the Commission in the 1997 reports, cannot find an appropriate justification, at least in legal terms. It is clear that the intention underlying these decisions was well justified in the need to ensure a higher degree of protection to human beings who suffer from the effects of armed conflicts and that, in this sense, the effort of providing an explanation for approaching IHL and HRL when determining the states' responsibility at a regional level deserves attention. But good will needs to find its place within the limits of pre-existing law and, in the absence of international tribunals specifically addressed to care for the respect of IHL, enlarging the competence of human rights courts requires careful thinking if the mechanism aspires to maintain the support of states.[79]

At this stage, a politically viable solution, being capable of complying both with this humanitarian interest and with the legal basis required by every mechanism for supervising human rights, should find its way without affecting and harming the protection of individuals or the trust of states.

Having explored the expressions used in decisions and reports to deal with IHL, it seems that neither the verb *apply* nor the verb *violate* have been suitable to describe the wished incorporation of IHL in cases analyzed by the Court or the Commission. In the future, then, instead of talking of a *joint application* or of *overlapping* (which may induce to think that *both* branches of law are equally applicable), it might be more appropriate to describe the implementation of IHL in terms of an *interpretative reference* or a *contextualizing guideline*.

My personal opinion, finally, is that these criteria would progressively enrich the work of the Commission as well as the jurisprudence of the Court – and potentially of other bodies pertaining to other regional systems that may profit from this experience – by permitting the indirect inclusion of several references to humanitarian norms and principles without having the need to incorporate them into the relevant field of competence against the text of the constitutive treaties.

---

[79] Especially taking into consideration that the international community is still far from ensuring in a systematic way a specific protection of humanitarian rules, if we follow the opinion of Luigi Condorelli, *L'évolution des mécanismes visant à assurer le respect du droit international humanitaire*, in L'évolution du droit international. Mélanges offerts à Hubert Thierry 133 (1998).

Chapter X

"Collateral Damages" of Military Operations: Is Implementation of International Humanitarian Law Possible Using International Human Rights Law Tools?

*Giovanni Carlo Bruno**

1. *Introduction*

The aim of this contribution is to take part in the largely debated question whether effective remedy is provided for victims of violations of international humanitarian law (IHL).

Euphemistically, in cases in which respect and protection of the civilian population is not ensured, states tend to speak of "collateral damages," a military jargon designating the wounding or the killing of civilians and the damage of their private goods as a consequence of military operations.[1]

What is highly controversial is whether an individual right to compensation for damage may arise from the ascertainment of state responsibility for "collateral damages."

From 24 March to June 10, 1999 the North Atlantic Treaty Organization (NATO) conducted an air campaign against the Federal Republic of Yugoslavia (FRY) – Operation Allied Force. Although NATO has not released official estimates

---

* Giovanni Carlo Bruno is a Researcher in International Law at the Institute for International Legal Studies (*Istituto di Studi Giuridici Internazionali*) of the Italian National Research Council (*Consiglio Nazionale delle Ricerche*) – Napoli.
[1] In an Amnesty International report, it is said that "[b]roadly defined, collateral damage is unintentional damage or incidental damage affecting facilities, equipment or personnel occurring as a result of military action directed against a targeted enemy force or facilities. Such damage can occur to friendly, neutral, and even enemy forces." Amnesty International, NATO/FRY, Collateral Damage or Unlawful Killings: Violations of the Laws of War by NATO During Operation Allied Force, AI Index: EUR 70/18/00 (June 2000), *available at*: www.web.amnesty.org/ai.nsf/index/EUR700182000 (last visited April 20, 2007), para. 2, note 6. The same document clarifies that "collateral damage" is not a term used in international humanitarian law.

of civilians or combatants killed, media have stated that a high number of civilians died in NATO air raids.

Several applications have been lodged by relatives of Yugoslav nationals killed during the air campaign with domestic and international courts. The applicants believed that civil liability for the deaths of their relatives laid within state authorities.

This contribution deals with the *Varvarin* and the *Marković* cases, brought in German and Italian courts, respectively.

While in the *Varvarin* case, declared admissible in 2003, the compensation claim was not recognised, the Italian Supreme Court affirmed, in a preliminary ruling on jurisdiction in 2002, that Italian courts lacked jurisdiction in the *Marković* case. An application against Italy was then lodged with the European Court of Human Rights, which declared it partially inadmissible in 2003 and examined the merits of the case at the same time as the issue of admissibility in 2006.

In this book it has been often recalled that, despite their different historical backgrounds and their own normative specificities, the central concern of human rights law and humanitarian law is "human dignity."[2]

May such a "common ground" be a valid basis for assessing effective and valid compensation for damage to "alleged victims" of any "grave" violations of human rights and humanitarian law?

The two cases under examination are an outstanding example of the complexity of the problem of ensuring an effective remedy when provisions of international humanitarian law are breached. Neither domestic courts and tribunals, nor the intervention of the Strasbourg Court – the organ established to supervise and implement the European system of protection of human rights – offered a valid safeguard. Should we conclude that complementarity between the two systems, as far as the use of protection tools is concerned, is possible only theoretically?

---

[2] *See* the Section 1 – Chapter 1. In its Advisory Opinion of July 8, 1996 on the Legality of the Threat or Use of Nuclear Weapons, the International Court of Justice confirmed the convergence and complementarity of human rights and humanitarian law. Recognising the continuing applicability of human rights law in time of armed conflict, the judges of the World Court affirmed: "the protection of the International Covenant of Civil and Political Rights does not cease in times of war, except by operation of Article 4 of the Covenant whereby certain provisions may be derogated from in a time of national emergency. Respect for the right to life is not, however, such a provision. In principle, the right not arbitrarily to be deprived of one's life applies also in hostilities. The test of what is an arbitrary deprivation of life, however, then falls to be determined by the applicable *lex specialis*, namely, the law applicable in armed conflict which is designed to regulate the conduct of hostilities. Thus whether a particular loss of life, through the use of a certain weapon in warfare, is to be considered an arbitrary deprivation of life contrary to Article 6 of the Covenant, can only be decided by reference to the law applicable in armed conflict and not deduced from the terms of the Covenant itself." Legality of the Threat or Use of Nuclear Weapons, Advisory Opinion, July 8, 1996), I.C.J. Reports 1996, para. 25. *See*, in general, Vincent Chetail, *The Contribution of the International Court of Justice to International Humanitarian Law*, 85 Int'l Rev. Red Cross 235 (2003).

2. Violations of the Obligation of Protection of Civilian Population and Civilian Objects, Prohibition of Attacks Against Civilians, and Article 91 of the 1977 Additional Protocol to the Geneva Conventions

It can be useful to recall those provisions of the 1977 Additional Protocol to the Geneva Conventions of 1949 which are directly referred to in the two cases examined.

The distinction between combatants and non-combatants is one of "the cardinal principles" constituting the "fabric" of humanitarian law.[3]

According to Article 57 (1) AP I: "In the conduct of military operations, constant care shall be taken to spare the civilian population, civilians and civilian objects."[4] Further, Article 51(4) AP I purports to give a comprehensive definition of "indiscriminate attacks" prohibited in all forms of warfare.[5]

"Grave breaches" of the Protocol and the regime of state and individual responsibility are provided for in Articles 85 and 86; Article 91 states that

> A Party to the conflict which violates the provisions of the Conventions or of this Protocol shall, if the case demands, be liable to pay compensation. It shall be responsible for all acts committed by persons forming part of its armed forces.[6]

---

[3] The First Chamber of the International Tribunal for the former Yugoslavia stated that: "the rule that the civilian population as such, as well as individual civilians, shall not be the object of attack, is a fundamental rule of international humanitarian law applicable to all armed conflicts" (Prosecutor v. Martic, Case No. IT-95-11-R61, Decision of Trial Chamber I, para. 10 (Mar. 8, 1996)).

[4] Protocol Additional to the Geneva Conventions of 12 August 1949, and Relating to the Protection of Victims of International Armed Conflicts (Protocol I), June 8, 1977, 1125 U.N.T.S. 3 [hereinafter AP I]

[5] Indiscriminate attacks are:
  (a) Those which are not directed at a specific military objective;
  (b) Those which employ a method or means of combat which cannot be directed at a specific military objective; or
  (c) Those which employ a method or means of combat the effects of which cannot be limited as required by this Protocol; and consequently, in each such case, are of a nature to strike military objectives and civilians or civilian objects without distinction.
  It goes on to give two particular examples:
  the following types of attacks are to be considered as indiscriminate:
  (a) An attack by bombardment by any methods or means which treats as a single military objective a number of clearly separated and distinct military objectives located in a city, town, village or other area containing a similar concentration of civilians or civilian objects; and
  (b) An attack which may be expected to cause incidental loss of civilian life, injury to civilians, damage to civilian objects, or a combination thereof, which would be excessive in relation to the concrete and direct military advantage anticipated.
  Id.

[6] *Id.*

Scholars,[7] but also domestic case-law,[8] tend to consider these provisions – and Article 91 in particular – as being "non-self-executing," thus precluding them from being invoked before national courts by alleged victims of violations of the Conventions' provisions.

Another issue concerns the application of the above-mentioned provisions to intervention of military coalitions established under the auspices of international organizations. With regard to Operation Allied Force, in addition to the jurisdiction of the national courts of any state, there was the concurrent jurisdiction of the International Criminal Tribunal for the Former Yugoslavia (ICTY): grave breaches of the Geneva Conventions (Article 2) and other violations of the laws and customs of war (Article 3) committed by any person – regardless of nationality – since 1991 in any part of the former Federal Republic of Yugoslavia (Article 1) were under ICTY's jurisdiction.[9]

3. *The Varvarin Case*

On May 30, 1999, during NATO air raid, the bridge of the small Serbian town of Varvarin was struck, causing the death of ten civilians and seventeen seriously injured.

A group of 35 relatives of the victims brought an action in damage in the District Court (*Landesgericht*) of Bonn, arguing that German authorities bore responsibility for the modalities in which the air strike had been carried out. The Varvarin bridge was considered a military target; in the plaintiff's opinion, compensation for damages had to be awarded for the general support offered by Germany to NATO campaign, together with the absence of any opposition on the question of the inclusion of the Varvarin bridge among military targets.

In its judgment of December 10, 2003,[10] the District Court dismissed the case as a matter of principle, since it did not recognise any right on individuals

---

[7] See Frits Kalshoven, *State Responsibility for Warlike Acts of the Armed Forces: From Article 3 of the Hague Convention IV of 1907 to Article 91 of Additional Protocol I and Beyond*, 40 ICLQ 827 (1991); Yves Sandoz, *Les dommages illicites dans les conflits armés et leur réparation dans le cadre du droit international humanitaire*, 228 Int'l Rev. Red Cross 135 (1982). See also the observations of Riccardo Pisillo Mazzeschi, *Reparations Claims by Individuals for States Breaches of Humanitarian Law and Human Rights: An Overview*, 1 JICL 339 (2003).

[8] See Micaela Frulli, *When Are States Liable Towards Individuals for Serious Violations of Humanitarian Law? The Marković Case*, 1 JICL 406 (2003).

[9] The Committee Established to Review the NATO Bombing Campaign Against the Federal Republic of Yugoslavia, Final Report to the Prosecutor, 39 ILM 1257, 1272 (June 8, 2000), *available at* un.org/icty/pressreal/nato061300.htm (last visited April 20, 2007).

[10] Bridge of Varvarin case, Landgericht (LG) Bonn, 1 O 361/02, reproduced in 57 NJW 525 (2004) and in 2 HuV-I 111 (2004). On the decision *see* Noëlle Quénivet, *The Varvarin Case: The Legal*

to a compensation claim for violation of international humanitarian law. In the Court's opinion, neither public international law nor German law supported the plaintiffs' arguments.

The traditional conception of international law as the "law of the community of states" barred any legal entitlement of subjects different from states to a reparation claim; an exception to this regime could be found in human rights law, where a direct action of individuals before courts to pursue their claims had been provided for. Once ascertained that the system of the European Convention on Human Rights had to be considered an exception, the judges affirmed that reparation for violations of international law – including humanitarian law – could be obtained only through diplomatic protection of the home state.[11]

Moreover, the German law on state liability was held to be inapplicable to the armed acts under scrutiny.[12]

Thus, following the approach of the Federal Court of Justice (*Bundesgerichtshof*) in the 2003 judgement in the *Distomo* case,[13] the District Court dismissed the case.

The Köln Regional Court (*Oberlandesgericht*), in its appellate ruling of July, 28 2005,[14] while confirming that international humanitarian law did not provide for a direct individual claim, recognized that an individual right to claim official responsibility of the state had to be acknowledged even for war crimes. Such a right emerged from recent developments of public international law, not only in the area of protection of fundamental human rights, but also in the practice of punishment of individuals who had committed "grave breaches" of the Geneva conventions.[15]

Nonetheless, the Regional Court denied that the civil liability for the deaths and wounded in Varvarin laid with the German authorities. A wide margin of appreciation on issues of foreign policy had to be guaranteed to the Government. The principle that they "need to know" applicable to NATO decision making did not entail in itself any responsibility on Germany, since government officials had trusted NATO decisions on being fully in conformity with international law.[16]

Standing of Individuals as Subjects of International Humanitarian Law, 3 Journal of Military Ethics 181 (2004).

[11] *Id.* paras 122 ff.

[12] *Id.* paras 133 ff.

[13] Bundesgerichtshof, Case No. III ZR 245/98, Decision, June 26, 2003, reproduced in 56 NJW 3488 (2003).

[14] Oberlandesgericht (OLG) Köln, 7 U 8/04, *available at* www.olg-koeln.nrw.de (last visited 20 April 2007).

[15] Paras 18 ff. of the text published in www.olg-koeln.nrw.de/home/presse/archiv/urteile/2004/7U008–04u.pdf (last visited Sept. 10, 2007).

[16] Paras 23 ff., p. 26 of the text published in www.olg-koeln.nrw.de/home/presse/archiv/urteile/2004/7U008–04u.pdf.

The final decision of the Federal Court of Justice was rendered on November 2, 2006.[17] It countered substantially the arguments of the Regional Court, affirming again that individual victims of violations of humanitarian law had no right to reparation neither under German law nor under international law. Only diplomatic protection was applicable to such cases, since states, and not individuals, might bring reparation claims.

Furthermore, the Court affirmed that no breach of conduct by German soldiers or authorities could be established. In fact, Germany supported the NATO air strikes without the direct intervention of German soldiers and only offered technical assistance via its planes. Consequently the Court dismissed the case. No further application by the plaintiffs has been lodged with German courts.

4. *The Marković Case*

The second case under examination is the *Marković* case, which is closer to the core point of our analysis on whether human rights machinery can be useful to ensure the application of international humanitarian law.

The case originated in an application lodged with the Rome District Court (*Corte d'Appello di Roma*) by ten applicants, all citizens of Serbia and Montenegro.[18] The applicants believed that civil liability for the deaths of their relatives for events occurred during the NATO air strikes on the territory of the Federal Republic of Yugoslavia from March 24, to June 8, 1999 (Operation Allied Force) laid down with the Italian Prime Minister's Office and Ministry of Defence and with the Command of NATO's Allied Forces in Southern Europe ("AFSOUTH").

The act under scrutiny before the District Court was the bombing of the RTS building in Belgrade, which took place on April 23, 1999; the partial collapse of the building caused the death of sixteen people, including five relatives of the applicants.

Italy provided the air bases from which the aircraft that bombed Belgrade and the RTS took off. It was argued by the applicants that the unlawful act that had caused the alleged damage should be regarded as having been committed in Italy, inasmuch as the military action had been organised on Italian territory and part of it had taken place there; in their opinion, the Italian courts had jurisdiction to hear the case on the basis of the Italian Criminal Code.[19] Moreover, several articles

---

[17] Bundesgerichtshof, III ZR 190/05, Nov. 2, 2006.
[18] The text of the summons of May 31, 2000 have been reproduced in Elena Sciso (ed.), L'intervento in Kosovo. Aspetti internazionalistici ed interni 399 (2000) [hereinafter Sciso].
[19] Article 6 of the Italian Criminal Code states that "Chiunque commette un reato nel territorio dello Stato e' punito secondo la legge italiana. Il reato si considera commesso nel territorio dello

of Additional Protocol I offered a valid support of their claim: the bombing of the RTS building constituted a conduct of war not allowed by the 1977 Protocol, mainly because the building had to be considered as a non-military objective and because the act was intentionally addressed against civilians.[20]

The defendants sought a preliminary ruling from the Court of Cassation on the question of jurisdiction (*regolamento preventivo di giurisdizione*), under Article 41 of the Italian Code of Civil Procedure; they argued that Italian courts had no jurisdiction to hear the case.[21] They maintained that no action against the Italian state could be brought before courts for acts performed in the exercise of state authority (*iure imperii*).[22] Therefore no basis could be provided for the guarantee of an abstract alleged personal right to obtain compensation for damage for acts carried out in the exercise of such authority.

The Court of Cassation, sitting as a full court (*Sezioni Unite*), found that the Italian courts had no jurisdiction.[23] Its ruling brought to an end the proceedings in the Rome District Court.

Stato, quando l'azione o l'omissione, che lo costituisce, e' ivi avvenuta in tutto o in parte, ovvero si e' verificato l'evento che e' la conseguenza dell'azione od omissione." (Anyone who commits an offence on the territory of the State shall be punished in accordance with Italian law. The offence will be regarded as having been committed on the territory of the State if all or part of the act or omission at the origin of the offence or all or some of the consequences of such act or omission occurred there.)

[20] *See*, in particular, paras 32–34 of the application. In addition, they argued that the same act violated Article 174 of the Italian military criminal code applicable in time of war (*codice penale militare di guerra*), which provides for the punishment of the commanding officer authorising or ordering, *inter alia*, the use of means or acts of war contrary to law and international treaties. According to the petitioners, the responsibility consequent from the above mentioned acts had to be attributed to Italy, both because as a NATO Member state it concurred in determining the conducts of war, and because the war action started on the Italian territory.
In the plaintiffs' opinion, the London Agreement of June 19, 1951 between the Parties of the NATO regarding the status of their armed forces – executed in Italy with law n. 1335 of Nov. 30, 1995 – was also applicable to the case. In particular, the claim was said to have arisen "out of acts or omissions of members of a force or civilian component done in the performance of official duty, or out of any other act, omission or occurrence for which a force or civilian component is legally responsible, and causing damage in the territory of the receiving state to third parties, other than any of the Contracting Parties" (Article VIII(5) of the Agreement). For the text of the Agreement, *see* www.nato.int/docu/basictxt/b510619a.htm (last visited Sept. 10, 2007).

[21] The text of the application of October 16, 2000 has been reproduced in Sciso, *supra* note 17, at 407 ff. *See* Franco Cipriani, *Regolamento di giurisdizione (I) Diritto processuale civile*, in Enciclopedia Giuridica (Vol. XXVI, 1991).

[22] With reference to the 1951 London Agreement, it was denied that it could be applicable to the case, since Article VIII(5) applies only to damage caused in the receiving state.

[23] Corte di Cassazione (sezioni unite), June 5, 2002, n. 8157 (order) *Presidenza Consiglio Ministri c. Marković e altri*, *in* Rivista di diritto internazionale 800 (2002). Large excerpts of the English version of the Order can be found at para. 18 of Marković, *supra* note 18.

According to the Court, the reasons of its decision had to be found in the peculiarity of the act under examination. The *Marković* and other cases concerned an issue of state responsibility deduced from an act of war, in particular aerial war, considered among modalities of war conduct. Now, the Court continued,

> [t]he choice of modalities of war conducts has to be included among Governmental acts. The said acts constitute an expression of a political function, and the Constitution attributes such function to a specific organ [the Government]. The nature of the political function is so peculiar that it cannot be provided for the existence of a situation of protected interest aimed to give or to deny a specific content to acts related to such function.[24]

On this point, it concluded that "[w]ith respect to the said acts, no judge can have the power of challenging the way in which the [political] function is carried out."[25]

As for international humanitarian law, and in particular Articles 35(2), 48, 49, 51, 52, 57 AP I, as well as the European Convention of Human Rights (ECHR) (Articles 2 and 15),[26] the *Corte di Cassazione* emphasised that, although the above-mentioned provisions concerning the conduct of hostilities were aimed at protecting civilians in case of attacks, they could not be considered as self-executing

> in that, being international rules, they govern relations among sovereign States only. Accordingly, such conventions autonomously provide for, at the international level, the procedures to ascertain violations, the sanctions to be applied against the responsible State (art. 91 of the First Protocol, art. 41 of the Convention), and the identification of courts or tribunals which can assess such responsibility.[27]

Turning then to the internal laws executing the international treaties in question, the *Corte* added that they

> do not contain any express rule allowing alleged victims to claim damages deriving from a violation of international law by a contracting State, before the latter's State tribunals directly. Provisions of this kind cannot be considered as implicitly introduced in the domestic legal order through the execution given to an international treaty as a whole.[28]

The rationale of this contention was that, according to the *Cassazione*, it would not have been in any case possible to recognise the judicial protection of individual interests against activities performed in connection with a state's political function.[29]

---

[24] *Id.* para. 2.
[25] *Id.* para. 2.
[26] European Convention for the Protection of Human Rights and Fundamental Freedoms (Nov. 4, 1950), 213 U.N.T.S. 221 [hereinafter ECHR].
[27] Marković Court of Cassation, *supra* note 24, para. 3.
[28] *Id.* para. 3.
[29] With regard to the London Agreement of 1951, the *Corte di Cassazione* excluded its relevance to the case. Motivations alleged to support that finding were not completely clear. Arguably, the

4. The Marković Case Before the European Court of Human Rights

The Italian Supreme Court's order in the Marković affair was challenged before the European Court of Human Rights. The applicants complained in particular of a violation of Article 6 ECHR, taken together with Article 1, but also Articles 2, 10, 13 and 17 ECHR.

On June 12, 2003, the Strasbourg Court delivered a decision of partial inadmissibility, deciding to communicate the remainder of the application (concerning the alleged violation of Article 6) to the Italian government.[30] After having relinquished jurisdiction to the Grand Chamber, the European Court delivered on December 14, 2006 its judgment, in which it held that there had been no violation of Article 6 ECHR.[31]

The application showed some similarities with another application lodged with the European Court by the relatives of other victims of the NATO air strikes against those states, Parties to the ECHR, which were also NATO Members: the *Bankovic and Others* case.[32] And, in fact, they both dealt with the same incident.

The 2003 decision of partial inadmissibility of the *Marković* case was based by the Court mainly on the reasoning followed in the 2001 decision of the *Banković* case: the complaints concerning the essential rights guaranteed by the Convention were inadmissible, *ratione loci*, because alleged violations took place in a territory which in no way could be considered under the "effective control" of the respondent states.[33] Reference was made to Article 1 ECHR which states that "[t]he High

---

Court wanted to stress the difficulty in ascertaining who had caused the death of the victims and what kind of damage should exactly be repaired:
> Whereas Article VIII(5) of the London Convention establishes a procedure for assessing damages caused in relation to concrete and precisely defined offences, the bombing of the Belgrade TV, albeit conducted by planes which took off from the Italian territory, is but a part of a more complex and vast operation whose legality could not be tested in the light of the system envisaged by the London Convention.

Id. para. 4.

[30] Marković et autres c. Italie, requête n° 1389/03, Décision partielle sur la recevabilité (12 juin 2003) [hereinafter Marković (2003)]

[31] Marković v. Italy, Application No. 1398/03, Judgment (Dec. 14, 2006) [hereinafter Marković (2006)].

[32] Banković and Others v. Belgium and Sixteen Other Contracting States, Application No. 52207/99, Decision (December 19, 2001).

[33] *Id.*, para 59: "As to the "ordinary meaning" of the relevant term in Article 1 of the Convention, the Court is satisfied that, from the standpoint of public international law, the jurisdictional competence of a State is primarily territorial. While international law does not exclude a State's exercise of jurisdiction extra-territorially, the suggested bases of such jurisdiction (including nationality, flag, diplomatic and consular relations, effect, protection, passive personality and universality) are, as a general rule, defined and limited by the sovereign territorial rights of the other relevant States." *See*, Georg Ress, *Problems of Extraterritorial Human Rights Violations: The Jurisdiction of the European Court of Human Rights: The Bankovic Case*, 12 IYIL 51 (2002).

Contracting Parties shall secure to everyone within their jurisdiction the rights and freedoms" defined in the Convention. The Court went on stating that:

> dans l'affaire *Banković et autres*, elle [the Court] avait déclaré l'inexistence d'un "lien juridictionnel" au sens de l'article 1 de la Convention entre les personnes qui avaient été victimes de l'acte incriminé et les Etats défendeurs et avait conclu que l'action en cause n'engageait pas la responsabilité de ceux-ci au regard de la Convention. Sur la base de ce constat, elle avait jugé ne pas devoir examiner les autres questions de recevabilité soulevées par les parties.
>
> Elle estime en l'occurrence que les circonstances particulières de l'espèce, notamment la saisine des juridictions italiennes par les requérants, ne lui permettent pas de s'écarter de ladite jurisprudence.[34]

Applying the *Bankovic* case-law, the European Court, also in the *Marković* case, did not find any "jurisdictional link" between the victims of the act complained and the respondent state.[35] It then declared inadmissible the grounds on Articles 2, 10, 13 and 17 ECHR.

The 2006 judgment ascertained first that the application was not manifestly ill-founded; the Court noted that the issues of fact and law raised in the case required an examination of the merits.[36] The assessment of all the elements of the dispute led to the conclusion that the domestic proceedings in the Rome District Court, brought to an end *ipso jure* by the Supreme Court decision on jurisdiction, did not amount to a violation of Article 6 ECHR.[37]

The applicants maintained that their inability to sue the state for a compensation claim for the alleged violation of their rights as a consequence of an act of foreign policy such as an act of war amounted to recognition of an immunity, and therefore could be regarded as an arbitrary removal of the courts' jurisdiction to evaluate a whole range of civil claims.

In the opinion of the European Court of Human Rights, the said inability was only one of the "principles governing the substantive right of action in domestic law."[38] Any other hearing

> would only have served to protract the domestic proceedings unnecessarily because, even assuming that the Court of Cassation's decision did not automatically bring the proceedings pending in the Rome District Court to an end, the District Court

---

[34] Marković (2003), *supra* note 31, p. 6 of the text available at www.echr.coe.int (last visited September 10, 2007).
[35] *Id.*
[36] Marković (2006), *supra* note 32, para. 65.
[37] *See* Carlo Focarelli, *Il caso Marković dinanzi alla Corte europea dei diritti dell'uomo* 2 Studi sull'integrazione europea 43 (2007).
[38] Marković (2006), *supra* note 32, para. 114.

would only have had power to determine the nature of the impugned acts and, in the circumstances of the case, would have had no alternative but to dismiss the claim.[39]

This line of reasoning was considered unconvincing by one of the European Court Vice Presidents, Mr Costa; in his concurring opinion he affirmed that, in this case, it would had been

> simpler – and clearer – to apply the standard principles [that is] the right of access to a court is not absolute, but may be subject to implied limitations. Some of these limitations are inherent in the right of access to a court, for instance those arising out of State immunity in international law.[40]

Defining the issue as a state immunity, it would have been easier to declare that a "right" to reparation under the law of tort could be assessed before domestic courts.

6. *The Possibility of Using International Human Rights Tools to Ensure the Respect of International Humanitarian Law*

The two cases examined invite for some remarks.

The first remark concerns the "political function" (*acte de gouvernement*) argument. It is true that governmental activities involving the exercise of "authoritative powers in foreign matters" should in principle be performed even at the cost of sacrificing the right of individuals to seek a judicial protection of their interests. In effect, domestic legal orders provide for different forms of control on the legitimacy of political acts performed by the Executive.[41] However, it seems doubtful that judicial review of those activities should be absolutely ruled out, in particular when possible violations of fundamental human rights are at stake.[42] As stated also by the Institute of International Law, the possibility for national courts to review the Executive's conduct in the exercise of its "authoritative power in foreign matters" should not be on principle excluded, when such exercise of power is subject to a rule of international law.[43] Furthermore, Article 15(1) ECHR contains "one window" through which it is possible to evaluate whether a derogation from the right to life

---

[39] *Id.* para. 115.
[40] *Id.* Concurring Opinion of Judge Costa, paras 14–15.
[41] For the Italian legal system, *see* Alessandro Pizzorusso, *Controlli. III) Controlli costituzionali*, in Enciclopedia Giuridica (Vol. III, 1989).
[42] *See* the analysis of Natalino Ronzitti, *Azioni belliche e risarcimento del danno*, 85 Rivista di diritto internazionale 682, 685 (2002). On the use of the "political act" doctrine in Italian case-law, *see* the critical note of Paolo Picone, *Giurisprudenza italiana e diritto internazionale: il Repertorio 1987–1998*, 53 La Comunità internazionale 19, 28 (1998).
[43] *See* the text of the resolution on "The activities of national judges and the international relations of their state" approved in the Session of Milan on September, 7 1993 in 65 Yearbook of the Institute of International Law 319 ff. The resolution was based on the Reports submitted by Benedetto

enshrined in Article 2 has been rendered possible by a "lawful act of war."[44] The recent case-law of the European Court is showing the weakness of such evaluation, and the problem will not be overcome unless the "effective control approach" in the interpretation of the meaning of "jurisdiction of a state" is modified.[45]

Let us turn now to the arguments concerning the nature of "humanitarian" treaties. According to the Italian Supreme Court ruling in the *Marković* case, all treaties of that kind would possess a non self-executing character. However, this assumption cannot be totally shared.

The subject of direct applicability of human rights treaties – and of international conventions in general – by Italian judges cannot be dealt with in depth in this essay.[46] It has to be pointed out that, in general, sources of international law have been, and still are, used mainly to confirm and support domestic legislation.

Furthermore, the possibility of a direct application of such provisions before Italian courts and tribunal has been often prevented. As far as human rights treaties are concerned, two arguments have been used by judges: the "programmatic" nature of international norms, and the surviving idea of international law as a "law of diplomats." In the last years, with reference to the ECHR in particular, Italian judicial decisions are more and more open to its direct application.[47]

In both cases under examination, treaties on humanitarian law are considered to create rights and obligations "among states." In legal doctrine several authors maintain that reparation claims by individuals are provided for by Article 91 AP I. Recent practice, and also the two cases examined in this contribution, show a clear refusal of such an interpretation.

Conforti, *Preliminary Report*, 65 Yearbook of the Institute of International Law, 327 ff., 331 ff.; *Provisional Report, id.* at 371 ff., 382 ff.; and *Final Report, id.* at 428 ff., 437.

[44] *See* René Provost, International Human Rights And Humanitarian Law 332 (2002).

[45] On the issue of 'jurisdiction of State' in human rights treaties, *see* Pasquale De Sena, La nozione di giurisdizione statale nei trattati sui diritti dell'uomo (2001).

[46] *See* Francesco Francioni, *The Jurisprudence of International Human Rights Enforcement: Reflections on the Italian Experience, in* Enforcing Human Rights in Domestic Courts 15ff. (Benedetto Conforti & Francesco Francioni eds., 1997) [hereinafter Conforti & Francioni]; Tullio Scovazzi, *The Application by Italian Courts of Human Rights Treaty Law, in* Conforti & Francioni, *id.* at 57 ff.; Antonio Cassese, *Diritto internazionale*, 297–298 (Paola Gaeta ed., 2006); Benedetto Conforti, Diritto internazionale, para. 38.4 (2006).

[47] *See*, among the most recent judgments, Corte Costituzionale, n. 399 (Dec. 12, 1998); n. 388 (Oct. 22, 1999); Corte di Cassazione (sezione I civile), n. 6672 (July 8, 1998); Corte d'Appello di Roma (sezione lavoro), (order) (April 11, 2002); Corte di Cassazione (Sez. I penale), (Oct. 3, 2006), No. 32678 Somogyi (*see* the note of Fulvio Maria Palombino, in 14 IYIL 2006, forthcoming). On the relationship between ECHR and Italian legal system, *see* Giuseppe Cataldi, *Convenzione europea dei diritti dell'uomo e ordinamento italiano: un tentativo di bilancio, in* Divenire sociale e adeguamento del diritto: studi in onore di Francesco Capotorti 55 (1999).

Moreover, recent jurisprudence on "acts" committed during World War II aims to provide for an exception to state immunity from jurisdiction for reparation claims when "international crimes" are committed.[48]

The same is not true for breaches of international humanitarian law committed as a consequence of "measures" and "actions" carried out in operations under the direction and control of international organizations. The duty of states to comply with and to ensure international humanitarian law does not entail changing in the sphere of individual rights, although a progressive shift of attitude would be desirable.

To conclude, and at least as far as the *Marković* and *Varvarin* cases demonstrate, complementarity of international human rights law and international humanitarian law, as for the use of tools belonging to one system to ensure rights provided for in the other, is still far from being effective.

---

[48] *See* Corte di Cassazione (sezioni unite civili), Judgment, (March 11, 2004), No. 5044, Ferrini c. Repubblica Federale di Germania. *See* the note of Massimo Iovane, *The Ferrini Judgment of the Italian Supreme Court: Opening up Domestic Courts to Claims of Reparation for Victims of Serious Violations of Fundamental Human Rights*, 14 IYIL 165 (2004).

Chapter XI

The Role of the UN Security Council in Implementing International Humanitarian Law and Human Rights Law

Gregor Schotten* and Anke Biehler**

1. *Introduction*

Traditionally the implementation of human rights law (HRL) and international humanitarian law (IHL) is not considered to be within the primary responsibilities of the United Nations, (U.N.) Security Council. The Security Council is rather a highly political organ primarily charged to maintain international peace and security. As such, it is very different from classic implementation bodies like the U.N. treaty monitoring bodies under human rights treaties or the International Committee of the Red Cross as far as the implementation of IHL is concerned and which is independent from the U.N. system. This does not imply, however, that the Security Council has no role to play in implementing HRL and IHL. In an era of globalization in which conflicts and its effects pass not only beyond borders, but beyond regions; in which the concept of state sovereignty is eroding and in which the protection of individuals therefore becomes increasingly an international concern, the Security Council can only maintain international peace and security when it also takes (respect for) HRL and IHL into account.

This article analyzes the practice of the Security Council relating to HRL and IHL. It examines the development of this practice with special attention being paid to practice closely linked to the determination of a threat to international peace and security by the Security Council according to Article 39 U.N. Charter. The evaluation of the practice attempts to show its relevance in discussing the new concepts of "human security" and the "responsibility to protect." Finally,

---

* The views expressed in this article are those of the author alone and do not reflect the position of the ICRC.
** The views expressed in this article are those of the authors alone and do not reflect the position of the German Federal Foreign Office.

the impact of this practice upon the Security Council and for HRL and IHL in general is examined.

2. *Practice of the U.N. Security Council*

2.1. *Practice from 1945 to 1989*

2.1.1. *Human Rights Law*

The Security Council is the only organ of the United Nations which has no explicit authority to deal with human rights. At the time of its creation, human rights were considered strictly internal matters of the state and consequently outside the scope of the Security Council.[1] Security was solely regarded as state security, the latter being wholly separate from human rights.[2] During the Cold War the Security Council was most of the time incapable to act due to the use of the veto right of the two superpowers. Between its foundation in 1945 and the Six Day War in 1967, thus for the first 22 years of its existence, the Security Council did not pass a single resolution on humanitarian or human rights aspects of armed conflict.[3]

Following the hostilities between Jordan and Israel in June 1967, the Security Council adopted Resolution 237, which called upon the parties to the conflict to respect human rights (even) during war.[4] In the 1970s and 1980s the Security Council reluctantly started to become involved in the implementation of HRL. In some cases it addressed issues like humanitarian assistance or the problem of refugees, e.g. the 1971 conflict in Pakistan or the 1974 conflict in Cyprus. In the latter it also urged the parties to the conflict to protect the civilian population.[5] However, the Security Council remained silent in other major crises such as the Biafra conflict or the Vietnam War.

Even though not related to the question of human rights in armed conflict, it is necessary to mention the Security Councils work for the promotion of the principle of self-determination, mainly in Africa, and its condemnation of apartheid, when assessing its human rights engagement at the time.[6]

---

[1] Sydney Bailey, The UN Security Council and Human Rights 123 (1994) [hereinafter Bailey]; Joanna Weschler, *Human Rights, in* The UN Security Council. From the Cold War to the 21st Century 55 (David M. Malone ed., 2004) [hereinafter Weschler].
[2] Weschler, *id.* at 55.
[3] Theo A. van Baarda, *The Involvement of the Security Council in Maintaining International Humanitarian Law*, 12 NQHR 137, 138 (1994) [hereinafter van Baarda].
[4] S.C. Res. 237, U.N. Doc. S/RES/237 (1967) (June 14, 1967).
[5] *See* in detail van Baarda, *supra* note 3, at 138–139.
[6] *See* in detail Bailey, *supra* note 1, at 1–15.

2.1.2. International Humanitarian Law

Initially, it was not intended that the United Nations engaged in international humanitarian law – contrary to human rights – at all. The decision not to mention international humanitarian law in the Charter of the United Nations was due to the fact that it was feared that any involvement in the implementation of IHL could possibly be misinterpreted as an acknowledgement of the failure on the part of the United Nations to achieve its most important objective, the maintenance of international peace and security. Furthermore, to mention IHL was considered as partly undermining the fundamental prohibition of the use of force contained in Article 2(4) U.N. Charter.[7] For this reason the United Nations – similarly to the position it took on human rights – played no particular role in the implementation of IHL for the first twenty years of its existence.[8]

Nevertheless, the Security Council could not continue to overlook the reality of modern armed conflicts. It thus cautiously began to consider aspects of IHL more often since it first referred to IHL in 1967 with regard to the Six Day War.[9] In Resolution 307 (1971) the Security Council called upon the parties to the conflict in Pakistan to respect the Geneva Conventions.[10] In Resolution 436 (1978) the Security Council called upon all parties to the civil war in Lebanon to allow units of the ICRC into the area of conflict to evacuate the wounded and provide assistance.[11] This was the first time that the ICRC and its rights were explicitly mentioned in a Security Council resolution and also the first time that the Security Council dealt with an armed conflict of non-international nature. In its 1979 Resolution 446 the Security Council went even further as it directly called upon a state (Israel) to rescind particular measures which it considered as violating the law.[12]

During the first Gulf war between Iraq and Iran (1980–1988) the Security Council urged both warring parties to respect the Geneva Conventions. The date

---

[7] Laurence Boisson de Chazournes, *Les résolutions des organes des Nations Unies, et en particulier celles du Conseil de sécurité, en tant que source de droit international humanitaire, in* Les Nations Unies et le Droit International Humanitaire 150, 151 (Luigi Condorelli, Anne Marie La Rosa & Sylvie Scherrer eds., 1995) [hereinafter Condorelli] [hereinafter Boisson de Chazournes]; Christiane Bourloyannis, *The Security Council of the United Nations and the Implementation of International Humanitarian Law*, 20 Den. J. Int'l L. & Pol'y 335 (1992).

[8] *Id.* at 335.

[9] All resolutions regarding the implementation of the Geneva Conventions in territories occupied by Israel from 1967–1993 are listed by Bailey, *supra* note 1, at 76.

[10] S.C. Res. 307, U.N. Doc. S/RES/307 (1971) (Dec. 21, 1971). For the background of this resolution see Bailey, *supra* note 1, at 79.

[11] S.C. Res. 436, U.N. Doc. S/RES/436 (1978) (Oct. 6, 1978).

[12] S.C. Res. 446, U.N. Doc. S/RES/446 (1979) (Mar. 22, 1979). *See* in detail van Baarda, *supra* note 3, at 139.

of the respective Resolution 540 in 1983,[13] three years after the conflict started, shows that the Security Council only very reluctantly took the initiative to act on this conflict. Later on, both Iran and Iraq were condemned for the use of poison gas.[14] Finally, the Security Council called upon the parties to the conflict to respect the third Geneva Convention in Resolution 598 (1987).[15]

2.1.3. Evaluation

As shown, the engagement of the Security Council on IHL and HRL was rather limited until the end of the Cold War. The first phase before 1967 has been correctly characterized as "*tabula rasa*" period.[16] The 1970s and 1980s marked a period of very careful and somewhat reluctant engagement as far as the implementation of HRL and IHL is concerned. Many armed conflicts during this period in which serious violations of IHL and HRL were known, either did not provoke any action of the Security Council or were only dealt with at a very advanced stage (when it had become impossible to look away or to ignore it any longer) as it was the case with violations of IHL and HRL during the first Gulf war. Nevertheless, the number of resolutions considering IHL and HRL violations in armed conflict increased significantly during that period and the Security Council cautiously started to call upon violators of IHL to refrain from such practices.

2.2. Practice since 1989

The end of the Cold War liberated the Security Council from previous restraints linked to the right of veto and allowed it to become increasingly active in the implementation of IHL and HRL in armed conflict. Therefore IHL and HRL are no longer treated separately in the following section. The actions taken by the Security Council can be classified according to their content as calls to respect IHL and HRL, calls to ratify, implement and disseminate HRL and IHL, calls to respect specific norms, and calls to prosecute certain HRL and IHL violations. With regard to HRL and IHL the practice of the Security Council concerning the explicit determination of a "threat to peace" in the meaning of Article 39 U.N. Charter is particularly significant.

2.2.1. Calls to Ratify and Disseminate HRL and IHL

There are numerous calls upon states to ratify, implement, and disseminate IHL and HRL conventions. Resolution 1265 (1999), which is the first resolution dealing

---

[13] S.C. Res. 540, U.N. Doc. S/RES/540 (1983) (Oct. 31, 1983).
[14] S.C. Res. 582, U.N. Doc. S/RES/582 (1986) (Feb. 24, 1986).
[15] S.C. Res. 598, U.N. Doc. S/RES/598 (1987) (July 20, 1987).
[16] Baarda *supra* note 3, at 142.

explicitly with "Protection of Civilians in Armed Conflict", is exemplary in that regard:

> [The Security Council] Calls on States which have not already done so to consider ratifying the major instruments of international humanitarian law, human rights law, and to take appropriate legislative, judicial and administrative measures to implement these instruments domestically.[17]

2.2.2. Calls to Respect IHL and HRL in General

In a number of resolutions the Security Council calls for the respect of IHL and HRL in general. In the early 1990s the Security Council started to use the terms "demand" or "request" respect for IHL and HRL instead of "calling" for their respect, which is much more articulate than the previous wording of respective resolutions. Such appeals can be found in general resolutions not related to a specific conflict or in conflict related resolutions.

A good example for this is again resolution 1265 (1999):

> [The Security Council] urges all parties concerned to comply strictly with their obligations under international humanitarian law, human rights and refugee law, in particular those contained in the Hague Conventions of 1899 and 1907 and in the Geneva Conventions of 1949 and their Additional Protocols of 1977.[18]

Similar appeals can be found in resolutions related to the conflicts in Afghanistan,[19] Angola,[20] Armenia/Azerbaijan,[21] Ethiopia/Eritrea,[22] the former Yugoslavia,[23] the

---

[17] S.C. Res. 1265, U.N. Doc. S/RES/1265 (1999) (Sept. 17, 1999), preambular para. 8.

[18] S.C. Res. 1265, U.N. Doc. S/RES/1265 (1999) (Sept. 17, 1999), para. 4. *See also*: S.C. Res. 1296, U.N. Doc. S/RES/1296 (2000) (April 19, 2000) preambular para. 7 ["Protection of Civilians in Armed Conflict"]; S.C. Res. 16/4, U.N. Doc. S/RES/1674 (2006) (April 28, 2006), para. 6 ["Protection of Civilians in Armed Conflict"]; S.C. Res. 1261, U.N. Doc. S/RES/1261 (1999) (Aug. 30, 1999), para. 3 ["Children in Armed Conflict"]; U.N. Doc. S/PRST/2000/1 (Jan. 13, 2001), p. 1 ["Promoting Peace and Security: Humanitarian Assistance in Africa"]; S.C. Res. 1325, U.N. Doc. S/RES/1325 (2000) (Oct. 31, 2000) preambular para. 6 ["Role of Women in the Prevention and Resolution of Conflicts."].

[19] U.N. Doc. S/PRST/2000/12 (April 7, 2000), p. 1.

[20] S.C. Res. 834, U.N. Doc. S/RES/834 (1993) (June 1, 1993), para. 13; S.C. Res. 1212, U.N. Doc. S/RES/1212 (1998) (Nov. 25, 1998), para. 7; U.N. Doc. S/PRST 1999/26 (Aug. 24, 1999).

[21] S.C. Res. 822, U.N. Doc. S/RES/822 (1993) (April 30, 1993), para. 3.

[22] S.C. Res. 1227, U.N. Doc. S/RES/1227 (1999) (Feb. 10, 1999), para. 6; S.C. Res. 1320, U.N. Doc. S/RES/1320 (2000) (Sept. 15, 2000), preambular para. 3; U.N. Doc. S/PPRST/2001/4 (Feb. 9, 2001), p. 2.

[23] S.C. Res. 771, U.N. Doc. S/RES/771 (1992) (Aug. 13, 1992), para. 1; S.C. Res. 808, U.N. Doc. S/RES/808 (1993) (Feb. 22, 1993), preambular para. 3.

Democratic Republic of Congo,[24] Georgia,[25] Guinea-Bissau,[26] Liberia,[27] Rwanda,[28] Sierra Leone[29] and Somalia.[30] This number already shows that the Security Council is now much more often concerned with IHL and HRL related questions than during the era of the Cold War. It now treats a large number of different conflicts and in its respective resolutions frequently mentions IHL and HRL together.

2.2.3. Calls to Respect Certain Rules of IHL and HRL

Apart from general calls to respect IHL and HRL, the Security Council also called upon parties to a conflict to respect certain rules of HRL and IHL and condemned violations of specific rules by the parties of the conflict. In this regard the major focus of the Security Council are the rules related to the protection of civilians in armed conflict.

2.2.3.1. Protection of Civilians

As well as in statements relating to a particular conflict the Security Council also addressed the issue of protection of civilians in general resolutions and presidential statements, which are not related to a particular conflict. An example for a general statement is resolution 1674 (2006). The Security Council,

> recalls that deliberately targeting civilians and other protected persons as such in situations of armed conflict is a flagrant violation of international humanitarian law, reiterates its condemnation in the strongest terms of such practices and demands that all parties immediately put an end to such practices.[31]

Furthermore, it even stresses its readiness

> to respond to situations of armed conflict where civilians are being targeted or humanitarian assistance to civilians is being deliberately obstructed, including through the

---

[24] U.N. Doc. S/PRST/1998/26 (Aug. 31, 1998), p. 1; S.C. Res. 1258, U.N. Doc. S/RES/1258 (1999) (Aug. 6, 1999), para. 11; S.C. Res. 1291, U.N. Doc. S/RES/1291 (2000) (Feb. 24, 2000), para. 15; S.C. Res. 1341, U.N. Doc. S/RES/1342 (2001) (Feb. 22, 2001), para. 9; S.C. Res. 1355, U.N. Doc. S/RES/1355 (2001) (June 15, 2001), para. 16.
[25] S.C. Res. 1036, U.N. Doc. S/RES/1036 (1996) (Jan. 12, 1996), preambular para. 9.
[26] S.C. Res. 1233, U.N. Doc. S/RES/1233 (1999) (April 6, 1999), para. 11.
[27] S.C. Res. 1041, U.N. Doc. S/RES/1041 (1996) (Jan. 29, 1996), para. 6.
[28] S.C. Res. 812, U.N. Doc. S/RES/812 (1993) (Mar. 12, 1993), para. 8.
[29] S.C. Res. 1260, U.N. Doc. S/RES/1260 (1999) (Aug. 20, 1999), para. 14; S.C. Res. 1270, U.N. Doc. S/RES/1270 (1999) (Oct. 22, 1999), para. 15; S.C. Res. 1315, U.N. Doc. S/RES/1315 (2000) (Aug. 14, 2000), preambular para. 6.
[30] U.N. Doc. S/PRST 2001/1 (Jan. 11, 2001), p. 2.
[31] S.C. Res. 1674, U.N. Doc. S/RES/1674 (2006) (April 28, 2006), para. 3. Most recently *see also* S.C. Res. 1738, U.N. Doc. S/RES/1738 (2006) (Dec. 23, 2006), preambular para. 5.

consideration of appropriate measures at the Council's disposal in accordance with the Charter.[32]

As mentioned above, there are numerous examples of the practice concerning the protection of the civilian population in specific armed conflict.[33] It has to be underlined again that the Security Council often combines IHL and HRL in its statements. For example in Resolution 1019 (1995), the Security Council referred to the situation in Bosnia and Herzegovina and expressed its grave concern "at the reports... of grave violations of international humanitarian law and of human rights in and around Srebrenica, and in the areas of Banja Luka and Sanski Most, including reports of mass murder."[34] Another example is Resolution 1034 (1995) in which the Security Council condemned "in particular in the strongest possible terms the violations of international humanitarian law and of human rights... as described in the [Secretary-General's report]... and showing a consistent pattern of... large-scale disappearances."[35]

This practice proves an increasing interest of the Security Council towards the protection of civilians in armed conflict. This area of concern is closely related to questions concerning the maintenance of international peace and security and will be discussed below in more detail.

2.2.3.2. Protection of Women and Children in Armed Conflict
Aside from the general issue of protection of civilians in armed conflict, the Security Council has paid specific attention to the protection of women and children in armed conflicts, because they are considered to be particularly vulnerable civilians. In this context, it passed general resolutions on "women and peace and security"[36] and on "children in armed conflict."[37] In Resolution 1325 on women and peace and security adopted in 2000, the Security Council called on "all parties to armed conflict to take special measures to protect women and girls from gender-based violence, particularly rape and other forms of sexual abuse, and all other forms of violence in situations of armed conflict."[38]

---

[32] S.C. Res. 1265, U.N. Doc. S/RES/1265 (1999) (Sept. 17, 1999), para. 10.
[33] U.N. Doc. S/PRST/2001/6 (Mar. 2, 2001), p. 1 [Burundi]; S.C. Res. 1341, U.N. Doc. S/RES/1341 (2001) (Feb. 22, 2001), para. 14 [Democratic Republic of Congo]; S.C. Res. 688, U.N. Doc. S/RES/688 (1991) (April 5, 1991), para. 1 [Iraq].
[34] S.C. Res. 1019, U.N. Doc. S/RES/1019 (1995) (Nov. 9, 1995), preamble.
[35] S.C. Res. 1034, U.N. Doc. S/RES/1034 (1995) (Dec. 21, 1995), para. 2.
[36] The most important resolution in this respect is S.C. Res. 1325, *supra* note 18. *See also* U.N. Doc. S/PRST 2006/42 (Oct. 26, 2006).
[37] S.C. Res. 1314, U.N. Doc. S/RES/1314 (2000) (Aug. 11, 2000).
[38] S.C. Res. 1325, *supra* note 18, para. 10.

In Resolution 1314, also adopted in 2000, the Security Council emphasised the need to provide special protection for children in armed conflict and proposed a detailed list of (practical) measures to be taken.[39]

2.2.3.3. Humanitarian Access

Although not a new phenomenon, the denial of access of humanitarian assistance to victims of armed conflict in need increasingly became an issue during the last two decades. This was to be observed in particular in conflicts such as in the former Yugoslavia, Afghanistan, the Democratic Republic of Congo, Liberia, Sierra Leone, and Sudan, where access to the population in need was deliberately denied.

In its resolutions as well as in presidential statements the Security Council repetitively urged and demanded the parties to the conflict to grant immediate, full and unimpeded access for humanitarian personnel. Many of the relevant resolutions concern the conflict in the former Yugoslavia starting in 1992,[40] but there are also a number of resolutions regarding other conflicts.[41]

In Resolution 1265 (1999) the Security Council expressed its willingness to "adopt appropriate steps" as a possible reaction to the deliberate obstruction of humanitarian assistance.[42] By doing so, it established a practice of demanding access not only from the respective governments, but from "all parties concerned" including non-state actors. This reveals the increasing usage of the wording "all parties to the conflict" by the Security Council, by which non-state actors are equally addressed. This constitutes a milestone for the development of customary law as it helps to establish a rule according to which non-state actors are obliged to grant access for humanitarian assistance to people in need in the same way as states.[43]

---

[39] S.C. Res. 1325, *supra* note 18 paras 1–6.
[40] S.C. Res. 752, U.N. Doc. S/RES/752 (1992) (May 15, 1992), para. 8. See for example resolutions S.C. Res. 758, U.N. Doc. S/RES/758 (1992) (June 8, 1992); S.C. Res. 761, U.N. Doc. S/RES/761 (1992) (June 29, 1992); S.C. Res. 764, U.N. Doc. S/RES/764 (1992) (July 13, 1992); S.C. Res. 787, U.N. Doc. S/RES/787 (1992) (Nov. 16, 1992); S.C. Res. 819, U.N. Doc. S/RES/819 (1993) (April 16, 1993); S.C. Res. 836, U.N. Doc. S/RES/836 (1993) (June 4, 1993); S.C. Res. 998, U.N. Doc. S/RES/998 (1994) (June 16, 1994); S.C. Res. 1004, U.N. Doc. S/RES/1004 (1996) (July 12, 1996) or S.C. Res. 1009, U.N. Doc. S/RES/1009 (1996) (Aug. 10, 1996).
[41] See for example S.C. Res. 822, U.N. Doc. S/RES/822 (1993) (April 30, 1993), para. 3; S.C. Res. 853, U.N. Doc. S/RES/853 (1993) (July 29, 1993), para. 11 [Armenia and Azerbaijan]; U.N. Doc. S/PRST 1999/1 (Jan 7, 1999) [Sierra Leone]; S.C. Res. 1234, U.N. Doc. S/RES/1234 (1999) (April 9, 1999), para. 9; S.C. Res. 1291, U.N. Doc. S/RES/1291 (2000) (Feb. 24, 2000), para. 12; S.C. Res. 1355, *supra* note 24, para. 19 [Democratic Republic of Congo]; U.N. Doc. S/PRST 2001/4 (Feb 9, 2001), p. 2 [Ethiopia and Eritrea].
[42] S.C. Res. 1265, U.N. Doc. S/RES/1265 (1999) (Sept. 17, 1999), para. 10.
[43] Regarding further U.N. and other practice for this rule *see*: Jean-Marie Henckaerts & Louise Doswald-Beck (eds.), Customary International Humanitarian Law (Volume I: Rules) 194–195, (2005) [hereinafter CIHL]. On the customary obligation to grant access for humanitarian assistance in non-international armed conflicts *see*: CIHL, *id.* at 194–195; Gregor Schotten, *Der aktuelle Fall:*

2.2.4. Practice with Explicit Reference to a "Threat to Peace" in the Sense of Article 39 U.N. Charter

For the discussion of the role of the Security Council in implementing IHL and HRL, it is particularly important to analyse its practice with regard to an explicit mentioning of a "threat to peace;" in other words cases in which the Security Council drew a direct link to the maintenance of international peace and security. The founders of the U.N. Charter originally wanted to exclude IHL and HRL violations as possible threats to peace and security.[44] However, the reality of modern armed conflicts after the fall of the iron curtain changed this concept. The Security Council qualified a situation within a state as a threat to international peace for the first time in Resolution 688 (1991), in which it

> condemns the repression of the Iraqi civilian population in many parts of Iraq, including most recently in Kurdish populated areas, the consequences of which threaten international peace and security.[45]

In this resolution the Security Council still stressed the necessity of a transboundary element as a condition for a threat to international peace and security, in this case refugee flows into neighbouring countries. Only one year later, faced with the conflict in Somalia, the Security Council no longer insisted on such an element. It stated that

> the magnitude of the human tragedy caused by the conflict in Somalia, further exacerbated by the obstacles being created to the distribution of humanitarian assistance, constitutes a threat to international peace and security.[46]

Another important example for this development is Resolution 808 (1993) on the situation in former Yugoslavia in which the Security Council explicitly qualified "widespread violations of international humanitarian law" as a "threat to international peace and security." Resolution 808 led to the establishment of the International Criminal Tribunal for the former Yugoslavia.[47] The categorisation of widespread violations of IHL as threats to international peace and security can also be observed in resolutions concerning the situations in Rwanda,[48] Sierra Leone

---

Wiederholtes Verbot für Hilfsflüge durch die sudanesische Regierung – gibt es ein Recht auf Zugang für humanitäre Hilfsorganisationen im nicht-internationalen bewaffneten Konflikt?, 12 HuV-I 34, 34–36 (1999); Heike Spieker, *Twenty-Five Years after the Adoption of Additional Protocol II: Breakthrough or Failure of Humanitarian Legal Protection?*, 4 Yearbook of International Humanitarian Law 129, 150 (2001).

[44] Jochen A. Frowein & Nico Krisch, *Article 39, in* The United Nations Charter. A Commentary para. 19 (Bruno Simma ed., 2002) [hereinafter Simma].
[45] S.C. Res. 688, U.N. Doc. S/RES/688 (1991) (April 5, 1991), para. 1.
[46] S.C. Res. 794, U.N. Doc. S/RES/794 (1992) (Dec. 3, 1992), preambular para. 2.
[47] S.C. Res. 808, U.N. Doc. S/RES/808 (1993) (Feb. 22, 1993), preambular paras 5, 6, 8.
[48] S.C. Res. 827, U.N. Doc. S/RES/827 (1993) (May 25, 1993), preambular para. 3.

and the Democratic Republic of Congo.[49] This practice shows that the Security Council increasingly includes questions of individual security and the protection of individual rights in its actions to maintain international peace and security. Apart from that, Resolutions 808 and 827 which led to the creation of the two *ad hoc* tribunals for the former Yugoslavia and for Rwanda had an important impact on establishing individual criminal responsibility.[50]

The Security Council's debate on the "protection of civilians in armed conflict," which began in 1999 gave a new dynamic to the approach to link international peace and security with respect for fundamental principles of IHL and HRL. After the first debate on 12 February 1999 the President of the Security Council made the following declaration:

> The Security Council has considered the matter of protection of civilians in armed conflict. The Security Council expresses its grave concern at the growing civilian toll of armed conflict and notes with distress that civilians now...are increasingly directly targeted by combatants and armed elements.... Bearing in mind its primary responsibility for the maintenance of international peace and security, the Council affirms the need for the international community to assist and protect civilian populations affected by armed conflict.... The Council expresses its willingness to respond, in accordance with the Charter of the United Nations, to situations in which civilians, as such, have been targeted or humanitarian assistance to civilians has been deliberately obstructed.... The Council requests the Secretary-General to submit a report containing concrete recommendations to the Council...on ways the Council, acting within its sphere of responsibility, could improve the physical and legal protection of civilians in situations of armed conflict. The report should also identify contributions the Council could make towards effective implementation of existing humanitarian law.[51]

After several debates in 1999 and 2000 on the subject the Security Council passed three resolutions. In Resolution 1296 (2000) the Security Council

> underlines the importance of safe and unimpeded access of humanitarian personnel to civilians in armed conflicts..., invites States and the Secretary-General to bring to its attention information regarding the deliberate denial of such access in violation of international law, where such denial may constitute a threat to international peace

---

[49] For a detailed lists of resolutions see Michael Bothe, *Les Nations Unies et la mise en oeuvre du droit international humanitaire, in* Condorelli, *supra* note 7, at 227; Jochen Herbst, Rechtskontrolle des UN-Sicherheitsrates, 347 (1999) [hereinafter Herbst].

[50] Vera Gowlland-Debas, *The Functions of the United Nations Security Council in the International Legal System, in* The Role of Law in International Politics 296 (Michael Byers ed., 2000) [hereinafter Gowlland-Debas].

[51] U.N. Doc. S/PRST/1999/6 (Feb. 12, 1999).

and security, and, in this regard, expresses its willingness to consider such information and, when necessary, to adopt appropriate steps.[52]

This resolution constitutes a remarkable development, because the Security Council refers for the first time to a link between a violation of IHL and HRL (the deliberate denial of access) and a possible threat to peace without references to a specific conflict. Before, decisions whether a situation constituted a threat to international peace or security were always made with regard to a specific case. Resolution 1296 (2000) is a precedent inasmuch as it generally acknowledges that a violation of IHL (in this case the deliberate denial of humanitarian access to people in need) may constitute a threat to international peace and security. The deliberate denial of humanitarian access being a regular pattern of modern armed conflict, especially in non-international conflicts, gives hence this resolution important practical significance.

3. Evaluation

3.1. Concepts of "Human Security" and "Responsibility to Protect"

In order to evaluate the Security Council's practice, it has to be analyzed in the light of the ongoing discussion about the political concepts of "human security" and the "responsibility to protect."

The role and the practice of the Security Council concerning questions of IHL and HRL cannot be separated from an emerging new interpretation of sovereignty, state security, and international security during the last two decades. International peace and security today are understood in a way that extends far beyond the traditional concept of collective security. In contemporary interpretation genocide, ethnic cleansing, and other gross violations of IHL and HRL, including those encompassed within the state's own borders, are considered threats to international peace and security that require collective action.[53] Human rights, which were once considered to be subordinate to the Charter's main goal, peace and security, and IHL, which was deliberately not mentioned in the U.N. Charter, now seem to have shifted in priority and have itself become part of the U.N. function to maintain and enforce peace.[54]

---

[52] S.C. Res. 1296, U.N. Doc. S/RES/1296 (2000) (April 19, 2000), para. 8. This phrase is repeated recently in S.C. Res. 1674, U.N. Doc. S/RES/1674 (2006) (April 28, 2006), para. 26.
[53] Gowlland-Debas, *supra* note 50, at 286.
[54] Gowlland-Debas, *supra* note 50, at 287; Bertrand Ramcharan, The Security Council and the Protection of Human Rights 1 (2002) [hereinafter Ramcharan]; Karel Wellens, *The UN Security Council and New Threats to the Peace: Back to the Future*, 8 JCSL 15–16 (2003) [hereinafter Wellens].

The Security Council debates on the issue of "protection of civilians in armed conflict," which have led to Resolutions 1265 and 1296 also reflected upon the new concept of "human security." While in 1945 the concern was primarily turned towards creating a system of collective security against acts of aggression emanating from states against states, today's security architecture is also faced with acts of aggression from non state actors which are not necessarily directed against state security. In fragile or even failed states, in which state sovereignty is either very weak or has broken down entirely or in conflicts in which civilians are deliberately targeted by non-state actors or in an environment in which the distinction between civilians and combatants is no longer made, the protection of civilians becomes an international security issue as such situations frequently affect other states. "Human security" therefore acquired the same significance as state security has in order to maintain international peace and security.[55]

A similar concept to "human security" is the so called "responsibility to protect." This notion was developed by the International Commission on Intervention and State Sovereignty (ICISS), an independent panel of experts, which published a report entitled "The Responsibility to Protect" in 2001.[56] Later, the recommendations of the ICISS were incorporated in the report of the High-Level Panel on Threats, Challenges and Change.[57] Finally, U.N. Secretary-General Kofi Annan also took up the concept in his report "In Larger Freedom," which was addressed to the 2005 World Summit.[58] According to this concept, states have the primary responsibility to protect their populations. However, if they either fail to guarantee this protection or are unwilling to provide it, external intervention is justified to protect the endangered people(s).[59]

---

[55] Claude Bruderlein, *People's Security as a New Measure of Global Stability*, 83 Int'l Rev. Red Cross 353, 359–361 (2001); Manuel Fröhlich, *"Responsibility to Protect" – Zur Herausbildung einer neuen Norm der Friedenssicherung, in* Die Reform der Vereinten Nationen- Bilanz und Perspektiven 167, 169 (Johannes Varwick & Andreas Zimmermann, eds., 2006) [hereinafter Fröhlich]; Nico J. Schrijver, *The Future of the Charter of the United Nations*, 10 Max-Planck Yearbook of United Nations Law 10 (2006). On the concept of human security *see generally* Human Security Centre (ed.), The Human Security Report 2005. War and Peace in the 21st Century (2005).

[56] International Commission on Intervention and State Sovereignty (ed.), The Responsibility to Protect (2001).

[57] U.N. Doc. A/59/565 (2004): A More Secure World: Our Shared Responsibility, Report of the High-Level Panel on Threats, Challenges and Change. *Available at* www.un.org/secureworld/report.pdf (last visited July 30, 2007).

[58] U.N. Doc. A/59/565 (2004), *supra* note 57. U.N. Doc. A/59/2005 (Mar. 21, 2005) In Larger Freedom: Towards Development, Security and Human Rights for All. Report of the Secretary-General.

[59] Alex J. Bellamy, *Whither the Responsibility to Protect? Humanitarian Intervention and the 2005 World Summit*, 20 Ethics & International Affairs 143 (2006) [hereinafter Bellamy];

The recommendations of the ICISS, the High-Level Panel on "Threats, Challenges and Change," and U.N. Secretary-General Kofi Annan were exhaustively discussed at the 2005 World Summit. As a result, the U.N. General Assembly dedicated one paragraph of its "Summit Outcome Document" to this concept. Paragraph 139 states:

> The international community, through the United Nations, also has the responsibility to use appropriate diplomatic, humanitarian and other peaceful means, in accordance with Chapters VI and VII of the Charter of the United Nations, to help protect populations from war crimes, ethnic cleansing and crimes against humanity. In this context, we are prepared to take collective action, in a timely and decisive manner, through the Security Council, in accordance with the Charter....[60]

For the time being, this paragraph contains the consensual position of the U.N. member states on the concept of "the responsibility to protect." It reaffirms the active role of the U.N. Security Council to protect civilians against serious violations of IHL and HRL.

Considering the emerging principles of "human security" and "responsibility to protect" the important role of the Security Council in implementing IHL and HRL becomes more evident. The wording "through the Security Council" in the above mentioned "Summit Outcome Document" shows that the overwhelming majority of states supports a proactive role of the Security Council for the protection of civilians in armed conflict.

3.2. *Attitudes of U.N. Member States and the Secretary-General towards the New Role of the Security Council*

The Security Council's extended interpretation of Article 39 of the U.N. Charter and its readiness to take upon a more active role in ensuring respect for IHL and HRL have been discussed and welcomed by the large majority of U.N. member states and the U.N. Secretary-General.

> For example, in the 1999 debate of the Security Council's on "the protection of civilians in armed conflict" the acting Presidency of the European Union (Finland) stated: Massive and systematic breaches of human rights and international humanitarian law can constitute threats to international peace and security, and therefore demand the attention and action of the Security Council.... The protection of civilians is fundamental to the purposes and principles of the United Nations.... The Security Council has a special responsibility and special powers to authorize coercive action

---

Fröhlich, *supra* note 55, at 171; Ramesh Thakur, *The United Nations, Peace and Security*, 244 (2006).

[60] G.A. Res. A/60/L.1, U.N. Doc. A/60/L.1 (Sept. 15, 2005), para. 139.

when international peace and security are threatened as a result of systematic and widespread violations of international humanitarian law and human rights law....[61]

Similarly, the Brazilian representative stated:

> The Security Council can and must contribute to the effort of promoting a climate of compliance, that is, to halt flagrant and grave violations of universally accepted international humanitarian and human rights law.... The main challenge for the Security Council is to take measures within the purview of its mandate, to bring the dire reality of modern conflict closer to the lofty ideals enshrined in international humanitarian and human rights law.[62]

The representative of the United States of America further underlined:

> It [the Security Council] must strive to strengthen international protection of civilians, recognizing that the Council's task of maintaining peace and security could extend to the protection of individuals as well.[63]

U.N. Secretary-General Kofi Annan, asked to report on the protection of civilians in armed conflict by the Security Council, wrote four reports on the issue, in which he made a number of recommendations to the Security Council and also commented upon the role of the Security Council in this regard. As major recommendations the following can be noted:

> The protection of civilians in armed conflict would be largely assured if combatants respected the provisions of international humanitarian and human rights law.... I recommend that the Security Council: Urge Member States to ratify the major instruments of international humanitarian law and human rights law... In cases of non-compliance [with human rights and IHL obligations], consider using the enforcement measures contained in the Charter of the United Nations under Chapter VII, to induce compliance....[64]

The reactions of member states as well as the recommendations of the U.N. Secretary-General show that they support a more proactive role of the U.N. Security Council with regard to the implementation of IHL and HRL. Most member states seem to acknowledge an explicit link between serious violations of IHL and HRL and a possible threat to international peace and security and, consequently, seem to support interventions of the U.N. Security Council as a response to serious violations of IHL and HRL. One can therefore conclude that the member states as well as the Secretary-General espouse the new interpretation of Article 39 of the U.N. Charter.

---

[61] U.N. Doc. S/PV. 4046 (Sept. 17, 1999) (Resumption 1), p. 9.
[62] U.N. Doc. S/PV. 4109 (Mar. 9, 2000) (Resumption 1), p. 18.
[63] U.N. Press Release SC/6642 (Feb. 12, 1999), p. 9.
[64] U.N. Doc. S/1999/957 (Sept. 8, 1999), pp. 8–9.

3.3. Constraints

Despite the progress to be observed in the practice of the Security Council with regard to the implementation and enforcement of HRL and IHL, the practice also shows significant shortcomings. First of all the Security Council is a highly political organ. Its decisions are the outcome of political considerations, not legal reasoning. Even though, the Security Council may take legal arguments into account, it is not obliged to do so. Therefore, legal arguments will in most cases be subordinate to political considerations, which will always remain the determining factor.[65] In a decision whether or not to intervene, political (including financial) interests therefore supersede humanitarian or human rights interests.[66] The result is selective action of the Security Council, insofar as many massive and grave violations of IHL and HRL are not taken up by the Security Council and insofar as it regularly fails to adopt resolutions, because its member states cannot agree.[67] The case of the Sudan is particularly illustrative in this regard. Furthermore, the Security Council often does not list all violations in its resolutions, but only those that could be agreed upon by its members. Consequently, the absence of condemnations of violations of HRL and IHL weakens the rules which are violated but not mentioned because these violations do not seem to be "grave" enough in the view of the Security Council. Last, but not least, it has been criticised that the Security Council never emphasized respect for IHL in resolutions authorizing multinational forces to the use of force.[68]

4. Conclusions

4.1. Role of the Security Council

The Security Council is not only an actor calling for the respect of IHL and HRL, but it is also directly confronted with questions of IHL and IIRL in its own actions, e.g. when imposing sanctions or authorizing military intervention. It is therefore particularly interesting to analyze the impact of the Security Council's practice for its own actions.

---

[65] Wellens, *supra* note 54, at 48.
[66] Tono Eitel, *The UN Security Council and its Future Contribution in the Field of International Law. What May we Expect?* 4 Max-Planck Yearbook of United Nations Law 65 (2000).
[67] Stephen M. Schwebel, *The Roles of the Security Council and the International Court of Justice in the Application of International Humanitarian Law*, 27 N.Y.U. J. Int'l L. & Pol. 731, 747 (1994–1995).
[68] Boisson de Chazournes, *supra* note 7, at 158; James D. Fry, *The UN Security Council and the Law of Armed Conflict: Amity or Enmity?*, 38 Geo. J. Int'l L. 327, 335 (2006).

The Security Council is increasingly aware of the relevance of IHL and HRL for its own actions. As it establishes more U.N. peacekeeping and observer missions, it also increasingly endows them with a human rights component.[69] For example, the – at the time of writing – biggest U.N. peacekeeping force, MONUC in the Democratic Republic of Congo (DRC), has human rights offices all over the territory of the DRC. The tasks of the MONUC human rights officers are *inter alia* to monitor the human rights situation, to investigate human rights violations, and to assist the Congolese Government in ending impunity for serious violations of HRL and IHL and also to support the civil society's capacity to monitor and advocate human rights. According to the report of the U.N. Secretary-General on the MONUC Mission, it should "continue to cooperate with efforts to ensure that those responsible for serious violations of human rights and international humanitarian law are brought to justice."[70]

The large number of Security Council resolutions concerning the implementation of IHL and HRL also has direct implications for its commitment to IHL and HRL. Article 24(2) of the U.N. Charter provides that the Security Council shall act in accordance with the purposes and principles of the United Nations laid down in Articles 1 and 2 of the U.N. Charter. While "respect for human rights" is explicitly noted in Article 1(3) of the Charter; there is no reference to IHL in either Article 1 or 2. As already discussed above, this is due to the fact that at the time of the creation of the U.N. Charter, a reference to IHL was thought to endanger the credibility of the purpose of maintaining international peace and security because IHL is only applicable in a situation of armed conflict, which the Charter aimed at banning completely. Nevertheless, a contemporary interpretation of the U.N. Charter has to consider subsequent practice of the organization and its member states.[71] The extensive practice of the Security Council shown above seems to support an interpretation of Article 1(3) of the U.N. Charter according to which IHL is among the purposes of United Nations. The first reason for this is that IHL is frequently mentioned together with HRL. Secondly, the U.N. Charter is – like every treaty establishing an international organization – a "constitution of delegated powers."[72] The United Nations and its organs are only competent to act if its member states delegated their powers. Thus, when the Security Council regularly engages in calling for respect for IHL, when it condemns violations of

---

[69] Ramcharan, *supra* note 54, at 2.
[70] U.N. Doc. S/2007/156 (Mar. 20, 2007), Twenty-third Report of the Secretary-General on the United Nations Organization Mission in the Democratic Republic of the Congo, p. 13.
[71] See in detail Georg Ress, *Interpretation*, *in* Simma *supra* note 44, paras 26 ss.
[72] Thomas M. Franck, *The Security Council and "Threats to the Peace": Some Remarks on Remarkable Developments*, *in* Le développement du rôle du Conseil de Sécurité 83, 110 (René-Jean Dupuy ed., 1992).

IHL or even stresses its readiness to act in order to prevent serious violations of IHL, the latter obviously has to be considered by the Security Council as a matter within its competence and therefore among the purposes of the United Nations, e.g. Article 1(3) of the U.N. Charter.[73]

When serious violations of IHL and HRL constitute a threat to peace in the sense of Article 39 of the U.N. Charter and when the Security Council considers measures to prevent such violations in order to maintain international peace and security, one can argue that IHL and HRL also fall under Article 1(1) of the U.N. Charter. This interpretation is in line with the new concept of human security and derives from the resolution cited above. Consequently, one must not forget that the Security Council itself is bound by IHL and HRL norms. This has an enormous significance for the planning of sanctions or military interventions.

4.2. Development of IHL and HRL

Resolutions and presidential statements of the U.N. Security Council are considered to reflect international practice and *opinio juris* and thus to contribute to the establishment of customary international law.[74] Therefore, the Security Council's most important contribution for the further development of both IHL and HRL is the influence of its practice on the establishment of customary IHL and HRL norms. The influence of the Security Council has been particularly important for the development of customary rules for non-international armed conflict: firstly, the Security Council frequently addresses "all parties to the conflict", which includes non-governmental armed groups. Furthermore, by imposing sanctions against non-state actors or by directly addressing them (in resolutions) the Security Council contributes to a development in which accountability and responsibility of these actors are increasingly demanded. Concerning the content of certain customary rules of IHL, the Security Council reiterated and thereby reinforced the customary character of IHL rules such as the protection of civilians and further developed others such as the right to humanitarian access.

---

[73] Among the growing number of scholars supporting this view see for example: Hans Peter Gasser, *The International Committee of the Red Cross and the United Nations Involvement in the Implementation of International Humanitarian Law*, in Condorelli, *supra* note 7, at 262; Herbst, *supra* note 49, at 383; Gowlland-Debas, *supra* note 50, at 305; Toni Pfanner, *Application of International Humanitarian Law and Military Operations Undertaken under the United Nations Charter*, in Symposium on Humanitarian Action and Peace-keeping Operations 49, 58 (Umesh Palwankar ed., 1994); Marco Sassòli, *Sanctions and International Humanitarian Law – Commentary*, in United Nations Sanctions and International Law 241 (Vera Gowlland-Debas ed., 2001; Gregor Schotten, Wirtschaftssanktionen der Vereinten Nationen im Umfeld bewaffneter Konflikte – zur Bindung des Sicherheitsrates an individualschützende Normen 238 (2007).

[74] Boisson de Chazournes, *supra* note 7, at 151; CIHL, *supra* note 43, at xlvii.

Finally, by frequently citing IHL and HRL together, the Security Council contributed to the growing awareness that the two bodies of law are complementary and inter-dependent. Both are necessary to best protect human beings from the consequences of armed conflict. In this sense a merger of IHL and HRL can be observed in the practice of the Security Council.

4.3. Final Conclusions

The Security Council underlined the significance of IHL and HRL for peaceful relations among and within states in general by an increasing number of resolutions covering most aspects of IHL and HRL and by starting to interpret serious violations of IHL and HRL as threats to international peace and security within the meaning of Article 39 of the U.N. Charter. It also seems that the Security Council is convinced today that international security is closely linked to the respect for human rights and international humanitarian law. The Security Council also contributed to the further development of customary international (humanitarian) law. Finally, one can conclude from the Security Council's practice of resolutions that it considers HRL as well as IHL to be among the principles and purposes of the United Nations as defined in Articles 1 and 2 of the U.N. Charter, which are also binding on the Security Council itself and thus limit its actions.

In view of the recent practice of the Security Council relating to HRL and IHL, it is argued that the Security Council provided "impetus for the development of an international public policy through its collective responses to violations of fundamental norms, considered by it to be component of the security fabric."[75] The first indications of such a development can indeed be observed. However, a further and more sustainable development in this regard depends on whether Security Council decisions will become less selective in the future. Respect for IHL and HR are the essential components of a new contemporary understanding of international security, which includes (individual) human security as well as state security. In this concept the Security Council plays an essential role as the only body legitimately able to authorize military intervention in order to protect human beings from violations of IHL and HRL. However, this is a heavy burden, not easily accomplished. In order to maintain its credibility and legitimacy the Security Council will have to avoid "future Rwandas as well as future Kosovos,"[76] while it continues to play a proactive role in maintaining international peace and security by addressing serious violations of IHL and HRL and, if necessary, by showing an appropriate reaction, including military intervention.

---

[75] Gowlland-Debas, *supra* note 50, at 286. Similarly Wellens, *supra* note 54, at 69.
[76] Bellamy, *supra* note 59, at 143.

Last, but not least, it should be stressed that the Security Council's role in implementing IHL and HRL can only be complementary to the primary responsibility of states to implement HRL and IHL or to the bodies of international law specifically created to guard a respective body of law, in other words the International Committee of the Red Cross for IHL or the U.N. Human Rights Council for Human Rights.

Part D
The Protection of Specific Rights and Persons

Chapter XII

The Right to Life in International Humanitarian Law and Human Rights Law

*Noëlle Quénivet**

1. *Introduction*

The right to life is unquestionably one of the most basic or fundamental human rights. In all conventional international human rights instruments, the right to life stands as the first right that is to be protected by the state. It is also recognised as a customary human right as well as a norm of *jus cogens*.[1] Furthermore, in the European Convention on Human Rights[2] the right to life is one of the core rights and as stipulated by the European Court of Human Rights, it "ranks as one of the most fundamental provisions in the Convention."[3] Under the Convention, this right can not be detracted from even in times of emergency, as specified in article 15. In other words, "the human-rights-based normative framework...is predisposed to question any use of deadly force,"[4] for the use of force is *per se* in contravention of human rights law. However "the European Court of Human Rights has repeatedly interpreted the right to life guaranteed by the ECHR to apply to the context of military use of lethal force."[5] Already in 1997, some authors

---

* Dr. Noëlle Quénivet is a Senior Lecturer at the University of the West of England. She holds a LL.M. from the University of Nottingham (UK) and a Ph.D. from the University of Essex (UK).
[1] *See* e.g. Restatement of the Law Third: The Foreign Relations of Law of the United States (1987), para. 702.
[2] European Convention for the Protection of Human Rights and Fundamental Freedoms 213 U.N.T.S. 221 (Nov. 4, 1950) [hereinafter ECHR].
[3] Isayeva, Yusupova and Bazayeva v. the Russian Federation, Applications Nos. 57947/00, 57948/00 and 57949/00, Judgment, (Feb. 24, 2005), para. 168 [hereinafter Isayeva et al.] and Isayeva v. the Russian Federation, Application No. 57950/00, Judgment (Feb. 24, 2005), para. 172 [hereinafter Isayeva].
[4] Kenneth Watkin, *Controlling the Use of Force: A Role for Human Rights Norms in Contemporary Armed Conflict*, 98 Am. J. Int'l L. 17 (2004) [hereinafter Watkin].
[5] Francisco F. Martin, *The Unified Use of Force and Exclusionary Rules: The Unified Use of Force Rule Revisited: The Penetration of the Law of Armed Conflict by International Human Rights Law*, 65 Sask. L. Rev. 407 (2002) [hereinafter Martin 2002].

forecasted that "[t]he complaints that have emerged from the conflict in Turkey could be a foretaste of the future."[6]

This chapter examines the jurisprudence of the European Court of Human Rights in relation to the right to life in times of armed conflict, with a specific focus on a series of judgments delivered on February 24, 2005 relating to violations committed on the territory of the Chechen Republic in the Russian Federation. These particular rulings partially corroborate earlier judgments of the Court in relation to situations rising to (armed) clashes.

It is often questioned whether armed forces during conflicts (both international and non-international) are not only obliged to abide by international humanitarian law (IHL) but also by human rights law (HRL). Authors such as Heinschel von Heinegg argue that "the law of international armed conflict is especially designed to serve as binding guidelines for the armed forces engaged in combat operations. Hence, it would not make much sense to complicate the situation by demanding they also submit to the obligations provided for by human rights instruments."[7] However, other commentators such as Roberts contend that,

> [a]lthough the right to life is inevitably subject to certain limitations in times of war and insurgency, its existence can potentially provide a basis for those whose rights have been undermined (or their surviving relatives) to argue that an armed force acted recklessly, granted its obligations.[8]

In this case human rights law is applicable whenever armed force is being used, i.e. during any military operations.

This chapter explores the possibility that human rights bodies reach beyond the treaties that established them and draw upon the principles of the law of armed conflict. First, the application, *sub silentio*, of international humanitarian rules by the European Court of Human Rights[9] will be examined. Then the right to life as protected by the Convention will be analysed. Particular attention is paid to principles which are usually connected with IHL. As a caveat however, it must be stressed that it is not the aim of this chapter to determine whether IHL would be applicable to the cases adjudicated by the European Convention or to discuss whether international humanitarian law is the *lex specialis* as far as the right to life

---

[6] Aisling Reidy, Françoise Hampson & Kevin Boyle, *Gross Violations of Human Rights: Invoking the European Convention on Human Rights in the Case of Turkey*, 15 NQHR 173 (1997) [hereinafter Reidy, Hampson & Boyle].

[7] Wolff Heinschel von Heinegg, *The Rule of Law in Conflict and Post-Conflict Situations: Factors in War to Peace Transitions*, 27 Harvard Journal of Law and Public Policy 868–869 (2004) [hereinafter Heinschel von Heinegg].

[8] Adam Roberts, *Implementation of the Laws of War in Late-Twentieth-Century Conflicts*, *in* The Law of Armed Conflict: Into the Next Millennium 366 (Michael N. Schmitt & Leslie C. Green eds, 1998).

[9] *See* William Abresch, *A Human Rights Law of Internal Armed Conflict: The European Court of Human Rights in Chechnya*, 16 Eur. J. Int'l L. 742 and 746 (2005) [hereinafter Abresch].

is concerned.¹⁰ Rather it aims to compare principles found in IHL to the jurisprudence of the European Court of Human Rights and to examine whether human rights law provides a pertinent and arguably more accurate framework to gauge the lawfulness of military operations.¹¹

2. *The Application of International Humanitarian Law by the ECHR*

According to the ECHR, the Court can solely determine whether a state party to the said convention has violated its provisions. It is only competent to decide in the field of HRL and not of IHL. Consequently, the Court is not required by virtue of the European Convention on Human Rights to examine whether a state party also complies with the 1949 Geneva Conventions and the 1977 Additional Protocols or any IHL rule of customary nature. Unlike the American Commission on Human Rights,¹² the Court has consistently refused to apply IHL despite the fact that several applicants referred to this *corpus juris*.¹³ In several cases it has referred to the possible applicability of IHL; yet, it never applied it as such. In the *Cyprus v. Turkey* case, the Court conceded that the Geneva Convention III was applicable to prisoners of wars but, in fact, the Court did not use the Convention as a yardstick when examining the events and only adjudicated the matter on the basis of Article 5 ECHR.¹⁴

---

[10] In this regard, *see* the comments by the International Court of Justice: "the right not arbitrarily to be deprived of one's life applies also in hostilities. The test of what is an arbitrary deprivation of life…falls to determined by the applicable *lex specialis*, namely, the law applicable in armed conflict which is designed to regulate the conduct of hostilities." Legality of the Threat or Use of Nuclear Weapons, Advisory Opinion (July 8, 1996), I.C.J. Rep. 1996, para. 25 [hereinafter Advisory Opinion on Nuclear Weapons]; and "As regards the relationship between international humanitarian law and human rights law, there are thus three possible solutions: some rights may be exclusively matters of international humanitarian law; others may be exclusively matters of human rights law; yet others may be matters of both these branches of international law. In order to answer the question put to it, the Court will have to take into consideration both these branches of international law, namely human rights law and, as *lex specialis*, international humanitarian law." Legal Consequences of the Construction of a Wall in the Occupied Palestinian Territories, Advisory Opinion, (July 9, 2004), I.C.J. Rep. 2004, para. 106.

[11] For example, Doswald-Beck explains that the idea that IHL is the *lex specialis* "presupposes that IHL is crystal clear as to when and how force can be used in all situations of armed conflict. This is not the case." Louise Doswald-Beck, *The Right to Life in Armed Conflict: Does International Humanitarian Law Provide all the Answers?*, 89 Int'l Rev. Red Cross 881, 882 (2006).

[12] *See* Section 3 – Chapter 3.

[13] The only exception to the rule is the Engel case. Engel et al. v. The Netherlands, Applications Nos 5100/71; 5101/71; 5102/71; 5102/72, Judgment (June 8, 1976).

[14] Cyprus v. Turkey, Applications Nos 6780/74 and 6950/75, Judgment (May 26, 1975). *See also* Jochen A. Frowein, *The Relationship between Human Rights Regimes and Regimes of Belligerent Occupation*, 28 Israel Yearbook of Human Rights 10 (1999) and Aisling Reidy, *The Approach of*

Kleffner explains that "[u]sing international humanitarian law as a means of interpretation of human rights law is...[an indirect] way to achieve compliance with international humanitarian law."[15] However, as seen from the discussion above, it is not the aim of a human rights body such as the European Court of Human Rights to be involved in the implementation of IHL. But, as Watkin argues, "[t]hat highly developed system of accountability has much to offer in terms of limiting the impact of some forms of violence, especially when compared to the still evolving accountability framework under international humanitarian law."[16] Yet, it is clear from the jurisprudence of the European Court and Commission of Human Rights that both bodies, specifically designed to control the application of the European Convention on Human Rights, reject their role as guardians of IHL. This reluctance may be difficult to understand inasmuch as the Court is obliged by virtue of Article 15(1) ECHR to take into account any relevant international rules when interpreting the Convention in situations of a state of emergency.[17] The Court is, as per its founding document, compelled to adopt a contextual interpretation of the provisions enshrined in the Convention. However, since Article 15 has not been invoked by states when using force leading to death, this section of the article cannot be applied. Nevertheless, as the Court recalls, the Convention must be interpreted in the light of the rules set out in the 1969 Vienna Convention on the Laws of Treaties[18] and therefore in pursuance of the Vienna Convention's Article 31(3)(c), account must be taken of "any relevant rules of international law applicable in the relations between the parties."[19] However, in the same breath,

---

the European Commission and Court of Human Rights to International Humanitarian Law, (1998) 324 Int'l Rev. Red Cross 519 [hereinafter Reidy].

[15] Jann K. Kleffner, *Improving Compliance with International Humanitarian Law through the Establishment of an Individual Complaints Procedure*, 15 LJIL 241 (2002). The same opinion was expressed by Greenwood. Christopher Greenwood, *International Humanitarian Law*, *in* The Centennial of the First International Peace Conference 240–241 and 251–252 (Frits Kalshoven ed., 2000).

[16] Watkin, *supra* note 4, at 2. According to Heintze, the use of human rights bodies enables a better protection in times of non-international armed conflicts. Hans-Joachim Heintze, *Entscheidungen des Europäischen Menschenrechtsgerichtshofs als Politikersatz? Menschenrechtsverletzungen der Türkei vor dem EGMR*, *in* Menschenrechte: Bilanz und Perspektiven 444 (Jana Hasse, Erwin Müller & Patricia Schneider eds., 2002) [hereinafter Heintze 2002].

[17] "In time of war or other public emergency threatening the life of the nation any High Contracting Party may take measures derogating from its obligations under this Convention to the extent strictly required by the exigencies of the situation, provided that such measures are not inconsistent with its other obligations under international law." ECHR, *supra* note 2. For an appreciation of the Court's position in this regard, *see* Fanny Martin, *Le Droit International Humanitaire devant les Organes de Contrôle des Droits de l'Homme*, 1 Droits Fondamentaux 124–128 (2001).

[18] Golder v. United Kingdom, European Court of Human Rights, Judgment (Feb. 21, 1975), Series A, No. 18 (1975), para. 29.

[19] Vienna Convention on the Law of Treaties, 1155 U.N.T.S. 331 (May 23, 1969).

the Court has on numerous occasions shown that "it must remain mindful of the Convention's special character as a human rights treaty."[20]

For example, in the case *Isayeva et al.*[21] a USA-based NGO called *Rights International, the Centre for International Human Rights Law*, submitted written comments alleging that Common Article 3 of the Geneva Conventions was applicable. The submission further explains that the norms of IHL must "be construed in conformity with international human rights law governing the right to life and to human treatment."[22] Yet in spite of this call, the European Court of Human Rights does not refer to IHL at all in the instant case. It only analyses the situation with regard to the human rights enshrined in the European Convention and it uses IHL principles to interpret the right to life in the context of armed conflict.

The areas of commonality between HRL and IHL are however highlighted in several ECHR cases. Although "the internal use of force is normally dealt with under a human rights paradigm"[23] the European Court of Human Rights draws heavily upon principles of IHL pertaining to international and non-international armed conflicts. Hence, Watkin's comment that "human rights advocates will have to become more comfortable with both the scope of [international humanitarian law] and its application to conflict"[24] seems to be pertinent.

Noticeably, the European Court of Human Rights applies core principles of IHL without determining whether an armed conflict is indeed taking place. As Abresch explains, "the rules espoused by the ECtHR are not limited by any conflict intensity threshold; they form a single body of law that covers everything from confrontations between rioters and police officers to set-piece battles between rebel groups and national armies."[25]

This lack of determinacy may be the reason for the Court's reluctance to state expressly that it applies IHL. In fact, should the Court declare that it contemplates IHL as the *lex specialis*, then states could dispute that the Court first needs to demonstrate that an armed conflict of either international or non-international nature is taking place. The determination of the existence of such a conflict and further of its characterisation is often arduous.

By only examining the events according to human rights law, the European Court of Human Rights eludes the answer to this tricky question; for, it never refers to the

---

[20] Loizidou v. Turkey, Application No. 40/1993/435/514, Judgment, Merits, (Dec. 18, 1996), para. 43; Banković v. Belgium and 16 Other Contracting States, Application No. 52207/99, Admissibility Decision, (Dec. 12, 2001), para. 57.
[21] Isayeva et al., *supra* note 3, paras 161–167.
[22] Isayeva et al., *supra* note 3, para. 166.
[23] Watkin, *supra* note 4, at 2.
[24] Watkin, *supra* note 4, at 32.
[25] Abresch, *supra* note 9, at 742–743 and discussion on 752–757.

concept of "armed conflict," preferring to speak of "armed clash,"[26] "violent armed clashes,"[27] "armed combat,"[28] "armed resistance,"[29] and "illegal armed insurgency."[30] The word "armed conflict" only appears in relation to documents produced by the applicant.[31] The Court thus refuses to delve in the intricacies of the determination of the nature of the conflict.[32]

3. Justifying the Use of Force under Article 2 ECHR: The Principle of Necessity?

While the test set by the European Convention on Human Rights does not take into consideration the nature of the conflict, it does require the state to be able to justify the very use of force. In other words, the court must first examine the information presented by the parties and assess the situation on the ground. Second, the court must verify whether the use of force was justified in pursuance of Article 2(2). Third, this section examines the principle of necessity as established in IHL.

3.1. Grounds for Deciding on the Justification of the Use of Force

The European Court of Human Rights acknowledges that "[i]n the light of the importance of the protection afforded by Article 2, the Court must subject deprivations of life to the most careful scrutiny, taking into consideration not only the actions of State agents but also all the surrounding circumstances."[33] Consequently, the terminology employed by the Court in many judgments relating to the use of force can be characterised as very cautious, notably due to the lack of information.

---

[26] Ergi v. Turkey, Application No. 23818/94, Judgment, (July 28, 1998), paras 16; 20; 22; 79 [hereinafter Ergi].
[27] Id. para. 85.
[28] Id. para. 20.
[29] Isayeva et al., *supra* note 3, para. 27.
[30] Id. para. 178; Isayeva, *supra* note 3, para. 180.
[31] See e.g. "The Supreme Court's published case-law did not contain a single example of a civil case brought by a victim of the armed conflict in Chechnya against the state authorities." Isayeva et al., *supra* note 3, para. 140 and Isayeva, *supra* note 3, para. 148. Furthermore, the submission by the NGO Rights International constantly refers to a "non-international armed conflict." Isayeva et al., *supra* note 3, paras 162–167. The opinion of the NGO is again referred to in Isayeva, *supra* note 3, para. 167.
[32] For an evaluation of the Court's reluctance to address the issue of the determination of the nature of conflict, see Hans-Joachim Heintze, *Europäischer Menschenrechtsgerichtshof und Durchsetzung der Menschenrechtsstandards des humanitären Völkerrechts*, 12 ZRP 510 (2000).
[33] Isayeva et al., *supra* note 3, para. 170.

Both cases relating to the conflict in Chechnya are prime examples of how the Court deals with information it receives from the parties.³⁴ For example, the Court states that it "is prepared to accept" or that "the measures could *presumably* include employment of military aviation."³⁵ It transpires from such expressions that the Court wishes to clarify that it is generous in its appreciation of the situation on the ground.

Undoubtedly this position reflects the lack of information which the Court possesses and its inability to judge whether a military decision was appropriate. Firstly, the Court clarifies that "[i]n the absence of corroborated evidence that any unlawful violence was threatened or likely, the Court retains certain doubts as to whether the aim can at all be said to be applicable."³⁶ A second, yet related, ground is that given the circumstances, it is difficult to assess the situation on the ground. Hence, the decision is better left in the hands of the military or those in charge of the operations.³⁷ Indeed, "the Court will tend to assume the lawfulness of the decision to resort to the use of force."³⁸ It therefore appears that, to a certain extent, the European Court of Human Rights is implicitly taking into consideration the nature of warfare and, thereby, its uniqueness.

This blunt assumption may be criticised by those who are familiar with IHL mechanisms and in particular with international criminal law. Though, in a human rights context, one should bear in mind that ECHR bodies have little investigative powers and therefore must rely on the documents produced by the parties before the court.³⁹ A notable part of the rulings deals with the facts submitted by the claimant as well as by the governmental authorities. Included in the compilation of documents produced by the parties, one may find court cases, NGO reports⁴⁰ and reports from the Red Cross.⁴¹ When weighing the evidence, the European Court of Human Rights uses the standard of proof of "beyond reasonable doubt."⁴² As the Court explains "[s]uch proof may follow from the coexistence of sufficiently strong,

---

[34] Isayeva, *supra* note 3; Isayeva et al., *supra* note 3.
[35] Isayeva et al., *supra* note 3, para. 178. (author's emphasis)
[36] Isayeva et al., *supra* note 3, para. 181.
[37] A similar stance was adopted by the Court in the *Ozkan* case. Ozkan et al. v. Turkey, Application No. 21689/93, Judgment, (April 6, 2004), para. 306.
[38] Report of the Expert Meeting on the Right to Life in Armed Conflicts and Situations of Occupation, Geneva (Sept. 1–2, 2005), *available at* www.cudih.org/communication/droit_vie_rapport.pdf (last visited Sept. 4, 2007), at 12 [hereinafter Expert Meeting].
[39] In the past, the European Commission on Human Rights took up the initiative to search for the facts. *See* Joachim A. Frowein, *Fact-Finding by the European Commission on Human Rights*, *in* Fact-Finding Before International Tribunals 237–251 (Richard B. Lillich ed., 1992).
[40] Isayeva et al., *supra* note 3, paras 102–104.
[41] Isayeva et al., *supra* note 3, paras 46–49.
[42] Avsar v. Turkey, Application No. 25657/94, Judgment, (July 10, 2001), para. 282.

clear and concordant interferences or of similar unrebutted presumptions of fact."[43] Moreover, in cases where the facts are of utmost significance to determine whether a violation of the Convention has occurred, the Court must take great care in its assessment. It is aware that it cannot and should not act as a court of first instance, especially in cases relating to Article 2 of the Convention. In such cases, the Court must take extreme caution and "apply a particularly thorough scrutiny."[44]

Furthermore, "the scope of fact-finding... is particularly tested when the issue is not alone one of resolving a dispute between the applicant and the Government as to the occurrence of particular facts, but over the wider picture: the existence of a practice of which the applicant claims to be a victim."[45] This is particularly true in cases relating to armed conflicts.

Without doubt the two aforementioned cases are only representative of the general situation that reigned in 1999–2000 on the territory of Chechnya. "Every human life remains precious, but assessing when the taking of life may be justified is rarely undertaken on a scale of one or two victims."[46] In this context it is strenuous for the Court to understand a single case; instead the Court needs to consider the broader picture. The Court has nonetheless consistently rejected this pro-active role in investigating more general claims.[47]

3.2. Grounds to Justify the Use of Force

Although the right to life is encapsulated in Article 2(1) ECHR, this provision does not purport to protect life unconditionally. The need to maintain public order both on the domestic and international level is expressed in the exceptions to the rule.[48] "It is accepted that these exceptions enable the State to maintain law and order, a societal interest that outweighs an individual's right to life."[49] Indeed, deprivation of life can still be lawful provided it fulfils a certain purpose outlined in the second paragraph of the aforementioned article or if it falls under Article 15(2) ECHR concerning "lawful acts of war."[50] Article 15 is not relevant in this

---

[43] Isayeva et al., *supra* note 3, para. 172.
[44] Isayeva et al., *supra* note 3, para. 173.
[45] Reidy, Hampson & Boyle, *supra* note 6, at 171.
[46] Watkin, *supra* note 4, at 33.
[47] Reidy, Hampson & Boyle, *supra* note 6, at 172.
[48] Sometimes one may have the impression that the right to life is absolute in nature. Yet, "that normative structure must also account for the taking of life so as to maintain social order." Watkin, *supra* note 4, at 10.
[49] Rachel Harvey & Emilia Mugnai, *The Right to Life*, August 2002, available at <http://www.childrenslegalcentre.com/>, 9 June 2005, p. 17.
[50] "[T]he European Court of Human Rights' principle of evolutive interpretation demands that the ambiguous language of article 15 of the ECHR be construed to apply to international and non-international conflicts given the changing character of contemporary armed conflicts and

discussion because no state has ever called for its application, thus, relegating the issue of permissibility to the ambit of Article 2 ECHR.[51]

Lethal use of force can be applied to defend a person against unlawful violence, to arrest a person or prevent the escape of a detainee, and to suppress a riot or an insurrection. As the list is restrictive, lethal use of force must consequently be grounded in one of the aforementioned purposes. In addition, because the right to life is a core right, any possible justification for infringing this right must be interpreted in a restrictive manner.[52]

If the governmental authorities cannot find an alternative to the use of force, i.e. the individual(s) cannot be arrested by law enforcement authorities, then the European Court of Human Rights accepts that a state uses force.[53] This was clearly spelled out in the *McCann* case in which the Court explained that

> the authorities were bound by their obligation to respect the right to life of the suspects to exercise the greatest care in evaluating the information at their disposal before transmitting it to the soldiers whose use of fire-arms automatically involved shooting to kill.[54]

In the case of *Isayeva*, the Court recognised that the presence of large groups of armed fighters and their resistance to law-enforcement agencies justified the use of lethal force by the State agents of Russia.[55] Furthermore, this use of force is conditional. Indeed, other cases brought before the European Court reveal that if the individual who should be arrested does not represent a threat to other persons' life and "is not suspected of having committed a violent offence" then force cannot be justified.[56] In a nutshell, the person must represent a serious threat in order for the state to apply force.

Accordingly, the state must convincingly demonstrate that failing the possibility to arrest the wrongdoers, it uses force with the aim of suppressing an insurrection or defending individuals against unlawful violence. In such a context, the European Court of Human Rights acknowledges that the use of force can be justified to shield the general population.[57] The court also accepts that the situation on the

---

the emergence of civil-military operations in international peace-keeping and peace-enforcement operations." Martin 2002, *supra* note 5, at 453.

[51] Doswald-Back, *supra* note 12, at 883 and Abresch, *supra* note 9, at 745.
[52] McCann et al. v. United Kingdom, Application No. 18984/91, Judgment (Sept. 5, 1995), para. 147 [hereinafter McCann et al.]; Soering v. United Kingdom, Application No. 14038/88, Judgment, (July 7, 1989), para. 88.
[53] *See* the discussion in Abresch, *supra* note 9, at 743.
[54] McCann et al., *supra* note 52, para. 211.
[55] Isayeva, *supra* note 3, para. 180.
[56] Nachova v. Bulgaria, Application Nos 43577/98 and 43579/98, Judgment (July 6, 2005), para. 95.
[57] *See* discussion *infra*.

ground calls for exceptional measures and thus the use of planes against illegal armed groups may be justified.[58] The intention of such an operation may be to defend the local population against the illegal armed insurgency. One nevertheless wonders whether the governmental operation is undertaken to protect the population from *past*, *present* or *future* instances of unlawful violence carried out by non-state actors. This is unfortunately not discussed in detail by the Court.[59]

3.3. The Principle of Necessity

As rightly pointed out by the Expert Meeting on the Right to Life in Armed Conflicts and Situations of Occupation, one of the "main feature[s] of the law enforcement model is that, where possible, State officials must arrest rather than kill persons who are posing a threat."[60] From a more general human rights viewpoint, Martin observes that

> military authorities may use force against combatant or mixed combatant-civilian targets only if there is no other alternative to inflicting injury and suffering for achieving lawful objectives, both tactical *and* strategic.[61]

This formulation is close to the principle of necessity. Indeed, according to the principle of necessity enshrined in IHL[62] those attacking a particular target must prove that it is necessary for military purposes and that a definite military advantage will be gained from carrying out the operation:

> The principle of necessity in the law of armed conflict requires that, once a valid contingency is identified, alternative strategies be prospectively evaluated. Assuming various sufficient strategies, instruments and programmes should be selected on

---

[58] Isayeva, *supra* note 3, para. 180; Isayeva et al., *supra* note 3, para. 178.
[59] On this issue, *see* the discussion in Expert Meeting, *supra* note 38, at 17–18 [hereinafter Expert Meeting].
[60] *Id.* at 8.
[61] Martin 2002, *supra* note 5, at 406.
[62] A definition of military necessity is:
Military necessity permits a belligerent, subject to the laws of war, to apply any amount and kind of force to compel the complete submission of the enemy with the least possible expenditure of time, life, and money.... It permits the destruction of life of armed enemies and other persons whose destruction is incidentally unavoidable by the armed conflicts of the war; it allows the capturing of armed enemies and others of peculiar danger, but does not permit the killing of innocent inhabitants for purposes of revenge or the satisfaction of a lust to kill. The destruction of property to be lawful must be imperatively demanded by the necessities of war. Destruction as an end in itself is a violation of international law. There must be some reasonable connection between the destruction of property and the overcoming of the enemy forces.
In re List and Others, United Nations War Crimes Commission. Law Reports of Trials of War Criminals. Volume VIII, 1949, at 66.

the basis of which ones accomplish the necessary objectives with the least possible quanta of harm.[63]

The European Court of Human Rights never assessed whether military operations conducted by state authorities were carried out in order to gain a military advantage. This is certainly linked to the fact that the very notion of military advantage is one encapsulated in IHL and is therefore beyond the legal remit in which the European Court of Human Rights assesses violations of the ECHR. A second difference between the interpretation espoused by the Court and the principle of necessity is that the Court stresses that killing is only permitted if capturing "pose[s] too great a risk to the government's law enforcement officials or to other members of society."[64] In contrast to IHL, "there is no *per se* rule that insurgents may be targeted with lethal force."[65] According to IHL however, the incapability to arrest/capture the person is no pre-requisite to his/her killing. The pre-requisite under IHL is that the person is a combatant (in international armed conflict) or actively participates in the hostilities (in non-international armed conflict). An additional reason that explains the shyness of the Court to apply the principle of necessity is (as discussed earlier) that the Court scrutinises whether the aims followed by the state were legitimate, a test that does not exist in IHL but is required in pursuance of the European Convention on Human Rights. The Court speaks of "permitted aims"[66] while IHL knows of no such concept since it would encroach upon the principle of distinction between the *jus in bello* and the *jus ad bellum*.[67]

Thus although at first instance it appears as though the European Court of Human Rights is using *prima facie* the principle of necessity, a careful examination of the jurisprudence proves that this is in fact not the case. Consequently it seems that the European Court does not consider IHL as the *lex specialis* trumping HRL provisions in armed conflict.

4. *The Principles of Distinction and Proportionality*

Having decided that the use of force is indeed necessary given the circumstances, the Court must then turn to another criterion that must be satisfied, namely, that

---

[63] W. Michael Reisman & Douglas L. Stevick, *The Applicability of International Law Standards to United Nations Economic Sanctions Programmes*, 9 Eur. J. Int'l L. (1998), *available at* www.ejil.org/journal/Vol9/No1/art4.html (last visited June 10, 2005).
[64] Expert Meeting, *supra* note 38, at 10.
[65] Abresch, *supra* note 9, at 759.
[66] McKerr v. UK, Application No. 28883/95, Judgment (May 4, 2001), para. 22; Isayeva, *supra* note 3, para. 181; Güleç v. Turkey, Application No. 21593/93, Judgment, (July 27, 1998), para. 16 [hereinafter Güleç].
[67] Abresch, *supra* note 9, at 765.

the use of force must be strictly proportionate to the achievement of one of the aims specified in Article 2(2). Under IHL, the principle of proportionality, which only applies to mixed military-civilian targets, is harnessed upon the principles of distinction and discrimination.

In this context, it is rather surprising that the notions, which are implicitly or explicitly mentioned by the European Court of Human Rights, pertain to the domain of IHL and more specifically to the rules regarding targeting (principles of distinction and proportionality).[68] One may question whether the Court realises that it uses typically IHL concepts in its reasoning. Indeed, "these criteria come remarkably close to those used as targeting principles in humanitarian law."[69]

4.1. *The Principles of Distinction and Discrimination*

One of the cornerstones of IHL is the principle that all possible measures must be taken to distinguish between civilian persons and objects, and military objectives.[70] The cardinal principle of distinction between civilians and fighters/combatants[71] and between civilian objects and military objectives is enshrined in customary international law and is applicable both in international and non-international armed conflicts.[72] Primarily, in times of non-international armed conflicts the distinction between members of armed opposition groups (correctly referred to as persons who are "taking a direct part in hostilities") and civilians appears difficult to pinpoint[73] as "there is no reference point for the general distinction between persons authorised to participate directly in the hostilities and those to be protected as civilians."[74] It is symptomatic that although Additional Protocol II consistently uses this term it does not include a definition of the concept of "civilians" or

---

[68] "The controlled application of force is often referred to in modern military terminology as 'targeting'." Watkin, *supra* note 4 at 15.

[69] Tom Ruys, License to Kill? State-Sponsored Assassination under International Law, Institute for International Law, Working Paper No. 76, May 2005, *available at* www.law.kuleuven.ac.be/iir/nl/wp/WP76e.pdf (last visited June 9, 2005) [hereinafter Ruys].

[70] The ICJ also identified the principle of distinction as a cardinal principle of international humanitarian law. Advisory Opinion on Nuclear Weapons, *supra* note 10, para. 78.

[71] While fighters enjoy the status of "combatant" in international armed conflicts, they do not in non-international armed conflicts. "This is not due to any altruistic articulation by governments of the need to avoid using force against all persons during such conflicts, but rather because of their insistence that rebels must not in any shape or form benefit from any kind of international recognition." Doswald-Deck, *supra* note 12, at 889.

[72] Rule 1 in Jean-Marie Henckaerts, *Study on Customary International Humanitarian Law: A Contribution to the Understanding and Respect for the Rule of Law in Armed Conflict*, 857 Int'l Rev. Red Cross 24 (2005) [hereinafter Henckaerts].

[73] *Id.* at 16.

[74] Constanze von Oppeln, *Victim's Protection in International Law: The Normative Basis and a Look into the Practice*, 10 Eur. J. Crime Cr. L. Cr. J. 242 (2002).

"civilian population." This lack of clarity is reflected both in further treaties and international customary law.[75]

These concepts were used on several occasions by the European Court of Human Rights: "civilian houses",[76] "civilian areas",[77] "civilian population",[78] "a civilian,"[79] "civilians,"[80] "civilian life/lives,"[81] "civilian cars,"[82] "civilian vehicles,"[83] and "civilian casualties."[84] As a matter of fact, the choice of the noun or adjective of "civilian" by a human rights organ is rather frightening, for it negates the basic tenet of human rights law that all human beings are equal. HRL applies to both civilians and combatants/fighters, i.e. it does not know of this distinction.[85] Indeed, human rights are "literally, the rights that one has simply because one is a human being."[86] Another perplexing characteristic of many European Court of Human Right's judgments is that the Court has never imparted any definition of the terms "civilians," "combatants," and "fighters," thereby causing some confusion as to who falls into which category.

The fundamental distinction between civilians and combatants/fighters is important for the application of the principle of discrimination that holds that only combatants/fighters and military objectives can be targeted during an attack. Article 13 APII asserts that "the civilian population as such, as well as individual civilians, shall not be the object of attack…unless and for such time as they take a direct part in hostilities." This principle, which is of customary nature and

---

[75] *See* e.g. Expert Meeting, *supra* note 38; Second Expert Meeting Direct Participation in Hostilities under International Humanitarian Law, The Hague (Oct. 25–26, 2004), *available at* www.icrc.org/Web/eng/siteeng0.nsf/htmlall/participation-hostilities-ihl-311205/$File/Direct_participation_in_hostilities_2004_eng.pdf (last visited Sept. 4, 2007); Third Expert Meeting on the Notion of Direct Participation in Hostilities, Geneva (Oct. 23–25, 2005), *available at* www.icrc.org/Web/eng/siteeng0.nsf/htmlall/participation-hostilities-ihl-311205/$File/Direct_participation_in_hostilities_2005_eng.pdf (last visited Sept. 4, 2007). *See also* Doswald-Beck, *supra* note 12, at 889–890.
[76] Ergi, *supra* note 26, para. 10.
[77] *Id.* paras 45; 84.
[78] *Id. supra* note 18, paras 70; 72; 80; 81; Isayeva, *supra* note 3, para. 200; Isayeva et al., *supra* note 3, para. 199.
[79] Ergi, *supra* note 26, para. 79.
[80] Isayeva, *supra* note 3, paras 176, 182, 183, 189, 190, 193, 194, 195, 196, 197; Isayeva et al., *supra* note 3, paras 175, 177, 185, 187, 189, 191, 196, 202, 203, 215, 222, 233.
[81] Isayeva, *supra* note 3, paras 176, 199; Isayeva et al., *supra* note 3, para. 184.
[82] Isayeva, *supra* note 3, para. 195.
[83] *Id.* para. 196.
[84] *Id.* para. 198; Isayeva et al., *supra* note 3, paras 190, 191, 205.
[85] In contrast, in international humanitarian law "[a]n individual's rights change when his classification changes." Abresch, *supra* note 9, at 757.
[86] Jack Donnelly, Universal Human Rights in Theory and Practice 10 (2003).

applicable in non-international armed conflicts, was reasserted in the *Tadic* case before the ICTY.[87]

Although the Court has never explained that it is expressly drawing upon the principle of discrimination, it constantly refers to it when it declares that state agents must pay attention to the lives of civilians.[88] Again, the principle of discrimination seems to run counter to general human rights law inasmuch as it declares that the lives of some persons, i.e. civilians, are worth protecting while the lives of others, i.e. fighters/combatants, can be violated. To speak of the principle of discrimination in the context of HRL is unmistakably a *contradictio in terminis* since HRL is based on the idea that all human beings are equal and should be treated as such. To a certain extent, the Court disregards the rights of those who are labelled fighters or combatants in the name of the *lex specialis* rule which is predicated on the premise that lethal force will be used and individuals killed.[89]

4.2. *The Principle of Proportionality*

As stated earlier, the principle of proportionality is one of the criteria used to assess the legality of a state operation leading to the death of a person. In the opinion of the Court, the intentional deprivation of life can only be understood as the result of "the deliberate or intended use of lethal force."[90] This use of force should not be more than absolutely necessary for the achievement of one or more of the purposes laid down in Article 2(2). Often, when considering a case pertaining to the use of force, the Court speaks of the principle of proportionality rather than that of "absolute necessity",[91] the literal expression found in Article 2(2).[92] This is

---

[87] Prosecutor v. Dusko Tadic a/k/a "Dule", Decision on the Defence Motion for Interlocutory Appeal on Jurisdiction, Appeals Chamber, Case No. IT-94-1-AR72, (Oct. 2, 1995), para. 127.

[88] See *infra* discussion on the principle of proportionality and the planning of the operations.

[89] However, speaking of the right to life as encapsulated in the ICCPR, Greenwood explains that "[i]t has to be remembered that the taking of life is an inherent feature of armed conflict and it was neither the intention nor the effect of Article 6 to prohibit the use of force by states." Christopher Greenwood, *Rights at the Frontier – Protecting the Individual in Time of War, in* Law at the Centre: The Institute of Advanced Legal Studies at Fifty 285 (Barry Rider ed., 1999). Without delving much into details, it may be argued that the same holds true concerning Article 2 ECHR.

[90] Isayeva et al., *supra* note 3, para. 169 and Isayeva, *supra* note 3, para. 173.

[91] Güleç, *supra* note 66, para. 83; Ergi, *supra* note 26, para. 79. Yet, Martin argues that the current test of permissibility with respect to intended or predictable death under human rights law is a test of absolute necessity. Martin 2002, *supra* note 5, at 355, 364–367, 372, 395.

[92] It must be noted that other human rights instruments use the word "arbitrarily" rather than "absolutely necessary." International Covenant on Civil and Political Rights, G.A. Res. 2200A (XXI), 21 U.N. GAOR Supp. (No. 16) at 52, U.N. Doc. A/6316 (1966), Article 6(1), 999 U.N.T.S. 171; American Convention on Human Rights, O.A.S. Treaty Series No. 36, 1144 U.N.T.S. 123, entered into force July 18, 1978, reprinted in Basic Documents Pertaining to Human Rights in the Inter-American System, OEA/Ser.L.V/II.82 doc.6 rev.1 at 25 (1992), Article 4(1); African

probably due to the linkage between the wording "absolutely necessary" and the reference to the aims of the use of force as mentioned in Article 2(2) ECHR.[93] Indeed, "proportionality…demands a careful balance to be struck between the goal to be achieved and the means used to this end. The nature of the threat and the intention of the suspects must be weighed against the possible outcome."[94]

The usage of the word "proportionate" is a reminder of the principle of proportionality that is well established in customary IHL too, and is valid in times of international as well as non-international armed conflict.[95] It requires that any attack that distinguishes between civilian and military objects be proportionate to the direct and concrete military advantage to be gained by the attack.

In treaty law, this principle of proportionality is only found in relation to international armed conflict.[96] Furthermore, reference is only made in implicit terms. The principle of proportionality serves as a shortened version for attacks that are "excessive in relation to the concrete and direct military advantage anticipated" as contained in Article 57(2) AP I.[97] Often this is referred to as "incidental loss of civilians" or "collateral damage". Accordingly, IHL tolerates "the killing and wounding of innocent human beings not directly participating in an armed conflict, such as civilian victims of lawful collateral damage."[98]

The very notion of "incidental loss,"[99] which is specific to IHL and is only recognised as applicable in international armed conflict by virtue of treaty law and according to customary law in both international and non-international armed conflicts, was adopted by the ECHR in the *Ergi* case in which a civilian woman had been killed as a result of military operations in Turkey. In other words, the European Court applies the principle although there is neither an international armed conflict (in which case API would be applicable) nor a non-international

---

Charter on Human and People's Rights (June 27, 1981), Article 4, 1520 U.N.T.S. 217. As Paust notes "the 'absolutely necessary' standard used in McCann is clearly different from the 'arbitrarily deprived' standard used in the International Covenant, the American Convention, and the African Charter." Jordan J. Paust, *The Right to Life in Human Rights Law and the Law of War*, 65 Sask. L. Rev. 411, 417 (2002) [hereinafter Paust].

[93] Heintze 2002, *supra* note 16, at 454.
[94] Ruys, *supra* note 69.
[95] General Assembly, *Respect for Human Rights in Armed Conflicts*, U.N. Doc. 1/7218, (Dec. 19, 1968). Rule 14 in Henckaerts, *supra* note 72.
[96] The protection of civilians against effects of fighting in international armed conflicts is rudimentary and, hence, relies heavily on customary international law.
[97] "The use of the term 'excessive,' rather than proportional, in relation to civilian casualties was in response to strong objections by several states that the concept of proportionality was contrary to humanitarian principles and international law." Judith G. Gardam, *Proportionality and Force in International Law*, 87 Am. J. Int'l L. 406 (1993) [hereinafter Gardam].
[98] Theodor Meron, *The Humanization of Humanitarian Law*, 94 Am. J. Int'l L. 240 (2000).
[99] Ergi, *supra* note 26, para. 79.

armed conflict (in which case one may apply customary international law with precaution). The Court also adopts this approach in the cases relating to military operations carried out by Russia in Chechnya as it declares that any operation must be mounted "with a view to avoiding and, in any event, minimising, incidental loss of civilian."[100] This statement however is less controversial since one may contend that the events in Chechnya may be branded as a non-international armed conflict.[101] Yet, one would still need to establish that the concept of "collateral damage" or "incidental loss" is applicable in the context of a non-international armed conflict. Obviously the European Court of Human Rights is bridging the gap by applying IHL norms that are only used in international armed conflicts to all kinds of situations.

According to Heintze the choice of words used by the Court proves that it is aware that IHL is the *lex specialis*[102] and should be the ruling *corpus juris* when dealing with cases relating to armed conflicts.[103] This assertion however is flawed in two ways. First, it is not all that clear that the European Court of Human Rights is indeed using international humanitarian law as a *lex specialis* and, second, the proportionality test adopted by the Court is different from the one established in IHL.

Indeed, the prohibition of excessive incidental loss to civilians is difficult to translate into concrete rules[104] and so far no clear test has been ascertained neither in international humanitarian law[105] nor in international criminal law. It is therefore not surprising that the European Court is attempting to establish such a test on a case-by-case basis. Unfortunately, the Court does not support its reasoning by any theory and fails to provide a clear and standardized test. It simply questions in *Isayeva et al.* whether the principle of proportionality was observed when it was obvious

---

[100] Isayeva et al., *supra* note 3, para. 172 and Isayeva, *supra* note 3, para. 176.

[101] On the qualification of the conflict in Chechnya, *see* Noëlle Quénivet, *The Moscow Hostage Crisis in the Light of the Armed Conflict in Chechnya*, 4 YB Int'l Humanitarian L. 348–372 (2001).

[102] This principle holds that when two norms of international law collide, the more specific should be applied in order to assist in the interpretation of the more general rule.

[103] Hans-Joachim Heintze, *Zum Verhältnis von Menschenrechtsschutz und humanitärem Völkerrecht*, 4 HuV-I 179 (2003). *See also* Hans-Joachim Heintze, *On the Relationship between Human Rights Law Protection and International Humanitarian Law*, 856 Int'l Rev. Red Cross 796–798 (2004) [Heintze 2004].

[104] See the discussion in Dale Stephens & Michael W. Lewis, *The Law of Armed Conflict-A Contemporary Critique*, 6 Melb. J. Int'l L. 55 (2005).

[105] As Stephens notes "[the interpretation of the principle of proportionality] is notoriously ambiguous. The difficulty lies in quantifying what may be considered an acceptable loss of life vis-à-vis the value placed upon achieving the military objective." Dale Stephens, *Human Rights and Armed Conflict-The Advisory Opinion of the International Court of Justice in the Nuclear Weapons Case*, 4 Yale Human rights and Development L.J. 1, 19 (2001).

that a substantial number of civilian cars and persons were present on the road.[106] In *Isayeva* the Court does not make many comments as to the compliance with the principle of proportionality; rather it explores whether the Russian armed forces took enough precautionary measures to prevent civilian casualties and damages. The subjectivity of the test found in IHL[107] seems to translate into HRL too.

Second, the European Court of Human Rights explains that "a balance must be achieved between the aim pursued and the means employed to achieve it."[108] In contrast, in IHL a balance must be struck between the principle of humanity and the principle of military necessity.[109] The connection between military necessity and the aim pursued has been already discussed earlier and it has been demonstrated that although similar, they remain separate. Moreover, the relationship between the principle of humanity and "the means employed to achieve the aim" is more complex. Basically, the proportionality test employed by the European Court does not reflect the one known to IHL. In fact, one may liken the test to that relating to the use of weapons. This also explains why the Court often prefers to examine whether sufficient precautionary measures were adopted prior to the launching of the operation and whether the operation was conducted by using appropriate means and methods.

5. *Precautionary Measures*

A second yardstick to determine whether the use of force is no more than absolutely necessary is to assess whether the operation was planned and controlled by the authorities in such a manner that it would minimise recourse to lethal force. This approach adopted by the European Court of Human Rights can generally be associated to the concept of precautionary measures established in IHL.

5.1. *Planning and Control of the Operation*

A way to check whether a certain action is proportionate to the aim is to investigate the planning of the operation and the control by the authorities over the operation. Furthermore, as noted by Doswald-Beck "several cases before the ECHR have underlined a distinction between the planning of a police operation and the actual

---

[106] The number of civilian casualties is nevertheless unclear.
[107] Judith Gardam, *Proportionality as a Restraint on the Use of Force*, 20 Austl. Y. B. Int'l L. 161, 109 (1999).
[108] Isayeva, *supra* note 3, para. 181.
[109] *See* e.g. Eyal Benvenisti, *Human Dignity in Combat: The Duty to Spare Enemy Civilians*, 39 Isr. L. Rev. 81, 81 (2006).

use of force by police officers."[110] After the Chechen cases, Doswald-Beck's comment also seems pertinent to cases of force being used by military forces. The dual obligation of states relating to "planning" and "control" is based on the fact that

> states do not merely have a negative obligation regarding protection of the right to life in the sense of a duty to abstain from unlawfully killing human beings or impermissibly interfering with the right to life, but states also have a positive obligation to act to prevent its infringement by state or private actors.[111]

In addition, the European Convention on Human Rights unmistakably enounces in Article 1 that states "shall *secure* to everyone within their jurisdiction the rights and freedom defined [in the Convention]."[112] Read in conjunction with Article 2, this provision grants the Court the opportunity to scrutinise the planning and execution of military operations.

The test to verify whether force was lawfully used was initially laid down in the *McCann and others* v. *UK*: the planning and the control of an operation must be so as to minimise recourse to lethal force:

> In keeping with the importance of this provision in a democratic society, the Court must, in making its assessment, subject deprivations of life to the most careful scrutiny, particularly where deliberate lethal force is used, taking into consideration not only the actions of the agents of the State who actually administer the force but also all the surrounding circumstances including such matters as the planning and control of the actions under examination.[113]

Later the Court explains that

> Against this background, in determining whether the force used was compatible with Article 2, the Court must carefully scrutinise, as noted above, not only whether the force used by the soldiers was strictly proportionate to the aim of protecting persons against unlawful violence but also whether the anti-terrorist operation was planned and controlled by the authorities so as to minimise, to the greatest extent possible, recourse to lethal force.[114]

This stance was reiterated in the *Ergi* judgment which concerned the accidental killing of a woman during a military operation. The Court argued that the state had failed

---

[110] Doswald-Beck, *supra* note 12, at 885.
[111] Paust, *supra* note 92, at 414.
[112] ECHR, *supra* note 2 (emphasis added).
[113] McCann et al., *supra* note 52, para. 150.
[114] McCann et al., *supra* note 52, para. 194.

to take all feasible precaution in the choice of means and methods of a security operation mounted against an opposing group with a view to avoiding or, at least, minimising incidental loss of civilian life.[115]

As a consequence, "the responsibility of the State is not confined to circumstances where there is significant evidence that misdirected fire from State agents has killed a civilian,"[116] i.e. it does not only stem from the direct deprivation of life but also from failure to take all feasible precautions.[117]

According to Reidy, the aforementioned test "provides a secure framework for assessing whether killings are illegal under the laws of armed conflict."[118] Indeed, the two cases pertaining to the situation in Chechnya prove her point. The Court stresses that all operations must be undertaken "so as to minimise, to the greatest extent possible, recourse to lethal force."[119] In the case of *Isayeva* in particular, the European Court of Human Rights declares that the operation in Katyr-Yurt "was planned some time in advance";[120] while it notes in both cases that the Russian military should have foreseen the dangers and should have thus acted accordingly.[121] Furthermore, in *Isayeva*, the Court underlines that despite being in possession of all the relevant information on the situation on the ground, the authorities did not take into account the effects of the assault on the civilian population.[122] As a consequence, the Court finds that Russia relinquished its duty to plan the attack with the prerequisite care for the lives of the civilian population, and thereby violated article 2 ECHR.

The Court's reasoning is a strong reminder of the rules of IHL inasmuch as "[t]he principles of discrimination and proportionality in their general formulations guide military commanders planning attacks."[123] Although there is no conventional basis for requiring precautionary measures in attack in non-international armed conflicts,

---

[115] Ergi, *supra* note 26, para. 79.
[116] *See also* Ozkan et al. v. Turkey, *supra* note 40, para. 297.
[117] Isayeva, *supra* note 3, para. 176. *See* among others Kelly et al. v. United Kingdom, Application No. 30054/96, Judgment, (May 4, 2001), para. 129; Gül v. Turkey, Application No. 22676/93, Judgment, (Dec. 14, 2000), para. 78; Orhan v. Turkey, Application No. 25656/94, Judgment, (June 18, 2002), para. 326.
[118] Reidy, *supra* note 14.
[119] Isayeva et al., *supra* note 3, para. 171 and Isayeva, *supra* note 3, para. 175.
[120] Isayeva, *supra* note 3, para. 188.
[121] Isayeva, *supra* note 3, para. 187 and Isayeva et al., *supra* note 3, para. 189.
[122] Isayeva, *supra* note 3, para. 189.
[123] David S. Koller, *The Moral Imperative: Toward a Human Rights – Based Law of War*, 46 Harv. Int'l L.J. 237 (2005). One must however stress that "[i]t is a duty to act in good faith to take practicable measures, and persons acting in good faith may make mistakes." William J. Fenrick, *The Law Applicable to Targeting and Proportionality after Operation Allied Force: A View from the Outside*, 3 YB Int'l Humanitarian L. 77 (2000) [hereinafter Fenrick].

such a rule is now enshrined in customary international law and is applicable to any type of armed conflict:

> In the conduct of military operations, constant care must be taken to spare the civilian population, civilians and civilian objects. All feasible precautions must be taken to avoid, and in any event to minimise, incidental loss of civilian life, injury to civilians and damage to civilian objects.[124]

In other words, "the conduct of the attack itself must not be negligent and involve unnecessary civilian casualties."[125]

Another rule that pertains to the realm of IHL and is linked to precautionary measures is the issuance of a warning. This is also used by the Court. According to IHL, a means to minimise the civilian death toll is to provide adequate advance warning to the civilian population, unless circumstances do not permit so.[126] In other words, if the military situation allows for a warning to be issued, then the combatants/fighters must take reasonable efforts to do so in order to allow the civilian population to flee the targeted area. In *Isayeva*, the European Court of Human Rights declares that "it was at least open to [the relevant authorities] to warn the residents in advance."[127] Again the Court promulgates rules that are largely derived from IHL without explicitly referring to this *corpus juris*.

The Court also criticises the fact that the Russian authorities did not seem to be *controlling* the operation appropriately. Similarly it explains in the *Ergi* case that the failure of the authorities to adduce direct evidence on the planning proved that insufficient precautions had been taken.[128] Despite the dearth of information and the insurmountable discrepancies between the various testimonies and documents the European Court is convinced that a mistake was made as far as the timing of the strikes was concerned. It declares that it is impossible that by the time the planes fired the missiles the pilots did not see the convoy of civilians.[129] According to IHL, the attack should have been cancelled or suspended since it became apparent that the target was of civilian nature and that the principle of proportionality would not be respected.[130] From the wording in the judgment transpires that the European Court of Human Rights does not explicitly but implicitly refer to this

---

[124] Rule 15 Henckaerts, *supra* note 72, at 25.
[125] Gardam, *supra* note 97, at 407. In Gardam's opinion, this is the third way to assess whether the principle of proportionality was complied with.
[126] Rule 20 in Henckaerts, *supra* note 72, at 25.
[127] Isayeva, *supra* note 3, para. 187.
[128] Ergi, *supra* note 26, para. 81.
[129] Isayeva et al., *supra* note 3, para. 194.
[130] Rule 19 in Henckaerts, *supra* note 72, at 25. In the Djakovica incident which occurred during the NATO bombing in 1999, the pilots having noticed that the convoy included civilians stopped the attack. ICTY Office of the Prosecutor, Final Report to the Prosecutor by the Committee Established to Review the NATO Bombing Campaign Against the Federal Republic of Yugoslavia (June 8, 2000), reproduced in (2000) International Legal Materials 1257–1283. For an appraisal

rule. It explores all the documents and testimonies before it draws the conclusion that the aerial operation was not carried out in pursuance of Article 2 ECHR[131] because of the authorities' failure to plan and *execute* the strikes with the requisite care for civilian lives.

5.2. *Indiscriminate Attacks*

Another approach to determine whether the operation and the ensuing deaths were "absolutely necessary" is to peruse the means and methods used inasmuch as they reveal whether the attack was indiscriminate and disproportionate. Indeed, as Gardam explains, a means to assess whether the principle of proportionality is respected is to examine the means and methods of attack.[132] Fenrick corroborates this in his stipulation: "the principle of proportionality is implicitly contained in Article 51 of Additional Protocol I, which prohibits indiscriminate attacks."[133] Furthermore, in giving advice to legal advisers of the USAF concerning the lawfulness of an attack, Heintzelman and Bloom state that "where the proposed target is a military objective, help is needed only in developing a means of attack that meets the criteria of proportionality."[134]

According to international customary law indiscriminate attacks are outlawed in non-international armed conflicts. Such attacks are defined as those "which are not directed at a specific military objective," "which employ a method or means of combat which cannot be directed at a specific military objective" or "which employ a method or means of combat the effects of which cannot be limited as required by international humanitarian law."[135]

Already in the *Ergi* judgment, the European Court of Human Rights "was unable to avoid checking the compatibility of the weapons systems with both international human rights *and* humanitarian law."[136] A day earlier, the Court had examined the case lodged by *Güleç*,[137] whose son had been killed by shots fired from a tank during a violent demonstration, and had come to a similar conclusion. The Court ruled that the use of force must be proportional to the aim and the means used. In *Güleç*, the use of battlefield weapons to quell a riot was deemed disproportionate even more so as the armed forces in charge of the suppression of the demonstration were equipped with the necessary equipment to fight off demonstrators.

---

of the Djakovica incident, see Eric David, *Respect for the Principle of Distinction in the Kosovo War*, 3 YB Int'l Humanitarian L. 99–101 (2000).

[131] Isayeva et al., *supra* note 3, para. 194.
[132] Gardam, *supra* note 97, at 407.
[133] Fenrick, *supra* note 123, at 58.
[134] Harry L. Heintzelman & Edmund S. Bloom, *A Planning Primer: How to Provide Effective Legal Input in to the War Planning and Combat Execution Process*, 37 AFLR 21 (1994).
[135] Rule 12 in Henckaerts, *supra* note 72, at 25.
[136] Heintze 2004, *supra* note 103, at 810 (emphasis in original).
[137] Güleç, *supra* note 66.

This test was also adopted in the cases relating to the military operations carried out by the Russian armed forces in Chechnya. In *Isayeva et al.* the Court first observes that "[t]he military used an extremely powerful weapon."[138] It then examines the weapon employed as well as its effects and concludes that "[a]nyone who had been on the road at that time would have been in mortal danger."[139] Clearly, the Russian military employed a weapon whose effects and impact on the population they could not limit.

The Court adopts a similar reasoning in *Isayeva* as it notices that the authorities decided in favour of a strong means to assail the armed opposition group despite the fact that the deployment of such a weapon occurred in a populated area.[140] In the opinion of the Court, the military authorities did not take into account the danger of such a means. Similarly, in the *Blaškić* case, the ICTY had declared that the mere use of indiscriminate weapons in a populated area can be contemplated as a deliberate assault on civilians.[141]

In *Isayeva*, after analysing the information at hand, the Court concludes that the assessment of the plan of the operation was not a "comprehensive evaluation of the limits of and constraints on the use of indiscriminate weapons within a populated area."[142] Similar wording is also used by Fenrick who explains that in IHL "[a]t a minimum, [this principle] requires major improvements in targeting where a massive and comprehensive analysis is needed to create a target base tailored to minimize the risk of collateral damage – ideally before military action –...."[143] The correlation between the interpretation by the European Court of Human Rights of the principle of proportionality and the prohibition of indiscriminate attacks as enshrined in IHL is therefore plainly established. As Reidy rightly asserts "[t]he Court's reference to means and methods in the conduct of military operation is one of the clearest examples of the Court borrowing language from international humanitarian law when analysing the scope of human rights obligations."[144]

6. Conclusion

The jurisprudence of the European Court highlights the latest developments that have brought HRL and IHL to converge. The blurring of the demarcation line between the two *corpus juris* is essentially obvious in situations amounting to non-

---

[138] Isayeva et al., *supra* note 3, para. 195.
[139] Isayeva et al., *supra* note 3, para. 195.
[140] Isayeva, *supra* note 3, para. 189.
[141] Prosecutor v. Blaškić, Case No. IT-95-14-T, Judgment, (March 3, 2000).
[142] Isayeva, *supra* note 3, para. 189.
[143] Fenrick, *supra* note 123, at 75.
[144] Reidy, *supra* note 14.

international armed conflict. "But rather than a confusing blend of various bodies of law, this confluence is creating a coherent law of internal armed conflict."[145] Without explicitly recognising that it is appraising the compliance of states with the core principles of IHL in non-international armed conflicts, the European Court of Human Rights is in fact referring to the main principles of the *lex specialis*.[146] Nevertheless, the Court diverges with regards to the interpretation of certain concepts and fills the gaps. Thus, Article 2 is able to provide a legal framework to assess military conduct in terms of precaution, proportionality, and necessity. What is remarkable is that the Court applies the detailed provisions applicable in times of international armed conflict to situations of non-international armed conflict.[147] Consequently one may speak of a kind of reconceptualisation of the lawful use of force in situations of armed conflict. Yet, as Sperotto puts it,

> [i]n refusing to use international humanitarian law explicitly, the Court avoids fuelling any criticism for applying that discrete body of law, which falls outside the scope of the Convention and which requires expertise some could sustain the Court does not master. Furthermore, by openly discussing issues traditionally belonging to international humanitarian law, the Court cannot be accused of regarding itself as a separate little empire.[148]

As a result, one may maintain that in assessing whether a situation amounts to a violation of Article 2(2) ECHR the Court is strongly *inspired* by principles of IHL but yet fills in the gaps left by IHL when it deems that this *corpus juris* is unclear. As Doswald-Beck avers, "both branches of law try to protect people from unnecessary violence to the degree possible whilst respecting the perceived needs of society."[149]

---

[145] Alex G. Peterson, *Order out of Chaos: Domestic Enforcement of the Law of Internal Armed Conflict*, 171 Mil. L. Rev. 42 (2002). In contradistinction, Heinschel von Heinegg argues that "[i]f [the members of the armed forces] were obliged to also comply with human rights, the applicable law would become rather complicated an, in many cases, inoperable." Heinschel von Heinegg, *supra* note 7, at 872.

[146] Heintze 2002, *supra* note 16, at 446.

[147] Alexander Orakhelashvili, The Interaction between Human Rights and Humanitarian Law: A Case of Fragmentation, International Law and Justice Colloquium, New York University (Feb. 26, 2007), at 21–22, available at <iilj.org/research/documents/Orakhelashvili.pdf>, (last visited Sept. 6, 2007).

[148] Federico Sperotto, Violations of Human Rights during Military Operations in Chechnya, Working Paper No. 41 (Feb. 1, 2007), available at <www.du.edu/gsis/hrhw/working/2007/41-sperotto-2007.pdf> (last visited Sept. 5, 2007).

[149] Doswald-Beck, *supra* note 12, at 903.

Chapter XIII

Protection of Women in International Humanitarian Law and Human Rights Law

Anke Biehler*

1. Introduction

1.1. Background

The issue of women affected by armed conflict has received increasing attention of the international community in the last 15 years or so. The initial reason for this were the mass rapes and other very serious, systematic violations of both international humanitarian law and human rights law in the former Yugoslavia within the framework of the so-called ethnic cleansing, which caused an international outcry. This international storm of protest subsequently led to the creation of the International Criminal Tribunal for Yugoslavia (ICTY) by the Security Council in 1993.[1] Serious violations of human rights of women during the Rwandan Genocide in 1994 also made people worldwide aware of the problem and consequently led to the creation of the International Criminal Tribunal for Rwanda (ICTR).[2] Sexual violence against women during armed conflict is still an issue today as the example of Darfur in Sudan or the Kivu region in the Democratic Republic of Congo show.

Awareness for the issue of women in armed conflict being risen, it since continued to be discussed on the international level such as on the Vienna World Conference on the status of Human Rights 1993, the Beijing World Conference on Women 1995, and the Beijing +5 Conference 2000 as well as by the United Nations General Assembly and the United Nations Commission on Human Rights. In October 2000 the United Nations Security Council also called in its resolution 1325 on "Women, Peace and Security" upon all parties to armed conflict

---

* The views expressed in this article are those of the author and do not reflect the position of the ICRC.
[1] S.C. Res. 827 (1993), U.N. Doc. S/RES/827 (1993) (May 25, 1993) [hereinafter ICTY Statute].
[2] S.C. Res. 955 (1994), U.N. Doc. S/RES/955 (1994) (Nov. 8, 1994) [hereinafter ICTR Statute].

"to respect fully international law applicable to the rights and protection of women and girls" and invited the Secretary General to carry out a study on the issue.[3] The subject has continued to be discussed inside the UN System as well as outside.[4] The International Committee of the Red Cross (ICRC), for example, conducted a study in which it describes the effects of armed conflict on women – which are different from the way men experience armed conflict – and also published guidelines based on the results of the study on how to practically protect women and girls in armed conflict.[5] The Inter-Agency Standing Committee, an inter-agency forum for the coordination, policy development, and decision-making involving the key humanitarian U.N. and non-U.N. partners such as the International Committee of the Red Cross and the International Federation of the Red Cross, lately also developed guidelines for gender-based violence interventions in humanitarian settings, which are currently being field tested.[6]

At last, when thinking about women in war and their protection of its effects, one must realize that women are not only mothers and housewives, but also politicians, doctors, community leaders, researchers etc. and that they experience conflict in many different ways ranging from active participation as combatants to being targeted as a member of the civilian population. Therefore women in armed conflict must not automatically be categorized as "vulnerable" or "victims" and protection of women in armed conflict includes much more than mere protection from sexual violence.[7]

This contribution examines how the two fields of public international law in question (IHL and HRL) provide specific protection for women in armed conflict situations today giving special emphasis to their different purposes and objectives. It is then discussed which influence the so-called soft law has on the issue, how the available enforcement mechanisms are functioning, and whether IHL and HRL

---

[3] S.C. Res. 1325 (2000), U.N. Doc.S/RES/1325 (Oct. 31, 2000), paras 9 and 16.
[4] For the discussion within the U.N. Security Council see its documents S/PRST/2001/31 (Oct. 31, 2001); S/2002/1154 (Oct. 16, 2002); S/PRST/2002/32 (Oct. 31, 2002); S/2004/814 (Oct. 13, 2004); S/PRST/2004/40 (Oct. 28, 2004); S/PRST/2005/52 (Oct. 27, 2005); S/PRST/2006/42 (Nov. 8, 2006), S/PRST/2007/5 (March 7, 2007).
[5] Charlotte Lindsey, Women Facing War, ICRC Study on the Impact of Armed Conflict on Women (2001); *see also* ICRC, Addressing the Needs of Women Affected by Armed Conflict: An ICRC Guidance Document (2004).
[6] Inter-Agency Standing Committee, Guidelines for Gender-based Violence in Humanitarian Settings, Focusing on the Prevention of and Response to Sexual Violence in Emergencies, *available at* www.humanitarianinfo.org/iasc/content/subsidi/tf_gender/gbv.asp#feedback (last visited April, 26, 2007).
[7] Charlotte Lindsey, *The Impact of Armed Conflict on Women, in* Listening to the Silences: Women and War 35 (Helen Durham & Tracey Gurd eds., 2005) [hereinafter Lindsey 2005]; *see also* Report of the Secretary-General on Women, Peace and Security, U.N. Doc. S/2002/1154 (Oct. 16, 2002), para. 13.

protect women in armed conflict adequately. Finally, the relationship between IHL and HRL with regard to the specific protection of women in armed conflict today is analyzed in order to identify whether and how recent developments indicate a merger of the two traditionally distinguished fields of law.

1.2. *Relation of IHL and HRL*

In order to assess the rules protecting women in armed conflict, it is crucial to identify which provisions of international humanitarian law and human rights law are applicable in which situation and whom they are binding. In principle, human rights law (HRL) is at all times applicable, i.e. in times of peace as well as in times of armed conflict. It regulates the relationship between a state and individuals, including – and specifically targeted on – the own nationals of the respective state. Except for the most essential human rights such as the right to life, the prohibition of torture or cruel, inhuman or degrading treatment, slavery and servitude, many human rights instruments nevertheless allow states to derogate certain rights in times of public emergency.[8] Contrary to this international humanitarian law (IHL) is only applicable in times of armed conflict and cannot be "derogated" or "suspended" In order to identify the applicable IHL codification(s), it needs to be determined in each case whether a conflict is of international, non-international or internal character. IHL furthermore only protects individuals, which fall under the definition of "protected persons" of the respective applicable Geneva Convention (GC)[9] and their Additional Protocols (AP).[10] IHL hence does not provide protection for a state's own nationals.[11] Another major difference between IHL and HRL is – at least from the traditional point of view – that human rights law binds only

---

[8] *See* for example Article 4, International Covenant on Civil and Political Rights, G.A., Res. 2200A/XXI, (Dec. 16, 1966), 52, U.N. Doc. A/6316 (Dec. 19, 1966), 999 U.N.T.S. 171, (entry into force on Mar. 23, 1976) [hereinafter ICCPR].

[9] The Geneva Convention for the Amelioration of the Condition of the Wounded and Sick in Armed Forces in the Field, Aug. 12, 1949, 75 U.N.T.S. 31, 32; Geneva Convention for the Amelioration of the Condition of the Wounded, Sick and Shipwrecked Members of the Armed Forces at Sea, Aug. 12, 1949, 75 U.N.T.S. 85, 86; Geneva Convention Relative to the Treatment to Prisoners of War, Aug. 12, 1949, 75 U.N.T.S. 135, 136 [hereinafter GC III]; Geneva Convention Relative to the Protection of Civilian Persons in Time of War, Aug. 12, 1949, 75 U.N.T.S. 287, 288 [hereinafter GC IV].

[10] Protocol Additional to the Geneva Conventions of August 12, 1949, and Relating to the Protection of Victims of International Armed Conflicts, June 8, 1977, 1125 U.N.T.S. 3 (entered into force Dec. 7, 1978) [hereinafter AP I]; Protocol Additional to the Geneva Conventions of 12 August 1949, and relating to the Protection of Victims of Non-International Armed Conflicts (Protocol II), June 8, 1977, 1125 U.N.T.S. 609 [hereinafter AP II].

[11] *See* Article 79 ff. GC IV, *supra* note 9 dealing with the internment of civilians as well as Jean Pictet (ed.), Commentary IV Geneva Convention 372 (1952) [hereinafter Pictet]. *See also* Robert Kolb, *The Relationship between International Humanitarian Law and Human Rights Law: A Brief History*

states.¹² This means that non-state actors such as armed opposition groups, who may under certain conditions be parties to an armed conflict according to IHL and are thus bound by the latter, do not have to comply with HRL.

Last, but not least, human rights are rights of (all) individuals, who themselves have the right to complain about violations of their human rights. Consequently, HRL often provides additional protection of the individual whose rights have been violated through enforcement mechanisms established by the human rights instruments as such. These are judicial or quasi-judicial bodies overseeing the implementation of the respective HR instruments to which individuals may directly complain and who can issue binding decisions to the state concerned. IHL, however, is only binding on the parties to an armed conflict and attributes no rights to the individual victims of armed conflict. Consequently, there are no enforcement mechanisms to which individuals can complain in order to ensure that the states, respectively the parties of an armed conflict, comply with IHL during an armed conflict.¹³ It can thus be concluded that IHL and HRL are generally complementary and that a parallel application of the two fields of law is possible. In case, however, an applicable IHL provision contradicts an also applicable HRL provision, international humanitarian law is to be considered as *lex specialis* to human rights law.¹⁴

2. International Humanitarian Law

2.1. Principles

In international humanitarian law all persons not directly participating in armed conflict are entitled to the same protection – be it as persons *hors de combat*, as civilians or as prisoners of war. Thus, women are principally granted the same protection as men. This means that the general principles of IHL such as the fact that it is applicable to all protected persons without discrimination, that all protected

---

of the 1948 Universal Declaration of Human Rights and the 1949 Geneva Conventions, 324 Int'l Rev. Red Cross 409 (1998).

[12] This view is increasingly debated nowadays. For more details *see* for example Andrew Clapham, Human Rights Obligations of Non-State Actors (2006) or Philip Alston (ed.), Non-State Actors and Human Rights (2005).

[13] For reasons of complying with IHL *see* Knut Ipsen, Völkerrecht § 70 (2004) [hereinafter Ipsen]. Individuals, who do not comply with IHL or HRL provisions, may be subject to criminal prosecution in case the non-compliance constitutes a war crime or a crime against humanity.

[14] Legality of the Threat or Use of Nuclear Weapons, Advisory Opinion (July 8, 1996), 1996 ICJ Rep. 226, para. 25 [hereinafter Nuclear Weapons Advisory Opinion]; Legal Consequences of the Construction of a Wall in the Occupied Palestinian Territory, Advisory Opinion (July 9, 2004), 2004 ICJ Rep. 136, para. 105.

persons must be treated humanely, that persons not directly participating in hostilities have to be protected against its effects and the restrictions and prohibitions on the use of specific weapons are applicable to women as they are to men.[15]

IHL furthermore prohibits discrimination on the basis of, *inter alia*, sex in the sense that no "adverse distinction founded on sex" is allowed.[16] This is, however, not a prohibition of differentiation of men and women, but allows differentiation as long as it is favorable as the wording "women shall be treated with all consideration due to their sex" shows.[17] Even though the term consideration is not clearly defined, it is understood to include concepts such as the "weaker" physiological constitution of women, i.e. honor, modesty, pregnancy, and child-birth.[18] The reason for this rule is that formal equality can easily be turned into injustice if special circumstances relating to the different needs (here: of women) could not be taken into account.[19]

2.2. *Specific Protection of Women*

In addition to the general prohibition of discrimination IHL provides special provisions for the protection of women against the effects of armed conflicts in recognition of their particular medical and physiological needs, which are not always, but often, related to their child-bearing role and are the reason for women's particular vulnerability compared to men.[20]

About forty of the approximately 560 articles in the four Geneva Conventions of 1949 and the two Additional Protocols of 1977 are considered to be of particular importance to women. The protection of women in the treaties of international humanitarian law and thus in international and non-international armed conflict has been extensively described and discussed.[21] It is therefore not necessary to

---

[15] Concerning the general principles of IHL *see* for example Hans-Peter Gasser, International Humanitarian Law: An Introduction (1993).
[16] Article 12 GC I and II, *supra* note 9; Article 16 GC III, *supra* note 9; Article 27 GC IV, *supra* note 10, Article 75 AP I, *supra* note 10; and Article 4 AP II, *supra* note 10.
[17] Article 12 GC I and II, *supra* note 9; Article 14 GC III, *supra* note 9 *See* also Jean-Marie Henckaerts & Louise Doswald-Beck, Customary International Humanitarian Law (Vol. 1, 2005), Rule 88 [hereinafter CIHL].
[18] Pictet (ed.), *supra* note 11, Article 12.
[19] Françoise Krill, *The Protection of Women in International Humanitarian Law*, 249 Int'l Rev. Red Cross 337, 339f (1985) [hereinafter Krill].
[20] For the impact of armed conflict on women, *see* Lindsey 2005, *supra* note 5. *See* also Judith Gardam & Michelle Jarvis, Women, Armed Conflict and International Law 19–51 (2001) [hereinafter Gardam & Jarvis].
[21] Krill, *supra* note 16; Helen Durham, *International Humanitarian Law and the Protection of Women, in* Listening to the Silences: Women and War 95 (Helen Durham & Tracey Gurd eds., 2005) [hereinafter Durham]; *see* also Kelly Dawn Askin, War Crimes Against Women 243–250 (1997).

enumerate all the articles providing specific protection to women in the Geneva Conventions and the Additional Protocols again exhaustively. Nevertheless, many of the principles, who were initially intended for international armed conflict as they derive from the Geneva Conventions and Additional Protocol I (and to a lesser extent from Additional Protocol II), have become customary international law as state practice shows that states comply with these rules because the *opinio juris* considers them as binding.[22] This fact, that many principles of the Geneva Conventions became customary international law, extends their scope of application beyond international armed conflict to non-international armed conflict. In this contribution it is therefore examined, which of the principles specifically protecting women have become customary international humanitarian law and are hence applicable in all armed conflicts – regardless of their qualification as international, non-international or internal. Generally, it is required to examine state practice and the *opinio juris* as thoroughly as possible in order to determine whether a rule has become customary international law. For customary international humanitarian law, however, the ICRC recently collected all available state practice and discussed with numerous well-known experts from all over the world, which principles of IHL derive from this practice. It published the results of this research in an extensive two volumes and three books study.[23] This contribution cannot possibly re-examine state practice with such knowledge and in such detail. Therefore it will instead refer to the ICRC study on customary international humanitarian law, in which the rules as well as the underlying state practice is discussed in great detail.

2.2.1. *Prohibition of Rape and Sexual Violence*

Although it needs to be stressed that sexual violence in armed conflict is not exclusively suffered by women, the overwhelming majority of its victims are female. The prohibition of rape and all forms of sexual violence therefore is one of the most important rules for the specific protection of women in armed conflict. Article 27(2) of the GC IV states that "Women shall be especially protected against any attack on their honor, in particular against rape, enforced prostitution, or any form of indecent assault." Even though the term "honor" has repeatedly – and correctly – been criticized to trivialize the crime of rape, which is much more than an attack on the honor of women, the provision must be seen as a product of the time of drafting the Geneva Conventions in the nineteen-forties, which nevertheless contains a binding prohibition of rape and sexual violence.[24] This prohibition

---

[22] On the requirements for the development of customary international law *see* ICJ in the Continental Shelf (Libyan Arab Jamahiriya v. Malta) Case (June 3, 1985), ICJ Reports 1985, p. 13, para. 29 and also the Nuclear Weapons Advisory Opinion, *supra* note 14, para. 253.
[23] CIHL, *supra* note 17. For more information on how the study was conducted see its introduction, Vol. I pp. xxv–li.
[24] Durham, *supra* note 21, at 98.

was supplemented in 1977 by Article 75(2)(b) of AP I, which states that "outrages upon personal dignity, in particular humiliating and degrading treatment, enforced prostitution and any form of indecent assault" are prohibited. Article 76(1) of AP I complements this provision by providing that women "shall be the object of special respect and shall be protected in particular against rape, forced prostitution and any other form of indecent assault;" while Additional Protocol II also prohibits rape in non-international armed conflict (Article 4(2)(e)). In line with the treaty provisions of international humanitarian law, the ICRC established in rule 93 of its study on customary international humanitarian law that "Rape and other forms of sexual violence are prohibited" and supports this perception by numerous examples for state practice and *opinio juris*.[25]

In addition to being prohibited as such, rape and sexual violence are also "outrages upon personal dignity, in particular humiliating and degrading treatment" and therefore constitute a violation of common Article 3 to the Geneva Conventions.[26] "Torture, cruel or inhuman treatment and outrages upon personal dignity" are furthermore prohibited in customary international humanitarian law as rule 90 of the ICRC study states, which also refers to decisions of the ICTY according to which rape can constitute torture.[27]

The significance of the fact that rape and sexual violence are not only prohibited as such, but also constitute "torture" or "inhuman treatment," lies in the fact that the latter are covered by the respective "grave breaches" – provisions of the Geneva Conventions and therefore constitute war crimes in international armed conflict.[28] In non-international armed conflict "rape" and "sexual violence" are as "torture" or "degrading treatment" violations of common Article 3 to the Geneva Conventions and consequently also have to be prosecuted.[29]

---

[25] CIHL, Vol. I – Rule 93, Vol. II – Chapter 32, Section G.

[26] Theodor Meron, *Rape as a Crime under International Humanitarian Law*, 87 am. J. Int'l l. 1993, 424–428 (1993) [hereinafter Meron].

[27] CIHL, *supra* note 25 Vol. I – Rule 90. For state practice *see* Vol. II – Chapter 32, Section D. The prohibition of torture is furthermore one of the few undisputed *jus cogens* rules, *see* e.g. Regina v. Bow Street Metropolitan Stipendiary Magistrate ex parte Pinochet Ugarte (No. 3)(2000) 1 AC 147, 198; 119 ILR (2002), p. 135 and the Prosecutor v. Furundzija, Case No. IT-95-17/1, Trial Chamber, (Dec. 10, 2002), para. 2.

[28] *See* Article 8(2)(b)(xxii) Rome Statute of the International Criminal Court. Rome Statute of the International Criminal Court, adopted on July 17, 1998 by the U.N. Diplomatic Conference of Plenipotentiaries on the Establishment of an International Criminal Court, entered into force, July 1, 2002, U.N. Doc. A/CONF.183/9 (1998) [hereinafter Rome Statute]. *See also* Meron, *supra* note 26, at 424–428.

[29] Article 8(2)(c)(v) Rome Statute, *supra* note 28.

2.2.2. Need to Respect Specific Protection, Health, and Assistance Needs of Women

Rule 134 of the ICRC study on customary international humanitarian law provides that: "The specific protection, health and assistance needs of women affected by armed conflict must be respected." Similar provisions are contained in each of the four Geneva Conventions as well as the first Additional Protocol.[30] Obviously, the specific needs of women differ according to the circumstances they are living in – e.g. displaced, in detention or at home, but always have to be respected. This provision includes protection against sexual violence (see above a.) as well as separation from men for women in detention (see below c.) and is supposed to ensure that women "receive medical, psychological and social assistance," when necessary.[31] The respect for specific protection, health, and assistance needs of women also includes particular care for pregnant women and mothers of young children, especially nursing or breast feeding mothers. Similarly to the respective provisions in the Geneva Conventions and the Additional Protocols, this rule is furthermore interpreted as to include an obligation to avoid the pronouncement of the death penalty on pregnant mothers or mothers having dependent infants for offences related to the armed conflict and to prohibit its execution on such women.[32]

2.2.3. Women in Detention

Women can be deprived of freedom during armed conflict for a huge variety of reasons. They can be detained as civilian internees, as prisoners of war, as security detainees or for reasons which are not related to the conflict. The four Geneva Conventions and the Additional Protocols contain a number of provisions generally relating to detention, especially the conditions of detention. First and foremost, a detention place, irrespective of whether it holds civilian detainees or prisoners of war – which need to be hold separately –[33] must be safe.[34]

With regard to specific protection of women in detention rule 119 of the ICRC study on customary humanitarian law states in accordance with Article 75(5) of AP I that: "Women who are deprived of their liberty must be held in quarters separate from those of men, except where families are accommodated as family units, and must be under the immediate supervision of women."[35] Looking at this provision,

---

[30] Article 12(4) GC I and II, *supra* note 9; Article 14(2) GC III, *supra* note 9; Article 27 GC IV, *supra* note 9; Article 8(a) AP I, *supra* note 10.

[31] CIHL, *supra* note 25, Vol. I – Rule 134.

[32] Articles 38 and 50 GC IV, *supra* note 9; Article 76(2) AP I, *supra* note 10; Article 6(4) AP II, *supra* note 10.

[33] Article 84 GC IV, *supra* note 9.

[34] Articles 19 and 23 GC III, *supra* note 9; Article 83 GC IV, *supra* note 9, CIHL, *supra* note 25, Vol. I – Rule 121.

[35] CIHL, *supra* note 25 Vol. I, Vol. II – Chapter 37, Section B. *See* also Article 97(4), Article 108 (2) GC III, *supra* note 9, Articles 76(4) and 124(3) GC IV, *supra* note 9.

it goes without saying that the specific protection, health and assistance needs of women affected by armed conflict – as discussed above under b. in detail – also apply to women in detention.

2.2.4. *Other Rules of Particular Importance to Women*
In addition to the rules of customary international humanitarian law, which are explicitly providing specific protection for women, other rules, which do not directly address the needs of women, are also of tremendous importance for women. For example, in addition to the protection of persons not directly participating in armed conflict, IHL contains regulations on the methods and means of warfare, including the prohibition of certain kinds of weapons. These provisions limit the use of force in armed conflict. The basic rule in this regard is the principle of distinction between civilians and combatants and between civilian objects and military objectives allowing attacks only against military objectives. Furthermore, these regulations prohibit indiscriminate attacks, being defined as those who are not directed at a particular military objective; weapons that cause "superfluous injury or unnecessary suffering," and do not allow methods which cause "widespread, long-term and severe damage to the natural environment."[36] While these rules are not primarily addressing women, they are of particular significance to them as women form the major part of the civilian population during armed conflict and are, thus, particularly concerned by the effects of hostilities.[37] This contribution, however, focuses on the specific protection of women in IHL and HRL. The question of how the regulations on the means and methods of warfare protect women is therefore – despite its importance to women as victims of armed conflict – not discussed in more detail.

Another concept of customary international humanitarian law, which is crucial for women in particular, is the maintenance of the family unit. The well-being of the family is important to all persons, not only women. However, it is most important for children to remain with their families, mostly at least their mothers as their primary care-givers, whose well-being is directly linked to that of their children. Furthermore, people affected by armed conflict tell *unisono* that not knowing what happened to loved ones is harder than knowing about the death of a loved one. In this regard rule 105, that reads: "Family life must be respected as far as possible"

---

[36] As far as international armed conflict is concerned *see* Articles 35, 48, 51 and 55 AP I, *supra* note 10; for non-international armed conflict *see* Articles 13 and 14 AP II, *supra* note 10. *See* also in detail Stefan Oeter, *Methods and Means of Combat*, *in* The Handbook of Humanitarian Law in Armed Conflicts 105–204 (Dieter Fleck ed., 1995). For details on the means and methods of warfare in customary international humanitarian law *see* CIHL, *supra* note 25, Vol. I – Part I. – The Principle of Distinction and Part IV. – Weapons.

[37] ICRC, An ICRC Guidance Document "Addressing the Needs of Women Affected by Armed Conflict" 20 (2004).

needs to be mentioned first. This provision is interpreted as to protect (1) the maintenance of the family unit, (2) the contact between family members and (3) the provision of information on the whereabouts of family members. In case of displacement rule 131 provides a similar provision to maintain family unity in as much as "all possible measures must be taken ... that members of the same family are not separated."[38] Last but not least, rule 117 requires all parties to a conflict to "take all feasible measures to account for persons reported missing as a result of armed conflict" and to "provide their family members with any information it has on their fate." This rule, which is already contained in the Fourth Geneva Convention and Additional Protocol I,[39] derives from the right of families to know what has become of their loved ones, and has to begin as soon as possible, which means at the very latest from the end of hostilities. Having examined how women are protected in IHL, the protection accorded to women in HRL also needs to be examined.

3. Human Rights Law

3.1. Doctrine

Human rights are rights all human beings possess solely because they are human. The history of HRL basically began only in the 20th century and is, thus, much shorter than that of IHL. Among the most important human rights instruments are the Universal Declaration of Human Rights (1948),[40] which influenced, although not binding, the emanation of customary international human rights law, and the two 1966 Covenants on Civil and Political Rights and on Social, Economic and Cultural Rights.[41] The first two instruments contain provisions for the basic protection of individuals such as the rights to life, humane treatment and freedom, the prohibition of slavery and torture as well as judicial guarantees. It goes without saying that – if not derogable respectively not derogated, see above A. 2. – these rules warranting basic protection of the individual are of particular significance to women in armed conflict, especially because they provide protection from the state of whom they are nationals.

---

[38] CIHL, *supra* note 25 Vol. I – Rules 105 and 131.
[39] Article 26 GC IV, *supra* note 9 and Article 32 AP I, *supra* note 10.
[40] Universal Declaration of Human Rights, G.A. Res. 217A(III), U.N. Doc. A/810 (1948) [hereinafter UDHR].
[41] International Covenant on Civil and Political Rights, G.A. Res. 2200A (XXI), 21 U.N. GAOR Supp. (No. 16) at 52, U.N. Doc. A/6316 (1966), 999 U.N.T.S. 171 [hereinafter ICCPR]; International Covenant on Economic, Social and Cultural Rights, opened for signature Dec. 16, 1966, 993 U.N.T.S. 3 (entered into force Jan. 3, 1976) [hereinafter ICESCR].

Furthermore, as a principle, discrimination on the basis of, *inter alia*, sex is prohibited in HRL like it is in IHL. All major human rights instruments contain respective provisions requiring (legal) equality between men and women.[42] Women are consequently entitled – theoretically – to the same rights and the same protection as men in HRL. However, it has repetitively been examined and found that even though women enjoy equality before the law, they still remain disadvantaged in society compared to men. Worldwide, women still cannot use their human rights to participate in society and politics like men do. As a consequence women earn less money, are less able to decide about their lives and generally have less access to resources (education, health care, legal aid, and financial means) than men. Furthermore, because of their sex and the associated lower status in most societies, women and girls are particularly affected by the adverse effects of armed conflict. The general vulnerability of women in armed conflict is, thus, the direct result of the discrimination and disadvantage women are subjected to in many areas of life.[43] The realization of this state of affairs contributed to numerous efforts to empower women in the sense of "human rights are women's rights," in the last two decades in order to enable women to profit of their human rights in the same way as men do.[44]

3.2. *Human Rights Protecting Women in Armed Conflict*

The specific human rights protection of women in armed conflict raises two different questions. Firstly, one must examine which human rights are of particular importance for women and whether their applicability brings added value to the protection of women in armed conflict. The other question concentrates on the aims of the instruments for the protection of human rights of women in general and whether they are designed to improve the situation and protection of women during armed conflict.

3.2.1. *Human Rights of Particular Significance for Women in Armed Conflict*
Human rights of particular significance for women in armed conflict are those which extend the protection of women provided by IHL, either substantively or by expanding the scope of application. In this regard rights protecting individuals

---

[42] *See* for example Article 2 UDHR, *supra* note 40; Article 2 ICCPR, *supra* note 40; Article 3 ICESCR, *supra* note 40.
[43] Fourth World Conference on Women, Action for Equality Development and Peace, Beijing Declaration and Platform for Action, U.N. Doc. A/Conf.177/20 (Oct. 17, 1995), para. 135.
[44] The slogan "Women's rights are human rights" goes back to a statement of Hilary Rodham Clinton at the United Nations Fourth World Conference on Women, Beijing, China dated Sept. 5, 1995, *available at* americanrhetoric.com/speeches/hillaryclintonbeijingspeech.htm (last visited May 10, 2007).

from arbitrary or excessive state action and thus the so-called civil and political rights are particularly important. Among these rights are the prohibitions of torture and inhuman or degrading treatment such as sexual violence and the right to life, freedom and safety of the person. Other principles, like equality before the law, can also become very critical for women in armed conflict situations, e.g. when they suddenly become heads of households. As already discussed above some of the civil and political rights principles can be derogated in emergency situations. This has serious consequences in international armed conflict because a state's own nationals do not fall under the protection provided by the four Geneva Conventions and Additional Protocol I.[45] It may also have some relevance in non-international armed conflict in which a state's own nationals may become the "enemy."[46] Nevertheless, most of the civil and political rights principles, the so-called first dimension rights, are also reflected in IHL as shown above.

In addition, social, economic, and cultural human rights like the right to food, the right to health, the right to adequate living conditions including clean water supply, and the right to education can become crucial to women in armed conflict situations. In modern human rights law these rights have the same significance as civil and political rights.[47] However, the wording of the International Covenant on Economic, Social and Cultural Rights (ICESCR) shows that states are very reserved to guarantee certain minimum standards. Member states for example "recognize the right of everyone to the enjoyment of the highest attainable standard of physical and mental health," but in order to "achieve the full realization of this right" it is sufficient to create conditions "which would assure to all medical service and medical attention in the event of sickness."[48] Furthermore, it must not be forgotten that social, economic, and cultural human rights are difficult to enforce in poor countries even under peaceful conditions. In an armed conflict situation, which is very volatile and unpredictable, it therefore becomes almost impossible to respect or to simply refer to these rights in practice. The same applies even more with regard to collective human rights of the so-called third generation like for example the right to peace, development, and a healthy environment. It can thus be concluded that even though these human rights are meaningful to women in armed conflict situations and could – at least theoretically – improve their protection against the effects of the conflict, especially social, economic, and cultural rights and collective human rights are almost impossible to enforce in such situations. Civil and political rights, however, play an important role in complementing the protection of women provided by IHL. Moreover, the full respect of the human rights of

---

[45] Common Article 2 GC, *supra* note 9; Article 1(3) AP I, *supra* note 10.
[46] Additional Protocol II, however, protects "all persons affected by an armed conflict," thus including the own nationals of a respective state.
[47] Ipsen, *supra* note 13, § 48 No. 38.
[48] Article 12 ICESCR, *supra* note 40.

women, which are – as discussed – still not fully implemented everywhere, might make women less vulnerable to the effects of armed conflict.

3.2.2. *Convention on the Elimination of Discrimination against Women (CEDAW)*

The main instrument for the special protection of the human rights of women is the 1979 Convention on the Elimination of Discrimination against women (CEDAW)[49] and its 1999 optional protocol.[50] The reason for the establishment of the treaty was the realization that even though formal equality had been warranted for some time in most western countries, women still did not enjoy equal opportunities, but continued to be widely discriminated against.[51] Having identified this *status quo* in many, if not most countries of the world, the CEDAW attempts to enable women to have the same access as men to chances in life by prohibiting all kinds of discrimination against women. This includes "any distinction, exclusion or restriction made on the basis of sex which has the effect or purpose of impairing or nullifying the recognition, enjoyment or exercise by women, irrespective of their marital status, on a basis of equality of men and women, of human rights and fundamental freedoms in the political, economic, social, cultural, civil or any other field."[52] It is crucial to note that the original CEDAW is exclusively aimed at states, which "condemn discrimination against women in all its forms, agree to pursue by all appropriate means and without delay a policy of eliminating discrimination against women,"[53] but does not give immediate or even enforceable rights to individual women. For example, states are obliged to ensure that women in rural areas have adequate living conditions, including sanitation and water supply, but the concerned women suffering from a lack of access to clean water cannot directly file a complaint to get clean water. In addition, CEDAW does not contain specific provisions on violence against women. Nevertheless, the Committee on the Elimination of Discrimination against Women, the monitoring body of CEDAW, adopted in 1992 a general recommendation on "Violence against Women", in which it refers explicitly to the human right of women "not to be subject to torture, or cruel, inhuman or degrading treatment or punishment."[54]

---

[49] Convention on the Elimination of All Forms of Discrimination Against Women, G.A. Res. 34/180, U.N. GAOR, 34th Sess., Supp. No. 46, U.N. Doc. A/34/36 (Sept. 3, 1981) [hereinafter CEDAW].

[50] Optional Protocol to the Convention on the Elimination of All Forms of Discrimination Against Women, U.N. Doc. A/RES/54/4 (Oct. 15, 1999).

[51] *See* preamble CEDAW, *supra* note 49.

[52] Article 1 CEDAW, *id.*

[53] Article 2 CEDAW, *id.*

[54] U.N. Committee on the Elimination of Discrimination Against Women (CEDAW), Eleventh Session, General Recommendation 19, U.N. Doc. CEDAW/C/1992/L.1/Add.15 /1992 (Jan. 20–30, 1992), especially para. 7(b) [hereinafter General Recommendation 19].

The only enforcement mechanism foreseen by the convention is a regular reporting duty about progress made with regard to the implementation of the convention. The enforcement of CEDAW is therefore much more difficult than it is for instruments such as the ICCPR or the ICESCR, which codify individual rights. The 1979 CEDAW is thus a rather weak human rights instrument as far as enforcement is concerned. However, the 1999 optional protocol to the CEDAW introduced the possibility of individual complaints to the Committee on the Elimination of all forms of Discrimination against Women. Nevertheless, it needs to be noted that while CEDAW enjoys recognition by most states of the world, its optional protocol was only ratified by 87 states at the time of writing this article.[55]

To conclude, the CEDAW (including its optional protocol) is the first and the only human rights instrument, which attempts to change pre-existing societies and their social structures in favor of women. This contributes to the protection of women in armed conflict in the sense that the empowerment of women and equal status of women in society makes them less vulnerable to the adverse effects of armed conflict. The implementation of the CEDAW can therefore have a preventive effect before and after an armed conflict. However, it must be stressed that the aim of the CEDAW, which is to change societies in favor of women, also shows very clearly that human rights law and international humanitarian law do not share the same aims with regard to the protection of women: HRL attempts to give women equal status in society while IHL "only" aims at protecting women from the effects of armed conflict.

3.2.3. *Soft Law Protecting Women in Armed Conflict*

Besides treaty law, women are also protected from the effects of armed conflict by a range of so-called "soft law" documents. To what is referred to as "soft law" indicates non-binding instruments, (political) statements or provisions that are not "law" of itself, but require particular attention because of their political importance in international legal development.[56] The sheer number of U.N. Security Council resolutions and presidential statements of the Security Council as well as reports of the U.N. Secretary General to the Security Council reflects the increasing value attached to the topic of women in armed conflict.

---

[55] *See* www.un.org/womenwatch/daw/cedaw/states.htm and www.un.org/womenwatch/daw/cedaw/protocol/sigop.htm (last visited June 9, 2007).

[56] "Soft law" refers to non-binding instruments, (political) statements or provisions that are not "law" of itself, but require particular attention because of their political importance in international legal development. Malcolm N. Shaw, International Law 110–112 (2003).

3.2.3.1. Approaches Prior to 1990

In 1968 the International Conference on Human Rights in Teheran addressed the issue of human rights and armed conflict for the first time.[57] It was the impetus for the discussion of the topic of women and children in armed conflict during the 1970, 1972, and 1974 sessions of the Commission on the Status of Women. These deliberations culminated in 1974 in the adoption of the U.N. General Assembly Declaration on the Protection of Women and Children in Emergency and Armed Conflict.[58] Even though the 1974 General Assembly Resolution basically only reaffirmed pre-existing legal provisions and failed to mention the problem of sexual violence during armed conflict, its significance lies in the fact that the situation of women in armed conflict was recognized for the first time by the international community, that made some effort to improve the situation of women in armed conflict.[59] However, following the 1974 General Assembly Declaration the international community gave no further consideration to the issue. Not even the 1985 World Conference to Review and Appraise the Achievements of the U.N. Decade for Women: Equality, Development, and Peace explicitly acknowledged violence against women as a human rights issue.[60]

3.2.3.2. Approaches by UN Human Rights Bodies after 1990

The issue of women in armed conflict only re-emerged on the international agenda in the early 1990s, in which the already mentioned mass-rapes during the armed conflict in former Yugoslavia and the genocide in Rwanda made the international community aware of the issue. At the same time a worldwide campaign for justice for women, euphemistically referred to as "comfort women," who had been forced into sexual slavery by the Japanese military during World War II, raised attention within the U.N. system to questions of women in armed conflict situations, especially focusing on sexual violence.

Influenced by the increased attention on the issue, the U.N. Committee on the Elimination of Discrimination against Women, the monitoring body of CEDAW, adopted a general recommendation on "Violence against Women" in 1992.

---

[57] Human Rights in Armed Conflicts. Resolution XXIII, adopted by the International Conference on Human Rights. Teheran (May 12, 1968).
[58] Declaration on the Protection of Women and Children in Emergency, G.A. Res. 3318, U.N. Doc. A/RES/3318 (XXIX), (Dec. 14, 1974); *see also* Commission on the Status of Women, Resolution XXIII (1974), and ECOSOC Resolution 1861 (LVI), U.N. Doc. ECOSOC Res. 1861 (LVI), (May 16, 1974).
[59] Gardam & Jarvis, *supra* note 20, at 142.
[60] *See* Report of the World Conference to Review and Appraise the Achievements of the UN Decade for Women: Equality, Development and Peace, Nairobi, July 15–26, 1985 also known as Nairobi Forward-Looking Strategies for the Advancement of Women. *Available at* www.un.org/womenwatch/confer/nfls/Nairobi1985report.txt (last visited June 25, 2007).

This recommendation is not mandatory but a directive for the interpretation of CEDAW. It explicitly mentions *inter alia* the human rights of women to life, not to be subject to torture or to cruel, inhuman or degrading treatment or punishment; the right to equal protection according to humanitarian norms in time of international, non-international or internal armed conflict; the right to ... security of person; and the right to equal protection under the law as possibly being affected by gender-based violence and thus discrimination within the meaning of Article 1 of CEDAW.[61] One year later, in 1993, the U.N. World Conference on Human Rights for the first time recognized violence against women as a human rights issue in the Vienna Declaration and Program of Action: "Violations of the human rights of women in situations of armed conflict are violations of the fundamental principles of international human rights and humanitarian law. All violations of this kind, including in particular murder, systematic rape, sexual slavery, and forced pregnancy, require a particularly effective response."[62] In the same year, the U.N. General Assembly adopted the Declaration on the Elimination of Violence against Women, which expresses concern that "women in situations of armed conflict are especially vulnerable to violence" and identifies one of the three main categories of violence against women as that perpetrated or condoned by states.[63]

However, the approaches in the early 1990s concentrated almost exclusively on (sexual) violence against women in armed conflict as part of the broader campaign to eradicate violence against women. Although this raised awareness for the issue of sexual violence in armed conflict, almost all other ways in which women are affected by armed conflict were overlooked. This changed with the Beijing World Conference on Women in 1995. For the first time that conference acknowledged formally that the general vulnerability of women in armed conflict situations (compared to men) is due to their "status in society and their sex."[64] Women are thus particularly affected by armed conflict, because they are widely discriminated and disadvantaged in many areas of life. In addition, the Beijing Conference identified "women and armed conflict" as one of the twelve critical areas of concern in need to be addressed by the international community as well as civil society and called to "take strategic action" on "effects of armed or other kinds of conflict on women, including those living under foreign occupation."[65] Furthermore, the

---

[61] General Recommendation 19, para. 7.
[62] World Conference on Human Rights, Vienna Declaration and Programme of Action. Vienna, June 14–25, 1993, U.N. Doc. A/Conf.157/24 (Oct. 13, 1993), para. 38.
[63] Declaration on the Elimination of Violence Against Women, G.A. Res. 48/104, UN. Doc. A/RES/48/104 (Feb. 23, 1994), preamble and Article 2.
[64] Fourth World Conference on Women, Action for Equality, Development and Peace, Beijing Declaration and Platform for Action, U.N. Doc. A/Conf. 177/29 /1995 (Oct. 17, 1995), para. 135.
[65] *Id.* para. 44.

significant number of civilian female and child victims of armed conflict as well as the frequency of violations of fundamental principles of international human rights and humanitarian law[66] of particular importance for women were pointed out, namely the suffering of women living in poverty, particularly in rural areas, as well as the effects of indiscriminate attacks, especially the consequences of the presence of landmines.[67] Nevertheless, sexual violence in armed conflict remained a central focus at the Beijing Platform for Action.[68] Altogether, it can be said that the Beijing Conference contributed significantly to the development of the acknowledgement that women are particularly affected by armed conflict.

The Commission on the Status of Women (CSW), being responsible to coordinate the follow-up of the Beijing Conference, subsequently considered the issue of women in armed conflict in 1998. The emphasis was again on the prevalence of sexual violence during armed conflict and its consequences as well as on the necessity of gender expertise in all mechanisms dealing with armed conflict and issues of redress.[69] In 2000, the U.N. General Assembly held a special session on "Women 2000: Gender Equality, Development and Peace for the Twenty-First Century" in order to review the progress made since the Beijing Conference five years earlier. However, even though the outcome document refers to the increased recognition that women and men are differently affected by armed conflict and lists the two *ad hoc* criminal tribunals and the creation of the Statute of the International Criminal Court as achievements in the area, it contains only very general and vague recommendations and does not comprise a clear strategy.[70] In 2005, the CSW again considered the follow-up of the Beijing Declaration and Platform of Action and the Outcome Document of the 2000 special session of the General Assembly. However, the respective declaration of the CSW and the report of the session only reaffirm the Beijing Declaration and Platform for Action adopted at the Fourth World Conference on Women and the outcome of the twenty-third special session of the General Assembly without examining the progress made with regard to the issue of women and armed conflict and do not make any new recommendations.[71]

---

[66] *Id.*para. 133.
[67] *Id.* paras 131, 138.
[68] *Id.* para. 131.
[69] 42nd Session of the Commission on the Status of Women (CSW), U.N. Doc. E/CN.6/1998/12 (Mar. 2–13, 1998).
[70] Follow-up to the Fourth World Conference on Women and full implementation of the Beijing Declaration and Platform for Action and the outcome of the twenty-third special session of the General Assembly, UN Doc. A/RES/55/71 (Feb. 8, 2001); *see also* Gardam & Jarvis, *supra* note 20, at 169f.
[71] Declaration adopted by the Commission on the Status of Women at its 49th Session, U.N. Doc. E/CN.6/2005/L.1 (March 3, 2005), Report on the 49th session, U.N. Docs. E/2005/27 and E/CN.6/2005/11 (Feb. 28–Mar. 22, 2005).

3.2.3.3. Actions of the UN Security Council

The incidents during the conflict in former Yugoslavia not only furthered the campaign to eliminate violence against women, but also made the issue of sexual violence a distinct one in the U.N. system. It notably linked systematic sexual violence and rape of women to international peace and security, to which the whole system of the United Nations and especially the Security Council were incited to respond.[72] "Appalled by reports of the massive, organized and systematic detention and rape, in particular of Muslim women, in Bosnia and Herzegovina" the Security Council demanded all camps for women to be immediately closed in 1992 and continued to condemn the rape of women in the former Yugoslavia in a number of subsequent resolutions.[73] The Security Council also requested the U.N. Secretary General to establish a Commission of Experts to investigate violations of IHL in the former Yugoslavia.[74] In its final report the commission specifically focused on the use of sexual violence for ethnic cleansing, but could not conclusively establish the use of rape as a strategy of warfare.[75] Nonetheless, the two Security Council resolutions establishing the International Criminal Tribunal for the Former Yugoslavia (ICTY) refer to sexual violence and rape.[76] This shows that the extent of sexual violence during the conflict in the former Yugoslavia played a significant role in the creation of the ICTY as a response to the gross violations of IHL and HRL, which constituted a threat to international peace and security in the eyes of the Security Council.

Similarly, following the 1994 conflict in Rwanda there were many reports about sexual violence against women on a massive scale.[77] Like it did in the case of former Yugoslavia the Security Council requested the Secretary General to establish a Commission of Experts to investigate violations of IHL in Rwanda. However, the final report of this Commission only referred to sexual violence in limited terms inasmuch as it basically contains allegations of sexual violence compiled by NGOs rather than its own findings on the issue.[78] Consequently, the resolution creating the

---

[72] For the role of the UN Security Council in implementing IHL and HRL and the significance of this development *see* Chapter XI.
[73] S.C. Res. 798, U.N. Doc. S/RES 798 (Dec. 18, 1992), *see* for example also S.C. Res. 820, U.N. Doc. S/RES 820 (April 17, 1993); S.C. Res 827, U.N. Doc. S/RES/827 (May 25, 1993); S.C. Res. 1019, U.N. Doc. S/RES/1019 (Nov. 9, 1995).
[74] S.C. Res. 780, U.N. Doc. S/RES/780 (Oct. 6, 1992).
[75] Final Report of the Commission of Experts Established Pursuant to Security Council Resolution 780 (1992) U.N. Doc. S/1994/624 (1994), (May 27, 1994) [hereinafter Final Report].
[76] S.C. Res. 808, U.N. Doc. S/RES/808 (Feb. 22, 1993) and S.C. Res. 820, U.N. Doc. S/RES/820 (May 25, 1993).
[77] For example *see* Binaifar Nowrojee, Shattered Lives: Sexual Violence during the Rwandan Genocide and its Aftermath, New York, Human Rights Watch, 1996.
[78] Final Report *supra* note 75.

International Tribunal for Rwanda (ICTR) in order to restore international peace and security does not refer to sexual violence unlike the respective resolution establishing the ICTY.[79] The different reactions of the Security Council to the conflicts in former Yugoslavia and Rwanda despite similar facts show that predominantly political considerations and not legal arguments are decisive for its practice.

In 2000, the U.N. Security Council dealt for the first time with the issue of women, peace, and security as such and not only in relation to a particular armed conflict as it did previously. In its respective resolution 1325 the Security Council expressed concern that "particularly women and children, account for the vast majority of those adversely affected by armed conflict" and reaffirmed "the need to implement fully international humanitarian and human rights law that protects the rights of women and girls during and after conflicts."[80] It therefore called upon all parties to armed conflict to comply with the respective obligations under HRL and IHL protecting women, including those of international criminal law and "to take special measures to protect women and girls from gender-based violence, particularly rape and other forms of sexual abuse…" It also called to take the particular needs of displaced women, especially in camps for refugees and internally displaced persons into account. Furthermore, the need to end impunity for international crimes, "including those relating to sexual and other violence against women and girls" was emphasized.[81] The Security Council consequently invited the U.N. Secretary-General to study *inter alia* the impact of armed conflict on women and girls and to submit the respective report to the Security Council.[82] The Secretary-General submitted the requested report in 2002 pointing out that "women do not enjoy equal status with men in any society," that violence and discrimination against women existing prior to conflict "will be exacerbated during conflict" and that women are "disproportionately targeted in contemporary armed conflicts."[83] In the section on the impact of armed conflict on women the report also mentions the vulnerability of women to violence, in particular sexual violence and its consequences, before identifying the particular consequences of armed conflict on the everyday life of women and during displacement.[84] Furthermore, the legal framework protecting women in armed conflict, especially the principle

---

[79] S.C. Res. 955 (1994), U.N. Doc. S/RES/955 (Nov. 8, 1994).

[80] S.C. Res. 1325 (2000), U.N. Doc. S/RES/1325 (Oct. 31, 2000), preamble.

[81] *Id.* paras 9, 10, and 11.

[82] *Id.* para. 16. The resolution as well as all subsequent reports and presidential statements also focus on how to improve the involvement of women, their specific needs, views and the resources they offer in peace processes and UN peace-keeping operations.

[83] Report of the Secretary-General on Women, Peace and Security, U.N. Doc. S/2002/1154, (Oct. 16, 2002), paras 5 and 6 [Report on Women].

[84] *Id.* paras 7–15.

of non-discrimination and the provisions of international criminal law relevant for the prosecution of sexual violence is explained. The Secretary General *inter alia* consequently recommended recognizing "the extent of the violations of the human rights of women and girls during armed conflict…"[85] The report furthermore condemns these violations and calls to "take all necessary measures to bring to an end such violations" and to ensure legal expertise on issues specifically concerning women, including sexual violence in a gender-sensitive way.[86] The Security Council in the following resolution condemned again *inter alia* all violations of the human rights of women and requested the Secretary General to submit a follow-up report two years later.[87] The 2004 U.N. Secretary General's report on women, peace, and security states, with regard to the humanitarian response to the needs of women and especially displaced women, that gender perspectives are increasingly incorporated in humanitarian interventions but that their inclusion still needs to be strengthened at field level. Concerning the prevention and response to gender-based violence the 2004 report states that "[t]hus far, the international community has not been able to prevent acts of violence against women from occurring during armed conflict"[88] and that "(a)lthough the occurrence of violence against women in armed conflict is now increasingly acknowledged and widely documented, our collective response, as measured against the magnitude of this violence, remains inadequate."[89] The Secretary General therefore recommends applying increased pressure to cease all violations of the human rights of women, ending impunity for international crimes, and ensuring gender-expertise of human rights (and other) monitors and of international and national courts.[90] The report also mentions the issue of sexual exploitation and abuse by humanitarian and peacekeeping personnel, which is condemned in very strict terms.[91] As a response the Security Council requested the Secretary General to prepare an action plan, with time lines, for the implementation of Resolution 1325 across the U.N. system.[92] This U.N. system-wide Action Plan was included in the 2005 report of the Secretary General on women, peace, and security for the period between 2005 and 2007. It mainly concentrates on who concretely does which with regard to the implementation

---

[85] *Id.* para. 15, Action 1.
[86] *Id.* para. 25, Action 3–6.
[87] U.N. Doc. S/PRST/2002/32 (Oct. 31, 2002).
[88] Report of the Secretary General on Women and Peace and Security, U.N. Doc. S/2004/814 (Oct. 13, 2004), para. 74 [hereinafter Report on Women 2004].
[89] *Id.* para. 76.
[90] *Id.* para. 87.
[91] Report on Women 2004, *supra* note 88, paras 99–103.
[92] U.N. Doc. S/PRST/2004/40 (Oct. 28, 2004).

of resolution 1325 and gender mainstreaming the U.N. system.[93] The Security Council subsequently acknowledged the report and requested follow-up reports,[94] the first of which was delivered in October 2006. It elaborated on the development of guidelines of the Inter-Agency Standing Committee on gender-mainstreaming humanitarian assistance and *inter alia* with regard to the integration of measures preventing and responding to gender-based violence within various sectors of society such as health, education, and justice.[95] Finally, in its latest presidential statements of November 2006 and March 2007 the Security Council requested the Secretary General to continue monitoring the action plan and decided again "to remain actively seized of the matter."[96]

3.2.3.4. Evaluation of the Soft Law Concerning the Protection of Women in Armed Conflict

As mentioned above, despite the fact that all the above-mentioned resolutions, reports, statements, and declarations deal with general issues relating to women in armed conflict rather than focus on sexual violence, they are not legally binding. Nevertheless, these documents can be considered as the expression of the opinion of the international community inasmuch as they show the increasing awareness of the international community on the issue of the protection of women in armed conflict and the subsequent development in the U.N. practice. While the protection of women in armed conflict was on the agenda in the early 1970s resulting in the 1974 "Declaration on the Protection of Women and Children in Emergency and Armed Conflict", it had been almost forgotten until the early 1990s. Since, it has – as shown – continuously been discussed. One can also observe a shift in the emphasis concerning the situation of women in armed conflict. While the actions of the Commission on Human Rights as well as those of the Security Council since 1990 at first concentrated almost exclusively on questions related to sexual violence in armed conflict, the approach within the U.N. system concerning women in armed conflict is now much broader. With the realization of the 1995 Beijing World Conference that women are particularly affected by armed conflict, because of their underprivileged status in society, the U.N. system began to adopt a broader approach not exclusively focusing on sexual violence in armed conflict, but also intending to empower women before, during, and after armed conflict in order to make them less vulnerable to its effects. This approach is much more

---

[93] Report of the Secretary General on Women and Peace and Security, U.N. Doc. S/2005/636 (Oct. 10, 2005).
[94] U.N. Doc. S/PRST/2005/52 (Oct. 27, 2005).
[95] Report of the Secretary General on Women and Peace and Security, U.N. Doc. S/2006/770 (Sept. 27, 2006) III. A. 4. and 7. *See* also *id.* footnote 6 for the guidelines of the Inter-Agency Standing Committee.
[96] U.N. Docs S/PRST2006/42 (Oct. 26, 2006) and S/PRST/2007/5 (Mar. 7, 2007).

comprehensive as it intends to tackle the causes of the particular vulnerability of women. It shows that the international community has acknowledged the real causes of the particular vulnerability of women and believes that the only possible sustainable approach is to ensure that women become less vulnerable to the effects of armed conflict. As a result, women would need less "protection" in legal terms. The Security Council Resolution 1325 and all subsequent reports and statements are exemplary in this regard. They not only contribute to the development of customary international law, but also show and support comprehensive political and social approaches and developments to lessen the effects of armed conflict on women preventively.

The actual significance of the presented soft law, for which the focus was in accordance with the title of this contribution on the protection of women in armed conflict, lies foremost in the involved political pressure to comply and enforce the discussed legal norms protecting women. Nevertheless, it must not be forgotten that in U.N. practice, in which 'soft law' originates overwhelmingly, political considerations reflecting state interests, rather than legal arguments, most often play a decisive role. A comparison between the responses of the Security Council to the conflicts in the Former Yugoslavia and Rwanda illustrates the point.[97] Last, but not least, even though 'soft law' contributes to the development of customary international law, it is not binding on states and cannot be actively enforced unless violations of international humanitarian law or human rights law relating to women are characterized as a threat to international peace and security by the Security Council. Having looked at the protection of women in two traditionally distinct bodies of law (IHL and HRL), it also needs to be examined which mechanisms are available in order to enforce the protection accorded to women and how effective they are.

4. *Enforcement Mechanisms and their Effectiveness*

4.1. *Human rights enforcement mechanisms within the UN System*

Human rights treaties usually establish three types of supervisory procedures: periodic reports to be submitted by states, inter-state complaints, and individual requests. As already mentioned above, however, the original CEDAW for example only foresees periodic reports. In addition, there are also monitoring mechanisms established by the Economic and Social Council (ECOSOC) such as resolution 1235 (1967),[98] resolution 1503 (1970)[99] as well as the system of thematic or country

---

[97] For more details on this problem *see* Chapter XI.
[98] ECOSOC Res. 1235 (XLII), U.N. Doc. E/4393 (June 6, 1967).
[99] ECOSOC Res. 1503 (XLVIII), U.N. Doc. E/4832/Add.1 (May 27, 1970).

Special Rapporteurs, which evolved in the Commission on Human Rights as well as the High Commissioner for Human Rights established in 1993.[100] With regard to the protection of women in armed conflict the system of Special Rapporteurs is of some significance, for, other enforcement mechanisms are regularly not functioning in times of armed conflict. For example, the discussion of the so-called "comfort women" in the U.N. Commission on Human Rights and the Working Group on Contemporary Forms of Slavery culminated in 1994 in the appointment of a Special Rapporteur on "Questions of Systematic Rape and Sexual Slavery and Slavery-like Practices During Wartime" in order to show the recognition of the crimes suffered by the "comfort women." In the 1998 final report the Special Rapporteur reiterated "the call for a response to the use of sexual violence and sexual slavery during armed conflict," emphasized "the true nature and extent of the harms suffered by women who are raped, sexually abused and enslaved by parties to an armed conflict," and examined "prosecutorial strategies for penalizing and preventing international crimes committed against women during armed conflict."[101] The report also focused on the issue of redress for the victims but, concretely, achieved almost nothing for the women concerned.[102]

Another Special Rapporteur, whose work is crucial for the protection of women in armed conflict, is the one on "Violence against Women, including its Causes and Consequences." Her mandate included examining violence against women in armed conflict situations and she *inter alia* focused on sexual violence during armed conflict and the treatment of refugee women in her preliminary report, while the emphasis of her final report was violence perpetrated or condoned by states or their actors against women in custody, refugee or internally displaced women, and women in armed conflict.[103]

The two country Special Rapporteurs also to be mentioned in this context are the Special Rapporteur on the situation of Human Rights in the Territory of the Former Yugoslavia and the Special Rapporteur for Rwanda. The Special Rapporteur for the Former Yugoslavia initialized in January 1993 an investigation of rape that was later found to have been used as an instrument of ethnic cleansing in

---

[100] Antonio Cassese, International Law 386ff (2005).
[101] Comtemporary Forms of Slavery. Systematic Rape, sexual slavery and slavery-like practices during armed conflict. Final Report submitted by Ms. Gay J. Mc Dougall, U.N. Doc. E/CN.4/Sub.2/1998/13 (June 22, 1998), para. 9–11; *see also* Preliminary Report U.N. Doc. E/CN.4/Sub.2/1996/26 (July 16, 1996).
[102] Gardam & Jarvis, *supra* note 20, at 230–332.
[103] Preliminary Report submitted by the Special Rapporteur on violence against women, its causes and consequences, Ms Radhika Coomaraswamy, in accordance with Commission on Human Rights Res. 1994/45, U.N. Doc. E/CN.4/1995/42 (Nov. 22, 1994); Report of the Special Rapporteur on violence against women, its causes and consequences in accordance with Commission on Human Rights Res. 1997/44, U.N. Doc. E/CN.4/1998/54 (Jan. 26, 1998).

Bosnia-Herzegovina and Croatia.[104] The Special Rapporteur for Rwanda found that rape "was systematic and was used as a 'weapon' by the perpetrators of the massacres."[105] While the reports of the listed thematic and country special rapporteurs certainly influenced the 'soft law' development on the protection of women in IHL and HRL, they nevertheless had no immediate effect for the victims of the human rights violations described in the respective reports. Special Rapporteurs are therefore predominantly a tool to make serious widespread human rights violations known and to put pressure on the respective perpetrating state, but have little effect on the abuses themselves.

4.2. *International Criminal Law*

The serious and systematic violations of international humanitarian and human rights law in the former Yugoslavia and Rwanda also contributed to the development of international criminal law since the early 1990s. The large scale of serious violations of humanitarian law and human rights including systematic sexual violence and rape in the former Yugoslavia was considered by the Security Council as a threat to international peace and security. It consequently created the International Criminal *ad hoc* Tribunal for the former Yugoslavia (ICTY) under Chapter VII of the U.N. Charter as a measure to restore international peace and security.[106] Similarly, the massive and systematic violations of IHL and HRL during the 1994 conflict in Rwanda led to the creation of the International Criminal *ad hoc* Tribunal for Rwanda (ICTR) on the basis of Chapter VII of the U.N. Charter and upon the request of the Rwandan government.[107] While the Security Council explicitly referred to sexual violence in its resolution establishing the ICTY, no such reference to sexual violence against women in its resolution establishing the ICTR despite systematic rape of women during the Rwandan conflict. Nevertheless, both statutes articulate crimes in connection with systematic sexual violence, albeit in a limited manner.[108] However, this did not restrain the two *ad hoc* tribunals from delivering groundbreaking judgments against perpetrators of rape and sexual violence during

---

[104] *See* Report of the Secretary-General on Rape and Abuse of Womenn the Territory of the Former Yugoslavia, U.N. Doc. E/CN.4/1994/5 (June 30, 1993) and Report on the Situation of Human Rights in the Territory of the Former Yugoslavia, U.N. Doc. E/CN.4/1993/50 (Feb. 10, 1993).

[105] Report on the situation of human rights in Rwanda submitted by Ms. René Degni-Ségui, Special Rapporteur under paragraph 20 of resolution S-3/1 of 25 May 1994, U.N. Doc. E/CN.4/1996/7 (June 28, 1995), para. 16.

[106] S.C. Res 808 (1993), U.N. Doc. S/RES/808 (Feb. 22, 1993), preamble para. 11 and S.C. Res. 823 (1993), U.N. Doc. S/RES/823 (May 25, 1993), preamble para. 3.

[107] S.C. Res. 955 (1994), U.N. Doc. S/RES/955 (Nov. 8, 1994).

[108] Article 5 ICTY-Statute – Crime Against Humanity and Article 4 ICTR-Statute – Violation of Article 3 common to the Four Geneva Conventions of 1949.

the two conflicts concentrating on the leaders of such crimes.[109] In this regard the *Kunarac* judgment of the ICTY, in which rape was considered as a crime against humanity (for which the accused were found guilty), and the *Akayesu* case of the ICTR, in which rape was branded genocide (for which the accused was convicted), need to be mentioned.[110]

Unlike the statutes of the two *ad hoc* criminal tribunals the Statute of the International Criminal Court (ICC) has a broader and more complete range of sexual and gender based crimes within its mandate which is to prosecute war crimes, crimes against humanity, and genocide worldwide. So far, however, at the time of writing there has been no conviction by the ICC.

However, given the scale of sexual violence during the conflicts and the very limited number of judgments by the *ad hoc* Tribunals, even though they constitute milestones, it is clear that until now the overwhelming majority of perpetrators remain unpunished. Thus, the real significance of international criminal law in general and the above-mentioned judgments in particular is on the one hand the recognition it gives to the victims and on the other hand the symbol set by showing that the international community considers rape and sexual violence as unacceptable behavior in armed conflict whose perpetrators need to be punished.

Yet, the necessary and indispensable fight against impunity for the perpetrators of such crimes is only one aspect in order to stop violations of international humanitarian law protecting women and of women's human rights. With regard to sexual violence in armed conflict it is even more crucial to immediately stop such practices by (almost) any means and to take care of the victims of sexual violence and other violations. Despite the progress made with the creation of the ICC by the Rome Statute, international law, however, continues to have very little means to enforce rules of IHL like the prohibition of rape. Even though rape in armed conflict always constitutes a war crime, and assuming the jurisdiction of the ICC as given, the court only has limited resources and cannot judge every single perpetrator, but only the most important ones. Therefore, impunity and the lack of general prevention ("Generalprävention") of such crimes will remain the necessary consequence, if the respective state is unable or unwilling to effectively enforce these rules through the means of its local authority – which also includes municipal centers local women can turn to in case of a threat or danger – and to prosecute these crimes on the grassroots level. These conditions are unfortunately for many practical reasons most difficult to fulfill in an armed conflict situation. Moreover,

---

[109] Kelly D. Askin, *The Jurisprudence of International War Crimes Tribunals: Securing Gender Justice for some Survivors*, in Listening to the Silences: Women and War (Helen Durham & Tracey Gurd eds, 2005).

[110] Prosecutor v. Kunarac, Case No. IT-96-23-TQ IT-96-23/1-T, Judgement, Trial Chamber, (Feb. 22, 2001); Prosecutor v. Kunarac, Case No. IT-96-23-Q IT-96-23/1A, Judgement, Appeals Chamber, (June 12, 2002); Prosecutor v. Akayesu, Case No. ICTR-96-4-T, Judgement, (Oct. 2, 1998).

the attempt to raise awareness via measures such as the dissemination of the laws of war to all parties of a conflict, and especially to the persons giving orders, is enmeshed with many practical problems. One of the issues relates to the difficulty to reach and train those persons who are likely to commit such crimes.

5. *Adequate Protection of Women in IHL and HRL*

It is sometimes argued by feminist scholars that IHL reflects the general discrimination against women in society and that its provisions therefore generally exacerbate their unequal status in society.[111] However, IHL being only applicable during conflict and aiming to protect women against effects of armed conflict, it is bound to use the *status quo* in any given country or context as a starting point in order to provide protection for women in armed conflict. Given that IHL only aims at protecting women in as far as they are victims of war, it does not attempt to change pre-existing social structures or societies – be they as unfair and unequal as they may. The critique that IHL reflects a "wrong," even an archaic picture of women in IHL, although based on the correct analysis that women are not only "victims," therefore shows that the – very limited – aims of IHL have not been taken into account. Even though this can be seen as disadvantaging women in the sense that IHL does not support women to obtain an equal status in society and equal chances in life (e.g. economically, independently, concerning self-determination), because their views are ignored, the aim of IHL – unlike HRL as discussed – is solely to protect women as victims of armed conflict and not to change society.

It has also often been argued that progress concerning women's rights in armed conflict during the last decades has almost exclusively been made with regard to women's human rights, not with regard to their protection in IHL.[112] Looking at the number of written resolutions, statements, and papers this is certainly true as it is more visible than any progress concerning women's protection in international humanitarian law. However, it must not be forgotten that the treaty provisions of IHL protecting women are older than most applicable HRL provisions and must be seen as a product of the time they were drafted in. Moreover, written IHL being made for the exceptional circumstances of armed conflict is more static and therefore less flexible than many areas of human rights law, which are under constant revision by the U.N. bodies concerned. For example, it took years to even agree on a third Additional Protocol introducing an additional emblem. Therefore, progress with regard to the specific protection of women in IHL can only exist in developing the interpretation of the respective rules – and progress in this regard is to be observed.

---

[111] Gardam & Jarvis, *supra* note 20, at 134.
[112] Gardam & Jarvis, *supra* note 20, at. 135–176, esp. 175f.

The most striking example for this is the interpretation of rape and sexual violence as discussed above as "torture" or "inhuman" or "cruel treatment" as a grave breach of the Geneva Conventions and a violation of common Article 3 as reflected in the Rome Statute of the International Criminal Court.

6. Conclusion

It has been proved that, even though HRL and IHL both aim to protect the fundamental rights of women as human beings, their specific aims with regard to women are completely different. Whereas IHL "only" attempts to protect women against the effects of armed conflict, HRL aims at enabling women to participate as much as men in public life and to create equal opportunities for them. Consequently, the protection they provide has to differ as much as the objectives of the provisions of the two different bodies of public international law. With regard to the protection of women in armed conflict they are, thus, not identical nor congruent in the sense that even though closely related they do not provide the same protection of women, nor are their enforcement mechanisms identical. Instead, the two bodies of law influence and complement each other, while their primary aims remain different. Nevertheless, considering that the reason women are particularly affected by armed conflict lies in the fact that they are discriminated and disadvantaged and thus have a lower status in almost any society than men, HRL aiming to improve the status of women in society can significantly contribute in making women less vulnerable to the effects of armed conflict. By empowering women to take an equal role in society and hence by making women less vulnerable to armed conflict HRL is furthermore crucial in post-conflict situations.

It has also been shown that IHL and HRL provide adequate legal protection for women in armed conflict, but that – although significant progress concerning the enforcement of legal regulations of IHL and HRL protecting women in armed conflict has been made – there still remains much more to be done in enforcing these rights. It is for example unbearable that sexual violence is still commonplace in today's armed conflicts like in Darfur (Sudan), the eastern provinces of the Democratic Republic of Congo, and the Central African Republic. As discussed above, these problems are only to a minor extent legal, but predominantly political and practical and cannot be solved academically from the outside. Unless the existing rules of IHL protecting women in armed conflict are politically and practically enforced in a way that perpetrations become the exemption rather than being the rule and have proven insufficient, new international laws protecting women in armed conflict are unnecessary.

Chapter XIV

Protection of Children in International Humanitarian Law and Human Rights Law

*Vesselin Popovski**

> To kill the big rats, you have to kill the little rats
> Radio Mille Collines, Rwanda, April 1994

1. *Introduction*

Children are the most vulnerable part of the population. This is true both in time of war and in time of peace. In time of armed conflict children are exposed to death, destruction, evacuation, separation from home and parents, starvation, physical and psychological trauma. Being a vulnerable group, they need special measures of protection in war, in addition to the measures for adult civilians. As most wars today are not between armies defending territorial borders, but intra-state conflicts, children among other civilians suffer disproportionately. In time of peace children also face enormous risks and become frequent victims of terrorism, organized crime, human trafficking, sexual abuse, prostitution, pornography etc. They have to endure also the harsh consequences of poverty, infectious diseases, environmental pollution, earthquakes, tsunami, floods and similar disasters.

The international humanitarian law (IHL) has gradually developed specific measures of protection of children in time of armed conflict. In parallel, the human rights law (HRL) has built up on the rights of the child, applicable in all time. The landmark 1989 Convention of the Rights of the Child (CRC)[1] was negotiated, signed and ratified in a record-breaking time. Regional human rights law regimes have also continuously elaborated a child-rights approach. In another advancement, the United Nations principal organs – General Assembly, Security Council, Secretary-General (and his Special Representative for Children) – adopted and enforced various measures, among them the reduction and elimination

---

* Dr. Vesselin Popovski. United Nations University, Tokyo. All opinions are personal.
[1] Convention on the Rights of the Child, G.A. Res. 44/25, Annex, 44 U.N. GAOR Supp. No. 49, U.N. Doc. A/44/49 (Nov. 20, 1989) (entered into force Sept. 2, 1990) [hereinafter CRC].

of recruitment and use of child soldiers. Most recently the recruitment of child soldiers and other crimes against children have gradually been criminalized in international law and prosecuted in international criminal tribunals.[2]

This chapter will present and compare the child-related developments in the codification and implementation of IHL and HRL. It will show similarities and controversies in the advancement of the child agenda in the two branches of international law, and demonstrate opportunities for mutual interplay. IHL and HRL historically originated through different concerns, forums and conventions, but have one major commonality – they both deal with the protection of victims. Still they are different: IHL applies in time of armed conflict; HRL applies in all times. IHL is a contract between states and regulates how to fight wars; HRL is a contract between states and citizens how to live in peace. IHL protects the civilians (children included) of the enemy state; HRL protects a state's own nationals. Finally, IHL requires individual responsibility of perpetrators, HRL demands states' responsibility for violations against individuals. In IHL states (prosecutors) sue individuals; in HRL individuals sue states.

The two branches, however, are not entirely separate circles. The boundary between "armed conflict" and "peace" became slimmer today in the age of terrorism, domestication of armed conflict, and increased role of non-state actors. Some human rights are restricted during armed conflict. And some crimes against humanity are no longer necessarily connected to an armed conflict, and can be prosecuted without the need to establish their nexus to war.

The chapter will explore the connections between IHL and HRL with regard to children and present both the positive developments towards complementarity and the still existing gaps. The codification of the protection of children is particularly illustrative of a convergence between IHL and HRL. HRL continuously evolved to be regarded as an instrument for universal protection of children both in time of war and peacetime. The law on the rights of the child, such as the 1989 Convention (Articles 38 and 39), or the African Charter on the Rights and Welfare of the Child (Article 22)[3] encompass obligations to respect the rules of IHL. As a result, these texts can be regarded as instruments of both IHL and HRL. The codification of IHL and HRL however was not followed by parallel implementation. The enforcement mechanisms available within IHL appear stronger than those within HRL, because IHL has a longer history and its violations by their very nature were taken more seriously and prosecuted. And on the opposite, although "softer" in

---

[2] Karin Arts & Vesselin Popovski (eds), International Criminal Accountability and the Rights of Children (2006) [hereinafter Arts & Popovski].
[3] African Charter on the Rights and Welfare of the Child, O.A.U. Doc. CAB/LEG/24.9/49, (1990) (entered into force Nov. 29, 1999) [hereinafter African Charter on the Rights and Welfare of the Child].

implementation, the HRL is more emblematic of the best interests of the child, respecting the young people's vulnerability and immaturity as a distinct value; whereas IHL regard children just as another group to be protected in warfare and only if this does not compromise military necessity.

The establishment of the International Criminal Court (ICC)[4] is a strong signal of the association between IHL and HRL inasmuch as the scope of crimes under the Statute cover both war and peace situations. The merger of IHL and HRL can be further exemplified with the developing prohibition of the recruitment of child soldiers. This practice has been gradually addressed and restricted in IHL (Article 77 of Additional Protocol I (AP I); similarly condemned and prohibited in HRL (Article 38 of CRC; in ILO[5] and others); condemned and combated through UN Security Council resolutions[6] and UN Secretary-General's Reports;[7] addressed and criminalized in international criminal law being declared a new category of war crime in the Rome Statute for the ICC.[8] It is of particular interest to observe that the crime of recruitment of child soldiers is the one that emerges very often in the scope of charges issued by the Prosecutor in the first cases of the work of the ICC.[9]

The overlap between IHL and HRL could be beneficial, but it could also be problematic. There is a need to identify possible gaps in protection, make sure that children do not fall in these gaps, and that each branch does not overestimate the other. IHL and HRL should complement each other and, where necessary interplay with other regimes (refugee law) as to offer full protection and best care for all children, in all circumstances, in all times.

---

[4] Rome Statute of the International Criminal Court, July 17, 1998, U.N. Doc. A/CONF. 183/9, (1998) [hereinafter Rome Statute].
[5] Convention Concerning the Prohibition and Immediate Action for the Elimination of the Worst Forms of Child Labour, June 17, 1999, ILO No. 182 [hereinafter ILO Convention].
[6] S.C. Res. 1261 (1999), S.C. Res. 1314 (2000); S.C. Res. 1332 (2000), S.C. Res. 1341 (2001), S.C. Res. 1335 (2001), S.C. Res. 1379 (2001), S.C. Res. 1460 (2003), S.C. Res. 1539 (2004), S.C. Res. 1612 (2005).
[7] Children and Armed Conflict: Report of the Secretary-General, U.N. Doc A/55/163-S/2000/712, (July 19, 2000); Children and Armed Conflict: Report of the Secretary-General, U.N. Doc. A/56/342-S/2001/852, (Sept. 7, 2001); Children and Armed Conflict: Report of the Secretary-General, U.N. Doc. S/2002/1299, (Nov. 26, 2002); Children and Armed Conflict: Report of the Secretary-General, U.N. Doc. A/58/546-S/2003/1053, (Nov. 10, 2003); Children and Armed Conflict: Report of the Secretary-General, U.N. Doc. A/59/695-S/2005/72, (Feb. 9, 2005).
[8] Rome Statute, *supra* note 4, Article 8 (b) (xxvi) and (c) vii).
[9] Prosecutor v. Thomas Lubanga Dyilo, Indictment, ICC-01/04–01/06; Prosecutor v. Joseph Kony, Vincent Otti, Raska Lukwiya, Okot Odhiambo and Dominic Ongwen, Indictment, ICC-02/04–01/05.

2. Codification of IHL With Regard of Children

Children suffer severely from armed conflicts.[10] In a recent account:

> more than 2 million children have died as a direct result of armed conflict, and more than three times that number have been permanently disabled or seriously injured. An estimated 20 million children have been forced to flee their homes, and more than 1 million have been orphaned or separated from their families. Some 300.000 child soldiers – boys and girls under the age of 18 – are involved in more than 30 conflicts worldwide.[11]

Children's suffering however has not triggered much attention in IHL until the last decade of the 20th century. The 1899 and 1907 Hague Convention did not distinguish between adults and children, expecting that children would simply benefit from the general protection provided for non-combatants in armed conflict. It was presumed for example that, even if not specifically mentioned, children would be protected by measures such as Chapter I, Section II of the 1907 Hague Convention "Means of injuring the enemy, sieges, and bombardments."[12]

The first child-oriented steps in IHL were made with the 1949 Geneva Conventions. Two texts in the Third Convention, relative to the Treatment of Prisoners of War (POW)[13] refer to age as a reason for privileged treatment – Article 16 "Equal Treatment" and Article 49 "Labour of POW." The first creates an exception from equality (privilege) that may be accorded by reason of age; the second demands to take consideration the age when utilizing POWs' labour. The Fourth Geneva Convention relates to civilians in general, but it included also specific texts on children,[14] that can be seen as an embryo of a child-oriented development in IHL. An embryo indeed, rather than a baby "as these provisions are pretty limited and insufficient". Carolyn Hamilton correctly pointed that the failure to obtain either more specific language, or even a Fifth Convention, "has had serious consequences for children caught up in armed conflict."[15] Article 24 of the Fourth Geneva

---

[10] Graça Machel, The Impact of War on Children: A Review of Progress since the 1996 United Nations Report on the Impact of Armed Conflict on Children (London, Hurst 2001).
[11] UNICEF Humanitarian Action Report 2005, *available at* www.unicef.org/emerg/index_HAR.html (last visited April 6, 2007).
[12] Convention Respecting the Laws and Customs of War on Land (Oct. 18, 1907), 36 Stat. 2277, 1 Bevans 631.
[13] Geneva Convention Relative to the Treatment of Prisoners of War (Aug. 12, 1949), 75 U.N.T.S. 135 [hereinafter GC III].
[14] *See* ICRC website summary table of provisions of IHL applicable to children in war www.icrc.org/Web/Eng/siteeng0.nsf/htmlall/5FfLJ5/$FILE/ANG03_04a_tableauDIH_TOTAL_logo.pdf?OpenElement (last visited April 6, 2007).
[15] Carolyn Hamilton, *Armed Conflict: the Protection of Children under International Law*, available at www.essex.ac.uk/armedcon/international/comment/Text/paper001.htm (last visited April 6, 2007).

Convention ensures "that children under fifteen, who are orphaned or are separated from their families as a result of the war, are not left to their own resources... The parties to the conflict must facilitate the reception of such children in a neutral country for the duration of the conflict."[16] This entirely child-oriented article is limited only to those children, deprived of their parents – it does not cover all other children who may similarly need survival, maintenance, education, etc. The drafters of the Fourth Convention did not approach the child as a vulnerable person, they showed more concern with family break-ups, with parents (or parties in conflict) losing their children through improper evacuation or poor care.

Another provision in the Fourth Convention, fully related to children, Article 50 obliged the occupying power to facilitate the proper working of all institutions devoted to the care and education of children, listing in great detail all steps that need to be taken. Article 51 excludes persons under eighteen from any circumstances that might necessitate them to be enlisted and compel to labour by occupying power. Article 68 excludes from the death penalty children under eighteen at the time of the offence. This has not been the practice in some national courts until very recently.[17] All these provisions, however, suffer from the same shortages, as the previous ones – they apply only to "protected persons" or civilian population in occupied territories; and the protection does not cover all indirect, and even direct, effects on children from the conduct of military hostilities.

The Additional Protocols (AP) to the Geneva Conventions try to fill these gaps. Article 77 AP I establishes the principle of special protection of children: "Children shall be the object of special respect and shall be protected against any form of indecent assault. The Parties to the conflict shall provide them with the care and aid they require, whether because of their age or for any other reason."[18] The principle of special care for children is extended to apply in non-international armed conflicts in Article 4 AP II.[19] Here is a full list of the child-related measures of protection in IHL:

---

[16] Geneva Convention IV Relative to the Protection of Civilian Persons in Time of War (Aug. 12, 1949), 75 U.N.T.S. 287 (entered into force Oct. 21, 1956) [hereinafter GC IV].

[17] On March 1, 2005 the ruling by the US Supreme Court in Roper v Simmons declared the imposition of capital punishment for crimes committed by juveniles under 18 "cruel and unusual punishment," therefore contradicting the 8th Constitutional amendment. The USA became the last country in the world abolishing the capital punishment for juvenile offenders. *See* William Schabas, *The Rights of the Child, Law of Armed Conflict and Customary International Law: A Tale of Two Cases*, *in* Arts & Popovski, *supra* note 2, 19–35 [hereinafter Schabas].

[18] Protocol Additional to the Geneva Conventions of 12 August 1949, and Relating to the Protection of Victims of Non-International Armed Conflicts (Protocol I), June 8, 1977, 1125 U.N.T.S. 3 [hereinafter AP II].

[19] Protocol Additional to the Geneva Conventions of 12 August 1949, and Relating to the Protection of Victims of Non-International Armed Conflicts (Protocol II), June 8, 1977, 1125 U.N.T.S. 609 [hereinafter AP I].

1. Establishment of hospital and safety zones (Article 14 GC IV);
2. Evacuations during armed conflict; release and return after conflict (Articles 17, 24(2), 49(3), 78, and 132(2) GC IV; Article 78 API; Article 4(3)(e) AP II);
3. Priority in care, for example in delivery of food, medical supplies, clothing (Articles 23, 38, 50(5) and 89 GC IV;
4. Family reunification (Articles 24, 25, 26, 49(3), 50, 82 GC IV; Article 78 AP I; Article 4(3b), 6(4) AP II);
5. Education (Article 24(1), 50, 94 GC IV; Article 78(2) AP I; Article 4(3)(a) AP II);
6. Special care of detained or interned children (Articles 76(5), 82, 85(2), 89, 94, 119(2), 132 GC IV; Article 77(3) and (4) AP I; Article 4(3)(d) AP II);
7. Immunity from death penalty (Article 68(4) GC IV; Article 77(5) AP I; Article 6(4) AP II).

In addition to the above, AP I and AP II developed a prohibition of the participation of children in armed hostilities in any capacity – from assisting combatants to members of armed forces.[20] If children are nevertheless recruited and take part in hostilities, they are recognized as combatants and accordingly, in the event of capture, are entitled to POW status under the Third Geneva Convention.

However, even these developments are still short of a comprehensive child-rights approach. One may argue that whatever progress could be made in IHL, this *lex specialis* would always remain limited as inherently compromising between military necessity and humanitarian aspirations. There might be little hope that IHL can ever protect children from becoming "non-excessive collateral damage." Notoriously, in some recent military hostilities, the number of children's casualties remained very high. UNICEF and "Save the Children" reported that between 40 and 45 percent of the civilian victims during the hostilities between Israel and Hezbollah in South Lebanon in August 2006 were children.[21]

The codification of IHL has absorbed slowly and insufficiently the child-related norms that have been gradually elaborated in HRL. For example the Geneva Conventions could have incorporated more language, or spirit, from the child-oriented 1924 Declaration of Geneva,[22] or the 1942 Children's Charter.[23] Similarly the AP I and II could have borrowed more from the 1959 Declaration on the Rights of the

---

[20] Article 77 AP I, *supra* note 19, and Article 4(3)(c) AP II, *supra* note 18.
[21] Kim Sengupta, "Help Save the Children, Victims of War", Independent, Aug. 3, 2006.
[22] Geneva Declaration of the Rights of the Child, adopted Sept. 26, 1924, L.N.O.J. Spec. Supp. 21, at 43 (1924) [hereinafter Geneva Declaration 1924].
[23] A Children's Charter in Wartime. Children in Wartime No. 2. Children's Bureau Publication No. 283, Washington 1943.

Child.[24] The major principle in the child-rights philosophy – the best interests of the child as primary consideration in all actions – is not spelled anywhere in IHL. Another major principle in the rights of the child – the non-discrimination – in fact could be even in conflict with the measures of protection in IHL that extend to certain categories of victims, but do not extend to others.

The truth is that IHL directs states towards the protection of civilians (and imprisoned or wounded soldiers) of the enemy, rather than of its own population. There is a natural explanation to this – states should protect their own population at any time in all circumstances – this is customarily obvious and does not need extra spelling in war-law Convention. But when it comes to children (or other vulnerable groups) the lack of sufficient attention in IHL and the discrimination between protecting some groups of children, but not others, becomes problematic.

3. Implementation of IHL and Protection of Children

The codification is only a small part in international law – the real test for norms and rules comes when they have to be ratified and applied by states, when the obligations need to be monitored and enforced through sanctions imposed on the violators. The implementation of IHL has intrinsically suffered from the fact that this *lex specialis* has to be applied against the thresholds of military necessity; it always co-exists with the extraordinary excesses of the armed conflicts. One can even argue that IHL is not "humanitarian" as the protection of non-combatants arises not so much from humanitarianism, but rather from a calculation; that it would be militarily advantageous to evacuate non-combatants from the battlefield and concentrate on targeting the military strength of the enemy.

The implementation of IHL suffers also from attempts of some states to desactivate Common Article 3 by not recognizing that hostilities on their territories amount to non-international armed conflict – among others Israel (West Bank, Gaza); India (Kashmir); Russia (Chechnya). Due to these problems concerning the implementation of IHL children continue to suffer from armed conflict in many ways, as indicated in Graça Machel's report.[25] In recent conflicts notorious anti-child methods, such as starvation of population; forceful deportation; separation of

---

[24] Declaration of the Rights of the Child, G.A. Res. 1386 (XIV), 14 U.N. GAOR Supp. (No. 16) at 19, U.N. Doc. A/4354 (1959).

[25] Graça Machel, Promotion and Protection of the Rights of Children: Impact of Armed Conflict on Children, U.N. Doc. A/51/306, (Aug. 26, 1996). For comprehensive analysis, *see* Françoise Hampson, Legal Protection Afforded to Children under IHL, *available at* www.essex.ac.uk/armed-con/international/comment/Text/paper002.htm (last visited April 6, 2007).

men from women and children; mass rape, including of young girls; child soldiers' recruitment etc. have been on the rise.[26]

The suffering of children in armed conflicts has been gradually given consideration, particularly after Graça Machel's report, and one result is the developing child-rights approach in the practice of domestic and international criminal courts and in the actions taken by different organs of the United Nations. In international criminal law the pioneer case of considering the age of the victims as an aggravating factor in the sentencing is *The Prosecutor v. Kunarac, Kovac and Vukovic* heard before the International Criminal Tribunal for former Yugoslavia (ICTY). Three Serb soldiers were prosecuted for rape, torture, enslavement and outrages upon personal dignity of women and young girls kept in detention centres in Foca, Bosnia. Many of the victims in this case were girls below eighteen, and during the process the Prosecutor repeatedly emphasized this aggravating factor. The judges took it into account and the Trial Judgement "considered the young age of some of the victims of the offences committed by Dragoljub Kunarac as an aggravating factor."[27] It also "considered in aggravation the fact that the offences had been committed against particularly vulnerable and defenceless women and girls."[28] The judges took the same view against Kovac: "the Trial Chamber considered as aggravating circumstances the age of the victims when the offences were committed...against several particularly vulnerable and defenceless girls and a woman was considered in aggravation" (paragraphs 874 and 875). Judge Florence Mumba told Kovac when sentencing him:

> Particularly appalling and deplorable is your treatment of 12-year-old A.B., a helpless little child for whom you showed absolutely no compassion whatsoever, but whom you abused sexually in the same way as the other girls. You finally sold her like an object, in the knowledge that this would almost certainly mean further sexual assaults by other men. You knew that any chance of her being re-united with her mother, whose immense grief the Trial Chamber had to countenance in the hearing, would thus become even more remote than it already was. At the time of trial, some 8 years later, the child had never been seen or heard of again. The treatment of A.B. is the most striking example of your morally depraved and corrupt character.[29]

---

[26] *See, e.g.*, Nick Danziger' account "Children at War", *available at* www.redcross.int/EN/mag/magazine2003_3/4–9.html (last visited April 6, 2007).

[27] Prosecutor v. Kunarac et al., Case Nos. IT-96-23-T & IT-96–23/1-T, Judgment, (Feb. 22, 2001) para. 864.

[28] *Id.*, para. 867.

[29] Kunarac, Kovac and Vukovic case, Judgement of Trial Chamber II, Press Release No. JL/P.I.S./566-e, (Feb. 22, 2001), *available at* www.un.org/icty/pressreal/p566-e.htm (last visited April 9, 2007).

The aggravating factor was also applied against Vukovic[30] for the rape of a fifteen years old girl. The defence at the appeal in *Kunarac et al.* tried to challenge the age of victims as aggravating circumstance, referring to the 1977 Penal code of the former Yugoslavia that allow to aggravate sentences only when the age of victims is below fourteen. Also it referred to the consensual age for marriage in the former Yugoslavia to be sixteen years old, not eighteen (a cynical argument, having in mind the difference between "repeated rape" and "marriage.") The Appeals Chamber rejected this defence and in an excellent reminder of the power of IHL, it reaffirmed that the Trial was referring to "the status of women and children who are specifically accorded protection under the Geneva Conventions and other IHL instruments in times of armed conflicts." In that light, "it was reasonable to conclude that the callous attacks on defenseless women merited specific assessment."[31] The Appeals Judgement confirmed that:

> The Trial Chamber has considered the defense expert witness's evidence with regard to the sentencing practice of the former Yugoslavia for the offence of rape, which shows that the youth of victims of sexual crimes constituted an aggravating circumstance in that practice. The witness confirmed in court that the rape of young girls under eighteen years of age led to aggravated sentences in the former Yugoslavia. In the view of the Appeals Chamber, the expert evidence did not contradict the prevailing practice in the former Yugoslav Republic of Bosnia and Herzegovina and was rightly considered by the Trial Chamber in this regard. There still was an inherent discretion of the Trial Chamber to consider a victim's age of 19 years as an aggravating factor by reason of its closeness to the protected age of special vulnerability. No doubt it was for this reason that the Trial Chamber spoke of different ages as relatively youthful. The Trial Chamber was right to distinguish between crimes committed in peacetime and in wartime. Young and elderly women need special protection in order to prevent them from becoming easy targets. The Appeals Chamber finds that the Trial Chamber was not in error by taking into account the young age of victims specified in the Trial Judgement. This part of the ground of appeal therefore fails.[32]

The judgments in *Kunarac et al.* are strong developments of child-oriented international law. They refer to norms and instruments of IHL (Geneva Conventions, vulnerability in wartime, need for special protection for children) and HRL (CRC, best interests of the child). An interesting moment is that the Appeal Chamber did not adopt a strict delimitation of various age levels that may exist in different laws with regard of children's maturity, responsibility, and vulnerability. Instead, it re-confirmed the discretion of the judges to regard victims at nineteen and

---

[30] Prosecutor v. Kunarac et al., Case Nos. IT-96-23-T & IT-96–23/1-T, Judgment, (Feb. 22, 2001) para. 879.
[31] Prosecutor v. Kunarac et al., Case No. IT-96-23 & IT-96–23/1A, Judgment, Appeals Chamber (June 12, 2002).
[32] *Id.*

twenty as close to the conventional protected age and award them the special care status, where necessary. David Tolbert, Deputy Prosecutor at ICTY, recognized that this is a "significant step in the direction of further protecting children, and provides a strong precedent on which the ICC and other courts and tribunals can build."[33] The practice of International Criminal Tribunal for Rwanda (ICTR) also considered aggravated sentencing for crimes when there were among the victims many children.[34]

In addition to aggravated sentencing for crimes against children, the practice of the international criminal tribunals focused on developing special measures of protection for child victims and witnesses, along with other vulnerable groups. The Rules and Procedures of the tribunals allow child witnesses to be accompanied by a parent, guardian, relative or friend for the whole duration of their travel to the court, their stay and travel back home. Further, the Victims and Witnesses Sections in these tribunals are equipped to provide constant special care, counselling and other protection. Moreover, specific measures were developed for victims and witnesses of sexual assault and gender crimes.[35]

The Victims and Witnesses Sections of the two *ad hoc* tribunals (ICTY, ICTR) developed measures protecting the privacy of child victims through the use of pseudonyms, face and voice distortion; closed sessions without media; use of closed circuit TV so that defendants cannot see the witnesses. The ICC went even further, adopting an approach closer to the civil law enhancement of rights of victims, and for the first time in international criminal law history the victims (children including) are allowed to have their own legal representation, subject to the discretion of the court. Still, there is a road to go ahead – a next step could be to ensure that in every case that involves child victims, a legal representative for the child is appointed, and paid for through the court's budget or through the national legal aid system. Unfortunately, the statistics suggest that despite these measures of protection, children generally are reluctant to testify and give evidence as witnesses.[36] Rule 90(b) of the ICTY Statute[37] and a similar Rule 66(2) in the ICC Statute relieve children from the necessity to make a solemn declaration to

---

[33] David Tolbert, *Children and International Criminal Law: The Practice of the ICTY*, in Arts & Popovski, *supra* note 2, at 153.

[34] For example Prosecutor v. Akayesu, Case No. ICTR-96-4-T, Judgment, (Sept. 2, 1998).

[35] Binaifer Nowrojee, *Making the Invisible War Crime Visible: Post-Conflict Justice for Sierra Leone's Rape Victims*, 18 Harv. Hum. Rts J., 85 (2005).

[36] *See* Sam Garkawe, Improving the Treatment of Child Victims during the Criminal Justice System, at the Conference Making Children's Rights Work: National and International Perspectives, Nov. 18–20, 2004, *available at* www.ibcr.org/PAGE_EN/2004%20Conference%20documents/Garkawe_ENG.pdf (last visited April 6, 2007).

[37] Statute of the International Criminal Tribunal for the Former Yugoslavia, S.C. Res. 827, U.N. Doc. S/RES/827 (May 25, 1993) [hereinafter ICTY Statute].

tell the truth. Still they have the choice to make such a non-binding declaration, if they wish. The ICC goes even a step further inasmuch as it provides that a child's testimony cannot be excluded solely because of the lack of a solemn declaration.

The practice of the Special Court for Sierra Leone (SCSL) made a further strong contribution to the child-related measures listed above. As far as many of the charges by the Prosecutor included crimes against children, the SCSL can be seen as a model of children rights' protection, at least in theory. In one of its first pronouncements in *Prosecutor v. Norman* the Appeals Chamber ruled that the recruitment of children under fifteen into armed forces or using them in combat is prohibited in customary international law, and also subject of individual criminal responsibility.[38] The importance of the *Norman* case has been emphasized in the law literature,[39] including by some officials involved such as Jeffrey Robertson, President Judge (with dissenting opinion), David Crane, Chief Prosecutor, and William Schabas, Commissioner of the TRC Sierra Leone.[40] The SCSL has also significantly advanced the protection of child victims and witnesses.[41]

4. Development of the Rights of the Child in HRL

As a consequence of the rise in crimes committed against children in time of peace the child-related HRL has gradually developed. In 1924 the Geneva Declaration adopted by the League of Nations required that "the child must be the first to receive relief in times of distress" and "must be protected against every form of exploitation."[42] In 1959 the U.N. General Assembly adopted the Declaration of the Rights of the Child. It consists of ten general principles and pays specific attention to the child as a vulnerable person, who "by reason of his physical and mental immaturity needs special safeguards and care, including legal protection."[43] The Declaration established the principle of "best interests of the child" (paragraphs 2 and 7). It spells the right of the child from birth to have a name and a nationality

---

[38] Prosecutor v. Samuel Hinga Norman, Case No. SCSL-2004-14-AR72(E), Decision on Preliminary Motion Based on Lack of Jurisdiction (Child Recruitment) (Appeals Chamber, May 31, 2004).

[39] *See* Matthew Happold, *International Humanitarian Law, War Criminality and Child Recruitment: The Decision of the Special Court for Sierra Leone in Prosecutor v Samuel Hinga Norman*, 18 LJIL 283–297 (2005).

[40] *See* Schabas, *supra* note 17, at 19–36 and David Crane, *Strike Terror No More: Prosecuting the Use of Children in Times of Conflict – The West African Extreme, in* Arts & Popovski, *supra* note 2, at 119–132.

[41] *See* Ann Michels, *As if it was Happening Again: Supporting Especially Vulnerable Witnesses, in Particular Women and Children, at the SCSL, in* Arts & Popovski, *supra* note 2, at 133–146.

[42] Geneva Declaration 1924, *supra* note 29.

[43] United Nations Declaration on the Rights of the Child, G.A. Res. 1386 (XIV), para. 4, U.N. Doc. A/4354 (Nov. 20, 1959).

(paragraph 3) and the entitlement to free and compulsory education (paragraph 7). The Declaration protects against neglect, cruelty, exploitation, and traffic (paragraph 9). It also requires the establishment of a minimum age (not specified) for employment and prohibits the engagement of a child "in any occupation or employment which would prejudice his health or education, or interfere with his physical, mental or moral development."[44] This text, although not binding law, could be regarded as an early expression of the United Nations' concern with the use of children in armed forces.

In 1974 the U.N. General Assembly adopted the Declaration on the Protection of Women and Children in Emergency and Armed Conflict, raising a gender-based awareness about the suffering of the most vulnerable groups of the population.[45] This Declaration, reflecting the time of its adoption, deplores the colonial and racist foreign domination "cruelly suppressing the national liberation movements and inflicting heavy losses and incalculable suffering on the population under their domination, including women and children."[46] The Declaration demands that "all forms of repression and cruel and inhuman treatment of women and children, including imprisonment, torture, shooting, mass arrests, collective punishment, destruction of dwellings and forcible eviction, committed by belligerents in the course of military operations or in occupied territories shall be consider criminal."[47] This text is an example of accumulation of customary prohibition of gender crimes, that was later inserted also into the UN Torture Convention,[48] the CRC, the jurisdiction of the international criminal tribunals etc. One minus in the 1974 Declaration is that it does not specify children as a vulnerable group, distinct from adults in armed conflict (a similar gap is found in the Geneva Conventions). It rather expresses a consciousness "for the destiny of mothers, who play an important role in society, in the family and particularly in the upbringing of children."[49] At that time more attention was paid to civilians in armed conflict and to women as a discriminated group.

Children became the centre of international attention with the adoption of the CRC in 1989, followed by a record-fast entry into force and near universal ratification, has become both a benchmark and a trigger for developing measures

---

[44] *Id.*

[45] Declaration on the Protection of Women and Children in Emergency and Armed Conflict, G.A. Res. 3318, U.N. GAOR 29th Sess., Supp. No. 31, U.N. Doc. A/9631 (Dec. 14, 1974) [hereinafter Declaration on the Protection of Women and Children].

[46] *Id.*

[47] *Id.*

[48] Convention Against Torture and Other Cruel, Inhuman or Degrading Treatment or Punishment, G.A. Res. 46, at 197, U.N. GAOR, 39th Sess., Supp. No. 51, U.N. Doc. A/39/51 (Sept. 28, 1984).

[49] Declaration on the Protection of Women and Children, *supra* note 45.

of protection of children. The Convention defines a child as "any human being below the age of eighteen years"[50] (Article 1) and covers all fundamental rights. The CRC recognizes and establishes the central purpose of survival and development of children, and determines three major principles – non-discrimination of age; children's participation; and the best interests of the child. These purposes and principles in their totality represent a comprehensive child-rights approach in international law. However, states made many reservations to the CRC that rendered low some of its benefits.

The CRC contains provisions relating to armed conflict – Articles 38 and 39 – *de facto* manifesting a tendency of a merger of IHL and HRL. However, some texts disappoint as they just repeat obvious previous obligations; for example Article 38(4) CRC requests only that "States Parties shall take all feasible measures to ensure protection and care of children who are affected by an armed conflict."[51] Someway recognizing Article 38's weakness, the Committee on the Rights of the Child chose the topic of children in armed conflict to start its first session.

Other provisions in the CRC also reiterate rights and protection that were already developed in IHL – reunification of families, education, protection from displacement, severe labour, or severe penalties, death penalty including. For example, according to Article 9 states are obliged to ensure that there is no separation of a child and parents against their will. Under Article 32 states must protect children from "work that is likely to be hazardous or to interfere with the child's education, or to be harmful to the child's health or physical, mental, spiritual, moral or social development."[52]

At the 1990 UN World Summit where the ambitious "World Declaration on the Survival, Protection and Development of Children in the 1990s"[53] and a "Plan of Action" were adopted.[54] These two documents, however, had a limited impact on children in armed conflict because they only spelled a general need for protection and made no specific recommendations. The 1993 World Conference on Human Rights in Vienna presented a more solid initiative since it recommended a study on the impact of armed conflict on children. Article 50 of the final document (Vienna Declaration)[55] proposed to the U.N. Secretary-General to "initiate a study into means of improving the protection of children in armed conflicts. Humanitarian norms should be implemented and measures taken in order to protect and facilitate assistance to children in war zones. Measures should include protection for children

---

[50] Article 1, CRC, *supra* note 1.
[51] CRC, *supra* note 1.
[52] *Id.*
[53] World Declaration on the Survival, Protection and Development of Children, *available at* www.unicef.org/wsc/declare.htm (last visited April 9, 2007).
[54] Plan of Action, *available at* www.unicef.org/wsc/declare.htm (last visited April 9, 2007).
[55] Vienna Declaration and Program of Action, U.N. Doc A/CONF.157/23 (July 12, 1993).

against indiscriminate use of all weapons of war, especially anti-personnel mines. The need for aftercare and rehabilitation of children traumatized by war must be addressed urgently."[56]

This is how the Graça Machel's report came to existence – as a shocking revelation of horrific abduction and forcible recruitment of child soldiers, dreadful sexual exploitation and other appalling crimes against children all over the world. A strong feature of the report is that it does not spare the names of countries where the notorious practices occurred. The report made far-reaching recommendations, underlying the need for creation of implementation mechanisms involving various actors – governments, regional arrangements, U.N. bodies, international treaties, World Health Organization, Bretton Wood institutions, ICRC, inter-institutional mechanisms, civil society. As a first step it suggested the establishment of a Special Representative of the Secretary-General on Children and Armed Conflict. In September 1997 Olara Otunnu (Uganda) was appointed for this post, in April 2006 he was succeeded by Radhika Coomaraswamy (Sri Lanka). This Office engages in various tasks voicing children's rights and advocating concrete steps to stop their violations in armed conflict. The Office co-operates with many organs within and outside the United Nations to reduce the abuse of children, release and rehabilitate child soldiers as well as achieve a complete cessation of recruitment and use of children in armed conflict.

In October 2002 the General Assembly adopted a document entitled "A World Fit for Children"[57] summarizing most of the achievements of the decade since the first World Summit for Children. In September 2005 the World Summit Outcome Document from the 60th Session of the General Assembly reaffirmed its commitment to the promotion and protection of the right and welfare of children.[58] It called upon States to take effective measures to prevent the recruitment and use of children in armed conflict by armed forces and groups and to prohibit and criminalize such practices.

5. Regional Human Rights Law

The 1950 European Convention for Human Rights (ECHR)[59] developed some interesting child-related case law through its Court's practice. In few cases the European Court for Human Rights considered violations of the ECHR against children

---

[56] *Id.* para. 50.
[57] UNICEF, A World Fit for Children: Outcome Document of the Special Session, A/RES/S-27/2, *available at* www.unicef.org/specialsession/wffc/ (last visited April 9, 2007).
[58] *Available at* www.un.org/summit2005 (last visited April 9, 2007).
[59] European Convention for the Protection of Human Rights and Fundamental Freedoms (Nov. 4, 1950), 213 U.N.T.S. 221.

in time of armed conflict – in fact applying HRL in situations that could not have been addressed within IHL, because states (e.g., Turkey, Russia) do not recognize the non-international armed conflicts that are taking place on their territory (e.g., Kurdistan, Chechnya). In *Aydin v. Turkey* the Court recognises that the rape of a seventeen years old girl is an "especially grave and abhorrent form of ill-treatment" that leaves "deep psychological scars which do not respond to the passage of time as quickly as other forms of physical or mental violence"[60] and accordingly finds an Article 3 (torture) violation. The lawyers of the applicant, emphasizing her sex, age and vulnerability, had indeed requested the Court "to find that the deliberately inflicted and calculated physical suffering and sexual humiliation of which she was the victim was of such severity as to amount to an additional act of torture."[61]

In *Isayeva et al. v. Russia* the European Court for Human Rights deals with a situation even closer to IHL – an actual military hostility. Though it accepts that the situation in Chechnya calls for exceptional measures under Article 15 ECHR and the attack was a legitimate response to an insurgency, the indiscriminate bombing of a road along which a large number of civilians – including children – were known to be travelling was found as a violation of Article 2 pertaining to the right to life.[62]

The ECHR case law is a good example of a cumulative approach with regard of children – HRL was successfully applied in situations where IHL could not have been applied for certain reasons. In fact many Kurdish, Chechen or IRA cases filed in the European Court for Human Rights are IHL-related. The same can be said for Bankovic, Behrami (a child) and other petitions against NATO countries for the 1999 bombing of Yugoslavia.[63] Obviously, one deficiency remains that the HRL incriminate states and does not go after individual perpetrators.

The already mentioned Article 15 ECHR allows for derogation from the Convention in situations when the life of the nation is threatened by war or other public emergencies. However, some human rights cannot be derogated even in time of war – arbitrary killing, torture, denial of religious freedom are absolutely prohibited in any circumstances, at any time. The 1969 American Convention on

---

[60] Aydin v. Turkey, European Court of Human Rights, Application 25660/94, Judgment, (July 10, 2001).
[61] *Id.*
[62] Isayeva, Yusupova and Bazayeva v. Russia, Applications 57947/00, 57948/00 & 57949/00, Judgment, (Feb. 24, 2005).
[63] Bankovic and Others v. Belgium and Sixteen Other Contracting States, 2001-XII Eur. Ct. H.R. 333. Further, it must be noted that the ICTY declined to prosecute war crimes by NATO in Yugoslavia, *see* The committee established to review the NATO bombing campaign against the federal republic of Yugoslavia, final report to the prosecutor, 39 I.L.M. 1257, 1272 (June 8, 2000), *available at* un.org/icty/pressreal/nato061300.htm (last visited April 9, 2007).

Human Rights also lists non-derogable rights (Article 27[64] and similar provision exists in International Covenant on Civil and Political Rights (Article 4).[65] These examples suggest that one needs to address overlaps and grey zones between IHL and HRL and ensure that children are not denied protection in case of a grey zone. In this context it is worth reminding the Martens Clause,[66] quoted properly in the 1990 Abo Turku Declaration to cover situations when IHL and HRL may not be sufficient to offer protection: In "cases not covered by human rights and humanitarian instruments, all persons and groups remain under the protection of the principles of international law derived from established custom, from the principles of humanity and the dictates of public conscience."[67]

6. *Prohibition of Recruitment of Child Soldiers in IHL and HRL*

In the context of a potential merger of IHL and HRL, it is interesting to compare the provisions on the prohibition of recruitment of child soldiers in the two branches of law. According to Article 38(2) CRC states "shall take all feasible measures to ensure that persons who have not attained the age of fifteen do not take a direct part in hostilities."[68] Paragraph 3 asks states to "refrain from recruiting any person who has not attained the age of fifteen into their armed forces. In recruiting among those persons who have attained the age of fifteen but have not attained the age of eighteen, States Parties must endeavour to give priority to those who are oldest."[69] These texts in HRL are very soft and wish-expressing, comparing to IHL since 12 years earlier in 1977 Article 4(3)(c) AP II already clearly demanded that "children who have not attained the age of fifteen shall neither be recruited in the armed forces or groups nor allowed to take part in hostilities."[70] Even more disappointing is the fact that the CRC does not raise the prohibition of recruitment of child soldiers to the age of eighteen; instead, it somehow oddly advised states to prioritize to the older, when recruiting children between fifteen and eighteen (Article 38(3)). How

---

[64] American Convention on Human Rights, signed Nov. 22, 1969, O.A.S.T.S. No. 36, O.A.S. Off. Rec. OEA/Ser. L/V/II.23, Doc. 21, Rev. 6 (Nov. 22, 1969), (entry into force on July 18, 1978).
[65] International Covenant on Civil and Political Rights, G.A., Res. 2200A/XXI, Dec. 16, 1966, 52, U.N. Doc. A/6316 (Dec. 19, 1966), 999 U.N.T.S. 171, (entry into force on Mar. 23, 1976).
[66] Martens clause, Hague Convention (II) with Respect to the Laws and Customs of War on Land and its annex: Regulation concerning the Laws and Customs of War on Land: 29 July 1899, 32 Stat. 1803, 1 Bevans 247, 26 Martens Nouveau Recueil (ser. 2) 949, 187 Consol. T.S. 429 (entered into force Sept. 4, 1900), preamble.
[67] *Declaration of Minimum Humanitarian Standards* (Adopted by Meeting of Experts at Human Rights Institute of Abo Akademi in Turku, Finland, U.N. Doc.E/CN.4/Sub.2/1991/55 (1990).
[68] CRC, *supra* note 1.
[69] *Id.*
[70] AP II, *supra* note 18.

can the same Convention declare "the best interests of the child", and advise how to recruit children between fifteen and eighteen, knowing that they can even be engaged in military hostilities?

Only a few months after the adoption of the CRC, the 1990 African Charter on the Rights and Welfare raised the prohibition of child soldiers' recruitment to eighteen.[71] In the same way as the CRC, it defines a child as "any human being below the age of eighteen" (Article 2),[72] but in Article 22, called "Armed Conflict", reminding obligations from IHL (paragraph 1), it demands states to "ensure that no child shall take a direct part in hostilities and refrain in particular, from recruiting any child" (paragraph 2). This became the first international legal text that prohibits the recruitment or direct participation in hostilities or internal strife of all children, including those above fifteen. The 26th International Conference of the Red Cross and Red Crescent in 1995 also recommends the age of eighteen as a limit for participation in armed forces.[73] The Council of Delegates adopted the Movement's plan of action, which in Commitment 1 decided to promote the principle of non-recruitment and non-participation in armed conflict of children under the age of eighteen. Also the 1999 ILO Convention No. 182[74] defines the "forced or compulsory recruitment of children for use in armed conflict" as one of the "worst forms of child labor" and asks ILO members to "take immediate and effective measures to secure the prohibition."[75]

The African Charter on the Rights and Welfare of the Child, the ICRC, and the ILO were instrumental in rising the minimum age of recruitment into armed forces from fifteen to eighteen and this was finally fixed in the 2000 Optional Protocol to the CRC on the involvement of children in armed conflict.[76] The Optional Protocol to the CRC generally strengthens the protection of children in armed conflict and can be seen as a pioneer example of adopting a treaty text in HRL that entirely addresses an issue relevant exclusively to the IHL. This Protocol may be regarded so far as the best example of a potential merger of HRL and IHL with regard of children. However, because of the reservations made by some states, the enforcement of the Optional Protocol to the CRC in some circumstances is still weak.[77]

---

[71] African Charter on the Rights and Welfare of the Child, *supra* note 3.
[72] *Id.*
[73] Documents *available at* www.icrc.org/Web/Eng/siteeng0.nsf/html/conf26 (last visited April 9, 2007).
[74] ILO Convention, *supra* note 5.
[75] *Id.*
[76] Optional Protocol to the Convention on the Rights of the Child on the Involvement of Children in Armed Conflict, G.A. Res. 54/263, Annex I, U.N. Doc A/RES/54/263 (May 25, 2000) (entered into force Feb. 12, 2002) [hereinafter Optional Protocol].
[77] For critical view *see* Marsha Hackenberg, *Can the Optional Protocol for the Convention of the Rights of the Child Protect the Ugandan Child Soldier*, 10 Ind. Int'l & Comp. L. Rev 417 (2000).

The Optional Protocol to the CRC distinguishes between forceful recruitment and voluntary recruitment. It ensures that members of armed forces who have not attained the age of eighteen do not take a direct part in hostilities (Article 1) and that persons who have not attained the age of eighteen are not compulsory recruited (Article 2).[78] Article 3 deals with voluntary recruitment and imposes the following restrictions: states that permit voluntary recruitment into their armed forces under the age of eighteen years shall maintain safeguards to ensure, as a minimum, that:

a) Such recruitment is genuinely voluntary;
b) It is carried out with the informed consent of the person's parents or legal guardians;
c) Such persons are fully informed of the duties involved in such a military service;
d) They provide reliable proof of age prior to acceptance into national military service.[79]

One can criticize the distinction between compulsory and voluntary recruitment, arguing that children below eighteen cannot be considered as joining "genuinely" the armed forces. Children are vulnerable to various kinds of threatening or rewarding pressures. They may have "volunteered" because they are poor, orphaned, denied education and have not much of other options left in their lives or were simply bought out or promised heavens. Others may have "volunteered" because of a threat, or because of a pride not to be seen as unpatriotic. One can also question generally the need at all for such a distinction – does it really matter what rationales or what amount of pressure may have had driven children to enlist "voluntarily"? What the international law needs to regulate is not the type of child soldiers' recruitment, but the total negative impact of wars on all children. Why not simply offer everyone below eighteen only non-military education and only non-military jobs? And once children become eighteen, they can join the armed force, if they want to volunteer.

The danger of keeping the distinction between forceful and voluntary is that child soldiers' recruiters will continue to play on the sense of national duty, on revenge for past grievances, or on economic tools – and these will continue to work for many orphans, or others who have not much of a choice to ensure basic safety. I would argue that any situation of child recruitment is in itself abnormal, as there is always an amount of pressure – anybody below eighteen in normal circumstances should be in a school or in a traineeship, and not consider joining armed forces. If the age of adult maturity and responsibility to take decisions is established at eighteen (in

---

[78] Optional Protocol, *supra* note 80.
[79] *Id.*

some circumstances even higher) any recruitment to armed forces below that age should be seen as lacking properly cognisant consent.[80] Moreover having in mind that child soldiers are not simply enlisted and recruited, but because of their still under-developed sense of fear, they are often urged into engagement in war combat and even into committing war crimes.[81]

Article 4 of the Optional Protocol to the CRC is an important advance as it extends the prohibition to non-state armed group, making for them illegal "under any circumstances, to recruit or use in hostilities persons under the age of eighteen."[82] Article 6 of the Optional Protocol demands that states take all feasible measures to ensure that children recruited or used in hostilities are demobilized and accord all appropriate assistance for their physical and psychological recovery and social re-integration.

Article 8 (2) (xxvi) of the Rome Statute for the ICC classified "conscripting or enlisting children under the age of fifteen into the national armed forces or using them to participate actively in hostilities"[83] as a war crime both in international and in internal armed conflict. The establishment of the ICC provided an independent judicial mechanism of accountability for this crime. In January 2002 the Special Court for Sierra Leone was established by an agreement between the UN and the government of Sierra Leone. Article 4(c) of its Statute incorporates *mot-a-mot* the same war crime from the Rome Statute of the ICC. In a further advancement of the criminalization of the use of children in armed forces, on May 31, 2004 in the mentioned above case *Prosecutor v. Norman* the SCSL stated even that the enlisting of child soldiers had been prohibited in customary international law and subject of individual criminal responsibility even before the adoption of the ICC Statute (July 1998), effectively from the beginning of the Special Court for Sierra Leone jurisdiction in November 1996.

7. *Conclusion*

This chapter presents the deficiencies in protecting children in time of war and in time of peace and demonstrates how the child-related IHL and HRL can overlap. It argues that states in time of armed conflict should not "forget" about broader children's rights and principles, developed in HRL. There is a merger of provisions, a merger of situations, a merger of scope of protection – in total, a merger

---

[80] *See* also Matthew Happold, Child Soldiers in International Law (2005).
[81] *See* more analysis in Peter Singer, Child Soldiers: Legal and Military Challenges in Confronting a Global Phenomenon (2005).
[82] Optional Protocol, *supra* note 80.
[83] Rome Statute, *supra* note 4.

of norms and rules applicable to all circumstances concerning children. But also there are differences between the two bodies of law: different *opinio juris*, different procedures, different targets, different monitoring and enforcement capacities. Both need to be kept in mind.

As far as children continue to suffer tremendously both in time of war and in time of peace, it is highly necessary to adopt a cumulative application of both IHL and HRL when children are concerned. Exactly because children are most vulnerable, any action should take into account their best interest, and the approach should be inclusive, rather than exclusive. The protection of children needs to be based not only on mutual recognition, but also on mutual re-enforcement of the norms and procedures of IHL and HRL.

The IHL community – military lawyers, strategists, planners, army officers – should accept the natural limits of IHL and not resist the incorporation of a child-rights approach from the CRC and the rest of HRL, when they make decisions or train soldiers. There is certainly further space for more effective implementation of IHL by all states, through the ratification and enforcement of the APs, and not contesting areas of application of IHL by narrowing the definition of non-international armed conflict, or discriminating the protection strictly to certain groups of civilians, but not to others. Apart from implementation of existing law, if there is a desire and commitment for further codification – a future conference on IHL may try to fill still existing gaps and adopt a "Fifth Convention" on the protection of various vulnerable groups within the civilian population.

The HRL community – activists, parliamentarians, diplomats, international legal scholars – should double their efforts to demand full application of the CRC principles of child protection. Human Rights and Children's NGOs should be further empowered through recognition, facilitation, and grants. Prosecutors, defense lawyers, and judges should follow from the emerging precedents and inject further child-oriented culture into the practice of international and domestic tribunals. The United Nations can think about the feasibility of establishing an independent body to monitor children's rights, particularly in time of armed conflict, but also, and not less important – during the long and hard years of post-conflict peacebuilding.

A fruitful exchange of child-related provisions and approaches between IHL and HRL can be instrumental to end notorious and criminal practices, such as recruiting child soldiers and disregarding children's suffering in armed conflict, and to promote and provide further measures of protection to help the most vulnerable group of people in all times and in all places – the children.

Chapter XV

Unaccompanied Minors and the Right to Family Reunification in International Humanitarian Law and Human Rights Law: The Iraqi Experience

*Kyriaki Topidi**

1. *Introduction*

> The car stopped at the makeshift checkpoint that cut across the muddy backstreet in western Baghdad. A sentry appeared. "Are you Sunni or Shia?" he barked, waving his Kalashnikov at the driver. "Are you with Zarqawi or the Mahdi army?" "The Mahdi army," the driver said. "Wrong answer," shouted the sentry, almost gleefully. "Get him!" The high metal gate of a nearby house was flung open and four gun-toting males rushed out. They dragged the driver from his vehicle and held a knife to his neck. Quickly and efficiently, the blade was run from ear to ear. "Now you're dead," said a triumphant voice, and their captive crumpled to the ground. Then a moment of stillness before the sound of a woman's voice. "Come inside boys! Your dinner is ready!"[1]

In recent legal history, a comprehensive legal framework has been developed with the intention to promote and protect the needs of unaccompanied children that become refugees or internally displaced persons (IDP) as a result of armed conflict. It would be premature to assume, however, that these developments have fully solved the matter.

Youth, as a social group, are understandably and predictably strongly affected by armed conflict. This negative experience becomes further enhanced for children in situations where they are separated from their families. As a preliminary remark, it should be acknowledged that while the effects of armed conflict are not always discernible and quantifiable in children, they remain present and multi-dimensional

---

* The author is a researcher at the Faculty of Law of the University of Lucerne (Switzerland), attached to the Chair of Comparative and Anglo-American Law.
[1] Michael Howard, *Children of War: The Generation Traumatised by Violence in Iraq*, The Guardian, Feb. 6, 2007.

to such an extent that it would be extremely ambitious for any legal or normative framework to pretend to tackle them holistically.[2]

For those separated from their families, the risk of abuse and exploitation almost mathematically increases. In that sense, the quality of the experiences does not differ fundamentally between unaccompanied IDP or refugee children in that they are both deprived of their primary role model, their parents.[3] In legal terms, however, internally displaced children do not benefit from the same level of protection that the status of refugee affords. The otherwise clear-cut legal distinction between IDPs and refugees appears, nevertheless, increasingly complicated to distinguish in its practice as both 'internal' and 'external' conflicts result often in refugee flows into the neighbouring countries.[4] Although there is no constant pattern in the way that children are affected by each type of conflict, statistically over 20 million children have been displaced by war within and outside their respective countries.[5] This figure serves well the purpose of indicating the size and urgency surrounding child displacement.

Against an admittedly gloomy picture, the aim of this chapter is to discuss the legal aspects of the protection of unaccompanied and separated children from both the viewpoint of international humanitarian law as well as of international human rights law. The main question addressed, through the comparative study of the two legal frameworks, will concern the compatibility and complementarities of the two regimes but also their responsiveness and adequacy for current humanitarian crises. Do the two regimes award similar or contradictory rights? Do they result in the creation of legal gaps? Or do they simply follow radically different orientations?

An ensuing third part of the analysis will attempt to demonstrate empirically the findings of the previous discussion. The field for such application will be the case of Iraq, where armed conflict has caught children for the third time in 20 years and where almost half of the population is under the age of 18.[6] Particular

---

[2] In conflict situations, where families are often torn apart and communities are displaced and divided, youth experience the political, social, economic and psychological effects of the war. These range form sexual abuse, grave psychological trauma to malnutrition, disease and lack of education. *See* United Nations, World Youth Report 2005: Young People Today and in 2015, Department of Economic and Social Affairs 141–152 (Oct. 2005) [hereinafter Word Youth Report 2005].

[3] For a similar view *see* Alain Aeschlimann, Displaced Children – Unaccompanied and Separated Children, Official Statement ICRC, Adding Colour to Peace-International Conference on Children Affected by Armed Conflict, Valencia, (Nov. 5–7, 2003), *available at* www.icrc.org/Web/Eng/siteeng0.nsf/html/64DJ58 (last visited April 2, 2007).

[4] Rachel Harvey, Children and Armed Conflict: A Guide to International Humanitarian and Human Rights Conflict 5 (June 2003) *available at* www.essex.ac.uk/armedcon (last visited April 2, 2007) [hereinafter Harvey].

[5] Harvey, *supra* note 4, at 6.

[6] UNICEF, At a Glance. Iraq, *available at* www.unicef.org/infobycountry/iraq.html (last visited April 3, 2007) [hereinafter At a Glance].

emphasis will be placed on the size and the consequences of the phenomenon of unaccompanied minors in Iraq. Finally, the fourth part of the chapter will conclude on the impact of the available frameworks on the legal standing and actual opportunities of unaccompanied and separated children to mend the rupture in their family ties that war has caused.

2. Protection of Separated Children during Armed Conflict and their Right to Family Reunification: The Current Legal Regime

The protection of displaced children extends primarily in two areas of international law: first, international humanitarian law (IHL) that deals with the rules and means of warfare, including the treatment of civilians in times of war and second, international human rights law (HRL) that seeks to regulate the treatment of individuals by states but is not necessarily restricted to times of peace (therefore also applicable during armed conflict).[7]

The scope *rationae personae* of this chapter extends to two categories of children, as mentioned previously: IDPs and refugees. The first category may be defined as persons under the age of 18 that have fled their home as a result of armed conflict but have chosen to resettle within the territory of their country, while the second category of children for similar reasons have actually crossed the national borders to seek refuge in another country. A third, broader term, 'separated children' encountered in policy documents characterizes the same categories of children but also those that may appear accompanied but in practice the accompanying adult is not able to assume responsibility for their care.[8] The advantage of this wider definition can be summarized in the fact that a larger number of children may benefit from international law protection. The term 'separated children' will only be used in this chapter if there is no substantial difference in the legal status of unaccompanied IDPs and refugee children in relation to the point made each time. Formally, however, and as the following part will show, IDPs are provided less protection by international law due to the fact that they remain under the jurisdiction of their originating state.

---

[7] Harvey, *supra* note 4, at 7.

[8] The concept of "separated children" is used for example by the NGO Save the Children in this sense. (Cf. Save the Children and The Separated Children in Europe Programme Position Paper on Returns and Separated Children (Sept. 2004), at 2 *available at* www.separated-children-europe-programme.org/separated_children/publications/reports/return_paper_final.pdf (last visited April 2, 2007). [hereinafter Save the Children Report]

2.1. International Humanitarian Law Provisions

Geneva Convention IV (GC IV)[9] is specifically relevant to children (and civilians more broadly) when victims of war and offers a net of general protection. Few obligations are imposed on state parties in order to protect children who are separated or orphaned.[10] The major legal weakness of GC IV lies in its scope of application: it applies to inter-state but not to intra-state conflicts.[11] In addition to GC IV, two additional protocols to the Geneva Conventions were adopted in 1997. The first (AP I) updated the rules applicable to the conduct of hostilities[12] while the second (AP II) laid down minimum guarantees specifically for internal conflicts.[13] AP I protects children against indecent assault and requires from states provisions of care and aid.[14] It also sets the minimum age for participation in the armed forces at

---

[9] Geneva Convention IV Relative to the Protection of Civilian Persons in Time of War, Aug. 12, 1949, 75 U.N.T.S. 287 (entered into force Oct. 21, 1956).

[10] Article 24(1) GC IV in particular stipulates: "The Parties to the conflict shall take the necessary measures to ensure that children under fifteen, who are orphaned or are separated from their families as a result of the war, are not left to their own resources, and that their maintenance, the exercise of their religion and their education are facilitated in all circumstances. Their education shall, as far as possible, be entrusted to persons of a similar cultural tradition."

[11] Common Article 3 to all four Geneva Conventions constitutes an exception to this limitation insofar as it obliges parties, even in situations of internal conflicts, to provide limited protection to civilians. It disposes: "In the case of armed conflict not of an international character occurring in the territory of one of the High Contracting Parties, each Party to the conflict shall be bound to apply, as a minimum, the following provisions:

(1) Persons taking no active part in the hostilities, including members of armed forces who *have* laid down their arms and those placed hors de combat by sickness, wounds, detention, or any other cause, shall in all circumstances be treated humanely, without any adverse distinction founded on race, colour, religion or faith, sex, birth or wealth, or any other similar criteria. To this end the following acts are and shall remain prohibited at any time and in any place whatsoever with respect to the above-mentioned persons:

(a) violence to life and person, in particular murder of all kinds, mutilation, cruel treatment and torture;
(b) taking of hostages;
(c) outrages upon personal dignity, in particular humiliating and degrading treatment;
(d) the passing of sentences and the carrying out of executions without previous judgment pronounced by a regularly constituted court, affording all the judicial guarantees which are recognized as indispensable by civilized peoples."

(2) The wounded and sick shall be collected and cared for...."

[12] Protocol Additional to the Geneva Conventions of August 12, 1949, and Relating to the Protection of Victims of International Armed Conflicts, June 8, 1977, 1125 U.N.T.S. 3 (entered into force Dec. 7, 1978) [hereinafter AP I].

[13] Protocol Additional to the Geneva Conventions of August 12, 1949, and Relating to the Protection of Victims of Non-International Armed Conflicts, June 8, 1977, 1125 U.N.T.S. 609 (entered into force Dec. 7, 1978) [hereinafter AP II].

[14] Article 77(1).

15 years old[15] and provides for some juvenile justice guarantees for children who commit a crime connected to warfare.[16]

Two broad categories of situations can be distinguished regarding population movements of children in the context of conflict: cases where children are sent abroad to allied or neutral countries in order to avoid the dangers of hostilities as part of an evacuation scheme and situations where children opt individually and independently to leave their country. Regarding the first case, Article 78 AP I calls for the evacuation of children from war-affected countries but only if compelling reasons impose it,[17] and specifies that separated children shall be reunited with their parents when the danger has passed.[18] It is also stressed that while away, children should continue their education.[19] The interpretation of Article 78(1) suggests that children who are nationals of the party to the conflict carrying out the evacuation are not included and thus the children concerned are those of enemy nationality, of refugees or of stateless persons.[20] At the same time, such an interpretation indicates that for children-nationals of the party to the conflict carrying out the evacuation, arrangements lie at the state's discretion and no specific rule or limitation applies. Forcible transfers from occupied territories are nevertheless prohibited under Article 49 GC IV but the same does not apply to voluntary transfers. Evacuations within occupied territories are possible only for the reasons pertaining to the security of the population or to military necessity. In the same vein, Article 49 (6) GC IV also prohibits the transfer by an occupying power of its own population into territory that it occupies. AP II largely reflects a similar content to AP I, yet is applicable only to the conduct of parties in non-international conflicts. Of particular relevance to

---

[15] Article 77(2) and (3).
[16] Article 77(4) and (5).
[17] Article 78(1) disposes. "No Party to the conflict shall arrange for the evacuation of children, other than its own nationals, to a foreign country except for a temporary evacuation where compelling reasons of the health or medical treatment of the children or, except in occupied territory, their safety, so require. Where the parents or legal guardians can be found, their written consent to such evacuation is required. If these persons cannot be found, the written consent to such evacuation of the persons who by law or custom are primarily responsible for the care of the children is required. Any such evacuation shall be supervised by the Protecting Power in agreement with the Parties concerned, namely, the Party arranging for the evacuation, the Party receiving the children and any Parties whose nationals are being evacuated. In each case, all Parties to the conflict shall take all feasible precautions to avoid endangering the evacuation."
[18] Article 78(3).
[19] Article 78(2).
[20] ICRC, Protocol Additional to the Geneva Conventions of 12 August 1949, and relating to the Protection of Victims of International Conflicts (Protocol I), 8 June 1977 – Commentary, points 3219–3222, *available at* www.icrc.org/ihl.nsf/WebPrint/470–750100–com?OpenDocument (last visited April 3, 2007).

this study is Article 4(3)(b) that stresses once more that "all appropriate steps shall be taken to facilitate the reunion of families temporarily separated."

For 'voluntary' departures of children belonging to the second category, the situation appears more complex. While family separation and family reunification are addressed, IHL provisions do not provide a definition of refugees. Accordingly, the legal status of the unaccompanied minor who crosses the border will depend on which country he or she chooses to flee to.[21]

Children population movements vary according to the situation in the country of departure to the one in the country where refuge is sought. This variation affects the level and kind of legal protection that the child will be afforded. The scope *ratione personae* of GC IV covers in Article 4 the persons, whether caught in conflict or under occupation, found in the hands of a party to the conflict of which they are not nationals. More specifically, it is possible to distinguish four different categories of situations:[22] first, nationals fleeing hostilities in their own state and seeking refuge to another state-party to the conflict are protected under IHL and in particular Article 44 GC IV. Second, for refugees fleeing from a country not involved in a conflict to a country at war with a third state, once more the GC IV applies. The third situation covers refugees who flee to a country not involved in conflict. These individuals are only covered by the 1951 Refugee Convention. Finally, for refugees to a state not involved in international conflict but facing an internal conflict, GC IV (in particular common Article 3) and the AP II, if relevant, apply. Very broadly, to enjoy protection under IHL, and more particularly GC IV, a refugee must flee to a country that is also part to the conflict but if he or she decides to flee to a country which is not involved in any international or internal conflict, the only available protection will be outside the strict remit of IHL, namely the 1951 Convention relating to the status of refugees, which provides narrow protection to children.[23]

2.2. *International Human Rights Law Provisions*

Contrary to IHL that counts a few decades of development of legal protection for children caught in warfare, international human rights law has only recently created legally binding obligations for states with regards to children. The Convention on the Rights of the Child (CRC), adopted in 1989, represents the most

---

[21] Article 78(2) will nevertheless apply to children – asylum seekers, especially regarding their right to continuing education.
[22] For further analysis of the four situations *see* Harvey, *supra* note 4, at 38–39.
[23] Convention relating to the Status of Refugees, adopted on July 28, 1951, 189 U.N.T.S. 150, into force April 22, 1954.

salient component of this evolution.[24] For the purposes of the Convention, a child is defined in Article 1 as "every human being below the age of eighteen years." As the first legally binding international instrument of its kind, it contains a full range of human rights with the accent on the special care and protection that children need in a variety of situations.[25] In this spirit, the Convention embraces four core principles to guide its actions and desired effects: non-discrimination prohibiting any discrimination on the basis of the status of the child being unaccompanied or refugee or asylum seeker,[26] devotion to the best interests of the child for every decision impacting on the child's life,[27] the right to life, survival, and development including protection from violence and exploitation and especially trafficking,[28] and finally respect for the views of the child.[29]

In general terms, the CRC's scope of application is not restricted to the protection of children in times of armed conflict but extends also in times of peace. The only exception to this rule is Article 38 that refers to the absence of a duty of states to protect children during hostilities.[30] The Convention applies to both IDPs and refugee children without discrimination of any kind (Article 2 CRC). This Article echoes Article 22 of the 1951 Refugee Convention whereby refugees must receive the 'same treatment' as nationals in education. Given the congruence of CRC with the 1951 Refugee Convention on this specific point, the former – widely ratified – will guarantee the rights of refugee children in the field of education even when a state has not ratified any refugee treaty.

More relevant to the topic of this chapter is Article 39 CRC that although related to the post-conflict care of children, disposes that "States Parties shall take all appropriate measures to promote physical and psychological recovery and social integration of a child victim of... armed conflict." The Article in question touches upon one of the most problematic areas or child displacement but does so in a fairly general manner.

---

[24] Convention on the Rights of the Child, G.A. Res. 44/25, Annex, 44 U.N. GAOR Supp. No. 49, U.N. Doc. A/44/49 (Nov. 20, 1989) (entered into force Sept. 2, 1990).

[25] The Preamble of the CRC clearly states in that respect that "as indicated in the Declaration of the Rights of the Child [adopted by the General Assembly on November 20, 1959], 'the child, by reason of his physical and mental immaturity, needs special safeguards and care, including appropriate legal protection, before as well as after birth'."

[26] Article 2.

[27] Article 3.

[28] Article 6.

[29] Article 12.

[30] This provision also retains the age of 15 years as a threshold for the recruitment of child soldiers and their direct participation in hostilities. Article 38(1) nevertheless contains a "bridging" provision with IHL legal texts by requiring the "respect for rules of IHL...which are relevant to the child."

Other provisions of the CRC, albeit not specifically related to armed conflict situations, address the distinctiveness of the case of unaccompanied minors and their right to family reunification in the following way: Article 9 CRC imposes a duty on state parties to prevent the separation of a child form his/her parents against their will, as a pre-emptive measure, with the exception of cases where this separation is necessary for the best interests of the child, reminiscing of Article 78 AP I under IHL (i.e. in cases of abuse or neglect). Complementing Article 9, Article 10 adds that when separation eventually occurs, any application by a child of his/her parent(s) to enter or leave a state party for the purposes of family reunification should be dealt with in a "positive, human and expeditious manner" and with "no adverse consequences for the applicants and for the members of their family." Once more, reference and comparison with Article 4(3)(b) AP II cannot be easily escaped.

Furthermore, the CRC reiterates the quest for special protection and assistance by states parties in Article 20 but specifically and explicitly for children "temporarily or permanently deprived of his or her family environment." This constitutes a crucial provision that is rich in content and heavy in obligations for states parties as it concerns a vast number of areas where it can find application.[31] Alternative care, in accordance with national laws, should be provided by state parties (Article 20(2) of CRC) with due regard to the child's ethnic, religious, cultural, and linguistic background (Article 20(3) of CRC). With respect to unaccompanied children who are at the same time seeking refugee status, Article 22(1) of CRC insists on the need for them to receive appropriate protection and humanitarian assistance in accordance with the rights set forth in the Convention, particularly in their attempts to reunite with families (Article 22(2) of CRC). Further state obligations *vis-à-vis* these children also cover the right to an adequate standard of living (Article 27 of CRC) appropriate to their physical, moral, and mental development, full access to education in accordance with Articles 28, 29(1)(c), 30 and 32 of CRC without any discrimination, in particular for girls as well as prevention of trafficking, abuse, violence, and exploitation (Articles 34–36 of CRC), read in conjunction with Article 20 of CRC.

At the level of implementation, the CRC, despite its wide ratification, has not been respected, as anticipated, by state parties. This often results in a *de facto* situation where the rights of children are rated as secondary concerns against the primary concern of survival, as the case study on Iraq will further demonstrate below.

---

[31] *See* point 3 of this chapter for a fuller discussion of the type of issues brought up in policy documents where Article 20 CRC can be implemented.

2.3. International Policy Considerations and Developments: Translating Children's 'Needs' into 'Rights'

A significant number of policy documents, some of them with declared persuasive force, have stimulated the debate on the need of enhanced legal protection for children, particularly those separated from their families, in warfare. They have been called to provide some background to the existing legal provisions, indicating the appropriate interpretation and extent that these norms should be given. While it is beyond the scope of this Article to provide a full account of all these documents, some of them merit special mention due to their impact and/or content.

The Machel Report, following GA resolution 48/157 of December 20, 1993 was the first contemporary comprehensive assessment of the human rights situation of war-affected children.[32] The concerns of unaccompanied children were covered in the report with emphasis put on the misperceptions surrounding these children as being available for adoption before any serious efforts are made to reunite them with their families. The report stressed the need to establish an agency in order to protect these children against any attempt to damage their family links.[33] Very pertinently, the Machel Report also recommended the creation of the position of a Special Representative of the Secretary General for children and armed conflict, which was later followed.[34] In parallel, it should be noted that in 1992 the Representative of the Secretary General on Internally Displaced Persons was also appointed at the request of the United Nations Commission on Human Rights.

In the light of the highlighted nature of the topic of children and armed conflict, six Security Council resolutions were subsequently adopted: resolution 1261, affirming that the protection of children caught in armed conflict was clearly a topic within the remit of action of the Security Council,[35] resolution 1314 that renewed calls for action and pointed at systematic violations of IHL and HRL,[36] resolution 1379 that established a link between armed conflict and HIV/AIDS and incited to the drawing of a list of state parties that use children as soldiers in violation of their international obligations,[37] resolution 1460 that pushed towards the actual implementation of the available tools and recommendations calling for an 'era of application' that even today remains disturbingly limited.[38] Additionally, resolution 1539 urged the Secretary General to devise an action-plan for systematic

---

[32] The Secretary-General, Report of the Expert of the Secretary-General: Impact of Armed Conflict on Children, delivered to the General Assembly, U.N. Doc. A/51/306, para. 7 (Aug. 26, 1996) (prepared by Graça Machel).
[33] Id. paras 69–74.
[34] G.A. Res. 51/77, U.N. Doc A/51/49, para. 35 (Dec. 12, 1996).
[35] S.C. Res. 1261, U.N. Doc. S/RES/1261 (Aug. 30, 1999).
[36] S.C. Res. 1314, U.N. Doc. S/RES/1314 (Aug. 11, 2000).
[37] S.C. Res. 1379, U.N. Doc. S/RES/1379 (Nov. 21, 2001).
[38] S.C. Res. 1460, U.N. Doc. S/RES/1460 (Jan. 30, 2003).

monitoring as well as a monitoring mechanism on the situation of children[39] and finally resolution 1612 in fact created this monitoring and reporting mechanism along with a Working Group of the Council on children and armed conflict.[40]

As for remedial measures for violations of IHL and HRL in this area, international practice so far retains reliance on post-conflict prosecutions within international *ad hoc* tribunals, as the examples of Rwanda and former Yugoslavia show.[41] The degree of efficiency of this solution is of course open to debate, especially when applied to children. Further to these general texts, more specific policy documents replicated separately the situation of unaccompanied IDPs and refugee children with the appropriate recommendations.

2.3.1. *Internally Displaced Unaccompanied Children*

If "it is fair to say that the international community is more inclined than it is prepared, both normatively and institutionally, to respond effectively to the phenomenon of internal displacement,"[42] the effectiveness of the current provisions is limited in providing adequate levels of protection and assistance to such individuals. In order to compensate for this void, a set of Guiding Principles were devised by the United Nations addressing the specific needs of children IDPs. Intended as a persuasive statement, these principles refer to internally displaced children as beneficiaries of special assistance and protection due to the specificity of their needs, reproducing the contents of CRC.[43] More specifically, however, they protect these children against attacks to their physical and mental integrity,[44] prohibit their recruitment in hostilities,[45] and impose an obligation on state authorities to guarantee their education.[46] Principles 16, 17, and 28 respectively organize tracing of family, prevention of separation to the extent possible, and, in cases of separation, return and resettlement. Despite complementing the current legal frameworks,

---

[39] S.C. Res. 1539, U.N. Doc. S/RES/1539 (April 22, 2004).

[40] S.C. Res. 1612, U.N. Doc. S/RES/1612 (July 26, 2005). Priority in monitoring would receive the following violations: recruiting and use of child soldiers, killing and maiming children, rape and other forms of grave sexual violence against children, illicit exploitation of natural resources, abduction of children and denial of humanitarian access to children. (*see* Children and Armed Conflict: Report of the Secretary-General, U.N. SCOR, 58th Sess., U.N. Doc. A/58/546-S/2003/1053 Corr. 2 (April 19, 2004)).

[41] Harvey, *supra* note 4, at 18.

[42] ESCOC, Comm'n on Hum. Rts., Guiding Principles on Internal Displacement, Addendum to the Report of the Representative of the Secretary-General, Submitted Pursuant to Commission Resolution 1997/39, U.N. Doc. E/CN.4/1998/53/Add.2, princ. 4 (Feb. 11, 1998) [hereinafter Guiding Principles on Internal Displacement].

[43] *Id.* Princ. 4 (2).

[44] *Id.* Princ. 11.

[45] *Id.* Princ. 13.

[46] *Id.* Princ. 23.

these guidelines have not been embraced by the states parties concerned by them, partly by reason of their weaker legal force and partly due to the width of the obligations they impose.

2.3.1.1 *Unaccompanied Children Seeking Asylum*
Similar guidelines were devised for separated children seeking asylum.[47] Drafted in accordance with the CRC, these guidelines parallel Article 3(1) of CRC on the absolute prioritization of the best interests of the child. The added value of these guidelines lays in the detailed analysis of the process of accommodating claims from unaccompanied children, from identification procedures including age assessment,[48] to registration by means of a child-friendly interview[49] and then to the appointment of an adviser/guardian able to represent the child's best interest and not jeopardize its fragile situation (e.g. by further abusing it),[50] the collection of information relevant to the child,[51] and finally attempts to trace the family.[52]

Regarding the asylum application *per se*, it is stressed that children seeking asylum should not be kept in detention, especially if unaccompanied.[53] In line with the CRC, the guidelines also address issues of access to health care and education.[54] Such children should benefit also from legal representation for their claim and their applications should be given priority. A case-by-case examination of each claim should take into consideration the particular circumstances of each child's story in a way to fall, wherever possible, within the scope of the 1951 Refugee Convention, so as to be awarded the desired refugee status.[55]

The final stage of such applications concerns the identification of a durable solution. Children are found either to qualify for asylum, in which case they are locally integrated or resettled in a third country on the grounds of family reunification,[56] or they are refused asylum, having therefore to return in their country of origin provided that their family has been traced, a suitable care-giver been found and the return is considered as in the best interest of the child.[57]

---

[47] UNHCR, Guidelines on Policies and Procedures in Dealing with Unaccompanied Children Seeking Asylum (Feb. 1997) [hereinafter Guidelines on Policies and Procedures in Dealing with Unaccompanied Children Seeking Asylum].
[48] *Id.* points 5.1 to 5.5. Two crucial stages are proposed: first finding out whether the child is in fact unaccompanied and second determining whether he or she is indeed an asylum seeker.
[49] *Id.* point 5.6.
[50] *Id.* point 5.7.
[51] *Id.* points 5.8–5.11.
[52] *Id.* point 5.17.
[53] *Id.* points 7.6-7.8.
[54] *Id.* points 7.9–7.14.
[55] *Id.* points 8.6-8.10.
[56] *Id.* point 9.1.
[57] *Id.* points 9.2–10.14.

In practice, a number of children never access asylum procedures either because they are ill-advised or unaware of the procedures. Even if they manage to lodge an application, a limited number of them are recognized as refugees, at least in European states, although there are equally few examples of enforced returns of child asylum seekers.[58] Status determination procedures in host countries also play a role against their recognition as refugees as they do not take into account the specific understanding and conception of fear of prosecution of unaccompanied children.[59] As for the preferred durable solution, the majority of asylum seekers remain in the country of asylum often with an indeterminate status lacking any long-term security.[60]

C. *Iraq's Displaced and Refugee Children: Case Study of a Humanitarian Crisis*

> I'm an 11-year-old boy who has never been to school – so I can neither read nor write. For the past two years I have been living on the streets of Baghdad, surviving on leftovers that I scavenge from garbage or by stealing from people and shop-lifting.... I'm an orphan and don't know who my parents are. Nor do I know if they are alive or dead. I was taken into an orphanage when I was four years old and since then different people have been taking care of me. They were not good people. During [former president Saddam Hussein] Saddam's time, police officers sometimes used to come and have sex with older boys. I ran away from the orphanage during the [US-led] invasion with another three boys in 2003. But three months ago they abandoned me as they discovered the world of drugs.[61]

According to United Nations estimates, 2.3 million Iraqis have fled violence in their country. The vast majority, around 1.8 million, have sought refuge in neighbouring countries such as Lebanon, Syria, and Jordan, while around 500,000 were internally

---

[58] Kate Halvorsen, *Separated Children Seeking Asylum: The Most Vulnerable of All*, 12 Forced Migration 34–36 (2002), *available at* www.fmreview.org/FMRpdfs/FMR12/fmr12.12.pdf (last visited Mar. 31, 2007) [hereinafter Halvorsen].

[59] These procedures often neglect for example the child's degree of mental development and maturity or the diverse expressions of fear and maltreatment penalizing the child whenever there is hesitation on the credibility of its story. (Cf. UNHCR, Refugee Children-Guidelines on Protection and Care (1994), in particular chapter 8.) Guidelines expressly suggest that in case of uncertainty the child should be given the benefit of the doubt (Cf. Committee on the Rights of the Child, General Comment No. 6: Treatment of Unaccompanied and Separated Children Outside Their Country of Origin, para. 31(i), U.N. Doc. CRC/GC/2005/6 (Sept. 1, 2005).

[60] Halvorsen., *supra* note 58 at 36.

[61] UN Office for the Coordination of Humanitarian Affairs, IRAQ: Fadhel, Iraq "Stealing Is the Easiest Job in Iraq Today", *available at* www.irinnews.org/HOVReport.aspx?ReportId=70046 (last visited Mar. 31, 2007).

displaced.⁶² Neither of these three countries are state parties to the 1951 Refugee Convention, a fact that along with the reduced support provided from international organisations and agencies underlines the difficulties faced by Iraqis, among them children as well, in their attempts to escape war. This sense of powerlessness reflected in the actions and omissions of local actors, the international community and donors has led to the politicization and militarization of any humanitarian activity by both Iraqi and international actors involved.⁶³

The effects of violence and insurgency on children have not been quantified and so far no corresponding information seems available.⁶⁴ It is hence very difficult at this stage of the conflict to assess the situation of unaccompanied children both within and outside Iraq. The United Nations High Commissioner for Refugees (UNHCR) is facing an escalating humanitarian crisis with fewer and fewer resources at its disposal. Moderate calculations by the Iraqi Ministry of Displacement and Migration suggest that about 40,000 children have been displaced within Iraq due to the ongoing sectarian violence resulting in their losing access to schools and medical care.⁶⁵ With regard to separated children, there are reports of individual cases which confirm diagnosis of clinical depression due to displacement.⁶⁶ Health assessment in the country has also indicated signs of acute malnutrition in children. Some efforts are geared towards the reactivation of the primary education system so as to allow displaced minors to overcome their security concerns and in a sense return to 'normality'⁶⁷ but the overall lack of security renders this task just as challenging.

---

⁶² Refugees International, Iraq: The World's Fastest Growing Refugee Crisis (Jan. 16, 2007), *available at* www.refugeesinternational.org/content/Article/detail/9679&output=printer (last visited April 1, 2007). Figures on IDPs and refugees vary. There are reports for example referring to over three million Iraqis being IDPs and refugees (cf. Andrew Harper, *Iraq's Neglected Humanitarian Crisis*, 27 Forced Migration 61, 61–63 (2007), *available at* http://www.fmreview.org/FMRpdfs/FMR27/42.pdf (last visited April 1, 2007)). The figures are therefore only used indicatively in this context.

⁶³ For a detailed discussion of the perceptions of humanitarianism in Iraq along with the crisis in the problematic donor environment *see* Greg Hansen, Coming to Terms with the Humanitarian Imperative in Iraq: Humanitarian Agenda 2015, Briefing Paper, Feinstein International Center, 2007, *available at* fic.tufts.edu/downloads/HA2015IraqBriefingPaper.pdf (last visited April 1, 2007). It is in fact interesting to note that the void of the appropriately scaled humanitarian presence is today filled by militias and parties that take up social functions in order to secure support and legitimacy (*Id.* at 7).

⁶⁴ Children and Armed Conflict: Report of the Secretary-General, U.N. SCOR, 61st Sess., U.N. Doc. A/61/529–S/2006/826, para. 41 (Oct. 26, 2006).

⁶⁵ UN Office for the Coordination of Humanitarian Affairs, IRAQ: Displaced Children Suffer Depression and Poor Health, *available at* www.irinnews.org/report.aspx?reportid=27074 (last visited Mar. 31, 2007).

⁶⁶ *Id.* the case of 12–year old Barek Ahmed.

⁶⁷ UNICEF Reports reflect the organization's concerns about education and health deterioration. *See* for example, At a Glance, *supra* note 6.

The displacement cycle is full of risk factors that affect each separated child in an individualized way. The limits of the law are hence obvious but still, faced with a humanitarian crisis of the size and type of Iraq, it is not difficult to single out the most crucial parameters that may influence (negatively) the already burdensome experience of displacement. It is noteworthy that most of these 'risk factors' equally concern refugee as well as internally displaced and returnee children, without major differences. These factors, as singled out recently cover all stages of displacement in most humanitarian crises situations. They also give a useful indication of the points where the implementation of IHL and HRL frameworks is failing.[68]

The first item on this list concerns the principle of best interests of the child which, although firmly established in legal terms, suffers from weak implementation. Individual states apply the principle relatively successfully in domestic cases but substantially more restrictively in immigration cases and durable situation decisions.[69] Registration and documentation issues constitute on the other hand one of the omissions of the system, as also mentioned previously. Mechanisms of identification of unaccompanied and separated children are also lacking. This last point, together with access to the appropriate legal and institutional mechanisms of the host state for refugee children, demand a certain degree of participation and good will on behalf of the states concerned. IHL and HRL can only influence that in a limited way by encouraging states to comply with the relevant legal texts and by putting some pressure on them to follow the rule of law and the available guidelines within the confines of international law and sovereignty principles broadly understood. In that respect, it is indicative for instance that the whole asylum process in most cases does not adapt to the specificities of unaccompanied children who even at that stage continue to face an increased risk of abuse and trafficking, despite the existence of comprehensive international legislation on the matter. All the above factors and constraints have found a clear application in the Iraqi case.

The current legal framework fails also to address post-conflict reintegration of Iraqi separated children who manage to return to their families. Incidents of sexual exploitation may still occur even on the way home.[70] Female children refugees are particularly prone to sexual exploitation by a variety of perpetrators such as border

---

[68] The factors outlined below are sourced from the recent observations of the Executive Committee of the High Commissioner's Programme, Children at Risk, U.N. Doc. EC/58/SC/CRP.7, (Feb. 22, 2007), at 3–4. See also UNHCR's 5 Priorities for Girls and Boys of Concern to UNHCR, *available at* www.unhcr.org/protect/PROTECTION/4398146f2.pdf (last visited Mar. 1, 2007).

[69] Save the Children Report, *supra* note 8, at 4. This report has observed this differentiation of legal standards in the context of several European Union member states.

[70] It should be noted that voluntary repatriation of Iraqis has significantly reduced in 2006 and originated primarily from Turkey and Iran. The facilitation and promotion of this solution is not favoured at the moment by the UNHCR due to instability in the country. (Cf. UNHCR, Resettlement of Iraqi Refugees, (Mar. 17, 2007) *available a:* www.unhcr.org/home/RSDLEGAL/45b626f04.pdf (last visited Mar.30, 2007), at 3 [hereinafter Resettlement of Iraqi Refugees 2007].

guards, humanitarian aid workers or fellow refugees.[71] Returnee figures suggest that the issue of resettlement in Iraq remains largely unresolved.[72] As a result, many refugees end up in internal displacement due to a lack of infrastructure such as housing, property disputes and insufficient livelihood means.[73] It is therefore paradoxical and indeed one of the perverse effects of the conflicts of law and politics, that although IHL and HRL standards encourage the return of children refugees and IDPs to their homeland as well as the subsequent reunification with their family left behind, that in the case of Iraq international organizations such as the UNHCR advise against such a return.[74] The low level of security is advanced as the main reason for the postponement as Iraqi authorities are for the moment unable to provide protection to their citizens, let alone the vulnerable category of separated children.

In the same context, one of the strongest concerns for separated children is education. The Iraqi case is particularly telling of the low level of access to education for both male and female children. Reconstruction efforts in post-conflict settings generally give precedence to primary school education but by no means cover the extended needs of these children.[75] While refugee children may in some cases profit from quality education that would not be otherwise available to them in host countries, internally displaced children face challenges in the educational context that could often amount to corporal punishment, exploitative labour conditions or physical abuse.[76] In the same vein, exclusive reliance on humanitarian aid – clearly insufficient in Iraq – extended stays in camps and poor health services darken even

---

[71] For a more detailed analysis of the risks of sexual exploitation *see* World Youth Report 2005, *supra* note 2, at 159–162.

[72] For 2005, an estimated 196,000 IDPs have returned. (Cf. International Displacement Monitoring Centre, IRAQ: Sectarian Violence, Military Operations Spark New Displacement, as Humanitarian Access Deteriorates (May 23, 2006), *available at* www.internal-displacement.org/ 8025708F004BE3B1/(httpInfoFiles)/5Ff5134F8672E698C125717700492CAC/$file/Iraq%20Overview%2023%20May%202006.pdf (last visited Mar. 30, 2007), at 216) [hereinafter Sectarian Violence, Military Operations Spark New Displacement]. As for refugees, the number suggested for 2005 by the UNHCR is 56,200 (Cf. UNHCR, 2005 Global Refugee Trends, 4, *available at* www.unhcr.org/statistics/STATISTICS/4486ceb12.pdf, (June 2006) (last visited April 4, 2007).

[73] Sectarian Violence, Military Operations Spark New Displacement, at 217. The main relevant "hard" and "soft" law provisions pointing at return and family reunification are Article 4(3) (b) AP II and Article 22(2) CRC on assistance for family reunification and principle 28 of the Guiding Principles on Internal Displacement (cf. *supra* note 40) as well as points 9.2–10.14 of the Guidelines on Policies and Procedures in Dealing with Unaccompanied Children seeking Asylum (cf. *supra* note 45).

[74] *Id.* at 231.

[75] *Id.* at 166.

[76] UNCHR, Return Advisory and Position on International Protection Needs of Iraqis outside Iraq, *available at* www.unhcr.org/cgi-bin/texis/vtx/home/opendoc.pdf?tbl=SUBSITES&id=45a252d92 (last visited Mar. 31, 2007) [hereinafter Return Advisory 2006].

further the picture for these children. Last but not least on the list of challenges that these children face, applicable mostly to refugee children, is the risk of discrimination and xenophobic treatment in countries of asylum and/or resettlement.[77] This is so despite the CRC provisions against discrimination (Article 2).

Durable solutions, although legally guided by the principles of family unity, are not always available to the same degree to all children concerned. Voluntary repatriation as a gateway to a return to normal life, not recommended at the moment concerning Iraq, prolongs the social and cultural rupture for refugee and IDP unaccompanied minors. Specifically for IDPs, repatriation should be understood as internal relocation from the region of their origin to another more secure region, usually from Southern or Central Iraq to Northern Iraq. A relocation of this kind, however, still does not address the threats of persecution or security risks allowing the desired return to normality.[78] Local settlement, on the other hand, requires careful planning and enhanced assistance to access food, health services and education, elements that are currently not available in Iraq. Further, resettlement involves the greatest upheaval, in particular if it is required for family reunification purposes. Iraqi refugees continue to be the victims of their situation in that respect as the international community as a whole and individual states separately largely resist their calls for help, leaving them in many cases with no options and alternatives.

The capacity of the family to receive a returning child is not taken into account, especially in cases where the family invested in sending the child abroad and relies on its income-earning capacity.[79] The legal framework clearly prioritizes family reunification but arguably fails to address its complexities. Factors such as the child's level of integration in the host country, for children refugees, is often determinant as the longer the time spent in the host country the more limited memories exist of the home country. Similarly, the possibility of family reunification should not come at the expense of any application of residence in a host country, precisely because a multitude of reasons affect a final decision to return. The need of separated

---

[77] According to the UNHCR, Syria, Jordan and Turkey are the countries of first asylum while Lebanon and Egypt are countries of secondary movement for Iraqis. The estimates of both the UNHCR and NGOs report 500.000–700.000 Iraqi refugees in Jordan and Syria, 10.000 in Turkey, 20.000–40.000 in Lebanon and 20.000–60.000 in Egypt (Cf. Resettlement of Iraqi Refugees 2007, *supra* note 58, at 1, 10). There are no age-specific statistics on resettlement for unaccompanied children available for the post 2003 period. Between 2001–2003, however, Iraq ranked third in the case of unaccompanied and separated children with 3.267 asylum applications to industrialized countries showing a preference for the U.K., Germany, the Netherlands, Switzerland, Sweden, Denmark and Greece. (Cf. UNHCR, Trends in Unaccompanied and Separated Children Seeking Asylum in Industrialized Countries, 2001–2003, July 2004, *available at* www.unhcr.org/statistics/STATISTICS/40f646444.pdf, at 11–14 (last visited Mar. 30, 2007)).

[78] *See* Return Advisory 2006, *supra* note 74 at 3.

[79] Save the Children Report, *supra* note 8, at 6.

children to be consulted and informed of the durable situation most appropriate for them remains a 'need' that has not been translated into a 'right' in practice, for Iraq as well as elsewhere.

While vulnerability is difficult to assess and compare, it cannot be easily disputed that unaccompanied children in Iraq face continuous challenges and threats. Resettlement is often perceived by Iraqis as the only available option because of fear to return home concerned about the possible revenge measures that might be carried against them. Resettlement rates remain nevertheless low.[80]

D. *Unaccompanied Children and Family Reunification: Evolving Legal Regime or Stagnant Reality?*

The experience of armed conflicts in the four corners of the globe has amply demonstrated that family separation is the beginning of a vicious circle that most often leads to child soldier recruitment, sexual exploitation, isolation from education and even significant deterioration of health.[81] There is reduced empirical documentation on the application of norms on family separation and its effects, despite an increasing number of legal texts and policy guidelines. This is partly due to cultural factors that influence reporting, as in many cases separation from the child's parents is not perceived as such if care is dispensed by the wider family. It is also due to the diversity of state responses to the issue of unaccompanied or separated children, in terms of content of rights, procedures of protection and asylum rules. At the same time, there is a generalized lack of effective methods of data collection that becomes relevant at various stages of the process, especially for undocumented children.[82]

The cardinal principle of the child's best interest despite being legally guaranteed cannot be easily translated into operational guidelines useful in decision-making and yet must be respected during the whole cycle of displacement.[83] But even when the implementation of certain rules is more obvious, as for instance in the case of the special duty of assistance provided to unaccompanied minors, it may

---

[80] UNHCR was able to resettle around 1,500 Iraqis in the last three years. (cf. Refugees International, Iraqi Refugees: Resettle the Most Vulnerable, Jan. 16, 2007, *available at* www.refugeesinternational.org/content/Article/detail/9774 (last visited Mar. 30, 2007)).

[81] For a similar comment in the context of the Sudanese conflict *see* Una Mc Cauley, *Separated Children in South Sudan*, 24 Forced Migration 52–55 (2005), *available at* www.fmreview.org/FMRpdfs/FMR24/FMR2429.pdf (last visited Mar. 30, 2007).

[82] Sarah Maloney, *Transatlantic Workshop on 'Unaccompanied/Separated Children: Comparative Policies and Practices in North America and Europe'*, 13 Journal of Refugee Studies 102, 105 (2000).

[83] *Id.* at 106.

materialize only through administrative regulations, influencing thus the legal intensity of the final outcome.[84]

From a strictly legal perspective, IHL and HRL provisions are largely harmonized and harmonizing with few exceptions. They suffer nevertheless from low implementation. Significant reliance is placed on the guidelines that fill in the gaps of the legislative frameworks. These guidelines, even if put forward as 'soft law' tools, tend to loose some of their persuasive force as their application depends on the goodwill of states. A typical illustration in this context is family tracing. There are no standardized models of follow-up for separated as well as reunified children in cases where immediate protection concerns arise. International standards on archiving the records of unaccompanied children could for example significantly raise the rate of success of family reunification.[85]

On the whole, it is not surprising to note the recurrent observation of experts in international *fora* of the increasing number of children in the precarious situation of being left alone as a consequence of violence or armed conflict.[86] While the available legal standards demonstrate coherence, a number of state parties have not always managed to follow the dynamics and evolutionary progress of these standards in each set of circumstances. The content of their legal obligations towards separated children is not in itself inadequate but it is rather the failure of states to adjust and even develop their protection mechanisms to and beyond the given standards, if this is required, that produces mediocre results.[87] This could explain also why Iraq today presents itself as such a dramatic humanitarian crisis as far as unaccompanied minors are concerned.

Moreover, the obligations deriving from GC IV, the Additional Protocols as well as the CRC have positive features.[88] State parties in most cases and for different reasons sidestep them and restrict themselves to a formalized negative reading of their duties. These positive obligations should range from measures preventing family separation to the extent possible, to identifying and protecting unaccompanied and separated children both within and at the borders of a state and finally to reunifying these children with their families, affording them a protection shield that follows them throughout their unpleasant and traumatizing cycle of displacement. It is perhaps in the acceptance of these positive duties that the stigma of family separation can be eliminated for some of these children.

---

[84] *Id.*
[85] Kirk Felsman, Alebel Derib & Stirling Cummings, *The Need for International Standards on Archiving the Records of Unaccompanied Children*, 15 Forced Migration 7 (2002), *available at* www.fmreview.org/FMRpdfs/FMR15/fmr15.2.pdf (last visited Mar. 30, 2007)
[86] Committee for the Rights of the Child, *General Comment No. 6*, 2005, at point 2.
[87] *Id.* at point 4.
[88] *Id.* at points 12–15.

Chapter XVI

Crossing Legal Borders: The Interface Between Refugee Law, Human Rights Law and Humanitarian Law in the "International Protection" of Refugees

Alice Edwards[*]

1. *Introduction*

International refugee law (IRL), international human rights law (IHRL), and international humanitarian law (IHL) are each discreet as well as inter-connected areas of international law. The 1951 Convention relating to the Status of Refugees[1] (1951 Convention) is commonly viewed by scholars, practitioners, and governments alike as the centerpiece of refugee protection, although it is increasingly accepted that it is supplemented by IHRL. In contrast, less attention has been paid to the role of IHL in displacement situations outside a few specific contexts, yet displacement is frequently the result of armed conflict and occupation, alongside persecution and other serious human rights violations. As a departure point, Article 5 of the 1951 Convention clearly allows for the application of other instruments to refugees that confer "rights and benefits."[2]

This article seeks to clarify the inter-relationship between IRL and these other branches of international law in attempting to understand their role in the "international protection" of refugees. It asks: What is "international protection" and where do refugee law, human rights law, and humanitarian law fit, if at all, within this legal concept? Divided into three parts, this article starts with an overview of the interface between IRL and IHRL, followed by IRL and IHL, while the third part takes a non-exhaustive look at the concept of "international protection" as it

---

[*] Alice Edwards is Lecturer at the University of Nottingham (United Kingdom). I would like to thank Fabrício Araújo Prado for his wonderful assistance with the research for this piece.
[1] 189 U.N.T.S. 137; entered into force April 22, 1954 [hereinafter 1951 Convention].
[2] *Id.* Article 5: "Nothing in this Convention shall be deemed to impair any rights and benefits granted by a Contracting State to refugees apart from this Convention."

has been applied in a range of contexts and the role played by these three distinct areas of law in giving meaning to it.

Throughout this article the definition of a "refugee" contained in Article 1 of the 1951 Convention as amended by its 1967 Protocol[3] is adopted, as well as wider definitions elaborated under applicable regional instruments. Article 1A(2) of the 1951 Convention as amended by the 1967 Protocol defines a "refugee" as any person:

> with a well-founded fear of being persecuted for reasons of race, religion, nationality, membership of a particular social group or political opinion who is outside the country of his [or her] nationality and is unable or, owing to such fear, is unwilling to avail himself [or herself] of the protection of that country.

Status may be denied on a number of grounds, including if there are serious reasons for considering that the applicant has committed a war crime or crime against humanity.[4] An almost identical definition of a "refugee" is incorporated in the 1950 Statute of the Office of the United Nations High Commissioner for Refugees[5] (UNHCR), with the exception that "membership of a particular social group" is not included as an asylum ground.[6]

In the African context, the definition of a "refugee" was expanded in 1969 to include persons who are compelled to leave their place of habitual residence due to "external aggression, occupation, foreign domination or events seriously disturbing public order in either the whole or part of the territory."[7] Likewise, the 1984 Cartagena Declaration recommends an enlargement of the definition of a "refugee" in the 1951 Convention to incorporate "persons who have fled their country because their lives, safety or freedom have been threatened by generalized violence, foreign aggression, internal conflicts, massive violation of human rights or other circumstances which have seriously disturbed public order."[8]

---

[3] 606 U.N.T.S. 267; entered into force Oct. 4, 1967.
[4] Article 1F(a), 1951 Convention, *supra* note 1.
[5] G.A. Res. 428(V), U.N. Doc. A/1775 (Dec. 14, 1950).
[6] Article 6(A)(ii), UNHCR Statute.
[7] Article 1(2), Organisation of African Unity (now African Union) Convention Governing the Specific Aspects of Refugee Problems in Africa, adopted by the Assembly of Heads of State and Government, Addis Ababa, Sept. 10, 1969; entered into force June 20, 1974. On the definition, *see* Alice Edwards, *Refugee Status Determination in Africa,* 14(2) Afr. J. Int'l & Comp. L. 204 (2006) [hereinafter Edwards (2006)].
[8] Cartagena Declaration on Refugees 1984, adopted by the Colloquium of the International Protection of Refugees in Central America, Mexico and Panama, Part III, para. 3. *See,* also, San José Declaration on Refugees and Displaced Persons, adopted by the International Colloquium in Commemoration of the "Tenth Anniversary of the Cartagena Declaration on Refugees", San José, Dec. 5–7, 1994; Mexico Declaration and Plan of Action to Strengthen the International Protection of Refugees in Central America, Mexico City, Nov. 16, 2004.

2. Refugee Law and Human Rights Law: the Same Legal Family?

Early intergovernmental arrangements on behalf of refugees under the League of Nations focused primarily on defining the legal status of refugees, organizing repatriation or resettlement, and providing relief.[9] The provision of consular assistance was added in 1928 by agreement.[10] The functions of the International Refugee Organization (IRO), the predecessor to the UNHCR, included repatriation, identification, registration and classification, legal and political protection, and transport, resettlement and re-establishment of persons of concern to the Organization.[11] According to Goodwin-Gill, "in the days of the IRO's demise, the major questions debated were *definitional* – just who should benefit from international action; and *functional* – what should be done for refugees, who should do it, and who should pay."[12]

The establishment of the UNHCR under its 1950 Statute pre-dated the passage of the modern human rights instruments, such as the International Covenants.[13] Nothing in the Statute refers to human rights specifically, although this can be implied into some of the expected activities of the UNHCR, such as the promotion of the conclusion and ratification of international conventions for the protection of refugees, as well as special agreements with governments calculated to improve the

---

[9] *See*, Guy Goodwin-Gill, The Refugee In International Law 208 (2nd ed., 1998), for an overview of the historical development of predecessor refugee agencies to the UNHCR [hereinafter Goodwin-Gill].

[10] 1928 Agreement concerning the functions of the representatives of the League of Nations High Commissioner for Refugees: 93 LNTS 2126, in Goodwin-Gill, *id.* at 209.

[11] Article 2, Constitution of the IRO, cited in Goodwin-Gill, *id.* at 210. The IRO operated until Feb. 28, 1952.

[12] Goodwin-Gill, *id.* at 211.

[13] This is a reference to the International Covenant on Civil and Political Rights 1966 (G.A. Res. 2200 A (XXI), 999 U.N.T.S. 171, U.N. Doc. A/6316 (Dec. 16, 1966); entered into force March 23, 1976) [ICCPR] and the International Covenant on Economic, Social and Cultural Rights 1966 (G.A. Res. 2200 A (XXI), 993 U.N.T.S. 3, U.N. Doc. A/6316 (Dec. 16, 1966)) [ICESCR]; entered into force Jan. 3, 1976). The other human rights instruments that make up the core seven treaties include the International Convention on the Elimination of All Forms of Racial Discrimination 1965 (G.A. Res. 2106 A (XX), 660 U.N.T.S. 195, U.N. Doc. A/6014 (Dec. 21, 1965); entered into force Jan. 4, 1969) [CERD]; Convention against Torture and Other Cruel, Inhuman or Degrading Treatment or Punishment 1984 (G.A. Res. 39/46, U.N. Doc. A/RES/39/46 (Dec. 10, 1984); entered into force June 26, 1987) [UNCAT]; Convention on the Elimination of All Forms of Discrimination against Women 1979 (G.A. Res. 34/180, U.N. Doc. A/RES/34/180 (Dec. 18, 1979); entered into force Sept. 3, 1981) [CEDAW]; Convention on the Rights of the Child 1989 (G.A. Res. 44/25, U.N. Doc. A/RES/44/25 (Nov. 20, 1989); entered into force Sept. 20, 1990) [CRC]; International Convention on the Protection of the Rights of Migrant Workers and Members of their Families (G.A. Res. 45/158, U.N. Doc. A/RES/45/158 (Dec. 18, 1990); entered into force July 1, 2003).

situation of refugees.[14] Clapham has argued that international organizations have human rights responsibilities, even if not specifically included in their mandates.[15] The Organization though post-dates the Universal Declaration of Human Rights 1948 (UDHR). In that declaration it was explicitly recorded that "Everyone has the right to seek and to enjoy in other countries asylum from persecution."[16] "At a minimum, Article 14 places the right to seek and to enjoy asylum within [a] human rights paradigm…"[17]

The Preamble to the 1951 Convention refers to the UN Charter and the UDHR, noting that these instruments "have affirmed the principle that human beings shall enjoy fundamental rights and freedoms without discrimination." The Preamble further notes that the United Nations has "manifested its profound concern for refugees and endeavoured to assure refugees the widest possible exercise of these fundamental rights and freedoms." Many substantive provisions were based on principles in the UDHR and the draft of what was to become the two International Covenants.[18] Lauterpacht and Bethlehem argue that human rights developments since the 1951 Convention are "an essential part of [its] framework… that must, by reference to the ICJ's observations in the *Namibia* case, be taken into account [at a minimum] for purposes of interpretation."[19]

---

[14] Article 8(a) and (b), UNHCR Statute.

[15] Andrew Clapham, Human Rights Obligations Of Non-State Actors 109 (2006) [hereinafter Chapham], citing the European Court of Human Rights in *Waite and Kennedy v. Germany* (2000) 30 EHRR 261, para. 67. *See also*, Report of the International Law Commission, 58th Session, U.N. Doc. A/61/10, para. 284–286 (2006).

[16] Article 14(1), UDHR. Article 14(2) provides: "This right may not be invoked in the case of prosecutions genuinely arising from non-political crimes or from acts contrary to the purposes and principles of the United Nations."

[17] Alice Edwards, *Human Rights, Refugees, and The Right "To Enjoy" Asylum*, 17 Int'l J. Ref. L. 293, 298 (2005) [hereinafter Edwards (2005)].

[18] *See*, Jane McAdam, The Refugee Convention as a Rights Blueprint for Persons in Need of International Protection, New Issues in Refugee Research, Research Paper No. 125, UNHCR, July 2006, 7, n.45 [hereinafter McAdam], referring to: "Comments on the Draft Convention and Protocol: General Observations", Annex II to Ad Hoc Committee on Statelessness and Related Problems; Draft Report of the Ad Hoc Committee on Statelessness and Refugees (16 Jan.–Feb. 1950), U.N. Doc. E/AC.32/L.38 para. 36 (Article 3 non-discrimination), para. 46 (Article 26 education) (Feb. 15, 1950); Ad Hoc Committee on Statelessness and Related Problems, "Refugees and Stateless Persons: Compilation of the Comments of Governments and Specialized Agencies on the Report of the Ad Hoc Committee on Statelessness and Related Problems" (Doc. E/1618) U.N. Doc. E/AC.32/L.40 (Aug. 10, 1950) 31 (France on Article 29(1) UDHR).

[19] Elihu Lauterpacht & Daniel Bethlehem, *The Scope and Content of the Principle of Non-Refoulement: Opinion*, in Refugee Protection In International Law: UNHCR Global Consultations On International Protection 75 (Erika Feller, Volker Türk & Frances Nicholson eds., 2003) [hereinafter Feller et al.].

In 1997, the UNHCR expressly stated in a policy document that "UNHCR stands for, and is entitled to invoke, the full array of rights, freedoms and principles related to refugee protection developed by the international community under the auspices of the UN or of regional organisations."[20] The Executive Committee of the High Commissioner's Programme in the same year "reiterate[d] ... the obligation to treat asylum-seekers and refugees in accordance with applicable human rights and refugee law standards as set out in relevant international instruments."[21] By that time, the right to asylum had been entrenched in a number of regional human rights instruments.[22]

At the 40th anniversary of the 1951 Convention, Michel Moussalli, then Director of the Division of International Protection at the UNHCR, stated, "It is regrettable that, within the framework of this existing body of international law, three areas of law [IRL, IHRL and IHL] have developed in parallel which could earlier have been linked more closely."[23] Ten years later, Erika Feller, then Director of the Department of International Protection, stated that, "[t]he refugee protection regime ... has its origins in general principles of human rights."[24] Moreover, the Executive Committee agreed in 2005 that refugee law is "informed by ... developments in related areas of international law, such as human rights and international humanitarian law bearing directly on refugee protection."[25] Human rights are further recognized as an important component of any complementary

---

[20] UNHCR, "UNHCR and Human Rights", AHC Memorandum AHC/97/325, Aug. 6, 1997.

[21] Executive Committee Conclusion No. 82 (XLVIII) on Safeguarding Asylum, para. (d)(vi) (1997). *See also*, EXCOM Conclusion Nos. 19 (XXXI), para. (e) (1980); 22 (XXXII), para. B (1981); and 36 (XXXVI), para. (f) (1985). *See further*, UNHCR, A Thematic Compilation of Executive Committee Conclusions on International Protection (2d ed. reprinted Sept. 2005), Ch. on Human Rights, 183–205 (*available at* www.unhcr.org/publ/PUBL/3d4ab3ff2.pdf (last visited March 3, 2007)).

[22] *See*, Article 22(9), 1969 American Convention on Human Rights, OAS Official Records, OEA/Ser. K/XVI/I.I, entered into force July 18, 1978; Article 22(9) provides a right "to seek and be granted asylum in a foreign country"; Article 12.3, 1981 African Charter on Human and Peoples' Rights, 21 ILM 59, entered into force Oct. 21, 1986; Article 12.3 provides: "Every individual shall have the right when persecuted to seek and obtain asylum in other countries in accordance with laws of those countries and international conventions." A notable exception is the 1950 European Convention for the Protection of Human Right and Fundamental Freedoms, ETS No. 5, Nov. 4, 1950, entered into force Sept. 3, 1953 [ECHR], which omits a right to asylum altogether.

[23] Michel Moussalli, *International Protection: The Road Ahead*, 3(3) Int'l J. Ref. L. 607, 614 (1991).

[24] Erika Feller, *International Refugee Protection 50 years on: The Protection Challenges of the Past, Present and Future*, 83 (843) Int'l Rev. Red Cross 581, 582 (2001). *See further*, UNHCR, Note on International Protection, U.N. Doc. A/AC/96/951, para. 4 (Sept. 13, 2001).

[25] EXCOM Conclusion No. 103 (LVI), Operational para. (c) (2005), Conclusion on the Provision on International Protection Including Through Complementary Forms of Protection.

protection granted,[26] although the Executive Committee cautions that parallel responses to refugees under complementary mechanisms, such as under IHRL, may undermine the existing refugee protection regime.[27]

Marking the 50th anniversary of the 1951 Convention, a Declaration of States' Parties was adopted unanimously in 2001. This document notes that the 1951 Convention, as amended by the 1967 Protocol, sets out human rights for refugees,[28] and recognizes "the importance of other human rights and regional refugee protection instruments…"[29] Operative Paragraph 2 of the Declaration refers to Article 14 of the UDHR and the "rights and freedoms of refugees." In the Agenda for Protection, the document that emerged following the Global Consultations on International Protection as part of a global strategy for future action, "human rights" is mentioned 11 times, while "international humanitarian law" is referred to only once (in relation to refugee children).[30] Consistent with this, the refugee definition has been interpreted by UNHCR and national asylum systems in light of human rights standards.[31]

---

[26] *Id.* Operational para. (n) provides: "Encourages States, in granting complementary forms of protection to those persons in need of it, to provide for the highest degree of stability and certainty by ensuring the human rights and fundamental freedoms of such persons without discrimination…"

[27] *Id.* Operational para. (k): "*Affirms* that measures to provide complementary protection should be implemented in a manner that strengthens, rather than undermines, the existing international refugee protection regime."

[28] Declaration of States Parties to the 1951 Convention relating to the Status of Refugees, Report of the Ministerial Meeting of States Parties to the 1951 Convention and/or 1967 Protocol relating to the Status of Refugees, U.N. Doc. HCR/MMSP/2001/10, Preambular para. 2 (Dec. 12–13, 2001), Geneva, [hereinafter 2001 Declaration of States Parties].

[29] 2001 Declaration of States Parties, *id.* Preambular para. 3.

[30] UNHCR, Agenda for Protection, UNHCR Executive Committee, 53rd session, U.N. Doc. A/AC.96/965/Add.1 (June 16, 2002). "Humanitarian" as a term is present throughout, although with a broader, more general meaning than in the context of IHL.

[31] UNHCR, 2001 Note on International Protection, *supra* note 24; UNHCR, Guidelines on International Protection No. 1: Gender-Related Persecution within the context of Article 1A(2) of the 1951 Convention and/or its 1967 Protocol relating to the Status of Refugees, U.N. Doc. HCR/GIP/02/01 (May 7, 2002); Guidelines on International Protection No. 2: "Membership of a Particular Social group" within the context of Article 1A(2) of the 1951 Convention and/or its 1967 Protocol relating to the Status of Refugees, U.N. Doc. HCR/GIP/02/02 (May 7, 2002); Guidelines on International Protection No. 6: Religion-Based Refugee Claims under Article 1A(2) of the 1951 Convention and/or the 1967 Protocol relating to the Status of Refugees, U.N. Doc. HCR/GIP/04/06, (April 28, 2004). *See further*, Rodger Haines, *Gender-Related Persecution*, in Feller et al., *supra* note 19, at 319; T. Alexander Aleinikoff, *Protected Characteristics and Social Perceptions: An Analysis of the Meaning of "Membership of a Particular Social Group"*, in Feller et al., *supra* note 19, at 263.

Complementarily to refugee-specific forums, the UN General Assembly has consistently called on states to respect the rights of refugees[32] and the United Nations Commission on Human Rights maintained an agenda item on refugees during its years of operation.[33] The new Human Rights Council has referred to refugees in a special session on the conflict in Lebanon in 2006, although it has yet to create a standing item in its regular sessions.[34] In addition, the human rights treaty monitoring bodies have admitted and heard claims under their individual petition systems from refugees and asylum-seekers.[35]

The 1951 Convention is both a status and rights-granting instrument. It enumerates a range of rights for refugees in Articles 3 to 34, yet increasingly, human rights law is seen and promoted as part of the international protection framework for refugees. Beyond the rhetoric, it is worth asking why human rights law is so appealing to refugees and asylum-seekers and their advocates, in preference, or in parallel, to refugee law.

First, the rights enumerated in the 1951 Convention are limited guarantees for refugees and asylum-seekers and are not the range of rights available to them under IHRL.[36] For example, there is no entrenched right to family life contained in either the 1951 Convention or the 1950 Statute;[37] nor is there a right to liberty.[38]

Second, the rights listed in the 1951 Convention are subject to, in the words of Hathaway, a complex "structure of entitlement" that provides for "enhanced rights as the bond strengthens between a particular refugee and the state party in which

---

[32] A range of G.A. resolutions on UNHCR can be found at: www.unhcr.org/cgi-bin/texis/vtx/doclist?page=excom&id=3b4f0ffa4 (last visited March 3, 2007). Most recent resolutions include G.A. Res. A/RES/61/137, (Jan. 25, 2007) and G.A. Res. A/RES/60/129, (Jan. 24, 2006).

[33] *See, e.g.*, United Nations Commission on Human Rights, Report of the Sixty-First Session (Mar. 14–Apr. 22, 2005), U.N. Doc. E/CN.4/2005/135 in which there were 70 references to "refugees."

[34] United Nations Human Rights Council, Report of the Human Rights Council on its Second Special Session on the Situation in Lebanon (Aug. 11, 2006), in which concern was raised for the outflow of refugees from the conflict, U.N. Doc. A/HRC/S-2/2 (Aug. 17, 2006).

[35] *See, e.g.*, Brian Gorlick, *Human Rights And Refugees: Enhancing Protection Through International Human Rights Law*, UNHCR New Issues in Refugee Research Working Paper No. 3, Oct. 2000, *available at* www.unhcr.org/research/RESEARCH/3ae6a0cf4.pdf (last visited March 3, 2007); O. Andrysek, *Gaps in International Protection and the Potential for Redress through Individual Complaints Procedures*, 9(3) Int'l J. Ref. L. 392 (1997) [hereinafter Andrysek].

[36] Edwards (2005), *supra* note 17, at 303.

[37] The Final Act of the 1951 United Nations Conference of Plenipotentiaries on the Status of Refugees and Stateless Persons recommends to governments to take measures to protect the refugee's family. *See*, Edwards (2005), *supra* note 17, at 308–319 (for an overview of protections of family life under IHRL versus IRL).

[38] *See*, Ophelia Field & Alice Edwards, Alternatives to Detention of Asylum-Seekers and Refugees, Legal and Protection Policy Research Series, U.N. Doc. POLAS/2006/03, UNHCR (April 2006), *available at* www.unhcr.org (last visited March 3, 2007).

he or she is present."³⁹ That is, not all rights contained in the 1951 Convention apply to recognized refugees; and only a few overtly apply to asylum-seekers.⁴⁰ IHRL, in contrast, is applicable to all persons on the basis of their shared humanity (with limited exceptions)⁴¹ and must be applied following principles of non-discrimination. In this way, IRHL is not nationality-based, but jurisdiction-based.⁴² Article 3 of the 1951 Convention, in contrast, provides that states parties must apply the Convention provisions without discrimination only as to "race, religion or country of origin."

The third advantage of having recourse to IHRL is that should a state fail to respect its human rights obligations, appropriate redress mechanisms may be available,⁴³ whereas apart from writing a letter of complaint to the UNHCR or exercising rights under domestic law, no such mechanisms exist under IRL.

Fourth, IHRL is particularly relevant with respect to non-state parties to the 1951 Convention and/or 1967 Protocol that are otherwise parties to various human rights instruments, as well as its role in developing international customary rules that apply to all states.⁴⁴

---

³⁹ James C. Hathaway, The Rights Of Refugees Under International Law 154 (2005). *See also*, Goodwin-Gill, *supra* note 9, at 305–307, in which he distinguishes four general categories on which the extent of a refugee's rights may be determined, namely "simple presence," "lawful presence," "lawful residence," and "habitual residence."

⁴⁰ These include non-discrimination (Article 3); non-penalization for illegal entry or stay (Article 31); and *non-refoulement* (Article 33).

⁴¹ Article 25 (right to participate in public life), ICCPR only applies to citizens; whereas the protection against arbitrary expulsion applies to aliens (Article 13, ICCPR). Similarly, exceptions may be made in relation to the granting of economic rights to non-nationals by developing countries, Article 2(3), ICESCR.

⁴² *See*, Human Rights Committee General Comment No. 15 on "The Position of Aliens under the Covenant", U.N. Doc. CCPR/C/21/Rev.1 (May 19, 1989), para. 2, in which it is stated that: "Thus the general rule is that each one of the rights of the [ICCPR and the ICESCR] must be guaranteed without discrimination between citizens and aliens." *See also*, Human Rights Committee, "General Comment No. 31: The Nature of the General Legal Obligation Imposed on States Parties to the Covenant", U.N. Doc. CCPR/C/21/Rev.1/Add.13 (Mar. 29, 2004); Committee on the Elimination of Racial Discrimination, General Recommendation XI on Non-Citizens, U.N. Doc. A/46/18 (Mar. 19, 1993); Loizidou v. Turkey, App. No. 15318/8923, Eur. H.R. Rep. 513 (Dec. 18, 1996), in which the Court stated at para. 52, "The obligation to secure...the rights and freedoms set out in the Convention, derives from the fact of...control [of territory.]" In relation to expanded understandings of State responsibility in recent case law, *see* G. Goodwin-Gill, Extra-Territorial Processing of Asylum Claims from a General International Law Perspective, Keynote address to Refugee Studies Centre International Conference on Refugees and International Law: Challenges to Protection, (Dec. 15–16, 2006), University of Oxford.

⁴³ Individual petition mechanisms are available under the ICCPR, UNCAT and the CEDAW. In order to exercise these rights, the individual petitioner must be in the territory of a State party that has accepted the jurisdiction of these treaty bodies to consider the case.

⁴⁴ Edwards (2005), *supra* note 17, at 299.

Fifth, "[t]he discrepancies between [the treatment of] refugees recognized under the 1951 Convention and the wider group of persons in need of international protection"[45] reinforce the relevance and importance of human rights instruments.[46]

Finally, IHRL applies to individuals prior to flight, during flight, and during refuge (depending of course on the state party concerned and/or whether the right has attained the status of custom). The operation of refugee law, on the other hand, starts with the act of seeking admission to the territory of an asylum state, and more usually after crossing an international border. Without IHRL, many individuals would remain in a legal vacuum until they manage to escape the persecutory conduct and reach safety in another country.

Clearly, IHRL is a device available to strengthen and to enhance existing standards of protection for refugees.[47] Erika Feller of the UNHCR has characterized the inter-linkages pragmatically, "To put it simplistically, to see the refugee problem as an issue of human rights law creates protection space."[48] But this is not to suggest that refugee law is made redundant by or is secondary to IHRL. For recognized refugees, IRL is *lex specialis* and contains specially tailored rights that are relevant to the refugee experience, including a range of detailed economic and social rights. McAdam argues that IHRL is in fact an inadequate complement to IRL in respect of persons who do not satisfy the refugee definition but who are nonetheless in need of international protection, as the former does not provide a legal status to such persons.[49] She argues further that this creates a protection hierarchy that has no legal justification.[50]

3. *Refugee Law and Humanitarian Law: Natural Allies?*

Much less has been said about the interface between refugee law and humanitarian law and even less regarding the place of IHL in relation to the "international

---

[45] *See*, UNHCR, *Note on International Protection*, U.N. Doc. A/AC.96/830 (Sept. 7, 1994), para. 21 (text also in 6 Int'l J. Ref. L. 679 (1994)).
[46] Andrysek, *supra* note 35, at 394.
[47] Edwards (2005), *supra* note 17, at 329.
[48] E. Feller, then Director of the Department of International Protection, UNHCR, *The Responsibility to Protect – Closing the Gaps in the International Protection Regime and the New EXCOM Conclusion on Complementary Forms of Protection*, Presentation to the "Moving On: Forced Migration and Human Rights" Conference, NSW Parliament House, Sydney, Australia, Nov. 22, 2005, *available at* www.unhcr.org [hereinafter Feller (2005)].
[49] McAdam, *supra* note 18, at 3.
[50] McAdam, *supra* note 18, at 3, referring to Guy S. Goodwin-Gill & Agnès Hurwitz, "Memorandum" in Minutes of Evidence taken before the EU Committee (Sub-Committee E) (April 10, 2002), in House of Lords Select Committee on the EU Defining Refugee Status and Those in Need of International Protection (The Stationery Office London) Oral Evidence 2–3.

protection" of refugees. In 1982, the Executive Committee of the UNHCR "*Stressed* the fundamental importance of respecting the relevant principles of international humanitarian law."[51] In emphasizing the "civilian and humanitarian character" of asylum, the Executive Committee in 1987 predicated its conclusion "on the rights and responsibilities of states pursuant to the Charter of the United Nations and relevant rules and principles of international law, including international humanitarian law."[52] Along the same lines in 1992, the Executive Committee:

> *Reaffirm[ed]* the primary nature of the High Commissioner's protection responsibilities which are performed as a non-political, humanitarian and social function within the framework of international refugee law and applicable regional instruments, with due regard for human rights and humanitarian law.[53]

In 1997, the Executive Committee re-emphasized the inter-linkages between the three branches of law to refugee protection, by "*Call[ing] on* States to take all necessary measures to ensure that refugees are effectively protected, including through national legislation, and in compliance with their obligations under international human rights and humanitarian law instruments bearing directly on refugee protection."[54] Reference to IHL has more specifically been raised by the Executive Committee in relation to the safety and security of humanitarian personnel,[55] child and adolescent refugees, in particular in relation to child recruitment into military forces,[56] improved cooperation between the UNHCR and the International Committee of the Red Cross (ICRC),[57] sexual exploitation of women and children,[58] mass influx situations,[59] and amnesties.[60]

In a presidential statement in 1999, the UN Security Council, under a general item entitled "Protection of civilians in armed conflict," "condemn[ed] attacks against civilians, especially women, children and other vulnerable groups, including also *refugees* and internally displaced persons, in violation of the relevant rules of international law, including those of international humanitarian and human rights law."[61] The General Assembly has, on a number of occasions, highlighted

---

[51] EXCOM Conclusion No. 27 (XXXIII) (1982), para. (a).
[52] EXCOM Conclusion No. 48 (XXXVIII) (1987).
[53] EXCOM Conclusion No. 68 (XLIII) (1992), para. (a). See also, EXCOM Conclusion No. 73 (XLIV) (1993), para. (a).
[54] EXCOM Conclusion No. 81 (XLVIII) (1997), para. (e). See also, EXCOM Conclusions No. 84 (XLVIII) (1997), para. (a); 94 (LIII) (2002); 98 (LIV) (2003).
[55] EXCOM Conclusion No. 83 (XLVIII) (1997).
[56] EXCOM Conclusions No. 84 (XLVIII) (1997), para. (a); 85 (XLIX) (1998), para. (k).
[57] EXCOM Conclusion No. 87 (L) (1999), para. (h).
[58] EXCOM Conclusion No. 98 (LIV) (2003), para. (c) (i) & (ii).
[59] EXCOM Conclusion No. 100 (LV) (2004).
[60] EXCOM Conclusion No. 101 (LV) (2004), para. (g).
[61] U.N. Doc. S/PRST/1999/6, para. 2 (Feb. 13, 1999) (emphasis added).

the inter-linkages between refugees, displacement and IHL in terms of averting flows of refugees and displaced persons, preventing the expulsion of refugees or asylum-seekers contrary to international law, and in relation to safeguarding the rights of refugee children from abuse and exploitation.[62] The ICRC has called the relationship between IHL and IRL a "two-way cross fertilization,"[63] although it is less apparent how IRL has influenced IHL than the other way around.

The relevance of IHL to refugees is evidenced by provisions that are specifically aimed at both the protection of refugees and at preventing displacement. In relation to control measures, refugees are not to be treated as "enemy aliens" exclusively on the basis of their nationality.[64] Nationals of the occupying power who had sought refuge in the territory of the occupied state (that is, refugees) shall not be arrested, prosecuted, convicted or deported, with some exceptions.[65] Under no circumstances shall a "protected person" be transferred to a country where he or she may have reason to fear persecution for his or her political opinions or religious beliefs.[66] Individual or mass forcible transfers and deportations are prohibited, except if the security of the population or imperative military reasons so demand.[67] Doing so in contravention of these safeguards is a war crime under the Rome Statute of the International Criminal Court 1998 (Rome Statute).[68] Similarly, the displacement of the civilian population is prohibited in non-international armed conflict, unless their security is at issue or imperative military reasons so demand.[69] Moreover, it is a war crime to willfully and in violation of the Geneva Conventions or Protocol

---

[62] *See*, e.g., G.A. Res. 48/139, Operative para. 3 (Dec. 20, 1993); G.A. Res. 52/103, Operative PP 5 & 16 (Dec. 12, 1997); G.A. Res. 53/125, Operative para. 18 (Dec. 9, 1998); G.A. Res. 54/146, Operative PP 4 & 19 (Dec. 17, 1999).

[63] Emanuela-Chiara Gillard, ICRC Legal Adviser, Official Statement to the International Association of Refugee Law Judges World Conference, Stockholm, April 23, 2004, Humanitarian Law, Human Rights and Refugee Law – Three Pillars, *available at* www.icrc.org/Web/eng/siteeng0.nsf/htmlall/6T7G86?OpenDocument&style=custo_print (last visited March 3, 2007).

[64] Article 44, Geneva Convention Relative to the Protection of Civilian Persons in Time of War, Aug. 12, 1949, 75 U.N.T.S. 287, 288 [hereinafter GC IV].

[65] Article 70, GC IV, *id*. Article 70 provides: "Nationals of the occupying Power who, before the outbreak of hostilities, have sought refuge in the territory of the occupied State, shall not be arrested, prosecuted, convicted or deported from the occupied territory, except for offences committed after the outbreak of hostilities, or for offences under common law committed before the outbreak of hostilities which, according to the law of the occupied State, would have justified extradition in time of peace."

[66] Article 45(3), GC IV, *supra* note 64.

[67] Article 49, GC IV, *supra* note 64.

[68] Article 8(2)(e)(viii), Rome Statute of the International Criminal Court, July 17, 1998, Article 8, 2187 U.N.T.S. 3, entered into force July 1, 2002 [hereinafter Rome Statute].

[69] Article 17, Protocol Additional to the Geneva Conventions of Aug. 12, 1949, and relating to the Protection of Victims of Non-International Armed Conflict (Protocol II), June 8, 1977 [hereinafter AP II].

I transfer parts of one's own population into the territory occupied, or deport or transfer all or parts of the population of the occupied territory within or outside that territory.[70] This crime is further recognized in the Rome Statute.[71]

In terms of jurisdictional limits, Jaquemet points out that IRL and IHL operate concurrently as well as successively.[72] When refugees are caught up in armed conflict, he notes that they are both refugees and conflict victims at the same time, and should theoretically benefit from "dual protection"[73] under both legal regimes. Refugees benefit as "protected persons" from the safeguards in the Fourth Geneva Convention[74] and Additional Protocol I[75] in the context of international armed conflict; while in non-international armed conflict, refugees can benefit from protection as "civilians not taking an active part in hostilities."[76] Article 5 of the 1951 Convention, as noted in the Introduction to this article, allows for, and foresaw, that other rights would be due to refugees apart from those contained within the Convention. The Geneva Conventions of 1949 are a case in point.

Yet, as states may provisionally derogate from all of the provisions of the 1951 Convention "in time of war or other grave and exceptional circumstances,"[77] IHL may be the only protection system available in such circumstances. Having said this, any measures introduced must be individually tailored and not collectively imposed.[78] In addition, IRL in the context of war is not as robust as IHL, as the former is based on an assumption that refugees are, with some exceptions, to be accorded the same treatment as aliens in general.[79] In the context of war, aliens are usually the first to experience limitations or restrictions on their rights. A further notable distinction between the two branches of law is that IHL contains protec-

---

[70] Article 85(4)(a), Protocol Additional to the Geneva Conventions of 12 August 1949, and Relating to the Protections of Victims of International Armed Conflicts (Protocol I), Article 75, opened for signature Dec. 12, 1977, U.N. Doc. A/32/144, Annex I, II, (1977) [hereinafter AP I].

[71] Article 8(2)(b)(viii), Rome Statute, *supra* note 68.

[72] Stéphane Jaquemet, *The Cross-fertilization of International Humanitarian Law and International Refugee Law*, 83(843) Int'l Rev. Red Cross 651, 652 (2001) [hereinafter Jaquemet].

[73] *Id.* at 652.

[74] Convention (IV) relative to the Protection of Civilian Persons in Time of War, Geneva, Aug. 12, 1949.

[75] AP I, *supra* note 70.

[76] AP II, *supra* note 69.

[77] Article 9, 1951 Convention, *supra* note 1: "Nothing in the present Convention shall prevent a Contracting State, in time of war or other grave and exceptional circumstances, from taking provisionally measures which it considers essential to the national security in the case of a particular person, pending a determination by the Contracting State that that person is in fact a refugee and that the continuance of such measures is necessary in his [or her] case in the interests of national security."

[78] *See*, Alice Edwards, *Tampering with Refugee Protection: The Case of Australia*, 15(2) Int'l J. Ref. L. 192, 195 (2003) (on limitations of Article 9, 1951 Convention, *supra* note 1).

[79] Article 7, 1951 Convention, *supra* note 1.

tions for individuals caught up in non-international armed conflict and who are at risk of violence by non-state actors,[80] whereas non-state actors are bound neither by refugee law nor by human rights law.[81]

In addition to the explicit protections offered by IHL to refugees in the context of armed conflict, IHL is also relevant to whether persons will satisfy the definition of a "refugee" in Article 1 of the 1951 Convention. When a victim of armed conflict is forced to leave his or her country because of being unable to obtain adequate protection from IHL, he or she may be entitled to the protection of international refugee law. Jaquemet argues that those grave breaches of IHL "constitute a substantial part of the refugee definition and become the factor triggering refugee protection."[82] In the 1992 version of its Handbook, UNHCR indicated that, with the exception of Africa, persons compelled to leave their country of origin as a result of international or national armed conflicts are "not normally considered refugees under the 1951 Convention or 1967 Protocol."[83] However, it did acknowledge that such conflicts "can result – and occasionally ha[ve] resulted – in persecution for one or more of the reasons enumerated in the 1951 Convention."[84] With the changing nature of many modern conflicts that have ethnic or religious dimensions,[85] the UNHCR has updated its position to acknowledge that: "it is nowadays widely recognised that war and violence may be used as instruments of persecution."[86] Additionally, IHL (and international criminal law) sets out what actions constitute war crimes

---

[80] Common Article 3, Geneva Conventions 1949, The Geneva Convention for the Amelioration of the Condition of the Wounded and Sick in Armed Forces in the Field, Aug. 12, 1949, 75 U.N.T.S. 31, 32; Geneva Convention for the Amelioration of the Condition of the Wounded, Sick and Shipwrecked Members of the Armed Forces at Sea, Aug. 12, 1949, 75 U.N.T.S. 85, 86; Geneva Convention Relative to the Treatment to Prisoners of War, Aug. 12, 1949, 75 U.N.T.S. 135, 136; Geneva Convention Relative to the Protection of Civilian Persons in Time of War, Aug. 12, 1949, 75 U.N.T.S. 287, 288.

[81] This statement ought to be distinguished from states bearing responsibility for the acts of non-state actors due to their failure to investigate, prosecute and/or punish alleged offenders as required by IHRL, or where states are unable or unwilling to offer protection against non-state harm in the case of IRL thereby giving rise to grounds for refugee status. Note, too, possible emerging exceptions to this general non-state actor rule argued in Clapham, *supra* note 15. *See further*, on distinctions between IRL and IHL, Rachel Brett & Eve Lester, *Refugee Law and International Humanitarian Law: Parallels, Lessons and Looking Ahead*, 83(843) Int'l Rev. Red Cross 713, 713 (2001).

[82] Jaquemet, *supra* note 72, at 652.

[83] UNHCR, *Handbook on Procedures and Criteria for Determining Refugee Status under the 1951 Convention and the 1967 Protocol relating to the Status of Refugees* (re-edited Jan. 1992, Geneva), para. 164 [hereinafter UNHCR Handbook].

[84] *Id.* para. 165.

[85] *See*, e.g., conflicts in Bosnia and Herzegovina, Rwanda, Burundi, Cote d'Ivoire, Somalia, and Sudan.

[86] UNHCR, The 1951 Convention relating to the Status of Refugees: Its Relevance in the Contemporary Context, para. 7 (Feb. 1, 1999). *See also*, Edwards (2006), *supra* note 7, at 231–232.

and crimes against humanity and as a result it has proven to be a crucial source of interpretative guidance in giving meaning to the same terms used in the context of who should be excluded from refugee protection under the 1951 Convention.[87] Equally, IHL is of interpretative guidance to the wider definition of a "refugee" under the OAU Convention.[88]

4. *The Concept of "International Protection": a Term of Art or Ambiguity?*

The scope or meaning of "international protection" is not well settled. In fact, the terms "protection," "refugee protection" and "international protection" are constantly and interchangeably used in the literature, but are rarely defined or clearly articulated. Notably, too, the term "protection" is used in the context of international human rights and humanitarian laws.[89] The term's origins lie in the 1950 Statute of the Office of the UNHCR, which states that the UNHCR is to provide "international protection" and to seek "permanent solutions for the problem of refugees."[90] Nowhere in the Statute is the term explicitly defined, although nine paragraphs of Article 8 are dedicated to identifying the activities that UNHCR is expected to engage in.[91] The list appears to be exhaustive, although the provisions

---

[87] Article 1F, 1951 Convention, *supra* note 1. On its interpretation, *see* UNHCR, Guidelines on International Protection No. 5: Application of the Exclusion Clauses: Article 1F of the 1951 Convention relating to the Status of Refugees, U.N. Doc. HCR/GIP/03/05 (Sept. 4, 2003).

[88] *See*, Edwards (2006), *supra* note 7.

[89] D.P. Forsythe refers to "humanitarian protection" in the context of individuals caught up in certain conflicts or man-made emergencies: David P. Forsythe, *Humanitarian Protection: The International Committee of the Red Cross and the United Nations High Commissioner for Refugees*, 83(843) Int'l Rev. Red Cross 675 (2001).

[90] Article 1, Ch. I, UNHCR Statute.

[91] Article 8, UNHCR Statute provides: The High Commissioner shall provide for the protection of refugees falling under the competence of his [or her] Office by:
(a) Promoting the conclusion and ratification of international conventions for the protection of refugees, supervising their application and proposing amendments thereto;
(b) Promoting through special agreements with Governments the execution of any measures calculated to improve the situation of refugees and to reduce the number requiring protection;
(c) Assisting governmental and private efforts to promote voluntary repatriation or assimilation within new national communities;
(d) Promoting the admission of refugees, not excluding those in the most destitute categories, to the territories of States;
(e) Endeavouring to obtain permission for refugees to transfer their assets and especially those necessary for their resettlement;
(f) Obtaining from Governments information concerning the number and conditions of refugees in their territories and the laws and regulations concerning them;

are particularly broad to be able to include a whole range of activities not initially foreseen. In addition, Article 9 allows for the potential expansion of UNHCR's mandate according to resolutions of the General Assembly;[92] and this has occurred from time to time.[93] The term does not appear in its longer form in the 1951 Convention, although the term "protection" is found in Article 1 (the refugee definition) and in the Preamble, which notes that "it is desirable...to extend the scope of and the protection accorded by such instruments by means of a new agreement." Outlined below are a range of contexts, albeit non-exhaustive,[94] in which the term (or variations upon it) has been applied.

4.1. *"Protection" in the Refugee Definition*

Apart from reference to "international protection" in UNHCR's Statute, the concept of "protection" (in its narrower form) appears in Article 1 of the 1951 Convention (the definition clause) and has been the subject of intense scrutiny by the academy. Two divergent understandings have emerged, and its meaning is far from agreed. Relying on the drafting history of the 1951 Convention and general principles of treaty interpretation, writers such as Grahl-Madsen,[95] Weis,[96] Jaeger,[97]

(g) Keeping in close touch with Governments and inter-governmental organizations dealing with refugee questions;
(h) Establishing contact in such manner as he [or she] may think best with private organizations dealing with refugee questions;
(i) Facilitating the co-ordination of the efforts of private organizations concerned with the welfare of refugees.

[92] Article 9, UNHCR Statute provides: "The High Commissioner shall engage in such additional activities, including repatriation and resettlement, as the General Assembly may determine..."

[93] For example, in 1974, the G.A. asked UNHCR to provide legal assistance to stateless persons (G.A. Res. 3274 (XXXIX) (Dec. 10, 1974)) and in 1996, it mandated the agency to promote the avoidance and reduction of statelessness (G.A. Res. 51/75 (Dec. 12, 1996)) Similarly, in 1998, the G.A. mandated the UNHCR to play a role in relation to internally displaced persons (G.A. Res. 48/116, para. 12 (Mar. 12, 1994)).

[94] E.g. this article does not address the issue of "temporary protection". *See*, instead, Erik Roxström & Mark Gibney, *The Legal and Ethical Obligations of UNHCR: The Case of Temporary Protection in Western Europe* 37, *in* Problems Of Protection: The Unhcr, Refugees, And Human Rights (Niklaus Steiner, Mark Gibney & Gil Loescher eds, 2003).

[95] Atl Grahl-Madsen, Protection for the Unprotected, Lecture at the Association of Attenders and Alumni of The Hague Academy of International Law, XXth Congress, Oslo, May 13–18, 1968, as cited in Antonio Fortin, *The Meaning of "Protection" in the Refugee Definition*, 12(4) Int'l J. Ref. L. 548, 557 (2001) [hereinafter Fortin].

[96] Paul Weis, Nationality And Statelessness In International Law (1956) [hereinafter Weis].

[97] Gilbert Jaeger, Status and International Protection of Refugees, Summary of Lectures of the International Institute of Human Rights, Strasbourg, 9th Study Session (1978) [hereinafter Jaeger], as cited in Fortin, *supra* note 95, at 557.

and Fortin[98] consider that the term "protection" in Article 1 refers to the inability or unwillingness of an individual to avail him or herself of the *diplomatic* protection of his or her country of nationality. According to Weis, diplomatic protection is understood as:

> a right of the State, accorded to it by customary international law, to intervene on behalf of its own nationals if their rights are violated by another State, in order to obtain redress.[99]

Jaeger similarly stated:

> The refugee...cannot claim the consular or diplomatic protection of his [or her] country of origin and does not benefit, in the absence of international protection, from bilateral or multilateral treaties between States. This difference in status between the ordinary alien and the refugee, justifies the concept of the refugee as an "unprotected alien".[100]

In his comprehensive article on this issue, Fortin refers to the explicit statement by the Acting President of the Conference of Plenipotentiaries, in which the 1951 Convention was adopted, as having stated:

> it clearly emerged...that what was primarily contemplated was the protection of so-called *de facto* stateless persons or refugees, in other words, persons, who for certain reasons, found themselves outside the borders of the countries of which they were legally nationals, and who either could not or did not wish to avail themselves of the diplomatic protection of those countries.[101]

---

[98] Fortin, *supra* note 95.
[99] Weis, *supra* note 96, at 35. *See*, Article 5, Vienna Convention on Consular Relations 1963, 596 U.N.T.S. 261, done at Vienna April 24, 1963; entered into force Mar. 19, 1967, for a list of consular functions, including "protecting in the receiving State the interests of the sending State and its nationals" (Article 5(a)); "issuing passports and travel documents to nationals of the sending State" (Article 5(d)); "helping and assisting nationals, both individuals and bodies corporate, of the sending State" (Article 5(e)); "acting as notary and civil registrar and in capacities of a similar kind" (Article 5(f)); "safeguarding the interests of nationals...of the sending State in cases of succession" (Article 5(g); "safeguarding, within the limits imposed by the laws and regulations of the receiving State, the interests of minors and other persons lacking full capacity who are nationals of the sending State" (Article 5(h)); "representing or arranging appropriate representation of nationals of the sending State before tribunals and other authorities of the receiving State" (Article 5(i)); "extending assistance to vessels and aircraft" (Article 5(k) & (l)); "performing any other functions entrusted to a consular post by the sending State which are not prohibited by the laws and regulations of the receiving State" (Article 5(m)).
[100] Jaeger, *supra* note 97, as cited in Fortin, *supra* note 95, at 557.
[101] Mr. Humphrey, Statement of Acting President, Conference of Plenipotentiaries on the Status of Refugees and Stateless Persons, Summary of Record of the First Meeting: U.N. Doc. A/CONF.2/SR.1, para. 5, as cited in Fortin, *supra* note 95, at 563.

Under this first approach, therefore, refugees were considered in need of "international protection" in another state because they did not enjoy the diplomatic protection of their country of nationality to make claims on their behalf. In this way, refugees were considered "unprotected persons"[102] and therefore entitled to special status.

A contrary view, espoused principally by Hathaway and more recently adopted in the jurisprudence in a number of jurisdictions,[103] is that the term "protection" in Article 1 of the 1951 Convention is to be understood to mean "internal protection" in the sense that the individual's state of nationality is unable or unwilling to protect victims or potential victims of persecution.[104] Out of this analysis, the idea of "surrogate" or "substitute" protection has emerged, such that it is argued that the drafters of the treaty intended only to provide protection "against a risk of serious harm that is demonstrative of a breakdown of national protection."[105] That is, an individual who has a well-founded fear of being persecuted must nonetheless demonstrate that the state is unable or unwilling to protect him or her against such persecution; rather than the individual being unable or unwilling to avail him or herself of the diplomatic protection of his or her country of nationality. "The [internal protection approach] is concerned with prevention of persecution in the country of origin; the [diplomatic protection approach] with enforcement of equal rights against the country of refuge."[106]

The "national protection" approach has contributed to the legitimization of the application of notions such as "internal flight, relocation or protection alternatives" to refugee status determination;[107] and arguably is influenced by recourse to human rights standards that speak in terms of due diligence obligations on the part of the state.[108] The differing emphasis has also been said to determine the acceptability of claims to refugee status involving non-state actors of persecution, although the

---

[102] Fortin, *supra* note 95, at 548 & 552.
[103] *See*, further and for caselaw, Daniel Wilsher, *Non-State Actors and the Definition of a Refugee in the United Kingdom: Protection, Accountability or Culpability?* 15(1) Int'l J. Ref. L. 68 (2003) [hereinafter Wilsher].
[104] James C. Hathaway, The Law Of Refugee Status (1991) [hereinafter Hathaway].
[105] Penelope Mathew, James C. Hathaway & Michelle Foster, The Role of State Protection in Refugee Analysis, Discussion Paper No. 2 Advanced Refugee Law Workshop, International Association of Refugee Law Judges, Auckland, New Zealand, Oct. 2002, 15(3) Int'l J. Ref. L. 444, 448–451 (2003) [hereinafter Mathew et al.].
[106] Wilsher, *supra* note 103, at 71.
[107] *See*, James C. Hathaway & Michelle Foster, *Internal Protection/Relocation/Flight Alternative as an Aspect of Refugee Status Determination, in* Feller et al., *supra* note 19, at 357. Cf. UNHCR, Guidelines on International Protection No. 4: "Internal Flight or Relocation Alternative" within the context of Article 1A(2) of the 1951 Convention and/or 1967 Protocol relating to the Status of Refugees, U.N. Doc. HCR/GIP/03/04 (July 23, 2003).
[108] Mathew et al., *supra* note 105, at 449.

UNHCR has denied that this is material and argues instead that the two approaches are not in effect contradictory.[109] Hathaway asserts that the harm feared must amount to "the sustained and systematic denial of core human rights."[110]

4.2. "Protection" versus "Asylum"

The term "protection" is frequently conflated with the concept of "asylum;" neither term having achieved a concise definition. The concept of "asylum" derives in its modern form from Article 14 of the UDHR,[111] although this provision did not impose an obligation on states to "grant" asylum.[112] The 1967 Declaration on Territorial Asylum,[113] the outcome of various failed attempts to agree a binding treaty, reiterates that the granting of asylum is an "exercise of sovereignty."[114] It affirms, however, that state discretion is curtailed by the obligation of *non-refoulement*, including in relation to rejection at the frontier.[115] Moreover, the right to seek asylum was reinforced by the inclusion of a specific prohibition on *refoulement* in the 1951 Convention[116] and it is now generally accepted that it forms part of customary international law.[117] Kneebone has stated that "... protection can be construed as the *non-refoulement* obligation in Article 33 of the [1951] Convention."[118] The *non-refoulement* prohibition has been buttressed by IHRL guarantees, in particular the absolute prohibition on return to torture.[119] In addition, regional human rights treaties recognize a right to be *granted* asylum.[120]

---

[109] UNHCR, Note on Interpreting Article 1 of the 1951 Convention relating to the Status of Refugees, UNHCR Geneva, PP 37 & 19 (April 2001).

[110] Hathaway, *supra* note 104, at 108.

[111] EXCOM Conclusion No. 82 (XLVIII) (1997), para. (b) "reaffirms that the institution of asylum...derives directly from the right to seek and enjoy asylum set out in Article 14(1)."

[112] Richard Plender & Nuala Mole, *Beyond the Geneva Convention: Constructing a* de facto *Right of Asylum from International Human Rights Instruments, in* Refugee Rights And Realities: Evolving International Concepts And Regimes 81 (Frances Nicholson & Patrick Twomey eds., 1999) [hereinafter Plender].

[113] G.A. Res. 2312 (XXIX) (Dec. 14, 1967). *See also*, Report of the U.N. Conference on Territorial Asylum, U.N. Doc. A/CONF.78/12 (Apr. 21, 1977).

[114] Article 1(1), 1967 Declaration on Territorial Asylum.

[115] Article 3(3), 1967 Declaration on Territorial Asylum: "No person [entitled to invoke Article 14 of the UDHR] shall be subjected to such measures as rejection at the frontier or, if he [or she] has already entered the territory in which he [or she] seeks asylum, expulsion or compulsory return to any State where he [or she] may be subjected to persecution."

[116] Article 33, 1951 Convention, *supra* note 1.

[117] *See, e.g.*, 2001 Declaration of States Parties, *supra* note 28, at Preambular para. 4.

[118] Susan Kneebone, *The Pacific Plan: The Provision of "Effective Protection"?*, Advance Access published on 29 Sept. 2006, Int'l J. Ref. L. 696, 698 (2006).

[119] Article 3, UNCAT; Article 7, ICCPR; Article 3, ECHR.

[120] *Supra* note 22.

According to a 1988 UN report, "asylum" consists of several elements: to admit a person to the territory of a state, to allow the person to remain there, to refuse to expel, to refuse to extradite, and not to prosecute, punish or otherwise restrict the person's liberty.[121] In its narrowest sense, asylum is, therefore, entry and admission, and guarantees against *refoulement* to persecution. A wider reading incorporates the rights contained in the 1951 Convention (noting that these become applicable at different stages of refugeehood) and other human rights guarantees.[122] Hathaway has recently opined that Articles 2–34 of the 1951 Convention contain the content of protection.[123] In many ways the terms are used interchangeably, based on an understanding that states parties are responsible for granting asylum; whereas UNHCR is responsible for supervising states in doing so under its "international protection" functions.[124] Having said this, it is in the broader sense that the lines of demarcation between the two terms (asylum and protection) can become blurred.

4.3. *"Protection" versus Assistance*

A further variation or qualification on the meaning of "protection" is the preference of some scholars and governments to distinguish it from what is termed "assistance" (or relief).[125] Historically, relief was part of the package contained in various League of Nations' agreements, whereas the mandate of the International Refugee Organization saw a shift to the identification of specific tasks, including "legal and political protection." Similarly, the Statute of the UNHCR does not mention the provision of relief or assistance explicitly. Instead, it states that the role of the UNHCR is to "facilitate" or to "coordinate" the activities of private organizations in relation to the "welfare" of refugees.[126] In other words, the original mandate of the UNHCR was non-operational.

The 1990s witnessed a shift in the approach (or reach) of UNHCR from an agency principally engaged in interventions with governments to afford minimum

---

[121] Chama L.C. Mubanga-Chipoya, Final Report, *The Right to Leave any Country, including His Own, and to Return to His Country*, U.N. Doc. E/C.4/Sub.2/1988/35, paras 103–106 (June 1988).

[122] *See*, e.g., Terje Einarsen, *The European Convention on Human Rights and the Notion of an Implied Right to de facto Asylum*, 2 Int'l J. Ref. L. 361 (1990); Plender, *supra* note 112, at 81.

[123] James C. Hathaway, Why 'Effective Protection' is Neither, Opening Speech to the University of Melbourne Law School Conference on "Effective Protection", 23 Feb. 2007 [hereinafter Hathaway 2007]. As Article 2 of the 1951 Convention imposes obligations on refugees to respect the laws of the asylum country and public order measures, I tend not to conceive it as part of the protection owed to the refugee, but rather the duties owed by the refugee to the asylum state.

[124] Article 35, 1951 Convention, *supra* note 1 and Article 8, UNHCR Statute.

[125] *See*, for an overview of UNHCR's evolving role in humanitarian assistance and development, Jeff Crisp, Mind the Gap! UNHCR, Humanitarian Assistance and the Development Process, UNHCR Working Paper No. 43, May 2001 [hereinafter Crisp].

[126] Article 8(i), UNHCR Statute.

rights to refugees (that is, so-called "legal or diplomatic protection") to an operational body that itself became engaged in activities that stretched beyond the diplomatic, such as resettlement, repatriation, and assistance.[127] According to Crisp, "UNHCR was transformed from a refugee organization into a more broadly-based humanitarian agency."[128]

Structurally today, the UNHCR is divided into two main departments: International Protection and Operations. The latter is not always understood or perceived to be part of the former, in spite of statements on integrating the two under the overarching banner of "International Protection."[129] The recent appointments of two Assistant High Commissioners, one dedicated to operations, the other to protection, arguably reinforce this division.

The UNHCR has indicated that "[strengthening protection] involves the provision of technical support, including training, of advisory services, of specialized expertise, and of financial and *material assistance*."[130] Nowhere in these documents is "protection" or "international protection" explained, although states are recognized as being "primarily responsible for providing protection to refugees,"[131] with UNHCR filling a secondary or substitute role. UNHCR has further elaborated that as far as its mandate is concerned, international protection "encompasses a range of concrete activities, covering both policy and operational concerns."[132] In particular, the UNHCR has stated that "the challenge of international protection is to secure admission, asylum, and respect by States for basic human rights, including the principle of *non-refoulement*."[133]

Under a human rights framework that embraces both civil and political as well as economic, social, and cultural rights as indivisible and interdependent,[134] the

---

[127] Guy Goodwin-Gill, International Protection and Assistance for Refugees and the Displaced: Institutional Challenges and United Nations Reform, Paper presented at the Refugee Studies Workshop, "Refugee Protection in International Law: Contemporary Challenges", Oxford, April 24, 2006, 3 [Goodwin-Gill (2006)].

[128] Crisp, *supra* note 125. *See*, also, UNHCR, The State Of The World's Refugees: In Search Of Solutions 19–55 (1995).

[129] See, e.g., EXCOM Conclusions Nos. 82 (XLVIII), para. (a) (1997).

[130] UNHCR, Strengthening Protection Capacities in Host Countries, 3d Meeting of the Global Consultations on International Protection, U.N. Doc. EC/GC/01/19, para. 5 (April 19, 2002) (emphasis added).

[131] *Id.* para. 7.

[132] UNHCR, Note on International Protection, Executive Committee of UNHCR's Programme, U.N. Doc. A/AC.96/930, para. 4 (July 7, 2000).

[133] *Id.* para. 9.

[134] *See*, Vienna Declaration on Human Rights and Programme of Action, World Conference on Human Rights, para. 5 (1993), which states: "All human rights are universal, indivisible and interdependent and interrelated. The international community must treat human rights globally in a fair and equal manner, on the same footing, and with the same emphasis."

provision of assistance (e.g. food, blankets, and shelter) constitutes fulfillment of basic human rights responsibilities under, for example, the ICESCR; and that "assistance" is (or ought to be) an integrated component of rights-protection. Certainly, the 1951 Convention contains economic rights, including rights to social security, employment, rationing, housing, and social security;[135] and national human rights decisions have confirmed these obligations, including holding that the denial of both rights to work and to social security can amount to degrading treatment or infringe human dignity.[136] Whether the UNHCR is deemed the agency most appropriately placed to delivery this assistance or whether it ought to revert to a more strictly defined mandate is open to discussion.[137] What is not open to discussion is that such assistance must be provided to refugees, and if an "international protection" framework aids its delivery, then assistance ought to fall within this broader reference to protection.

4.4. "International Protection" Obligations and Non-Refugees

Developed to apply to refugees and stateless persons following the Second World War, "international protection" as a term is now additionally used to apply to individuals who do not satisfy the strict legal requirements of the refugee definition in the 1951 Convention.[138] In 2005, the Executive Committee indicated that there are persons who "may not be eligible for refugee protection but who may be in need of international protection,"[139] suggesting that "international protection" is broader in scope than "refugee protection," or for that matter refugee law, and encompasses obligations under other branches of international law, such as protection against return to torture.[140] In fact, in 1982, the UNHCR noted a "widening

---

[135] Chs. III and IV, 1951 Convention, *supra* note 1.
[136] E.g., R (Limuela, Tesema & Adam) v. Secretary of State for the Home Department [2005] UKHL 66 (United Kingdom House of Lords decided that denying the right to social security and the right to work could amount to "degrading treatment" and contravened Article 3 ECHR); Minister for Home Affairs v. Watchenuka and Another (2004) 1 All SA 21 (SA Sup Crt, Nov. 28, 2003) (South African Supreme Court of Appeal ruled that issuing a blanket prohibition on employment to all asylum-seekers, without offering social benefits, amounted to a breach of the constitutional right to human dignity, as among those excluded would be persons who had no other means of survival.).
[137] *See*, e.g., Goodwin-Gill (2006), *supra* note 127.
[138] It is noted that this is not an issue in the African context; nor in parts of the Americas. In the European Union context, *see* Council Directive 2004/83/EC on minimum standards for the qualification and status of third country nationals or stateless persons as refugees or as persons who otherwise need international protection and the content of the protection granted (Apr. 29, 2004)
[139] *See*, e.g., EXCOM Conclusion No. 103 (LVI) (2005), *supra* note 25, Preambular para. 6.
[140] *See*, Article 3, UNCAT; Article 7, ICCPR; Article 3, ECHR. *See*, in particular, Chahal v. United Kingdom, App. No. 22414/93, 23 Eur. H.R. Rep. 413 (Nov. 15, 1996).

of the concept of persons entitled to international protection," but raised concern about the "growing disparity between the liberal way in which the concept of persons entitled to benefit from international protection is now perceived and the restrictive manner in which the refugee definition is being applied."[141] In other words, the expansion of international protection obligations has, in some instances, simply meant a transfer of persons from one legal regime to another, lesser one. Those persons who are categorized as in need of international protection short of satisfying the refugee definition rely wholly on international human rights standards for protection, whereas refugees are able to benefit from dual protection under both IRL and IHRL. In both cases, IHL would apply in the context of armed conflict, but specific provisions relevant to refugees, as identified above, may not apply to all persons.

4.5. *"Effective Protection"*

Attempts have been made to further qualify the concept of "protection" as "effective protection."[142] "Effective protection" has most notably been associated with the introduction of increasingly restrictive asylum control measures by some industrialized countries, for example, the return or transfer of asylum-seekers to alternative places of "protection" (or "safe third countries"). In this context, Legomsky includes the availability of fundamental human rights as a prerequisite to establishing that "effective protection" is available elsewhere.[143] The UNHCR has argued that respect for fundamental human rights is a minimal requirement to any such returns.[144] But

---

[141] UNHCR, Note on International Protection, U.N. Doc. A/AC.96/609/Rev.1, para. 18 (Aug. 26, 1982).

[142] *See*, Stephen H. Legomsky, Secondary Refugee Movements and the Return of Asylum Seekers to Third Countries: The Meaning of Effective Protection, UNHCR Legal and Protection Policy Research Series, PPLA/2003/01, (Feb. 2003), 52–81, in which he outlines the elements of "effective protection" as: (1) Advance consent to readmit and to provide a fair refugee status determination; (2) No refoulement to persecution in the third country; (3) Assurance that the third country will respect 1951 Convention rights; (4) Respect for international and regional human rights standards; (5) Assurance that the country will provide a fair refugee status determination; (6) Third country is a party to the 1951 Refugee Convention; (7) Availability of a durable solution in the third country [hereinafter Legomsky].

[143] *Id.* Cf. Amnesty International, UK/EU/UNHCR: Unlawful and Unworkable – Amnesty International's Views on Proposals for Extra-territorial Processing of Asylum Claims, AI Index: IOR 61/004/2003 (June 18, 2003).

[144] UNHCR, Summary Conclusions on the Concept of "Effective Protection" in the Context of Secondary Movements of Refugees and Asylum-Seekers, Lisbon Expert Roundtable, Dec. 9–10, 2002, issued Feb. 2003, para. 15(b) stated: "The following elements, while not exhaustive, are critical factors for the appreciation of 'effective protection' in the context of return to third countries.... (b) There will be respect for fundamental human rights in the third State in accordance with applicable international standards, including but not limited to the following:

it is difficult to reconcile human rights standards and return issues, as IHRL does not (or has not yet) prohibited the return or transfer of individuals to all forms of human rights violations. Likewise, asylum is not granted in respect of each and every human rights violation, only those that amount to persecutory conduct and otherwise fall within the refugee definition.[145]

At a 2002 expert roundtable organized by the UNHCR, a list of "critical factors" were identified that ought to be "appreciated" (as opposed to respected) by states contemplating the return of asylum-seekers to third countries for the processing of their claims. Among them, respect for fundamental human rights was noted, in particular that return should not occur where there is a real risk of return to torture or to cruel, inhuman or degrading treatment, threats to life, or deprivation of liberty without due process.[146] Feller has asserted that " '[e]ffective protection' is not a term of art, although rather unfortunately it is becoming one."[147] She argues that "effective protection" must be "quality protection,"[148] although the approach of many states would seem to equate "effective protection" with "minimum protection" and to import varying standards of protection that are acceptable depending on where the asylum-seeker is to be sent and processed. Hathaway argues that the concept of "'effective protection' is a linguistic ruse," finding no source for the terminology in the 1951 Convention, and further noting that "if there is such a thing as 'effective protection', one presumes that there must also be 'ineffective protection.' "[149]

4.6. *Emerging Norm of a "Responsibility to Protect"*

More recently, in the context of the UN Secretary-General's High-Level Panel on Threats, Challenges and Change, the term "protection" found a further, expanded

---

- There is no real risk that the person would be subjected to torture or to cruel, inhuman or degrading treatment or punishment in the third State;
- There is no real risk to the life of the person in the third State;
- There is no real risk that the person would be deprived of his or her liberty in the third State without due process." [hereinafter UNHCR Summary Conclusions 2002]

See, Legomsky, *supra* note 142.

[145] Only the serious human rights violations would satisfy the "persecution" element of the refugee definition; *See*, UNHCR, Note on Interpreting Article 1 of the 1951 Convention relating to the Status of Refugees, UNHCR Geneva, April 2001.

[146] UNHCR Summary Conclusions 2002, *supra* note 144, at para. 15 (e), (f), and (g). Other proposed criteria included that the third State had acceded to international refugee and human rights instruments, that fair and efficient asylum procedures were in place, and that the individual would have access to means of subsistence to maintain an adequate standard of living.

[147] Erika Feller, *Asylum, Migration and Refugee Protection: Realities, Myths and the Promise of Things to Come*, Advance Access published on Nov. 8, 2006, Int'l J. Ref. L. 510, 528 (2006).

[148] *Id.* at 529.

[149] Hathaway 2007, *supra* note 123.

meaning within what the Panel endorsed as "the emerging norm of responsibility to protect civilians in large-scale violence."[150] From a refugee perspective, UNHCR has endorsed the concept, stating that "[the concept of a 'responsibility to protect'] is…a most useful frame…within which to promote a more flexible and less discretionary approach to addressing the many protection gaps which still confront delivery of protection to persons of our concern."[151] "In other words, [the UNHCR hopes] to give genuine form to, and real outcomes flowing, from the notion of the 'responsibility to protect'."[152] Whether this new and emerging responsibility will frame the issue of protection, or be placed alongside general principles of international protection and IRL, IHRL and IHL, remains to be seen.

5. Conclusion

This article has attempted to highlight, albeit cursorily, a range of different usages of the term "international protection" (and variations upon it) in the refugee context, and to understand the roles that IRL, IHRL and IHL play, if any, in the construction of that legal concept. Clearly, the inter-linkages between these three areas of law are extensive; and yet areas of distinction are also notable. The recognition in the 1951 Convention that other rights may apply to refugees beyond those within it is a logical point of departure.[153] IHRL is an important complement to what have proven to be, at times, inadequate refugee safeguards, especially in the context of asylum-seekers or those who do not meet the narrowly constructed refugee definition in Article 1 of the 1951 Convention; while IHL continues to operate even should a state party to the 1951 Convention derogate from those provisions in time of war. Moreover, both IHRL and IHL have been sources of guidance as to who qualifies as a refugee under the 1951 Convention and/or under regional instruments.

It is evident that IRL, IHRL, and IHL are all important components of the protection of refugees, but they do not have the same terms of reference, nor do they necessarily cover the same physical territory or protect the same individuals.

---

[150] This notion was previously referred to as "humanitarian intervention". *See*, "A more secure world: our shared responsibility – Report of the High-Level Panel on Threats, Challenges and Change", U.N. Doc. A/59/565 (Dec. 2, 2004); U.N. Report of the Secretary-General, "In Larger Freedom: towards development, security and human rights for all", U.N. Doc. A/59/2005 (Mar. 21, 2005). *See also*, earlier report of the International Commission on Intervention and State Sovereignty, "The Responsibility to Protect", Dec. 2001; UNHCR, Note on International Protection, U.N. Doc. A/AC.96/1008, paras 35 & 72 (July 4, 2005); Feller (2005), *supra* note 48.
[151] Feller (2005), *supra* note 48.
[152] *Id.*
[153] Article 5, 1951 Convention, *supra* note 1.

In crude form,[154] IRL applies either at the time of seeking admission to the territory of a foreign state or after crossing a border; IHRL applies on all sides of the border; and IHL applies within states to a conflict. Refugee law applies to refugees and noting the declaratory status of refugee status, it ought also apply to asylum-seekers pending a determination of their claims; human rights law applies to all persons, with a few exceptions; and humanitarian law applies to specific categories of "protected persons."

Although it is accepted that these three branches of international law share areas of convergence as well as areas of deviation, it is not settled whether IHRL and IHL simply inform the concept of "international protection," or whether, alongside IRL, they define its parameters. In 2000, UNHCR recognized that its own "... international protection function has evolved greatly over the past five decades from being a surrogate for consular and diplomatic protection to ensuring the basic rights of refugees, including their physical safety and security."[155] The Organization further acknowledged that "a plethora of varying notions of protection have emerged recently in international debate."

In an attempt to "demystify protection and clarify its content", UNHCR stated that, "International protection is not an abstract concept. It is a dynamic and action-oriented function...with the goal of enhancing respect for the rights of refugees and resolving their problems."[156] One approach argues that only organs of the international community, such as the UNHCR, engage in "international protection."[157] States, in comparison, are said to engage in national protection in performance of their international obligations[158] or, in other words, surrogate or substitute protection.[159] But, today, the language is far more blurred than this would evince; and the emphasis placed on international burden and responsibility sharing[160] means that "protection," regardless of how it is modified by state practice, is a joint effort of both states, that have primary responsibility, and the UNHCR, which has secondary.[161]

---

[154] These distinctions are subject to whether a State has ratified the relevant treaty, has entered a reservation against a particular provision, or a provision or treaty has attained the status of customary international law or *jus cogens*.

[155] UNHCR, Note on International Protection, Executive Committee of UNHCR's Programme, U.N. Doc. A/AC.96/930, para. 2 (July 7, 2000).

[156] *Id.* para. 4. *See also*, EXCOM Conclusion No. 95(LIV) (2003), para. (b): The "international protection is both a legal concept and at the same time very much an action-oriented function."

[157] Fortin, *supra* note 95, at 568.

[158] *Id.* at n. 65.

[159] Mathew et al., *supra* note 105.

[160] *See*, e.g., EXCOM Conclusion Nos. 11 (XXIX), para. (e) (1978); 22(XXXII) (1981); 67 (XLII) (1991); 85 (XLIX) (1998); 90 (LII) (2001); 93 (LIII) (2002).

[161] *See*, e.g., EXCOM Conclusion No. 81 (XLVIII), para. (d) (1997): "*Emphasizes* that refugee protection is primarily the responsibility of States, and that UNHCR's mandated role in this regard cannot substitute for effective action, political will, and full cooperation on the part of States."

The increasingly restrictive, selective, and nuanced applications of the range of terms that cover the protection of refugees, whether in longer or shorter forms, has led to a situation of ambiguity in international discourse. Determining the scope and meaning of these terms is not purely an academic exercise; nor should the inter-linkages between these three laws be seen simply as a curiosity of the international legal system. Rather, it must be remembered that gaps, uncertainty, and disagreements that exist within the international system, alongside efforts to resolve them, can have a real impact on the lives of refugees.

Part E
Specific Situations

Chapter XVII

Fair Trial Guarantees in Occupied Territory – the Interplay between International Humanitarian Law and Human Rights Law

Yutaka Arai-Takahashi[*]

1. *Overview*

This chapter analyzes the emerging normative framework of fair trial guarantees in occupied territory, which can be discerned through the interaction between international humanitarian law (IHL) and international human rights law (IHRL). The aim is to explore the rights of the accused in criminal proceedings before a military tribunal of the occupying power (so-called occupation courts) and to assess the extent to which and how due process rights can apply to them.

Individuals accused or convicted in occupied territory can benefit from the fair trial guarantees enlisted in the Fourth Geneva Convention (GC IV)[1] and Article 75(4) of Additional Protocol I (API).[2] Articles 65–77 GC IV recognize fair trial guarantees for "protected persons" (within the meaning of Article 4), who are accused of offences against penal/security laws in occupied territory. Common Article 3 GCs contains a general clause of fair trial guarantees applicable at all times. The chapeau of Article 75(4) AP I furnishes the rights of the accused to "an impartial and regularly constituted court respecting the generally recognised principles of regular judicial procedure." This is elaborated in ten sub-paragraphs constituting the catalogue of minimum fair trial guarantees.[3] Article 75 AP I embodies

---

[*] Dr. Yutaka Arai-Takahashi is Senior Lecturer at the Law Department of the University of Kent (United Kingdom).
[1] Geneva Conventions Relative to the Protection of Civilian Persons in the Times of War, Aug. 12, 1949, 75 U.N.T.S. 287, 288 [hereinafter GC IV].
[2] Protocol Additional to the Geneva Conventions of 12 August 1949, and Relating to the Protection of Victims of International Armed Conflicts (Protocol I), opened for signature Dec. 12, 1977, U.N. Doc. 12. 1977, U.N. Doc. A/32/144, Annex I, II, (1977), *reprited in* 16 I.L.M. 1391 (1977) [hereinafger AP I].
[3] Compare Article 67 ICC Statute. Rome Statute of the International Criminal Court, July 17, 1998, U.N. Doc. A/CONF. 183/9, (1998) [hereinafter ICC Statute].

"fundamental guarantees" for those who do not benefit from more favourable treatment under the GCs or AP I.

Article 75 AP I is, therefore, a "legal safety net,"[4] now part of customary international law.[5] Both Articles 75(4) AP I and common Article 3 GCs are reflective of basic human rights law.[6] Contrary to the view expressed in the *travaux préparatoires*,[7] their scope of application is not limited to persons deprived of liberty.[8] They apply instead to *all* persons,[9] irrespective of their status, including a party's own nationals[10] and unprivileged belligerents captured in a battlefield.[11]

IHL contains more progressive elements of due process rights than IHRL. The rights of the accused are expressly recognised in the GC IV, Article 75(4) AP I and their customary counterparts. By contrast, no fair trial guarantees are expressly

---

[4] Hans-Peter Gasser, *Protection of the Civilian Population*, in The Handbook of Humanitarian law In Armed Conflicts 281 (Dieter Fleck ed., 1995).

[5] IACmHR, Report on Terrorism and Human Rights, OEA/Ser.L/V/II.116, Doc. 5 rev. 1 corr. 22 Oct. 2002, *available at* www.cidh.org/Terrorism/Eng/toc.htm (last visited Sept. 12, 2007), paras 64 and 257.

The US government has considered Article 75 as part of the customary rules embodied in Protocol I: Us Army, Operational Law Handbook 5ff (2002); Michael J. Matheson, *The United States Position on the Relation of Cusotmary International Law to the 1977 Protocols Additional to the 1949 Geneva Conventions*, 2 Am. U. J. Int'l L. & POL'Y 419, 427–428 & 432 (1987). *See also* Christopher J. Greenwood, *Customary Law Status of the 1977 Geneva Protocols*, in Humanitarian Law of Armed Conflict: Challenges Ahead: Essays in Honor of Frits Kalshoven 93, 103 (Astrid J.M. Delissen & Gerard J. Tanja eds., 1991).

[6] Gasser, *supra* note 4, at 233.

[7] *See* Official Records of the Diplomatic Conference on the Reaffirmation of International Humanitarian Law Applicable in Armed Conflicts, Geneva (1974–1977) [hereinafter Official Records], Vol. XV, (Federal Political Department 1978], at 406–461, CDDH/407/Rev. 1, paras 41–42 (Report of Committee III). Id. at 460, CDDH/407/Rev. 1, para. 41. This restrictive scope of application *ratione personae* was proposed by Australia and the United States, CDDH/III/314, reported in Official Records, Vol. III, at 292; and Official Records, Vol. XV, at 40, CDDR/III/SR.43, para. 80 (statement by Mr. de Stoop of Australia). In contrast, for a broader personal scope of application of Article 75, see Official Records, Vol. XV, CDDH/III/SR. 43, para. 74 (statement by Mr. Condorelli of Italy).

[8] Michael Bothe, Karl J. Partsch & Waldemar A. Solf, New Rules for Victims of Armed Conflicts 463 (1982) [hereinafter Bothe et al.].

[9] Jean-Marie Henckaerts & Louise Doswald-Beck, Customary International Humanitarian Law (hereinafter Study), Vol. I, at 352–374, Rules 100–102.

[10] See Civilians Claims Eritrea's Claims 15, 16, 23 & 27–32, Eritrea Ethiopia Claims Commission, Dec. 17, 2004, 44 ILM 601, 608 (para. 30) & 617 (para. 97) (2005).

[11] For the argument that even battlefield unprivileged belligerents can be covered by the protections of GC IV, on the basis that the combat zone has been transformed into an occupied territory, or that they were transferred to occupied part of the territory, *see*: Knut Dörmann & Laurent Colassis, *International Humanitarian Law in the Iraq Conflict*, 47 German Ybk I. L. 292, 322–327 (2004).

classified as non-derogable under Article 4 of the ICCPR.[12] The drafters of the Additional Protocols (APs) enumerated ten due process rights under Article 75(4) AP I for the purpose of precluding state parties invoking the derogation clause under Article 4 ICCPR.[13] At the Diplomatic Conference in Geneva (1974–1977), the Dutch Delegate, referring to Article 4 ICCPR, made clear that draft Article 65 (now Article 75) was intended to make many of the due process guarantees recognised in the ICCPR applicable even in time of war.[14]

Notwithstanding this, the combined effectiveness of the rights guaranteed under GC IV and Article 75(4) AP I is insufficient. Many IHL provisions remain unelaborated. Despite the detailed elaborations of the rights contained under Article 75(4) AP I, *specific* elements of the rights concerning the means of defence are expressly recognised only in Articles 71–73 GC IV, the personal scope of application of which is confined to protected persons in occupied territories.[15] It is therefore crucial to identify customary IHL rights equipped with a broader material and personal scope of application.

All fair trial guarantees under treaty-based IHL rules find parallels in IHRL. To what extent and under what conditions may the jurisprudence and doctrine on corresponding rights under IHRL be invoked to fill the gaps of treaty-based IHL? Problems arise with respect to rights yet to be recognised as non-derogable under IHRL. In what ways can specific elements and principles fleshed out in relation to *derogable* rights in non-emergency circumstances be regarded as customary rules? In particular, can these elements be transposed to the context of occupation and international armed conflict?[16]

It is important to highlight three objectives that can be fulfilled by the complementary role of IHRL practice and doctrine: (i) clarification of the meaning of fair trial guarantees that remain unarticulated under IHL; (ii) elaboration of specific

---

[12] International Covenant on Civil and Political Rights, G.A. Res. 2200A [XXI], 21 U.N. GAOR (Supp. No. 16) at 52, U.N. Doc. A/6316 (Dec. 16, 1966), 999 U.N.T.S. 171, entered into force Mar. 23, 1976 [hereinafter ICCPR].

[13] Bothe et al., *supra* note 8, at 464.

[14] *Official Records*, Vol. XV, Summary Record of the 43rd Meeting (April 30, 1976), at 28, CDDH/III/SR.43, paras 16–17, the statement of Mr Schutte (Netherlands).

[15] Along the same line, Olivier argues that IHL "is, by its very nature, discriminatory" in that only those pertaining to the protected groups are covered by this body of law. Clémentine Olivier, *Revising General Comment No. 29 of the United Nations Human Rights Committee: About Fair Trial Rights and Derogations in Times of Public Emergency*, 17 Leiden J. Int'l L. 405, 408 (2004).

[16] Heike Krieger, *The Relationship Between Humanitarian Law and Human Rights Law in the ICRC Customary Law Study*, 11 JCSL 265, 285–286 (2006). However, contrary to her suggestion, the Study's reference in its Vol. II (and not in Vol. I) to the case of European Court of Human Rights decided in non-emergency circumstances (Van Leer v. the Netherlands, Judgment, Feb. 21, 1990)) is designed more as a reference point only: Study, Vol. II, Part 2, at 2351, para. 2715; and Vol. I (2006), Rule 99, at 350 (the right of a person arrested to be informed of the reasons for arrest).

elements of fair trial guarantees; and (iii) supplementing of additional prerequisites for fair trial guarantees. Clearly, it is justifiable to use guidelines derived from IHRL to obtain clarity in relation to the elements already embodied in GCs and Article 75(4) AP I. In contrast, to integrate as part of customary IHL entirely new elements of fair trial guarantees, which are developed in the doctrine and the case law of IHRL *in non-emergency circumstances,* requires special caution in not overstepping the material scope of application of *lex lata* by incorporating elements of *lex ferenda*. One must duly weigh the normative status, relevance, and weight, as well as the scope of application of principles enunciated by the monitoring bodies of IHRL to extraordinary situations faced by occupation courts.

2. *Normative Status and Weight of Evidence for Ascertaining Customary International Law*

2.1. *The Structure of Analysis*

The methodology of harnessing effective convergence between IHL and IHRL to deduce customary IHL rules on the rights of the accused can be disaggregated into three processes: (i) the identification of customary law status of the rules contained in IHL treaty provisions concerning fair trial guarantees; (ii) the ascertainment of whether corresponding IHRL rules are non-derogable and thus applicable in any circumstances, including occupation; and (iii) the evaluation of whether, in what ways and to what extent, the elements and principles elaborated by IHRL monitoring bodies can be transposed to IHL.

2.2. *Identification of Customary Law Status of Fair Trial Guarantees in IHL Treaty Provisions*

2.2.1. *Overview*
All the fair trial guarantees described as customary IHL by the ICRC's Customary International Humanitarian Law Study (hereinafter Study) are, except for the right of appeal, embodied in Articles 65–77 GC IV and Article 75 AP I. The customary law status of the due process rights safeguarded in GC IV is beyond doubt. Meron argues that most rules embodied in the GCs are the prime examples of treaty rules accepted as reflecting customary principles without even need to examine concordant practice.[17] The question is rather whether their personal scope of application is broadened to encompass all accused persons. With respect to

---
[17] Theodor Meron, The Humanization of International Law 381 (2006) [hereinafter Meron 2006].

Article 75(4) AP I, what remains unclarified is the extent to which customary law status can be attributed to rights implicitly derived from the general phrase "the generally recognized principles of regular judicial procedure". For the purpose of analysing customary law, the distinction must be drawn between the ten specific requirements expressly embodied in this provision and additional elements that are implied rights.

2.2.2. *The Customary Law Status of the Elements of the Rights of the Accused under Article 75(4) AP I*

It may be contended that the declaratory nature of the judicial guarantees recognised in Article 75(4) AP I dispenses with inquiries into the interaction between treaty-based rules and customary norms, without much further ado. Even so, the ascertainment of this correlation must be considered essential to the extent that this provides guidance on the mechanism and the validity of deducing additional guarantees as implied rights from a treaty provision. The examination touches upon the question of the "entangled strands of treaty and custom" in a more than tangential manner.[18]

In the *North Sea Continental Shelf Cases*, the International Court of Justice (ICJ) recognised the possibility of a treaty norm generating a customary rule. It stated that:

> [t]here is no doubt that this process [the process of a treaty provision generating new customary law] is a perfectly possible one and does from time to time occur.[19]

Whether a particular IHL provision can be described as a "norm-creating provision" ought to be evaluated against benchmarks suggested in that case.[20] According to the ICJ, the relevant treaty provision:

> should, at all events potentially, be of a fundamentally norm-creating character such as could be regarded as forming the basis of a general rule of law."[21] Still, the Court added a caveat that the process of a treaty rule yielding customary law "is not lightly to be regarded as having been attained.[22]

---

[18] Oscar Schachter, *Entangled Treaty and Custom*, *in* International Law at a Time of Perplexity: Esssays in Honour of Shabtain Rosenne 718 (Yoram Dinstein ed., 1989).
[19] 1969 ICJ Rep 41, para. 71 (Feb. 20). *See also* Gerald Fitzmaurice, *Some Problems Regarding the Formal Sources of International Law, in* Symbolae Verzijl 157 (1958) (emphasis in original) [hereinafter Fitzmaurice].
[20] 1969 ICJ Rep 41, para. 71(Feb. 20) (concerning Article 6 of the 1958 Geneva Convention on the Continental Shelf, which contains the equidistance principle for the delimitation of continental shelves).
[21] *Id.* para. 72.
[22] *Id.* para. 71.

Villiger argues that the two yardsticks, "fundamentally-norm generating character" and "general rule of law," are instrumental in understanding the mechanism of a treaty provision developing into custom.[23] These two yardsticks call for the capacity of a norm to regulate *pro futuro*.[24] The rules embodied in ten sub-paragraphs of Article 75(4) AP I, one of the axiomatic provisions of the "law-making" treaty (*traité loi*), can be considered to meet these two requirements. When discussing the possibility of ascribing customary law status to a treaty rule, Schachter distinguishes between codification treaties and "treaty rules resulting from widely politicized debates and bloc voting." He suggests that the application of the criteria of State practice and *opinio juris* varies, depending on: (i) the nature of the convention; (ii) the relationship of the convention to "basic values;" (iii) the process by which the convention came into existence.[25]

Apart from the "fundamentally norm-creating character", the other criterion is "a very widespread and representative participation in the convention," which "include[s] that of States whose interests were specially affected."[26] This evinces that if many "States with priority in contributing to the creating of customary international law...object to the formation of a custom, no custom can emerge."[27] While this requirement *might* pose a potential problem for the customary law formation of some API provisions, it is clearly satisfied in relation to Article 75 AP I, which was adopted by consensus.

Even if a treaty provision like Article 75(4) AP I serves as a vehicle for a "customary law generator," the crucial question is the verification of evidence of evolving customary norms in relation to states *not* parties to AP I.[28] In the *North Sea Continental Shelf Cases*, the ICJ emphasised the need to leave aside the practice of contracting parties (and of states that would shortly become parties) *inter se*, since these "were...acting actually or potentially in the application of the Convention [the Geneva Convention on the Continental Shelf]. From their action no inference could legitimately be drawn as to the existence of a rule of customary international

---

[23] Mark E. Villiger, Customary International Law and Treaties 177–178 (2d ed. 1997) [hereinafter Villiger].
[24] *Id.* at 177–179.
[25] Oscar Schachter, *Remarks in Disentangling Treaty and Customary Law*, 81 ASIL Proc. 158, 159 (1987).
[26] 1969 ICJ Rep 41, para. 73 (Feb. 20).
[27] Yoram Dinstein, *The ICRC Customary International Humanitarian Law Study*, 36 Israel Y.B. Hum. Rts. 1, 13 (2006) [hereinafter Dinstein].
[28] Robert Cryer, *Of Custom, Treaties, Scholars and the Gavel: The Influence of the International Criminal Tribunals on the ICRC Customary Law Study*, 11 JCSL 239, 244 (2006) [hereinafter Cryer]; Dinstein, *supra* note 27, at 10; and Villiger, *supra* note 23, at 183.

law..."²⁹ Here lies the methodological conundrum.³⁰ In view of the large number of states parties to AP I, to evaluate the practice and *opinio juris* of states *dehors* the framework of this treaty, with focus on conduct and legal views of non-parties *inter se* (as well as on those of state parties vis-à-vis third parties), becomes highly intractable.³¹

With respect to the due process guarantees of Article 75(4) AP I, it is safe to observe that by the time of the adoption of AP I in 1977, i.e. one year after the entry into force of ICCPR, all were established as customary law in *non-emergency* circumstances. However, the applicability of most of them to extraordinary situations like international armed conflict and occupation was yet to be recognised. As discussed, the ten specific elements of the rights of the accused were enumerated with a view to fending off the possibility that states parties to AP I might call into play the derogation clause of Article 4 ICCPR. This shows that many of these elements were perceived as innovations.³² Uncertainty remains as to the extent of codificatory elements.³³

It is clear that most of the procedural elements under Article 75(4) AP I have hardened into customary law after the adoption of this treaty. The fluid and haphazard manner in which customary rules evolve makes it impossible to pinpoint the precise juncture at which such customary rules have been shaped and consolidated. The crux of the matter is that at present they all are declaratory of customary IHL.

---

[29] *North Sea Continental Shelf* Cases, 1969 ICJ Reps, para. 76 (Feb. 20). *See also* the US Department of State, *US Initial Reactions to the ICRC Study on Customary International Law*, Nov. 3, 2006.

[30] This is what is often referred to as "Baxter's paradox." For details, *see* Richard R. Baxter, *Multilateral Treaties as Evidence of Customary International Law*, 41 Brit. Y.B. Int'l L. 275, 282–283 (1965–1966).

[31] Villiger, *supra* note 23, at 183–184. *See also* Dinstein, *supra* note 27, at 10.

[32] No debut, at least two rules, the prohibition of collective punishment and the principle of *nullum crimen nulla poena sine lege* which are contained in sub-paragraphs (b) and (c) respectively, were deemed as codificatory at the Diplomatic Conference on Humanitarian Law in 1973–1977. Von Glahn suggests that many of the rights of the accused were primarily based on the experience during WWII and considered innovative at the time of 1949. Gerhard von Glahn, The Occupation of Enemy Territory – A Commentary on the Law and Practice of Belligerent Occupation (1957) [hereinafter von Glahn].

[33] Zappalà argues that the right to be presumed innocent or any equivalent guarantee was not recognized by the Nuremberg and the Tokyo Military Tribunals. Salvatore Zappalà, *The Rights of the Accused*, *in* The Rome Statute of the International Criminal Court: A Commentary 1319, 1341 (Antonio Cassese, Paola Gaeta & John R.W.D. Jones eds, 2002).

2.2.3. Additional Elements of the Rights of the Accused, Which Can Be Derived from Article 75(4) AP I, and the Ascertainment of Corresponding Customary Rules

It can be proposed that the ten fair trial guarantees contained in Article 75(4) AP I be construed as merely exemplary, so that this open-ended list be supplemented by more detailed elements recognised as inalienable under IHRL. The general phrase "the generally recognized principles of regular judicial procedure" in its chapeau is accompanied by the wording "which include the following." Similarly, common Article 3 GCs stresses the minimum requirement of "affording all the judicial guarantees which are recognized as indispensable by civilized peoples." These provisions are couched in general terms without stringent conditions for their application. Even so, there remains a problem of *how* to identify additional elements that can be "grafted" onto the treaty provision of Article 75(4) AP I without overstepping the bounds of teleological interpretation. Some authors argue that "[i]t is legitimate to have recourse to the corresponding provisions of the Covenant [ICCPR] in order to define which principles of regular judicial procedure are generally recognized."[34] Yet, when advocating the "borrowing" of specific fair trial requirements from Article 14, they fail to delve into the relationship between IHL and IHRL.

This chapter proposes that the general phrase "the generally recognized principles of regular judicial procedure" be interpreted in the light of corresponding customary rules. Within this analytical framework, this general phrase provides a vehicle through which customary international law can be called into play to cement the relationship between IHL and IHRL. The next step is to examine the extent to which the development of fair trial rights in the IHRL context has impacted upon customary IHL. It is assumed that the proposed interpretation remains within the framework of the conventional norm, and that it is not intended as a modification of a declaratory treaty rule by new customary international law. There is no conflict between a component element of the conventional rule and a new element of the customary rule.[35] Still, it should be remarked that there is no clear-cut demarcation line between interpretation and modification. Villiger provides a cogent argument on this matter:

> parties may, in their interpretation, gradually wander from the original text towards a different content and thereby modify the rule.... Modificatory practice via adaptation may eventually constitute a new customary rule.[36]

Nevertheless, there is need for raw empirical data. The state practice and *opinio juris* must indicate that additional rights of accused applicable in occupied territory are no longer in *statu nascendi* but clearly embedded in the premises of customary

---

[34] Bothe et al., *supra* note 8, at 464.
[35] For a detailed analysis of this issue, *see* Villiger, *supra* note 23, at 193–223.
[36] *Id.* at 213.

rules, and that the material scope of application of such rules covers extraordinary situations like occupation. To argue that the general phrase used in Article 75(4) AP I is declaratory of customary law so as to obliterate *individuated* inquiries into customary law status of each of new elements is unpersuasive. In undertaking an empirical survey, there may be an obstacle to identifying sufficient degree of state practice and *opinio juris* relating to fair trial guarantees that are apposite in specific context of occupation. In response, it can be argued that in contrast to other areas of international law, the standard of evidence applied by international tribunals for ascertaining the material and psychological elements may not be stringent under IHL.[37]

2.3. *Ascertainment of Non-Derogability*

Apart from Article 27(2) ACHR, which only generally describes the judicial guarantees essential to the protection of non-derogable rights as inalienable, none of the fair trial guarantees embodied in IHL provisions is classified as non-derogable in IHRL. This does not handicap the methodology of integrating detailed elements from the case law and the doctrinal discourse developed in the IHRL context. A preliminary observation is that the derogable rights are not automatically to be suspended in time of occupation or other public emergencies. Their continued applicability is not affected unless and until an occupying power duly invokes the derogation clause and satisfies the necessary conditions, including notification. Assuming that the occupant meets such conditions, two further arguments need to be explored.

First, it may be asked whether the customary law equivalents of fair trial guarantees embodied in Articles 71–73 GC IV and Article 75(4) AP I have their scope of application *ratione materiae (*and *ratione personae)* extended to cover all accused persons in any circumstances relating to armed conflict and occupation. With respect to the customary law concomitant of Article 75(4) AP I, may it be claimed that its material scope goes beyond the situations defined in Article 1 AP I so as to encompass non-international armed conflict, including that taking place in occupied territory? The fact that the list of fair trial guarantees under Article 6 AP II[38] is truncated in half has not debarred the ICRC's Customary IHL Study from

---

[37] Frederic L. Kirgis, *Custom on a Sliding Scale*, 81 Am. J. Int'l L. 146, 149 (1987) [hereinafter Kirgis]; Theodor Meron, Human Rights and Humanitarian Law as Customary Law 44–45 (1989) [hereinafter Meron 1989]; *id. supra* note 17, at 380–381; Anthea E. Roberts, *Traditional and Modern Approaches to Customary International Law: A Reconciliation*, 95 Am. J. Int'l L. 757, 764–766, 772–774, 778–779, 790 (2001) [hereinafter Roberts].

[38] Note that at the Diplomatic Conference at Geneva (1974–1977), Committee III adopted draft Article 65 (now Article 75) AP I by incorporating into it the elements of Articles 6 and 10 of draft AP II. *Official Records*, Vol. XV, at 460, para. 40.

asserting this conclusion. With regard to the rights of the accused under Articles 71–73 GC IV, they may be described as "the core of the due process guarantees" under GC IV, which amount to "general principles of law" within Article 38(1)(c) ICJ Statute and hence are opposable to all states.[39] Alternatively, it can be contended that the customary law equivalent of these treaty-based rules has their scope of application expanded to cover persons other than protected persons.

Second, under IHRL the non-derogable nature of many fair trial guarantees is supported by the case-law and the documents of IHRL monitoring bodies. For identifying inalienable elements in IHRL, the ICRC's Customary IHL Study relies on the HRC's General Comment No. 29 and the IACmHR's Report on Terrorism and Human Rights, both of which have articulated supplementary catalogues of non-derogable rights. Useful insight may also be obtained from the AfCHPR's soft-law documents specifically dealing with fair trial guarantees.[40]

The General Comment 29 stresses that "certain elements of the right to a fair trial" are explicitly guaranteed under IHL.[41] It contends that "the principles of legality and the rule of law" underpin the safeguards relating to derogation under Article 4, and that even during armed conflict and occupation, "fundamental requirements of fair trial" must be guaranteed.[42] Nevertheless, caution is needed. The Committee's reference to core elements of due process guarantees is confined to three procedural safeguards: (i) access to a court in case of criminal proceedings; (ii) the presumption of innocence; and (iii) the right to *habeas corpus* or *amparo*, namely, the right to take proceedings before a court to have the lawfulness of detention determined without delay.[43] As an alternative, reliance can be made on the Report on Terrorism and Human Rights. This gives the most liberal current to the expanded scope of non-derogable rights.

---

[39] Meron 1989, *supra* note 37, at 49–50. He refers specifically to three rules: the *nullum crimen, nulla poena sine lege* principle (Article 65); the general principles of criminal law, in particular the proportionality of a penalty to an offence (Article 67); and the requirement that "[n]o sentence shall be pronounced by the competent courts of the Occupying Power except after a regular trial" (Article 71).

[40] See, for instance, *Principles and Guidelines on the Right to a Fair Trial and Legal Assistance in Africa*, adopted at the 33rd Ordinary Session, Niamey, Niger (May 15–29, 2003).

[41] HRC, General Comment 29, States of Emergency (Article 4), U.N. Doc. CCPR/C/21/Rev.1/Add. 11 (2001), Aug. 31, 2001 (adopted on July 24, 2001), para. 16.

[42] *Id.*

[43] *Id.*

2.4. Methodology to Transpose Specific Elements and Principles from the Documents and Case Law of IHRL Monitoring Bodies

2.4.1. Overview

The ICRC's Study draws considerably on documents and case-law of IHRL monitoring bodies to identify elements proffering building blocks for constructing its customary IHL framework. Its approach to fair trial guarantees is nonetheless wanting in two respects. First, it fails to determine the normative status and weight of such sources.[44] Second, it does not address the questions whether, and if so, to what extent, it is methodologically defensible to transfer the elements and principles developed in relation to those fair trial guarantees which are yet to be declared non-derogable even in the documents or the case-law of IHRL monitoring bodies.

2.4.2. The Normative Significance of the Case-law of the Monitoring Bodies of IHRL in Ascertaining Customary International Law

It is necessary to diagnose the normative status and weight of the case-law for the purpose of identifying customary international law. Inquiries are firstly made into the decisions of international tribunals as a "quasi-formal source" or "formally material source" of international law in the sense described by Fitzmaurice.[45]

Pursuant to Article 38(1)(d) ICJ Statute, judicial decisions are subsidiary means of identifying international law. Even though there is no common-law doctrine of binding precedent or *stare decisis*, the decisions of international tribunals serve as an authoritative source of developing international law.[46] They play a highly influential role in identifying (if not generating) customary international law.[47] After discussing that the Court's decisions have helped formulate or clarify "varying degrees of crystallisation" of rules of international law, and established "a kind of fixed 'jurisprudence'", Hersch Lauterpacht argues that "this general recognition of the persuasive force of judicial precedent" indicates "the method and the spirit in which the Court may be counted upon to approach similar cases."[48] Similarly,

---

[44] For the same criticism in the context of international criminal law, *see* Cryer, *supra* note 28, at 252.

[45] Fitzmaurice, *supra* note 19, at 173 and 176.

[46] *See* Oppenheim's International Law: Vol. I: Peace, 41, para. 13 (Robert Y. Jennings & Arthur Watts eds, 9th ed, 1992) (footnotes omitted).

[47] Shahabuddeen notes that the decision of the ICJ can only recognize the emergence of a new customary rule which is at the final stage of crystallization. Mohamed Shahabuddeen, Precedent in the World Court 72 (1996). In contrast, *see* Robert Y. Jennings, *The Judiciary, International and National, and the Development of International Law*, 45 Int'l Comp. L. Q. 1, 3 (1996).

[48] Hersch Lauterpacht, The Development of International Law by the International Court 18 (1958).

Schwarzenberger claims that the subjective impartiality of judges, "an international outlook which represents the world's main legal systems and high technical standards" are the three hallmarks that accord the ICJ the prominent place in "the hierarchy of the elements of law-determining agencies." Even so, his support for regional or *ad hoc* courts in such a hierarchy is more mitigated.[49] Rousseau furnishes a crucial insight into the ascertainment of customary law through decisions of judicial bodies. He argues that

> ...les règles qui se dégagent des décisions judiciaries ne s'imposant pas en tant que décisions jurisprudentielles, mais uniquement comme éléments de la coutume lorsqu'elles sont suffisamment constants pour paraître refléter l'assentiment générale des Etats....[50]

Nguyen Quoc Dinh recognises that in view of their elements of coherence, continuity and legitimate expectation (*sécurité juridique*) the decisions of international tribunals can be given more authoritative weight than academic opinions.[51] Nevertheless, this is not sufficient to make the jurisprudence in general as a veritable source of international law.[52]

To return to the case-law of the HRC, its role as the supervisory body of the universal human rights treaty in providing cogent evidence of customary law rights cannot be underrated. First, the HRC members serve on an individual capacity. Second, the individual complaints (and inter-state complaints that have never been utilised) must be screened through the rigorous process of admissibility decisions based on established procedural grounds. Third, in examining the merits of petitions, the HRC supplies coherently reasoned opinions, which are attended by separate and dissenting opinions. These features bear striking resemblance to judicial decisions. Similar observations can be made about the opinions of the AfCmHPR and the IACmHR. Despite their limited geographical scope of application, their intrinsic quality, ought not to be overlooked.

2.4.3. *The Normative Significance of the Documents of IHRL Monitoring Bodies in Ascertaining Customary International Law*

Equally, authoritative weight can be ascribed to the supervisory organs of IHRL treaties, including the HRC's General Comments. Pursuant to Article 40(4) ICCPR, the HRC is authorised to transmit such general comments as it may see fit to the states parties and, together with copies of state reports, to ECOSOC.

---

[49] *See also* Georg Schwarzenberger, International Law as Applied by International Courts and Tribunals, vol. I, 30 (3rd ed, 1957).
[50] Charles Rousseau, Droit International Public, Tome I, 368–369 (1970).
[51] This is supported by Fitzmaurice, *supra* note 19, at 174–175.
[52] Nguyen Quoc Dinh – Droit International Public, 389–390, para. 265, (Patrick Daillier & Alain Pellet ed., 5th ed, 1994).

They are purported to elucidate the nature of obligations on states parties, elaborate the scope of protection of rights, and supply suggestions concerning cooperation between states parties in applying ICCPR provisions.[53]

Two arguments can be put forward. First, the General Comments can be considered as a "subsequent practice in the application of the treaty which establishes the agreement of the parties regarding its interpretation" within the meaning of Article 31(3)(b) of the Vienna Convention on the Law of Treaties. It is possible to argue that the state parties to the ICCPR have agreed to "delegate" to the monitoring body (HRC) the power of clarifying the meaning of this treaty.[54] Nowak describes the General Comments as evidentiary of "the most authoritative interpretation" of the ICCPR's provisions.[55] Second, it is possible to contend that the General Comments being the fruits of elaborate doctrinal discourse of the leading experts on IHRL, their status and weight as a material source of international law are comparable to, but more authoritative than, the writings of leading publicists. Similar observations can be said about the IACmHR's Report on Terrorism and Human Rights.[56] In accordance with Article 41 ACHR, the mandate of the IACmHR includes the preparation of reports as it considers advisable in performing its duties and the submission of an annual report to the General Assembly of the OAS. However, the Report is the product of a regional human rights body. Clearly, where it is invoked to support customary law status of specific elements or their non-derogable nature, care must be taken not to read its evidential value in universal context without separate evidence traceable outside the OAS mechanism.

Having analysed the methodology of recruiting specific elements of due process guarantees from IHRL practice into IHL, the examinations now turn to elements that are identifiable both in IHL and IHRL through customary law. As explained, the analysis divides elements expressly articulated in sub-paragraphs of Article 75(4) AP I and those implicitly derived from the general terms used in its chapeau.

---

[53] Manfred Nowak, UN Covenant on Civil and Political Rights – CCPR Commentary 746–748 (2d ed. 2005), paras 61–64 [hereinafter Nowak].

[54] Orakhelashvili argues that "Where treaties provide for a supervisory body entrusted with the function of interpretation and application of the treaty, it follows naturally that it is not only the practice and attitudes of the contracting states that matter, but also the attitudes expressed by the supervisory body itself." Alexander Orakhelashvili, *Restrictive Interpretation of Human Rights Treaties in the Recent Jurisprudence of the European Court of Human Rights*, 14 Eur. J. Int'l L. 529, 535–536 (2003).

[55] Nowak, *supra* note 53, at Introduction, XXII, para. 6.

[56] *See also* The *Cleveland Principles of International Law on the Detention and Treatment of Persons in Connection with the "Global War on Terror"*, drafted by experts on Nov. 7, 2005 at Case Western Reserve University School of Law.

3. The Elements of the Rights of the Accused Expressly Contained in Article 75(4) Ap I

3.1. Overview

Any individual accused in occupied territory is beneficiary of the fundamental principles of criminal law, starting with the principle of *nullum crimen nulla poena sine lege*.[57] Nine other fair trial guarantees are expressly recognized in Article 75(4) AP I: the right to be presumed innocent; the right to be informed of the nature and the cause of accusation; the right to trial by an independent, impartial and regularly constituted court; the right of the accused to be present at the trial; the right to examine and to have examined witnesses; the right not to be compelled to testify and the protection against coerced confessions; the right to be informed of available remedies and time-limits; *ne bis in idem*; and the right to public proceedings. This section focuses on the right to trial by an independent, impartial and regularly constituted court, and *ne bis in idem*.

3.2. The Right to Trial by an Independent, Impartial and Regularly Constituted Court

3.2.1. Overview

Individuals accused of offences against penal/security laws in occupied territory have a right to be tried by an independent, impartial and regularly constituted court.[58] The ICRC Study describes this right as part of customary IHL.[59]

Article 66 GC IV requires occupation courts to be "properly constituted, non-political military courts."[60] Reference to "military courts" under Article 66 of GC IV does not debar civilians serving on such courts. The only condition is that they must be subordinate to direct military control and authority.[61] At the Diplomatic Conference of Geneva in 1949, the reference to "civil courts" in the Stockholm draft text of Article 66 of GC IV (draft Article 57) was deleted on two grounds. First, the Committee III, which was responsible for drafting the Civilians Convention,

---

[57] Article 75(4)(c) AP I, *supra* note 2; and second sentence of Article 65 and the first sentence of Article 67 GC IV, *supra* note 1. The prohibition of retroactive application of criminal law is designated as non-derogable in ICCPR (Article 4), ACHR (Article 27) and ECHR (Articles 7 and 15).

[58] Article 75(4) chapeau AP I, *supra* note 2; common Article 3 GCs; and Article 66 GCIV, *supra* note 1.

[59] Study, *supra* note 9, Vol. I, at 354–356.

[60] At the Diplomatic Conference of Geneva in 1949, the expression "properly constituted" was substituted for the original word "regular", which was considered insufficient to denote the requirement of adequate safeguard: *Final Record of the Diplomatic Conference of Geneva of 1949* (hereinafter, *Final Record*), Vol. II-A, (Bern: Federal Political Department), at 833.

[61] von Glahn, *supra* note 32, at 116.

felt that this expression would implicitly allow the occupying power to extend part of its civil legislation to occupied territory. Second, civil courts were considered more susceptible to politics than military courts.[62]

The second sentence of Article 66 GC IV states that "[c]ourts of appeal shall preferably sit in the occupied territory." This does not obligate the occupying power to set up a system of appeal. The second sentence of Article 73(2) GC IV clarifies that in the absence of appeal procedures, the convicted persons are entitled to petition against the finding and sentence to the "competent authority" of the occupant. The theatre commander of the occupant (or a military governor) can act as such "competent authority."[63]

3.2.2. Non-Derogability under the Practice of IHRL

IHRL practice and doctrine elucidate the meaning of independence and impartiality, while providing additional prerequisites for a "regularly constituted court." IHRL treaties guarantee the right to a "competent" tribunal,[64] or a tribunal "established by law" while specifically requiring elements of independence and impartiality.[65] Yet, this right does not belong to the catalogue of non-derogable rights expressly mentioned under the derogation clauses. Its peremptory character, however, was recognised by case-law and the document of some IHRL monitoring bodies. The IACmHR's Report on Terrorism and Human Rights specifically affirms that the elements of independence and impartiality must be guaranteed in all circumstances.[66] In the *Civil Liberties Organisation and Others v. Nigeria*, the AfCmHPR enunciated that Article 7 of the African Charter, which guarantees, *inter alia*, "the right to be tried… by an impartial court or tribunal," embodies a non-derogable right.[67] On the other hand, in the more universal context of ICCPR, the HRC has stopped short of specifying elements of independence and impartiality in its enlarged parameters

---

[62] *Final Record, II-A, supra* note 60, at 765 and 833.
[63] von Glahn, *supra* note 32, at 117.
[64] Article 14(1) ICCPR, *supra* note 12; Article 8(1) American Convention on Human Rights, O.A.S. Treaty Series No. 36, 1144 U.N.T.S. 123, entered into force July 18, 1978, reprinted in Basic Documents Pertaining to Human Rights in the Inter-American System, OEA/Ser.L.V/II.82 doc.6 rev.1 at 25 (1992) [hereinafter ACHR]; Article 40(2)(b)(iii) Convention on the Rights of the Child, Nov. 20, 1989, 1577 U.N.T.S. 3 [hereinafter CRC].
[65] Article 14(1) ICCPR, *supra* note 12; Article 6(1) Convention for the Protection of Human Rights and Fundamental Freedoms, 213 U.N.T.S. 222, entered into force Sept. 3, 1953, as amended by Protocols Nos 3, 5, 8, and 11 which entered into force on Sept. 21, 1970, Dec. 20, 1971, Jan. 1, 1990, and Nov. 1, 1998 respectively [hereinafter ECHR]; Article 8(1) ACHR, *supra* note 64; Articles 7(1)(d) and 26 African Charter on Human and Peoples' Rights, June 27, 1981, 21 ILM 58 (1982) [hereinafter AfCHPR]; Article 40(2)(b)(iii) CRC, *supra* note 64.
[66] IACmHR, Report on Terrorism and Human Rights, *supra* note 5, paras. 245, 247.
[67] AfCmHPR, Civil Liberties Organization and Others v. Nigeria, 218/98, Decision (April 23–May 7, 2001), para. 27.

of inalienable rights, invoking only the general phrase "fundamental principles of fair trial" or "fundamental requirements of fair trial."[68]

3.2.3. The IHRL's Complementary Role

The complementary role of IHRL is instrumental in elucidating specific procedural elements of this right that must be provided by occupation courts. The words "properly constituted...courts" under Article 66 GC IV or the term "regularly constituted court" under common Article 3 GCs and Article 75(4) AP I are unarticulated. By drawing on the practice of IHRL, the ICRC's Customary IHL Study stresses that the wording "regularly or property constituted" should be interpreted as requiring the courts to be established in accordance with the laws and procedures already in force in the country concerned.[69]

With regard to independence, the survey of the practice of IHRL suggests that this demands a judicial organ to be able to make decisions free from any influence from the executive.[70] As regards impartiality, the *subjective* impartiality requires judges to be free from preconceptions on the case *sub judice* (especially, the guilt of the accused or any other prejudice or bias against him/her) and to act in a manner that does not promote the interests of one of the parties.[71] In addition, objective impartiality demands that the tribunals or judges must offer sufficient guarantees to remove any legitimate doubt about their impartiality.[72]

---

[68] UNHRC, General Comment No. 29, paras. 11, 16.

[69] Study, Vol. I, *supra* note 9, at 355.

[70] UNHRC, 468/1991, CCPR/C/49/D/468/1991, Bahamonde v. Equatorial Guinea, Views, (Oct. 20, 1993), para. 9.4. For the jurisprudence of AfCHPR, see AfCmHPR, Centre for Free Speech v. Nigeria, 206/97, Decision (Nov. 15, 1999), paras 15–16. For the case-law of the ECHR, see ECtHR, Belilos v. Switzerland, Judgment (April 29, 1988), A 132, para. 64; Findlay v. UK, Judgment (Feb. 25, 1997), para. 73. *See also* Inter-AmCmHR, Annul Report 1992–1993, Inter-AmCmHR, Doc. OEA/Ser.L/V/II. 83 Doc.14 (March 12, 1993), Javier v. Honduras Case 10.793, Report No. 8/93, Inter-AmCHR, OEA/Ser.L/V/II.83 Doc. 14, at 93 (1993), para. 20; and Inter-AmCmHR, Garcia v. Peru, Report No. 1/95, OEA/Ser.L/V/II.88 rev.1, Doc. 9, at 71 (1995) (Feb. 17, 1995), Case 11.006 (Peru), Report, Section VI(2)(a).

[71] *See* Australia, Military Court at Rabaul, Ohashi and Six Others case, Judgment (March 20–23, 1946), Law-Reports of Trials of War Criminals, The United Nations War Crimes Commission, Vol. V, at 25–31 (1948); and UNHRC, Karttunen v. Finland, Views, No. 387/1989 (Oct. 23, 1992), U.N. Doc. CCPR/C/46/D/387/1989; 1 IHRR 79, at 83, para. 7.2.

[72] AfCHPR, Constitutional Rights Project v. Nigeria, 60/91, Decision (March 13–22, 1995), para. 14; Malawi African Association and Others v. Mauritania, 54/91, Decision (May 11, 2000), (2001) 8 IHRR 268, at 282–283, para. 98. For the case-law of the ECHR, see ECtHR, Piersack v. Belgium, Judgment (Oct. 1, 1982), A 53, paras 28–33; De Cubber v. Belgium, Judgment (Oct. 26, 1984), A 86, paras 24–26; Findlay v. UK, Judgment (Feb. 25, 1997), para. 73. For the jurisprudence of ACHR, *see* IACmHR, Raquel Martí v. Peru, Case 10.970, Report No. 5/96 (March 1, 1996), OEA/Ser.L/V/II.91 Doc.7 at 157, Section V(B)(3)(c).

3.3. Ne bis in idem *(the Freedom from Double Jeopardy)*

Article 75(4)(h) AP I safeguards the right not to be prosecuted or punished by the same Party for an offence in respect of which a final judgement acquitting or convicting that person has been previously pronounced under the same law and judicial procedure (the *non bis in idem* or *ne bis in idem* principle). This right must be recognised as a minimum guarantee for any persons convicted for offences related to the armed conflict. With special regard to protected persons in occupied territory (or in the territory of a party to the conflict), Article 117(3) GC IV recognises that they may not be punished more than once for the same act or on the same charge (count).[73] This right is fully recognised by international criminal law[74] and IHRL.[75] Its non-derogable nature is yet to be fully endorsed in the context of IHRL, except for the IACmHR's Report on Terrorism and Human Rights.[76]

This principle does not prohibit the resumption of a trial justified by exceptional circumstances,[77] or the prosecution of the same offences in different states.[78] Such exceptional circumstances for revisions of conviction or sentence[79] are allowed on two grounds: (i) discovery of new evidence, which was unavailable at the time of the trial; and (ii) fundamental defect in previous proceedings.[80] Further, in case occupation courts are equipped with the appeal system, prosecutorial appeals

---

[73] Article 117(3) GC IV, *supra* note 1.
[74] ICC Statute, *supra* note 3, Article 20(2); Article 10(1), S.C. Res. 827 (1993), U.N. Doc. S/RES/827 (1993) (May 25, 1993) [hereinafter ICTY Statute]; Article 9(1), S.C. Res. 955 (1994), U.N. Doc. S/RES/955 (1994) (Nov. 8, 1994) [hereinafter ICTR Statute]; Article 9(1) *See* Agreement on the Establishment of a Special Court for Sierra Leone, UN-Sierra Leone (Jan. 16, 2002), U.N. Doc. S/2002/246, annex, app. 2 (to which the Statute of the Special Court is attached); Sierra Leone, Special Court Agreement, 2002 (Ratification) Act, Act No. 9 (Mar. 29, 2002) [hereinafter Statute of the Special Court for Sierra Leone].
[75] Article 14(7) ICCPR, *supra* note 12, Article 8(4) ACHR, *supra* note 64; Article 4 Protocol 7 to ECHR, *supra* note 65. *See also* EU Charter of Fundamental Rights, Article 50.
[76] IACmHR, Report on Terrorism and Human Rights, *supra* note 5, para. 261(a).
[77] UNHRC, General Comment No. 13 (April 12, 1984), para. 19.
[78] UNHRC, A.P. v. Italy, No. 204/1986, Admissibility Decision (Nov. 2, 1987), U.N. Doc. Supp. No. 40 (A/43/40) at 242, para. 7.3.
[79] *See* Article 84 ICC Statute, *supra* note 3.
[80] Christine Van den Wyngaert & Tom Ongena, *Ne bis in idem Principle, Including the Issue of Amnesty*, in Cassese, et al. (eds), *supra* note 33, Ch. 18.4. 705–729, at 722 [hereinafter Van den Wyngaert & Ongena]. Similarly, Article 4(2) of Protocol No. 7 to ECHR allows the reopening of the case if there is evidence of new or newly discovered facts, of if there has been a fundamental defect in the previous proceedings that could affect the outcome of the case.

against both convictions and acquittals[81] are not considered to run counter to this principle.[82]

The *ne bis in idem* principle entails crucial implications on the jurisdictional relationship between the occupation court and the ICC. Special regard must be had to specific exceptions to this principle provided in Article 20(2) and (3) ICC Statute. Starting with Article 20(2), it is highly unlikely that the *res judicata* effect of the ICC vis-à-vis national courts (what Van der Wyngaert and Ongena call "downward *ne bis in idem*")[83] has serious ramifications on the occupation court. In relation to the meaning of *idem*, it must be noted that Article 75(4)(h) AP I mentions "offence," and not "conduct." As commented by Wyngaert and Ongena, in the vertical relationship between national courts and the ICC,[84] an individual convicted for "core crimes" by the ICC can be retried for the same acts in proceedings before the local court or the occupation court in occupied territory on the basis of "ordinary crimes." Further, these courts sitting in occupied territory are not bound to take into account the sentence already pronounced by the ICC for the same conduct.[85]

In the scenario contemplated in Article 20(3) ICC Statute,[86] the *ne bis in idem* principle is inapplicable in two circumstances: (i) where it serves to shield a person from criminal responsibility, as in the case of sham trials; and (ii) where the proceedings were marred by irregularity (namely, absence of independence or impartiality) flouting due process guarantees *and* were conducted in a manner inconsistent with an intent to bring the person concerned to justice, as in the case of partisan justice.

Unlike the ICTY and ICTR Statutes,[87] the ICC Statute does not expressly recognise, as an exception to the *ne bis in idem* principle, that it is possible to try a person who has been tried by a national court for an act constituting war crimes, but only with respect to ordinary crimes.[88] The present writer argues that in occupied territory, if an act of the person who has been tried only for offences against penal/security laws in occupied territory involves war crimes, the occupying power is obligated under customary international criminal law to prosecute

---

[81] *See* Article 81 ICC Statute, *supra* note 3.
[82] While in common law countries, such appeals are deemed as derogation from this principle, in civil law countries this is not considered even as an exception to it. Van den Wyngaert & Ongena, *supra* note 80, at 722.
[83] *Id.* at 722–723.
[84] *Id.* at 723–724.
[85] *Id.* at 724.
[86] *Id.* at 724–726.
[87] Article 10(2)(a) ICTY Statute, *supra* note 74; and Article 9(2)(a) ICTR Statute, *supra* note 74.
[88] The drafters considered this exception too ambiguous. Van den Wyngaert & Ongena, *supra* note 80, at 725–726.

him/her for war crimes based on the same act.[89] Indeed, what Article 75(4)(h) AP I prohibits is the re-trial for an offence "under the same law."

4. The Elements of the Rights of the Accused, which are Implied from the General Terms Under Article 75(4) Ap i

4.1. Overview

Apart from the fair trial guarantees expressly recognized under Article 75(4) API, three specific rights can be considered implicit under this provision. These include the right to trial without undue delay and the right to appeal. Further, Article 75(4)(a) API refers to "all necessary rights and means of defence" only in a general manner. Can the general term "all necessary rights and means of defence" be interpreted as a basis for deducing specific rights? The following examinations start with the methodology of inferring rights relating to means of defence.

4.2. The Rights Relating to Means of Defence

Article 72(1) GC IV recognises five specific rights concerning means of defence of persons accused in occupied territory: (i) the right to present evidence necessary to the defence; (ii) the right to call witnesses; (iii) the right to be assisted by a qualified advocate or counsel of their own choice; (iv) the right of the advocate or the counsel to visit the accused freely; and (v) the right of the advocate or the counsel to enjoy the necessary facilities for preparing the defence. Article 123(2) guarantees the rights of the internee, which include: (i) the right to be given an opportunity to explain his/her conduct and to defend him/herself; (ii) the right to call witnesses; and (iii) the right to have recourse to the services of a qualified interpreter.

In contrast to the relatively elaborate requirements embodied in Article 72(1) GC IV, Article 75(4)(a) AP I adverts to the entitlement of the accused to "all necessary rights and means of defence" only in a general manner. Indeed, at the Diplomatic

---

[89] A new trial is necessary even if war crimes elements fall outside the scope of grave breaches under GCs and API, *and* the catalogue of "other serious violations of laws and customs" applicable to international armed conflict. It is possible to argue that the catalogue of war crimes under customary international law does not overlap the list embodied in Article 8 ICC Statute. This assumption can be supported by the inclusion of Article 10 ICC Statute, which reads that "[n]othing in this Part shall be interpreted as limiting or prejudicing in any way existing or developing rules of international law for purposes other than this Statute." *See* U.S. Department of State, *supra* note 29, Comment on Rule 157. Paust goes even so far as to argue that all violations of laws of war amount to war crimes over which there is universal jurisdiction. Jordan J. Paust, *The United States as Occupying Power over Portions of Iraq and Special Responsibilities under the Laws of War*, 27 Suffolk Transnat'l L. Rev. 1, 13 (2003).

Conference at Geneva (1974–1977), there was a proposal to insert more specific reference to means of defence,[90] but this was not accepted. Five specific rights can be inferred from the general wording: (i) the right to defend oneself or to be assisted by a lawyer of one's own choice; (ii) the right to legal assistance; (iii) the right to sufficient time and facilities to prepare the defence; (iv) the right of the accused to communicate freely with a counsel; and (v) the right to the assistance of an interpreter or a translator.

When seeking guidance from IHRL practice, one must bear in mind that none of these rights has yet been recognised as inalienable in the treaty provisions, and in the case-law or the documents provided by the IHRL monitoring bodies. Indeed, the HRC's General Comment No. 29 fails to single out any specific right of defence in its catalogue. It is by reference to the progressive twist provided by the IACmHR in its Report on Terrorism and Human Rights that the acquisition of the non-derogable status can be confirmed.[91] The appraisal of the rights relating to means of defence focuses only on the the right to sufficient time and facilities to prepare the defence.

4.2.1. *The Right to Sufficient Time and Facilities to Prepare the Defence*

The accused in occupied territory has the right to "necessary facilities" for preparing the defence, without, however, adverting to "sufficient time" (Article 72(1) GCIV). The practice of national military laws mostly follows this provision, so that the material scope of this right is limited only to facilities (to the exclusion of temporal element).[92] In contrast, both IHRL[93] and international criminal law[94] fully endorse the right to both physical and temporal elements (facilities and time).

The present writer proposes that the requirement of necessary facilities for the defence as embodied in Article 72 GC IV be taken as embracing the temporal element. This interpretation needs to be attended by the argument that the corresponding customary norm equipped with the same material elements has already been shaped and grafted onto the treaty norm (Article 72 GC IV) under IHL. The

---

[90] *See* the proposal made by the Netherlands and Switzerland, CDDH/III/317 (April 29, 1976), as reported in: *Official Records*, Vol. III, at 294. *See also Official Records*, Vol. XV, at 29 and 31 Summary Record of the 43rd Meeting (April 30, 1976), CDDH/III/SR.43, paras. 21, 31.

[91] IACmHR, Report on Terrorism and Human Rights, *supra* note 5, para. 247 (the right to defend oneself or to be assisted by a lawyer of one's own choice; the right to legal assistance; the right to sufficient time and facilities to prepare the defence; and the right to the assistance of an interpreter or translator).

[92] *Id.* Vol. II, part 2, at 2435–2439.

[93] Article 14(3)(b) ICCPR, *supra* note 12; Article 6(3)(b) ECHR, *supra* note 65; Article 8(2)(c) ACHR, *supra* note 64.

[94] Article 67(1)(b) ICC Statute, *supra* note 3; Article 21(4)(b) ICTY Statute, *supra* note 74; Article 20(4)(b) ICTR Statute, *supra* note 74; Article 17(4)(b) Statute of the Special Court for Sierra Leone, *supra* note 74.

cogency of such argument can be reinforced by the express recognition of this right in IHRL treaty provisions and soft law,[95] as well as in the Statutes of international criminal tribunals. Still, whether Article 72 GC IV may be deemed as a provision of "norm-generating character" in the sense articulated by the ICJ in the *North Sea Continental Shelf Cases* remains ambivalent, in view of the limited scope of application *ratione materiae* (occupied territory) and *ratione personae* (protected persons).

In its Principles and Guidelines on the Right to a Fair Trial and Legal Assistance in Africa, the African Commission on Human and People's Rights delineated factors determinative of the adequacy of time for preparation of a defence. These include: (i) the complexity of the case; (ii) the defendant's access to evidence; (iii) the length of time laid down by rules of procedure prior to particular proceedings; and (iv) prejudice to the defence.[96]

4.3 *The Right to Trial without Undue Delay*

Article 71(2) GC IV recognises the right to be tried "as rapidly as possible." The right to trial without undue delay is fully established in both IHRL and international criminal law.[97] Nevertheless, it is handicapped in two respects. First, the catalogue of procedural safeguards under Article 75(4) AP I does not include it. Unless the customary law equivalent is considered as broader in the scope of application, this raises the question of its applicability to persons other than protected persons. Second, the HRC's General Comment No. 29 or documents prepared by other monitoring bodies of IHRL fail to confirm its inalienable status. Even the most liberal IACmHR, in its Report on Terrorism and Human Rights, concedes that the right to a hearing within a reasonable time can be derogated from in case of emergency.[98] However, the Report emphasises that a delay exceptionally longer than would otherwise be acceptable in non-emergency situations can be recognised only pursuant to two specific conditions: (i) the delay must be subordinated "at all times" to judicial review; and (ii) it must not be prolonged or indefinite.[99]

---

[95] See Principle 18(2), Body of Principles for the Protection of All Persons under Any Form of Detention or Imprisonment [hereinafter Body of Principles on Any Form of Detention or Imprisonment].

[96] AfCmHPR, Principles and Guidelines on the Right to a Fair Trial and Legal Assistance in Africa, May 15–29, 2003, Provisions Applicable to Proceedings Relating to Criminal Charges, para. 3(c).

[97] Articles 9(3) and 14(3)(c) ICCPR, *supra* note 12; Article 40(2)(b)(iii) CRC, *supra* note 64; Articles 5(3) and 6(1) ECHR *supra* note 65; Article 8(1) ACHR, *supra* note 64; Article 7(1)(d) AfCHPR, *supra* note 65. *See also* Principle 38, Body of Principles on Any Form of Detention or Imprisonment, *supra* note 95; EU Charter of Fundamental Rights, Article 47.

[98] IACmHR, Report on Terrorism and Human Rights, *supra* note 5, paras. 253 and 262(c).

[99] *Id.* para. 262(c).

The first condition requires two comments germane to occupation courts. In the first instance, the Report fails to specify the frequency of review in case the trial becomes lengthy, if not protracted. Second, clearly, the requirement that accused persons who are detained pending trial must be given the right to seek *judicial* review needs to be distinguished from the requirement provided in Article 78(2) GC IV. According to that, periodic review of protected persons who are interned or administratively detained without criminal charge in occupied territory can be undertaken by administrative board.[100]

In assessing the customary law status of this right based on national military manuals or relevant national laws, the ICRC's Customary IHL Study's methodological rigour may be questionable. The actual empirical examples cross-referenced by Vol. I and cited in Vol. II of the Study are not thoroughly consistent with the Study's assertion that the right to trial without delay is set forth in "several" military manuals and included in "most, if not all, national legal systems."[101] Admittedly, these data may be seen as referring only to the most exemplary ones. In respect of national laws, apart from the Kenyan constitutional provision whose non-derogable status remains unexplained, the data cited in Vol. II relate to the laws of three countries which criminalise violations of the provisions of GC IV. Yet, these national laws contemplate the personal scope of application equivalent to that of Article 71 GC IV.[102]

The customary law status of GC IV, including even those provisions which were considered as progressive development of law in 1949, is fully established. It would only be a small incremental step to claim that the right which corresponds to the right contained in Article 71 GC IV has evolved into customary IHL, and that its personal scope of application is broad enough to cover *any* individual persons who are accused of offences relating to international armed conflict.

Be that as it may, valuable insight can be obtained from the case-law of IHRL. The reasonableness in the length of time must be calculated from the time of the charge to the final judgment, including the appeal.[103] According to the case-law of the ECHR and the ACHR, the relevant factors include: (i) the complexity of the case; (ii) the behaviour of the accused; and (iii) the diligence of the authorities.[104]

---

[100] Article 78(2) GC IV refers to "a competent body" for the purpose of review, *supra* note 1.

[101] Study, *supra* note 9, Vol. II, Part 2, at 2447, paras. 3316–3324 (reference to the military manuals of Argentina, Australia, Canada, Columbia, New Zealand, Spain, and US). *Id.* at 2447.

[102] Study, *supra* note 9, Vol. II, Part II, at 2447–2448, paras. 3324–3327.

[103] UNHRC, General Comment No. 13 (1984).

[104] *See inter alia*, ECtHR, Wemhoff v. Germany, Judgment (June 27, 1968), A7, para. 12; König v. Germany, Judgment (June 28, 1978), A 27, paras 101–111; Letellier v. France, Judgment (June 26, 1991), A207, para. 35; Tomasi v. France, Judgment (Aug. 27, 1992), para. 102; IACtHR, Genie Lacayo Case (Jan. 19, 1997), Series C No. 30, para. 77; IAmCmHR, *see* Case 11.245

The evaluation of the diligence of the authorities must necessarily take into account the extraordinary situations of occupation.

4.4. *The Right to Appeal*

Both Article 73 GC IV and Article 75(4)(j) AP I stop short of expressly recognising the right of appeal. The phrase "provided for by the laws applied by the court" suggests that Article 73(1) does not require the occupying power to guarantee the right of appeal against sentence in all circumstances.[105] Along this line, the ICRC's Commentary on AP I states that convicted persons must be fully advised of available judicial (appeal or petition) or other remedies (such as pardon or reprieve),[106] and of the time limits for such remedies, without, however, expressly referring to the right of appeal as such. The failure fully to embrace the right of appeal can be explained by the fact that when APs were adopted, the majority of the states had yet to recognise the right of appeal in their laws.[107]

On the basis of its survey, the ICRC's Customary IHL Study concludes that "the influence of human rights on this issue is such that it can be argued that the right of appeal proper–and not only the right to be informed whether appeal is available–has become a basic component of fair trial rights in the context of armed conflict."[108] Nevertheless, the Study's assertion is not backed by empirical evidence in a rigorous manner.

The Study refers to national constitutional provisions[109] which do not mention their non-derogable status. With respect to IHRL, the Study refers to the pertinent provisions of the treaties,[110] but all of them, except for the African Charter, are expressly stated as being susceptible to suspension in time of emergencies. Among the work of the supervisory bodies of IHRL, again, only the IACmHR's Report on Terrorism and Human Rights confirmed its non-derogability.[111] The national military manuals cited by the Study are in tune with the wording of Article 73

(Argentina), Report (March 1, 1996), para. 111; Report on Terrorism and Human Rights, *supra* note 5, para. 234.

[105] New Zealand's Military Manual (1992), §1330(3); and U.K. Ministry of Defence, The Manual of the Law of Armed Conflict 297, para. 11.70 (2004).

[106] ICRC's Commentary on AP I, at 885, para. 3121.

[107] *Id.*

[108] Study, *supra* note 9, Vol. I, at 369–370.

[109] *Id.* Vol. II, Part II, at 2484–2485, paras 3604–3605.

[110] Article 14(5) ICCPR, *supra* note 12; Article 40(2)(b)(v) CRC, *supra* note 64; Article 2(1) Protocol 7 to the ECHR, *supra* note 65; Article 8(2)(h) ACHR, *supra* note 64; Article 7(1)(a) AfCHPR, *supra* note 65.

[111] The Report considers the non-derogability of the right to appeal as a possibility. IACmHR, Report on Terrorism and Human Rights, *supra* note 5, para. 261(c)(v).

GC IV, as they tend to reproduce the wording of this stipulation. They stop short of expressly recognising the right of convicted persons to appeal as such. *Some* national military manuals referred to in the Study relate only to the right to appeals of convicted *prisoners of war*,[112] and not of civilians and unprivileged belligerents held and convicted in occupied territory. These appraisals suggest that to assert the right of appeal for *all* convicted persons as fully established in customary IHL remains somewhat far-fetched within the framework of positive law. Surely, this observation does not negate the possibility that this right can be evolving into customary IHL.

If the appeal procedure is instituted for occupation courts, Article 73(2) GC IV requires the occupying power to comply with the penal procedural rules embodied in Part III, Section III, including elaborate fair trial guarantees for the accused persons under Articles 71–73 GC IV.[113] Any time-limit for appeals in case of death penalty or imprisonment of two years or more must not run until the protecting power receives the notification of the judgement.[114]

5. *Conclusion*

The foregoing appraisal explored how the assertive convergence between IHL and IHRL helped shape an emerging framework of due process guarantees in occupied territory. It deployed the concept of non-derogability of human rights norms as a key to concurrent identification of detailed principles relating to the rights of the accused in both IHL and IHRL. The underlying assumption is that all the fair trial guarantees of non-derogable nature are customary. Within the interactive relationship between treaty-based rules and corresponding customary norms, the latter can assist elaborate elements to be read into the general terms employed in the former, such as the chapeau of Article 75(4) AP I.

Many argue that the intrinsic moral values articulated by specific human rights norms are crucial to determining their non-derogable status.[115] Surely, the very foundation of democracy and the rule of law may be jeopardised by an infringement or suspension of many elements of fair trial guarantees.[116] As examined, it is plausible that the conclusion reached by the ICRC's Study relating to non-

---

[112] Study, *supra* note 9, Vol. II, Part 2, at 2483–2484 (Argentina and Hungary).
[113] Article 73(2) GC IV, *supra* note 1.
[114] Article 74(2), 4th sentence, GC IV, *supra* note 1.
[115] Koji Teraya, *Emerging Hierarchy in International Human Rights and Beyond: From the Perspective of Non-Derogable Rights*, 12 Eur. J. INt'l L. 917, 921–922 (2001) [hereinafter Teraya].
[116] Olivier, *supra* note 12, at 415. Nevertheless, the IACtHR stated that "It is neither possible nor advisable to list all the possible 'essential' judicial guarantees that cannot be suspended under Article 27(2)." IACtHR, Judicial Guarantees in States of Emergency (Arts 27(2), 25 and 8 of

derogability of some judicial guarantees has been swayed by deductive reasoning.[117] This issue is closely intertwined with the method of identifying customary international law. Ascertainment of customary international law is traditionally premised on inductive reasoning, which focuses on empirical data to extrapolate a general norm.[118] As evidenced by the ICJ in the *Nicaragua* case,[119] in relation to norms invested with intrinsically fundamental values and authority such as the non-use of force and many catalogues of human rights, there has been a tendency to bend prerequisites of the traditional methodology by shifting emphasis on the "elusive and rather ephemeral" notion of *opinio juris* rather than on tangible state conduct.[120] This often goes in tandem with the deductive approach that places special importance on normative (rather than descriptive) part of *opinio juris*. Such an approach is certainly not free from controversy.[121] Deduction is susceptible to subjective reasoning,[122] which is undertaken under the "preponderant" influence of a few powerful states.[123]

The idea of international law cannot be segregated from the dialectical and dynamic process of international society re-conceiving itself through accommodating and integrating consciousness emanating from diverse and competing value-systems.[124] It is against the backdrop of such a value-laden process of the modern international society that the notion of non-derogability has been yielded to rationalise an emerging hierarchy or verticalisation of international norms.[125] The paper has sought to establish a solid methodology that can provide greater effectiveness in guaranteeing rights of all accused persons in occupied territory. Through its disaggregated analysis, it has responded to some of the methodological

---

the American Convention on Human Rights), Advisory Opinion OC-9/87, Oct. 6, 1987, Inter-Am.Ct.HR (Ser.A) No. 9 (1987), para 40.

[117] It ought to be noted that the IACmHR's Report on Terrorism and Human Right, which the *Study* has heavily relied on in this regard, fails in itself to provide guidelines for ascertaining non-derogability of rights of the accused.

[118] Bruno Simma & Philip Alston, *The Sources of Human Rights Law: Custom, Jus Cogens, and General Principles*, 12 Aust. YBIL 82, 88–89 (1988–1989) [hereinafter Simma & Alston].

[119] Military and Paramilitary Activities in and against Nicaragua (Nicaragua v. US), Merits, 1986 ICJ Reps 14, at 99–104, paras 188–195 (June 27).

[120] *See*, for instance, Kirgis, *supra* note 37, at 149.

[121] Roberts, *supra* note 37, at 763–764.

[122] Meron notes that "the characterisation of some rights as fundamental results largely from our own subjective perceptions of their importance." Theodor Meron, *On a Hierarchy of International Human Rights*, 80 Am. J. Int'l L. 1, 8 (1986).

[123] Meron 2006, *supra* note 17, at 377. *See also* Simma & Alston, *supra* note, at 88, 94, 96. They propose that search for universal human rights should focus on the notion of general principles along a strictly consensualist line. *Id*. at 102–108. *See also* Martti Koskenniemi, *The Pull of the Mainstream*, 88 Mich. L.R. 1946, 1951 (1990).

[124] Philip Allott, Eunomia: New Order for a New World 110 (1990).

[125] Teraya, *supra* note 193, at 937.

questions left unanswered by the ICRC's Study in determining the customary law rights of the accused persons while endorsing and reinforcing most of the Study's outcomes.

Chapter XVIII

Terrorism in International Humanitarian Law and Human Rights Law

*Roberta Arnold**

1. *Introduction*

Following September 11, 2001 the international legal and political community witnessed the rise of the new concept of "global war on terror." The United States responded with the use of force against Afghanistan first and Iraq afterwards, intending to find those responsible and to eradicate the phenomenon in so-called "rogue states." High numbers of suspects were jailed, very often without being granted procedural guarantees like the right to know the charges against them or to have a legal counsel, as enshrined in international human rights law (HRL) instruments and humanitarian law (IHL). These two legal branches were misused in order to argue that although the detainees were "combatants" in the sense of IHL, thereby not qualifying for rights attached to civilians, due to their "unlawful" participation in combat they were not eligible to prisoner of war (POW) status under the Third Geneva Convention (GC) of 1949.[1] They were simply "terrorists" to be kept in a legal limbo, for an undetermined period of time, at least until the "war on terror" would be over. Those captured in Afghanistan were taken to a U.S. military detention facility in Guantanamo Bay, Cuba. Those captured in Iraq, occupied with the argument that it was a rogue state in which Saddam Hussein was hiding weapons of mass destruction, were kept in even worse conditions, as proven by the pictures of Abu Ghraib. Perhaps an improvement in the Abu Ghraib case, with respect to Guantanamo Bay, was the recognition that the four Geneva Conventions of 1949 in this latter case applied and that there had been a clear breach of the prohibition of torture. This was indeed an improvement since a major debate

---

* Dr.iur (Bern), LLM (Nottingham), Former Legal Adviser at the Swiss Department of Defence, Laws of Armed Conflict Section. Legal officer within the Swiss armed forces. This paper is based in particular on the contents of the author's book. The ICC as a New Instruments for Repressing Terrorism (2004) [hereinafter Arnold].
[1] Geneva Convention Relative to the Treatment to Prisoners of War, Aug. 12, 1949, 75 U.N.T.S. 135, 136 [hereinafter GC III].

that arose in the aftermath of 9/11 was about the applicable legal regime to this type of situations.

The aim of this chapter is to discuss the human rights implications of this new approach, holding that terrorism is a phenomenon to be fought with military strategies rather than traditional criminal law mechanisms. According to the path chosen there may be severe differences in relation to the rights applicable to the law enforcement agencies, the jurisdiction of the courts, the status of the detainees and even the mechanisms a state may resort to, to defend itself. According to whether a situation is tantamount to a state of "war" (or armed conflict, a technical term preferred in international law), or peacetime, an act may qualify as a legitimate act of warfare or as a terrorist act. This very much also depends on the nature of the target – military or civilian – and the status of the attacker. Within the framework of an ongoing armed conflict, if an attacker fulfils the combatant criteria under Article 4(A)(2) GC III and aims at a military target, the attack will constitute a legitimate act of warfare, no matter whether it was launched by a member of the regular armed forces of a state or a guerrilla group. A highly debated issue in this regard, for instance, was the qualification of the attack on the Italian Carabinieri (who are members of the Italian armed forces) in November 2003 in Nassirya. Under the laws of war, in fact, only attacks which are *primarily* aimed at *civilian* targets or the side effects of which (collateral damages) are disproportionate are unlawful. Thus, only those attacks which are primarily aimed at terrorising the *civilian* population qualify as acts of terrorism under IHL.[2] In peacetime, instead, every attack, independently from whether launched a military or civilian installation, if aimed at forcing a government or an international organisation to meet specific political demands, constitutes terrorism in the ordinary sense. Thus, the standards differ. Moreover, in wartime, attackers who are not eligible for combatant – and POW – status, by default are to be considered civilians to be charged not only for unlawful methods of warfare, but also for the mere fact of having participated in combat. Unlike combatants, in fact, civilians, under IHL, are not allowed to engage in war and for this they may be tried according to ordinary criminal law applicable

---

[2] *See* Article 51(2) Protocol Additional to the Geneva Conventions of 12 August 1949, and Relating to the Protections of Victims of International Armed Conflicts (Protocol I), opened for signature Dec. 12, 1977, U.N. Doc. A/32/144, Annex I, II, (1977), *reprinted in* 16 I.L.M. 1391 (1977) [hereinafter AP I] and Articles 4 and 13 Protocol Additional to the Geneva Conventions of 12 August 1949, and Relating to the Protection of Victims of Non-International Armed Conflicts, opened for signature: Dec. 12, 1977, 1125 UNTS 609 [hereinafter Additional Protocol II] and Article 33 Geneva Convention Relative to the Protection of Civilian Persons in Time of War, Aug. 12, 1949, 75 U.N.T.S. 287, 288 [hereinafter GC IV]. The details are discussed in Arnold, *supra* note *.

to civilians in peacetime, rather than IHL.[3] Although in both cases – peacetime and wartime – human rights play a crucial role, the aim of this chapter is to discuss in what measure, according to whether the repression of terrorism shall be viewed as an armed conflict subject to IHL or as the repression of an ordinary crime occurring in peacetime, their scope of application may differ.

In the lengthy "dispute" between the United Kingdom and the Irish Republican Army in Northern Ireland, for instance, the solution was to declare a "state of emergency," rather than an armed conflict, thereby maintaining the laws applicable in peacetime and, at the same time, having the possibility, according to international standards, to limit or suspend the application of specific human rights. A state of war was never declared, as this would have implied the application of IHL and the recognition of combatant status to the IRA, granting them more privileges, particularly in relation to detention, interrogation, etc,. A similar approach was followed by Germany and Italy with regard to the Red Brigades and the Red Army Faction in the 1970s–1980s. Their members were tried according to the applicable criminal laws and procedures. The Bush administration, instead, decided to resort to military force to apprehend and repress those suspected of membership in Al-Qaeda, the international criminal organisation that has allegedly orchestrated the September 11th and other terror attacks.[4]

One of the reasons was probably dictated by the lack in the United States – contrary to the United Kingdom – of applicable emergency laws, due to constitutional limitations. Faced with the impossibility to detain suspects of terrorism without specific charges for an undetermined period of time, the ideal solution seemed to resort to IHL, which permits to retain enemy combatants until the end of the hostilities, without a specific charge. But their detention as POWs would have implied too many privileges, reason for which it was decided to label them as "unlawful combatants," thwarting their right to invoke POW status.

The Guantanamo Bay situation provides a good overview of the restrictions on the human and procedural rights of suspects of terrorism following 9/11, which is partly derived from the confusion about the applicable regime. Related to that, as highlighted by the Abu Ghraib scandal, is the issue of the legitimacy to resort to torture during interrogations.

In order to discuss the application of human rights to suspects of terrorism, section B defines *who* the terrorists are and the applicable legal regime to them. Section C discusses the "state of emergency," during which some human rights may be derogated from, whereas Section D examines the prohibition on the use

---

[3] This aspect is also discussed in Roberta Arnold, *The Liability of Civilians under IHL's War Crimes Provisions*, 5 YB Int'l Humanitarian L. 344 (2002).
[4] See *The Terror Attack in Amman, Jordan, available at* edition.cnn.com/2005/WORLD/meast/11/10/jordan.blasts/index.html (last visited Oct. 22, 2007).

of torture and its scope. Section E discusses the United States' attitude towards the status of the suspects of terror, whereas Section F considers the European position. Conclusions are drawn in Section G.

2. What is Terrorism?

2.1. A Working Definition

There is no universally accepted legal definition of terrorism, yet.[5] In some people's view, terrorism is a subjective notion, which "exists in the mind of the beholder, depending upon one's political views and national origins."[6] However, the media and the average man, when using this term, seem to think of violent and intimidating acts – usually directed against innocent targets – aimed at coercing a government or a community to comply with the perpetrators' political requests. May this common understanding provide the basis for a universal *legal* definition of "terrorism"? Perhaps[7] IHL may provide a solution. "Acts of terrorism" are referred to in Article 33 GC IV, Article 51(2) AP I and Articles 3 and 14 AP II. They indicate an act of violence in breach of the principles of military necessity, proportionality, and distinction, which is primarily aimed at spreading fear among the civilian population.[8] This definition contains the same elements of the definition commonly used: innocent victims (civilians) as targets, a violent act as conduct and a political end as triggering reason which, however, in contrast with the Machiavellian motto, does not justify the means. One of the core principles of IHL, in fact, is proportionality.[9] The four Geneva Conventions of 1949 amount to customary law and have been universally accepted. Therefore, it could be argued that the meaning of "terror" under IHL may provide the basis for a universal legal definition. Since it is beyond the scope of this paper to discuss the legal definition of terrorism, the one previously referred to is going to be used as a "working" definition in this paper.

---

[5] Elizabeth Chadwick, Self-Determination, Terrorism and the International Humanitarian Law of Armed Conflict 2 (1996); Andreas Zimmermann, *Commentary to Article 5: Crimes within the Jurisdiction of the Court, in* Commentary on the Rome Statute of the International Criminal Court 97, 99 (Otto Triffterer ed., 1999).
[6] Robert A. Friedlander, *Terrorism, in* Encyclopaedia of Public International Law 371, 372 (Rudolf Bernhardt ed., 1981).
[7] Arnold, *supra* note 1, at 69ss.
[8] Arnold, *supra* note 1, at 71ss.
[9] Jean Pictet, Commentary to the IV Geneva Convention 45 (1958); Arnold, *supra* note 1.

2.2. The Fight vs. Terrorism vs. the War on Terror

According to whether we qualify the repression of terrorist acts as a "fight" or a "war" the application of two different legal regimes may be implied.

The first expression recalls the criminal and procedural law mechanisms undertaken by the German, Italian, and British regimes in the 1970s-1980s to eradicate terrorist movements like the Red Army Faction (RAF), the Red Brigades or the IRA. In fact, terrorism is not a new phenomenon. To overcome the problem of a lacking universal definition of terrorism, a piecemeal approach was adopted by the international legal community,[10] a strategy that resulted into the enacting of numerous anti-terrorism conventions since 1963.[11] These, however, have several deficiencies, such as the limited scope of application, the failure to provide for universal jurisdiction, the blurring of terrorist acts with political offences, the subjection to extradition law rules, the failure to address state terrorism, and the lack of control mechanisms.[12] Some of these were evidenced, for instance, in the *Lockerbie Case*,[13] when Libya refused to extradite to the United States and the United Kingdom two suspects on the basis of the extradition law rule that a state cannot be compelled to extradite its own citizens.

Some of these problems, however, may be overcome by considering these as acts of warfare subject to IHL. As long as they are primarily aimed at civilian targets, terrorist acts are considered war crimes under Article 33 GC IV, Article 51(2) AP I and Articles 4 and 13 of AP II.[14] These provisions, however, have a limited scope of application: a) they only apply in times of armed conflict, i.e. situations which have a higher intensity of violence than mere riots and internal disturbances; b) they generally address civilians as protected persons.[15] Under IHL, acts of terror are

---

[10] See the information provided by UNDOC (United Nations Office on Drugs and Crime), *available at* www.unodc.org/unodc/en/terrorism.html (last visited Oct. 22, 2007). Stefan Sohm, *Die Instrumentalisierung des Völkerrechts zur Bekämpfung des internationalen Terrorismus*, 4 HuV-I 164, 170 (1999). For a list of the conventions, *see* Extract from the Report of the Secretary-General on Measures to Eliminate International Terrorism, DOC. A/57/183, as updated on December 10, 2002, *available at* www.un.org/law/terrorism/terrorism_table_update_12-2002.pdf (last visited Oct. 22, 2007).

[11] In the sense that they have a global – rather than a regional – geographical scope of application. This term, however, does not imply that they are universally binding.

[12] For details *see* Arnold, *supra* note*.

[13] *See* Roberta Arnold, *Terrorism and IHL: A Common Denominator?*, *in* International Humanitarian Law and the 21st Century's Conflicts: Changes and Challenges 5, 9 (Robert Arnold & Pierre Antoine Hildbrand ed., 2005).

[14] The four 1949 GCs and the 1977 AP I apply to international conflicts (the latter including self-determination wars). The 1977 AP II only applies to non-international conflicts between a state and the insurgents and Article 3 common to the four GCs applies to all types of non-international conflicts.

[15] Arnold, *supra* note 1, at 147ss.

per se legitimate, as long as they do not *primarily* target *civilians* and do constitute a military advantage. The political motivation, on the other hand, is not directly relevant. Thus, according to the circumstances, the qualification of an act and the status of the perpetrator and the potential victim may change. Consequently, also the applicable human rights may vary. As it will be discussed later, in fact, there are some human rights that may restricted in a state of emergency. However, the latter is not to be confused – or abused – to label what in reality is a permanent status of "war." Moreover, there are some human rights which are better protected in times of war, under IHL, than in peacetime, under human rights instruments. The aim of the following section is to discuss the relationship between these two legal branches with regard to the protection of human rights (of detainees in particular) and to analyse in what measure their scope of protection differs.

2.3. *Human Rights Law and International Humanitarian Law: Two Different Applicable Legal Regimes?*

HRL and IHL have long been regarded as two distinct branches of law. Only in 1968, at the Tehran Conference on Human Rights, their relationship was raised for the first time. Three theories emerged. According to the integrationist theory, the two are merged in a unique body of law, whereas under the separatist theory they are totally unrelated. The complementarist theory, on the other hand, the one accepted universally and supported by the International Committee of the Red Cross (ICRC), maintains that they are distinct and separate, but nevertheless complementary to each other.[16] The rationale is that IHL was specifically drafted to take into consideration the reality and brutality of war. In times of armed conflict it becomes a soldier's duty to kill the enemy, therefore requiring a derogation from the protection of the general right to life, enshrined in human rights instruments. For the same reason a combatant, unlike a civilian, cannot be considered a criminal for having engaged in combat or having killed an enemy. The same approach cannot be shared under HRL, which was specifically drafted for times of peace. It is for this reason that when the situation escalated towards a conflict, not having reached the threshold, yet, a state of emergency may be declared under which some human rights may be derogated from. IHL, instead, shall apply only once a certain intensity of the fighting has been reached, normally requiring the intervention of the armed forces to sedate it. In times of war it is also unconceivable to grant to everyone, in particular the members of the armed forces, the same freedom of expression, counterbalanced by the need to keep certain activities secret, etc. at the same time, however, there are some human rights which are so fundamental

---

[16] On this *see also* Legal Consequences of the Construction of a Wall in the Occupied Palestinian Territory, Advisory Opinion (July 9, 2004), 2004 ICJ Rep. 163, paras 104ss.

to find application under all circumstances, including times of armed conflict. As such, these rights are restated in the four Geneva Conventions of 1949 and their two Additional Protocols of 1977, which have the status of *lex specials* in relation to HRL instruments. In this sense, the two branches are complementary to each other.

For example, IHL, in particular Article 13 GC III and Common Article 3, offers protection to certain persons like detainees or sick and wounded former combatants. According to these two provisions, POWs must be treated humanely at all times. Any act by the "Detaining Power" causing their death is a serious breach. A prisoner who, for operational reasons, cannot be held, must be released. The judicial guarantees of detainees are provided for in Articles 99–100. Furthermore, *incommunicado* detention is a breach of a POW's right to stay in touch with the external world (Articles 69–77). POWs shall further be enabled to write to their families and to the Central Prisoners of War Agency (Article 70 in conjunction with Article 123). They shall be allowed to send and receive letters, cards (Article 71) and parcels (Article 72). To withhold a POW as a "bargaining chip" is further a serious violation of Article 118. Another fundamental provision, which draws from HRL, is Article 75 AP I, which has customary law status. It protects fundamental guarantees such as the prohibition of violence to life and health (physical and mental), in particular murder and torture, humiliating and degrading treatment, the taking of hostages, collective punishments, and unjustified delayed release. All these rights are to be protected at *all times*, under *all circumstances*. A comparative table can be drawn between the rights of detainees provided by IHL and HRL instruments:[17]

	ECHR[18]	ICCPR	III GC	AP I	Art. 3	AP II
Right to Life	Art. 2	Art. 6	Art. 13	Art. 75(2)	Para. 1	Art. 4(2)
Torture and Inhumane Treatment	Art. 3	Art. 7	Art. 13–14	Art. 75(2)	Para. 2	Art. 4(2)
Hostage Taking	Art. 3	Art. 7	Art. 13–14	Art. 75(2)	Para. 1	Art. 4
Legality, Non-Retroactivity	Art. 7	Art. 15	Art. 99	Art. 75(4)	Para. 1	Art. 6(2)
Right to Fair Trial	Art. 6	Art. 14	Art. 99–108	Art. 75(4)	Para. 1	Art. 6(1–5)
Freedom of Thought, Conscience, Religion	Art. 9	Art. 18	Art. 33–37/120			

---

[17] For details *see* Roberta Arnold, *Human Rights in Times of War: The Protection of POWs and the Case of Ron Arad*, 5 H.R.L.R. 8 (2000) and El Kouhene, Les garanties fondamentales de la personne en droit humanitaire et droits de l'homme 117 (1986).

[18] Convention for the Protection of Human Rights and Fundamental Freedoms, (Nov. 4, 1950), 213 U.N.T.S. 221 (entered into force Sept. 3, 1953) [hereinafter ECHR].

Unlike IHL, which provides for non-derogable and universal rights, with customary status, applicable at all times, when there is an armed conflict, Article 4 ICCPR provides for the *possibility* of derogating from some of its provisions.[19] In a state of emergency, which will be discussed in the next paragraph, only Articles 6, 7, 8, 11, 15, 16 and 18,[20] are excluded from the right of derogation (Article 10, instead, which deals with detainees, is not exempt). Under IHL, e.g., unlike under HRL, family rights are non-derogable.[21]

A further advantage is that whereas human rights violations can only be invoked against a state, IHL violations can be charged against individuals, as proven by the numerous cases brought in front of international tribunals like the ICTY,[22] ICTR[23] or, more recently, the ICC.[24]

3. *The State of Emergency*

According to the dictionary,[25] a state of emergency is a:

> governmental declaration that may suspend certain normal functions of government, may work to alert citizens to alter their normal behaviors, or may order government agencies to implement emergency preparedness plans. It can also be used as a rationale for suspending civil liberties. Such declarations usually come during a time of natural disaster, during periods of civil unrest, or following a declaration of war. In some countries, the state of emergency and its effects on civil liberties and governmental procedure are regulated by the constitution or a law that limits the powers that may be invoked during an emergency or rights suspended (e.g. Art. 2-B Executive Law of New York state) It is also frequently illegal to modify the emergency law or Con-

---

[19] International Covenant on Civil and Political Rights, G.A. Res. 2200A (XXI), 21 U.N. GAOR Supp. (No. 16) at 52, U.N. Doc. A/6316 (1966), 999 U.N.T.S. 171 [hereinafter ICCPR],

[20] No derogation is allowed to Article 6 (right to life), Article 7 (torture), Articles 8(1) and 8(2) (slavery), Article 11 (imprisonment for inability to fulfil a contractual obligation), Article 15 (no retroactivity of penal provisions), Article 16 (right to recognition as a person before the law) and Article 18 (right to freedom of thought, conscience and religion).

[21] International Committee of the Red Cross, Human rights and the ICRC: International Humanitarian Law 3 (1993). However, it will be discussed later that according to the U.N. Human Rights Committee also those provisions which are not enlisted under Article 4 contain some elements considered to be non-derogable.

[22] Statute of the International Criminal Tribunal for the Former Yugoslavia, S.C. Res. 827, U.N. Doc. S/RES/827 (May 25, 1993) [hereinafter ICTY Statute].

[23] Statute of the International Criminal Tribunal for Rwanda, S.C. Res. 955, U.N. Doc. S/RES/955 (November 8, 1994) [hereinafter ICTR Statute].

[24] Rome Statute of the International Criminal Court, U.N. Doc. 2187 U.N.T.S. 90, entered into force July 1, 2002 [hereinafter ICC Statute].

[25] *Available at* www.answers.com/%22state%20of%20emergency%22 (last visited Oct. 22, 2007).

stitution during the emergency (e.g. Basic Law of the Federal Republic of Germany, Chapter X, Article 115e, section 2).

A state of emergency is fairly uncommon in democracies and is rather used by dictatorial regimes and prolonged indefinitely as long as the regime lasts. In some circumstances, martial law is also declared, allowing the military greater powers. It is generally declared at times of overwhelming danger, when certain normal standards of procedure need to be abrogated and replaced by others. For example, it may be declared in cases of disturbances and demonstrations, including violent ones, or natural catastrophes, internal or international armed conflict. Not every disturbance or catastrophe, however, qualifies as a public emergency that threatens the life of the nation. In these exceptional cases, measures can be declared which may derogate from certain human rights provisions, on condition that: a) the situation must amount to a public emergency threatening the life of the nation and b) the state party must have officially proclaimed a state of emergency. These measures must be limited to the period of time which is strictly required by the situation and the state which declares it must provide for a well-considered justification of both the declaration of a state of emergency and of the specific measures which have been taken on this basis.

In order to limit the authority to derogate from human rights, certain guarantees have been declared as non-derogable. These include the right to life; the prohibition of torture; the principle of legality in the field of criminal law; and the freedom of thought, conscience, and religion among others. For example, in relation to Article 4 ICCPR, the U.N. Human Rights Committee recognized that also those provisions of the Covenant that are not listed in Article 4(2) contain certain elements that cannot be subject to lawful derogation. Examples are provided by the treatment of all persons deprived of their liberty with humanity and with respect for the inherent dignity of the human person; the prohibitions against hostage taking, abductions, or unacknowledged detention; the international protection of minority rights; the prohibition of propaganda for war or in advocacy of national, racial, or religious hatred that would constitute incitement to discrimination, hostility, or violence; and procedural guarantees and safeguards related to, for example, fair trials.

Similarly, at the Conference on the Human Dimension of the CSCE in Copenhagen in 1990, the participating OSCE member states adopted a document reaffirming that any derogation from human rights obligations during a state of emergency must remain strictly within the limits provided for by international law.[26]

---

[26] Copenhagen Document, para. 25. Further considerations for the conditions for the justifiability of any derogation include that measures not involve discrimination solely on the grounds of race, colour, sex, language, religion, social origin, or of belonging to a minority (Copenhagen Document, para. 25.4).

The authority to declare a state of emergency depends on a country's domestic legislation. In the United Kingdom this is usually vested in the monarch or a Senior Minister. According to the *Civil Contingencies Act 2004*, this is allowed if there is a serious threat to human welfare or the environment or in case of war or terrorism. The emergency may last for seven days unless confirmed by Parliament.

In other systems the authority may be vested in the Parliament or the Head of State.[27] For example in the United States, it is the chief executive who is typically empowered with it. The President, a governor of a state, or even a local mayor may declare a state of emergency within his/her jurisdiction. This seems to be relatively rare at the federal level, but quite common at the state level, in response to, e.g., natural disasters. Under these circumstances, individuals may be arrested without cause, private places may be searched without warrant, or private property may be seized without immediate compensation or a chance to prior appeal. U.S. courts seem to be rather lenient in allowing almost any action to be taken in the case of such a declared emergency, if it is reasonably related. For example, *habeas corpus* is the right to challenge an arrest in court. The U.S. Constitution says, "The Privilege of the Writ of Habeas Corpus shall not be suspended, unless when in Cases of Rebellion or Invasion the public Safety may require it."

In Canada, the state of emergency is defined in the *National Emergencies Act* as "an urgent and critical situation of a temporary nature that exceeds a province's ability to cope and that threatens the welfare of Canadians and the ability of the Canadian government to preserve the sovereignty, security and territorial integrity of Canada" and it can be declared by the Prime Minister and the Cabinet. It can last up to 90 days, at which point it can be extended.[28]

Review of a state of emergency may be undertaken by the U.N. Human Rights Committee.[29] In fact, HRL instruments often provide for control mechanisms

---

[27] *Available at* encyclopedia.laborlawtalk.com/State_of_Emergency (last visited Oct. 22, 2007).

[28] Info *available at* http://www.cbc.ca/news/background/stateofemergency/ (last visited Oct. 22, 2007). In this case the government may, at its discretion: regulate or prohibit travel when it is deemed necessary for health and safety reasons; remove people and their possessions from their homes; use or dispose of non-government property at its discretion; authorize and pay persons to provide essential services that are deemed necessary; ration and control essential goods, services and resources; authorize emergency payments; establish emergency shelters and hospitals; assess and repair damaged infrastructure; convict or indict those who contradict any of the above.

[29] Concluding Observations of the Human Rights Committee: Ireland, U.N. Doc CCPR/C/79/Add.21, July 3, 1993, para. 11. "The Committee expresses special concern over the continuation of the state of emergency declared with the adoption of the Emergency Powers Act in 1976. The Committee notes with concern that the Emergency Powers Act, particularly section 2 thereof, provides excessive powers to law enforcement officials. The Committee also expresses its concern with respect to the Special Court established under the Offences Against the State Act of 1939. It does not consider that the continued existence of that Court is justified in the present circumstances. The measures referred to above are of a character that normally fall to be notified under article 4

(e.g. the Human Rights Committee in relation to the ICCPR, or the Committee on Torture in relation to the Convention Against Torture).[30] At political level, pressure may be also exercised by organisations like the OSCE[31] or the European Union. OSCE participating states, for example, committed themselves to inform the OSCE Secretariat of a decision to declare or lift a state of emergency.[32] With respect to this, the 1992 Concluding Document of Helsinki assigns an important task to the ODIHR to act as a clearing house regarding information on states of emergency.[33] This commitment also requires a participating state to inform of the OSCE of any derogation made from international human rights obligations.

According to paragraph 28.1. of the Moscow Document, a state of public emergency may not be used to subvert the democratic constitutional order or to destruct internationally recognized human rights and fundamental freedoms. Moreover, citizens of the concerned states must be promptly informed by the measures taken (para. 28.3). These must also ensure that the normal functioning of legislative bodies will be guaranteed to the highest possible extent during a state of public emergency (para. 28.5).

Another option may be the intervention of the U.N. Security Council. Indeed, should a state abuse its right to declare the state of emergency, and thereby pose a threat to international peace and security, the Security Council may intervene on the basis of Chapter VII of the U.N. Charter. Internal crisis and human rights abuses have long been considered an internal matter not allowing external interferences on the basis of the principle of state sovereignty. However, if this situation may pose a threat to international stability, an intervention may be justified, as in the case of the Rwandan genocide. In some cases, should a state of emergency lead to gross human rights violations and crimes against humanity, it is conceivable that, likewise, a case may be referred to the International Criminal Court by the Security Council.

All this information on state emergency is also very important to determine whether we are still acting within the framework of peace- or wartime. According to the four GCs of 1949, IHL shall not apply to isolated and sporadic acts of violence such as riots. There is a lower threshold that needs to be achieved, requiring

---

of the Covenant. The Committee notes, however, that the State party has failed to inform other States parties of any state of emergency through the Secretary-General of the United Nations, as required under article 4, paragraph 3, of the Covenant."

[30] Convention against Torture and Other Cruel, Inhuman or Degrading Treatment or Punishment, G.A. Res. 39/46, [annex, 39 U.N. GAOR Supp. (No. 51) at 197, U.N. Doc. A/39/51 (1984)], entered into force June 26, 1987 [hereinafter CAT].

[31] *See* Office for Democratic Institutions and Human Rights, *available at* www1.osce.org/odihr/13485.html (last visited Oct. 22, 2007).

[32] 1991 Moscow Meeting of the Conference on the Human Dimension, para. 28.10.

[33] Helsinki Document, 1992, para. 5b.

a specific intensity of the violent activities. The state of emergency is normally declared within the framework of peacetime when, however, urgency provisions need to be enacted. This, however, does not bring into play IHL, yet. Those caught committing acts of urban guerrilla, therefore, may be labeled as terrorists to be subjected to ordinary criminal law provisions, including, as it will be discussed later, emergency law provisions and administrative detention provisions.

4. *Torture as a Special Case*

Torture captured the public opinion's attention particularly after the disclosure of the images of the Iraqi prisoners abused by U.S. privates at the Abu Ghraib detention facility in Baghdad. Pursuant to the *Taguba Report*,[34] between October and December 2003 "numerous incidents of sadistic, blatant, and wanton criminal abuses" were inflicted on several detainees. Since then, the question has arisen whether torture, in extreme cases, should be allowed to extract important information from terrorist suspects, which may save hundreds of lives. The granting to the executive of the authority to decide what may constitute torture and to set the limits, however, carries with it a high risk of arbitrariness, which, in relation to a breach as serious as torture cannot be accepted. For this reason, several important international instrument ban torture under *all* circumstances. Among these are the Geneva Conventions of 1949, their Additional Protocols of 1977 and the 1985 UN Convention against Torture. The latter established the U.N. Committee against Torture as a control mechanism. It defines torture in Article 1[35] and declares that no state of emergency, other external threats, nor orders from a superior officer or authority may be invoked to justify its use. Each state is obliged to provide training to law enforcement personnel and the military on torture prevention, keep

---

[34] A report prepared by Maj.Gen. Antonio M. Taguba on alleged abuse of prisoners by members of the 800th Military Police Brigade at the Abu Ghraib Prison, Baghdad. It was ordered by Lt. Gen. Ricardo Sanchez, Commander of Joint Task Force 7, the senior U.S. military official in Iraq, following persistent allegations of human rights abuses at the prison. *Available at* news.findlaw.com/hdocs/docs/iraq/tagubarpt.html#ThR1.3 (last visited Oct. 22, 2007).

[35] "For the purposes of this Convention, torture means any act by which severe pain or suffering, whether physical or mental, is intentionally inflicted on a person for such purposes as obtaining from him or a third person information or a confession, punishing him for an act he or a third person has committed or is suspected of having committed, or intimidating or coercing him or a third person, or for any reason based on discrimination of any kind, when such pain or suffering is inflicted by or at the instigation of or with the consent or acquiescence of a public official or other person acting in an official capacity. It does not include pain or suffering arising only from, inherent in or incidental to lawful sanctions.

This article is without prejudice to any international instrument or national legislation which does or may contain provisions of wider application."

its interrogation methods under review, and promptly investigate any allegations that its officials have committed torture during official duties. At present sixty five nations have ratified the Convention and sixteen more have signed but not yet ratified it.[36] The prohibition of torture has acquired customary law status[37] and breaches thereof may also constitute – given the circumstances – a war crime or a crime against humanity under Articles 7[38] and 8 ICC Statute.[39] Similarly, the ICTY confirmed in *Furundžija*[40] that the prohibition of torture is an absolute right, which can never be derogated from, even in times of emergency. In Israel, there has been a period in which the "ticking bomb theory" was supported, holding that lighter forms of torture, such as shaking, were allowed during the interrogation of suspects of terrorism if this was going to prevent foreseeable attacks planned in the near future. However, this procedure was ruled out as being unlawful by Israel's High Court of Justice on September 6, 1999.[41]

5. *The Attitude of the Bush Administration and the American Courts*

With the "global war on terror," the Bush administration seems to have preferred military to traditional law enforcement mechanisms to identify, locate, and arrest suspects of terrorism. This approach has not been particularly efficient. Osama Bin Laden, with other key players in the realm of terror, are still on free foot. The military is not adequately trained and structured to deal with a phenomenon which has

---

[36] The United States ratified it on October 21, 1994, but on June 3, 1994, the U.N. Secretary-General received a communication from the U.S. Government requesting, in compliance with a condition set forth by the U.S. Senate, in giving advice and consent to the ratification of the Convention, and in contemplation of the deposit of an instrument of ratification of the Convention by the U.S. Government, that a notification should be made to all present and prospective ratifying Parties to the Convention to the effect that: "…nothing in this Convention requires or authorizes legislation, or other action, by the United States of America prohibited by the Constitution of the United States as interpreted by the United States." Further details can be found at the OHCHR Website, *available at* www.ohchr.org/english/countries/ratification/9.htm#N11 (last visited Oct. 22, 2007).

[37] *See* Prosecutor v. Furundzija, Case No. IT-95-17/1, Trial Chamber, (Dec. 10, 1998), paras 137ss [hereinafter Furundzija].

[38] Under Article. 7 ICC Statute, "'Torture' means the intentional infliction of severe pain or suffering, whether physical or mental, upon a person in the custody or under the control of the accused; except that torture shall not include pain or suffering arising only from, inherent in or incidental to, lawful sanctions." Rome Statute, *supra* note 24.

[39] *Id.*

[40] Furundzija, *supra* note 37, paras 144ss.

[41] For a report on the case *see* Jerrold Kessel, *Israel Supreme Court bans interrogation abuse of Palestinians*, 6.9.1999, CNN, *available at* edition.cnn.com/WORLD/meast/9909/06/israel.torture/ (last visited Oct. 22, 2007).

traditionally belonged to competences of the police. By trying to repress terrorism with the occupation of so-called rogue states, not only have the United States acted in breach of several public international law principles (e.g. state sovereignty), but have also brought into play the laws of armed conflict to regulate a situation these were not foreseen for. Although the 9/11 attack should have been responded to with traditional mechanisms of international cooperation in criminal matters, by virtue of the occupation of Afghanistan and Iraq, the U.S. armed forces are now engaged in a conflict where the adversaries are a mixture of terrorists from the pre-invasion phase (Al Qaeda, e.g.), and regular combatants who have come into play to respond to the invasion. This means that those apprehended *after* the occupation of Iraq and Afghanistan, who have been fighting in conformity with IHL, in fulfilment of the combatant status criteria under Article 4(A)(2) GC III, shall be granted POW status. The problem, however, is that POWs enjoy several privileges. For instance, they cannot be compelled, when questioned, to give other information than surname, first names and rank, date of birth, and army, regimental, personal or serial number, or failing this, equivalent information (Article 17 GC III). POWs, in fact, are *not* criminals. They can only be charged with breaches of the laws of war, not with mere participation in combat. The latter is considered a crime only if committed by civilians, who are not allowed engaging in the hostilities. Another difference is that POWs facing a trial for war crimes retain their status.[42] The reason for the United States to label the Guantanamo detainees as "unlawful combatants" seems to be due to the fact that according to general criminal procedural law, a suspect against whom no specific charges can be brought, shall be released within 48 hours. This would have obviously constituted a problem in relation to the detainees held in Guantanamo. POWs, instead, may be retained until the end of the hostilities even if no specific charge is brought against them, since their detention is not aimed at punishing them for criminal conduct, but at preventing them from rejoining the enemy forces. In the Guantanamo case, therefore, the attempt is to consider the "war on terror" a conflict under Article 2 common to the Geneva Conventions of 1949, permitting the detention of suspects of terrorism until its end. The *en bloc* qualification of the Guantanamo detainees as combatants, therefore, without making distinctions between those belonging to Al Qaeda and those to the Taleban, permits the U.S. administration to circumvent the 48-hour problem. However, recognition of combatant status for these detainees pursuant to Article 4(A)(2) GC III would imply their eligibility to POW status, which is not in the interest of the United States. For this reason the new term "unlawful combatant" was coined,

---

[42] It should be noted, however, that abidance by the laws of war is a constitutional criterion for POW status in relation to members of irregular armed groups, whereas it is simply a declaratory criterion for members of regular armed forces. More on this can be found in Arnold, *supra* note 1, *see* chapter on terrorism as a war crime.

in order to grant neither POW rights, nor those attached to civilians, including traditional criminal law and criminal procedural law.

The alternative (and correct) solution would have been to consider detained members of Al Qaeda as civilians to be tried according to domestic and international anti-terrorism legislation. In these circumstances and option permitting to circumvent the above-mentioned problem of the 48–hour deadline for bringing specific charges would have been to resort to administrative detention, as done in the United Kingdom or Israel. However, due to constitutional limitations, this option was not available in the United States. Administration detention, as described by the Israeli NGO "B'tselem," is:

> detention without charge or trial, authorized by administrative order rather than by judicial decree. It is allowed under international law, but, because of the serious injury to due process rights inherent in this measure and the obvious danger of abuse, international law has placed rigid restrictions on its application. Administrative detention is intended to prevent the danger posed to state security by a particular individual. However, Israel has never defined the criteria for what constitutes "state security."[43]

Administrative detention raises several issues relating to human rights, but at least it is allowed under international law. One should ask about the *malus minor*: to keep detainees in a legal vacuum, with *no* rights at all, or to hold them in administrative detention, with derogation only from *some* rights?

With respect to Guantanamo Bay, the U.S. Supreme Court made an important ruling in *Rasul* v. *Bush*[44] on June 28, 2004. Reference was made to the law authorising President George W. Bush to use:

> all necessary and appropriate force against those nations, organisations or persons he determines planned, authorised, committed or aided the terrorist attacks... or harbored such organisations or persons,

on the basis of which the detention facility of Guantanamo Bay was established.[45] The case concerned two Australian detainees (Mamdouh Habib and David Hicks), who had filed petitions in U.S. federal courts for writs of *habeas corpus*, requesting, among others, release from custody, access to counsel, and freedom from interrogation. The petitions were dismissed by the U.S. District Court for want of jurisdiction, on the basis of *Eisentrager* precedent holding that:

> [a]liens detained outside the sovereign territory of the United States [may not] invoke a petition for a writ of *habeas corpus*.[46]

---

[43] *Available at* www.btselem.org/English/Administrative%5FDetention/ (last visited Oct. 22, 2007).
[44] 542 US 1 (2004); 72 USLW 4596 (2004).
[45] Authorisation for the Use of Military Force, Public Law 107–40, paras 1–2, US Stat 224.
[46] Johnson v. Eisentrager 339 US 763 (1950).

The decision was reversed by the Supreme Court, which remitted the case to the federal courts. By rejecting the argument that the U.S. executive cannot be held answerable in courts for the detention off-shore of alleged terrorists, the Supreme Court upheld the rule of law and avoided the creation of a legal vacuum in Guantanamo Bay.

Another important ruling was released on January 19, 2005 by the U.S. District Court for the Court of Columbia in *Khalid* v. *Bush*. The Petitioners in *Khalid*, 7 foreign nationals, 5 Algerian-Bosnians, one Algerian, and one Frenchman, were captured *outside* Afghanistan (6 in Bosnia and one in Pakistan). They challenged their detention under U.S. and international law and asked the court to issue a writ of *habeas corpus*. The Court concluded that "[…] no viable legal theory exists by which it could issue a writ of habeas corpus under these circumstances," recalling the U.S. Supreme Court's decision in *Rasul*. It further stated that:

> the petitioners are asking this court to do something no federal court has done before: evaluate the legality of the Executive's capture and detention of non-resident aliens, outside the U.S. during a time of armed conflict,

suggesting ignorance of the ruling in *Rasul*.[47] Regarding non-U.S. nationals held in Guantanamo, the *Rasul* court found that U.S. courts have jurisdiction to hear the detainees' petition. Yet, in *Khalid*, the Court seems to have come to a different conclusion.

On November 8, 2004, in *Hamdan*, the same District Court had come to a diametrically opposed outcome. The dispute may have been solved by the U.S. District Court for the District of Columbia *In re Guantanamo Detainees Cases*, held on January 31, 2005. As mentioned, the first case, decided by Judge Robertson (*Hamdan*, November 8, 2004) found in favour of the detainees. The second, decided by Judge Leon (*Khalid*, January 19, 2005) found in favour of the government. The third, instead, found in favour of the detainees.[48] The Court analysed the "due process clause" of the 5th amendment to the U.S. Constitution, adopting the reasoning of the Supreme Court in *Rasul*, i.e. that the Guantanamo base is to be considered as part of U.S. sovereign territory where the 5th Amendment applies to all the detainees kept there, be these U.S. or non-U.S. nationals. The Court followed also the Supreme Court's reasoning in *Hamdi*. It found that the U.S. government's argument that the detainees could be held as long as the "war against terrorism"

---

[47] For an analysis see Bernard Dougherty, Severe Setback in the Battle for Rights of Guantanamo Detainees, Bofaxe No. 290E, Feb. 18, 2005, *available at* www.ruhr-uni-bochum.de/ifhv/publications/bofaxe/x290E.pdf (last visited Oct. 22, 2007).

[48] Bernard Dougherty, Unnamed Detainees at Guantanamo; Decision for the Detainees. Score before the District Court now: 2–1 in favour of the Detainees, Bofaxe No. 292E, March 1, 2005, *available at* www.ruhr-uni-bochum.de/ifhv/publications/bofaxe/x292E.pdf (last visited Oct. 22, 2007).

continued, could amount to a life sentence, providing sufficient interest for the detainees to litigate their detention and to be given notice of the reasons thereof. The Court also found that the CSRT (Combatant Status Review Tribunal) did not grant the detainees a fair opportunity to review their status because: 1. they were not provided assistance of counsel; 2. they were not provided with sufficient notice of the factual basis for their detention because certain evidence was not disclosed to them; and 3. some of the evidence against them may have been obtained by torture or other coercion.

In this ruling, specific attention was given to the GC III, particularly Articles 4 and 5,[49] according to which, in case of doubt, someone shall be treated as a POW until a decision on the status is made by a competent tribunal. In agreement with *Hamdan*, the Court found that the GCs are self-executing and that President Bush's early determination that there is no doubt that the detainees are not entitled to POW status did not qualify as a judgement by a competent tribunal under Article 5.

However, most recently, on October 28, 2005, the Inter-American Commission on Human Rights, in its ruling on the Extension of Precautionary Measures (No. 259) regarding Detainees in Guantanamo Bay, Cuba, observed, *inter alia*, that, notwithstanding the Supreme Court decision in *Rasul* v. *Bush*, according to the information available to it:

> nearly half of the Guantanamo detainees have not been given effective access to counsel or otherwise provided with a fair opportunity to pursue a habeas corpus proceeding in accordance with the Supreme Court's ruling, despite the fact that the purpose of habeas is intended to be a timely remedy aimed at guaranteeing personal liberty and humane treatment.

It concluded that the situation at Guantanamo continues to be of an urgent character, and asked that the United States provide information concerning compliance with its precautionary measures, together with the additional information requested, within 30 days.[50]

The Commission further requested that the US:

1. take the immediate measures necessary to have the legal status of the detainees at Guantanamo Bay effectively determined by a competent tribunal;
   - take all measures necessary to thoroughly and impartially investigate, prosecute and punish all instances of torture and other mistreatment that may be perpetrated

---

[49] Of particular relevance is Article 5, stating that "The present Convention shall apply to the persons referred to in Article 4 from the time they fall into the power of the enemy and until their final release and repatriation.

Should any doubt arise as to whether persons, having committed a belligerent act and having fallen into the hands of the enemy, belong to any of the categories enumerated in Article 4, such persons shall enjoy the protection of the present Convention until such time as their status has been determined by a competent tribunal." GC III, *supra* note 2 (emphasis added).

[50] *See* www.asil.org/pdfs/ilibmeasures051115.pdf (last visited Oct. 22, 2007).

against the detainees at Guantanamo Bay, whether through methods of interrogation or otherwise, and to ensure respect for the prohibition against the use in any legal proceeding of statements obtained through torture, except against a person accused of torture as evidence that the statement was made;
– take the measures necessary to ensure that any detainees who may face a risk of torture or other cruel, inhuman or degrading treatment if transferred, removed or expelled from Guantanamo Bay are provided an adequate, individualized examination of their circumstances through a fair and transparent process before a competent, independent and impartial decision-maker. Where there are substantial grounds for believing that he or she would be in danger of being subjected to torture or other mistreatment, the State should ensure that the detainee is not transferred or removed and that diplomatic assurances are not used to circumvent the State's non-refoulement obligation.

The United States reiterated its position that the Commission's jurisdiction and competence do not extend to the laws and customs of war or to issuing requests for precautionary measures against non-states parties to the American Convention. It further contended that there was a requirement of exhaustion of domestic remedies and, *inter alia*, that as of September 27, 2005, 160 habeas proceedings involving 292 detainee petitions had been filed with U.S. courts. It noted that these proceedings included *Hamdan* v. *Rumsfeld*, 415 F. 3d 33 (DC Cir. 2005) and *In re Guantanamo Detainees*, 355 F. Supp. 2d 311 (D.D.C. 2005), resulting in conflicting conclusions as to whether non-resident aliens have the right to challenge their detention under the U.S. Constitution, under customary international law or under international treaties. It further observed that a consolidated appeal to the U.S. District Court for the District of Columbia is pending and that there have been administrative proceedings at Guantanamo Bay, including proceedings before Combatant Status Review Tribunals, initiated in July 2004, charged with determining whether detainees are properly classified as enemy combatants.

With respect to allegations of torture regarding the Guantanamo detainees, the United States observed that its Department of Defense denied these and restated its commitment to treating the prisoners humanely. It submitted that as of December 2004, the U.S. government had documented eight instances of infractions resulting in different actions ranging from admonishment to court-martial. It further contended that the facility at Guantanamo is continually open to the International Committee of the Red Cross (ICRC) and foreign and domestic media.

The petitioners, in their submissions to the Commission, alleged that there are still about 225 detainees who have been denied access to counsel and that the U.S. military has interfered with their right to a confidential attorney-client relationship. They further alleged that the assurances provided by the U.S. government have proven unreliable; reports by the ICRC, statements by U.S. government officials, government memoranda leaked to the media and media reports indicate, on the contrary, that the detainees have been subjected to beatings, sleep deprivation, sensory deprivation, exposure to extreme temperatures and prolonged isolation, and that such treatment has been approved at the highest levels of authority of the United States. It was further noted that detainees have also been transferred to countries with deplorable human rights records and no guarantees that these will refrain from torture. In response to the U.S. position that the Commission had no jurisdiction to deal with this case, the Commission concluded that it has the authority to adopt precautionary measures in respect of non-state parties to the American Convention and to consider and apply IHL. It also stated that the principle of exhaustion did not apply to the precautionary measures, for such measures are "intended to reinforce and complement, rather than replace, domestic jurisdiction."

In sum, the U.S. jurisprudence proves that a distinction needs to be drawn between IHL and HRL, in that the former has a stronger hold, providing for non-derogable rights under all circumstances with customary status. With human rights it is easier to argue that these may be derogated from for reasons of state emergency. However, by qualifying the fight against the global threat of terrorism as a "war," the U.S. government is now facing a "boomerang" effect, finding itself bound by more stringent provisions. In this sense, it can be argued that thanks to IHL, core human rights are better anchored and have a stronger chance to be – if not respected – at least enforced if invoked in a court. With the creation of several international tribunals, breaches of core human rights may qualify as war crimes or crimes against humanity and also be brought as charges against *individuals*, rather than states. It shall be recalled, in fact, that human rights violations may only be invoked vertically, whereas breaches of IHL or the commission of crimes against humanity can now be invoked also horizontally.

6. *The Attitude of the European Organs and the European Courts*

As mentioned in the introduction, terrorism is not a new phenomenon and several judicial instruments and decisions have already been enacted. For example the United Kingdom, faced with the terrorist threat posed by the IRA, enacted several anti-terrorism laws.[51] In 2000, it passed the *Terrorism Act* and in 2001 the *Criminal Justice and Police Act*, extending police powers. It made a derogation to Article 15 ECHR and adopted more intrusive surveillance measures. Particularly in response to the anti-terrorism policy adopted in Northern Ireland, several cases were brought to the European Court of Human Rights, particularly in relation

---

[51] Eg. the Northern Ireland (Emergency Provisions) Acts 1973–98 (UK), the Criminal Justice (Terrorism and Conspiracy) Act 1998 (UK) and the Prevention of Terrorism (Temporary Provisions) Acts (UK), in continuous use between 1974 and 2001. The Terrorism Act 2000 (UK) which came into force in February 2001.

to the right to derogate from certain human rights. Article 15 ECHR provides that "[a] country cannot derogate by adopting measures that are inconsistent with other obligations under international law"[52] and that "No derogations may be made from rights contained in the Convention Articles."[53] For instance in *Lawless v. Republic of Ireland [No. 3]*,[54] which concerned the case of an Irish citizen who had been detained without trial by Irish (rather than British) authorities for five months in 1957, on the basis of his alleged activities as a member of the IRA, the court held that the Irish government was justified in declaring a public emergency and acting as it did.

Between 1957 and 1975, the United Kingdom gave notice of derogation from Article 5 ECHR in order to use extra-judicial powers to deprive suspects of liberty for interrogation, detention and as a preventative measure. On a complaint by Ireland, the European Court found various breaches, particularly in relation to the obligation to preserve access to judicial review. Some contraventions were held to be within a permissible derogation. However, in respect of instances of inhuman treatment and torture, which were found, derogation was not permitted by the Convention. To this extent, the complaint by Ireland was upheld.[55]

Another issue related to the question of who bore the onus of establishing justification of the reasonableness of the measures adopted by a national government to combat terrorism, as required under Article 5(1), in *Fox and Others v. United Kingdom*[56] the European Court concluded that:

> the respondent government has to furnish at least some facts or information capable of satisfying the Court that the arrested person was reasonably suspected of having committed the alleged offence.

The European Court has recently dealt also with the Basque separatist movement (ETA) in Spain. Following 9/11 the European Union, in December 2001 and

---

[52] Art. 15(1) ECHR, *supra* note 18.
[53] Article 2 ECHR (Right to Life), Article 3 ECHR (Prohibition on Inhuman Treatment and Torture), Article 4(1) ECHR (Prohibition on Slavery and Servitude), Article 7 ECHR (Retroactive Laws), *id.*
[54] Lawless v. Republic of Ireland [No. 3], Application No. 332/57, (July 1, 1961).
[55] Republic of Ireland v. United Kingdom, (1978) 2 EHRR at 107. *See also* Hon Justice Michael Kirby AC CMG, National Europe Centre Canberra, The Australian National University, Nov. 11, 2004, Robert Schuman Lecture on "Terrorism and the Democratic Response: A Tribute to the European Court of Human Rights" [hereinafter Kirby].
[56] Fox, Campbell and Hartley v. United Kingdom, Applications Nos 18/1989/178/234–236, (Aug. 30, 1990). On the application of human rights in the "war against terrorism" *see also* The Queen (on the application of Hilal Abdul-Razzaq Ali Al-Jedda) – and – Secretary of State for Defence, commented by James Johnston, *IHL v. Human Rights: The Al Jedda Case and Issues Arising from an Operational Perspective, in* Law Enforcement in Peace Support Operations (Roberta Arnold ed., 2007).

June 2003 acceded to Spain's request to proscribe ETA as a terrorist organisation. Batasuna, the political wing of ETA, was dissolved by order of Spain's highest civil court. An appeal to the Constitutional Court of Spain was rejected in January 2004. On March 17, the Spanish Supreme Court unanimously decided to declare Batasuna a terrorist, and therefore illegal, organization. The de-legalization meant that Batasuna, Euskal Herritarrok and Herri Batasuna were erased from the registry of political parties; that they would not be able to participate in any elections; that none of their activities (meetings, publication, propaganda, electoral process) was to be permitted; and that their patrimonial assets were to be sold off and the proceeds used for social or humanitarian activities. In September 2003 the Basque government initiated a claim against the Spanish government at the European Court. The claim alleged that the Law of Political Parties, used as a base to de-legalize Batasuna, violates fundamental rights. In November, the European Court officially received the cases of 221 Batasuna candidates who were not allowed to stand for office.[57] On February 5, the Court rejected the claim, saying that the case was "inadmissible" for technical reasons.[58] However, the European Court, in its jurisprudence, has acknowledged that European states have a "margin of appreciation" when dealing with terrorism.[59]

As it can be seen, there are not many cases dealing with the issue of the restriction of human rights of detained suspects of terrorism. As a consequence, the debate is still open. The burden will be on international lawyers to act as watchdogs over politicians, who often decide about the laws to be enacted and implemented, and who may be misled in thinking that the end may justify the means, even when dealing with derogations from fundamental human rights.

---

[57] Country Reports on Human Rights Practices – 2003, Released by the U.S. Department of State's Bureau of Democracy, Human Rights, and Labor, Feb. 25, 2004, *available at* www.state.gov/g/drl/rls/hrrpt/2003/27865.htm (last visited Oct. 22, 2007); BBC News World Edition, *Spain Maintains Basque Party Ban*, Jan. 17, 2004, *available at* news.bbc.co.uk/2/hi/europe/3405211.stm (last visited Oct. 22, 2007).

[58] On this aspect *see also* Thomas Ayres, *Batasuna Banned: The Dissolution of Political Parties under the European Convention of Human Rights*, 27 B.C. Int'l & Comp. L. Rev. 99 (2004). *See also* Information released by the Bureau of Democracy, Human Rights, and Labor, Feb. 28, 2005, *available at* www.nationbynation.com/Spain/Human.html (last visited Oct. 22, 2007).

[59] *See also* Kirby, *supra* note 55 and Kenneth Dobson, *The Spanish Government's Ban of a Political Party: A Violation of Human Rights?*, 9 New Eng. J. Int'l & Comp. L. 637, 639 (2003). *See* Council Regulation 2580/01, Dec. 28, 2001 on Specific Restrictive Measures Directed Against Persons and Entities with a View to Combating Terrorism, Article 2(3), 2001 O.J. (L 344) 2, *available at* europa.eu.int (last visited Oct. 22, 2007). *See also EU Blacklists Basque Party*, BBC News, June 5, 2003, *available at* news.bbc.co.uk/1/hi/world/europe/2965260.stm (last visited Oct. 22, 2007).

7. Conclusions

With the launching of the "new war on terror" the U.S.-led coalition seems to have preferred the use of armed force to repress and prevent a crime which, until recently, belonged to the police and law enforcements' sphere of competences. This attitude, however, may have had a "boomerang" effect. It is not a coincidence, that neither the United Kingdom, Israel, nor any other state faced with major terrorist threats in the past has ever attempted to qualify these situations as an "armed conflict." Spain and Turkey, for instance, have always considered ETA and the PKK as criminal movements to be dealt with internally. Similarly the United Kingdom has always considered the IRA as a terrorist group, not as an irregular armed group. The reason is that the qualification of these situations as non-international armed conflicts would have implied the application of IHL and its cumbersome provisions. IHL provides for very strict rights to detainees. Combatants in enemy hands shall be granted POW status and not considered criminals. Fighting is their job, and as long as an attack, no matter how scary and bloody it may be, is not primarily aimed at terrorising the civilian population, it shall not be considered a criminal act. This is where the "boomerang effect" and the dilemma of the states engaged in the global war on terror emerge since their aim is not to regard those they are fighting against as combatants entitled to POW status, but as common criminals. But to take this approach, it would have been necessary to conduct the fight against terrorism within the framework of international criminal law, resorting to law enforcement agencies like the police and international criminal cooperation mechanisms, like extradition. The problem, however, is that HRL applicable in peacetime, unlike IHL, provides that those held captive shall be released within 48 hours if no specific charges are brought against them. How could it be determined exactly, whether those held in Guantanamo were members of the Taleban, entitled to POW status, or members of Al Qaeda – i.e. terrorists – individually involved in the planning and commission of the 9/11 attacks and alike, within 48 hours? This was simply impossible. Thus the idea was to resort to IHL and the provision according to which a POW may be retained until the end of the hostilities. But the major mistake was not to distinguish between the detention of a POW, who shall be prevented from rejoining the enemy forces, and the detention of a criminal, who shall be punished for having committed a specific crime. Consequently, even the human rights regimes may differ. POWs are obviously entitled to better treatment in terms of contact with the external world, interrogation, visits, etc… This is why the U.S. courts correctly came to the conclusion that to hold a common suspect of terrorist acts in detention until the end of the so-called "war on terror," when this undertaking shall not be manned as an armed conflict, was tantamount to a life-long sentence, requiring the application of specific human rights.

The "war on terror" and the deriving jurisprudence show the strong bond and complementary of HRL and IHL. IHL, given the circumstances, may provide for better treatment. Another advantage is that breach of the fundamental human rights enshrined in IHL, such as those mentioned in Article 75 AP I and Common Article 3 GCs, constitute grave breaches subject to *mandatory* universal jurisdiction that may be brought against individual perpetrators.

To lead the fight against terrorism as a war in a strict sense of the term, subject to the rules of IHL, turns out to be counterproductive since they are not fashioned to deal with prolonged detention of criminal suspects and, quite on the opposite, pose strict limitations on the right of interrogation.

A better solution would have been to improve international criminal law instruments, particularly extradition rules and emergency laws regulating, among others, administrative detention. Although the latter has been the subject of much criticism, it is certainly a better solution than no provision at all, and one which, at least, is subject to review by international control mechanism like the U.N. Committee of Human Rights and accepted under international law.

Chapter XIX

Judging Justice: Laws of War, Human Rights, and the Military Commissions Act of 2006

*Christian M. De Vos**

1. *Introduction*

On November 13, 2001, two months after the terrorist attacks of September 11th, President George W. Bush issued a Presidential Military Order (PMO) authorizing that those who have "engaged in, aided or abetted, or conspired to commit, acts of international terrorism"[1] – "enemy combatants" in the administration's parlance[2] – be tried, at his discretion, by military commission. Based largely on a similar order issued by President Franklin D. Roosevelt in July 1942, the PMO cited the "danger to the safety of the United States and the nature of international terrorism" as justification for the commissions, permitting a swifter justice reflective of the fact that it would not be "practicable" to apply the principles of law and rules of evidence otherwise available under domestic criminal law during a time of war.

---

* Christian M. De Vos is a Staff Attorney with the United States Court of Appeals for the Second Circuit. He is a 2007 graduate of the American University, Washington College of Law and holds an MSc in Theory and History of International Relations from the London School of Economics and Political Science. The views expressed herein are those of the author and do not represent the views or policies of the Second Circuit.
[1] Military Order of November 13, 2001: Detention, Treatment, and Trial of Certain Non-Citizens in the War Against Terrorism, 3 C.F.R. 918 (2001 comp.); 66 Fed. Reg. 57, 833 (Nov. 16, 2001), *available at* www.whitehouse.gov/news/releases/2001/11/20011113–27.html (last visited May 29, 2007).
[2] The phrase "enemy combatants" is not based on a formal reading of the Geneva Conventions. The term itself, and its corollaries (e.g., "unlawful combatant" and "unprivileged combatant") has little currency as a term of art in the law of war; rather, the category has principally developed through U.S. jurisprudence. *See* Ex Parte Quirin, 317 U.S. 1, 30–31 (1942) ("By universal agreement and practice the law of war draws a distinction between the armed forces and the peaceful populations of belligerent nations and also between those who are lawful and unlawful combatants. Lawful combatants are subject to capture and detention as prisoners of war by opposing military forces. Unlawful combatants are likewise subject to capture and detention, but…they are subject to trial and punishment by military tribunals for acts which render their belligerency unlawful.")

Despite the Bush administration's efforts to justify and later modify the commissions, they nevertheless came under significant political criticism and legal scrutiny. This scrutiny culminated in the U.S. Supreme Court's decision of June 29, 2006 in the case of *Salim Ahmed Hamdan v. Donald Rumsfeld*, in which a 5–3 majority held that the President did not have the authority to establish the commissions absent congressional authorization. Further, a plurality found them to be procedurally deficient under both the Uniform Code of Military Justice and the 1949 Geneva Conventions.[3] Particularly significant to the latter determination was the Court's affirmation that Common Article 3 of the Geneva Conventions[4] applied to the conflict with Al Qaeda, and is binding on the President and his subordinates. Whereas the Bush administration had long maintained that the Conventions had "no legal applicability to members or affiliates of Al Qaeda, a terrorist organization that is not a state and has not signed the...Conventions,"[5] Justice Stevens, writing for the plurality, found that Common Article 3, though "falling short of full protection under the Conventions," nevertheless affords "some minimal protection

---

[3] *See* Hamdan v. Rumsfeld, 126 S. Ct. 2749 (2006) [hereinafter Hamdan v. Rumsfeld]. Hamdan, a Yemeni citizen, was captured during the course of hostilities in Afghanistan in November 2001 and was subsequently transferred to the U.S. Naval Station in Guantanamo Bay. On July 3, 2003, President Bush determined there was reason to believe Hamdan (who had admitted by affidavit to being Osama bin Laden's personal driver between 1996 and 2001) was a member of the Al Qaeda network, and designated him for trial before a military commission. In April 2004, Hamdan's civilian defense counsel, Professor Neal Katyal of Georgetown University Law Center and Lieutenant Commander Charles Swift, filed a petition for a writ of *habeas corpus*, which was granted in part by District Court Judge James Robertson on November 8, 2004. Following Judge Robertson's decision, the government sought an expedited appeal before the U.S. Court of Appeals for the D.C. Circuit. On July 15, 2005, a three-judge panel (including now Chief Justice John Roberts) unanimously reversed the District Court, holding that the PMO was proper as a function of the president's constitutional authority as Commander in Chief and by virtue of the Authorization for the Use of Military Force, which granted congressional authorization to commence military operations against those responsible for the attacks of 9/11. Additionally, the Court held that a non-citizen detainee could not seek enforcement of claimed rights under the Third Geneva Convention in U.S. courts. On November 7, 2005, Hamdan's petition for certiorari was granted by the Supreme Court. *See* Jonathan Mahler, *The Bush Administration vs. Salim Hamdan*, N.Y. Times Magazine, Jan. 8, 2006.

[4] The Geneva Convention for the Amelioration of the Condition of the Wounded and Sick in Armed Forces in the Field, Aug. 12, 1949, 75 U.N.T.S. 31, 32 [hereinafter GC I]; Geneva Convention for the Amelioration of the Condition of the Wounded, Sick and Shipwrecked Members of the Armed Forces at Sea, Aug. 12, 1949, 75 U.N.T.S. 85, 86 [hereinafter GC II]; Geneva Convention Relative to the Treatment to Prisoners of War, Aug. 12, 1949, 75 U.N.T.S. 135, 136 [hereinafter GC III]; Geneva Convention Relative to the Protection of Civilian Persons in Time of War, Aug. 12, 1949, 75 U.N.T.S. 287, 288 [hereinafter GC IV].

[5] Press Release, Dep't of Justice, Statement of Mark Corallo on the Hamdan Ruling (Nov. 8, 2004), *available at* www.usdoj/opa/pr/2004/November/04_opa_735.htm (last visited May 29, 2007).

to all individuals involved in an armed conflict... and applies as a matter of treaty obligation to the conflict against Al Qaeda."[6] Notably, such protections include Common Article 3's prohibition on "the passing of sentences... without previous judgment pronounced by a regularly constituted court affording all the judicial guarantees which are recognized as indispensable by civilized peoples."[7] President Bush's proposed commissions, the Court held, failed to afford such guarantees.

As a result of the *Hamdan* ruling, congressional hearings were held throughout the summer of 2006 on the appropriate procedures for the military commissions, as Congress and the White House sought to establish standards that would represent a so-called "middle ground" for trying terror suspects, i.e., commissions that would be compliant with Common Article 3 but not obstructive of the desire for swift justice. After much debate, these hearings culminated in the Military Commissions Act of 2006 (MCA),[8] which President Bush signed into law on October 17, 2006.[9] It is the legality of this Act under international law that is the focus of this chapter, which argues that the standards it establishes for the trial of "enemy combatants," though a moderate improvement over the 2001 PMO, continue to violate in significant respects both international humanitarian law (IHL) and human rights law. Although some of the more egregious deficiencies of the earlier commissions have been remedied as a result of the legislative process, significant flaws remain, including an overly broad definition of combatancy; the admission of evidence obtained through coercion amounting to, if not torture, at least inhuman treatment; the continued ability to deny "classified evidence" to an accused's counsel; the stripping of independent judicial oversight, particularly the right of *habeas corpus*; and, perhaps most significantly, the apparent isolation of the commission's legal framework from domestic courts-martial and, indeed, from international law itself.

2. *Human Rights and Humanitarian Law: The U.S. Position*

In examining the MCA's deficiencies this chapter adopts the position that any interpretation of rights and duties during periods of armed conflict must refer to both human rights and humanitarian law. Significantly, the United States contests this view but, as other contributions in this collection have persuasively argued,

---

[6] Hamdan v. Rumsfeld, *supra* note 3, at 2796.
[7] *Id.* at 2795.
[8] Military Commissions Act of 2006, Public Law 109–336, 120 Stat. 2600 (Oct. 17, 2006), *available at* frwebgate.access.gpo.gov/cgi-bin/getdoc.cgi?dbname=109_cong_bills&docid=f:s3930enr.txt.pdf (last visited May 29, 2007) [hereinafter MCA].
[9] "President Bush Signs Military Commissions Act of 2006" (Oct. 17, 2006), *available at* www.whitehouse.gov/news/releases/2006/10/20061017–1.html (last visited May 29, 2007).

this separation theory is increasingly at odds with a growing body of international jurisprudence[10] and persuasive legal authority,[11] which endorses the complementary application of both bodies of law. In contrast, the United States maintains that human rights law and international humanitarian law are "conceptually distinct" and argues that attempts to merge them invite conflict and ambiguity.[12] In the context of the detainees at Guantanamo Bay, for example, the U.S. position has been that because it is "engaged in a continuing armed conflict against Al Qaida [sic]…the law of war applies to the conduct of that war and related detention operations, and…the International Covenant on Civil and Political Rights, by its express terms, applies only to 'individuals within its territory and subject to its jurisdiction.'"[13]

The view that the provisions of human rights treaties are inapplicable during armed conflict or do not apply extraterritorially is an anomaly adhered to by an increasingly limited number of states. Indeed, the U.N. Human Rights Committee,

---

[10] *See e.g.*, Legal Consequences of the Construction of a Wall in the Occupied Palestinian Territories, Advisory Opinion, (July 9, 2004), I.C.J. Reports 2004, para. 106 (holding that the protections offered by human rights conventions apply extraterritorially and do not cease in times of armed conflict, "save through the effect of provisions for derogation of the kind to be found in article 4 of the [ICCPR].") *See also* Human Rights Committee, General Comment No. 29 (2001), HRI/GEN/1/Rev.7, para. 3 ("During armed conflict, whether international or non-international, rules of international humanitarian law become applicable and help, in addition to the provisions…of the Covenant, to prevent the abuse of a State's emergency powers.") [hereinafter General Comment No. 29]; General Comment No. 31 (2004), para. 11 ("While in respect of certain Covenant rights, more specific rules of [IHL] may be specifically relevant for the purposes of the interpretation of Covenant rights, both spheres of law are complementary, not mutually exclusive.") *But see* "General Comments of the United States on Basic Principles and Guidelines on the Right to a Remedy for Victims of Violations of International Human Rights and Humanitarian Law" [hereinafter "General Comments of the U.S."] (Aug. 15, 2003), *available at* geneva.usmission.gov/press2003/1508Statement%20on%20International%20Humantiarian%20Law.html (last visited May 29, 2007) (asserting the U.S. position that "the mandate of the Human Rights Commission does not extend to the laws of war.")

[11] *See e.g.*, The Berlin Declaration: The ICJ Declaration on Upholding Human Rights and the Rule of Law in Combating Terrorism, adopted by the International Commission of Jurists (Aug. 28, 2004), Principle No. 11, *available at* www.icj.org/IMG/pdf/Berlin_Declaration.pdf (last visited May 29, 2007) (declaring that "[d]uring times of armed conflict and occupation states must apply and respect the rules and principles of both international humanitarian law and human rights law. These legal regimes are complementary and mutually reinforcing.")

[12] *See* "General Comments of the U.S.," *supra* note 10 (reiterating the "firm belief" of the U.S. government that by attempting to address IHL the Principles "create conflict in a well-developed area of law conceptually distinct from international human rights law").

[13] *See Situation of Detainees at Guantanamo Bay*, U.N. Doc. E/CN.4.2006/120 (Feb. 27, 2006) [hereinafter Special Rapporteurs Report], Annex II, at 53 (Letter of Jan. 31, 2006 addressed to the Office of the High Commission for Human Rights by Ambassador Kevin Edward Moley, Permanent Representative of the United States of America).

the Inter-American Commission on Human Rights, and the European Court of Human Rights have all determined that their respective human rights treaties apply extraterritorially and in times of armed conflict.[14] The United States, however, has been one of the most persistent objectors to this position.[15] As Michael Dennis of the U.S. Department of State's Office of the Legal Adviser has argued:

> The obligations assumed by states under the main international human rights instruments were never intended to apply extraterritorially during periods of armed conflicts. Nor were they intended to replace the *lex specialis* of international humanitarian law. Extending the protections provided under international human rights instruments to situations of international armed conflict and military occupation offers a dubious route toward increased state compliance with international norms.[16]

Notably, notwithstanding Dennis' rejection of the applicability of human rights to armed conflict, at the time it ratified the International Covenant on Civil and Political Rights (ICCPR) the United States did not enter any reservations or "declarations of understanding" contrary to Article 4 of the treaty, which sets forth those category of rights non-derogable under any circumstance.[17]

---

[14] *See e.g.*, General Comment No. 31, *supra* note 10, para. 10 ("[A] State party must respect and ensure the rights laid down in the Covenant to anyone with the power of effective control of that State party, *even if not situated within the territory of the State party*") (emphasis added); Issa and Others v. Turkey, App. No. 31821/96, 2004–V Eur. Ct. H.R. 629 (Nov. 16, 2004), para. 71 ("[A] State may also be held accountable for violation of the Convention rights and freedoms of persons who are in the territory of another State but who are found to be under the former State's authority and control through its agents operating – whether lawfully or unlawfully – in the latter State"); Report on Terrorism and Human Rights, Inter-Am. Comm. H.R., OEA/Ser.L/V/II.116 (Oct. 22, 2002), para. 44, n. 14, *available at* www.cidh.org/Terrorism/Eng/toc.htm (last visited May 29, 2007) ("[A] state's human rights obligations are not dependent upon a person's nationality or presence within a particular geographic area, but rather extend to all persons subject to that state's authority and control.") [hereinafter Report on Terrorism and Human Rights].

[15] *See e.g.*, United States v. Verdugo-Urquidez, 494 U.S. 259, 268–71 (1990) ("Indeed we have rejected the claim that aliens are entitled to Fifth Amendment rights outside the sovereign territory of the United States.")

[16] Michael Dennis, *Application of Human Rights Treaties Extraterritorially in Times of Armed Conflict and Military Occupation*, 99 Am. J. Int'l L. 119, 141 (2005).

[17] These rights include the right to life (Article 6), the prohibition on torture and inhuman treatment (Article 7), the prohibition on slavery and servitude (Article 8), the prohibition on imprisonment for failure to fulfill a contractual obligation (Article 11), the prohibition on prosecution for offenses which were not crimes when committed (Article 15), the right to recognition as a person before the law (Article 16), and freedom of thought, conscience, and religion (Article 18). *See* International Covenant on Civil and Political Rights, Article 4(2), G.A. Res. 2200A (XXI), 21 U.N. GAOR (Supp. No. 16) at 52, U.N. Doc. A/6316 (Dec. 16, 1966), 999 U.N.T.S. 171, entered into force Mar. 23, 1976 [hereinafter ICCPR]. As affirmed by the Human Rights Committee, the rights to an independent and impartial tribunal and to *habeas corpus* are also now considered non-derogable. *See* General Comment No. 29, *supra* note 10, para. 16 (noting that certain elements of a fair trial are "explicitly guaranteed under international humanitarian law during armed conflict" and find-

Thus, while accepting the primacy of international humanitarian law as *lex specialis*,[18] the arguments developed herein reject the U.S. interpretation of IHL's relationship with human rights law and urges that any assessment of military commission's (il)legality is incomplete without also considering the more sophisticated human rights jurisprudence that has developed with respect to fair trial standards. Failure to consider both these bodies of law risks further obscuring the minimum fair trial standards that the commissions ought to adhere to and that Common Article 3 is, in fact, meant to protect.

3. *A History of Military Commissions and* Hamdan v. Rumsfeld

Military commissions in the United States are distinct from a court martial, which is a military panel usually set up to try members of the U.S. military for violations of the Uniform Code of Military Justice (UCMJ), the congressional code of military criminal law applicable to U.S. military members worldwide.[19] Instead, commissions are special courts that exercise concurrent jurisdiction with courts-martial[20] and are convened to adjudicate what the government considers to be "extraordinary" cases, often involving violations of the laws of war or other offenses (including acts of terrorism) that may be authorized by statute.

The first military commissions were established in 1847 to address undisciplined action and other misconduct by American troops during the Mexican-American War. They were later used during the Civil War to address crimes and military

---

ing "no justification for derogation from these guarantees during...emergency situations"), *cf.* Gonzalez del Rio v. Peru, Communication No. 263/1987, U.N. Doc. A/48/40 (1992) (holding that the right to trial by an independent and impartial tribunals is "an absolute right that may suffer no exception.")

[18] Gabor Rona defines *lex specialis* as a term "used to indicate any specific branch of law that is triggered by special circumstances. [It] prevails over *lex generalis*, or generally applicable law." See Gabor Rona, *Interesting Times for International Humanitarian Law: Challenges from the "War on Terror,"* 27 Fletcher Forum of World Affairs, 55, 70, n. 3 (Summer/Fall 2003). *See also* Legality of the Threat or Use of Nuclear Weapons, Advisory Opinion, (July 8, 1996), I.C.J. Reports 1996, para. 25 (holding that while "the right not arbitrarily to be deprived of one's life applies also in hostilities. The test of what is an arbitrary deprivation of life... falls to determined by the applicable *lex specialis*, namely, the law applicable in armed conflict which is designed to regulate the conduct of hostilities.")

[19] *See* Uniform Code of Military Justice, *available at* www.army.mil/references/UCMJ (last visited May 29, 2007) [hereinafter UCMJ].

[20] In 1920, Congress amended then Article 15 (now Article 21) of the UCMJ to provide military commissions with concurrent jurisdiction over courts-martial, a move that was intended to restrict such commissions in light of how they had "repeatedly and improperly assumed jurisdiction over offenses better handled by courts-martial" during the Civil War. Louis Fisher, Military Tribunals & Presidential Power: American Revolution to the War on Terrorism 122 (2005).

offenses that fell outside the jurisdiction of courts-martial and existing civil courts, though the Supreme Court sharply curtailed the use of these commissions at the war's end.[21] It was not until World War II, beginning with the case of *Ex parte Quirin*, that commission were later resurrected and used most extensively for the prosecution of war crimes.[22] Congressional scholar Louis Fisher notes:

> Military commissions have traditionally been used as an emergency measure by a commander in the field to fill a temporary gap created by the absence of a civilian court or court-martial jurisdiction. They have typically occurred in a zone of combat operations or occupied territory, have generally adhered to the procedures used in courts-martial, and have never singled out a broad class of non-citizens.[23]

Unfortunately, the commissions authorized by President Bush stray far from these three edicts. While a review of legal precedents indicates that the president's authority to try war criminals by military tribunal is now well settled,[24] both the 2001 Presidential Military Order and the congressionally authorized Military Commissions Act depart in significant respects from the UCMJ and the minimum standards of Common Article 3.

Why is this significant? Under Article 102 of the Third Geneva Convention, "[a] prisoner of war can be validly sentenced only if the sentence has been pronounced by the same courts according to the same procedure as in the case of members of the armed forces of the Detaining Power, and if, furthermore, the provisions of the present Chapter have been observed."[25] Thus, for those detained as prisoners

---

[21] In the 1866 case of *Ex parte Milligan*, for example, the Court forbade the use of military commissions for civilians so long as federal courts were "open and unobstructed." Ex parte Milligan, 71 U.S. 2 (1866) at 121.

[22] *See generally* Louis Fisher, Nazi Saboteurs on Trial (2005); Pierce O'Donnell, In Time of War: Hitler's Terrorist Attack on America (2005).

[23] Brief of Louis Fisher as *Amicus Curiae* Supporting Petitioner, Hamdan v. Rumsfeld (2005) (No. 05–184), at 2.

[24] *See e.g.*, Ex parte Quirin, *supra* note 2. Though criticism of *Quirin* has since argued that the decision was "deeply flawed," the Court continued to hear a series of martial law-related cases in the years that followed. *See* Brief of Legal Scholars and Historians as *Amici Curiae* Supporting Petitioner, Hamdan v. Rumsfeld (2005) (No. 05–184) (arguing that, as a result of judicial biases, conflicts of interests, presidential intimidation, a rush to judgment, and lack of reliable authority, *Quirin* is "poisoned precedent" and incompatible with "a modern sense of justice;") Hamdi v. Rumsfeld, 542 U.S. 507, 569, 124 S.Ct. 2633, 2669 (2004) (Scalia, J., dissenting) (noting that *Quirin* "was not this Court's finest hour.") Of particular significance was In re Yamashita, 327 U.S. 1, 20–24 (1946) (upholding the jurisdiction of a military commission to try Japanese General Yamashita for war crimes because the Articles of War only conferred courts-martial jurisdiction over U.S. military personnel and its affiliates) and Johnson v. Eisentrager, 339 U.S. 763, 777–779 (1950) (holding that German soldiers who had been tried and convicted by an American military commission sitting in China for crimes committed there were not constitutionally protected by the Fifth Amendment and did not have a right to bring a writ of *habeas corpus* in U.S. courts).

[25] GC III, *supra* note 4, Article 102.

of war (POW) by the United States the proper forum for any prosecution must adhere to the same standards as those applied to members of the U.S. military, i.e., the UCMJ.[26] By contrast, unprivileged combatants "can be tried and punished under the criminal law of the detaining power for their unprivileged belligerency, even if their hostile acts complied with the law of war."[27]

In *Ex Parte Quirin*, the Supreme Court glossed over the issue of whether commissions were legally required to follow the same procedures laid down for courts-martial.[28] In *Hamdan*, however, this question was unavoidable and the Court answered it in the negative: the military commissions convened by President Bush lacked "the power to proceed" because their structures and procedures violated the UCMJ and Common Article 3.[29] In so doing, the Court adopted a balancing test to conclude that the principle of uniformity of trial procedures applies to military commissions, and that any departure from such uniformity must be "tailored to the exigency" requiring it.[30] Accordingly, the Court endorsed the "practicability" standard enunciated in UCMJ Article 36(b), meaning the government would have to show that it would be "impracticable" to apply the rules of courts-martial to the proposed commissions.[31]

As for the commissions' compliance with the fair trial requirement of Common Article 3, the Court declined to articulate what the standards for such a trial

---

[26] Article 84 GC III exclusively provides for trial by military court, unless the Detaining Power's laws also

> [P]ermit civil courts to try a member of [its] armed forces...in respect of the particular offense alleged to have been committed by the prisoner of war. In no circumstances whatever shall a prisoner of war be tried by a court of any kind which does not offer the essential guarantees of independence and impartiality as generally recognized, and in particular, the...rights and means of defense provided for in Article 105. *Id.* Article 84.

[27] Robert K. Goldman, *Report of the Independent Expert on the Protection of Human Rights and Fundamental Freedoms while Countering Terrorism*, U.N. Doc. E/CN.4/2005/103 (Feb. 7, 2005), n. 18.

[28] At the time *Quirin* was decided Article 38 of the UCMJ provided that "nothing contrary to or inconsistent with" the Code could be prescribed. Article 36 now provides in part that "Pretrial, trial, and post-trial procedures...in courts-martial, military commissions and other military tribunals...may be prescribed by the President by regulations which shall, so far as he considers practicable, apply the principles of law and the rules of evidence generally recognized in the trial of criminal cases in the United States district courts, but which may not be contrary to or inconsistent with this chapter." *See* UCMJ, *supra* note 19, Article 36. *See also* Madsen v. Kinsella, 343 U.S. 341, 347 (1952) ("In the absence of attempts by Congress to limit the President's power...he may, in time of war, establish and prescribe the jurisdiction and procedure of military commissions.")

[29] Hamdan v. Rumsfeld, *supra* note 3, at 2772–2775.

[30] *Id.* at 2756.

[31] *Id.* ("Without reaching the question whether any provisions of Commission Order No. 1 is strictly 'contrary to or inconsistent with' other provisions of the UCMJ, we conclude that the 'practicability' determination the President has made is insufficient to justify variances from the procedures governing courts-martial.")

would be, although the plurality opinion noted that "they must be understood to incorporate at least the barest of those trial protections that have been recognized by customary international law," including Article 75 of Protocol I.[32] Significantly, the plurality also cited provisions of the ICCPR as evidence of other international instruments to which the United States is a party and whose protections echo those set forth in Article 75.[33] While the Court acknowledged that Common Article 3, by its nature, is an imprecise standard, noting "its requirements are general ones, crafted to accommodate a wide variety of legal systems... *requirements* they are nonetheless."[34] It is to these requirements under both international humanitarian law and human rights law that the following section now turns.

4. *"Impartial and Independent": The Right to a Fair Trial and the Military Commissions Act of 2006*

> In order to determine whether a court has been properly appointed, set up, or established, it is necessary to refer to a body of law that governs such matters. I interpret Common Article 3 as looking to the domestic law of the appointing country because I am not aware of any international law standard regarding the way in which ... a court must be appointed, set up, or established[.]
>
> — Justice Alito, *Hamdan v. Rumsfeld*[35]

The right to a fair trial as a norm of international human rights law dates back at least until the adoption of the Universal Declaration of Human Rights in 1948 and the codification of that right in the relevant provisions of the International Covenant on Civil and Political Rights.[36] Since the ICCPR's ratification, a significant international jurisprudence has developed elaborating the meaning of the

---

[32] *Id.* at 2797.
[33] *Id.* at 2797, n. 62. ("Other international instruments to which the United States is a signatory include the same basic protections set forth in Article 75. *See, e.g.*, [ICCPR], Article 14, para. 3(d)... setting forth the right of an accused "[t]o be tried in his presence, and to defend himself in person or through legal assistance of his own choosing.")
[34] *Id.* at 278 (emphasis in original). By contrast, Justice Alito, in dissent, indicated he was "not aware of any international law standard regarding the way in which such a [properly appointed] court must be appointed, set up, or established." *Id.* at 2851.
[35] *Id.* at 2851 (dissenting opinion).
[36] ICCPR, Articles 14, 15, *supra* note 17. *See also* Universal Declaration of Human Rights, Article 11, G.A. Res. 217A(III), U.N. Doc. A/810 (1948) ("1. Everyone charged with a penal offence has the right to be presumed innocent until proved guilty according to law in a public trial at which he has had all the guarantees necessary for his defence. 2. No one shall be held guilty of any penal offence on account of any act or omission which did not constitute a penal offence, under national or international law, at the time when it was committed. Nor shall a heavier penalty be imposed than the one that was applicable at the time the penal offence was committed.")

right to a fair trial. In particular, the Human Rights Committee (HRC) has been required to issue many decisions interpreting Articles 14 and 15 of the Covenant, which are the principal provisions on the right to a fair trial. Article 14(1) of the ICCPR states that in criminal proceedings "everyone shall be entitled to a fair and public hearing by a competent, independent and impartial tribunal established by law," and further provides comprehensive protections to a defendant, guaranteeing the presumption of innocence,[37] the right to appeal,[38] the right to counsel of an accused's choice, to call and examine witnesses, and freedom from compelled self-incrimination.[39] As affirmed by the HRC, many of these rights are now considered non-derogable, particularly the right to an independent and impartial tribunal and the right to *habeas corpus*.[40] The Basic Principles on the Independence of the Judiciary also recognizes that everyone shall have the right to be tried by "ordinary courts or tribunals using established legal procedures. Tribunals that do not use the duly established procedures...shall not be created to displace the jurisdiction belonging to the ordinary courts or judicial tribunals."[41]

Unlike human rights law, which is broadly tailored, international humanitarian law's provisions for a fair trial are more detailed and depend on both the status of the accused and the nature of his/her crimes. Prisoners of war, for instance, benefit from the customary law of combatant immunity; as such, they may only be prosecuted for violations of the laws of war or crimes unrelated to the hostilities. Articles 82 to 108 of the Third Geneva Convention outline the protections that accompany

---

[37] ICCPR, *supra* note 17, Article 14(2).
[38] *Id.* Article 14(5).
[39] *Id.* Article 14(3). ("In the determination of any criminal charge against him, everyone shall be entitled to the following minimum guarantees, in full equality: (a) To be informed promptly and in detail in a language which he understands of the nature and cause of the charge against him; (b) To have adequate time and facilities for the preparation of his defence and to communicate with counsel of his own choosing; (c) To be tried without undue delay; (d) To be tried in his presence, and to defend himself in person or through legal assistance of his own choosing; to be informed, if he does not have legal assistance, of this right; and to have legal assistance assigned to him, in any case where the interests of justice so require, and without payment by him in any such case if he does not have sufficient means to pay for it; (e) To examine, or have examined, the witnesses against him and to obtain the attendance and examination of witnesses on his behalf under the same conditions as witnesses against him; (f) To have the free assistance of an interpreter if he cannot understand or speak the language used in court; (g) Not to be compelled to testify against himself or to confess guilt.")
[40] General Comment No. 29, *supra* note 10. *See also* The Siracusa Principles on the Limitation and Derogation Provisions of the ICCPR, 7 Hum. Rts. Q. 1, 3 (1985), Principles 70(e)-(g) (declaring that any person charged with an offense should be entitled to a fair trial by a "competent, independent and impartial court established by law.")
[41] Basic Principles on the Independence of the Judiciary, endorsed by G.A. Res. 40/32 (Nov. 29, 1985) and G.A. Res. 40/146 (Dec. 13, 1985), Principle No. 5, *available at* www.unhchr.ch/html/menu3/b/h_comp50.htm (last visited May 29, 2007) [hereinafter Basic Principles on the Independence of the Judiciary].

the prosecution of such crimes,[42] including the right to counsel of the accused's choice and the right to call witnesses.[43] Under the Fourth Geneva Convention, judicial proceedings against civilians, particularly those living in occupied territory, are governed by Articles 71 to 76 and include many of the same provisions as those for POW's.[44]

As noted earlier, those who do not benefit from the protections of the Third or Fourth Convention, particularly unprivileged or enemy combatants, are nevertheless entitled, to the extent its provisions embody customary law, to the protections outlined in Article 75 of Additional Protocol I (AP I).[45] Article 75(4), in particular, requires that proceedings adhere to the standards of an "impartial and regularly constituted court respecting the generally recognized principles of regular judicial procedure," e.g., the presumption of innocence and freedom from self-incrimination.[46] Notably, the former guarantee is absent from the Third and

---

[42] GC III, *supra* note 4, Articles 82–108.

[43] *Id.*, Article 105 ["Rights and means of defence"].

[44] GC IV, *supra* note 4, Articles 71–76 (granting accused persons the right to present evidence necessary to their defense, call witnesses, be assisted by a qualified advocate of their choice [Article 72], and the right of appeal [Article 73]).

[45] Protocol Additional to the Geneva Conventions of 12 August 1949, and Relating to the Protections of Victims of International Armed Conflicts (Protocol I), Article 75, opened for signature Dec. 12, 1977, U.N. Doc. A/32/144, Annex I, II, (1977), *reprinted in* 16 I.L.M. 1391 (1977) [hereinafter AP I].

[46] *Id.*, Article 75(4). Article 75(4) provides in full:
No sentence may be passed and no penalty may be executed on a person found guilty of a penal offence related to the armed conflict except pursuant to a conviction pronounced by an impartial and regularly constituted court respecting the generally recognized principles of regular judicial procedure, which include the following: (a) The procedure shall provide for an accused to be informed without delay of the particulars of the offence alleged against him and shall afford the accused before and during his trial all necessary rights and means of defence; (b) No one shall be convicted of an offence except on the basis of individual penal responsibility; (c) No one shall be accused or convicted of a criminal offence on account of any act or omission which did not constitute a criminal offence under the national or international law to which he was subject at the time when it was committed; nor shall a heavier penalty be imposed than that which was applicable at the time when the criminal offence was committed; if, after the commission of the offence, provision is made by law for the imposition of a lighter penalty, the offender shall benefit thereby; (d) Anyone charged with an offence is presumed innocent until proved guilty according to law; (e) Anyone charged with an offence shall have the right to be tried in his presence; (f) No one shall be compelled to testify against himself or to confess guilt; (g) Anyone charged with an offence shall have the right to examine, or have examined, the witnesses against him and to obtain the attendance and examination of witnesses on his behalf under the same conditions as witnesses against him; (h) No one shall be prosecuted or punished by the same Party for an offence in respect of which a final judgement acquitting or convicting that person has been previously pronounced under the same law and judicial procedure; (i) Anyone prosecuted for an offence shall have the right to have the judgement pronounced publicly; and (j) A convicted person shall be advised on conviction of his judicial and other remedies and of the time-limits within which they may be exercised.

Fourth Conventions. The commentary to Article 75 notes that the genesis of this article was motivated by the "expressed concern that a minimum of protection should be granted in time of armed conflict to *any person* who was, for one reason or another, unable to claim a particular status, such as that of prisoner of war, civilian internee... wounded, sick or shipwrecked."[47] In particular, the Commentary notes:

> Article 75, even more than common Article 3 of the Geneva Conventions, which was called a "mini Convention," constitutes a sort of "summary of the law" particularly in the very complex field of judicial guarantees, which will certainly facilitate the dissemination of humanitarian law and the promulgation of its fundamental principles.[48]

Thus, although AP I did not draw up a systematic list of persons intended to be covered by Article 75, those Al Qaeda combatants designated for trial by the U.S. commissions, as persons unable to claim a status other than POW or civilian internee, should nevertheless fall within the scope of the Article's protection.

Notably, while the the United States has ratified neither of the Convention's Additional Protocols, its objections to AP I were never on the grounds of Article 75. Indeed, as Professors Robert Goldman and Brian Tittemore have argued, "[t]he core provisions of Article 75 should also be considered to constitute a part of customary international law binding on the United States."[49] The United States itself has not objected to this position. Michael Matheson, then Deputy Legal Adviser to the U.S. Department of State, noted in 1987 that the U.S. government recognized the fair trial protections of Article 75(4) as declaratory of customary law[50] and, as such, binding on the United States.[51]

---

[47] Yves Sandoz, Christophe Swinarski, Bruno Zimmerman, eds., Commentary on the Additional Protocols of 8 June 1977 to the Geneva Conventions of 12 August 1949, paras 2927–2928 (1996) (emphasis added).

[48] *Id.* at 865.

[49] Robert K. Goldman & Brian D. Tittemore, *Unprivileged Combatants and the Hostilities in Afghanistan: Their Status and Rights Under International Humanitarian and Human Rights Law*, American Society for International Law: Task Force on Terrorism (Dec. 2002), at 38, *available at* www.asil.org/taskforce/goldman.pdf (last visited May 29, 2007) [hereinafter Goldman & Tittemore]. *See also* Jean-Marie Henckaerts & Louise Doswald-Beck, Customary International Humanitarian Law, Volume 1: Rules 352 (2005) (Rule 100 establishes that a fair trial is a norm of customary international law applicable in both international and non-international armed conflicts) [hereinafter Henckaerts & Doswald-Beck].

[50] Michael Matheson, *The United States' Position on the Relation of Customary International Law to the 1977 Protocols Additional to the 1949 Geneva Conventions*, 2 Am. U. J. Int'l L. & Pol'y 419, 427–428 (1987) ("We support in particular the fundamental guarantees contained in article 75... and that no sentence be passed and no penalty executed except pursuant to conviction pronounced by an impartial and regularly constituted court respecting the generally recognized principles of regular judicial procedure.")

[51] *See e.g.,* The Paquete Habana 175 U.S. 677, 700 (1890) (declaring that "international law is part of [U.S.] law.")

In light of the foregoing, it is plain that human rights law and humanitarian law can be mutually instructive in establishing the standards for a "regularly constituted court" under the terms of Common Article 3. Unlike other situations of armed conflict – where the rules of humanitarian law might be less subject to interpretation and apply more easily as *lex specialis* – there is a "marked convergence" between both these bodies of law in establishing minimum fair trial protections for privileged and unprivileged combatants.[52] As Professor Christopher Greenwood notes, "[t]here is no reason why... recourse should not be had to human rights law in order to gain a better understanding of what are the essential guarantees [of independence and impartiality]."[53] Unfortunately, crucial aspects of the MCA indicate no such understanding.

4.1. *Definition of "Unlawful Enemy Combatant"*

As an initial matter, the scope of the MCA's definition of an "enemy combatant" is dangerously sweeping. Section 948a of the Act, which defines the class of defendants subject to the commissions, diverges substantially from Article 4 of the Third Geneva Convention. Whereas the Convention's determination of POW status defines combatancy in terms of one's affiliation with a country's armed forces or other militia/volunteer corps,[54] the commission's personal jurisdiction removes any requirements for proximity to the battlefield itself and includes individuals who have "purposefully and materially supported hostilities against the United States or its co-belligerents," including specifically members of the Taliban and Al Qaeda.[55] The second prong of the definition appears to delegate to the President or Secretary of Defense unrestricted power to deem *anyone* an "unlawful enemy combatant." All it requires is that a Combatant Status Review Tribunal (CSRT), which was established in the wake of *Hamdi v. Rumsfeld*, or "another competent

---

[52] Goldman & Tittemore, *supra* note 49, at 51.
[53] *See* Christopher Greenwood, *Rights at the Frontier: Protecting the Individual in Time of War*, in Law at the Centre: The Institute of Advanced Legal Studies At Fifty, 277–293 (Barry Rider, ed., 1999) (supporting the concurrent application of human rights law and the law of war in the cases of occupied territory, prisoner treatment, and trials).
[54] GC III, *supra* note 4, Article 4 (for example, Article 4(A)(2) provides that members of other militias or volunteer corps may receive prisoner of war status if they are shown to be under a responsible command, wear a "fixed, distinctive sign," carry their arms openly, and obey the laws of war).
[55] MCA, *supra* note 8, para. 948a(1)(A)(i). Why members of the Taliban are included as "enemy combatants" remains unclear, as the Bush administration later recanted its position that Taliban soldiers, unlike Al Qaeda fighters, were not protected by the Geneva Conventions.

tribunal" makes such a determination.⁵⁶ Nothing is said about the substantive criteria that these tribunals should apply.

Two potential problems arise in the context of these definitions. First, while many legal scholars acknowledge the category of the "unprivileged" or "illegal" combatant, it should be noted that the term itself remains contested. Many commentators have criticized the use of such an intermediate category of combatants, as it finds no textual support in the Conventions themselves.⁵⁷ Setting this debate aside, however, even more troubling is the reliability of the standards currently employed, particularly by the CSRT's, for determining who qualifies as an "enemy combatant." While this is the ostensible role of the review tribunals, the compliance of these proceedings with due process standards is even more questionable than the military commissions.⁵⁸ Detainees appearing before a CSRT are not allowed to call witnesses (unless the witnesses are other Guantanamo detainees), may not have attorneys present, and are presumed guilty of being an enemy combatant based on evidence that they are not allowed to see. One recent study found that the U.S. government did not produce any witnesses in any CSRT hearings and did not present any documentary evidence to the detainee prior to his hearing in ninety-six percent of the cases.⁵⁹ Eight-nine percent of the time no evidence was even presented on the detainee's behalf.⁶⁰ The implications of the CSRT's proce-

---

⁵⁶ *See* Hamdi v. Rumsfeld, *supra* note 24 (holding that due process requires that enemy combatants be given a meaningful opportunity to contest the factual basis for their detention).

⁵⁷ *See e.g.*, Knut Dörmann, *The Legal Situation of "Unlawful/Unprivileged Combatants*, 849 Int'l Rev. Red Cross 45, 49 (2003) (arguing that if the detainees are not POW's, they must be accorded civilian status under GC IV, on the theory that Article 5's reference to "protected persons" must encompass unlawful combatants). Article 51(3) AP I also appears to anticipate a category of hostile civilians (providing for suspension of their protection from international targeting "for such time as they take direct part in hostilities"), buttressing the view that the Conventions reject divesting civilian status "in favour of permitting temporary derogation of the protections associated with the civilian class." Mark David Maxwell & Sean M. Watts, *'Unlawful Enemy Combatant': Status, Theory of Culpability, or Neither?*, 5 J. Int'l Crim. J. 19, 22 (2007).

⁵⁸ The CSRT process is also subject to "competency" standards under IHL. *See* GC III, *supra* note 4, Article 5 ("Should any doubt arise as to whether persons, having committed a belligerent act and having fallen in to the hands of the enemy, belong to any of the categories enumerated in Article 4, such persons shall enjoy the protection of the present Convention until such time as their status has been determined by a competent tribunal.")

⁵⁹ *See* Mark Denbeaux & Joshua Denbeaux, No-Hearing Hearings: An Analysis of the Proceedings of the Government's Combatant Status Review Tribunals at Guantánamo, at 1 (SSRN Electronic Paper Collection: Seton Hall Public Law Research Paper Series) (Dec. 2006), *available at* papers.ssrn.com/sol3/papers.cfm?abstract_id=951245 (last visited May 29, 2007).

⁶⁰ *Id.* at 3. *See also* Tim Golden, *For Guantanamo Review Boards, Limits Abound*, N.Y. Times, Dec. 31, 2006 (noting that examination of the CSRT's suggests that "they have often fallen short, not only as source of due process.... but also as a forum to resolve questions about what the detainees have done and the threats they may pose.")

dural shortcomings are thus profound, as they raise the serious risk of improperly categorizing detainees as "enemy combatants" based on limited, often unverified information.[61]

In addition to this risk, the MCA's incorporation of a "material support" provision greatly expands the scope of combatancy in ways that fundamentally redefine the law of war and the Geneva Conventions. As Jack Beard notes, "[t]he distinction between combatants and civilians is a cardinal principle of the law of war, serving to ensure that armed conflicts are waged solely between and against combatants and not against the civilian population."[62] Yet the MCA's expansive definition of "unlawful enemy combatant" obscures this distinction,[63] thereby posing a threat to the fair trial rights of not only those detained at Guantanamo, but to any non-U.S. citizen whose connections to the "War on Terror" may be attenuated at best. Indeed, the Supreme Court in *Hamdan* recognized such a risk of attenuation when the plurality also held that, contrary to the 2001 PMO, conspiracy was not cognizable as a war crime triable by military commission; rather, it was an inchoate offense extrinsic to the law of war.[64] In spite of this admonition, the MCA nevertheless reincorporates that very crime.[65]

4.2. *Right to Confront Evidence*

A critical point in the Supreme Court's ruling in *Hamdan* was that, under the 2001 PMO, an accused could be denied the right to be present at trial, a provision the Court considered "the barest of those trial protections that have been recognized by customary international law."[66] While the MCA remedies this exclusion to some degree, the Act is nevertheless troublesome as it continues to permit the

---

[61] If an accused is improperly categorized, then two alternatives prevail: either he is a lawful combatant, i.e., a prisoner of war protected by GC III and subject to court martial under the UCMJ or a civilian, subject to civilian immunity.

[62] Jack M. Beard, *The Geneva Boomerang: The Military Commissions Act of 2006 and U.S. Counterterror Operations*, 101 Am. J. Int'l L. 56, 60 (2007).

[63] *See* Aryeh Neier, *The Military Tribunals on Trial*, 49(2) N.Y. Rev. of Books, Feb. 14, 2002 (arguing that, under the 2001 PMO, an "Irish-American immigrant who participated in a fund-raising event for widows and orphans of those killed in the struggle in Northern Ireland could be hauled before a military tribunal for aiding or abetting international terrorism.")

[64] Hamdan v. Rumsfeld, *supra* note 3, at 2779. ("[T]he offense alleged must have been committed both in a theater of war and *during*, not before, the relevant conflict. But the deficiencies in the time and place allegations also underscore indeed are symptomatic of the most serious defect of this charge: The offense it alleges is not triable by law-of-war military commission.")

[65] MCA, *supra* note 8, para. 950v(b)(28). Indeed, none of the 28 specific crimes listed in para. 950v(b) of the MCA require a nexus with armed conflict, suggesting that the Act may potentially have much wider application.

[66] Hamdan v. Rumsfeld, *supra* note 3, at 2797.

assertion of a "national security privilege,"[67] a potentially far reaching provision that protects classified "sources, methods, or activities," if the disclosure of such information "would be detrimental to the national security."[68] As such, the military judge may: authorize the deletion of specified items from documents or substitute a summary for such information;[69] permit the introduction of classified evidence without disclosing "the sources, methods, or activities" by which it was acquired, assuming it is "reliable;"[70] and review a trial counsel's objection on the grounds of national security privilege, on an *ex parte* basis, at any time "to any question, line of inquiry, or motion to admit evidence."[71] All of these provisions contradict international humanitarian law[72] and the Supreme Court's admonition in *Hamdan* that "an accused, must, absent disruptive conduct or consent, be present for his trial and must be privy to the evidence against him."[73]

Admittedly, the question of how to handle sensitive or classified information at trial is not to be taken lightly and has been confronted before by other international criminal tribunals.[74] Human rights law, under the "equality of arms" doctrine,

---

[67] MCA, *supra* note 8, para. 949d(f)(1). In U.S. criminal law, the government has occasionally asserted a "state secrets" privilege akin to the MCA's national security privilege which, until recently, has met with little success in U.S. courts. Most courts have held that due process requires the government to drop charges against an accused if the evidence it seeks to withhold is necessary to conduct a proper defense. As the Supreme Court explained in United States v. Nixon, 418 U.S. 683, 709 (1974):

> The very integrity of the judicial system and public confidence in the system depend on full disclosure of all the facts, within the framework of the rules of evidence. To ensure that justice is done, it is imperative to the function of courts that compulsory process be available for the production of evidence needed either by the prosecution or by the defense.

Similarly, in courts-martial under the UCMJ the government can assert a national security privilege; if the accused requests access to the classified information the government can seek to satisfy the request by offering sanitized/redacted documents, an unclassified alternative, a stipulation to relevant facts, or limited disclosure under secure conditions. If, however, the government's refusal to disclose the information would "materially prejudice a substantial right" of the accused then the convening authority or military judge must dismiss the charge. *See* Richard V. Meyer, *When a Rose is Not a Rose: Military Commissions v. Courts-Martial*, 5 J. Int'l Crim. J., 48, 57 (2007).

[68] *Id.* para. 949d(f)(1)(A).
[69] *Id.* para. 949d(f)(2)(A).
[70] *Id.* para. 949d(f)(2)(B).
[71] *Id.* para. 949d(f)(2)(C).
[72] AP I, *supra* note 45, a Article t. 75(4)(g) ("Anyone charged with an offence shall have the right to examine, or have examined, the witnesses against him and to obtain the attendance and examination of witnesses on his behalf under the same conditions as witnesses against him.")
[73] Hamdan v. Rumsfeld, *supra* note 3, at 2758. The Court did note, however, that "express statutory provision," which the MCA undoubtedly is, could be a basis for restricting disclosure of the information used to convict a person. *Id.* at 2798.
[74] *See e.g.*, Rome Statute of the International Criminal Court, Article 72, adopted on July 17, 1998 by the U.N. Diplomatic Conference of Plenipotentiaries on the Establishment of an International

provides that parties must be treated in a manner ensuring their procedurally equal position during the course of a trial,[75] although redaction, summarization, and the substitution of classified documents are all measures that have been previously implemented.[76] As such, it is not necessarily a violation of the right to a fair trial that these methods be permitted as alternatives to full disclosure where absolutely necessary. More troublesome, however, is the propensity with which the security privilege has already been invoked in previous terrorism prosecutions, often with little explanation or justification, and the fact that the privilege may be invoked with no opportunity for defense counsel to confront the evidence.[77] Indeed, this problem abuts a further criticism as to whether the commissions can properly be considered politically independent, not only because the military justice system is part of the executive branch,[78] but because the commissions are effectively struc-

---

Criminal Court, entered into force, July 1, 2002, U.N. Doc. A/CONF.183/9 (1998) [hereinafter Rome Statute] (outlining a three-step procedure for when a state or individual believes that disclosure of information would prejudice its national security interests, including authority to refer non-cooperative states to the Assembly of States Parties or, if the Security Council originally referred the matter to the Court, to the Security Council). *See also* Prosecutor v. Blaskic, IT-95–14–AR108*bis*, Judgment on the Request of the Republic of Croatia for Review of the Decision of Trial Chamber II, paras 63–66 (Oct. 29, 1997) (stating that "to allow national security considerations to prevent the [ICTY] from obtaining documents that might prove of decisive importance would be tantamount to undermining the very essence of [its] functions," but *ex parte* procedures before a judge to determine the legitimacy of a state's objections are allowed).

[75] Manfred Nowak, U.N. Covenant on Civil and Political Rights: CCPR Commentary 321 (2d ed., 2005) ("The most important criterion of a fair trial is the *principle of "equality of arms"* between the plaintiff and respondent or the prosecutor and defendant.") (emphasis in original). *See also* Prosecutor v. Tadic, IT-94-1-A, Judgment (Jul. 15, 1999), para. 52 ("This principle means that the Prosecution and the Defence must be equal before the Trial Chamber."); *cf.* Robinson v. Jamaica, Communication No. 223/1987, U.N. Doc. A/44/40 (1989) (requiring that prosecution and defense be treated equally in a criminal trial and, where a Jamaican court had refused the accused an adjournment in order to arrange for legal representation, admonishing the court not to act in a way that gives the prosecution an advantage over the defense).

[76] *See* Laura Moranchek, *Protecting National Security Evidence While Prosecuting War Crimes: Problems and Lessons for International Justice from the ICTY*, 31 Yale J. Int'l L. 477, 489 (2006) (noting that the ICTY did allow for "some kinds of redacting information before it was passed to the defense.") [hereinafter Moranchek]

[77] *See e.g.*, Susan Burgess, *Cases without Courts: The State Secrets Privilege Keeps some Claims from ever Being Heard*, 30 The News Media & The Law (Summer 2006) (noting that research of reported cases reveals that the privilege has been invoked in 18 cases since Sept. 11, 2001), *available at* www.rcfp.org/news/mag/30–3/prr-caseswit.html (last visited May 29, 2007). *See generally* Louis Fisher, In The Name of National Security: Unchecked Presidential Power and the *Reynolds* Case (2006).

[78] *See e.g.*, Olo Bahamonde v. Equatorial Guinea, Communication No. 468/1991, U.N. Doc. CCPR/C/49/D/468/1991 (1993) (noting "that a situation where the function and competencies of the judiciary and the executive are not clearly distinguishable or where the latter is able to control or direct the former" is incompatible with the notion of an independent and impartial tribunal

tured to be both prosecutor and executioner.[79] As one commentator has noted, assertion of the security privilege may have been appropriate in forums like the ad hoc tribunals, "where no one state has an interest in conviction and controls the prosecution, the procedural rules, the evidence, and the judges."[80] No such protections exist with the military commissions.

Linked to the national security privilege, the MCA also establishes an expansive exception for hearsay evidence, permitting it so long as the proponent of the evidence "makes known to the adverse party, sufficiently in advance to provide [him] with a fair opportunity to meet the evidence, the intention of the proponent to offer the evidence, and the particulars of [it] (including...general circumstances under which the evidence was obtained)."[81] Evidence is presumptively admissible unless it can be demonstrated that it is "unreliable or lacking in probative value."[82] Several commentators have rightly noted that the admission of hearsay evidence does not necessarily violate human rights norms,[83] as many continental law systems admit what would be considered hearsay in U.S. courts. Indeed, these hearsay provisions of the MCA ironically mark a rare foray into comparative law, an effort otherwise at odds with the Act's hostility to international legal standards.[84] Nevertheless,

---

within Article 14(1) of the ICCPR); *cf.* Inter-Am. Ct. H.R., Castillo Petruzzi v. Peru, Judgment, May 30, 1999, Ser. C., No. 52, para. 130 (faulting military court proceedings where the armed forces, "fully engaged in the counter-insurgency struggle, are also prosecuting persons associated with insurgency groups.")

[79] *See* Basic Principles on the Independence of the Judiciary, *supra* note 41, Principle No. 2 ("The judiciary shall decide matters before them impartially...without any restrictions, improper influences, inducements, pressures, threats or interference, direct or indirect, from any quarter or for any reason;") *cf.* Guidelines on the Role of Prosecutors, adopted by the Eighth United Nations Congress on the Prevention of Crime and the Treatment of Offenders, Guideline No. 10, available at www.unhchr.ch/html/menu3/b/h_comp45.htm (last visited May 29, 2007) ("The office of prosecutors shall be strictly separated from judicial functions.")

[80] Moranchek, *supra* note 76, at 501 (emphasis in original).

[81] MCA, *supra* note 8, para. 949a(b)(2)(E)(i).

[82] *Id.*, para. 949a(b)(2)(E)(ii). Section 949a(b)(2)(F) further provides that the military judge "shall exclude any evidence the probative value of which is substantially outweighed – "(i) by the danger of unfair prejudice, confusion of the issues, or misleading the commission; or "(ii) by considerations of undue delay, waste of time, or needless presentation of cumulative evidence."

[83] *See e.g.*, Jeffrey Addicott, *The Military Commissions Act: Congress Commits to the War on Terror*, Jurist at 3, *available at* jurist.law.pitt.edu/forumy/2006/10/military-commissions-act-congress. php (last visited May 29, 2007) (defending the MCA's evidentiary provisions and dismissing its "ethnocentric" critics, whose "views are quickly dispelled when one considers the day-to-day activity of most European criminal courts where hearsay is regularly considered...Even the International Criminal Court allows hearsay.")

[84] MCA, *supra* note 8, sec. 6(a)(2) ("No foreign or international source of law shall supply a basis for a rule of decision in the courts of the United States in interpreting the prohibitions enumerated in subsection (d) of such section 2441.") *See also* David Scheffer, *Introductory Note to Military Commissions Act of 2006*, 45 ILM 1241 (2006) (noting that "[s]uch extraordinary censorship of what

the standards for reliability that the MCA adopts remain perilously low. Both the Human Rights Committee and the Inter-American Commission have indicated that the right to examine witnesses can never be dispensed with yet,[85] under the MCA, interrogators could be permitted to testify to statements made by other detainees (in Guantanamo or elsewhere) against the accused, without providing the opportunity for that detainee to be cross-examined. Likewise, documents submitted based solely on the assertion of general national security reasons could be denied to the accused or significantly altered with minimal judicial oversight. Thus, notwithstanding the MCA's affirmation of an accused's right to be present at trial, the broad sweep of its hearsay provisions and the failure to set forth more narrowly defined exceptions for the national security privilege continue to imperil the confrontation right of defendants.

4.3. *Admissibility of Evidence Obtained through Coercion*

Certainly one of the most problematic provisions of the MCA includes the very low standard of admissibility for statements made prior to the passage of the Detainee Treatment Act on December 30, 2005.[86] Human rights law[87] and, more recently,

---

judges and justice may rely upon to interpret and enforce Common Article 3 is unprecedented in U.S. law and jurisprudence.")

[85] *See e.g.*, General Comment No. 29, *supra* note 10; *see also* Report on Terrorism and Human Rights, *supra* note 14, para. 238 ("The effective conduct of a defense additionally encompasses the right of the person concerned to examine or have examined witnesses against him or her and to obtain the attendance and examination of witnesses on his or her behalf, under the same conditions as opposing witnesses.")

[86] Detainee Treatment Act 2005, Title X of the Department of Defense Appropriations Act, 2006, H.R. 2863 (hereinafter DTA). The passage of the DTA, which was meant to eliminate the geographical exception the U.S. had previously read into Article 16 of the UN Convention Against Torture (obligating states to prevent "cruel, inhuman and degrading treatment") is an important first step in reversing efforts to sever the crime of torture from inhuman treatment. On its face, the DTA applies to all U.S. personnel everywhere, without regard to whom they are interrogating. *But see* Charlie Savage, *Bush Could Bypass New Torture Ban*, Boston Globe, Jan. 4, 2006 (noting that the President issued a "signing statement" to the DTA, reserving authority to interpret the ban on inhuman treatment and interrogation techniques "in the context of his broader powers to protect national security").

[87] United Nations Convention Against Torture and Other Cruel, Inhuman or Degrading Treatment or Punishment, Article 15, G.A. Res. 39/46, annex, 39 U.N. GAOR Supp. (No. 51) at 197, U.N. Doc. A/39/51 (1984), entered into force June 26, 1987 (requiring state parties to "ensure that any statement which is established to have been made as a result of torture shall not be invoked as evidence in any proceedings") [hereinafter CAT], *accord* ICCPR, *supra* note 17, Article 7 ("No one shall be subjected to torture or to cruel, inhuman or degrading treatment or punishment.") *See also* A and Others v. Secretary of State for the Home Department, United Kingdom House of Lords 71 (Dec. 8. 2005) (interpreting Article 15 CAT as imposing a blanket exclusionary rule that

important decisions by international criminal tribunals[88] are clear as to the excludability of evidence obtained by torture and other coercive methods. Moreover, it is highly doubtful whether the wide discretion given to military judges for assessing coerced testimony is consistent with Common Article 3's parallel prohibition on torture and "outrages upon personal dignity." By contrast, under the MCA, a significantly lower "totality of the circumstances" standard is to be applied to all statements where the degree of coercion is disputed.[89]

The MCA's vague test for admissibility is thrown into sharp relief when compared to its related provision in the UCMJ, which clearly states that "[n]o statement obtained...through the use of coercion, unlawful influence, or unlawful inducement may be received in evidence against him in a trial by court-martial."[90] Moreover, despite the MCA's purported exclusion of evidence obtained through torture as well as cruel and inhuman treatment (CIDT), its definition of CIDT diverges substantially from the standards of other international courts. Whereas CIDT is "constituted by an intentional act or omission which causes serious mental or physical suffering or injury or constitutes a serious attack on human dignity,"[91] the MCA ominously defines "serious pain or suffering" as bodily injury involving at least one of the following: substantial risk of death, extreme physical pain, burns or physical disfigurement of a serious nature, or significant loss or impairment of the function of a bodily member.[92] The use of such vague and permissive standards is particularly dangerous in the context of Guantanamo Bay, given that the period preceding passage of the DTA was also the most notorious with respect to U.S. interpretations of the prohibition on torture (notably the 2002 Department of

---

applies to all judicial proceedings and endorsing a "balance of probabilities" standard in assessing whether information relied on by the state was obtained by torture).

[88] *See e.g.*, Prosecutor v. Musema, Case No. ICTR-96-13-T, Judgment and Sentence, paras 38–39 (Jan. 27, 2000) ("As a general principle, the Chamber attaches probative value to evidence according to its credibility...As the Chamber has noted above, the probative value of evidence is based upon an assessment of its reliability.")

[89] MCA, *supra* note 8, paras. 948r(c) and 948r(d). For statements obtained prior to the DTA's passage, if the military judge finds that the "totality of the circumstances renders the statement reliable and possessing sufficient probative value," and that the "interests of justice" would be served by its admission, then it may be admitted. Post-DTA statements are similarly subject to a "totality of the circumstances" test, however, the definition of coercion is broadened to include "cruel, inhuman, or degrading treatment" as defined by the DTA. *See id.*, para. 948r(d)(1)-(3).

[90] UCMJ, *supra* note 19, Article 31(d).

[91] Prosecutor v. Delalic et al., Case No. IT-96-21-A, Appeals Chamber Judgment, para. 424 (Feb. 20, 2001).

[92] MCA, *supra* note 8, at para. 950v (12)(B) and Sec. 6(b)(2)(D). *See also* Christian M. De Vos, *Mind The Gap: Pain, Purpose, and the Difference Between Torture and Inhuman Treatment*, 14(2) Hum. Rts. Brf. 4–10 (arguing that the "gap" between torture and inhuman treatment is being exploited by wrongly focusing on the severity of treatment and degree of pain suffered as the principal distinction between the two categories).

Justice memorandum by the Office of Legal Counsel, which set forth an extremely high threshold for torture).[93]

4.4. *Suspension of* Habeas Corpus

As the Detainee Treatment Act (DTA) had earlier sought to do, the MCA effectively strips U.S. courts of jurisdiction over *habeas corpus* claims filed by detainees.[94] Human rights law strictly guards the right of *habeas corpus* and, as such, the MCA's stripping of it flies in the face of a wealth of jurisprudence affirming its non-derogability.[95] As Professors Goldman and Tittemore have also noted, "Where [the regulations and procedures under international humanitarian law prove inadequate to properly safeguard the minimum standards of treatment of detainees] . . . human rights supervisory mechanisms, including *habeas corpus* . . . may necessarily supersede international humanitarian law."[96]

That the MCA strips U.S. courts of *habeas* jurisdiction is all the more troubling in light of other provisions that fly in the face of human rights norms, including the right to a speedy trial, which the Act specifically withholds.[97] Thus, detainees can be held in confinement indefinitely with no fundamental right to a speedy trial, and no recourse to *habeas corpus* as an essential safeguard for ensuring their fair

---

[93] Memorandum from U.S. Dept. of Justice, Office of Legal Counsel, Office of the Assistant Attorney General, to Alberto R. Gonzales, Counsel to the President, Re: Standards of Conduct for Interrogation Under 18 U.S.C. sections 2340–2340A, (Aug. 1, 2002), *available at* www.gwu.edu/~nsarchiv/NSAEBB/NSAEBB127/02.08.01.pdf (last visited May 29, 2007) (defining torture as "[I]ntense pain or suffering of the kind that is equivalent to the pain that would be associated with serious physical injury so severe that death, organ failure, or permanent damage resulting in a loss of significant body function will likely result.")

[94] MCA, *supra* note 8, sec. 7(a) (amending Section 2241 of U.S.C. Title 28 by inserting the following subsection: "(e)(1) [N]o court, justice, or judge shall have jurisdiction to hear or consider an application for a writ of habeas corpus filed by or on behalf of an alien detained by the United States who has been determined by the United States to have been properly detained as an enemy combatant or is awaiting such determination.")

[95] *See e.g.,* Inter-Am. Ct. H.R., Habeas Corpus in Emergency Situations (Articles 27(2) and 7(6) of the American Convention on Human Rights), Advisory Opinion OC-8/87, Jan. 30, 1987, Ser. A, No. 8, P 33 (describing *habeas* as a judicial remedy "designed to protect personal freedom or physical integrity"); *cf.* Prosecutor v. Barayagwiza, Case No. ICTR-97–19-AR72, Appeals Chamber Decision, para. 88 (Nov. 3, 1999) (stating that *habeas corpus* is "a fundamental right and is enshrined in international human rights norms.") *See also* General Comment No. 29, *supra* note 10, para. 16 (describing the remedy as a non-derogable norm of international human rights law).

[96] Goldman & Tittemore, *supra* note 49, at 47.

[97] MCA, *supra* note 8, para. 948b(d)(1)(A) ("The following provisions of this title shall not apply to trial by military commission under this chapter . . . Section 810 [article 10 of the Uniform Code of Military Justice], relating to speedy trial, including any rule of courts martial relating to speedy trial.")

treatment.⁹⁸ Importantly, the Act also extends its *habeas* stripping provisions not only to those detained at Guantanamo Bay, but all claims "filed by or on behalf of an alien detained by the United States who has been determined... to have been properly detained as an enemy combatant or is awaiting such determination."⁹⁹ In other words, the provision encompasses all non-citizens, including permanent legal residents of the United States, and applies even if they are on U.S. territory. Although the DTA grants the D.C. Circuit Court authority to review the administrative proceedings held at Guantanamo, given how narrowly drawn the scope for such review is, it is hardly a commensurate remedy.¹⁰⁰

As a matter of U.S. constitutional law, the question as to whether enemy combatants enjoy a constitutional right to *habeas corpus* (as opposed to a statutory right), remained unanswered by the Supreme Court's opinion in *Rasul v. Bush*¹⁰¹ and will likely be an essential basis for judicial review of the MCA. At the time of writing, however, the Court had already rejected a petition for certiorari to review the matter,¹⁰² after a divided panel of the U.S. Court of Appeals upheld the MCA's *habeas* stripping provisions.¹⁰³ In the interim, the Act continues to entrench a detention

---

⁹⁸ *See e.g.*, Inter-Am. Ct. H.R., Castillo Paez Case, Judgment, Nov. 3, 1997, Ser. C., No. 34, para. 83 ("The purpose of habeas corpus is not only to guarantee personal liberty and humane treatment, but also to prevent disappearance or failure to determine the place of detention, and, ultimately, to ensure the right to life.")

⁹⁹ MCA, *supra* note 8, sec. 7(a).

¹⁰⁰ Indeed, the government has argued that the DTA does not permit the Circuit Court to engage in any fact-finding; rather, it is limited to reviewing the CSRT "record" only, to determine "whether [it] followed appropriate procedures." Petitioners may not introduce nor may the Court consider extrinsic evidence controverting the record, e.g., evidence that statements used against petitioners were obtained through torture or coercion.

¹⁰¹ Rasul v. Bush, 542 U.S. 466, 124 S.Ct. 2686 (2004) (holding that U.S. federal courts, under 28 U.S.C. section 2241, have *habeas corpus* jurisdiction over legal claims brought by persons detained at Guantanamo Bay).

¹⁰² The Court's denial of review was not explained, however, Justices Stevens and Kennedy authored a separate statement explaining that they were declining review in order for detainees to first exhaust their other "available remedies," i.e., the DTA and MCA. They added that the Court's denial of review did not amount to an expression of "any opinion" on the merits of the detainee claims. Justices Breyer, Souter and Ginsburg dissented from the denial. Boumediene v. Bush and Odah v. United States, 549 U.S. ___ (2007), *available at* www.supremecourtus.gov/opinions/06pdf/06–1195Stevens.pdf (last visited May 29, 2007). Following the Supreme Court's denial, the Justice Department filed a motion on April 19, 2007 to dismiss all pending *habeas corpus* cases.

¹⁰³ Boumediene v. Bush, Nos. 05–5062 (D.C. Cir., Feb. 20, 2007). Both the majority decision and dissent proceeded on the assumption that the MCA was not a formal constitutional "suspension" of the *habeas* writ; rather it was a jurisdictional revocation that the majority considered not constitutionally protected for non-citizens detained abroad as "enemy combatants." In dissent, Judge Judith Rogers argued that application of the *habeas* statute to Guantanamo detainees was consistent with the historical reach of the writ. Judge Rogers also argued that the CSRT's and

regime inconsistent with both the requirements of IHL and international human rights norms.

4.5. *Right to Appeal*

The narrow parameters of an accused's right to appeal further imperil the "equality of arms" doctrine essential to human rights. While human rights law leaves a degree of flexibility to the organization of appellate proceedings in a state's legal orders, it is nonetheless recognized as a "condition for the realization of fair trial and due process."[104] Under the International Criminal Court's Statute, for instance, both the prosecutor and accused are entitled to appeal for procedural errors, as well as errors of fact or law.[105] A convicted person is also entitled to appeal on "any other ground that affects the fairness or reliability of the proceedings or decision."[106]

Notably, the MCA permits trial counsel before the commission to take an interlocutory appeal to the Court of Military Commission Review for "any order or ruling of the military judge"[107] (e.g., that terminates proceedings, excludes evidence, or relates to the protection of classified information and the exclusion of the accused from portions of the proceedings), while the defense is given no such right. For the accused there is no review until the commission reaches a verdict, whereas the U.S. can seek an immediate appeal on any unfavorable decision. Moreover, the Court of Review's reviews may only be made with respect to matters of law; procedural complaints may not form a basis for appeal.[108] As one commentator has noted, "[u]nder the pressure of a possible interlocutory appeal by the United States, one could see a military judge reversing a decision pursuant to the discretion given."[109]

---

the MCA's provisions for limited review of their decisions were not constitutionally adequate substitutes for *habeas corpus*; she noted that they permit the introduction of coerced evidence, that detainees are not entitled to counsel at status hearings, or to see classified evidence used against them. *Id.*, Dissent Op. at 21–23.

[104] Salvatore Zappala, Human Rights in International Criminal Proceedings 158 (2003) [hereinafter Zappala]. *See also* Inter-Am. Ct. H.R., Abella v. Argentina, Report No.55/97, OEA/Ser.L/V/II.98, d\Doc. 7 rev. para. 261 (1998) (considering that to guarantee the full right of defense, appeals should include a "material review of the interpretation of procedural rules …. where the right to defense was rendered ineffective, and also with respect to the interpretation of the rules on the weighing of evidence.") [hereinafter Abella v. Argentina]

[105] Rome Statute, *supra* note 74, Articles 81–85.

[106] Zappala, *supra* note 104, at 173.

[107] MCA, *supra* note 8, para. 950d(a).

[108] *Id.*, para. 950f(d) ("In a case reviewed by the Court of Military Commission Review under this section, the Court may act only with respect to matters of law.").

[109] Benjamin Davis, *'All the Laws But One': Parsing the Military Commissions Bill*, Jurist at 12, *available at* jurist.law.pitt.edu/forumy/2006/09/all-laws-but-one-parsing-military.php (last visited May 29, 2007).

5. Conclusion

It is not difficult to see how these central provisions of the MCA recall Georges Clemenceau's famous phrase that "Military justice is to justice what military music is to music." But it need not be this way. Although one may critique the decision of the U.S. government to invoke a law of war paradigm in the context of a largely rhetorical "War on Terror," that it has elected to do so means the U.S. is equally bound to respect the rights this legal regime demands. This regime is, quite obviously, regulated by humanitarian law but it is also supplemented by the obligations that flow from both customary international law and applicable human rights treaties. As James Stewart notes, "[i]nternational human rights standards are also of vital importance, both as a means of defining the terms of the judicial guarantees enshrined in [Article 75 of AP I] and as an independent and complementary body of rules simultaneously applicable during armed conflict."[110]

Unfortunately, the U.S. continues to endorse the increasingly indefensible position that the human rights guaranteed in treaties to which it is a party are not applicable extraterritorially or during a time of war, and that to abide by the ICCPR would lead to the "absurd result [of] ... unlawful combatants [receiving] more procedural rights than would lawful combatants under the Geneva Conventions."[111] Such an interpretation, however, misstates the relationship between humanitarian law and human rights; it assumes that the latter displaces the former when, in fact, human rights norms *complement* the law of war, "in order to support, strengthen and clarify [its] analogous principles."[112] By its very design humanitarian law supports a restricted scope of rights for unprivileged combatants, which is precisely why this chapter has not argued that commissions are an illegitimate forum for prosecutions or that certain actions for which POWs are immunized may not be the basis for prosecuting "enemy combatants." But human rights law, also by its very design, does not make the distinctions that IHL does and, as such, its norms should inform the procedural and substantive laws that make up any "regularly constituted court," including those of military commissions.

Despite the attempted isolation of the provisions of the Military Commissions Act from other relevant sources of law,[113] the separationist view endorsed by the U.S. is untenable. Just as human rights courts are increasingly extending their

---

[110] James G. Stewart, *The Military Commissions Act's Inconsistency with the Geneva Conventions: An Overview*, 5 J. Int'l Crim. J. 26, 29 (2007).
[111] Special Rapporteurs Report, *supra* note 13, at 54.
[112] Henckaerts & Doswald-Beck, *supra* note 49, at 299.
[113] MCA, *supra* note 8, sec. 6(a)(2).

supervisory functions to include international humanitarian law,[114] so too must humanitarian law consider those fundamental human rights necessary to protect its guarantees of due process. Congress cannot make military commissions compliant with Common Article 3 by mere legislative fiat, as it has attempted to do through the MCA.[115] Attention should instead focus on a coordinated application of international humanitarian law and human rights law that "takes into account the exceptional nature of [terrorist] violence, and at the same time respects the basic human rights to which individuals are entitled in all circumstances."[116] The right to a fair trial, whatever the crime, is such a basic right and precisely because IHL is less tailored as to its scope, reference to human rights norms is both appropriate and necessary. America ignores them at its own peril.

---

[114] *See e.g.*, Abella v. Argentina, *supra* note 104 (where the Inter-American Commission affirmed, for the first time, that it was competent to invoke international humanitarian law and apply its rules to state parties to the American Convention).

[115] MCA, *supra* note 8, para. 948b(f) (declaring that "A military commission established under this chapter is a regularly constituted court...for purposes of common Article 3 of the Geneva Conventions.")

[116] Brian D. Tittemore, *Guantanamo Bay and the Precautionary Measures of the Inter-American Commission on Human Rights: A Case for International Oversight in the Struggle Against Terrorism*, 6 Hum. Rts. L. Rev. 378, 401 (2006).

Chapter XX

Targeted Killings and International Law: Law Enforcement, Self-defense, and Armed Conflict

*Michael N. Schmitt**

1. *Introduction*

In 1991, United Air Force Chief of Staff General Michael Dugan's admission that Coalition air forces were targeting Saddam Hussein during Operation Desert Storm provoked a controversy that led to his eventual dismissal. U.S. officials denied, rather unconvincingly, that they hoped to kill the Iraqi President.[1]

A mere eight years later, NATO repeatedly targeted Slobodan Milosevic during Operation Allied Force. The missions, albeit framed in the broader context of command and control warfare, raised few eyebrows. By the fall of 2001, Coalition forces were openly hunting for the elusive Taliban leadership during Operation Enduring Freedom, a targeted killing campaign widely reported, and acknowledged by Coalition spokespersons, in the press. Then, in March 2003, President George Bush actually moved the Operation Iraqi Freedom launch time forward when intelligence assets located Saddam Hussein at Doha Farms outside Baghdad. The ensuing aerial attack failed, as did a further 50 air strikes against various Iraqi leaders. Even non-governmental organizations such as Human Rights Watch acknowledged the legality of targeting specific individuals, only expressing concern regarding how some of the missions had been carried out.[2] Clearly, the "operational

---

* Michael N. Schmitt is Charles H. Stockton Professor of International Law at the United States Naval War College (USA).
[1] On the subject, and the state of the law at the time, *see* Michael N. Schmitt, *State Sponsored Assassination in International and Domestic Law*, 17 Yale J. Int'l L. 609 (1992).
[2] Human Rights Watch, Off-Target: The Conduct of War and Civilian Casualties in Iraq (Dec. 2003), *available at* hrw.org/reports/2003/usa1203 (last visited May 13, 2007). For a different view of the strikes that is, in part, critical of the Human Rights Watch assessment, *see* Michael N. Schmitt, *The Conduct of Hostilities During Operational Iraqi Freedom: An International Humanitarian Law Assessment*, 6 YB Int'l Humanitarian L. 73 (2003).

code" governing individual targeting had evolved dramatically in the dozen years since Operation Desert Storm.[3]

Beyond traditional state-on-state conflict, both the United States and Israel have embraced the "targeted killings" of individual terrorists as an effective tactic and an overarching counter-terrorism strategy. U.S. operations in this regards are growing increasingly aggressive and frequent. They initially captured international attention in 2002 when a CIA-operated Predator unmanned aerial vehicle employed a Hellfire missile to destroy a vehicle in which Qaed Senyan al-Harthi, a senior al-Qaeda operative, was riding in Yemen. The United States conducted the attack with the cooperation of Yemen's intelligence agencies.[4] In another well-known example, the United States conducted an air strike four years later against Amyan al-Zawahiri, al-Qaeda's second in command, in a remote area of Pakistan. This time, U.S. forces mounted the operation without the consent of the state of situs, at least according to public pronouncements from President Pervez Musharraf.[5] And on several occasions in 2007, U.S. AC-130 gunships targeted senior al-Qaeda members in Somalia during the Somali government's campaign to recapture control of the country, particularly Mogadishu, from radical Muslim militia forces.[6]

Even more widely known, and condemned, is Israel's policy of targeted killings. It is a response to terrorism that is decades old for Israel.[7] Israel adopted the policy following the infamous massacre of its athletes at the 1972 Munich Olympics. In the aftermath of the murders, Israeli commandos tracked down and killed the Palestinians involved. They conducted similar operations against Palestinian terrorist leaders in a number of Arab countries. Future Israeli leaders such as Moshe Yaalon (future Chief of Staff of the Israel Defense Forces) and Ehrud Barak (future Prime Minster) participated.

---

[3] The operational code is the unofficial, but actual normative system governing international actions. It is discerned in part by observing the behaviour of international elites. An operational code contrasts with a "myth system," the law that, according to such elites, purportedly applies. On the distinction, *see* W. Michael Reisman & James Baker, Regulating Covert Action: Practices, Contexts and Policies of Covert Action Abroad in International and American Law 23–24 (1992); W. Michael Reisman, Jurisprudence: Understanding and Shaping Law 23–35 (1987); Michael N. Schmitt, *The Resort to Force in International Law: Reflections on Positivist and Contextual Approaches*, 37 A. F. L. Rev. 105, 112–119 (1994).

[4] *Profile: Ali Qaed Senyan al-Harthi*, BBC News World Report (Nov. 5, 2002), *available at* news.bbc.co.uk/2/hi/middle_east/2404443.stm (last visited May 13, 2007); Anthony Dworkin, *The Yemen Strike*, Nov. 14, 2002, *available at* www.crimesofwar/onnews/news-yemen.html (last visited May 13, 2007) [hereinafter Dworkin].

[5] Katrin Bernhold, *Musharraf Condemns U.S. Strikes in Pakistan*, Int'l Herald. Trib., Jan. 27, 2006, at 7.

[6] Michael R. Gordon & Mark Mazzetti, *U.S. Joined Ethiopians in Somalia Campaign*, Int'l Herald. Trib., Feb. 24, 2007, at 1.

[7] *See* discussion, e.g., in Daniel Byman, *Do Targeted Killings Work?*, For. Aff., Mar./Apr. 2006, at 95.

In the 1980s and early 1990s, Israel targeted Hezbollah, killing its Secretary-General, Shiek Abbas Musawi. During the 1990s, most Israeli operations focused on the Palestinians. For instance, in 1995 Israeli operatives killed Fathi Shikaki, leader of the Palestinian Islamic Jihad (PIJ).

The incidence of targeted killing grew dramatically after the start of the second intifada in 2000. Between 2000 and 2005, Israel, pursuant to its "policy of targeted frustration," killed nearly 300 members of organizations such as Hamas, PIJ, and the Al Aqsa Martyrs Brigade.[8] By 2004, Israeli had expanded the scope of attacks to political leaders, an approach marked by the March helicopter strike against the wheelchair bound political leader of Hamas, Shiek Ahmed Yassin. Some 150 civilians were killed in the attacks, and hundreds were wounded.

This article explores the legality of targeted killings.[9] In doing so, it distinguishes between targeted killings as law enforcement, self-defense, and armed conflict. A major complicating factor in determining the applicable law in a particular situation is that no universally accepted dividing line exists between peace and armed conflict. Consider transnational terrorism. The International Committee of the Red Cross (ICRC) takes a generally restrictive approach to international armed conflict, requiring the existence of a belligerent state on both sides.[10] Transnational terrorism, standing alone, would not qualify. By contrast, the Israeli Supreme Court looks to the geographical aspects of conflict, defining an international armed conflict as one that "crosses the borders of the State."[11] By this interpretation, transnational terrorism qualifies. And while the ICRC views non-international armed conflict as restricted to civil wars, rebellions, and the like,[12] the U.S. Supreme Court recently characterized the global war on terrorism as "not international" because of the absence of a belligerent state on each side of the conflict.[13] Complicating matters, some commentators argue, employing traditional notions of the *jus ad bellum*, that counter-terrorist military operations unaffiliated with an ongoing armed conflict fall within the purview of the law of self-defense, but do not directly implicate the

---

[8] HCJ 796/02, The Public Committee against Torture v. Israel, para. 2 [hereinafter Public Committee].

[9] Although numerous excellent articles have addressed aspects of the subject, the most comprehensive treatment of the subject is Nils Melzner, Targeted Killing under the Normative Paradigms of Law Enforcement and Hostilities, unpublished doctoral dissertation of the University of Zürich (forthcoming, 2007) [hereinafter Melzner].

[10] ICRC Official Statement, The Relevance of IHL in the Context of Terrorism, July 21, 2005, *available at* www.icrc.org/web/eng/siteeng0.nsf/html/terrorism-ihl-210705 (last visited May 13, 2007).

[11] Public Committee, *supra* note 8, para. 18.

[12] *See*, e.g., Jean de Preux, Commentary: III Geneva Convention Relative to the Treatment of Prisoners of War 35–36 (1960).

[13] Hamdan v. Rumsfeld, 126 S. Ct. 2749 (2006).

corpus of law applicable during armed conflict, primarily international humanitarian law (IHL).

Determining whether any particular conflict is international, non-international or neither lies well beyond the scope of this article. Rather, it explores the normative regimes applicable to each of the three circumstances in which targeted killings are likely to occur. Since each involves differing prescriptive norms, an operation lawful in one may not be in another. As will become apparent, there is no one size fits all body of law governing targeted killings.

2. *Law Enforcement Targeted Killings*

Targeted killings conducted during peacetime fall into two categories – those conducted in a situation to which the law of self-defense does not apply and those to which it does (discussed *infra*). In the former, traditional law enforcement restrictions apply. Any law enforcement lethal killing not justifiable under both international human rights law and domestic law will be "extrajudicial" and, thus, unlawful.

Domestic norms regarding the use of deadly force by law enforcement authorities vary from state to state. However, the United Nations Office of the High Commissioner for Human Rights issued what is effectively a model standard in 1990. The Basic Principles on the Use of Force and Firearms by Law Enforcement Officials provides that:

> Law enforcement officials shall not use firearms against persons except in self-defense or defense of others against the imminent threat of death or serious injury, to prevent the perpetration of a particularly serious crime involving grave threat to life, to arrest a person presenting such a danger and resisting their authority, or to prevent his or her escape, and only when less extreme means are insufficient to achieve these objectives. In any event, intentional lethal use of firearms may only be made when strictly unavoidable in order to protect life.[14]

Some states also authorize the use of deadly force to protect critical infrastructure. Whatever the state-specific standards, any use of deadly force by a state's agents contravening them will self-evidently be unlawful. In the first instance, therefore, a state's own laws govern whether its law enforcement, military, or intelligence authorities may lethally "target" an individual.

International human rights norms further restrict a state's resort to potentially deadly law enforcement methods.[15] Most treaties safeguarding civil rights protect

---

[14] UNHCR, 1990, U.N. Doc. A/CONF.144/28/Rev.1, prov. 9, *available at* www.unhchr.ch/html/menu3/b/h_comp43.htm (last visited May 13, 2007).

[15] For an insightful discussion of these norms, and indeed the subject of targeted killings more generally, *see* David Kretzmer, *Targeted Killings of Suspected Terrorists: Extrajudicial Executions or Legitimate Means of Defense?*, 16(2) Eur. J. Int'l L. 171 (2005) [hereinafter Kretzmer].

the "inherent right to life" as non-derogable. Typically, they express the prohibition in terms of "arbitrary" deprivation of life. Article 6(1) of the International Covenant on Civil and Political Rights, which provides that "[n]o one shall be arbitrarily deprived of his life," is paradigmatic.[16] Those instruments not adopting the "arbitrary" formulation reach, in general terms, the same result. For instance, Article 2 of the European Convention on Human Rights (ECHR) prohibits intentional deprivation of life except when, *inter alia*, "absolutely necessary" in the "defence of any person from unlawful violence."[17]

Violation of these standards occurs if the deadly force employed violates one of two (or both) requirements applicable to all State uses of force in situations short of armed conflict – necessity and proportionality. Also underpinning the *jus ad bellum* notion of self-defense (discussed *infra*), in the context of human rights they require that deadly force be used only as a last resort and only in situations presenting grave danger to others.

Necessity mandates the use of other than forceful measures if they are available and reasonably likely to achieve the legitimate ends sought. Proportionality requires that when force is necessary, authorities use only that degree required to achieve the objective. Thus, for example, if peaceable arrest is feasible in a given situation, force may not be used. It would be unnecessary, even when acting to prevent the death of others. By the principle of proportionality, if the arrest can only be effected forcefully, no more force may be used than reasonably called for in the attendant circumstances.

One can easily imagine situations in which the intentionally lethal use of force meets the necessity and proportionality criteria. Consider a suicide bomber present in a crowded area. Authorities may have to employ intentionally lethal force to keep him from activating his explosive device. This reality underpinned the shoot-to-kill policy adopted by British police in response to the July 2005 London bombings. They implemented the policy the very day after the attacks when shooting to death Brazilian Jean Charles de Menezes in the Stockwell Tube Station. Despite evoking controversy, the police actions made operational sense, and pass legal muster, in light of the tactics adopted by the London bombers. The European Court of

---

[16] International Covenant on Civil and Political Rights, G.A. Res. 2200A (XXI), 21 U.N. GAOR Supp. (No. 16) at 52, U.N. Doc. A/6316 (1966), 999 U.N.T.S. 171 [hereinafter ICCPR]. *See also* American Convention on Human Rights, O.A.S. Treaty Series No. 36, 1144 U.N.T.S. 123, Aticle 4, entered into force July 18, 1978, *reprinted in* Basic Documents Pertaining to Human Rights in the Inter-American System, OEA/Ser.L.V/II.82 doc. 6 rev. 1 at 25 (1992) [hereinafter ACHR]; African Charter on Human and Peoples' Rights, Article 4, June 27, 1981, O.A.U. Doc. CAB/LEG/67/3 rev. 5, *reprinted in* 21 I.L.M. 58 (1982) [hereinafter ACHPR].

[17] Convention for the Protection of Human Rights and Fundamental Freedoms, 213 U.N.T.S. 222, Articles 2(1), 2(2) entered into force Sept. 3, 1953, as amended by Protocols Nos 3, 5, 8, and 11 which entered into force on Sept. 21, 1970, Dec. 20, 1971, Jan. 1, 1990, and Nov. 1, 1998 respectively [hereinafter ECHR]. The two other situations are preventing the escape of someone who has been detained and quelling riots or insurrections.

Human Rights case *McCann* illustrates a related scenario. Litigation arose when British forces in Gibraltar shot-to-kill three Irish Republican Army terrorists whom they believed would detonate a car bomb if they realized arrest was imminent. The Court held that the actions did not violate Article 2 ECHR.[18]

It is often necessary and proportionate to target a specified terrorist to prevent his attack elsewhere. Typically, this occurs when authorities cannot arrest him with a sufficient degree of certainty, such that they can thereby foil future attacks. For instance, the terrorist may be located at a place that authorities cannot reach, or at least not reach without forewarning the terrorist. The area may be remote, as in the case of Federally Administered Tribal Areas in northwest Pakistan along the Afghan border, or one that authorities do not effectively control, such as certain Sunni strongholds in Iraq.

Given the principles of necessity and proportionality, the law requires more than mere inability to arrest. Authorities may only act based on reliable and substantial evidence that the terrorists will strike in the future and they must reasonably conclude there will be no future viable opportunity to prevent the anticipated act(s) of terrorism. Of course, since a presumption of innocence attaches in law enforcement operations, they must also have a reliable and substantial belief that their target is in fact a terrorist intent on executing terrorist acts.

Ultimately, then, a targeted killing will comport with human rights norms only if the authorities harbour a reasonable belief, in the circumstances holding at the time, that they are acting in the last possible window of opportunity to prevent a terrorist attack that is almost certainly going to be perpetrated by their target(s). Absent such conditions, the action will comprise an unlawful extrajudicial killing.

3. Self-defense Targeted Killings

In many cases, terrorists operate from other countries. The model set forth above, however, applies only to areas over which a state exercises full law enforcement jurisdiction, generally the territory of the state itself. If terrorists who threaten state A are located in state B, only state B may conduct law enforcement activities at the magnitude of targeted killings.[19] This limitation does not deprive a state of its ability to protect itself from terrorists situated abroad, for a separate and distinct

---

[18] McCann et al. v. United Kingdom, Application No. 18984/91, Judgment (Sept. 5, 1995), para. 149 (1995). However, the Court found that the United Kingdom violated the article by failing to conduct sufficient planning to identify alternatives.

[19] Note that they may have the authority to use deadly force in another country. The best example is the right of military forces to conduct law enforcement activities in their camps pursuant to status of forces agreements. Said authority extends to the use of deadly force to protect individuals in the camps and to protect critical assets, such as classified material and weapons.

basis for counter-terrorist operations during "peacetime" (situations short of armed conflict) exists, the law of self-defense.

Before turning to the *jus ad bellum* law of self-defense, note that the applicability of human right norms to extraterritorial operations has been questioned in the European Court of Human Rights (ECtHR). In *Bankovic*, the Court rejected jurisdiction over a case brought against NATO states party to the European Convention on Human Rights for the wrongful deaths of individuals killed when NATO aircraft attacked the Radio Televizije Srbije (Radio-Television Serbia, "RTS") headquarters in Belgrade during Operation Allied Force.[20] The ECtHR held that since the NATO states concerned did not exercise effective control of the relevant territory and its inhabitants (Belgrade) at the time of the attack, the Convention did not apply. The Human Rights Commission subsequently adopted a more liberal position, broadening jurisdiction to those in the "power" of a Party and expressly extending application into periods of armed conflict.[21] Moreover, as David Kretzmer has noted,

> [w]hile a state party's *treaty* obligations are a function of the scope of application defined in the particular treaty, some of the substantive norms in human rights treaties that have been ratified by the vast majority of states in the world have now become peremptory norms of customary international law. The duty to respect the right to life is surely one of these norms.[22]

Regardless of one's position on the extraterritorial scope of human rights norms (whether treaty-based or customary), the debate has *de minimus* impact on self-defense operations (outside an armed conflict paradigm), for, as will be seen, the criteria applicable to such operations yield essentially the same result.

The threshold question is whether the law of self-defense applies to counter-terrorist operations. Article 51 U.N. Charter sets forth the standard: "Nothing in the present Charter shall impair the inherent right of individual or collective self-defense if an armed attack occurs against a Member of the United Nations, until the Security Council has taken measures necessary to maintain international peace and security."[23] Note that the defensive acts may be either individual or collective. Other states may act in concert with a victim state (or even alone in defense of that state) when the victim state seeks assistance.[24] Thus, any defensive

---

[20] Banković v. Belgium and 16 Other Contracting States, Application No. 52207/99, Admissibility Decision, (Dec. 12, 2001), 16 were killed and 16 wounded in the attack.
[21] General Comment No. 31: The Nature of the General Legal Obligation Imposed on States Parties to the Covenant, May 26, 2004, U.N. Doc. CCPR/C/21/Rev.1/Add.13.
[22] Kretzmer, *supra* note 15, at 184–185.
[23] U.N. Charter, Article 51.
[24] The requirement that the State under attack make a request for assistance was acknowledged by the Military and Paramilitary Activities in and against Nicaragua (Nicaragua v. U.S.A.), Merits, 1986 I.C.J. Reports (June 27), 14, [hereinafter Nicaragua Case].

action allowed to the target state may also be conducted by a state coming to its assistance, including targeted killings.

Traditionally, scholars and practitioners viewed this prescriptive scheme as designed to allow states the opportunity to defend against armed attacks by other states. Defense against non-state entities fell within the ambit of the law enforcement measures described *supra*. Indeed, when the United States launched air strikes in 1986 against Libyan based-terrorist targets (Operation El Dorado Canyon) in response to the terrorist bombing of a Berlin discothèque frequented by U.S. military personnel, the international community expressed outrage. The U.N. General Assembly "condemned" the operation as "a violation of the Charter of the United Nations and international law," a view echoed by Secretary General Javier Perez de Cueller.[25] Only traditional allies Israel and the United Kingdom publicly supported El Dorado Canyon.

Yet, a careful reading of Article 51 reveals no limitation to state-conducted attacks. This left the way open for revisionist interpretation of the law of self-defense. By September 12, 2001, the day after the al-Qaeda attacks in the United States, states appeared ready to accept a dramatically different operational code, one by which states may respond to terrorists mounting large scale attacks with military action pursuant to the law of self-defense. On that day, the Security Council passed the first in a series of resolutions, 1368, recognizing the right of individual and collective self-defense in the case.[26] Two weeks later, it did the same in Resolution 1373.[27] Regional organizations such as NATO and the Organization of American States also treated the terrorist attacks as activating the right of self-defense,[28] as did the scores of states that offered verbal, material, and military support.

No state practice in the aftermath of the American-led strikes on Al-Qaeda and the Taliban that began on October 7, 2001, indicated anything but continuing acceptance of the notion that large-scale terrorist operations constituted "armed attacks" under Article 51.[29] The Security Council adopted resolution after resolution reaffirming 1368 and 1373, thereby implicitly endorsing the Coalition mili-

---

[25] G.A. Res. 41/38 (Nov. 20, 1986); Elaine Sciolino, *Attack on Libya: The View from Capital Hill*, N.Y. Times, April 16, 1986, at A7. Note that the targets included Libyan government facilities, a fact that no doubt added to international outrage.

[26] S.C. Res. 1368, U.N. Doc. S/RES/1368 (2001) (Sept. 12, 2001).

[27] S.C. Res. 1373, U.N. Doc. S/RES/1373 (2001) (Sept. 28, 2001).

[28] Press Release, NATO Statement by the North Atlantic Council (Sept. 12, 2001); Terrorist Threat to the Americas, Res. 1, 24th Meeting of Consultation of Ministers of Foreign Affairs, OAS Doc. RC.24/RES.1/01 (Sept. 21, 2001).

[29] *See*, generally, Michael N. Schmitt, *Counter-terrorism and the Use of Force in International Law*, 32 Isr. Y.B. Hum. Rts. 53–116 (2002), *reprinted in* International Law and the War of Terror 7 (Fred Borch and Paul Wilson eds., 2003).

tary actions as consistent with the law of self-defense.[30] Even China, Russia, Arab states such as Egypt, and the Organization of the Islamic Conference endorsed the Operation Enduring Freedom.[31]

The new parameters of the operational code appeared settled until July 2004, when the International Court of Justice issued its Advisory Opinion on *Legal Consequences of the Construction of a Wall in the Occupied Palestinian Territories*.[32] There, the majority asserted that Article 51 did not apply to the case because Israel had not asserted that the terrorist attacks the wall was built to thwart were imputable to a foreign state. The opinion seemed mired in the past, particularly the Court's earlier judgment in *Military and Paramilitary Activities in and against Nicaragua*. In *Nicaragua*, it had found that actions of irregulars could constitute an armed attack if they had been "sent by or on behalf" of a state and if the "scale and effects" of their actions "would have been classified as an armed attack...had it been carried out by regular armed forces."[33] In other words, state action or direction was necessary to activate the right to respond to attacks by a non-state actor.

The decision wrongly ignored the effect of recent state practice on the law of self-defense, a point made by Judges Higgins, Kooijmans, and Buergenthal.[34] In rejecting the majority's flawed opinion, they relied on the points made above; 1) the absence in Article 51 of any requirement for a state to have mounted the armed attack, and 2) the Council's treatment of the "9/11" terrorist attacks as falling within the article's scope. The ill-reasoned majority opinion represents an unfortunate anomaly in the post-9/11 normative environment.

There was agreement, however, that the law of self-defense only applied to attacks mounted from outside a state (unless imputable to another State).[35] The judges drew differing conclusions as to the effect of this principle in the *Wall* case, but consensus on the principle existed. By their (correct) interpretation, self-defense does not apply to classic domestic terrorism; hence, the distinction drawn in this article between domestic law enforcement and self-defense.

---

[30] E.g., S.C. 1378, U.N. Doc. S/RES/1378 (2001) (Nov. 14, 2001) S.C. Res. 1383, U.N. Doc. S/RES/1383 (2001) (Dec. 6, 2001); S.C. Res. 1386, UU.N. Doc. S/RES/1386 (2001) (Dec. 20, 2001) S.C. Res. 1390, U.N. Doc. S/RES/1390 (2002) (Jan. 16, 2002).

[31] Sean D. Murphy, *Contemporary Practice of the United States Relating to International Law*, 96 Am. J. Int'l L. 237, 248 (2002); Daniel Williams, *Islamic Group Offers U.S. Mild Rebuke*, Wash. Post, Oct. 11, 2001, at A21 (the rebuke expressed concern that the United States not extend operations against states other than Afghanistan).

[32] Legal Consequences of the Construction of a Wall in the Occupied Palestinian Territory, Advisory Opinion (July 9, 2004), 2004 ICJ Rep. 163 [hereinafter Palestinian Wall].

[33] Nicaragua Case, *supra* note 24 at para. 195.

[34] Palestinian Wall, *supra* note 32, Separate Opinion of Judge Higgins, para. 33; Separate Opinion of Judge Kooijmans, para. 35; Declaration of Judge Buergenthal, para. 6.

[35] *Id*. para. 139; Higgins, para. 34; Buergenthal, para. 6.

If it is permissible to use force in self-defense against terrorist groups, then it is obviously permitted to target individual terrorists. To argue that knowing the identity of a target precludes attack would approach absurdity. There are limits. If an operation based on the right of self-defense lacks a nexus to an armed conflict (recall the debate over whether counter-terrorism is armed conflict discussed *supra*), there are three normative requirements conditioning exercise of the right – necessity, proportionality, and immediacy. On repeated occasions, the International Court of Justice has recognized the first two.[36] The third (and the others) derives directly from 19th century *Caroline* incident and the ensuing exchange of diplomatic notes between the United States and United Kingdom.[37] Together, they comprise the keystones of the law of self-defense.

As noted, necessity requires that there be no viable option other than force to deter or defeat the imminent armed attack. For counter-terrorist operations not occurring during armed conflict, this criterion poses the greatest obstacles. Should law enforcement measures (or, for that matter, other non-forceful options) likely suffice to deter future attacks, their existence would preclude defensive targeted killings as unnecessary. Of course, a rule of reason must prevail. Planners may consider the risk to the authorities executing arrests when assessing their viability. So too may they consider its likelihood of success, for if the target(s) escapes, they may have lost their only opportunity to thwart future terrorist attacks. Because self-defense operations take place outside the victim state's territory and often depends on the cooperation of unreliable local authorities, this factor will often be determinative.

Adding to the complexity, planners may further factor in the potential consequences of failure. For instance, if static anti-terrorist measures at the site of the anticipated terrorist attack are strong, defenders must shoulder greater risk of an unsuccessful arrest failure, for example, than if they do not know the situs or time of the prospective attack. Similarly, it is appropriate to factor in the likely gravity of the anticipated terrorist attack(s). In the case of an expected small-scale attack, planners must bear greater risk of arrest failure than in one involving weapons of mass destruction (WMD). By contrast, in WMD attacks, targeted killing will generally be justified in all cases except where the likelihood of success in attempting to arrest or otherwise frustrate the terrorists approaches certainty.

---

[36] Nicaragua Case, *supra* note 24, para. 194; Legality of the Threat or Use of Nuclear Weapons, Advisory Opinion, 1996 I.C.J. Rep. 226 (July 8), para. 41; Oil Platforms (Iran v. US), Merits, 2003 I.C.J. Rep. 161 (Nov. 6), para. 51.

[37] In which U.S. Secretary of State Daniel Webster, without objection from the United Kingdom, opined that the "necessity of self-defense" must be "instant, overwhelming, leaving no moment for deliberation." 30 British & Foreign State Papers 193 (1843), *reprinted in* R.Y. Jennings, *The Caroline and McLeod Cases*, 32 Am. J. Int'l L. 82, 89 (1938).

Proportionality limits the degree of defensive force employed to that reasonably required to foil an anticipated armed attack or defeat an ongoing one. The question is not whether force may be used (as in necessity), but rather how much. Thus, whereas necessity requires consideration of non-forceful measures as an *alternative* to forceful ones, proportionality mandates consideration of non-forceful measures as a *factor* in reducing the degree and nature of forceful actions necessary.

In the case of terrorism, proportionality generally involves consideration of forceful measures used in concert with non-forceful ones. For example, to defeat a particular attack, it may be necessary to kill only the individual assigned to execute it, but not his co-conspirators, such as those making the bomb. Of course, planners must assess the anticipated terrorist actions comprehensively. In the posited scenario, the co-conspirators, were they to escape, would likely plan future operations that the victim state may not be as well-placed to deter. If so, striking all the members of the terrorist cell may be justified, even though not mandated by the need to thwart the particular imminent attack in question. In this sense, the principles of necessity and proportionality operate synergistically.

Indeed, one might argue that the principle of proportionality, in certain circumstances, mandates a targeted killing. Consider a terrorist cell operating from a village across the border. One option is crossing into the neighboring country with ground forces to seize control of the village, either to engage the terrorists or effect their arrest. However, if intelligence reveals that the organization's leadership will be meeting at a known location, a surgical attack would be less invasive, less violent, and less disruptive to the civilian population than a major ground force movement. It would also be more likely to achieve the intended objective, disruption of planned terrorist attacks.

As to execution of any particular individual targeted attack, it would generally be naïve to demand application of a precise quantum of force in fulfillment of the proportionality criterion, since gradations beyond the arrest-deadly force dichotomy tend towards operational impracticability. Resultantly, the *jus ad bellum* proportionality principle seldom operates in the context of an individual strike.

The third self-defense criterion is immediacy. It is irrelevant to ongoing attacks, for once an attack is underway, the victim state can obviously defend itself. Rather, immediacy bears on either anticipatory or *ex post facto* defensive actions.

Traditionally, the notion was understood temporally – time proximity to the anticipated armed attack. Should the pending attack not meet the *Caroline* criterion of "instant, overwhelming, leaving no moment for deliberation," defensive action would be unlawful.[38] It would also be unlawful if taking place too long after an armed attack; a tardy response is retaliatory, not defensive.

---

[38] *See* text *id.*

This approach made sense in the context of classic warfare, in which attacks emanated from states. It allowed for diplomacy and other non-forceful measures to have the greatest opportunity to succeed; the law recognized and facilitated the possibility that states, presumptively rational actors who seek to avoid armed conflict and usually act lawfully, might strike an 11th hour deal averting war. Moreover, surprise is difficult to achieve in conventional military actions. Armed forces must usually mobilize, move towards the border, and perform other activities likely to be noticed by the other side. Even in modern conflict, with aircraft that can strike from afar and missiles that can traverse continents in minutes, complete surprise remains elusive, for there will typically be an increase in political tensions, while corresponding observable tactical preparations, such as an aircraft stand-down, take place. With "bolts out-of-the-blue" the exception, the risk of waiting to act defensively until the launch of an attack was imminent seemed acceptable.

Transnational terrorism generates an entirely different paradigm. As noted in the 2002 National Security Strategy, "[r]ogue states and terrorists do not seek to attack us using conventional means. They know such attacks would fail. Instead, they rely on acts of terror and, potentially, the use of weapons of mass destruction – weapons that can be easily concealed, delivered covertly, and used without warning."[39]

Because it rendered the traditional approach to immediacy impractical and risky, this nascent reality led the United States to adopt the doctrine of pre-emption.[40] In the first place, it hardly makes sense for states to assume risk in the irrational hope that negotiations with terrorists might avert a planned attack. Moreover, potential terrorist attacks present an exceptionally high risk because, unlike a state-based attack, there is unlikely to be any advance indication of its location and timing (indeed, absent complete surprise, a terrorist attack enjoys little possibility of success). Thus, terrorist attacks are difficult to either defend against or mitigate (by taking measures such as evacuating the civilian population). Finally, whereas organized military operations previously presented a threat of a greater scale than terrorist attacks, the accessibility of weapons of mass destruction to non-state actors has neutralized the difference. Today, a terrorist attack could result in a level of death and destruction far exceeding that of a conventional military attack.

Since law must always operate with sensitivity to the context in which it applies, the operational code can no longer revolve around temporal proximity to an impending attack. Instead, the post-9/11 code forces an examination of the exis-

---

[39] White House, The National Security Strategy of the United States of America 15 (2002). *See* also Joint Chiefs of Staff, The National Military Strategy (2004); Department of Defense, The National Defense Strategy (2005); White House, National Security Strategy (2006).

[40] The pre-emption was retained in the current U.S. National Security Strategy. 2006 NSS, *id*. On US strategies and international law *see* Michael N. Schmitt, *US Security Strategies: A Legal Assessment*, 27 Harv. J.L. & Pub. Pol'y 737–763 (2004); Michael N. Schmitt, *Preemptive Strategies and International Law*, 24 Mich. J. Int'l L. 513–448 (2003).

tence of options. A perceptive recognition of this shift appeared in the 2004 report of the High Level Panel appointed by the Secretary-General to assess the future of the U.N. system.[41] Although claiming not to reinterpret Article 51, the panel, in describing when it would be inappropriate to act in self-defense, stated that in the face of non-imminent or non-proximate threats, "arguments for *preventive* military action, with good evidence to support them, ... should be put to the Security Council, which can authorize such action if it chooses to. If it does not so choose, there will be, by definition, *time to pursue other strategies*, including persuasion, negotiation, deterrence and containment – and to visit again the military option."[42] Read carefully, it becomes apparent that the amount of time between anticipatory response and pending attack matters less than the existence of alternatives to the use of defensive force. The Panel rejected preventive actions (i.e., actions in the face of only a threat), but not preemptive ones (where the threat has matured into a planned attack that necessitates defensive action).

Thus, a number of conditions precedent must coincide before the right to take forceful action in self-defense crystallizes:

1. The prospective attacker must be reasonably believed to have *ability* to conduct an armed attack;
2. The prospective attacker must be reasonably believed to have the *intent* to conduct an attack;
3. Non-forceful *alternatives* to deter an attack must be exhausted or unavailable; and
4. Defensive action represents the *last chance* to mount an effective defense against an armed attack.

In other words, self-defense is permissible only in the last window of opportunity a state has to effectively defend itself against an attack that is highly likely to occur.

Note that the knowledge criterion is expressed in terms of a reasonable belief that a terrorist group is going to conduct *an* attack (or attacks), not a particular attack. To impose a more stringent knowledge requirement would deprive a state of any meaningful opportunity to defend itself against terrorism. After all, secrecy plays a seminal role in virtually all terrorist planning; indeed, a terrorist will cancel any attack he believes may have been compromised.

This approach would, in certain circumstances, permit targeted killings well in advanced of a planned terrorist strike. Terrorists operate in a difficult to penetrate shadowy world. Yet, mere membership in a terrorist group usually suffices as evidence of a terrorist's intention to conduct attacks. That is the organization's

---

[41] United Nations, A More Secure World: Our Shared Responsibility, Report of the High Level Panel on Threats, Challenges and Change (Dec. 2, 2004).
[42] *Id.* para. 190 (emphasis added).

foundational purpose. Further, terrorist attacks are difficult to effectively defend against at the time of attack because their location and timing are seldom known in advance. These factors coalesces into the reality that when a state gets a known terrorist in the cross-hairs, it may well represent the last opportunity to foil future attacks. Of course, the state's conclusion that it must act immediately should be based on a reasonable assessment of the evidence and no reasonably available and viable options may still exist.

The immediacy criterion of self-defense also affects when defensive operations may be mounted following an attack. At a certain point, based on the circumstances, a response is so remote that it is less defensive than retaliatory. But terrorism operates in a different dynamic than state-on-state conflict. While, a significant peaceful period following hostilities suggests the return to non-violent (albeit perhaps not friendly) relations between states previously at war, the same logic does not apply to terrorists. Since a terrorist group's purpose is to conduct violent attacks, it will typically disband once it no longer harbors such an intention (or transform itself into a political organization that seeks to engage in non-violent political processes).[43]

This logic leads to a dramatic simplification of the immediacy criterion. Once a terrorist group has conducted its first attack (thereby demonstrating ability and intent), it has effectively launched a "campaign" that negates the need to apply the immediacy criterion to future attacks. The victim state does not know where or when future attacks will take place, but it does know, by virtue of the existence of a group formed to conduct them, that attacks will be attempted. Restated, since states exist for purposes other than conducting hostilities, it may not be necessarily assumed that an individual armed attack is but one in a series of attacks constituting an on-going campaign. By contrast, with transnational terrorist organizations that is the only logical conclusion to be drawn from the group's continued post-attack existence. This being so, immediacy will seldom serve as an obstacle to a post-terrorist attack targeted killing of a terrorist.

The final major issue regarding defensive targeted killings involves when they can be conducted in another state's territory (operations on one's own territory were dealt with *supra* in the section on law enforcement). By the principle of necessity, if state authorities where the terrorists are located (sanctuary state) can effectively arrest them or otherwise foil future attacks, and they are willing to do so, a defensive targeted killing by the victim state would be unlawful. If the sanctuary state cannot effectively mount such an operation, then it should consent to a targeted killing of the terrorist on their territory executed by the victim-state (assuming lesser means of neutralizing them are not viable). The paradigmatic example is the 2002

---

[43] As in, some claim, Hamas and the Irish Republican Army. However, such transformations are exceedingly rare; it would be reasonable to impose a rebuttable presumption that a terrorist organization had not become purely political.

CIA-operated Predator strike against Al-Qaeda operative Qaed Senyan al-Harthi in Yemen, which was conducted with the cooperation of Yemeni intelligence.[44]

More complex legally is the situation where a sanctuary state cannot or does not take action to neutralize the threat and does not grant permission to the victim state to mount operations on its territory. Territorial inviolability is one of the foundational principles of international law; it is enshrined in Article 2(4)'s prohibition on the use of force,[45] which the International Court of Justice has labeled a cornerstone of the Charter.[46] On the other hand, the victim state's right of self-defense is equally weighty.

The collision of two rights in international law need not present an either-or dilemma. Rather, a fair accommodation of the underlying purposes of each is preferred, at least when possible. An appropriate balancing in this situation would first require the victim state to demand that the sanctuary state police its territory. Ensuring one's territory is not used to the detriment of other States is a legal duty of long-standing, famously set forth by John Basset Moore in the 1927 Permanent Court of International Justice case *The S.S. Lotus*: "It is well settled that a State is bound to use due diligence to prevent the commission within its domain of criminal acts against another nation or its people."[47] The International Court of Justice addressed the issue in its very first case, *Corfu Channel*, holding that Albania bore responsibility for the presence of mines in the channel that struck two British warships transiting the strait in innocent passage.[48] The British subsequently swept Corfu Channel over Albanian objections. Although the Court found the action improper because "respect for territorial integrity is an essential foundation of international relations," it held that Albania's "failure to carry out its duties after the explosions, and the dilatory nature of its diplomatic notes" were "extenuating

---

[44] *Profile: Ali Qued Senyan al Harthi*, BBC News World Report, Nov. 5, 2002, *available at* news.bbc.co.uk/2/hi/middle_eat/2404443.stm (last visited May 13, 2007); Dworkin, *supra* note 4.

[45] *See also* Declaration on Principles of International Law Concerning Friendly Relations and Cooperation Among States in Accordance with the Charter of the United Nations: "Every State has a duty to refrain in its international relations from the threat or use of force against the territorial integrity or political independence of any State, or in any other manner inconsistent with the purposes of the United Nations. Such a threat or use of force constitutes a violation of international law and the Charter of the United Nations and shall never be employed as a means of settling international issues." G.A. Res. 2625 (XXV), U.N. GAOR, 25th Sess., Supp. No. 28, at 121, U.N. Doc. A/8028 (1970). The resolution was adopted by acclamation.

[46] Case Concerning Armed Activities on the Territory of the Congo (Democratic Republic of the Congo v. Uganda), Judgment (Dec. 19, 2005), I.C.J. Rep. 2005, para. 148.

[47] S.S. Lotus (France v. Turkey) 1927 P.C.I.J. (ser. A) No. 10, at 4, 8 (Moore, J. dissenting on other grounds). In support, Moore cited the U.S. Supreme Court case United States v. Arjona, 120 U.S. 479 (1887).

[48] Corfu Channel Case (U.K. v. Albania), Merits, (Apr. 9, 1949) 1949 I.C.J. Rep. 4.

circumstances."[49] Thus, *Corfu Channel* highlights both the duty to police one's territory and the fact that the right of territorial integrity is conditional.[50]

The Security Council has spoken to the issue as well. The most significant and unambiguous example, Resolution 1373, came in the aftermath of the September 11th attacks. It required States to

> [t]ake the necessary steps to prevent the commission of terrorist acts, including by provision of early warning to other States by exchange of information; [d]eny safe haven to those who finance, plan, support, or commit terrorist acts, or provide safe havens; and [p]revent those who finance, plan, facilitate or commit terrorist acts from using their respective territories for those purposes against other States or other citizens.[51]

Numerous soft law instruments also apply the duty directly to situations involving terrorism. The 1954 Draft Code of Offences against the Peace and Security of Mankind characterizes "[t]he organization, or the encouragement of the organization, by the authorities of a state, of armed bands within its territory or any other territory for incursions into the territory of another state, or the toleration of the use by such bands in its own territory, or the toleration of the use by such armed bands of its territory as a base of operations or as a point of departure for incursions into the territory of another State" as an offence against "the peace and security of mankind."[52] The General Assembly echoed this prescription in its 1970 Declaration on Principles of International Law of International Law Concerning Friendly Relations and Co-operation among States in accordance with the Charter of the United Nations[53] and the 1994 Declaration on Measures to Eliminate Terrorism.[54]

Thus, both the victim state's right of self-defense and the sanctuary state's duty to police its territory temper the latter's right of territorial integrity. Combined, they permit the non-consensual penetration of sanctuary state territory to conduct defensive operations, including targeted killings.

However, since the right of territorial integrity remains intact, the victim state's right to mount such operations is limited. Before any intrusion, the victim state must demand compliance by the sanctuary state with its policing obligations, giving it sufficient time to fulfill them. Defensive realities drive sufficiency. For instance, if a key terrorist operative might evade capture unless immediate defensive targeting

---

[49] *Id.* at 22, 57.

[50] Especially since the right of innocent passage pales beside the right of self-defense in legal gravitas.

[51] S.C. Res. 1373, *supra* note 27.

[52] Draft Code of Offences against the Peace and Security of Mankind, [1954] 2 Y.B. Int'l L. Comm. 150, U.N. Doc. A/CN.4/SER/A/1954/Add.1.

[53] GA Res. 2625 (XXV), UU.N. Doc. A/8028 (1971) (Oct. 24, 1970).

[54] Declaration on Measures to Eliminate International Terrorism, paras 4–5, Annex to G.A. Res. 49/60, U.N. Doc. A/RES/49/60, at 5(a) (Dec. 9, 1994).

occurs, there may not be enough time to notify the sanctuary state and allow it to launch its own operations. On the other hand, if a terrorist training camp is being operated on sanctuary state territory, there will likely be ample time to notify the sanctuary state and give it the opportunity to act.

State practice illustrates the norm. Indeed, the foundational case in the law of self-defense presented exactly such a scenario. In the *Caroline* incident, the British government repeatedly asked the United States to put an end to use of its territory by insurgents during the 1837 Mackenzie Rebellion. Only when the United States failed to act did British forces cross into the United States to capture and destroy the ship, which was used to support the rebels.

More recently, Operation Enduring Freedom was preceded not only by post-9/11 US demands on the Taliban to cooperate in eradicating the al-Qaeda presence in Afghanistan,[55] but also by three years of Security Council pre-9/11 demands to do so.[56] Operation Change Direction, the Israeli defensive strike against Hezbollah in 2006, was likewise preceded, over some six years, by both Security Council and Israeli demands that the Lebanese armed forces move south into territory from which Hezbollah was attacking Israel.[57] Whether the Lebanese Army lacked the wherewithal to control southern Lebanon or simply decided not to, Israel had undeniably afforded Lebanon sufficient time to act before conducting its own counter-terrorist operations. When it did, criticism was less about the fact that Israel had acted than about how.[58]

If a sanctuary State either cannot act or does not act within a reasonable period following demands it meet its international obligations, extraterritorial counter-terrorist operations into its territory are permissible, including targeted killings. As they are based in the law of self-defense, the necessity, proportionality, and immediacy criteria bound all aspects of the ensuing actions. Applied to the operation as a whole, they require that any intrusion into a third states territory be limited in scale and scope to that required to end the imminent threat posed by the terrorists and that forces withdraw as soon as that goal is achieved. Targeted

---

[55] Address before a Joint Session of the Congress of the United States, Response to the Terrorist Attacks of September 11, 37 Weekly Compilation of Presidential Documents 1347, 1347 (Sept. 20, 2001); President's Radio Address, 37 Weekly Compilation of Presidential Documents 1429, 1430 (Oct. 6, 2001).

[56] S.C. Res. 1193, U.N. Doc. S/RES/1193 (1998) (Aug. 28, 1998); S.C. Res. 1214, U.N. Doc. S/RES/1214 (1998) (Dec. 8, 1998); S.C. Res. 1267, U.N. Doc. S/RES/1267 (1999) (Oct. 15, 1999); S.C. Res. 1333, U.N. Doc. S/RES/1333 (2000) (Dec. 19, 2000); S.C. Res. 1363, U.N. Doc. S/RES/1363 (2001) (July 31, 2001).

[57] *See*, e.g., S.C. Res. 1680 (2006) (May 17, 2006); S.C. Res. 1655 (2006) (Jan. 31, 2006); S.C. Res. 1583 (2005) (Jan. 28, 2005); S.C. Res. 1559 (2004) (Sept. 2. 2004); S.C. Res. 1310 (2000) (July 27, 2000).

[58] Statement of Secretary-General to Security Council, U.N. Doc. S/PV.5492 (July 20, 2006).

killings consistent with the restrictions described earlier in this article, and meeting the overall necessity, proportionality, and immediacy constraints of the operation within which they occur, are lawful.

4. *Targeted Killings During Armed Conflicts*

The third normative scenario in which targeted killings may occur is "armed conflict," a legal term of art. The existence of an armed conflict negates the requirement for the *jus ad bellum* "proportionality" and "necessity" analyses that apply in situations short of armed conflict.[59] Rather, as will be discussed, the mere status of an individual as either a combatant or direct participant in hostilities renders him targetable.

Once violence rises to the level of "armed conflict," international humanitarian law applies. Armed conflicts may be either international or non-international. However, with regard to the law governing targeted killings, the distinction is not determinative, for the customary law of targeting is, in relevant part, identical in both forms of conflict. There is, however, a debate within the international law community over whether human rights law applies during armed conflict, and if so to what extent.[60] Assuming *arguendo* that it does, the *lex specialis*, IHL, determines the arbitrariness of an individual "deprivation of life" through targeted killing; thus, whether it applies or not, there is no difference in practical result.

The law governing the attack of individuals derives from the core principle of distinction. Article 48 AP I restates the customary norm applicable in both international and non-international armed conflict: "In order to ensure respect for and protection of the civilian population and civilian objects, the Parties to the conflict shall at all times distinguish between the civilian population and combatants and between civilian objects and military objectives and accordingly shall direct their operations only against military objectives."[61] Article 51(2), equally a restatement

---

[59] Note that the terms proportionality and necessity were previously used in their *jus ad bellum* context. Confusedly, they exist in international humanitarian law with a completely different meaning.

[60] Palestinian Wall, *supra* note 32, para. 106; see also Nicaragua Case, *supra* note 24, para. 25.

[61] Protocol Additional to the Geneva Conventions of August 12, 1949, and Relating to the Protection of Victims of International Armed Conflicts, June 8, 1977, article 48, 1125 U.N.T.S. 3 (entered into force Dec. 7, 1978) [hereinafter AP I]. In the Nuclear Weapons Advisory Opinion, the International Court of Justice recognized distinction as one of two "cardinal" principles of the law of armed conflict, the other being unnecessary suffering. Nuclear Weapons, *supra* note 36, para. 78. For treaty law in non-international armed conflict, *see* Geneva Convention Relative to the Treatment to Prisoners of War, Aug. 12, 1949, article 3, 75 U.N.T.S. 135, 136 [hereinafter GC III] (each of the four 1949 Geneva Conventions contains the identical article) [CA3]; Protocol Additional to the Geneva Conventions of 12 August 1949, and relating to the Protection of Victims of Non-International Armed Conflicts (Protocol II), June 8, 1977, Article 13, 1125 U.N.T.S. 609 [hereinafter AP II]. For customary law restatements, *see* Jean-Marie Henckaerts & Louise

of customary law in both international and non-international armed conflict, operationalizes the general principle for individuals: "The civilian population as such, as well as individual civilians, shall not be the object of attack."[62]

By mandating distinction between civilians and combatants, and extending protection from attack to the former, the principle implicitly permits the targeting of combatants, either as individuals or in groups. In international armed conflict, combatancy is often defined by reference to Article 4 GC III, which deals with entitlement to prisoner of war status. Combatants include members of the armed forces, militias and other volunteer corps that; 1) are commanded by person responsible for the conduct of subordinates; 2) dress in a manner allowing them to be distinguished from civilians; 3) carry weapons openly; and 4) conduct operations in accordance with the laws and customs of war.[63]

Critics of this approach note that Article 4 only identifies those eligible for prisoner of war status, not those susceptible to lawful attack.[64] They prefer reference to the express definition found in Article 43 AP I:

1. The armed forces of a Party to a conflict consist of all organized armed forces, groups and units which are under a command responsible to that Party for the conduct or its subordinates, even if that Party is represented by a government or an authority not recognized by an adverse Party. Such armed forces shall be subject to an internal disciplinary system which, inter alia, shall enforce compliance with the rules of international law applicable in armed conflict.
2. Members of the armed forces of a Party to a conflict (other than medical personnel and chaplains covered by Article 33 of the Third Convention) are combatants, that is to say, they have the right to participate directly in hostilities.[65]

Doswald-Beck, Customary International Humanitarian Law (Vol. 1, 2005), Rule 1 [hereinafter CIHL].; Michael N. Schmitt, Charles H.B. Garraway, & Yoram Dinstein, The Manual on the Law of Non-International Armed Conflict: With Commentary (2006), para. 1.2.2., *reprinted in* 36 Isr. Y.B. Hum. Rts. (2006) (Special Supplement) [NIAC]. In *Tadić*, the International Criminal Tribunal for Yugoslavia Appeals Chamber also found the principle of distinction to be customary law in non-international armed conflict. Prosecutor v. Tadic, Decision on The Defense Motion For Interlocutory Appeal on Jurisdiction, Appeals Chamber, Case IT-94-1 (Oct. 2, 1995), paras. 122, 127.

[62] AP I, *supra* note 61, Article 51(2). *See also* CA3, *supra* note 61; CIHL, *supra* note 61, Rule 6; NIAC, *supra* note 61, 2.1.1.1.
[63] GC III, *supra* note 61, Article 4. *See also* Hague Convention Respecting the Laws and Customs of War on Land, with Annex of Regulations, Oct. 18, 1907, 36 Stat. 2277; T.S. 539; The Geneva Convention for the Amelioration of the Condition of the Wounded and Sick in Armed Forces in the Field, Aug. 12, 1949, Article 13, 75 U.N.T.S. 31, 32 [hereinafter GC I]; Geneva Convention for the Amelioration of the Condition of the Wounded, Sick and Shipwrecked Members of the Armed Forces at Sea, Aug. 12, 1949, Article 13, 75 U.N.T.S. 85, 86 [hereinafter GC II].
[64] *See* Melzner, *supra* note 9, at 392–393.
[65] The ICRC's Customary International Humanitarian Law Study adopts this approach. CIHL, *supra* note 61, Rules 3–5.

The difference between the two approaches affects whether individuals complying with Article 43 standards but not those of Article 4 enjoy combatant immunity and prisoner of war status, but has little bearing on their targetability. This is because advocates of the Article 4 approach characterize someone meeting only Article 43's standards as a targetable "unlawful combatant." Therefore, to the extent that an individual meets the Article 43 threshold of being a member of organized armed forces under command responsible to a Party, he will be fully targetable either as a combatant or as an unlawful combatant, depending on one's perspective.

In non-international armed conflict, the notion of combatants makes little sense. Recall that combatancy entitles members of the armed forces to immunity for their (lawful) hostile acts and prisoner of war status. Neither applies to rebels in a non-international armed conflict; no law sanctions their use of force and upon capture they are treated as criminals under domestic law. Some scholars and practitioners have therefore adopted the term "fighters" to distinguish rebel forces from civilians.[66] But despite these differences, targeting principles are constant in both international and non-international armed conflict. Both combatants in international armed conflict and members of dissident armed groups in non-international armed conflict (who are not *hors de combat* or otherwise specifically protected and regardless of the position they occupy in the chain of command) may be attacked throughout the duration of an armed conflict.

Instead, differences of opinion exist over the targeting of other than combatants or members of dissident armed groups. The legality of such actions depends on whether the targets are direct participants in hostilities. With regards to international armed conflict, Article 53(3) AP I, sets forth the norm, one accepted as customary: "Civilians shall enjoy the protection afforded by this section, unless and for such time as they take a direct part in hostilities."[67] An analogous norm applies in non-international armed conflict. Common Article 3 to the four 1949 Geneva Conventions prohibits violence against "[p]ersons taking no active part in the hostilities," while Article 13(3) AP I, provides civilians protection "unless and for such time as they take a direct part in hostilities." There is no substantive distinction between the terms "active" and "direct" in the context of participation.[68]

A civilian who directly participates in hostilities thereby loses his protection from direct attack and becomes individually targetable. But what acts rise to the level of direct participation? As a general matter, direct participation must be distinguished from mere participation in the war effort. The former includes such activities as

---

[66] NIAC, *supra* note 61, para. 1.1.2. The ICRC retains the term "combatants."
[67] CIHLS *supra* note 61, Rule 6.
[68] The International Criminal Tribunal for Rwanda has correctly opined that the terms "active" and "direct", as used with reference to participation in hostilities, are synonymous. The Prosecutor v. Akayesu, Case No. ICTR-96-4-T (1998), para. 629.

attacking the enemy, its materiel or facilities; sabotaging enemy installations; acting as members of a gun crew or artillery spotters; delivering ammunition; or gathering military intelligence in the area of hostilities. It would not include, general contributions to the war effort, such as soliciting contributions, conducting media campaigns or engaging in political decision-making related to the conflict (e.g., a parliamentarian who votes for funding of the war effort).

Difficult cases lie between these extremes. The official ICRC *Commentary* to Additional Protocol I explains that "[d]irect participation in hostilities implies a direct causal relationship between the activity engaged in and the harm done to the enemy at the time and place where the activity takes place."[69] It goes on to describe direct participation as "acts which by their nature and purpose are intended to cause actual harm to the personnel and equipment of the armed forces."[70] Similarly, the commentary to AP II notes that in non-international armed conflict the notion of direct participation "implies that there is a sufficient casual relationship between the act of participation and its immediate consequences."[71]

Scholars and practitioners differ over how such descriptions play out in individual cases.[72] The best approach assesses the criticality of the civilian's actions to the direct application of violence against the enemy forces.[73] As suggested elsewhere:

> [T]he civilian must have engaged in an action that he knew would harm (or otherwise disadvantage) the enemy in a relatively direct and immediate way. The participation must have been part of the process by which a particular use of force was rendered possible, either through preparation or execution. It is not necessary that the individual foresaw the eventual result of the operation, but only that he knew their participation was indispensable to a discrete hostile act or series of related acts.[74]

This standard would encompass, for instance, those who direct, plan, and execute acts of violence; provide key logistical support, such as transportation of weapons and explosives to the battlefield (or place of attack); offer sanctuary to those executing an attack immediately preceding an attack; hide attackers immediately after an attack; gather, analyze, and disseminate tactical or operational level intelligence; and provide communications services for an attack. It would also extend to

---

[69] Commentary on the Additional Protocols of 8 June 1977 to the Geneva Conventions of 12 August 1949 (Yves Sandoz, Christophe Swinarski and Bruno Zimmerman eds., 1987), para. 1678.
[70] *Id.* para. 1942.
[71] *Id.* para. 4787.
[72] The TMC Asser Institute and the ICRC have sponsored a number of expert meetings to explore the subject. Reports thereof are at www.icrc.org/Web/eng/siteeng0.nsf/html/participation-hostilities-ihl-311205.
[73] Michael N. Schmitt, *Humanitarian Law and Direct Participation in Hostilities by Private Contractors or Civilian Employees*, 5 Chi. J. Int'l L. 511, 534–535 (2005).
[74] *Id.* At 533.

civilian leaders who engage in direct participation, for instance by ordering specific military missions.[75]

A second issue presented by direct participation surrounds the meaning of the "unless and for such time" phrase. The commentary to Article 53(3) AP I notes that several delegations felt that direct participation includes "preparations for combat and the return from combat," but that "[o]nce he ceases to participate, the civilian regains his right to the protection."[76] The Additional Protocol II commentary similarly provides that the direct participant loses protection "for as long as his participation lasts. Thereafter, as he no longer presents any danger for the adversary, he may not be attacked."[77] Such explanations have led to what is known as the "revolving door" debate. In other words, does the law permit a civilian to be a guerrilla by night and a farmer by day by "passing through the door"?

Although some argue it does, a rule that a person, having attacked the other side and intending to engage in further such attacks in the future, can acquire immunity from attack simply by making it home would seem counter-intuitive. Many attacks are carried out without much opportunity for the party attacked to engage the attacker. A contemporary example is the use of roadside bombs. In such cases, the only opportunity to strike the attacker may come once he has returned home, or has been located using means, such as telephone intercepts.

The only operationally reasonable interpretation of the "for such time" phrase is treating the direct participant as a valid military objective until he unambiguously opts out through extended nonparticipation or an affirmative act of withdrawal. Although it may be difficult to determine when the direct participant has ceased participating, it is reasonable to impose any risk of mistake on him; after all, he participated with no right to do so. Lawful combatants who enjoy a privilege to participate should not be required to (illogically) assume that an individual who has previously attacked them has opted out of the fight simply because he is not active at the moment.

Once it has been determined that an individual may be attacked because he is a combatant (international armed conflict), fighter (non-international armed conflict), or direct participant (both), an attacker must comply with additional requirements governing all attacks. The first is *jus in bello* principle of proportionality, not to be confused with the *jus ad bellum* proportionality principle in the law of self-defense. The principle, customary law in both international and non-international armed conflicts and codified in AP I, prohibits as indiscriminate

---

[75] On the issue of targeting leadership, *see* Michael N. Schmitt, *Fault Lines in the Law of Attack*, in Testing the Boundaries of International Humanitarian Law 277, 286–290 (Susan Breau & Agnieszka Jachec-Neale eds., 2006).
[76] Commentary, *supra* note 69, paras 1943–44.
[77] *Id.* para. 4789.

"an attack which may be expected to cause incidental loss of civilian life, injury to civilians, damage to civilian objects, or a combination thereof, which would be excessive in relation to the concrete and direct military advantage anticipated."[78] Therefore, even if the individual in question may lawfully be targeted, the harm that would likely result to civilians and civilian objects (incidental injury and collateral damage respectively) during the attack may not be excessive in relation to what the attacker hopes to achieve military by killing him.

One must be cautious in applying this rule to targeted killings. Such attacks are often unsuccessful, as in all 50 of those conducted during Operation Iraqi Freedom, many of those launched in Afghanistan during Operation Enduring Freedom, and the failed attempts to kill Slobodan Milosevic during Operation Allied Force. An unsuccessful attack (i.e., one yielding no military advantage) that injures or kills civilians or damages or destroys civilian objects does not necessarily violate the proportionality norm (as critics sometimes appear to believe).[79] Rather, the legal questions are: 1) what did the attackers reasonably *expect* to achieve militarily if the attack was successful, and 2) what harm to civilians and civilian property did the attackers reasonably *expect* the attack to cause in the circumstances prevailing at the time?

Assuming the attacker sensibly concludes that the targeted killing will not result in excessive incidental injury and collateral damage, a second grouping of preconditions applies – precautions in attack. Most are considered customary. Article 57 AP I, which codifies them, provides, in relevant part:

1. With respect to attacks, the following precautions shall be taken:
    (a) those who plan or decide upon an attack shall:
        (i) do everything feasible to verify that the objectives to be attacked are neither civilians nor civilian objects and are not subject to special protection but are military objectives within the meaning of paragraph 2 of Article 52 and that it is not prohibited by the provisions of this Protocol to attack them;
        (ii) take all feasible precautions in the choice of means and methods of attack with a view to avoiding, and in any event to minimizing, incidental loss of civilian life, injury to civilians and damage to civilian objects;
        (iii) refrain from deciding to launch any attack which may be expected to cause incidental loss of civilian life, injury to civilians, damage to civilian objects, or a combination thereof, which would be excessive in relation to the concrete and direct military advantage anticipated;
    (b) an attack shall be cancelled or suspended if it becomes apparent that the objective is not a military one or is subject to special protection or that the attack

---

[78] Protocol I, *supra* note 61, Articles 51, 57. *See also* CIHL, *supra* note 61, Rules 14, 19; NIAC, *supra* note 61, para. 2.1.1.4.

[79] *See* generally discussion in Michael N. Schmitt, *Conduct of Hostilities during Operational Iraqi Freedom: An International Humanitarian Law Assessment*, 6 Y.B. Int'l Hum. L. 73 (2003).

may be expected to cause incidental loss of civilian life, injury to civilians, damage to civilian objects, or a combination thereof, which would be excessive in relation to the concrete and direct military advantage anticipated;

(c) effective advance warning shall be given of attacks which may affect the civilian population, unless circumstances do not permit.

...

3. When a choice is possible between several military objectives for obtaining a similar military advantage, the objective to be selected shall be that the attack on which may be expected to cause the least danger to civilian lives and to civilian objects.

Applied to targeted killings, these prescriptive norms require the attacker to use all reasonably available human and technical assets to both verify that the target is who the attacker believes him to be and to assess likely collateral damage and incidental injury that the strike might cause. An attacker is not required to exhaust only those verification capabilities that make operational sense in the circumstances. Planners must also select the target, choose the weapons (means)[80] and employ the tactics (methods)[81] likely to cause the least incidental injury or collateral damage, although he need only select from among those yielding a comparable likelihood of mission success. They need not consider any which would decrease likelihood of success to an operationally unacceptable level (a determination often driven by the importance of the individual targeted). Of course, if, as the attack is underway, an attacker realizes that it will cause excessive collateral damage and incidental injury, he must cancel the attack (or modify it). Typically, this occurs when the attacker observes unexpected civilians in the target area. Lastly, although there is a requirement to warn the civilian population of an impending attack, the "unless circumstances do not permit" escape clause will usually negate the need to do so in a targeted killing since advance notice would guarantee the absence of the target.

Targeted killings conducted during an armed conflict pursuant to IHL are limited to the territory of the belligerents and the high seas.[82] A neutral state bears responsibility under the law of neutrality for ensuring belligerents do not base operations from their territory or use it as a sanctuary.[83] Should it nevertheless so be used, the opposing belligerent must, time and circumstances permitting, demand that the neutral act to put an end to its enemy's use of neutral territory. Only if the neutral cannot or does not comply with this legitimate demand may the belligerent conduct operations to put an end to the misuse of neutral territory. The scope and nature of such operations must reflect that purpose. In a sense,

---

[80] E.g., unguided weapon, guided weapon, weapons of differing explosive force, air launched weapon, ground-based weapon, ground troops, etc.

[81] E.g., altitude of attack, direction of attack, time of attack, location of attack, etc.

[82] Hague Convention (V) Respecting the Rights and Duties of Neutral Powers and Persons in Case of War on Land, Article 1, 36 Stat. 2310 (1907). Hague V is considered largely declaratory of customary international law.

[83] *Id.* Article 5.

therefore, belligerent operations into neutral territory operate analogously to the self-defense operations into third states discussed *supra*.

Recently, targeted killings during armed conflict have been subjected to judicial scrutiny in Israel. Among the tactics employed by the Israelis to counter terrorism is "the policy of targeted frustration," in which "security forces act in order to kill members of terrorist organizations involved in the planning, launching, or execution of terrorist attacks against Israel."[84] Israel also refers to targeted killings as "preventative strikes."

In December 2006, the Israeli Supreme Court, sitting as the High Court of Justice, issued its decision in *The Public Committee against Torture* v. *Israel*, the first direct judicial treatment of targeted killings,[85] Court President (emeritus) Aharon Barak wrote the lead opinion in the case (with which Vice President Eliezer Rivlin and President Dorit Beinisch concurred). Although its characterization of the conflict as international is questionable,[86] the analysis of the application of IHL to targeted killings during an armed conflict is incisive.

Barak focused on the status of those targeted in an approach similar to that set forth *supra*. He began by exploring whether individuals belonging to the terrorist groups against which Israel is fighting qualify as combatants under the classic Article 4 formula (which is also contained in The Hague Regulations of 1907 and the First and Second Geneva Conventions).[87] They do not, their failure to conduct "operations in accordance with the laws and customs of war" representing the most glaring departure from the requirements.[88]

If they are not combatants, are they "civilians"? Barak adopts the traditional view that there are but two customary law categories of actors during an international armed conflict – combatants and civilians. The Israeli government asserted that a third category, unlawful combatants, exists, one consisting of those individuals who "take an active and continuous part in an armed conflict, and therefore should be treated as combatants."[89] Many scholars and practitioners, as well as the United States government, support the existence of the third category.[90] However, Barak,

---

[84] Public Committee, *supra* note 8, para. 2.
[85] *Id.*
[86] *Id.*, sec. A. *See also* HCJ 9293/01 Barake v. The Minister of Defense, 56(2) PD 509; HCJ 3114/02 Barake v. The Minister of Defense 56(3) PD 11; HCJ 3451/02 Almandi v. The Minister of Defense, 56(3) PD 30; Ajuri v. The Military Commander of the Judea and Samaria Area, 56(6) PD 352, 358.
[87] *See* fn 63 *supra* and accompanying text.
[88] After all, the *modus operandi* of such organizations is to attack civilians and civilian property, violations of the "cardinal" distinction principle.
[89] Public Committee, *supra* note 8, para. 27.
[90] *See*, e.g., Yoram Dinstein, The Conduct of Hostilities under the Law of International Armed Conflict (2004), at ch. 2 [hereinafter Dinstein]; Military Commissions Act, sec. 948a, PL 109–336, 120 Stat. 2600, Oct. 17, 2006.

noting that "[t]he question before us is not one of desirable law, rather one of existing law," rejects the assertion, finding it "difficult...to see how a third category can be recognized in the framework of the Geneva and Hague Conventions."[91] For him, such individuals are "civilians who are unlawful combatants."

Civilians or not, they are legally susceptible to attack. The decision turned on the notion of direct participation. It found the principle (codified in Article 53 of AP I) that civilians who directly participate in hostilities forfeit their protection from direct attack to constitute customary international law. The Barak opinion expressly endorses the ICRC's Customary International Humanitarian Law Study's assertion to that effect.[92] It further cites Common Article 3's grant of protection to those "taking no active part in hostilities"; the Statute of the International Criminal Court's criminalization of attacks on civilians not taking a direct part in hostilities;[93] the International Tribunal for the Former Yugoslavia's holding in *Strugar* that Article 51 restated customary international law;[94] and inclusion of the norm in such military manuals as those of England, France, Holland, Austria, Italy, Canada, Germany, the United States, and New Zealand.[95]

In analyzing direct participation, Barak first addresses its scope, usefully reminding readers that participation includes "hostilities against the civilian population of the state."[96] Barak then distinguishes between direct and indirect participation, since IHL only strips civilians engaged in the former of their protection. No accepted articulation of the distinction exists. Although some commentators have argued for a narrow interpretation of "direct," hoping to protect as many individuals as possible from attack, Barak implicitly rejects this simplistic approach, citing a more sophisticated rationale for adopting a liberal approach.

> Gray areas should be interpreted liberally, i.e., in favor of finding direct participation. One of the seminal purposes of the law is to make possible a clear distinction between civilians and combatants. Suggesting that civilians retain their immunity

---

[91] Public Committee, *supra* note 8, para. 28. It should be noted that Vice President Rivlin was somewhat hesitant about dismissing the possibility of a third category, citing, in particular, the work of Professor Yoram Dinstein on the subject (Dinstein, *supra* note 90, at 29–30). However, he did not find the issue determinative because, by Barak's approach, the "unlawful combatant" can be targeted as a direct participant. Rivlin concurrence, para. 2.

[92] CIHL, *supra* note 61, Rule 6.

[93] Rome Statute of the International Criminal Court, July 17, 1998, Article 8(2)(b)(i)–(ii), 2187 U.N.T.S. 3 [hereinafter ICC Statute].

[94] Prosecutor v. Strugar, Trial Chamber Decision on Jurisdiction, Case No. IT-01-42-T, (June 7, 2002), paras 17–21; Strugar, Appeals Chamber Decision on Jurisdiction, Case No. IT-01-42-T, (Nov. 22, 2002), para. 9. *See also* Prosecutor v. Tadic, Appeals Chamber Decision on Jurisdiction, Case No. IT-94-1, (Oct. 2, 1995), para. 127; Prosecutor v. Blaskic, Appeals Chamber Judgement, Case No. IT-95-14, (July 29, 2004), paras 157–158.

[95] Public Committee, *supra* note 8, para. 30.

[96] *Id.* para. 33.

even when they are intricately involved in a conflict is to engender disrespect for the law by combatants endangered by their activities. Moreover, a liberal approach creates an incentive for civilians to remain as distant from the conflict as possible – in doing so they can better avoid being charged with participation in the conflict and are less liable to being directly targeted.[97]

Activities that qualify include collecting intelligence; transporting combatants to and from the hostilities; operating weapons, supervising their operation, or controlling their use, even if distant from the "battlefield"; transporting ammunition; serving as voluntary human shields; and planning, ordering, and directing hostilities. Those not qualifying include expressing sympathy for hostilities without participating in them, selling food or medicine to unlawful combatants, failing to prevent an incursion by one of the parties, offering general strategic analysis to combatants, distributing propaganda and granting monetary aid.

On the temporal aspect of direct participation, the Israeli Government argued that the "for such time" text in Article 51(3) was not customary. Although the Court as a whole disagreed, Barak's opinion interprets the article in the manner suggested *supra*, thereby locking the revolving door, a result palatable to the Government. He swiftly dispenses with the easy case, that of an individual who participates on a single occasion or only very sporadically. Once that individual is no longer participating and is unambiguously detached from hostilities, civilian protection returns. Barak also quickly, but correctly, dismisses the more controversial case of the participant who is a member of a group of illegal combatants.

> [A] civilian who has joined a terrorist organization which has become his "home", and in the framework of his role in that organization he commits a chain of hostilities, with short periods of rest between them, loses his immunity from attack 'for such time' as he is committing the chain of acts. Indeed, regarding such a civilian, the rest between hostilities is nothing other than preparation for the next hostility.[98]

Barak suggests this characterization reflects customary international law.

For situations between the extremes, Barak proposes a case-by-case approach. Although not offering a definitive standard, he usefully points out operational factors planners should consider. As required by the precautions in attack norms discussed *supra*, information on which the attack is based must be "most thoroughly verified," specifically as to "the identity and activity of the civilian who is allegedly taking part in the hostilities."[99]

---

[97] *Id.* para. 34, citing Michael N. Schmitt, *Direct Participation in Hostilities and 21st Century Armed Conflict*, in Crisis Management and Humanitarian Protection: Festschrift fur Dieter Fleck 505 (Horst Fischer ed., 2004).
[98] Public Committee, *supra* note 8, para. 39.
[99] *Id.* para. 40.

But then Barak and the Court impose a requirement not based in IHL, that "a civilian taking a direct part in hostilities cannot be attacked at such time as he is doing so, if a less harmful means can be employed."[100] Under IHL, combatants and direct participants may be attacked even if they could be captured, at least as long as they have not surrendered or are otherwise *hors de combat*. In mandating this requirement, the Court looked to the Israeli domestic law principle of proportionality, by which "trial is preferable to the use of force."[101] Since this requirement is Israeli-specific, it need not be adopted by other states engaged in armed conflicts, although, as noted, it applies in situations of domestic targeted killings and targeted killings occurring during operations conducted pursuant to the law of self-defense (falling short of armed conflict).

A third requirement mandated by the decision also derives from domestic policy – performing an *ex post facto* investigation into the "precision of the identification of the target and the circumstances of the attack."[102] While an investigation might be well-advised as a matter of policy during low-intensity conflict, it would generally be impractical to conduct one into every strike executed in a high intensity armed conflict. Instead, IHL only requires investigations into possible war crimes.[103]

The final requirement acknowledged by the Court is that discussed *supra*, proportionality. Civilians are often incidentally injured or killed and civilian property collaterally damaged or destroyed during lawful targeted killings. But only when such consequences, anticipated at the time of planning and execution, qualify as "excessive" does the targeted killing of a combatant or direct participant become prohibited. As Barak notes "[t]he State's duty to protect the lives of its soldiers and civilians must be balanced against its duty to protect the lives of innocent civilians harmed during attacks on terrorists."[104]

5. Conclusion

The subject of "targeted killings" has become highly politicized and emotive. This reality has tended to impede objective assessments of the law governing such strikes. In fact, the relevant international law is rather straight forward.

---

[100] *Id.*
[101] *Id.*
[102] *Id.*
[103] Indeed, by the principle of command responsibility, a commander is criminally responsible for the war crimes of his subordinates if he fails to "submit the matter to the competent authorities for investigation and prosecution." ICC Statute, *supra* note 93, Article 28.
[104] Public Committee, *supra* note 8, para. 46.

Domestic operations must comply with human rights norms that govern all law enforcement activities employing deadly force. In general, such activities are only lawful when necessary to prevent loss of life or grievous injury. Beyond the borders of a state, the international law of self-defense governs strikes directed at specified individuals. The criteria of necessity, proportionality, and immediacy determine whether, when, how, and where a defensive targeted killing may be conducted. Finally, IHL becomes operative once an armed conflict is underway. Pursuant to IHL, only combatants (and members of dissident armed groups) or civilians directly participating in hostilities may be attacked. Although disagreement surrounds several aspects of direct participation, the tactic of targeted killing raises few unique issues in this regard. As with any other attack, a targeted killing must comply with the *jus in bello* principle of proportionality, and those executing the attack must take the requisite precautions in attack. The sole judicial treatment of targeted killings, that by the Israeli Supreme Court in *The Public Committee against Torture*, captures the relevant IHL with precision, as well as appropriate sensitivity to the context in which it applies.

Chapter XXI

Implementing the Concept of Protection of Civilians in the Light of International Humanitarian Law and Human Rights Law: The Case of MONUC

Katarina Månsson*

1. Introduction

When planning for MONUC deployments in the field, do you take into consideration reports by MONUC Human Rights Division in terms of the human rights situation?
  I'm not sure about it, I think there should be, because we have to fulfil our mandate and it is part of that, wherever possible, if we have the capacity to take action in that regard. At [the] least, if we cannot send deployments, we can send patrols for areas just to cover. Because we are here to protect the population.

  You would say that this is your main mandate?
  Yes, to protect the vulnerable populations and to put an end to impunity.[1]

This excerpt from an interview with a military official at MONUC (United Nations Mission in the Democratic Republic of the Congo) Headquarters in Kinshasa highlights the centrality of the concept of protection of civilians in what currently

---

* Katarina Månsson is a doctoral candidate at the Irish Centre for Human Rights, National University of Ireland, Galway. She holds a Master's degree in political science (Lund University, Sweden) and a European Master's Degree in Human Rights and Democratization (EIUC, Italy) and has work experience from the Raoul Wallenberg Institute of Human Rights and Humanitarian Law, the European Commission and the Office of the High Commissioner for Human Rights. The author would like to thank Prof. David Kretzmer, Dr. Ray Murphy and an anonymous reader at the Peacekeeping Best Practices Section of the United Nations Department of Peacekeeping Operations (DPKO) for commenting on earlier drafts of this article. The views expressed herein are solely those of the author who remains responsible for any errors it may contain.
[1] Interview, Human Rights and Civil Affairs Officer, MONUC Force Headquarters, Kinshasa, May 2006.

amounts to the largest U.N. peace operation.[2] It also reflects the increased importance attached to human rights concerns within peace operations, not the least within the military. MONUC was the second U.N. peace operation to be formally mandated, under Chapter VII of the U.N. Charter, to "protect civilians under imminent threat of physical violence."[3] Since then, five U.N.-led peace missions and four operations led by regional organizations have followed suit, authorizing the use of military force to protect civilians.[4]

At a political level, consensus on civilian protection as an inviolable norm in international peace and security-related matters appears undisputed. The "responsibility to protect," in cases of genocide, war crimes, ethnic crimes, and crimes against humanity, was universally acclaimed in the 2005 World Summit.[5] In February 2006, the U.N. Under Secretary-General for Peacekeeping Operations, Mr. Jean-Marie Guéhenno, referred to the protection of civilians as an additional "core principle" of U.N. peacekeeping.[6] This article addresses the latter situation, using MONUC as a case study, with the aim of evoking debate around two controversial issues on which little consensus exist: The practical implementation of the concept of civilian protection ("operationalization") and the legal parameters under international human rights law (HRL) and international humanitarian law (IHL) that imbue such peacekeeping activities. In particular, the article purports at understanding how peacekeeping mandates of protecting civilians may be interpreted in the light of U.N. member states' legal obligations under IHL and HRL. Given the present

---

[2] *See* Democratic Republic of the Congo, MONUC, Facts and Figures (Feb. 2007), *available at* www.un.org/Depts/dpko/missions/monuc/facts/html (last visited Sept. 15, 2007).

[3] The United Nations Mission in Sierra Leone (UNAMSIL) was the first U.N. peace operation to be formally mandated, under Chapter VII, to protect civilians under imminent threat of physical violence. *See* S.C. Res. 1270, U.N. Doc. S/RES/1270 (1999), at 14. MONUC was initially authorized to "protect civilians under imminent threat of physical violence," in the "area of deployment of its infantry battalions and as it deems within its capabilities." S.C. Res. 1291, U.N. Doc. S/RES/1291 (Feb. 24, 2000), at 8. It should be noted, however, that the first U.N. operation in the Congo (ONUC) and its mandate for the protection of law and order was interpreted as authorizing it "to deploy troops to protect civilians when they were threatened by tribal war or violence." Brian Urquhart, Hammarskjold 561 (1972).

[4] The U.N. missions are those in Liberia (UNMIL, U.N. Doc. S/RES/1509 (Sept. 19, 2003) at 3(j)); Côte d'Ivoire (ONUCI, U.N. Doc. S/RES/1528 (May 21, 2004), at 6(i)); Haiti (MINUSTAH, U.N. Doc. S/RES/1542 (April 30, 2004), at 7I(f)); Burundi (ONUBI, U.N. Doc. S/RES/1545 (May 21, 2004), at 5); Sudan (UNMIS, U.N. Doc. S/RES/1590 (March 24, 2005), at 16(i)). *See* Victoria K. Holt & Tobias C. Berkman, The Impossible Mandate? Military Preparedness, the Responsibility to Protect and Modern Peace Operations 87 (2006) [hereinafter Holt & Berkman].

[5] General Assembly, Res. 60/1. 2005 World Summit Outcome, U.N. Doc. A/RES/60/1 (Oct. 24, 2005) para. 139.

[6] Statement addressed by Mr. Guéhenno to the Special Committee on Peacekeeping Operations, (Feb. 27, 2006).

limitations of the article and the ubiquitous complexities of the subject matter at hand, it must thus be read as an explorative exercise during which traditional legal interpretations and approaches may be challenged. Therefore, questions that are raised but left unanswered should be read as deliberate provocations that call for further research and empirical analysis.

For this purpose, the article first addresses the issues of applicability of IHL and HRL to U.N. peace operations and how the protection of civilians' mandate can be understood against these two legal frameworks. Subsequently, it analyses MONUC's operationalization of the concept by focusing on three areas: (i) *protection through respect* for IHL and HRL (peacekeepers' compliance); (ii) *protection through ensuring respect* for such standards by other actors (peacekeepers' influence); and (iii) *protection through "enforcing" respect* for IHL and HRL by other direct action (peacekeepers' activism). While emphasis will necessarily be on military activities, collaborative civil-military arrangements, in particular those between human rights and military actors, will be given special attention.[7]

2. U.N. Peace Operations, International Human Rights Law and International Humanitarian Law

The point of departure for any analysis on the relationship between the United Nations and IHL and HRL must be the Charter of the United Nations. First and foremost, promoting and encouraging respect for human rights is one of the United Nations' main purposes.[8] Secondly, its member states pledge "to take joint and separate action in cooperation with the Organization" for the achievement of that purpose.[9] According to its preamble, member states are determined to "reaffirm faith in fundamental human rights." The drafters of the Charter interpreted the preamble and purposes of the United Nations as its "ideology" and "raison d'être" respectively.[10] It has been suggested that the identification of human rights as a purpose of the United Nations entails a "constitutional requirement" of the

---

[7] This part is informed, *inter alia*, by interviews conducted during field research at MONUC Headquarters in Kinshasa in May 2006. The field research forms an integral part of the author's Ph.D. thesis on the integration of human rights in U.N. peace operations. 28 interviews were conducted with representatives from primarily MONUC Military, Human Rights and Police Divisions.
[8] Article 1(3) U.N. Charter.
[9] Articles 1(3) and 56 (in conjunction with Article 55(c) U.N. Charter.
[10] Verbatim minutes of third meeting of Commission I, U.N. Doc. 1167, I/10 (June 23, 1945), *in* Documents of the United Nations Conference on International Organization, San Francisco, 1945, Volume VI, General Provisions, 16 (1945).

United Nations to integrate human rights in all its activities.[11] In addition, the Charter provides that the adjustment and settlement of international disputes or situations should be conducted "in conformity with the principles of justice and international law."[12]

Taken together, thus, the Charter sets out both positive and negative obligations upon its member states and the Organization itself vis-à-vis human rights and, more broadly, international law. Whereas the Charter contains no explicit provision on peacekeeping, the drafters of the Charter envisaged "three possible varieties of armed force could be used by the Security Council" in order to preserve peace.[13] One was "national contingents under international command."[14] The founders of the Organization thus foresaw the deployment of troops under U.N. command and control as a possible tool by the Security Council to address a threat to or breach of the peace or an act of aggression. France even proposed, but failed, to include a provision that provided that "Nothing contained in this Chapter shall authorize the Organization to intervene in matters which are essentially within the domestic jurisdiction of the State concerned, *unless the clear violation of essential liberties and of human rights constitutes in itself a threat capable of compromising peace...*"[15]

In view of the above and mindful of the fact that the United Nations is a subject of international law, there is no doubt that U.N. peace operations should comply with the rules and principles of IHL and HRL and that they can be responsible for breaches of provisions of its core instruments.[16] Since the *enforcement* and *accountability* of such legal obligations by the United Nations is still wrapped in uncertainties, however, the analysis must also consider obligations of troop contributing member states under the same instruments in order to provide for a meaningful and comprehensive discussion.

---

[11] Karen Kenny, *Fulfilling the Promise of the UN Charter, Transformative Integration of Human Rights*, 10 Irish Studies Int'L Aff. 44 (1999).

[12] Article 1(1) U.N. Charter.

[13] Summary report of second meeting of Committee III/3 (May 7, 1945), U.N. Doc. 140/III/3/4 (May 8, 1949), *in* Documents of the United Nations Conference on International Organization, Volume XII, Commission III, Security Council (1945), at 278.

[14] *Id*.

[15] *See* Suggestions of Participating Governments for the Amendment of Chapter VIII, Section A, of the Dumbarton Oaks Proposals; Together with other Proposed Amendments Bearing on this Section, U.N. Doc. 207, III/2/A/3 (May 10, 1945), *in* Documents on the U.N. Conference, Vol. VI, General Provisions, 191, *supra* note 10 (emphasis added).

[16] *See* Ray Murphy, UN Peacekeeping in Lebanon, Somalia and Kosovo – Operational and Legal Issues in Practice 225 (2007). Also, draft article 3 on the responsibility of international organizations recognizes both negative and positive obligations of international organizations. *See* U.N. Doc. A/CN.4/L.632 (Jun. 4, 2003), para. 2.

2.1. *UN Peace Operations and International Human Rights Law*[17]

The U.N. transitional administrations in Kosovo and East Timor epitomize the complexities with respect to the relationship between the United Nations and international human rights law. Although the United Nations has exercised executive and legislative authority in both territories, the only official U.N. declaration in respect of its relationship to international human rights law has been that "all persons undertaking public duties or holding public office in Kosovo/East Timor shall *observe* internationally recognized human rights standards."[18] Thus, not even in situations where the Organization has exercised *de facto* state functions, has the United Nations, as of yet, declared internationally human rights instruments directly applicable to itself. This can partly be explained by the fact that the United Nations is not formally a party to any human rights instruments, partly because making human rights law apply directly to the United Nations would, in the case of Kosovo, provoke sensitive issues of state sovereignty. In view of such difficult legal and political aspects, the obligation of U.N. staff members to "observe" human rights standards has been adopted as kind of a compromise formula.[19]

The U.N. Committee on Human Rights, on the other hand, has stressed the existence of both positive and negative obligations of the United Nations. In its concluding observations on the implementation of the International Covenant on Civil and Political Rights (ICCPR) by UNMIK in Kosovo, the Committee held that "UNMIK, as well as PISG, or any future administration in Kosovo, are *bound to respect and to ensure to all individuals within the territory* of Kosovo and *subject to their jurisdiction* the rights recognized in the Covenant."[20] This obligation

---

[17] Given the present delimitation, the overview here is necessarily superficial. For a more exhaustive analysis on the topic, *see*, *inter alia*, Murphy, *supra* note 16, at 214–293; Boris Kondoch, *Human Rights Law and UN Peace Operations in Post-Conflict Situations*, *in* The UN, human rights and post conflict situations 33–41 (Nigel D. White & Dirk Klaasen eds, 2005); ICRC Report, Expert Meeting on Multinational Peace Operations, Applicability of International Humanitarian Law and International Human Rights Law to UN Mandated Forces (2003) [hereinafter ICRC Report].

[18] UNMIK Regulation No. 1999/24 enlists the following human rights instruments: the Universal Declaration on Human Rights (UDHR); the European Convention for the Protection of Human Rights and Fundamental Freedoms (ECHR); the two International Covenants on Civil and Political Rights (ICCPR) and on Economic, Social and Cultural Rights (ICESCR); the Convention on the Elimination of All forms of Racial Discrimination; the Convention on All Forms of Discrimination Against Women (CEDAW); the Convention Against Torture (CAT); and the Convention on the Rights of the Child (CRC) (emphasis added in quote). UNMIK Regulation No. 1999/24, Section 1.3. *See also* UNTAET Regulation 1999/1, Section 2.

[19] Interview, Anonymous, U.N. Headquarters, New York, October 2006. *See also* Report submitted by the UNMIK to the Human Rights Committee on the situation of human rights in the territory of Kosovo since June 1999, U.N. Doc. CCPR/C/UNK/1 (March 13, 2003) paras 123–124.

[20] Concluding Observations, U.N. Doc. CCPR/C/UNK/CO/1 (Aug. 14, 2006) para. 4 (emphasis added). It is worth recalling the wording of the Committee is almost identical to Article 2(1) ICCPR.

stems from a variety of legal sources, the Committee argued, primarily the Security Council mandate and U.N. regulations, but also, "from the Charter and other provisions of international law."[21] U.N. peace operations, in keeping with the draft Status of Forces Agreement (SOFA), are also under an obligation to respect "all local laws and regulations," thus potentially involving also relevant international human rights instruments.[22]

While issues of responsibility appear unquestionable, the difficulty resides in the enforcement of such responsibility given the very nature of the United Nations as an intergovernmental organization.[23] In view of the scandals of sexual abuse and exploitation committed by peacekeeping personnel, not the least in MONUC, important steps are however underway to address the issues. The most recent initiative taken in this regard is the draft *Convention on the Criminal Accountability of United Nations Officials and Experts on Mission* presented by a Group of Legal Experts and the establishment of an Ad Hoc Committee to consider this and other proposals.[24] This, however, concerns issues of individual criminal responsibility and not that of the accountability on the part of the United Nations in terms of implementation of international human rights standards.[25]

Just as the Group of Legal Expert focuses on the need to strengthen states' capacities to take legal action in cases of crimes committed by individual peacekeeping

---

International Covenant on Civil and Political Rights, G.A. Res. 2200A (XXI), 21 U.N. GAOR Supp. (No. 16) at 52, U.N. Doc. A/6316 (1966), 999 U.N.T.S. 171 [hereinafter ICCPR].

[21] Summary Record of the U.N. Human Rights Committee, U.N. Doc. CCPR/C/SR.2384 (Jul. 28, 2006), para. 38. It should be noted that the Committee "has consistently taken the view, as evidenced by its long-standing practice, that once the people are accorded the protection of the rights under the Covenant, such protection devolves with territory and continues to belong to them, notwithstanding change in government of the State party, including dismemberment in more than one State or State succession or any subsequent action of the State party designed to divest them of the rights guaranteed by the Covenant." The human rights obligations of UNMIK can thus also be understood in the light of this principle of "continuity of obligations" by successor States. *See* General Comment No. 26 of the U.N. Human Rights Committee, U.N. Doc. CCPR/C/21/Rev.1/Add.8/Rev.1, para. 4.

[22] Model Status of Forces Agreement for Peacekeeping Operations, Report of the Secretary-General, U.N. Doc. A/45/594 (Oct. 9, 1990), para. 6.

[23] Apart from the complexities identified above with respect to UNTAET and UNMIK, this also resides in the fact that United Nations and U.N. staff is protected by immunities and privileges and that the possibility of compensation and remedies by the United Nations remains limited.

[24] Report of the Group of Legal Experts on ensuring the accountability of United Nations staff and experts on mission with respect to criminal acts committed in peacekeeping operations, U.N. Doc. A/60/980 (Aug. 16, 2006), Annex III. *See also* U.N. Doc. A/RES/61/29 (Aug. 18, 2006).

[25] The crimes specified in the draft convention are murder, wilfully causing serious injury to body or health, rape and acts of sexual violence, sexual offences involving children, attempts to commit any of these crimes, as well as participation in any capacity, such as accomplice, assistant or instigator in any of these crimes. *See* draft Convention in U.N. Doc. A/60/980 (Aug. 16, 2006), Article 3.

personnel,[26] it is to the human rights obligations by member states contributing to U.N. peace operations we must turn for a more complete picture. Two outstanding elements figure in this respect: extra-territorial applicability of human rights law and effective control. The U.N. Human Rights Committee has determined that States parties to the ICCPR are under the obligation to respect and ensure the Covenant's provisions to "anyone within the power and effective control of a State party of that State party," including "forces constituting a national contingent of a State party assigned to a national peace-keeping or peace-enforcement operation."[27] In 1998, the Human Rights Committee expressed its concern about the behaviour of Belgian soldiers participating in UNOSOM II and acknowledged, in this respect, "that the State party has recognized the applicability of the Covenant in this respect and opened 270 files for purpose of investigation."[28]

While national as well as international case law has confirmed the *de jure* application of this principle,[29] the extra-territorial application of human rights instruments when states parties exercise effective control outside its territorial jurisdiction remains a "contentious issue."[30] Two regional human rights bodies are, however, currently examining specific cases of alleged human rights violations by peacekeeping forces and their outcome will hopefully bring further clarification on the subject matter.[31]

---

[26] *Id.* para. 44.
[27] General Comment No. 31, U.N. Doc. CCPR/C/2/1/Rev.1/Add.13 (2004), at 10.
[28] U.N. Doc. CCPR/C/79/Add.99 (Nov. 19, 1998), para. 14.
[29] *See* definition by the European Court of Human Rights in the case of Issa and Others v. Turkey, Application No. 31821/96, judgment, (Nov. 16, 2004), para. 69. *See also* Loizidou v. Turkey (Preliminary Objections), ECHR (1995) Series A, No. 310 (Feb. 23, 1995), para. 62 and the Inter-American Commission on Human Rights' judgement in Coard et al. v. United States, Case 10.951, Report No. 109/99, (Sep. 29, 1999). With respect to the International Covenant on Civil and Political Rights, applicable to individuals "within its territory and subject to its jurisdiction," the Human Rights Committee has welcomed the commitment by States parties as to its applicability to its armed forces when deployed as part of peacekeeping operations. See, for instance, the Committee's concluding observations with respect to Italy (U.N. Doc. CCPR/C/ITA/CO/5 (April 24, 2006), para. 3) and Norway (UN Doc. CCPR/C/NOR/CO/5 (April 25, 2006), para. 6. A case of particular importance in the case of the DRC is the judgement of the International Court of Justice (ICJ) in the Case concerning Armed Activities on the Territory of the Congo (DRC v. Uganda), (Dec. 19, 2005), 2005 ICJ Rep. 116 [hereinafter DRC v. Uganda]. For a more exhaustive list of cases, *see* Matteo Tondini, *How to Make International Organizations Compliant with Human Rights and Accountable for Their Violations by Targeting Member States*, paper presented at conference on "Accountability for Human Rights Violations by International Organizations," Brussels, Mar. 16–17, 2007. *See* fn. 138, at 20.
[30] ICRC Report, *supra* note 17, Executive Summary, at 4. The Bankovic decision, in particular, by the European Court of Human Rights delimited such extra-territorial reach of that Convention. *See* Murphy, *supra* note 16, at 287.
[31] First, in mid-2007, the Grand Chamber of the European Court of Human Rights considered the applications of Agim Behrami and Bekir Behrami v. France, (Application No. 71412/01) and of

The advantage with addressing state responsibility under international human rights law in the context of peacekeeping is that this body of law applies in all times[32] and that it allows for legal proceedings as to compensation and reparations.[33] Importantly in the case of MONUC, mandated to assist the Congolese Government in the promotion and protection of human rights,[34] the Human Rights Committee has asserted that "the contractual dimension of the [ICCPR] involves any State Party to a treaty *being obligated to every other State Party to comply with its undertaking under the treaty*."[35] This may be interpreted as a direct obligation of troop contributing and other states to ensure that their troops serving in peacekeeping operations respect the human rights of the population of the host country, likely to a state party to the Covenant. Another interesting determination of the Committee in terms of inter-state relations and human rights compliance is that "[t]o draw attention to possible breaches of Covenant obligations should, far from being regarded as an unfriendly act, be considered as a reflection of *legitimate community interest*."[36] In this context, could it not be perceived of an indirect obligation of peacekeepers to highlight human rights violations committed by the authorities of the host state in which they are deployed, with a view to ensure compliance by the host state?

The difficulties involved in considering human rights obligations of member states contributing to peacekeeping operations include that of the difficulty of assessing when and where peacekeepers exercise effective control, determining

---

Ruzhdi Saramati v. France, Germany and Norway, (Application No. 78166/01) and rendered a fairly controversial decision on their applicability. Second, subsequent to a request by a Haitian human rights NGO, Zanmi Lasante, the Inter-American Commission on Human Rights held a hearing regarding the human rights obligations of member states of the Organization of American States operating as peacekeeping troops in Haiti on March 3, 2006. See Todd Howland, *Peacekeeping and Conformity with Human Rights Law: How MINUSTAH Falls Short in Haiti*, 13 Int'l Peacekeeping 462–476 (2006).

[32] With the exception of public emergencies when States parties may derogate from their obligations under ICCPR. However, General Comment No. 29 of the Human Rights Committee should be borne in mind: "[E]ven during an armed conflict measures derogating from the Covenant are allowed only is and to the extent that the situation constitutes a threat to the life of the nation." U.N. Doc. CCPR/C/21/Rev.1/Add.11 (2001), para. 4. The principle that basic human rights, such as the right not to be arbitrarily deprived of one's life, apply also in times of hostilities was laid down by International Court of Justice in its Advisory Opinion on the *Legality of the Threat or Use of Nuclear Weapons. See* Legality of the Threat or Use of Nuclear Weapons, Advisory Opinion, (July 8, 1996), I.C.J. Reports 1996, para. 25 [hereinafter Nuclear Weapons Advisory Opinion].

[33] *See* DRC v. Uganda, para. 345(5).

[34] *See* U.N. Doc. S/RES/1565 (Oct. 10, 2004), para. 5(g).

[35] HRC, General Comment No. 31: Nature of the General Legal Obligation Imposed on States Parties to the Covenant, (May 26, 2004), U.N. Doc. CCPR/C/21/Rev.1/Add.13, para. 2.

[36] *Id.* (emphasis added).

responsibility, and the practical challenge of taking legal action and ensuring justice. Even more challenging and important in this context, is to determine when a *positive obligation* exists for member states to ensure human rights protection; that is (a) proactively act itself for protection and (b) proactively seek other State parties' (i.e. host state's) compliance with human rights.

Some of these loopholes can be addressed by considering the protective scheme as provided by IHL. Again, as determined by the Human Rights Committee, while the ICCPR "applies also in situations of armed conflict … more specific rules under IHL may be relevant for the purpose of the interpretation of Covenant rights[. Both] spheres of law are complementary, not mutually exclusive."[37] Also, international human rights law is generally considered to apply only to governments, while international humanitarian law applies also to armed groups, particularly relevant in peacekeeping contexts.[38]

2.2. U.N. Peace Operations and International Humanitarian Law

Contrary to international human rights law, the United Nations has officially declared, in a Secretary-General's Bulletin, that certain "fundamental principles and rules of international humanitarian law" are applicable to U.N. forces "when in situations of armed conflict they are actively engaged therein as combatants."[39] Protection of the civilian population is referred to as the first substantive of such rules and principles.[40] The Bulletin codifies earlier U.N. positions confirming the applicability of IHL to U.N. peacekeeping troops, for instance, when using weapons in self-defence.[41] It furthermore reinforces such declarations in terms of legal language (from "principles and spirit" to "rules") and scope (by recognizing the engagement by peacekeepers in "enforcement actions").[42] It thus clearly affirms the opinion of the International Committee of the Red Cross (ICRC) and other experts

---

[37] *Id.* para. 11. *See also* the reasoning by the ICJ on *lex specialis* in its Nuclear Weapons Advisory Opinion, *supra* note 32, para. 25.

[38] *See* Jean-Marie Henckaerts & Louise Doswald-Beck, Customary international Humanitarian Law, Vol. 1, Rules (2005), at 299 [hereinafter CIHL].

[39] Secretary-General's Bulletin, Observance by United Nations Forces of International Humanitarian Law, U.N. Doc. ST/SGB/1999/13 (Aug. 6, 1999), para. 1.1 [hereinafter Secretary-General's Bulletin].

[40] *Id.* para. 5.1.

[41] For instance, the U.N. Secretary-General wrote to states contributing with troops to the United Nations Interim Force in Lebanon (UNIFIL) that in such situations, the "principles and spirit of humanitarian law" as contained, *inter alia*, in the Geneva Conventions … [and] the Protocols … shall apply." The model SOFA includes an express provision of the obligation of U.N. forces to observe and respect the principles and spirit of international conventions applicable to the conduct of military personnel. *See* Murphy, *supra* note 16, at 262, 248.

[42] Secretary-General's Bulletin, *supra* note 39, para. 1.1.

that "[f]rom the moment that UN forces are involved in combat that reaches the threshold of an armed conflict, international humanitarian law applies."[43]

The Bulletin has been subject to justified criticism in that it "mixes law and policy" by avoiding to address the issue of whether U.N. peace operations become a party to the Geneva Conventions of 1949 and the two Additional Protocols of 1977.[44] By refraining from doing so, however, the United Nations is consistent with its official position that U.N. forces act on behalf of the international community why it can neither be considered a party or power to the Conventions.[45] While there is disagreement whether the participation of U.N. multinational forces *per se* renders an armed conflict "international" in character,[46] consensus seems to prevail that the moment U.N.-mandated forces *take action* against a state's forces, as in Somalia, the law of international armed conflict would apply. However, in instances where U.N. troops use force, *alongside the government of the host state* or independently against organized armed groups, as in the case of MONUC, the question remains "unsettled."[47] The ensuing uncertainty whether the law of non-international armed conflict would apply in such cases appears not to have been resolved. However, given the effect of the Secretary-General's Bulletin, the identification of customary rules of IHL[48] and the continuing application of HRL[49] suggest that peacekeepers never operate in a legal vacuum in regard to basic principles of IHL. The difficulty resides, rather, in determining when the threshold of an "armed conflict" has been reached.[50]

Given that the main responsibility of training rests with troop contributing countries, and mindful of the fact that states, also in U.N.-commanded forces like MONUC, retain a considerable degree of control over their forces, ultimately *de facto* responsibility for enforcement of IHL rests with states.[51] In this vein, Article 1 of the 1949 Geneva Conventions and the Additional Protocols of 1977 is of

---

[43] ICRC Report, *supra* note 17, at 1–2.
[44] *Id.* at 8. This is so, given the Bulletin's contradictory statement that IHL applies "when they are actively engaged therein as combatants," while this on the other hand "does not affect...their status as non-combatants."
[45] *See* Murphy, *supra* note 16, at 248.
[46] ICRC Report, *supra* note 17, at 11.
[47] *Id.*
[48] *See* CIHL, *supra* note 38. *See also* further below.
[49] This rule was indeed recognized as early as 1968 and 1970 in the General Assembly Resolutions on Respect for Human Rights in Armed Conflict and Basic principles for the protection of civilian populations in armed conflicts respectively. The latter specifies that "[f]undamental human rights, as accepted in international law and laid down in international instruments, continue to apply fully in situations of armed conflict." U.N. Doc. 2675 (XXV) (Dec. 9, 1970), para. 1.
[50] Murphy, *supra* note 16, at 242.
[51] *Id.* para. 245.

particular importance (read in conjunction with Article 89).[52] Article 1 sets out that "The High Contracting Parties undertake to *respect* and *ensure respect* for the present Convention in all circumstances." Both a negative as well as a positive obligation in terms of compliance are intended here. In the view of the ICRC, this article entails that States parties "should do *everything in their power to ensure* that [the Convention] is respected universally."[53] The drafters of the Geneva Conventions never defined closely what this means in terms of the positive obligation of ensuring respect by other parties – an aspect of particular relevance in this context.[54] The ICRC in its Commentary to the Conventions, however, makes an interesting interpretation:

> The limitations to such actions are obviously those imposed by general international law, particularly the prohibition on the use of force. *Even if the United Nations were to take coercive measures involving the use of armed force in order to ensure respect for humanitarian law*, the limitation would be that of the very respect due to this law in all circumstances.[55]

It may, perhaps daringly so, be suggested that this interpretation sanctions the possibility of U.N. peacekeeping forces to use force as a means to ensure respect of IHL, as long as measures for doing so remains within the limits of the same law. The ICRC furthermore considers that the obligation to "ensure respect" with respect to the Conventions and Protocol I on the Protection of Civilian Populations essentially anticipates measures for execution and supervision, i.e. that "all necessary measures" for the execution of the obligations be taken "without delay" and that the High Contracting Parties "*shall give orders and instructions to ensure... observance*" and supervise their execution.[56] Read in conjunction with Article 89 (Cooperation) AP I, the law of international armed conflict appears to provide a rather strong cause that states participating in U.N. peacekeeping forces

---

[52] The Geneva Convention for the Amelioration of the Condition of the Wounded and Sick in Armed Forces in the Field, Aug. 12, 1949, 75 U.N.T.S. 31, 32 [hereinafter GC I]; Geneva Convention for the Amelioration of the Condition of the Wounded, Sick and Shipwrecked Members of the Armed Forces at Sea, Aug. 12, 1949, 75 U.N.T.S. 85, 86 [hereinafter GC II]; Geneva Convention Relative to the Treatment to Prisoners of War, Aug. 12, 1949, 75 U.N.T.S. 135, 136 [hereinafter GC III]; Geneva Convention Relative to the Protection of Civilian Persons in Time of War, Aug. 12, 1949, 75 U.N.T.S. 287, 288 [hereinafter GC IV]. Protocol Additional to the Geneva Conventions of 12 August 1949, and Relating to the Protections of Victims of International Armed Conflicts (Protocol I), opened for signature Dec. 12, 1977, U.N. Doc. A/32/144, Annex I, II, (1977), *reprinted in* 16 I.L.M. 1391 (1977) [hereinafter AP I]. Emphasis added.
[53] ICRC, Commentary on the Additional Protocol of 8 June 1977 to the Geneva Conventions of 1949 (1986), at 35, para. 41 [Hereinafter Commentary 1].
[54] Other than by means of the examples provided in Articles 7 (Meetings) and Article 89 (Cooperation). *Id*. at 36–37, para. 46.
[55] *Id*. (emphasis added).
[56] Article 80(1) and (2) (emphasis added).

are under an obligation to ensure "through everything in their power" the protection of civilians as expressed in the Security Council mandate. This interpretation is reinforced in light of Article 89 AP I:

> In situations of *serious violations*[57] of the Conventions or of this Protocol, the High Contracting Parties undertake to act, *jointly or individually, in cooperation with the United Nations and in conformity with the United Nations Charter* (emphasis added).

According to the ICRC, this article "has as its purpose the ensuring of respect for the law, and more especially, the prevention of breaches being answered by further breaches."[58] Importantly, furthermore, in the interpretation of the ICRC, possible U.N. actions to which Article 89 refers may "consist of issuing an appeal to respect humanitarian law, just as well, for example, setting up enquiries on compliance with the Conventions and the Protocol and even, where appropriate, of coercive action which may include the use of armed force."[59]

The above reading of Article 1 and Article 89 AP I proposes that states contributing to U.N. peacekeeping forces are *de jure* under a dual obligation to (i) ensure other Contracting parties' respect for the Geneva Conventions and Protocol I and (ii) to prevent serious violations of international and non-international armed conflict,[60] particularly the protection of civilians. Therefore, obligations set out vis-à-vis the United Nations (given that the Secretary-General's Bulletin is binding upon troops under U.N. command)[61] as well as vis-à-vis Contracting Parties to Protocol I (in view of Articles 1 and 89) jointly represents a strong legal framework for U.N. peacekeeping troops.

2.2.1. Some Remarks on U.N. Peace Operations and International Human Rights and Humanitarian Law

In light of the above, it seems appropriate to suggest that it is by addressing the *dual and concomitant responsibilities and obligations* under IHL and HRL of both

---

[57] While the Diplomatic Conferences of the Geneva Conventions and the Additional Protocols did not specify the meaning of "serious violations," the ICRC considers such to encompass any conduct, both acts and omissions, contrary to the relevant instruments concerned and which are not included in "grave violations." ICRC outlines three possible categories which could fall under "serious violations:" (i) isolated instances of conduct...of a serious nature; (ii) conduct which...takes on a serious nature because of the frequency of the individual acts committed or because of the systematic repetition thereof or because of circumstances, (iii) "global violations," for example, military acts whereby a particular situation, a territory or a whole category of persons or objects is withdrawn from the application of the Convention or the Protocol. ICRC Commentary 1, *supra* note 53, at 1033.

[58] ICRC Commentary 1, at 1032.

[59] *Id.*

[60] *See* Common Article 3 GC, *supra* note 52.

[61] ICRC Report, *supra* note 17, at 2.

the United Nations and member states, that the legal obligations to ensure civilian protection and prevent violations thereof may best be considered. This approach also appears to be in line with the realities of U.N. peace operations, the dynamics of which are determined by the concerted pressures, resources, skills, and interests of the U.N. Secretariat, the Security Council and member states. In this respect, the Special Representative of the Secretary-General (SRSG) carries a key role in his/her capacity as Head of Mission. Importantly, the SRSG is "responsible for implementing [a] mission's mandate, and [for] developing strategies for achieving these goals using the political, institutional and financial resources available."[62]

Two documents further underscore the positive obligations inherent in that responsibility. First, according to the model SOFA, the Special Representative/Force Commander "shall take all appropriate measures to ensure the observance of all local laws and regulations."[63] Thus, even if states contributing to peace operations have not ratified the key instruments of IHL and HRL, they remain under the obligation to respect the provisions of the international instruments ratified by the host state. Also, MONUC, specifically,

> s'acquitte de sa mission dans la République démocratique du Congo dans le plein respect des principes et régles des conventions internationales relatives à la conduite du personnel militaire. Ces conventions internationales comprennent les quatre Conventions de Genève du 12 août 1949 et leurs Protocoles additionnels du 8 juin 1977 et la Convention internationale de l'UNESCO pour la protection des biens culturels en cas de conflit armé.[64]

Second, the Memorandum of Understanding concluded between the Office of the High Commissioner for Human Rights (OHCHR) and the Department of Peacekeeping Operations (DPKO) states that "the SRSG or Head of the peacekeeping operation shall ensure that all staff of the operation – whether civilian or military – are aware of, and abide by, international human rights and humanitarian law standards."[65] Read in the light of Article 1 GC and 89 AP I respectively, these

---

[62] United Nations, Handbook on United Nations Multidimensional Peacekeeping Operations, Best Practices Unit, Department of Peacekeeping Operations 9 (2003).

[63] Report of the Secretary-General, Model Status-of-Forces Agreement for Peace-Keeping Operations, U.N. Doc. A/45/594 (Oct. 4, 1990), para. 6. The DRC is a High Contracting Party to the Geneva Conventions as well as to the 1977 Additional Protocols, *available at*: www.icrc.org/ihl.nsf/Pays?ReadForm (last visited Sept. 15, 2007). *See also* Secretary-General's Bulletin, *supra* note 39, Section 3.

[64] Accord entre l'Organisation des Nations Unies et La République Démocratique du Congo concernant le Statut de la Mission de l'Organisation des Nations Unies en République Démocratique du Congo (SOFA, MONUC), signed on May 4, 2000 in Kinshasa, Article 6(a).

[65] Memorandum of Understanding between the Office of the High Commissioner for Human Rights and the Department of Peacekeeping Operations, Annex, para. 12. *See also* Secretary-General's Bulletin, *supra* note 39, Section 3.

documents assume further legal weight and importance. To identify mechanisms by which the SRSG's responsibility to implement a mission's mandate to protect civilian populations in line with the United Nations' and member state's legal obligations under HRL and IHL could be assessed and monitored, appears to be a key step to the realization of such duties.

3. Protection of Civilians in the Light of International Humanitarian and Human Rights Law[66]

Although a U.N. system-wide definition and understanding of "protection" in the context of peacekeeping is missing, the definition developed by the U.N. Inter-Agency Standing Committee (IASC) in 2001 stands out as one of the most authoritative. Protection is defined as encompassing "all activities aimed at ensuring full respect for the rights of the individual in accordance with the letter and spirit of the relevant bodies of law, i.e. human rights, humanitarian law and refugee law."[67] While cognizant that civilian protection addressed from a rights-based approach includes also other bodies of international law, in particular international refugee and criminal law,[68] focus here is on the most relevant provisions of (first) international humanitarian and (second) human rights law relative to the implementation of a Chapter VII-mandate to protect civilians under imminent threat of physical violence. As stated by the Secretary-General in his first report on the protection of civilians in armed conflict, "[t]he protection of civilians would be largely assured if combatants respected the provisions of international humanitarian and human rights law."[69]

3.1. International Humanitarian Law

The principle of protection of civilians is one of the most fundamental provisions of IHL and forms part of customary law.[70] Embodied in the principle of distinc-

---

[66] Given the present delimitation, this section presents a far from exhaustive list of provisions of relevance in this respect. It will focus on provisions that may be considered of key importance in the contexts similar to that in which MONUC operates.

[67] OHCHR Staff, *Protection in the Field: Human Rights Perspectives*, in Human Rights Protection in the Field 122 (Bertrand G. Ramcharan, 2006) [hereinafter OHCHR Staff].

[68] *Id.* at 123.

[69] Report of the Secretary-General to the Security Council on the Protection of Civilians in Armed Conflict, U.N. Doc. S/1999/957 (Sept. 8, 1999), para. 35. Reiterated by the Secretary-General in his fifth report on the same matter, *see* U.N. Doc. S/2005/740 (Nov. 28, 2005), para. 12.

[70] The ICJ in the Nuclear Weapons Advisory Opinion (*supra* note 32) laid down that the first of the "cardinal principles" of IHL was that "aimed at the protection of the civilian population and civilian objects and establishes the distinction between combatants and non-combatants; States

tion between combatants and non-combatants and between military and civilian objects, the principle has origins in both the 1899 Hague Convention No. II and 1907 Hague Convention No. IV.[71] Despite the recommendations in 1929 that "an exhaustive study should be made with a view of the conclusion of an International Convention regarding the condition and protection of civilians of enemy nationality in the territory of a belligerent or in territory occupied by a belligerent,"[72] it would take another 50 years before such instruments were formally adopted: The 1977 Additional Protocols I and II relating to the Protection of Victims of International Armed Conflicts and Non-International Armed Conflicts respectively.[73]

The 1949 Geneva Conventions do not address the issue of the protection of the civilian population as a whole, but rather provide protection for specific categories.[74] However, Part II of the IV Geneva Convention relative to the protection of civilian persons in time of war provides for a "general protection of populations against certain consequences of war."[75] By covering "the whole of the populations of the countries in conflict, without any adverse distinction based, in particular on race, nationality, religion or political opinion,"[76] the object of Part II was to bind belligerents to observe certain restrictions in their conduct of hostilities.[77] Commenting on its field of application, the ICRC stipulates that:

---

must never make civilians the object of attack…" para. 78. *See also* Mika Nishimura Hayashi, *The Principle of Civilian Protection and Contemporary Armed Conflict*, in The Law of Armed Conflict: Constraints on the Contemporary use of military force 106 (Howard M. Hensel ed., 2005). This article provides a good historical overview of the evolution of the principle of protection of civilians from the perspective of IHL.

[71] *See* Convention (II) with Respect to the Laws and Customs of War on Land and its annex: Regulations concerning the Laws and Customs of War on Land (July 29, 1899), Article 23(b), (c) and Article 25 and Convention (IV) respecting the Laws and Customs of Law on Land and its annex: Regulations concerning the Laws and Customs of War on Land, (Oct. 18, 1907), Article 23(b), (c) and Article 25.

[72] Final Act of the Diplomatic Conference (convened by the Swiss Federal Council), Geneva, (July 29, 1929), recommendation VI. In 1938, the International Law Association drew up the Draft Convention for the Protection of Civilian Populations Against New Engines of War, but states demonstrated no or little interest. *See* Hayashi, *supra* note 69, at 108.

[73] *See* Hayashi as to the reasons for such delay, *id.*

[74] The four Geneva Conventions of 12 August 1949 (GC I-IV) each deal with one category of people in special need of protection in times of armed conflict: GC I (wounded and sick in armed forces); GC II, 12 August 1949 (wounded, sick and shipwrecked members of armed forces at sea); GC III (Prisoners of War); GC IV (Civilian Persons in Times of War – civilians of enemy forces).

[75] This part applies to "the whole of the populations of the countries in conflict, without any adverse distinction based, in particular, on race, nationality, religion or political opinion, and are intended to alleviate the sufferings caused by war." Article 13 GC IV, *supra* note 52.

[76] *Id.*

[77] ICRC, Commentary, IV Geneva Convention 118 (1958) [hereinafter Commentary IV].

> In former times the need to protect the civilian population in wartime was not felt to the same degree as since more recent years. Military operations nowadays ... threaten the whole population. Consequently the provisions in Part II are *as general and extensive in scope as possible*... The provisions in Part II therefore apply not only to protected persons, i.e. to enemy or other aliens and to neutrals, as defined in Article 4, but *also to the belligerents' own nationals.*[78]

Of particular importance to the present context are Articles 15 and 16 of Part II. Article 15 deals with the establishment of "neutralized zones intended to shelter from the effects of war...civilian persons who take no part in hostilities." Military authorities were considered those in the "best position to take the necessary measures" so as to "ensure that those in danger as a result of the fighting are given speedy assistance."[79] Neutralized zones were envisaged to serve not only for the wounded and sick but also as "safety zones for civilians who take no part in hostilities," meaning the "whole of the population in the combat area."[80]

Article 16 provides for protection and respect of wounded and sick civilians, and the infirm and expectant mothers: this obligation is general and absolute from which no derogation is permitted.[81] The article also, however, provides a general obligation of protection for each Party to the conflict "to facilitate the steps taken to search for the killed and wounded, *to assist* the shipwrecked and *other persons exposed to grave danger, and to protect them against pillage and ill-treatment.*" "Other persons exposed to grave danger" covers, according to the ICRC Commentary, "any civilians who while not being either wounded or shipwrecked *are exposed to some grave danger as a result of military operations.*"[82] Thus, it would appear as if the GC IV, to which all MONUC troop contributing countries are party,[83] in the light of Articles 15 and 16, entails a wider scope for assisting, through protective measures, the civilian population "under imminent threat." It is also a most important provision in that it concerns a positive obligation to protect.

Articles 15 and 16 GC IV, applicable in international armed conflict, could thus be interpreted in the broad sense as envisaged by the ICRC. This way, they can be seen as constituting a crucial protective clause parallel to Common Article 3, applicable in non-international armed conflict. Common Article 3 sets out that persons "taking no part in hostilities" shall "in all circumstances be treated humanely, without any adverse distinction founded on race colour, religion or

---

[78] *Id.*
[79] *Id.* at 130.
[80] *Id.* at 130–131.
[81] *Id.* at 134.
[82] *Id.* at 136.
[83] *See* ICRC website, *available at* www.icrc.org/ihl/nsf/Pays?ReadForm (last visited Sept. 15, 2007).

faith, sex, birth or any other similar criteria."[84] To this end, the following acts are prohibited, at any time, at any place:[85]

(a) violence to life and person, in particular murder of all kinds, mutilation, cruel treatment and torture;
(b) taking of hostages;
(c) outrages upon personal dignity, in particular humiliating and degrading treatment;
(d) the passing of sentences and the carrying out of executions without previous judgment by a regularly constituted court…

The fact that Common Article 3 was intended to protect individual civilians rather than civilian populations as a whole (contrary to Article 15 and part II in general of GC IV) does not diminish its importance in the context of the DRC, rather the opposite.[86]

The absence of a clear prohibition of indiscriminate attacks against the civilian population as a whole in the Geneva Conventions was remedied in Additional Protocol I (applicable in international armed conflicts) which provides for the collective as well as individual protection of civilians. Article 51 sets out that the civilian population and individual civilians shall enjoy general protection against the dangers of military operations and that they shall not be the object of attack.[87] It furthermore prohibits "acts or threats of violence the primary purpose of which is to spread terror among the civilian population" as well as "indiscriminate attacks."[88] Likewise, civilian objects are protected from attacks.[89] Women and children are "objects of special respect:"[90] women shall be protected in particular against rape, forced prostitution and any other form of indecent assault; children against any form of indecent assault.

Additional Protocol II, applicable in non-international armed conflicts, provide for the same protections, with the exception of a clause on the prohibition of indiscriminate attacks against the civilian population.[91] The same instrument

---

[84] Article 3(I) GC IV, *supra* note 52.
[85] *Id*. Article 3(I), (a)–(d).
[86] It was suggested that one of the most serious incidents of human rights violations in the DRC are individual acts of violence committed by armed groups throughout the country. *See also* Hayashi, *supra* note 69, at 114.
[87] Article 51(1–2) AP I, *supra* note 52.
[88] *Id*. Article 51(3–4) AP I. Types of attacks which may be considered as indiscriminate are laid out in article 51, para. 5 (a–b).
[89] *Id*. Article 52 AP I.
[90] *Id*. Articles 76 and 77 AP I.
[91] Article 13(1–2) Protocol Additional to the Geneva Conventions of 12 August 1949, and relating to the Protection of Victims of Non-International Armed Conflicts (June 8, 1977) [hereinafter AP II].

extends the fundamental guarantees of Common Article 3 to by prohibiting, in addition, collective punishments, rape, enforced prostitution and any form of indecent assault, acts of terrorism, slavery, pillage, and threats to commit any of the foregoing acts.[92] It also provides that "measures shall be taken, if necessary, . . . to remove children temporarily from the area in which hostilities are taking place to a safer area within the country."[93]

The two sections in the Secretary-General's Bulletin dealing with "Protection of the civilian population" and "Treatment of civilians and persons hors de combat" constitute a merge of the above provisions of the two Protocols and the Geneva Conventions.[94] It provides a proactive obligation to U.N. forces "in its area of operations" to "take all necessary precautions to protect the civilian population, individual civilians and civilian objects under the dangers resulting from military operations." Given that the Bulletin is applicable in enforcement actions, it seems to provide a broader scope for action than provided for in Security Council mandates in that it does not restrict such measures to situations where civilians are "under imminent threat of physical violence." Its suggested non-binding nature vis-à-vis contributing states is of little concern in view of the above provisions which are directly applicable, *mutatis mutandis*, to the U.N. forces whose troop contributing states have ratified the Geneva Conventions and Additional Protocols.

3.2. *International Human Rights Law*

Given the delay in codifying the more elaborate and comprehensive prohibition on attacks against civilians and civilian populations in times of war, the United Nations has spelled out in several documents the continuing applicability of human rights during armed conflict.[95] The first "basic principle for the protection in armed conflict" identified by the General Assembly in 1970 were indeed "fundamental human rights, as accepted in international law and laid down in international instruments [which] continue to apply fully in situations of armed conflict."[96] That resolution furthermore spells out that the provision of international relief to civilian populations is in conformity with the humanitarian principles of the Charter of the United Nations, the Universal Declaration of Human Rights (UDHR) and

---

[92] *Id.* Part II Humane treatment, Article 4(2) Fundamental Guarantees AP II.
[93] *Id.* Article 4(3) (e) AP II.
[94] Secretary-General's Bulletin, *supra* note 39, Sections 5 and 7.
[95] *See*, in particular, Respect for Human Rights in Armed Conflicts, G.A. Res. 2444 (XXIII) (Dec. 9, 1968); Basic Principles for the Protection of Civilian Populations in Armed Conflicts, G.A. Res. 2675 (XXV) (Dec. 9, 1970); Respect for Human Rights in Armed Conflicts, G.A. Res. 2676 (XXV) (Dec. 9, 1970); Respect for Human Rights in Armed Conflict, G.A. Res. 2677 (XXV) (Dec. 9, 1970); Reports of the Secretary-General, Respect for Human Rights in Armed Conflict, U.N. Doc. A/7720 (Nov. 20, 1969), and U.N. Doc. A/8052 (Sept. 18, 1970), respectively.
[96] G.A. Res. 2675 (XXV) (1970), *supra* note 94, para. 1.

other international instruments in the field of human rights.[97] The conferences which later led to the drafting and elaboration of the two Additional Protocols were explicitly welcomed in the third General Assembly resolution on respect for human rights in armed conflict.[98] In this respect, the call for stronger provisions in IHL for the protection of civilians was in fact set against the existing human rights law framework: the preamble of the Charter;[99] the purpose of the United Nations to promote respect for human rights;[100] the obligation of member states to promote universal respect and observance thereof;[101] and the urge that member states strictly comply with the provisions of the existing international instruments concerning human rights.[102]

Key human rights provisions of relevance for the protection of civilians in situations of armed conflict in which U.N. forces are deployed may be identified as the following;[103]

– The principle of human dignity[104]
– The principle of non-discrimination[105]
– The right to life, liberty and security of person[106]
– The prohibition of slavery or servitude[107]
– The prohibition of torture or cruel, inhuman or degrading treatment or punishment[108]

In view of the principle of extraterritorial application of human rights instruments and the positive obligation of states parties to ensure compliance by other state parties,[109] these standards can be regarded as a the minimum human rights standards which member states contributing to U.N. forces must proactively seek to

---

[97] *Id.* para. 8; Universal Declaration of Human Rights, G.A. Res.217A (III), U.N. GAOR, 3d. Sess., pt. 1, at 71, U.N. Doc. A/810 (1948) [hereinafter UDHR].

[98] G.A. Res. 2676 (XXV) (1970), *supra* note 94, preamble; G.A. Res. 2677 (XXV) (1970), *supra* note 94, *see* preamble and para. 6.

[99] G.A. Res. 2676 (XXV) (1970), *supra* note 94, preamble.

[100] *Id.*

[101] *Id.*

[102] *Id.* para. 6.

[103] This is of no prejudice to the full scope of rights which are set forth in the main international human rights treaties. *See also* OHCHR Staff, *supra* note 66.

[104] Article 1 UDHR, *supra* note 18 preamble ICCPR, *supra* note 20. It should be noted that most of the main international human rights instruments assert this and the following principles. The limitation here to UDHR and ICCPR is based on their statuses as universally applicable (UDHR) and as the key instrument in terms of civil and political rights (ICCPR).

[105] Article 2 UDHR, *supra* note 18; Article 2 ICCPR, *supra* note 20.

[106] Article 3 UDHR, *supra* note 18; Articles 4, 6 and 9 ICCPR, *supra* note 20.

[107] Article 4 UDHR, *supra* note 18; Article 8 ICCPR, *supra* note 20.

[108] Article 5 UDHR, *supra* note 18; Article 7 ICCPR, *supra* note 20.

[109] *See* General Comment No. 31, U.N. Doc. CCPR/C7Rev.1/Add.13, para. 2.

protect. The ICCPR would, however, stand out as the most pertinent instrument with respect to the protection of civilians. In this respect, it is regretful that the Secretary-General's recommendation in 1999 that the Security Council "call on member states and non-state actors...to adhere to international humanitarian, human rights and refugee law, particularly the non-derogable rights enumerated in Article 4 of the ICCPR" has never been specifically acted upon.[110]

3.3. *A Merger for Peace Operations? Customary International Humanitarian Law*

Cognizant, however, of the practical difficulties and political sensitivities for a U.N. peace operation in identifying relevant obligations under IHL and HRL of different troop contributing countries, the identification of customary IHL standards by the ICRC is a welcome and complementary step of importance to this study. Such rules facilitate for both member states and the United Nations in ensuring consistency regarding awareness and implementation of the most relevant standards of IHL. This is particularly so as the "work of international organizations" is particularly referred to as one of the very purposes of specifying rules of customary IHL.

> [C]ustomary international law may also be of service in a number of situations where reliance on customary international law is required. This is especially relevant for the work of courts and international organisations...Customary international law is also re*levant to the work of international organizations* in that it *generally represents the law binding upon all member states*.[111]

It thus seems legitimate to propose that the United Nations and member states may wish to consider the dissemination of those customary rules of IHL relevant to the protection of civilians mandate among peacekeeping troops and other mission components. Apart from the obligation to distinguish between civilians and combatant and the prohibition of indiscriminate attacks,[112] eighteen "fundamental guarantees" appear as particularly important to this aim. The ICRC, when interpreting these rules, constantly refers to human rights law, documents, and case law. The importance of this mutually reinforcing cross-fertilization of both bodies of law is that they apply equally to all parties simultaneously, notwithstanding ratification status, declarations or reservations.[113] In the context of U.N. peacekeeping opera-

---

[110] Report of the Secretary-General to the Security Council on the Protection of Civilians in Armed Conflict, *supra* note 68, para. 36(2).
[111] CIHL, *supra* note 38, at xxix–xxx.
[112] *See* rules 1–6, in part 1, 2, 5 and 6, and rule 7. CIHL, *supra* note 38, at 3–40.
[113] *Id.* at 299. In the case of MONUC, the ratification status of the main troop contributing with respect to the Geneva Conventions and the two Additional Protocols display consistency in terms of the Geneva Conventions (ratified by all states), but variation in terms of ratification of the Additional Protocols I and II: Bangladesh, South Africa, Uruguay and Ghana have ratified both Protocols; Pakistan (signed both), Nepal, and Morocco (signed both) have ratified neither. It should be remembered that the DRC is a Contracting Party to all instruments.

tions and the mandate to protect civilians, the following customary fundamental guarantees stand out:

Rule 87: Civilians and persons *hors de combat* must be treated humanely;
Rule 88: Adverse distinction in the application of international humanitarian law based on race, colour, sex, language, religion or belief, political or other opinion, national or social origin, wealth, birth or other status, or on any other similar criteria, is prohibited;
Rule 89: Murder is prohibited;
Rule 90: Torture, cruel or inhumane treatment and outrages upon personal dignity, in particular humiliating and degrading treatment, are prohibited;
Rule 93: Rape and other forms of sexual violence are prohibited;
Rule 94: Slavery and the slave trade in all their forms are prohibited;
Rule 95: Uncompensated or abusive forced labour is prohibited.

The potential relevance of this set of rules to U.N. peacekeepers engaged in enforcement operations is further underscored in view of the customary rule the study identifies with respect to enforcement of such customary international humanitarian law: "States may not encourage violations of international humanitarian law by parties to an armed conflict. *They must exercise their influence, to the degree possible, to stop violations of international humanitarian law.*"[114] The two main forms of state practice which, according to the study, make this provision qualify as customary rule, include collective measures such as the "sending of peacekeeping or peace-enforcement troops."[115] Thus, the very practice of U.N. peacekeepers to prevent violations of the laws of armed conflict has contributed to the elaboration of a positive obligation, under customary humanitarian law, of states and international organizations to "exercise influence" to prevent and stop breaches of the same.[116] This, again, supports the thesis that the protection of civilians by U.N. peacekeepers be interpreted as the enforcement of member states' positive obligations under both IHL and HRL.

In view of the above, thus, there is ample evidence that the mandate to protect civilians can be interpreted as a responsibility of the United Nations and member states to implement their legal obligations under both IHL and HRL. ICRC's list of fundamental guarantees is useful in that they, in clear terms and explicit language, determine legal rules which applies to all, at all times, in all places. Also, importantly, they do not require determination of a conflict as international or non-international armed conflict in order to apply. Given that most U.N. peace operations deploy in situations of internal strife involving armed groups with clear

---

[114] *Id.* at 509 (emphasis added).
[115] *Id.*
[116] *See also* Secretary-General's Report to the Security Council on the Protection of Civilians in Armed Conflict, *supra* note 68, paras 44, 57.

military and political support from other states and non-state actors, this is most valuable.[117]

This is not to say that instruments of IHL and HRL have ceased in relevance. On the contrary, they remain at the core of legal obligations of sending states as well as the host state, and allow for legal action in case of non-compliance. The obligations of states under both sets of legal frameworks form, and should continue to do so, the basis when analysing positive and negative obligations inherent in the fundamental guarantees. Judging from the periodic reports of the Secretary-General on the issue of civilian protection, however, the emphasis of this legal dimension of the protection of civilians appears to have faded since 1999.[118]

4. Implementing the Concept of Civilian Protection: Monuc

It was only subsequent to the crisis in the town of Bunia in Eastern Congo in 2003, temporarily stifled by a temporary E.U.-led intervention known as Interim Multinational Emergency Force (IEMF) or Operation Artemis, that MONUC's mandate to use force to protect civilians under threat assumed real significance.[119] Building on IEMF's assertive presence and authority to act,[120] a 5,000 troop strong MONUC Ituri brigade deployed to the area under a new, reinforced Security

---

[117] *See*, for instance, the report from 2004 of the Secretary-General on MONUC: "The majority of human rights violations involve violations of the right to security and private property committed by the armed elements, militia members, foreign armed groups and State law enforcement agencies, who are also responsible for killings, torture and inhuman and degrading treatment, including the widespread practice of detaining prisoners in underground cells." U.N. Doc. S/2004/251, para. 46 (Mar. 25, 2004).

[118] A review of the Secretary-General's reports on the protection of civilians in armed conflict since 1999 (*see* U.N. Docs. S/1999/957; S/2002/1300; S/2004/431; S/2005/740) reveals that the strong wording and call by the Secretary-General in 1999 for action by the Security Council with respect to IHL and HRL is never repeated in subsequent reports. *See* U.N. Doc. S/1999/957, *supra* note 68, paras 30–32.

[119] For MONUC and the protection of civilians as well as the specific EU-led Operation Artemis, see the following literature: Alpha Sow, *Achievements of the Interim Emergency Multinational Force and Future Scenarios*, in Challenges of Peace Implementation, The UN Mission in the Democratic Republic of the Congo (Mark Malan and Joao Gomes Porto, 2004) at 209–232 [hereinafter Sow and hereinafter Malan & Porto]; Department of Peacekeeping Operations, Best Practices Unit, *Operation Artemis: Lessons of the Interim Emergency Multinational Force* (2004); Katarina Månsson, *Use of Force and Protection of Civilians: Peace Operations in the Congo*, 12 INt'l Peacekeeping 503–519 (2005); Holt & Berkman, *supra* note 4, at 155–179.

[120] U.N. Doc. S/RES/1484 (May 30, 2003), para. 1. The SC Resolution authorized IEMF, under Chapter VII, "to ensure... if the situation so requires it, to contribute to the safety of the civilian population."

Council mandate.[121] Contrary to the initial mandate from 2000, MONUC was now authorized to "use *all necessary means* to fulfil its mandate in Ituri district and, as it deems within its capabilities, in North and South Kivu,"[122] including the protection of civilians under imminent threat of physical violence. In 2004, the geographical as well as substantive scope of MONUC's Chapter VII mandate was further expanded; first, to encompass the DRC *in toto*, second, to include a mandate to support the Government of National Unity and Transition to, among other things, support operations to disarm foreign combatants and to assist in the promotion and protection of human rights.[123]

An interesting detail of this resolution is paragraph 6. It "[a]uthorizes MONUC to use necessary means, within its capacity and in areas where its armed units are deployed, to carry out the tasks listed in paragraph 4, subparagraphs (a) to (g) above, and in paragraph 5, subparagraphs (a), (b), (c), (e) and (f) above." This entails that whereas MONUC may resort to the use of force to, *inter alia*, protect civilians, disarm foreign combatants and contribute to the successful completion of the electoral process, it is not authorized to use the necessary means to fulfil its mandate to assist in the promotion and protection of human rights.[124] Formally speaking, thus, MONUC's protection of civilians mandate is not expressly couched in human rights terms or directly associated with MONUC's efforts to assist the Congolese authorities to protect and promote human rights.

Several factors may serve to explain this: First, there is still no agreed definition, let alone doctrine, of protection of civilians in a U.N. peacekeeping context.[125] One U.N. staff member referred to the need, as a matter of priority, for DPKO to develop a protection of civilians doctrine which spells out in generic terms what the concept means in practice.[126] Second, the size of the DRC is enormous. The extension alone of the Chapter VII mandate to the whole of the country *per se* raised expectations among the population which, in the words of the United Nations, "no external partner could ever fulfil."[127] In this respect, the UN Secretariat has stressed that "MONUC can not implement the transitional process on behalf of the Transitional Government, it can only assist."[128] Any notion of enforcing,

---

[121] U.N. Doc. S/RES/1493 (July 28, 2003), paras 25–27.
[122] *Id.* para. 26 (emphasis added). This should be contrasted with the mandate to "take necessary action" to, among other things, protect civilians," as provided for in U.N. Doc. S/RES/1291 (Feb. 24, 2000).
[123] U.N. Doc. S/RES/1565 (Oct. 1, 2004), para. 5(a) and (g).
[124] *Id.* para. 5(g).
[125] Holt & Berkman, *supra* note 38, at 110. However, there are efforts underway in DPKO Peacekeeping Best Practices Unit to establish best practices with respect to this particular issue.
[126] Phone interview, U.N. staff, Galway-Kinshasa, May 2006.
[127] *See* Report of the Secretary-General on the United Nations Organization Mission in the Democratic Republic of the Congo, S/2004/650 (Aug. 16, 2004), paras 59, 119.
[128] *Id.* para. 119.

literally speaking, respect for human rights through the use of force throughout the territory would inevitably have further raised immense expectation among the Congolese population.

In retrospective, another likely, and highly controversial, explanatory aspect relates to one of most contentious issues of the implementation of MONUC's mandate: its joint operations with the Congolese army, the *Forces Armées de la République Démocratique du Congo* (FARDC). Such joint operations are deployed primarily as a means to extend state authority throughout the territory of the DRC, to forcibly disarm foreign armed groups and to protect civilians.[129] Joint operations mostly entail MONUC acting in support of FARDC[130] and are undertaken "in the context of [MONUC's] protection of civilians mandate and to support the ongoing efforts to strengthen FARDC to enable them to carry out their responsibilities in this regard."[131] As the list of allegations of human rights violations committed by the FARDC in the course of such operations has grown dramatically and huge population displacements, even reprisals against civilians, have taken place as a consequence thereof,[132] MONUC has found itself in a highly difficult position. One MONUC staff member phrased the conundrum of interpreting its protection of civilians mandate in this context in the following way:

> In our rules of engagement, if we witness soldiers looting or raping, of course we stop these things from happening, but is it policy that our protection of civilians also applies against the national government authorities in that we are allowed to shoot if necessary to stop them?[133]

Had MONUC been formally mandated to use all necessary means to protect and promote human rights of the Congolese population, it could be argued that the answer, in theory, to this question would be a positive one. In practice, it would be

---

[129] *See* S.C. Res 1565 (Oct. 1, 2004), para. 5(c) and Report of the Secretary-General on the United Nations Organization Mission in the Democratic Republic of the Congo, U.N. Doc. S/2006/310 (May 22, 2006), para. 8.

[130] *See* for instance, Report of the Secretary-General on the United Nations Mission in the Democratic Republic of the Congo, S/2005/167 (Mar. 11, 2005), para. 79.

[131] *Id.*

[132] According to MONUC Human Rights Division's assessment of the human rights situation in the DRC from January 1 to June 30, 2006, 53 percent of all violations recorded by the Division were committed by the FARDC. The Division reports that "many of these violations have been committed in the context of ongoing military operations against militia groups who remain active in Ituri, North, and South Kivu and Katanga provinces." *See* The Human Rights Situation in the Democratic Republic of the Congo (DRC) [hereinafter The Human Rights Situation in the DRC], (July 27, 2006), at 8, 9, *available at*: www.monuc.org/downloads/HRD/_6_months_2006_report.pdf (last visited Sept. 15, 2007). Regarding reprisals on civilian population and massive displacement as a consequence of FARDC operations, *see* U.N. Doc. S/2006/310, paras 28 and 37–41.

[133] Interview, staff, MONUC, Kinshasa, May 2006.

impossible: it runs counter to the fact that MONUC is deployed at the invitation of the government and given its mandate to assist in support of the Government. Instead, MONUC has embarked on a three-fold strategy to ensure that the human rights costs arising from FARDC operations be mitigated: (i) strengthening civil and military coordination with FARDC; (ii) contingency planning for a humanitarian response to possible displacements before military operations are launched; (iii) actively pursue with the Government of the DRC its efforts to investigate and prosecute human rights abuses during these operations, with particular emphasis on holding commanders responsible.[134]

A more positive, and long-term approach, it may be argued, is thus to interpret the protection of civilians mandate from a HRL and IHL perspective by emphasising both negative and positive obligations deriving from both sets of legal frameworks on the part of MONUC troop contributing states and the Congolese authorities. Protection of civilians in the DRC largely concerns two questions: urgent issues such as massacres and individual acts of violence committed by armed groups.[135] In this respect, it has been opined that the real question evolving around the issue of protection of civilians mandate relates to how it can be conceived of and coined in human rights terms. It is felt that civilian protection in peacekeeping contexts was still considered as a matter of conflict resolution matter rather than a matter of human rights protection.

While we most commonly associate civilian protection with direct military action, MONUC's approach to the implementation of its mandate is an integrated one; "MONUC intervention should be multi-layered and homogenous, in the sense that all components are targeting the same objectives."[136] Below follows an attempt to identify some of the key activities undertaken by MONUC military and civilian components to implement its mandate to protect civilians and how they can be construed of in such a legal perspective.[137] As will be demonstrated, MONUC may be considered the key peace operation to have adopted the most proactive and assertive, and perhaps most creative, methods to implement that mandate.

---

[134] U.N. Doc. S/2006/310 (May 22, 2006), para. 49(a–c).
[135] Phone interview, U.N. staff, Galway-Kinshasa, May 2006.
[136] Sow, *supra* note 118, at 215. This approach was particularly tested from the outset in Ituri, where a multi-pronged "Ituri strategy" was prepared by MONUC in July 2003 in order to address key political, humanitarian, human rights, military, security and recovery issues in Bunia and Ituri over the short and medium term. *See* Henri Boshoff, *Overview of MONUC's Military Strategy and Concept of Operations, in* Malan & Porto, *supra* note 118, at 141.
[137] This does not, by any means, attempt to provide an exhaustive list of activities nor of obligations under IHL or HRL, but should rather be read as an initiative to further studies and research in the subject matter.

4.1. Civilian Protection through Respect by Peacekeepers (Peacekeepers' Compliance)

Peacekeepers, first of all, can contribute to strengthening civilian protection by refraining from acts of abuse, ill-treatment, exploitation, and harassment. The revelations of the sexual abuse and exploitation committed by MONUC civilian and military peacekeepers had such grave repercussions in terms of credibility and legitimacy that it almost made the "whole operation collapse" in 2004.[138] From January 1, 2004 to December 9, 2005, investigations against 278 personnel were carried out: As a result, 16 civilians, 16 Formed Police Units (FPU), and 122 military personnel were dismissed from the mission.[139] Under IHL and HRL, rape and other forms of sexual violence, especially against women and children who remain most vulnerable, is prohibited.[140] The 1999 SG's Bulletin also prohibits rape, enforced prostitution and any form of sexual assault, and humiliation and degrading treatment.[141]

Apart from the assault on the very human dignity of the victims subject to any abuse and exploitation, sexual or other forms of harassment and ill-treatment, there are two serious consequences with a wider impact on civilian protection: First, U.N. peacekeepers (military in particular) act as role models for FARDC soldiers. If acts of abuse are not acted against promptly and proactively by MONUC authorities, how can incentives to combat abuse, particularly by prosecution, committed by FARDC be expected to take hold? Second, U.N. peacekeepers loose credibility in the eyes of the local population whom they are supposed to protect. A serious implication of this is that MONUC may loose what constitutes its most important source of information, and is, as a result, left with poorer intelligence upon which to plan tactical operations, including those that could be of relevance to its civilian protection mandate.

4.2. Civilian Protection through "Ensuring Respect" (Peacekeepers' Influence)

The duty of U.N. peacekeepers to uphold the negative obligations as stipulated in IHL and HRL is of utmost importance. However, assisting, through pro-active measures, the host state in paying tribute to its own legal obligations is perhaps of greater importance. Such efforts are likely to have more long-term effect in terms of reinforcing state capacity and setting the groundwork for relationship between state

---

[138] Interview, staff, MONUC, Kinshasa, May 2006.
[139] Implementation of the Recommendations of the Special Committee on Peacekeeping Operations, U.N. Doc. A/60/640, Add.1, (Dec. 29, 2005), para. 42. *See also* Ray Murphy, *An Assessment of UN Efforts to Address Sexual Misconduct by Peacekeeping Personnel*, 13 Int'l Peacekeeping 534–537 (2006).
[140] *See*, for instance, Common Article 3(c) GC, *supra* note 52; Articles 76 and 77 AP I, *supra* note 52 Article 4(2) (Fundamental Guarantees) AP II, *supra* note 92.
[141] Secretary-General's Bulletin, *supra* note 38, para. 7.2.

authorities and its population based on respect and protection. The best "civilian protection" is enhancing sustainability of state authorities.[142] In MONUC, we may identify at least three methods undertaken by its military and civilian components to implement the mandate of civilian protection in this respect: joint operations and patrols; reporting and monitoring; and assisting in prosecution.[143] They can all be conceived of as states' obligations to *promote* respect for and observance of human rights and to *draw attention* to possible breaches of civilian and political rights (U.N. Charter/ICCPR), to *ensure respect* for the rules of IHL (Article 1 GC and AP I in conjunction with Article 89), and to *exercise their influence*, to the degree possible, *to stop violations of international humanitarian law* (Rule 144, customary international humanitarian law).

4.2.1. *Joint Patrols and Joint Operations with FARDC*

One weakness identified with the E.U.-led IEMF has been that it undertook too few foot patrols.[144] Once MONUC Ituri brigade took over, it has been assessed that, thanks to house searches carried out by Uruguayan and Bangladeshi contingents patrolling on foot, the violence decreased and a sense of security returned.[145] When such activities are undertaken jointly with FARDC soldiers, MONUC forces may perform a role model role through appropriate instructions, guidance, and their behaviour. A MONUC Commander explained the procedure of undertaking joint patrols with FARDC in his area of operation:

> Before the patrol starts, the patrol commander from the brigade, usually a captain, brief them on the route, the purpose of the patrol, what it is that they should not do in particular, [ensure] there is no harassment, no shooting unless you are ordered to do so. They are told the ground rules... At least, they are learning something, becoming more professional. The more they see, even how we dress, how we comport ourselves; if there is an incident, how we handle it... They will see that we just don't go around brutalizing people.[146]

Likewise, joint operations between MONUC and FARDC may have a similar positive effect. According to another MONUC Commander, the purpose of the

---

[142] In this respect, successful security sector reform, aiming at a fully integrated and functioning Congolese army and police respectively, is the best long-term protection for the civilian population. Secretary-General's report on the United Nations Mission in the Democratic Republic of the Congo, U.N. Doc. S/2005/167 (Mar. 11, 2005), correctly identified the continuous lack of payment for soldiers and policemen as the "greatest concern for security." para. 74.

[143] One could add two other key areas, training of state security forces and the overall security sector reform which are key measures crucial to civilian protection in a more long-term perspective.

[144] Sow, *supra* note 118, at 211.

[145] *Id.* at 211–212.

[146] Interview, MONUC Commander (I), Kinshasa, May 2006.

joint operations is two-fold: protect civilians and disarm.[147] Such robust operations have occurred primarily in the eastern part of the Congo, particularly in North and South Kivu in response to attacks by Forces Démocratiques de Libération du Rwanda (FDLR) and other armed elements on the local population. Joint MONUC-FARDC operations have included foot patrols, supported by activities of rapid reaction helicopter units, in an attempt to stabilize the situation.[148] Such close cooperation has revealed the significant weaknesses of FARDC such as "the training; equipping and other logistical support, in particular transportation; organisation; leadership; fighting ability and, above all, the conduct of Congolese army units' vis-à-vis the population."[149] The SRSG has raised this last issue with the President of the DRC, Joseph Kabila, and MONUC has compiled detailed information on serious misconduct on the part of the Congolese armed forces. A direct dialogue on relevant standards of HRL and IHL between MONUC and the Congolese authorities has thus been initiated as a consequence of cooperation between the two.[150]

4.2.2. Reporting and Monitoring

Such a dialogue has partly been rendered possible as a consequence of active monitoring of and reporting of the human rights record of FARDC and other Congolese security agencies. In terms of reporting, MONUC Military Division contends that it has reported on human rights as a separate heading since the outset of the mission.[151] More systematic reporting on human rights, based primarily on information gathered by military observers regarding complaints on FARDC, was initiated in February 2005 and culminated in a comprehensive report on FARDC in January 2006 (covering all 2005).[152] Representing a most interesting novelty in terms of civil-military cooperation in peacekeeping contexts, this reporting within the military on FARDC has developed into a system of joint reports on human rights by MONUC Human Rights Division and MONUC Military Division.[153] By

---

[147] Interview, MONUC Commander (II), Kinshasa, May 2006.
[148] Report of the Secretary-General on the United Nations Mission in the Democratic Republic of the Congo, U.N. Doc. S/2005/506 (Aug. 2, 2005), para. 33.
[149] Report of the Secretary-General on the United Nations Mission in the Democratic Republic of the Congo, U.N. Doc. S/2006/310 (May 22, 2006).
[150] Diplomatic dialogue, it should be remembered, was one of the "indirect methods" which could be adopted through a third Party for the purpose of the establishment of so-called "neutralized zones" or safety zones for civilians under Article 15 of the IV Geneva Convention. *See* Commentary IV, *supra* note 76, at 130.
[151] Interview, Human Rights and Civil Affairs Officer, MONUC Force Headquarters, Kinshasa, May 2006.
[152] *Id.*
[153] Interview, Human Rights Officer, MONUC, Kinshasa, May 2006. This system of joint reports had only been initiated a few months prior to field research in May 2006.

merging the military's monthly reports, based on reports from MONUC Military Observers, with the monthly reports of the Human Rights Division, consolidated monthly human rights report are handed over to the Congolese officials since the start of 2006.[154] The importance of a merged report rests in the fact that it allows for the Human Rights Division to ensure correct use of terminology and that the right definition of violations is used.[155] This new system was warmly commended by MONUC senior leadership who viewed it as an important tool to put pressure on the FARDC high command to take action against human rights perpetrators in its forces and, as a result, induce positive change.[156]

Reporting relies on proper monitoring *in situ*. MONUC Commander of Sector 5 (Maneima and the Kivus) in Eastern Congo set out that

> proper and complete military information picture...is a critical requirement for the successful conduct of operation [and] has been greatly enhanced by the deployment of troops on the ground as well as the increase in the number of military observer teams and their deployment to team sites in remote areas throughout the sector.[157]

The role played by Military Observers is key to this aim, not the least in terms of assembling information with significant human rights implications. For instance, they perform an indispensable role in areas where MONUC Human Rights Division has no field presence. One MONUC human rights officer described the Military Observers as "very good to go and check [out an incident] when we are not there, and then sending back messages that they think we should come."[158] Military observers have also played a role in locating and identifying vulnerable populations in need, upon which MONUC human rights officers are informed of their situation or by physically bringing them to the nearby human rights office.[159] Incidents have been prevented due to such information and can thus be perceived of as a collaborative method of protecting civilians.

Such an indirect human rights role of MONUC Military Observers, the "eyes and ears of the mission," is likely to be reinforced as a system of Military Observer Human Rights focal points is due to be put in place.[160] The idea is that such human rights focal points be briefed on basic human rights methodology by the nearby human rights field office, be instructed on how to collect basic information on human rights cases through an "incident form" which should be handed back to

---

[154] Including President Kabila and to the FARDC Force Commander.
[155] Interview, Human Rights Officer, MONUC, Kinshasa, May 2006.
[156] Interview, Senior Official, MONUC, Kinshasa, May 2006.
[157] Lawrence Smith, *MONUC's Military Involvement in the Eastern Congo (Maneima and the Kivus)*, in Malan & Porto, *supra* note 118, at 235.
[158] Interview, Human Rights Officer, MONUC, Kinshasa, May 2006.
[159] Phone interview, Military Observer, MONUC, Kinshasa-Beni, May 2005.
[160] Interview, Human Rights Officer, MONUC, Kinshasa, May 2006.

the closest human rights field office. Drafted by the Human Rights Division and developed jointly with MONUC Force HQ, such incident forms aim at educating all reporting sources within the Military, both military observers and troops, on how to report on a human rights incident. Again, MONUC appears to be setting groundbreaking precedent in the context of close cooperative arrangements between human rights officers and the military in peacekeeping operations which may have significant bearing on the protection of civilians.

4.2.3. *Protection through Prosecution*
Reliable information, in turn, is a prerequisite if military commanders and soldier be held to account for violations of IHL and HRL. Although the process may be slow, MONUC can today show pride in having assisted in the prosecution of several FARDC officers responsible for breaches of HRL and IHL.[161] A MONUC staff member explained the effect of firm action in arrest and prosecution. "The lesson from DRC Ituri is that arrests and the prosecutions were actually an effective tool in breaking the morale of the militia, breaking their backbone, by showing that the prosecution authority is universal and the lesson was that that impunity doesn't help, even in the name of disarmament."[162] MONUC, for instance, provided technical and logistical support and accompanied, for on-site hearings, the *Tribunal Militaire de Garnison de Mbandaka* and the lawyers of seven soldiers accused of committing mass rapes in December 2003 in Songo Mboyo.[163] Seven of the accused were sentenced to life for crimes against humanity (rape and looting), a verdict later upheld almost in full by the military Appeals Chamber.[164] MONUC Human Rights Division monitored the trial and the execution of the sentence pronounced. This and other successful legal actions against the military,[165] according to a MONUC human rights officer, send very important signals to the civilian population but also make the military justice system familiar and used to dealing with human rights cases. "Now you have a team [the *auditorat militaire*] that is motivated, for the first time they apply the Rome Statute. We made them feel proud that they were doing something new good in the DRC and they understood the role."[166]

---

[161] *See* in particular the case of Songo Mboyo, *The Human Rights Situation in the DRC, supra* note 131, at 11.
[162] Interview, staff, MONUC, Kinshasa, May 2006.
[163] *The Human Rights Situation in the DRC, supra* note 131, at 18.
[164] *Id.* 11.
[165] *Id.* at 11–12. In 2006, 42 soldiers were also sentenced by a military court in Mbandaka for murder and rape, as crimes against humanity, committed during a mutiny on July 3 to 4, 2005. See Report of the Secretary-General on the United Nations Mission in the Democratic Republic of the Congo, U.N. Doc. S/2006/759 (Sept. 21, 2006) para. 71.
[166] Interview, Human Rights Officer, MONUC, Kinshasa, May 2006.

Human Rights Mobile Teams, established under the Special Investigation Unit of the Human Rights Division with the purpose of reacting rapidly to serious incidents of human rights violations and tasked with in-depth investigations of such abuses in remote areas,[167] constitute yet another important feature of MONUC's overall mandate to protect civilians.[168] Dispatched as multi-disciplinary teams, they have not only documented human rights abuses by FARDC and militia groups and handed over names of suspects to the Congolese authorities for legal action,[169] but have been instrumental in having a preventive effect.[170] "[In terms of] early warning, effectiveness of investigation, outreach to the civilian population, and follow up of cases with previous judicial and military authorities it is really a good formula."[171] By depending on military escorts for most of the work, the mobile teams have also provided a means of demonstrating to MONUC Force what MONUC can accomplish in human rights matters.[172] In addition, in North Kivu, human rights mobile teams constitute "one of the main sources of information [for MONUC] because they really go out where the military is in control."[173] The high value of such information for the mission as a whole was confirmed by senior MONUC leadership, particularly due to its independence, impartiality and accuracy, and constituted an important means of exercising political pressure.

4.3. *Protection through "Enforcing Respect" (Peacekeepers' Activism)*

The above examples may be considered less controversial but also less "traditional" measures of implementing the protection of civilians mandate. Direct enforcement measures by military troops remains perhaps our standard perception of protection. Exact information as to the nature of such direct military action, understood as the use of force, is difficult to access (because of their rare occurrence?), why one necessarily has to broaden the scope of proactive measures which may result in enhanced security and safety for civilians. Two broad categories may be identified: (i) Deterrence and prevention through action and (ii) Presence, facilitating assistance, and other methods.

A senior MONUC official referred to the mission's approach to the protection of civilians as one which attempts "to bring together military and humanitarians [including human rights actors] to work together using, I think, rather uniquely,

---

[167] *The Human Rights Situation in the DRC, supra* note 131, at 18.
[168] The first Human Rights Mobile Team was established in North Kivu in 2005 and, following its successfulness, three other mobile teams were established in Katanga, Ituti and South Kivu in May 2006.
[169] *The Human Rights Situation in the DRC, supra* note 131, at 17–18.
[170] Interview, Human Rights Officer, MONUC, Kinshasa, May 2006.
[171] *Id.*
[172] Interview, Human Rights Officer, MONUC, Kinshasa, May 2006.
[173] *Id.*

our own military to protect civilians."[174] In this respect, the dominant approach appears to work according to a narrow definition of protection, i.e. as protection against violence in terms of *prevention* and *containment* so that the level of violence decreases.[175] In such perspective, protection is first and foremost a matter of military means, where the role of civilians is to draw the attention of the military what needs to be done or to help alert humanitarian actors. In practice, what this means, is respect for basic human rights and principles of IHL. As recalled by another MONUC official, "imminent threat of physical violence" in reality means "a threat of human rights abuses."[176] In the same breath, the same official underscored that it should always be borne in mind that protection of civilians is but one of several mandates bestowed on MONUC. Therefore, protection is not a matter of interpretation, but one of priority.[177]

4.3.1. *Deterrence and Prevention through Action*
Pursuant to the Bukavu crisis in summer of 2004, MONUC, in outlining its military concept of operations, determined that the efficiency of its military force deployment in South Kivu and other parts of eastern Congo depended on "its capacity to act as *a deterrent*, on the one hand, and as *a rapid reaction force*, on the other."[178] The Secretary-General asserted that the military capability of MONUC in Ituri, North, and South Kivu[179] must be one to deter challenges as those presented in Bukavu "while, at the same time, ensuring the protection of civilians who may be of risk."[180] It is interesting that the report avails of broader language than "imminent threat;" which seems to provide MONUC with a large margin of appreciation in interpreting its mandate.

From 2004 and beyond, the pre-emptive measures employed by a more robust MONUC to prevent attacks on civilian populations have involved forcible measures to disarm militia and dismantle their headquarters and other strongholds.[181] In Ituri, such methods of forcibly disarming militia groups have included distribution of flyers with the warning that unless they surrender their arms "you will be considered

---

[174] Interview, Senior Official, MONUC, Kinshasa, May 2006.
[175] As set out in the terms of reference of the so-called Protection Clusters, *see* below. Phone interview, UN staff, Galway-Kinshasa, May 2006.
[176] Interview, Senior Official, MONUC, Kinshasa, May 2006.
[177] *Id.*
[178] Report of the Secretary-General on the United Nations Mission in the Democratic Republic of the Congo, U.N. Doc. S/2004/650 (Aug. 16, 2004), para. 81 (emphasis added).
[179] For the main tasks of the MONUC force in North and South Kivu *see id.* para. 84.
[180] *Id.* para. 78.
[181] Report of the Secretary-General on the United Nations Mission in the Democratic Republic of the Congo, U.N. Doc. S/2005/167 (Mar. 15, 2005) paras 12, 15, 19.

as a criminal and you will be pursued."[182] In eastern Congo, the mission's rules of engagement have subsequently allowed MONUC to arrest and detain civilians and militia element found engaged in criminal acts.[183]

Large-scale cordon-and-search operations have been undertaken in Ituri to dismantle Front for National Integration (FNI) strongholds and in the Kivus to weaken FDLR or ex-FAR/Interahamwe presences, not seldom involving military clashes resulting in casualties on both sides.[184]

Other measures deter attacks against civilians in eastern Congo have included assistance by MONUC to organize community-based Village Vigilance Committees in South Kivu, an early warning system aimed at preventing attacks on the population.[185] A MONUC Commander referred to this early warning as a "911-number system" by which members of the local population call a specific number or by churches using bells or other association.[186] As a response, MONUC may use its quick reaction forces, with or without FARDC, using mortar rounds and by illuminating areas to deter harassment (so called "night flash operations.") The system was considered very successful.

In the spirit of GC IV, the "direct method" of establishing neutralized zones, or more appropriately "safety zones" for the civilian population, has been employed by MONUC. In the Kivus, for instance, to sustain a ceasefire between Rwanda and the Congolese Government, MONUC established a 10-kilometre-wide security zone in the Kanyabayonga/Lubero area to protect the civilian population and ensure access for the distribution of humanitarian assistance.[187] This security zone permitted some limited aid operations and facilitated the gradual return of some 150,000 internally displaced persons.[188]

4.3.2. *Presence, Facilitating Assistance, and other Methods*

Protection by the use of MONUC forces, it appears, is however done mostly by using their very presence as a stabilization factor and through patrolling, either by

---

[182] Andrew England, *UN Soldiers Talk Tough in Attempt to Pacify Congo*, Financial Times, Mar. 29, 2005.
[183] Roberto Ricci, *Human Rights Challenges in the DRC: A View from MONUC's Human Rights Section*, in Malan & Porto, *supra* note 118, at 100.
[184] Report of the Secretary-General on the United Nations Mission in the Democratic Republic of the Congo, U.N. Doc. S/2005/167 (Mar. 15, 2005), paras 19, 41, 78.
[185] Report of the Secretary-General on the United Nations Mission in the Democratic Republic of the Congo, U.N. Doc. S/2005/506 (Aug. 2, 2005) para. 33.
[186] Interview, Commander II, MONUC, Kinshasa, May 2006.
[187] Report of the Secretary-General on the United Nations Mission in the Democratic Republic of the Congo, U.N. Doc. S/2004/1034 (Dec. 31, 2004) para. 22.
[188] Report of the Secretary-General on the United Nations Mission in the Democratic Republic of the Congo, U.N. Doc. S/2005/167 (Mar. 15, 2005), para. 22.

vehicle, helicopter, or foot.[189] The case of Katanga is one case in point where violence and harassment of the local population by FARDC succumbed only after the deployment of MONUC forces. According to a senior MONUC official, Katanga represents the case "where even a small contingent of military troops can have an extraordinary pacifying effect, a) on the civilian population who look forward it, and b) [by putting] the military on their guard."[190] While the Katanga brigade was established primarily to secure the elections, reports of repeated serious human rights violations were mentioned as a key reason for its deployment.[191] As a general rule, the more patrols undertaken by MONUC, the more of a deterrent effect.[192]

MONUC forces have also provided military escort to facilitate humanitarian assistance and food delivery to vulnerable populations, particularly in the east, and provided protection to such operations. Another protection activity in which MONUC Military engage with the humanitarian community is through the Joint Protection Working Group. Established in November 2005 in North Kivu, by mid-2006 such Working Groups existed also in South Kivu, Ituri, and Katanga.[193] Co-chaired by MONUC and the United Nations High Commissioner for Refugees, it encompasses MONUC Military, Humanitarian Affairs, Police, Child Protection, Human Rights and other civilian components as well as UNICEF and other U.N. agencies and international NGOs. The Working Groups operate primarily at a provincial level as Protection Clusters with a focus of pursuing advocacy vis-à-vis the local authorities on the development of protection strategies. The focus is the use of MONUC forces to protect civilian population and to minimize the collateral damage of FARDC operations. To this aim the Clusters have initiated a so called "qualitative monitoring" system, the purpose of which is to exercise pressure on FARDC and the Congolese authorities by identifying gross trends and patterns of abusive behaviour.

Yet, another interesting pioneering protection mechanism in MONUC came with the establishment by the Human Rights Division of a so-called Protection Unit of Victims, Witnesses and Human Rights Defenders in 2005. The Unit originated from the need to protect witnesses to human rights investigations carried out by the Division and was formed against the question how MONUC's mandate (under Chapter VII) to protect civilians under imminent threat of physical violence could merge with that (under Chapter VI) to put an end to impunity.[194] The strategy is to

---

[189] Phone interview, U.N. staff, Galway-Kinshasa, May 2006.
[190] Interview, Senior Official, MONUC, Kinshasa, May 2006.
[191] *Id.*
[192] *See*, for instance, Report of the Secretary-General on the United Nations Mission in the Democratic Republic of the Congo, U.N. Doc. S/2006/759 (Sept. 21, 2006), para. 47.
[193] Phone interview, U.N staff, Galway-Kinshasa, May 2006.
[194] Interview, Human Rights Officer, MONUC, Kinshasa, May 2006.

protect individual civilians at risk of human rights violations through monitoring, follow-up on cases with authorities and making it known to potential perpetrators that the security of certain individuals is under surveillance.[195] This approach is almost the opposite that of the Protection Clusters' quantitative- and trend-focused strategy and is indicative of the fact that "protection" remains a highly contested concept which give rise to numerous interpretations and, consequently, activities within a peace operation.

5. Conclusion

As we move to the field, the theoretical linkages between the mandate to protect civilians, on the one hand, and IHL and HRL, on the other, appear to evaporate to a significant degree. Explicitly outlining legal obligations imply a corresponding process of identifying responsibility, alongside the necessary allocation of resources, political willingness, and prioritization over other mandated goals. There is good reason to believe that states have few incentives to embark on such identification process; it may even deter from contributing to peace operations. It must also be remembered that protection of civilians, generally, is still to be defined in doctrine. Peacekeeping missions, as is the case also in MONUC, have as of yet not identified any "best practices" with respect to the implementation of the protection of civilians mandate during the course of operations which could inform such a doctrine. Any future doctrine, it is hoped, should wish to adopt and embrace the legal framework provided by basic rules of HRL and IHL as a *constructive* point of departure. States should embrace such a framework as a *positive* instrument against which, with imagination and creativity, concrete methods can be extrapolated and subsequently implemented in the field.

However, signs of humanitarian and human rights law already penetrating through the window of the protection of civilians mandate are several.[196] A clear indication is the strengthened collaborative arrangements between military and human rights actors in the field, and MONUC may stand out as a pioneering "best practices" case study in this respect. The fact that MONUC military deployments have been made on the basis of reports of human rights violations documented by the mission's Human Rights Division is an important example in this respect. Another positive aspect of the cooperation between military and human rights actors

---

[195] *The Human Rights Situation in the DRC, supra* note 131, at 16.
[196] Reflected also in several reports of the Secretary-General on MONUC. *See* in particular U.N. Doc. S/2003/1098 (Nov. 17, 2003), para. 68; U.N. Doc. S/2004/251 (Mar. 25, 2004), para. 28; U.N. Doc. S/2006/310 (May 22, 2006), paras 43, 49.

is that it has generally been proactively linked to a political process of enhancing state authority and to efforts aiming at reinforcing capacities of the Congolese (military) justice system.

While shortcomings and flaws inevitably remain, the importance is that such process has been set in motion, and that HRL and IHL is *peu à peu* internalized by national authorities. Several interviewees stressed the supportive and positive attitude of MONUC Force Commander and senior MONUC leadership in this respect. This seems to underscore the abovementioned importance attached to identifying, and reinforcing the observance of, the obligations of the SRSG and Force Commander involved in their overall responsibility for the implementation of the mandate. They must ensure proper training, clear instructions and the allocation of adequate resources to enable a constructive, integrated approach aiming at a shared vision as to how protection of civilians mandate is to be realized.

It may be by framing member states' positive obligations, under international humanitarian law, to "ensure respect" by other state parties and, under international human rights law, to draw the attention of other states parties to comply with their obligations, that the protection of civilians mandate may most fruitfully be considered. This way, U.N. peace operations constitute a most interesting case study where the encounter between IHL and HRL is constructively merged, with positive short-term as well as long-term effects. Such an approach appears to constructively link the mutually reinforcing legal obligations under both legal frameworks to the overall process of consolidating state authority and building viable institutions responsible for upholding and respecting the rights of its population.

Conclusions

The new "war on terror" has gradually led to a misapplication of the foundations of international humanitarian law (IHL), in particular the provisions applicable to protected persons like Prisoners of War (POW). The question of the relationship between IHL and human rights law (HRL), which may provide for a "safety net", has therefore become more relevant than ever.

IHL and human rights lawyers have traditionally been rivals, with the first being considered utopian view holders of a peaceful world and the latter being viewed as ruthless realists who simply try to *set limits* to violence, which is considered intrinsic to human nature. However, since the 9/11 attacks, major deprivations of fundamental rights considered as non-derogable under IHL, have occurred. In order to justify these, suspects of terrorism have been labelled as "unlawful combatants", an unheard term under the Geneva Conventions of 1949, according to which a person shall either be considered a combatant or a civilian, and therefore be granted protection under the respective convention. This new term was coined in order to deprive detainees of any classification and, thus, any protection under IHL. IHL and HRL lawyers, in particular military lawyers, reacted with a joint outcry. It shall be recalled that the misapplication of IHL provisions, as operated in Guantanamo Bay and Abu Ghraib, does not only deprive the captives of their rights, but also jeopardizes the rights of the military forces detaining them. The aim of this book, as illustrated by N. Quénivet, was to discuss whether the new war on terror and this joint reaction to ensure that no person may be kept in a "legal vacuum", may be leading to a merger of HRL and IHL.

The outcome is that IHL and HRL are two distinct, though complementary, branches of law. They are not interchangeable, since in times of war the tolerated level of violence is higher than in peacetime, meaning that also the restrictions on the use of force – and the respect e.g. of the right to life, as indicated by J.M. Henckaerts – will considerably differ. As paradoxical as it may seem, due to the different aims of IHL and HRL, it may even be that with regard to specific issues IHL may be more "humane" than human rights. E.g. whereas in times of armed conflict "dum dum" bullets are prohibited, they may be used by the police in peacetime, particularly in hostage taking cases, when the victim's protection may justify the killing of the aggressor. In armed conflicts, though, the objective is not necessarily to kill the enemy, as mistakenly supported by some, but rather to place him/her "out of the game". This objective may be achieved by wounding or taking captive the enemy, but the idea is that he/she should be given the chance to get back to a normal life after the end of the conflict. This is why certain weapons, which cause unnecessary suffering or irreparable damages, are outlawed by IHL in times of armed conflict, although they are not in peacetime. In this given situation, thus, IHL provides for a better protection of the right to life. It may be even said that IHL is more "humane" than HRL and therefore, as reported by M. Odello, that there is a general trend towards "the humanization of international law".

This, as highlighted by Conor McCarthy, is particularly clear in times of (prolonged) military occupation, when the borderline between peace- and wartime may be blurred, as discussed by Vesselin Popovski: shall the occupying power respect the system and human rights applicable in the occupied state, or shall it "import" its domestic human rights provisions? Do human rights obligations apply extraterritorially? To what extent may this have an impact on IHL? The degree to which specific human rights may be enforced and promoted by the occupying forces will also depend on their degree of control over the occupied territory. According to Ruys & Verhoeven, the *Case concerning Armed Activities on the Territory of the Congo* unequivocally confirms the Court's finding in the *Palestinian Wall Case* that HRL applies whenever states *exercise* jurisdiction extraterritorially, even in times of armed conflict.

Another risk behind the "merger" of IHL and HRL in times of conflict is to miss their respective focus. As pointed out by Biehler, e.g. with regard to women their specific aims differ. Whereas IHL attempts to protect women against the effects of armed conflict, HRL aims at enabling them to participate in public life and get equal opportunities. Not even the enforcement mechanisms are identical. However, in Biehler's view, in both situations the inefficiencies in protecting women primarily lie in the political unwillingness of the parties. A key player is the UN Security Council which, as observed by Schotten & Biehler, has underlined the significance of IHL and HRL for peaceful relations among and within states in an increasing number of resolutions.

In conclusion, the discussions in this book suggest that IHL and HRL are two distinct categories, with their specific aims and fields of application. However, particularly in grey area situations like military occupation, insurgencies or the "new war on terror", their complementary application may guarantee the respect of the rule of law.

Index

Abu Ghraib   86, 91, 96, 97, 475, 477, 486
Afghanistan   58, 59, 70, 85, 86, 91, 96, 107, 250, 251, 313, 316, 475, 488, 490, 500, 510, 533, 541, 547
AFSOUTH   300
Akayesu Case   71, 83, 379, 392, 544
Angola   156, 313
Apartheid   227, 310
Armed clashes   332, 336
Armenia   313, 316
Aut dedere aut judicare   228, 234, 592
Aydin v Turkey Case   93, 397
Azerbaijan   313, 316

Bankovic Case   136ss, 149ss, 172, 175, 177, 179, 208, 261, 303, 304, 335, 397, 531, 561
Behrami Case   397, 561
Beijing + 5 Conference 2000   355
Beijing World Conference on Women 1995   355, 370, 375
Biafra conflict   310
Blaskic Case   82, 83, 352, 515, 550
Bosnia and Herzegovina   315, 372, 391, 433, 490

Central African Republic   381
Chechen Republic   36, 265, 332, 348, 397
Chechnya   23, 34, 36, 58, 215, 223, 250, 266, 292, 332, 336ss, 346, 349, 352, 353, 389, 397
Child soldiers   169, 181, 184, 189, 241, 384ss, 390, 396, 398, 399ss, 409, 412
Civil liberties organisation et al. vs. Nigeria Case   463
Civilians   4, 5, 45, 46, 53, 59, 69–70, 81, 96–98, 161, 163–164, 174, 178, 180, 201, 213–214, 240, 250, 274, 277, 283, 295ss, 301, 302, 313ss, 318, 320ss, 342ss, 350, 352, 357, 363, 383ss, 394, 397, 402, 405, 406, 430, 432, 440, 450, 462, 472, 475ss, 488ss, 505, 509, 512ss, 527, 543, 544, 547ss, 555ss, 561, 565ss, 569ss, 576ss, 582ss
Collateral damage   55, 201, 295ss, 345, 346, 352, 388, 476, 547–548, 588
Combatant (non)   11, 68, 69, 81, 97, 98, 106, 178, 297, 386, 389

Combatant   8, 11, 23, 59, 69, 70, 81, 89, 98, 192, 213, 214, 262, 274, 296, 297, 318, 320, 322, 340ss, 350, 356, 363, 388, 475ss, 481, 488, 492, 496, 499, 500ss, 506, 508, 510ss, 519ss, 542ss, 546, 549ss, 563ss, 568ss, 577
Comfort women   369, 377
Compensation   191ss, 215, 217, 248, 252, 295, 296, 297ss, 304, 484, 560, 562
Complementarity   1, 9, 12, 55, 202, 287, 296, 307, 384
Croatia   50–51, 127, 173, 378, 515
Customary law   2, 27ss, 43ss, 51–52, 54, 66, 82, 89, 111, 112, 116, 130, 202, 208, 226, 241, 242, 270, 316, 343, 345, 351, 450ss, 470, 474, 478, 481, 487, 508ss, 510, 542ss, 568
Cyprus   35, 83, 93, 139, 142ss, 173ss, 175, 177, 260, 310
Cyprus vs Turkey Case   35, 83, 93, 136ss, 151, 170, 173ss, 176, 261, 292, 333

Death penalty   66, 150, 187, 362, 387, 388, 395, 472
Democratic Republic of Congo   67, 156, 314, 316, 318, 324, 355, 381
Detention   21, 38, 51, 57ss, 68, 71, 73, 81ss, 91ss, 106ss, 137, 173, 177, 251, 258ss, 262, 362, 372, 390, 406, 413, 458, 469, 477, 481, 483, 486, 488ss, 496ss, 502, 512, 520
Diplomatic protection/immunity   11, 68, 234, 304ss, 388, 508, 513, 544, 546, 550, 551
Discrimination   17, 25, 31, 32, 45, 47, 51, 66, 70, 71, 76, 81, 83, 88, 129, 150, 188, 225, 243, 244, 257, 342ss, 349, 359, 365ss, 370ss, 380, 389, 395, 409, 410, 418, 423ss, 483ss, 449, 573
Displaced children   404, 405, 412, 417
Dissemination   49, 225, 252, 380, 510, 574
Distomo Case   299
Draft Articles on State Responsibility   168
Due process (see fair trial guarantees)   51, 66, 443, 449ss, 458, 461, 466, 472, 489ss, 512ss, 521, 523

Economic, cultural and social rights   206, 428, 441
Ergi case   345, 350

Eritrea   216, 313
Ethiopia   216, 313
Ethnic cleansing   319, 321, 355, 372, 377

Fair trial guarantees   6, 9, 45, 65ss, 255, 258, 449ss, 461, 467, 469ss, 481ss, 504ss, 510ss, 521, 523
FRY   295, 323

Gaza   121, 389
Genocide   17, 39ss, 47, 80, 227, 257, 319, 355, 369, 372, 379, 485, 556
Georgia   314
Grave breaches   80, 82, 201, 227ss, 251, 297ss, 341, 433, 467, 497
Guantanamo Bay   37, 58, 86ss, 92ss, 107, 174, 290, 475ss, 488ss, 500, 502, 512ss, 520
Guinea-Bissau   314, 464, 515
Güleç case   36, 341, 344, 351

Habeas corpus   262, 273, 458, 484, 489ss, 500, 508, 519ss
Human dignity   11, 30, 33, 57, 60, 72ss, 82ss, 94, 201, 204, 209, 221, 296, 441, 518, 573, 580
Human security   56, 310, 319ss
Humanitarian access   316, 319, 325, 412, 417

ICISS   320, 321
ICRC Customary Law Study   37, 270, 451, 454
Ill-treatment   60, 61, 73ss, 82ss, 91, 94, 98, 99, 397, 570, 580
IMT   230
IMTFE   230
India   74, 389
Indiscriminate attacks   60, 297, 351, 352, 363, 371, 571, 574
Inhuman, cruel or degrading treatment   4, 73ss, 80ss, 90ss, 361, 394, 494, 501, 503, 517, 518
Inter-American Convention on Human Rights   64, 74, 76, 95, 205, 284, 288
Internally displaced persons   69, 373, 377, 403, 404, 411, 412, 416, 417, 430, 435, 587
International conference on human rights in Teheran 1968   4, 29, 249, 369
International Federation of the Red Cross   356
Iran   311, 312, 417, 534
Iraq   58, 70, 86ss, 107, 121, 137, 144ss, 167ss, 175ss, 217, 250, 259, 261, 311ss, 403ss, 415ss, 450, 467, 475, 486, 488, 525, 530, 547

Isayeva Case   267, 292, 331, 335ss, 343ss, 351, 352ss, 397
Israel   4, 43, 138, 144, 169ss, 184, 189, 191, 195, 250, 310ss, 388, 389, 486, 487, 526ss, 532ss, 541, 549, 551ss
Italian Supreme Court   296, 303, 306

Jordan   90, 310, 414, 467, 477
Judicial guarantees   45, 67, 81, 253, 257, 364, 426, 453, 456ss, 472ss, 481, 501, 510, 522
Jurisdiction   33ss, 39, 41, 43, 71, 85, 89, 105, 107, 108, 133ss, 142ss, 152ss, 169ss, 185, 195, 203, 207ss, 228ss, 241ss, 257, 259, 260, 267, 270, 279, 286ss, 296, 298, 300, 301, 303ss, 307, 348, 379, 393, 401, 405, 428, 432, 437, 466, 476ss, 484, 489ss, 502ss, 511, 519, 520, 530ss, 543, 550, 558, 561
Jus cogens   47, 73, 111, 202, 209, 214, 287, 331, 361, 445, 473

Kashmir   389
Kovac Case   78, 390
Kunarac Case   78, 82, 83, 379, 390ss
Kurdistan   397

Lebanon   175, 311, 388, 414, 418, 427, 541, 558, 563
Liberia   49, 250, 314, 316, 556

Machel Report   386, 389, 390, 396, 411
Markovic Case   296, 298, 300ss
McCann Case   36, 62, 339, 345, 348, 530
Military advantage   69, 297, 340ss, 480, 547, 548
Military courts   187, 462ss
Military intervention   20, 122, 170, 174, 208, 323, 325, 326
Military objective   69, 297, 301, 342ss, 351, 363, 542, 546ss
Monitoring bodies   75, 309, 427, 452, 458ss, 468, 469
MONUC   166, 324, 555ss

Namibia Case   424
Nassirya   476
NATO air strikes   300, 303
Ne bis in idem   465ss
Nicaragua Case   27, 42, 43, 53, 158, 473, 531, 533, 534, 542
Nigeria   4, 255, 463, 464,
Non-derogable rights   4, 7, 25, 30, 37, 51, 54, 66ss, 184, 256ss, 267, 289ss, 398, 452, 483, 493, 503, 508, 519, 529, 574
Non-state actors   15, 28ss, 33, 39ss, 49, 54,

Index 595

178, 316, 320, 340, 358, 384, 424, 433, 436, 536, 574, 576
Norman Case 393
North Sea Continental Shelf Case 104, 112, 453ss, 469

Occupation 4, 12, 19, 23, 38, 68, 102, 105ss, 121ss, 455, 457ss, 466, 470ss, 488, 502ss
Operation Allied Force 295ss, 349ss, 525, 531, 547

Pakistan 310, 311, 490, 526, 530, 574
Peacekeeping 15, 21, 52, 260, 324, 374, 555ss, 574ss, 582, 584, 589
Poison gas 312
Principle of distinction 297
Principle of humanity 2, 7, 8, 15ss, 68, 256, 273, 288, 347, 379
Principle of necessity 68, 85, 89, 336ss, 340ss, 353, 385, 388ss, 407, 478, 529ss, 535ss, 553
Principle of proportionality 65ss, 248, 341ss, 344ss, 478, 529, 530, 535, 542, 546, 547, 552, 553
Prisoners of war 69ss, 109, 214, 216, 262, 386, 388, 481, 488, 491, 496, 475ss, 505, 506, 510ss, 522, 543, 544
Protected persons 70, 71, 81, 96, 163, 188, 213, 214, 239, 314, 357, 358, 387, 431, 432, 437, 445, 449, 451, 458, 465, 469, 470, 512, 570, 591

Redress 371, 377, 427, 428, 436
Refugees 69, 207, 213, 251, 310, 373, 403ss, 414ss, 421ss, 430ss, 440ss, 588, 591
Reparation 33, 91, 215, 217, 248, 297ss, 306ss, 562
Responsibility (state) 20, 47, 135, 138, 168, 195, 215, 217, 219, 228, 229, 249, 261, 295, 295, 302, 428, 562
Right of access to a court 305
Right of derogation 482
Right to appeal 467, 471, 472, 508, 521
Right to education 239, 366ss
Right to food 129ss, 239, 252, 366
Right to habeas corpus 262, 273, 458, 484, 489, 490, 491, 500, 501, 503, 505, 508, 519, 520, 521
Right to know the charges 475
Right to know family's whereabouts 364
Right to life 3, 7, 8, 11, 12, 17 25, 35, 36, 51, 56, 62, 67, 68, 102, 169, 184, 201, 205, 208, 252, 256ss, 263ss, 273, 277, 282, 283, 285, 289, 290, 305, 331ss, 347, 349, 351ss, 397, 409, 480ss, 494, 520, 529, 531, 573

Russian Federation 74, 176, 331, 332
Rwanda 28, 38, 156ss, 201, 218, 248, 314, 317, 318, 326, 355, 369, 372ss, 392, 412, 433, 482, 485, 544582, 587

Sanctions 48, 76, 213, 215, 302, 323, 325, 341, 389, 486, 487, 544, 565
Self-determination 23, 47, 148, 161, 190, 191, 310, 380, 478
Self-executing 205, 215, 298, 302, 306, 491
Separated children 404ss, 413ss
September 11th attacks 20, 21, 57, 74, 90, 98, 157, 158, 273, 304, 305, 396, 475, 477, 487, 492, 495, 499, 532, 540, 541
Sexual violence 35ss, 45, 83, 369ss, 377ss, 381, 412, 560, 575, 580
Sierra Leone 49, 218, 226, 248, 250, 314, 316, 317, 392, 393, 401, 464, 468, 556
Slavery 4, 25, 45ss, 51, 67, 256, 257, 273, 357, 364, 369, 371, 377, 482, 494, 503, 572ss
Soft law 50, 356, 368, 375, 376, 378, 417, 420, 458, 469, 540
Somalia 173, 314, 317, 433, 526, 558, 564
Special Court for Sierra Leone 218, 226, 393, 401, 465, 468
State sovereignty 20, 309, 320, 444, 485, 488, 559
Strasbourg Court 151, 207, 210, 296, 303, 435
Sudan 156ss, 250, 316, 317, 323, 381, 419, 433, 556
Syria 414, 418

Tadic Case 10, 41, 52, 71, 213, 226, 232, 344, 515, 543, 550
Targeting 8, 163, 314, 342, 349, 352, 389, 512, 525, 526, 540ss, 561, 579
Terrorism 15, 20ss, 57ss, 72, 74, 75, 80, 84, 85, 90, 93ss, 291, 383, 384, 450, 458, 461, 463, 465, 468ss, 475ss, 502ss, 506, 510, 515ss, 523, 526, 527, 530, 532ss, 540, 549, 572
Threat to peace 312, 317, 319, 325
Torture 4, 25, 35, 42ss, 51ss, 60, 67, 68, 70, 72ss, 80, 82ss, 90ss, 107, 108, 135, 136, 169, 175, 176, 181, 201, 205, 243, 244, 250, 256, 273, 284, 288, 289, 357, 361, 364, 366, 367, 370, 381, 390, 394, 397, 406, 423, 438, 441, 443, 475, 477, 478, 481ss, 491ss, 501, 503, 517ss, 549, 553, 559, 571ss
Turkey 35ss, 74, 83, 91, 136ss, 142, 149ss, 170, 175ss, 224, 226, 254, 259, 261, 265, 292, 332ss, 345, 349, 397, 416, 418, 428, 496, 503, 539, 561

Unaccompanied children   403, 410ss
United Kingdom   36, 62, 65, 66, 72ss, 90, 92, 114, 144ss, 164, 183ss, 207, 217, 224, 261, 334, 339, 349, 421, 437, 441, 449, 477, 479, 484, 489, 493ss, 517, 530ss
UNMIK   125, 218, 559, 560
UNTAET   125, 218, 559, 560
Use of force   339ss, 351, 353, 363, 473, 475, 528, 529, 532, 539, 544, 545, 552, 565, 576ss, 585

Varvarin Case   296, 298, 299, 307
Vienna World Conference on the status of human rights 1993   355

Vietnam   4, 310
Vukovic Case   390, 391

War crimes   39, 52, 92, 122, 199, 218, 224ss, 231ss, 244, 248, 249, 252, 272, 299, 321, 340, 359, 361, 379, 397, 401, 433, 464, 467, 477, 479, 488, 493, 505, 515, 552, 556
West Bank   121, 140, 389
World Summit 2005   64, 320, 396, 556

Yugoslavia   10, 28, 38, 73, 142, 164, 182, 201, 208, 218, 248ss, 272, 295ss, 300, 313, 316ss, 350, 355, 369, 372ss, 390ss, 397, 412, 482, 543, 550